Alternative Iran

Alternative Iran

Contemporary Art and Critical Spatial Practice

Pamela Karimi

Stanford University Press
Stanford, California

STANFORD UNIVERSITY PRESS
Stanford, California

Publication of this book has been aided by grants from the Millard Meiss Publication Fund of CAA and the Graham Foundation for Advanced Studies in the Fine Arts.

Printed in the United States of America on acid-free, archival-quality paper

Library of Congress Cataloging-in-Publication Data
Names: Karimi, Z. Pamela (Zahra Pamela), author.
Title: Alternative Iran : contemporary art and critical spatial practice / Pamela Karimi.
Description: Stanford, California : Stanford University Press, 2022. | Includes bibliographical references and index.
Identifiers: LCCN 2021051790 (print) | LCCN 2021051791 (ebook) | ISBN 9781503630017 (cloth) | ISBN 9781503631809 (paper) | ISBN 9781503631816 (ebook)
Subjects: LCSH: Dissident arts—Iran. | Arts—Political aspects—Iran. | Arts, Iranian—21st century.
Classification: LCC NX574.A1 K37 2022 (print) | LCC NX574.A1 (ebook) | DDC 700.955/09051—dc23/eng/20220517
LC record available at https://lccn.loc.gov/2021051790
LC ebook record available at https://lccn.loc.gov/2021051791

Cover design: Rob Ehle
Cover image: Av Theatre Group, *Melpomene*, directed by Babak Mohri. 2013. Old underground thermal bath, Tehran. Photograph by Jeremy Suyker.
Typeset by Motto Publishing Services in 11/15 Minion Pro

To Robert

The best companion

Contents

INTRODUCTION The Different Senses of the Alternative 1

1 **INVISIBILITY:** Art in Concealed and Loosely Covert Spaces 36

2 **ESCAPISM:** Critical Engagements with Remote Natural Sites 104

3 **EPHEMERALITY:** Temporal Interjections in the City 148

4 **IMPROVISATION:** Artful Curation and Spatial Reconfiguration in and out of Conventional Sites 214

EPILOGUE Alternative Iran: Allures and Aversions 292

Acknowledgments 317

Notes 323

Bibliography 385

Index 417

Alternative Iran

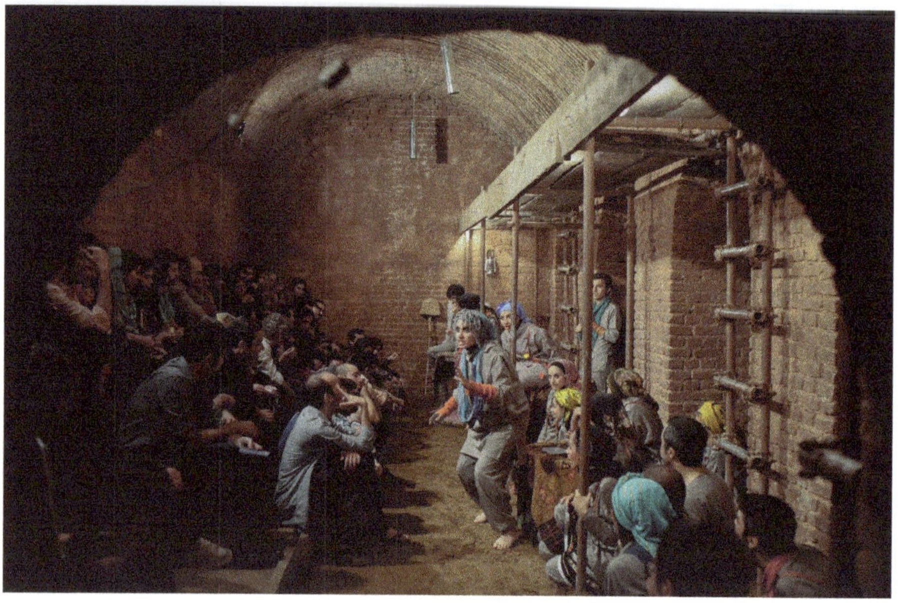

FIGURE I.1 Av Theatre Group, *Melpomene*, directed by Babak Mohri. 2013. Old underground thermal bath, Tehran. Photograph by Jeremy Suyker.

INTRODUCTION

The Different Senses of the Alternative

IN FEBRUARY 2015 I came across a photo-essay on "Iran's Underground Art Scene" circulating on social media. The work of French documentary photographer Jeremy Suyker, its cover image shows an experimental theater group performing in a disused underground thermal bath. I was struck by the spontaneity and expressiveness of the bodies of the performers interacting with their audience (fig. I.1).[1]

Looking at the people packed tightly into the abandoned subterranean vault, I was also reminded of the lived spaces of my childhood. During the Iran-Iraq war of the 1980s, my family took shelter in similar places. Some nights we slept under the main staircase in our house, clinging to the faint hope that the concrete structure would be the last thing to yield to the aftershock of an air strike. We lay jammed into the *stair* alcove, with the soffit so close it felt claustrophobic.

Following the 1979 Islamic Revolution that ousted Mohammad Reza Shah Pahlavi (hereafter, the Shah), the underground became part of the reality of our lives—and not only in the form of domestic bomb shelters. After school, I would go to a class convened by my art instructor, Ali Faramarzi (b. 1950),[2] on the fourth floor of the upscale Vanak Mall in northern Tehran. Tucked away at the end of a long corridor lined with administrative offices and storage spaces, the door of the class bore a small plaque that read "Faramarzi Art Studio." Over cups of steaming tea and Danish pastries, we would listen to extempore lectures on art history, Faramarzi holding rare and colorful art books in front of his chest to illustrate compositions, ideas, and techniques. I still remember the day in 1987 when he introduced us to Henri Matisse's *The Red Studio,* pointing to the ghost-like objects outlined in white lines in a French book. There was something uncanny about Matisse's use of the same color—an oxide red, or, more precisely, a blood red—for both the floor and the walls of the studio. Saturating the space, this blood red resonated with the war images that we saw on TV and in the propaganda murals and posters plastered all over the walls of our city.

Most of those who lost their university teaching posts because of their "Western" viewpoints or affiliation with the Shah's regime, which lasted from 1941 to 1979, had little choice but to give lessons in their homes (using public studio spaces as a formal place of education or a source of income was a challenging undertaking). Faramarzi's painting class, then, was presumably among only a handful that operated in a public space. His sculpture class was another matter, as he would recall years later. Based on their interpretation of Islamic texts, religious scholars had dictated that sculpture was a "forbidden medium," so "all teaching sessions involving three-dimensional art had to take place in a more secretive location"—in this case, the basement of the mall.[3]

With the cooperation of the mall security guard, Faramarzi managed to keep the location of his teaching sessions under wraps. But he still had to take precautions. Girls and boys attended on separate days, and the only way to learn about these after-school painting lessons was through word of mouth; classes were not publicized at all. Indeed, private art studios were only fully recognized by the government after the end of the Iran-Iraq war in 1988.[4] To obtain a license to teach, instructors had to follow specific rules outlined by the Ministry of Culture and Islamic Guidance (*Vezarat-e farhang va ershad-e eslami*; hereafter, MCIG).[5] This was the sociopolitical milieu in which my generation learned about Western art, a topic banned in the government-run educational system.

That late afternoon lesson on Matisse's *Red Studio* would be cut short by the earsplitting sound of air-raid sirens signaling the approach of Iraqi fighters. The lights went out and we rushed in a panic to the basement, running down the stairs in complete darkness with the thudding pulse of anti-aircraft fire all around us. As we sheltered near Faramarzi's stash of statues, I told a classmate how sorry I was that the *Red Studio* story had been interrupted. I was still feeling energized by the painting and wanted to know why Matisse had chosen to make his studio blood red. Appalled at my seeming unawareness of the danger we were in, she whispered, "We'll be lucky to get out of here alive."

Matisse's *Red Studio* and endless nights sleeping in shelters are not just my memories; they are microcosms of a shared experience that continues to this day. While no conventional wars have been fought on Iranian soil since 1988, the threat of war has remained ever-present. The practice of art follows a similar logic. While efforts have been made to legitimize all kinds of art, many forms continue to be deemed inappropriate; regularly monitored, censored, or even banned by the government, they are often consigned to informal and unofficial spaces. Although Suyker's photograph is of a sanctioned performance space, it nonetheless fully captures the mood that still prevails in Iran—the juxtapositions of excitement and fear, happiness and disappointment, stealth and openly passionate expression.

My reading of Suyker's photograph might be interpreted as subjective, but familiar and cultural factors also mobilize this personal experience. To appropriate Roland Barthes's words in *Camera Lucida*, Suyker's photograph works as "a sort of umbilical cord, [which] link[s] the body of the photographed thing to my gaze: light, though impalpable, is here a carnal medium, a skin I share with anyone who has been photographed."[6] The viewer relates to the photograph through personal experience, but at the same time the image can become an entry point into a shared cultural memory.[7]

In the same way, Iran's nongovernmental art and cultural scenes are not only sites of personal encounters but also part of the collective experience of its citizens, and particularly of the artist community. This book sets out to provide an entry point into this experience without catering to voyeuristic curiosity or emphasizing the allure of what is already perceived as stealthy, illegal activity.

From the Underground to the Alternative

Some writers and journalists, especially if they live outside Iran, refer to postrevolutionary sites of nonconformist and grassroots activities as *zirzamini* (literally, *of the underground*). Although the term is often associated with banned, Western-style music performances, it is also applied to other artistic and cultural events.[8] Azar Nafisi's best-selling memoir, *Reading Lolita in Tehran* (2003), helped bolster the global perception that all sorts of unofficial activities are taking place in Iran's domestic and concealed spaces. After being forced to leave her post as a university professor, the US-educated Nafisi conducted private classes in her apartment for students who wanted to learn more about world literature. Many of the books they analyzed were banned and could not be taught at the university. With its vivid description of the sharp contrasts between public and private life in Iran, *Reading Lolita* drew attention to the underground spheres formed by experts who were unable to work in public or operate within the state-controlled educational system.

While there were many such gatherings in Iran in the early years of the Islamic Republic, as well as a strong underground distribution network for foreign films and music, the black-and-white world depicted in Nafisi's book—where most genuine artistic expression must be performed in secret—could lead the reader to the false conclusion that everything is clear-cut in the daily lives of Iranians. In truth, most unconventional or even forbidden (*makrooh*) activities occur in more porous environments. Blake Atwood, who has written on the circulation of banned films and music in the 1980s and 1990s, believes that the underground in Iran must be treated more as a third space that brings together public and private pursuits, sometimes forcefully but more often casually.[9] In the years before the lifting of the ban in 1994, men specializing in film (*filmi*) or video (*videoie*) moved quietly through artist studios, graphic design offices, film circles, and architectural firms, renting out videocassettes of "artsy films" (*filmha-ye honari*).[10] These films, by the likes of Jim Jarmusch, Krzysztof Kieślowski, and Andrei Tarkovsky, would in turn influence postrevolutionary Iranian highbrow cinema. The robustness of the underground networks, combined with the relative openness of their operation, suggests the situation was muddier than is generally assumed.[11]

Art experts living in Iran are fully cognizant of the term *zirzamini*, or "underground," but interpret it in varying ways. In the theater, any performance not sanctioned by the MCIG tends to be labeled underground. As I will show in chapter 1, this unauthorized status may be due to a lack of desire to seek permission rather than a failure to secure it. In other words, restrictions imposed by the Islamic Republic are not the sole reason for the choice of alternative locations for theatrical performances. Deeply indebted to the teachings of the Polish experimental theater director Jerzy Grotowski, many theater experts in Iran choose unconventional locations for their performances, some of which may inadvertently exude an air of covertness or out-of-sightness, even when paperwork from the MCIG is in order.[12] Regarding "underground" music, with its potential to be distributed more widely, in both physical and virtual ways, music historian Nahid Siamdoust writes that the distinction between "underground" and "aboveground" is tenuous and depends on circumstances. As such, the concept "continues to mean a number of things. It often refers to music that crosses the boundaries of the publicly permitted as far as content, language, and musical form are concerned; it can also allude to a wide range of musical genres, depending on government restrictions."[13]

In the visual arts the definition of "underground" is even more fluid. Artist Rozita Sharafjahan (b. 1962), founding director of the MICG-authorized Azad Art Gallery (also known as *Tarrahan-e Azad* Gallery) in Tehran, claims the term is rarely used to describe unofficial and private art galleries in Iran. Instead, these private spaces with trusted audiences (carefully chosen from the curator's close circle of artist friends) are called "showrooms."[14]

In Tehran, one of the pioneers in the creation of unregistered, "alternative" art spaces is Fereydoun Ave (b. 1945), a Zoroastrian who went to school in England before studying theater arts in the United States, where he was part of New York's underground film movement and a longtime assistant and friend of Cy Twombly. From 1984 to 2010 Ave hosted the 13 Vanak Street space and a more private space in a converted Olympic-size pool at his house. But Ave himself did not perceive these spaces as underground showrooms or galleries, and says he found it unsettling when artists used such terms in unofficial invitations to their shows.[15] For Ave, a more appropriate way to describe them would be "experimental," "under the radar," "noncommercial," "nongallery," "nonexhibition," or "private clubs."[16] This kind of designation recognizes that even if there is an "underground" quality to any initiative outside the direct purview of the government, nothing is absolutely subterranean or covert.

In contemporary Iran, art practices ebb and flow in the interstices between realms of legality and illegality, visibility and nonvisibility, publicness and privacy, presence and absence, transparency and ambiguity. There is no consistent tradition with a fixed technique, or a single "appropriate" means of engaging in artistic practices. Rather, Iranian artists improvise in multiple ways, and even official protocols admit degrees of elasticity. Hamidreza Sheshjavani (b. 1975), a scholar in art economy (*eghtesad-e honar*), a newly established field in Iran's higher-education system, has defined four categories of art institution, each of which sponsors the arts in line with its own interests: executive (*hokoomati*), governmental (*dolati*), public (*omoomi*), and private (*khosoosi*).[17] This makes for complicated relations among Iranian art, politics, and economics. Art connected with the upper echelons of government, the executive, is often purely agitprop. Governmental art, by contrast, is not necessarily propaganda, although it is subject to strict rules governing its making and presentation. I experienced this for myself in August 2020, when I was invited to join the jury for an urban art competition for a governmental organization, Tehran Municipality's Beautification Bureau (*Sazman-e ziba sazi-e shahrdari-e Tehran*). As conversations progressed on a shared WhatsApp platform—the pandemic ruling out more direct contact—I saw how the independent curators and artists involved in the initiative became increasingly frustrated with the official editing of the language of the mission statement and the call to artists that outline concepts and methods of distributing funds. As this editing came more and more to resemble censorship, the artists and curators withdrew their support and the project collapsed.

While there are a few overlaps with governmental (*dolati*) initiatives, most of the art projects discussed in this book fit into Sheshjavani's categories of public (*omoomi*) and private (*khosoosi*). However, even within these two categories, there are different shades of public and private. Some artists proceed without authorization, but many others seek permission from Iran's MCIG, whose guidelines tend to fluctuate as a reflection of the composition of its leadership or the political atmosphere. The minister of culture and Islamic guidance is appointed by the elected president of the Islamic Republic and confirmed by Parliament. Often, the license for an event is issued by the ministry, only to be disregarded by the judiciary, which is under the control of the supreme leader. In addition, most things considered taboo in Iran are not legally proscribed, so within the rubric of the MCIG it is sometimes possible to take advantage of these legal gray areas to bypass the unwritten rules. There have also been paradigm shifts in methods of control and regulation. For example, when in the early 2010s theater became privatized, the ministry adopted a nontraditional method of issuing permissions, involving the nonnegotiable enforcement of regulations by non-MCIG agents (see chapter 1). The MCIG's August 2021 call for a complete renewal and further "Islamization" of the existing rules, under the watch of the newly elected president Ebrahim Raisi, was another major paradigm shift that shook the artist community to its core.

Whether sanctioned by the authorities or not, whether performed in open or closed locations, the examples showcased in this book reveal what I call a *loose covertness* across both art spaces and art practices.[18] The artists' occupation of unconventional sites, especially private homes and disused buildings, can be seen in relation to the alternative art scenes of the 1960s and 1970s Europe or America, or the renewed artistic interest in the abandoned buildings of postindustrial cities in North America and Europe. But a parallel—perhaps a more appropriate one—can also be drawn with the unconventional artistic practices of the Occupy Movement. While alternative and even oft-unauthorized, these art scenes are highly visible as vigorous challenges to the status quo within the urban contexts of developed countries. In Iran, however, artists operate in relative disguise, subject to censorship, surveillance, and ideological restrictions. Being visible in public—even for those who comply with the rules—often means being exposed to the relentless control of Iran's morality police. As such, artists often opt for loosely covert spaces.

Flying under the radar is something artists had to do in the Soviet Union as well, as Victor Tupitsyn relates in *The Museological Unconscious* (2009).[19] The sweeping, and often deadly, purges of the Stalin era were followed by a brief period of liberalization, cut short when the premier, Nikita Khrushchev, visited the thirtieth anniversary exhibition of the Moscow Artists' Union in 1962 and found, to his dismay, that some artists had felt emboldened to depart from "committed" and social realist themes. After this, the suppression of artists resumed in earnest, and many took their artistic practice to private spaces.[20] Tupitsyn describes how *kommunalka* (communal apartment) became a code word for many exhibitions. This "communal optic" registered the influence on art of characteristically Russian phenomena such as "communal living, communal perception, and communal speech practices." Tupitsyn analyzes the series of "anti-shows" organized in private apartments between 1982 and 1984 by the Moscow-based group APTART—the name is a play on "apartment art" and the Cyrillic transcription of the English word "art."[21] In doing so, he reveals a perceptual gap between Western and Russian views of what otherwise appears to be similar work. Within the communal space of a large apartment building, Tupitsyn writes, Russian artists created greater autonomy in relation to official institutions than their counterparts in the capitalist West.

If the *kommunalka*, the most characteristic form of living in the Soviet Union, provides a useful lens through which to view its unofficial art, then the story of Iranian art could also be told through the loose covertness that is one of the most prominent forms of daily life in Iran. In this book, when appropriate, and in line with the preferences of Iranian artists, I have drawn comparative examples mostly from Eastern Europe and the Soviet Union, out of a desire to initiate a dialogue between Iranian alternative art and other global models.

. . .

"Alternative" is the term I use throughout this book to describe Iran's artistic genres, in preference not only to underground but also to informal, unofficial, countercultural, oppositional, defiant, or activist. Informal (*gheyr-e rasmi*) is a word often applied to political graffiti, or to the young people who dance in the streets of Tehran to Western music played on portable stereos or iPhones. With its makeshift connotations, "informal" does not reflect the ethos of the work featured in this book, which is created by individuals who see themselves as professional artists rather than occasional political agents or activists. "Unofficial art," in turn, is a historically specific term in the literature of modern art, commonly referring to the context of the communist systems in which most art activities were funded by the state, and anything outside that system was deemed unofficial.[22]

The Anglo-Saxon term "counterculture" has fallen out of use since the 1960s, as Western societies have become less homogenous, fragmenting into an increasing number of subgroups, some interconnected and others isolated. However, in Iran—and in many other developing countries with authoritarian systems of governance—there is still a substantial divide between the mainstream and the counterculture. Theories and ideas regarding global countercultural movements remain pertinent to some of the trends addressed in this book, and in particular to the Iranian artists who have departed from the center and moved to remote areas, much like their 1960s American hippie counterparts.[23]

Oppositional and defiant art are terms that can refer to any prohibited approach, such as photographs with strong feminist connotations, for example, or sexually provocative paintings, or antireligious iconography. Many Iranian artists feel they are unable to display a large portion of their work for this reason. Evoking the equivalent Soviet term, "writing for the desk drawer," Jinoos Taghizadeh (b. 1971) refers to this body of work as "closet art" (*honar-e keshoyi*), while Houman Mortazavi (b. 1964) calls these art forms, for example his "untitled" watercolor series, his "under the bed" (*zirtakhti*) collection, that is, not viewable in public (fig. I.2).[24] The practice of concealing them aside, these works belong to the category of object-oriented art, a territory already explored by several esteemed art historians, notably Talinn Grigor, Shiva Balaghi, Fereshteh Daftari, Abbas Daneshvari, and Hamid Keshmirshekan.[25] This book has a different focus, addressing the wider spectrum of alternative art scenes, including critical engagements with site.

Activist is a term whose political connotations can overshadow the aesthetic merit of a work.[26] Moreover, not all art forms discussed in this book are defined by their opposition to the regime and its ideological apparatus. Some very young and passionate artists just want to experiment with unusual locations and unconventional forms of presentation, regardless of

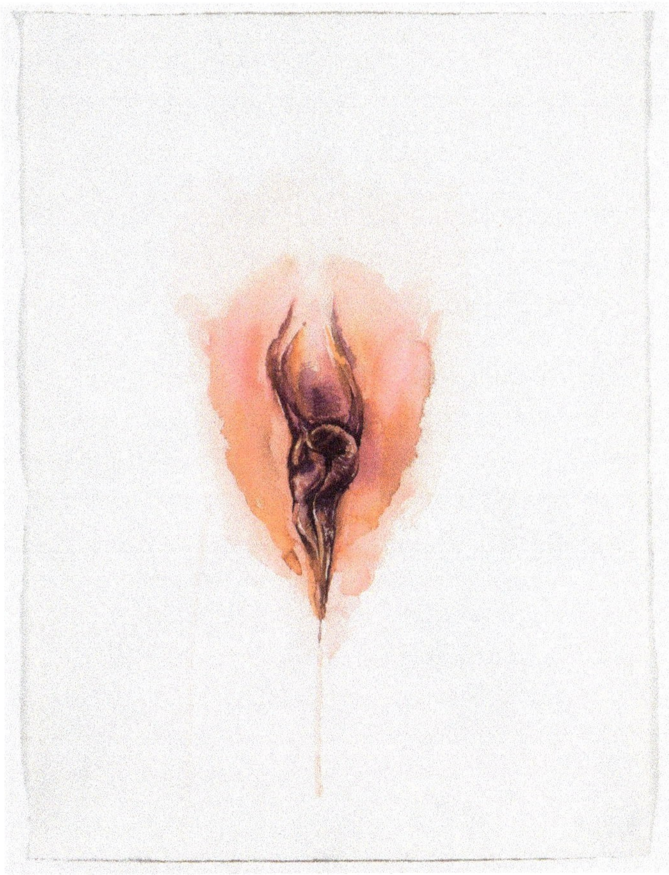

FIGURE I.2 Houman Mortazavi, *Untitled*, from the artist's *zirtakhti* collection. 2010. Tehran. Courtesy of Houman Mortazavi.

politics. Sometimes, the emphasis is simply on the aesthetic or therapeutic qualities of the art. In other cases, the shortage of official arts spaces means that artists and performers turn in desperation to ad hoc locations, participating in unofficial (and thus seemingly underground) activities not for political reasons but because they have nowhere else to go. While some alternative art forms appear to reject state-sanctioned ideologies and aesthetic sensibilities, others focus more on neoliberal economics, targeting powerful private entities or real estate developers involved in urban renewal plans.

When art is taken into unconventional locations, the parameters that define its essence and medium change. It gains an ephemeral and dematerialized character and, with it, the potential to transcend ideological boundaries and commercial pressures. From its inception, the aforementioned Azad Art Gallery has described itself as an alternative "space (*faza*) to create cutting-edge art." By sponsoring experimental art (*honar-e tajrobi*), it distances itself from the "narrow-minded *nouveaux riches* who always expect some conventional codes in Iranian art."[27] Similarly, in selecting the artists who presented at 13 Vanak, Fereydoun Ave favored those who were unable to show their art in official and registered spaces, either because of the subject matter or because the art was not the kind of commodity that could easily be sold in the regular art market.[28] Ave wanted to nurture and financially support conceptual artists, and especially those who were working outside the commercial system.[29]

The Ethos of Iran's Alternative Art

In this book, experimental music and theater are addressed insofar as their encounters with alternative sites are of significance. Architecture is explored when the design process is symptomatic of a search for the creation of alternative spaces for art and everyday life. Although focused only on the work of a selected group of renowned architects, my aim here is not merely to celebrate them but to follow what Ghanaian-British architect David Adjaye calls "a line of inquiry," and a way of thinking about initiating a dialogue between the public and the private through design.[30]

Most of the other art forms that I discuss in this book belong to the art-historical category of post-studio practices, which encompasses socially engaged art, interventionist art, participatory art, collaborative art, and community-based art and involves physical and intellectual engagement with a variety of agents on the ground.[31] As such, the art under study here is "dematerialized," a phenomenon rooted in 1960s countercultural practices, such as Happenings, that dissolved the boundaries between the production and consumption of art. In the mid-1960s, many alternative initiatives emerged in major cities like New York.[32] The broader, social dimensions of art were also theorized by philosophers, artists, and critics, among them Umberto Eco, Jean-Luc Nancy, Guy Debord, Joseph Beuys, and Paulo Freire. Art historian Lucy Lippard famously crystallizes this new way of looking at art—of rejecting the market system and engaging instead with spaces and things beyond the limited institutionalized spaces of art—in her *Six Years: The Dematerialization of the Art Object, 1966–1972.*[33]

While such a freeform approach to art and community life may seem to fit more easily into progressive Western societies, it is also plausible in the global South. In fact, Iran has a long tradition of communal and interactive art that reaches back to premodern times. Oriented toward experience rather than objects, many of these artistic expressions materialized in the form of religious ceremonies during the lunar month of Muharram, notably the *ta'ziyeh* passion plays that narrate the tragic and heroic martyrdom of Imam Hussain, grandson of the Prophet Muhammad, in the battle of Karbala in Iraq in Muharram of 680 CE.[34] *Ta'ziyeh* means "consolation," implying the blessing that performers are believed to obtain by dramatizing the events that led to the persecution of the Prophet's family. While symbolizing the spirit of resistance against tyranny, the ritual drama is also shaped by the active participation of ordinary people. Nonprofessional actors are invited to contribute as both performers and spectators, and the way the story unfolds is spontaneous and at times improvised. Hamid Dabashi writes that in *ta'ziyeh,* "[t]he stage is not really a stage, not because [those] who stage the *ta'ziyeh* are poor and cannot afford a proper amphitheater, but because the stage must be an extension of . . . ordinary realities. . . . Non-actors can frequent the stage easily, while the actors fall in and out of character without any prior notice."[35] Nor was participation in artistic expression limited to religious art and rituals. *Naqqali* (storytelling), *Shahnameh-khani* (reading of verses of the *Shahnameh*), *roohowzi* (layman entertainment performances), and *motrebi* (light music played on streets and at social events) were interactive and time-based entertainment art forms that, in their delivery, resonated with religious passion plays.[36] This collective approach even extended to the high-ranking professional (miniature) painters of the royal courts: while one mastered the portrayal of the human body, another would be an expert in depicting foliage or animals, and so on. In fact, until the modern period and increased interactions with Europe, it was rare to think of art as a solitary pursuit.

Just how Iranians kept these traditions alive is not so clear. Today, many performance artists and theater experts strongly oppose any connections with the *ta'ziyeh* while acknowledging the influence of experimental theater directors Peter Brook and Grotowski, who both traveled to Iran and performed there in the late 1960s and 1970s, during the Shiraz Arts Festival, launched by the Empress Farah and held annually from 1967 to 1977.[37] Ironically, both of those iconic directors were captivated by the dramatic possibilities of *ta'ziyeh* performances that were brought into the spotlight at the fourth festival, which revolved around the theme of the "ritual." As Brook explained:

> I saw in a remote Iranian village one of the strongest things I have ever seen in theater: a group of 400 villagers, the entire population of the place, sitting under the tree and passing from roars of laughter to outright sobbing—although they knew perfectly well the end of the story—as they saw Hussein in danger

> of being killed, and then fooling his enemies, and then being martyred. And when he was martyred, the theater form became truth.[38]

Brook would distill his experience into an experimental theater piece, *Orghast*, performed at the 1971 Shiraz Arts Festival, which was written entirely in a language invented by his collaborator, the poet Ted Hughes. As a contemporary review in the *New York Times* notes, the use of words that had no meaning—only rhythm, texture, tone—forced "the spectator to listen to the work as they would listen to music, and to watch the action as if it were a religious experience."[39] Grotowski, who visited Iran four times and closely followed the Shiite rituals, also used elements from the *ta'ziyeh* tradition to bond performers and audiences.[40] Theater historian Daniel Gerould has written of how Grotowski's actors became "celebrant[s] for the community of spectators, inciting them to take part in the rituals."[41]

Often Iranian performances, some featured in this book, draw on what the German dramatist Bertolt Brecht calls *Verfremdungseffekt* (*distancing effect* or simply *alienation*), the theatrical device that intentionally distances audiences from the fictive narrative and instead engages them in real activities. With the exception of a few, Iranian performers tend to deny the connection between the Brechtian distancing effect and the *ta'ziyeh*.[42] But several scholars, including Hamid Dabashi, have compared the dramatic value of distancing in conveying the strong moral principles associated with the *ta'ziyeh*, where performers do not "play roles" per se, but try to impersonate the protagonists and the antagonists.[43]

This cross-fertilization—from Shiite performances, to European avant-garde theater, and back again in contemporary performances in Iran—provides an insight into the complex spectrum of influences on Iranian art. *Ta'ziyeh* props and their methods of assembly—and in particular, the temporary structures hastily assembled for the annual rituals of the month of Muharram—have also proved to be a source of inspiration. As will be shown in chapter 4, the same "rushed" building style (*hey'ati*; literally, of a delegation—referring to a delegation of devout men who quickly construct large-scale, temporary religious paraphernalia), which has become a defining feature of agitprops in Iran is also used by artists to make sarcastic commentaries on urban propaganda.

. . .

In the last two decades of the Pahlavi dynasty, Iranian visual arts were increasingly dominated by ideas of personal expression and distinct authorship, both of which were indexed to financial value. However, there were still some instances of interactivity. *Dematerialized* and time-based art forms were introduced to Iranian art scenes during the Shiraz Arts Festival through artists such as John Cage, Merce Cunningham, and Robert Wilson. In 1966 the architect and artist Kamran Diba (b. 1937), Empress Farah's cousin, collaborated with the sculptor Parviz Tanavoli (b. 1937) and calligrapher Faramarz Pilaram (1937–1982) on *Clever Waterman* (*Ab-baz-e zebar dast*), a Dadaist-inspired multimedia installation (or what Diba himself refers to as *poochgaraie* or nihilism) involving water faucets and large-scale adaptations of a silhouetted diver whose body was animated by calligraphic inscriptions on the subject of water. The whole spectacle was set against the soundtrack of a Dadaist poem about water.[44] Invited guests at the opening of the show included, surprisingly, the staff of Tehran's Department of Water.[45] In 1976, Diba had some women in designer shoes stand on a mock winners' podium while Ahmad Aali (b. 1935) photographed them under the watchful eyes of audiences at the exclusive Zand Gallery.[46] That same year, as part of his activism during the Lebanese Civil War, Koorosh Shishegaran (b. 1944) appropriated Eastern European interactive mail art with a work titled *honar-e posti*.[47] In the decade-long run of the Shiraz Arts Festival, performance art (*honar-e ejra'ie*) or theater-like art (*honar-e te'atre gooneh*) gained a firm foothold in Iran.

After the revolution, compared to theater, music, and the Islamic "harmonious movement" performances (*harakat-e mowzoon*) that substituted for dance, visual art found it harder to engage with the community, despite the historical traditions of *interactivity*.[48] Throughout the 1980s, mural painting was probably the only visual art form that engaged a broader public—and even then, this engagement was one-sided, with passersby being mere spectators. Dematerialization and participation in art were more commonly found in private art scenes.

Regarding how unconventional forms of art became widespread as early as the 1980s, classical guitar performer and composer Saba Khozoie (b. 1966) further describes how hard it was to systematically learn conventional arts such as Western classical music. "Even during broadcast orchestra on TV, the cameras refused to focus on the musicians and the instruments they were playing. If the TV broadcasted a performance, they would do so by pairing the music with images of flowers, rather than focus on the performers themselves," Khozoie recalled.[49] These restrictions made it difficult for Iran's classical musicians to be innovative and progressive. But at the same time, such restrictions paved the way for alternative and subversive forms of music—fusion styles and rock and rap.

In the 1990s, a few exhibitions in rundown and ready-to-renovate homes revived forms of conceptual art (*honar-e mafhoomi*), performance art (*honar-e ejra'ie*), and ephemeral art (*honar-e mira*). While they were on display, these shows caught the attention of both casual visitors and high-profile art circles, but for various reasons—a lack of sponsorship, a shortage of film and photographic documentation, a dearth of press coverage—for a long time they failed to make their way into art history books.

In the early 2000s, under the reformist president Muhammad Khatami (in office 1997–2005), the Tehran Museum of Contemporary Art (TMoCA) and its progressive director, Alireza Sami-Azar (b. 1961), broke new ground with a series of cutting-edge exhibitions on conceptual art (*honar-e mafhoomi*) and new media art (*honar-e neo media*), in which artworks engaged the space of the museum. More exhibitions of site-oriented art (*honar-e makan mehvar*) and participatory art (*honar-e mosharekati*) followed in their wake.[50] By involving their own bodies and the bodies of their audiences, and by interacting with the built environment, Iranian alternative artists pushed the boundaries of conceptual art to make it more dematerialized and experience-based. In Iranian art circles, "dialogic" (*ta'amol garayi*) and "engaging" (*dargiri*) are the terms most commonly used to describe this participatory approach. For some Tehran-based art historians, interactive art (*honar-e ta'amoli*) can be defined as that which "allows a shared experience between the artist and the viewer . . . in unexpected (*gheir-e ghabel-e pishbini*) and open (*goshoodeh*) ways."[51]

Engaged Audiences and Affective Sites

Rather than being mere onlookers, audiences are frequently co-producers or participants in these alternative art forms. But the nature of the audience varies among the categories of experimental music or theater, performance art, and installation. The majority of those who can afford to apply for permits, purchase art materials, and produce nonconventional art that does not generate any income are from middle- and upper-class urban centers. The backgrounds of these artists are mirrored in the audience for their work, a small portion of the educated urban elite.

Theater, by contrast, attracts a much broader cross-section of society, especially in its traditional religious and vernacular forms.[52] My main focus in this book will be on the experimental style, increasingly embraced by directors and actors since the officially sanctioned privatization of theater in 2009. Although some experimental theater takes place in private, it is also staged in authorized private companies and public places, particularly in residual urban zones, to reach a wider audience. Graffiti art is likewise intended for a broad, public audience. The fact that it is officially condemned as "vandalism" also means it carries more political weight than other art forms. While the graffiti artists chosen for this study are highly skilled, the nature of their art obliges them to keep their distance from any form of elite art circle or institutionalized art.[53] Being political, sometimes they will present their work in private, in front of a small audience drawn exclusively from like-minded friends. Often, graffiti artists operate under tag names and pseudonyms and deliberately avoid proper documentation of their works. As they rarely respond to queries about their work or invitations to participate from academic circles, I was very fortunate to be able to interview some of them.

Many of the projects in this book contain an element of subversiveness. A few artists dare to be explicit in their message, even if descriptions and reviews of the artworks tend to be couched in rather nebulous terms. One such artist is Amir Mobed (b. 1974), who engages with gallery spaces in openly provocative ways. In 2011, he staged a famous "Opening" at a group show in Tehran's Siin Gallery in which he "censored" the artworks of his co-exhibitors. To get into the gallery, people had first to get past the artist, who was posted at the entrance, dressed as a militant security guard, complete with a bank robber's balaclava. Once inside, they found an installation of framed artworks, some of which depicted mundane and apolitical images—of flowers and butterflies, for example. Against a loud soundtrack of Qur'an recitations, Mobed then burst into the room and proceeded to censor the works by stapling sheets of black cloth onto the outer edges of the frames (fig. I.3). When audiences and other participating artists tried to stop him, he roughly pushed them aside, wielding the large stapler even more forcefully, so it began to sound like gunfire. Calculated to agitate and shock, the performance invited a reaction from its audiences. While fully aware of Mobed's intended message, some in attendance rushed to rip off the black cloth when the "censor" moved to other rooms. A few art critics celebrated the interventionist aspect of Mobed's performance, but this kind of blunt political message is rarely welcomed in Iran, even sometimes among those who strongly object to censorship.[54] Writing in 2013, Tehran-based art historian Helia Darabi (b. 1974) cast doubt on the directness (*rokgooyi*) and one-sidedness (*takgooyi*) of Mobed's method of delivery in this performance, although she appreciated the fact that he drew

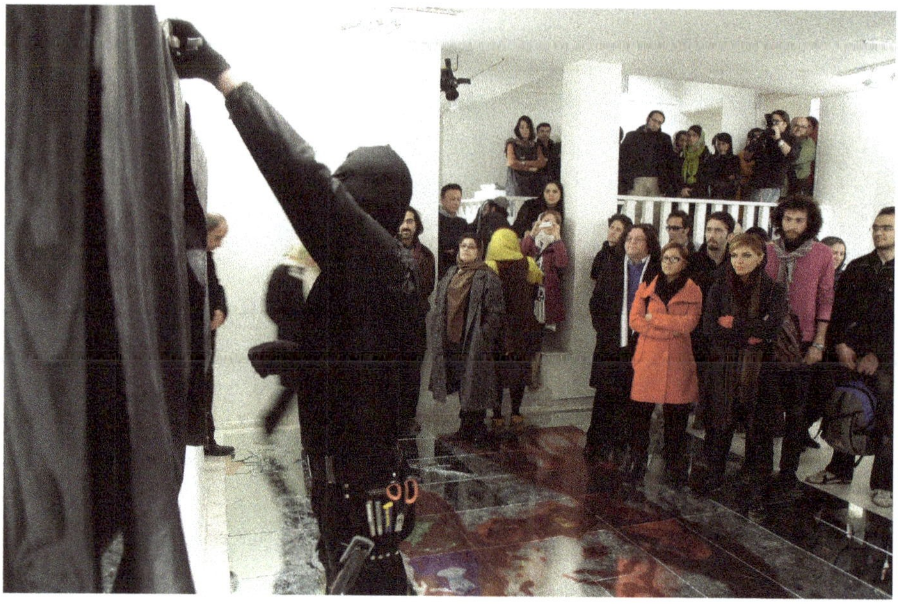

FIGURE I.3 Amir Mobed, *Opening*, performance featuring the artist as a "censor." 2011. Siin Gallery, Tehran. Photograph by Zarvan Rouhbakhshan. Courtesy of Amir Mobed.

attention to the pervasive systems of violence to which Iranians have become inured.[55]

Most subversive art projects that critically engage with space are subtler in tone than Mobed's "Opening." The political artwork may be out there, in plain sight, but its intentions will remain obscure. Artists often disguise their role, leading spectators to see the performance as an unstaged event. In this sense, many art performances resonate with what the Brazilian dramatist and political activist Augusto Boal called "Invisible Theater"—a form of performance whose seeming "ordinariness" enabled it to escape the attentions of the police during the repressive dictatorships in Brazil and Argentina. Often, political references are oblique. In her exhibition *Open Wiring* (*Sim-keshi-e roo kar*; an archaic, exposed wiring system equivalent to *knob-and-tube wiring* in the United States), which took place from November to December of 2015 at Tehran's O Gallery, artist Jinoos Taghizadeh featured, among others, the iconic nine-minute shot of the homesick Russian poet carrying a candle across a pool, from Tarkovsky's *Nostalghia* (1983). Taghizadeh recalled, "The struggle to keep the flame lit while poised between wind and water is a metaphor for our life in Iran. In one long, uninterrupted shot, it effortlessly captures the story of our struggles in coping with the simplest, futile (*bifaydeh*) even, tasks of everyday life."[56] Taghizadeh's remarks also evoke Tarkovsky's yearning for capturing the meaning of his own life under the Soviet regime and, hence, allude to the extent to which former Soviet and Eastern Bloc art speaks to a certain generation of Iranian artists.

Many artists in Iran who speak or write about politics in art do so in an abstract (*enteza'ie*) manner. For instance, when, in 2012, *MesoCity Tehran Workshop: Art, Ecology & the City* invited a team of architects and artists to reflect on the future of Tehran's *qanat*, an extensive derelict underground water network, some took the opportunity to explore the dark side of state-sanctioned rapid developments in the capital. Since the early 1990s these developments have extended the capital northward over the slopes of the Alborz Mountains, underneath which are the mother wells, the deepest and widest shafts located closest to the aquifer where the *qanat* originates. The wastewater of the northern inhabitants of Tehran goes straight into these channels and then directly into the historic downtown, where the soil is porous enough for water to penetrate the surface.[57] Thus, the *qanat* no longer functions as an irrigation system for natural groundwater but instead as a wastewater network, with destructive consequences.[58] A statement by participating artist Amir Hossein Bayani (b. 1977) reads: "The [simplest] view of the *qanat* narrates life and movement in the underground. . . . [W]ater, the liquid of life is constantly flowing in the underground, and all this happens away from the eyes of citizens on the surface. Thus, *the truth* is *not necessarily what lies in front of us*."[59] Bayani's statement about hidden water sources obliquely references the ways in which "truth" is handled in Iran. This tacit sardonic language is also evident in testimony about the art of Shahab Fotouhi (b. 1980), consisting of blue-colored dots on highways and bridges to mark the location of the *qanat* ducts. Regarding Fotouhi's demarcations, the organizer of the workshop, Paris-based architect Sara Kamalvand, writes, "Fotouhi insisted on the static atmosphere of the contemporary condition. By being constantly projected in the future, by living in a superficial world where everything has become as flat as an image, his blue spots on the ground create an unexpected event pushing the viewer in the present."[60] Because of the government's systematic neglect of ecological issues, which has escalated since the 2010s, recent engagement with environmental issues has taken on a political tone, if only tacitly. If the dissident tone in this approach readily resonates with many people, there are other ways of engagement with the environment whose politics is more layered and complex. As I show in chapter 2, sometimes engaging with natural places becomes a means to create opportunities for freedom of artistic expression rather than further the environmental discourse.

. . .

The subtle, multilayered engagement with politics is also evident from the local literature; for example, in the summer 2016 issue of the prominent Tehran-based journal *Herfeh honarmand* (The Career of the Artist), in which Iranian artists, critics, and art historians elaborate on the many ways art and politics are enmeshed. The articles cover a broad range of art forms that fall into the category of political art (*honar-e siyasi*), among them revolutionary art (*honar-e enghelabi*), ideological art (*honar-e ideologic*), formal art (*honar-e rasmi*), governmental art (*honar-e dolati*), social art (*honar-e ejtema'yi*), oppositional art (*honar-e moghavemati*), activist art (*honar-e konesh gara*), and protest art (*honar-e e'terazi*).[61] While most of the articles focus on the political themes and ideas depicted in object-based art (painting and sculpture), some contributors address the spatial aspects of art and politics—the same themes that inform my engagement with the political dimensions of alternative art in this book. For example, artist and art critic Samila Amir-Ebrahimi (b. 1950) refrains from addressing underground art culture in the Islamic Republic, but she does write on how social art (*honar-e ejtema'yi*) went underground (*zirzamin*) during the Pahlavi regime.[62] In another important contribution, based on a roundtable discussion organized by *Herfeh honarmand*'s editor-in-chief, Iman Afsarian (b. 1974), the prominent conceptual artist Barbad Golshiri (b. 1982) sets out to dispel the myth of the isolated artist (*honarmand-e monzavi*) promoted by formalist artists of previous generations, insisting on the value of engagement in public spaces and in society.[63] Here, too, Golshiri prefers a low-key approach. To paraphrase him: a political artist is not necessarily one who directly encounters some kind of interference from the authorities or is given a nudge (*sikh bokhoreh*) by the (morality) police—there are more subtle ways of being political.[64] On this issue, I align myself with Golshiri. Most of the art presented in this book was not made with express political aims, which is not to say that art which consciously engages with politics is not of interest to Iranian artists and their audiences, or to me in this study. More precisely, I want to shift the emphasis: rather than looking at objects and spaces through their semantic associations, I want to consider the practices of flow and circulation that propel art and the ways in which art provokes certain feelings and emotions. Rather than seeking the *literal* meaning of the art under study, I intend to look at how it becomes less *readable* and more *feelable* when it enters a certain sphere.[65]

Feelings triumph over logic in major decision-making processes in Iran. In a recent conversation with Ali Alizadeh, a London-based Iranian political analyst and media specialist, the Tehran-based journalist Habib Rahimpour Azghadi talked about how the Islamic Republic has tended, from the very outset, to justify its ideology through emotional (*hayejani*) rather than logical (*haghghani*) assertions.[66] Azghadi concluded that this approach has penetrated all forms of debate in Iran; all discussions, regardless of their political stripe, continue to be guided by emotional responses. The regime's propaganda continues to whip up "fleeting feelings" (*ehsasat-e lahzehyi*) among the masses.[67] "Emotional control" is the name anthropologist William Reddy gives to this form of political discourse—a means of exercising power over citizens. As he notes, "Emotions are of the highest political significance. Any enduring political regime must establish, as an essential element, a normative order for emotions."[68]

Correspondingly, through circulation and exchange, certain collective emotions gain in value and become more commonplace in society, and this phenomenon in turn influences the political directions of alternative art.[69] My study of such impulsive and emotional actions is aligned with cultural critic Sara Ahmed's assertion that "rather than seeing emotions as psychological dispositions, we need to consider how they work, in concrete and particular ways, to mediate the relationship between the psychic and the social, and between the individual and the collective."[70] Above all, rather than focusing on "feeling" as something that circulates only among living bodies, alternative art forms also attend to architectural spaces and the sites around them—spaces that can accumulate and circulate this affective currency.

. . .

Under the rubric of makeshift spaces (*fazahay-e jaygozin*), art historian Helia Darabi bases her definition of alternative art on the unconventional places in which it arises, highlighting site-specific art (*honar-e makan vijeh*) and site-oriented art (*honar-e makan mehvar*) as well as a number of informal sites, including both architecturally significant and informal places such as vacant homes and marginal urban spots.[71] Like Darabi, I believe these kinds of sites not only are alternative in and of themselves but also have an agency that paves the way for alternative (*jaygozin*) art forms. Moreover, the greater the interdependence between art and the space around it, the more the parameters we use to define conventional art institutions are called into question, opening up new possibilities for thinking about the relationship between art and architecture.[72]

What difference does it make for Iranian art to be critically engaged with space and site? Compare Mortazavi's exposé of the vagina from his *zirtakhti* collection, described earlier in this text, to Pooya Aryanpour's handling of the same subject matter in an actual public exhibition space. Aryanpour (b. 1971) is known for his provocative mirror work (*ayeneh kari*) sculptures, which often capture what he calls the display of profane images (*namayesh-e sovar-e ghabiheh*). Other artists before him, most notably Monir Shahroudy Farmanfarmaian (1922–2019), have used *mirror works* in their sculptures. For Shahroudy Farmanfarmaian, the *ayeneh kari* spaces act like a "living theater," and because of this visual effect she enthusiastically reproduced their images in her work.[73]

Starting in the Safavid period, *ayeneh kari* became associated with the inner sanctum of Shiite shrines (*imamzadeh*). Upon entering, one encounters a dazzling array of small, geometrical mirrors set in the walls and ceiling that presumably allow the believer to "transcend all particularities and realize the Self within all selves, to become not this person or that person but personhood as such, which also means becoming the perfect mirror of the Divine."[74] While *ayeneh kari* is found in palatial architecture as well, the use of mirror work in shrines is significantly different. There it takes the form of shattered pieces, so fractured that one's reflection is skewed, an urgency drawn from the teachings of the highest-ranking Shiite clerics, including Ayatollah Khomeini himself, that proscribe praying in front of portraits, including one's own image.[75]

With this backdrop in mind, Aryanpour proceeded to deconstruct the whole concept. In *Beautiful Virgin* (2015), he "reinvented *ayeneh kari* to contradict and subvert the original sacred associations by substituting the sacred with the earthly."[76] Rather than resisting the inherent function of *ayeneh kari*, he followed its logic, or what he calls "constant concealment" (*penhankari-e modavem*), providing "possibilities for distorting what is considered taboo."[77]

Aryanpour presented this work at the invitation of architect Faryar Javaherian (b. 1951), who organized the group exhibition *Picnic, Iranian Style* (*Pik nik-e Irani*) at the Golestan Palace Museum from September to November 2017.[78] Golestan Palace has several *ayeneh kari* rooms, including the throne room, which was chosen by Aryanpour for his gigantic *ayeneh kari* vagina-like piece. At the opening of the exhibition, the members of the palace museum staff and other officials did not notice the sly fusing of the sacred and the earthy, and they all admired the art and even took photos with

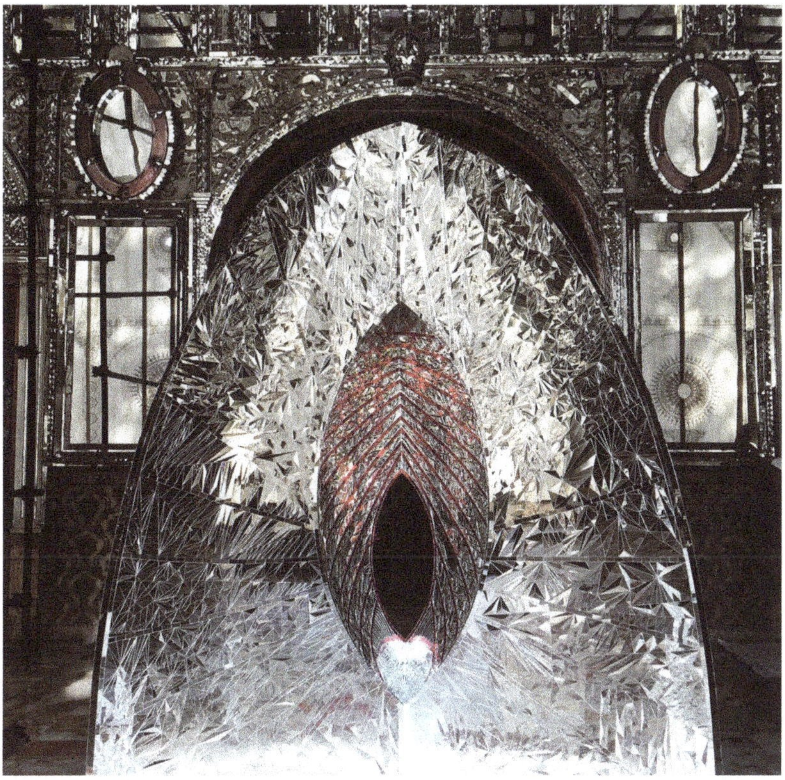

FIGURE I.4A Pooya Aryanpour, *Beautiful Virgin*. 2015. Tehran. Photograph by Sahar Safarian Baranlou. Courtesy of Pooya Aryanpour.

it. Not long after, however, someone spotted the visual reference, and palace staff rushed to place a shroud over the vagina. This addition prompted curiosity, leading visitors to remove the shroud to see the hidden part. Unable to relocate the piece because of its size and weight, officials then placed a divider in front of it to prevent further contact. In the exhibition's catalog, they darkened the center of the vagina, and on the website the piece was shown only partially. Thus was the fate of the artwork: from a sacred-seeming object to a profane one, and also an interactive art or performance piece, one that provoked various acts of censorship, self-censorship, and curiosity (figs I.4a/b).

The ferment around Aryanpour's art exemplifies the very means by which Iranian artists, censors, and viewers negotiate, redefine, or reconstruct new readings and offer participating viewpoints. Aryanpour's personal ways of thinking about the sacred and the profane did not constitute, as one staff member of the MCIG insisted, protest art (*honar-e e'terazi*);

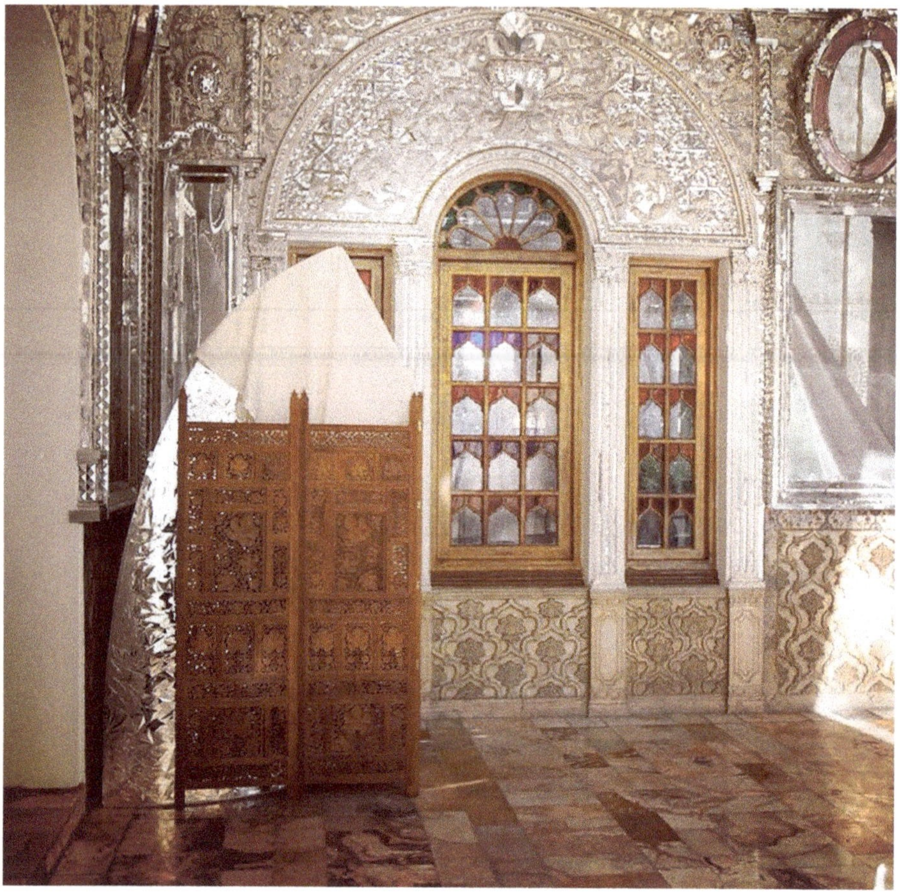

FIGURE I.4B Pooya Aryanpour. *Beautiful Virgin*, on display at the Golestan Palace Museum. 2017. Tehran. Photograph by Sahar Safarian Baranlou. Courtesy of Pooya Aryanpour.

rather, his art invited various agents and actors to interact with it and change its appearance and meaning as they saw fit. When approached for consent regarding usage of the shroud or the screen or the defacing of images of his work in subsequent publications, Aryanpour responded: "I couldn't care less; do as you wish and don't feel obliged to contact me again for every step of this process."[79] In this way, the artist allowed the art to take on an afterlife of its own. This complex and interwoven narrative of art and architecture shows the extent to which such pieces are more complicated than portable and frameable art intended for gallery and museum display or for sale at auctions. The tangled tale of Aryanpour's project, both expected and unexpected, sets the tone for many of the art projects that I present in this book.

Critical Spatial Practice

Through its focus on Iran's alternative art scenes, this book blends art with ideas about critical spatial practice—a term coined by architect and theorist Jane Rendell in 2003 to refer to practices situated at a three-way intersection: between art and architecture, public and private, theory and practice. While building on pioneering art-historical contributions, notably Rosalyn Deutsche's *Evictions: Art and Spatial Politics* (1996), Rendell's ideas are mainly informed by French critical spatial theory, and in particular by Michel de Certeau's *The Practice of Everyday Life* (1980) and Henri Lefebvre's *The Production of Space* (1974), which fused everyday spatial practices with notions of social transformation.[80] Extending the lineage of this work, critical spatial practice tests the boundaries between disciplines, questioning and transforming the social conditions of the sites of intervention.[81] Following Rendell, other theorists and practitioners have used the term and expanded its definition, drawing on a plethora of works by geographers like Edward Soja and David Harvey and by feminist scholars such as Liz Bondi, Doreen Massey, Linda McDowell, and Gillian Rose (among many others).[82] In 2011, at the peak of the Occupy Movement and the Arab Spring, Nikolaus Hirsch and Markus Miessen started a paperback series and a website, both titled *Critical Spatial Practice*, featuring the work of critics and practitioners who tie critical spatial practices in art and design to economic, political, and ecological issues.[83] The term "spatial," Markus argues, "is often misunderstood as something . . . that simply happens in space. However, . . . spatial could signify not only something that happens physically in three-dimensional space, but also something that has a certain scale and effect on space, such as policy or other forms of legal and nonlegal frameworks. The spatial always has an underlying structure to it . . . that governs it."[84] Similarly, it is within the broader framework of the "spatial" that I have contextualized most of the creative projects in this book.

While this book is informed by the literature relating to "critical spatial practice," it primarily engages with the ideas that guide the work of most of the protagonists featured here, namely, the critical spatial theories developed by twentieth-century French intellectuals. The groundbreaking contribution of Michel Foucault, one of Iran's favorite critical thinkers, centers on how power configures space—on how, for example, the spatial arrangement of streets disciplines the bodies of citizens. By extension, the theories of Lefebvre and de Certeau offer a means to examine the ways in which

Iranians resist certain rules and regulations, ultimately finding a way to participate in the production of spaces.

Since the Islamic Revolution, space in Iran has operated across multiple dimensions that can be framed according to Lefebvre's triad: lived space, physical or abstract space, and constructed space. The idea of "lived space" has been examined by contemporary Tehran-based sociologists, remarkably Abbas Kazemi (b. 1973), and by scholars outside Iran, notably Asef Bayat and Shahram Khosravi,[85] who have described how ordinary citizens, and especially young people, break the conventions of public life, allowing aspects of everyday life to "fall outside of or run counter to the scrutiny of power."[86] This book looks at "lived space" through a different lens. Rather than writing a history of ordinary people who use tactics of informality to transcend state-imposed regulations, I am interested in how nonviolent acts of civil disobedience manifest themselves in art venues, elegantly, and often deliberately, imagined and improvised by art experts and designers. Operating in a field of self-scrutiny, artists, performers, and architects are openly involved in the making of "lived space."

Physical space, or "abstract space" in Lefebvre's terminology, is constructed by various powerful agents such as the state, developers, urban planners, and architects. I will look at how "abstract space" is challenged not just by artists but by architects and curators who seek to undo "abstraction" and "alienation" through design solutions, proposing alternative modes of living, granting agency to the users of the space, and intervening within the existing spaces of the Islamic Republic. Overlaid on this are the constructed discourses of social space, invariably centered on religion and ideology. For example, the opening (or closure) of various art spaces, theaters, and museums has been continually debated since the onset of the revolution. Regardless of whether the particular spaces have survived, the critical discourses surrounding them endure. In contributing to such discourses, Iranian scholars naturally borrow from Lefebvre and other theorists, mining their works selectively, adopting some translated concepts and repudiating others to reinforce their argument. As architectural historian Esra Akcan has pointed out in her illuminating study of architectural concepts in translation, "the traditional humanist supposition that translation provides an evenly balanced cultural exchange between languages would hardly tell the full story of world exchanges."[87] Aidin Torkameh (b. 1987), a pioneering translator of key works of French and American critical spatial theory—including a number of Lefebvre's books and Mark Gottdiener's *The Social Production of Urban Space* (1985)—believes it is wrong to give word-for-word translations of certain concepts in the Iranian context. For example, while the European and American idea of *the right to the city* has been translated into Persian, word for word, as *haghgheh beh shahr*, there is no direct equivalent in Iran's urban life.[88] For Lefebvre, and for sociologists such as David Harvey and Anna Plyushteva, *the right to the city* relates not only to the individual's freedom to access urban spaces and resources but also to the possibility of being involved in the making and control of the city and its spaces.[89] While the Iranian government often touts the access to public space it provides its citizens, it does not allow them full participation in decision-making processes.

To these constructed meanings, we could add what some Iranian critics call "urban imaginaries" (*takhayyolat-e shahri*).[90] In the Iranian context, these are produced by two different agents. One is unique to Iran and comes from the regime's more progressive (but still loyal to the overall ideological apparatus) cohort. The other, as in Western capitalist societies, consists of powerful and wealthy individuals who have benefitted from a locally constructed economic system. Urban theorist Ananya Roy has called this system "homegrown neoliberalism"; in the official rhetoric of the Islamic Republic, it is referred to as *khosoolati* economics—a portmanteau of *khosoosi* (private) and *dolati* (governmental).[91] While in office from 2013 to 2021, President Hassan Rouhani repeatedly used the word *khosoolati* to criticize the privatizations that had taken place under his predecessors. The *khosoolati* system grants special powers to bypass the law (*ghodrat-e fara-ghanooni*).[92] Some individuals are exempt from paying taxes. Others are allowed to keep both their public identities and their financial records secret.[93] The privatization of the economy has enriched agents in companies with close ties to the Iranian government; for example, the branches of Iran's nationalized oil industry.[94] Looking for somewhere to invest their huge profits, many of these agents choose urban development, focusing on solutions geared toward short-term financial gains rather than long-term infrastructural changes with more widespread benefits.

. . .

Many developments in the urban fabric of Tehran, especially in the wake of the 2009 political uprising, or Green Movement, appear on the surface to be straightforward urban renewal projects. According to Tehran-based critic Pouria Jahanshad (b. 1974), however, most of the changes are security-discipline oriented (*amniati-enzebati*), designed to give the morality police greater control over people's interactions as they navigate through public space.[95] For its part, the government likes to present these efforts under the rubric of organizing or structuring (*sazmandahi* or *samandahi*) or beautification (*zibasazi*), with the latter aptly spearheaded by the Tehran Municipality's Beautification Bureau.

As sociologist Nazanin Shahrokni argues in relation to the creation of all-women public parks in Tehran, the politics of gender segregation in the Islamic Republic has moved in recent decades from "excluding" or "prohibiting" women to "including" or "providing" for their presence. As Shahrokni sees it, this shift is largely driven by the government's desire to regulate its own citizens more efficiently.[96] She uses the term "*differential exclusion and inclusion*" to describe these efforts at control, reflecting the constant state of flux in government policies and the ways in which ordinary people resist them.[97] Art, too, has been subject to the same flux of government policies and attempts at control. In this case, it has given rise to what I refer to as the *predatory aestheticization* turn. A careful analysis of the careers of artists and stakeholders in the alternative arts shows a distinct aptitude for continuously *disrupting* rather than *disseminating* the ideology of the prevailing regime, even among those who indirectly benefit from government support. Often, too, powerful, wealthy private agents in Iran will subtly challenge the system from within, either by endorsing controversial artists or by participating in radical curation and spatial reconfiguration of art spaces.

Regardless of regimes of sponsorship, and like their contemporary global counterparts, alternative artists in Iran "critique the sites into which they intervene" and challenge "the disciplinary procedures through which they operate"—to frame their work in the terms of Rendell's critical spatial practice.[98] The decisive modalities through which they engage with critical spatial practice include escaping, curating, choreographing, improvising, planning (temporally), reconfiguring (spatially), and negotiating (verbally). Akin to artists in the restrictive sociopolitical atmosphere of the former Soviet Union, Iranian alternative artists engage critically with space, and they do so across venues that are neither closed nor open—neither entirely illegal nor completely within the purview of the state and powerful stakeholders. Instead, these spaces operate in *loose covertness*. Such improvised forms of engagement with art, space, and audiences have in turn informed my research methodologies.

Improvised Research Tactics

In placing non-Western artists at its core, this book contributes to the emerging discourse of a "decolonized" art history. However, decolonization is not only a matter of telling different stories and making people aware of them. It is also about the ways in which we approach these narratives; how we help historically underrepresented subjects to fully "appear," to borrow from art historian Nicholas Mirzoeff.[99] This mode of "appearing," as I will show in this book, cannot be limited to that which is visible or invisible; rather, it includes that which is related to more complicated social contexts, such as the domains of the palpable, affects, and emotions. Instead of focusing on just one artist, a single theory, or a fixed methodology, the book engages with a wide spectrum of artists—both prominent artists and those on the fringe—and with the ways a multitude of audiences, from professionally trained critics to laypersons, respond to their work.

Some of the makers featured in this book self-censor, others deliberately avoid systematic presentation or documentation. Their work is developed outside the usual temporal or spatial organizations (biennials, annual juried shows, museums, reputable galleries, etc.) that serve the art market's demand for accumulation or the Islamic Republic's urge to control. Alternative art is consequently forced out of the timeline assigned to conventional art. Some of the photographs, maps, and drawings reproduced here could only be found in the personal archive of the artist or designer. Many were presented online at some point, only to be removed when there was a shift in the political atmosphere.

Like the occupants of Foucault's panopticon, the inhabitants of Iran's art scenes have become self-regulating, even when nobody is hearing, or watching.[100] Most critics consider it their duty to turn a blind eye to the artist's true intentions and instead divert attention to a more convenient viewpoint. Whether in Persian or English, many locally published art reviews and art statements prefer not to address issues in a direct manner. A comparison of the descriptions of the work of the South African artist Richard Penn illustrates the point. As an artist-in-residence in Tehran in October 2012, Penn produced a large wall painting, *No Signal, Tehran*, composed of parallel bands of diverse shades of gray, black, and brown, seemingly overlaid with a smattering of blood stains. The catalog published in Tehran opines: "That something is happening or may already have occurred is apparent but not clear. Something is getting through. 'No Signal' is as powerful as a signal as any other; it is inevitably hiding within its chaos."[101]

By contrast, the statement on the artist's own website reads: "The Tehran streets are filled with martyr murals funded by the state which celebrate soldiers (fictional or real) who gave their lives for the regime especially in their wars with Iraq. It is such a violent form of communication. . . . I had the idea of making a large wall mural to stand as a marker of the filters and blockages and isolationism that is the government's policy in Iran."[102] Distrust of the Ministry of Culture and Islamic Guidance alters ways of writing about art inside Iran; therefore, to interpret the textual materials as accurately as possible, I have occasionally compared them with texts published outside Iran or with oral interviews with multiple interlocutors.

. . .

The early stage of this research was conducted inside Iran. Going to places and talking directly to the agents of the alternative art scenes was for me a kind of "sensuous scholarship," to use Paul Stoller's term—an attempt to profoundly reawaken my own body by "demonstrating how the fusion of the intelligible and the sensible can be applied to scholarly practices and representations."[103] Seeking to describe a place so that its presence can be felt, I rested my hand on the dilapidated staircase of an abandoned building, then climbed those stairs into a lingering smell of newsprint and ink that wafted from the walls, which were covered with thousands of newspapers; I experienced the refreshing coolness of tucked-away basement galleries in the scorching summer heat; I squeezed into a tiny exhibition space, part of an audience that awkwardly arranged itself around cheaply made metal buckets filled with hay against the backdrop of a larger-than-life donkey.

A large part of the material in this book is derived from personal interviews with more than a hundred experts. While not all of the interviews are directly addressed in these pages, in their entirety they shaped my thinking and arguments. Over the course of six years, I tracked down most of the interviewees via Persian or English publications, through word of mouth, or on social media. In a few instances, I have withheld names to protect the identities of political activists. Most artists, however, were eager to share their ideas and experiences and gave their consent to be cited properly.

Additionally, these experts offered all kinds of textual, audio, and visual materials, from professional recordings to their own snapshots and videos of people interacting with art—the kind of wealth of information that cannot be absorbed by one person on a single visit. Through my interviews with curators, gallerists, artists, and even viewers, I was then able to build up a picture of the intricacy of each encounter. The complex narratives and varied viewpoints enriched my writing, allowing me to describe the *experience* of art, even though I have not encountered most of the artworks firsthand.

Having talked informally with almost every artist, architect, musician, curator, and theater expert featured here, I was able to develop an informed sense of their influences and sources of inspiration. Officially, all aspects of university curricula and programming are overseen by the Islamic government; professors in the arts and humanities rarely depart from the prescribed textbooks, out of fear of being questioned or even removed from their positions. Despite this, Iranian art experts are well versed in global and particularly Western art history and critical theory, thanks to the tremendous efforts made outside the university context. Scores of important books are translated into Persian. In Tehran there are several independent institutions, such as Arya, Bidar, Mah-e Mehr, Chaharsoo, Karnameh, Shamseh, and Porsesh, that offer classes not only on Western theory and philosophy but also on critical art history, including queer practices that are considered taboo in the official education system. While these independent and alternative institutions must be sanctioned by the MCIG, none fully abide by the ministry's rules. The reason they get away with it, according to Tehran-based art historian and instructor Hamid Severi (b. 1958), is that they "do not have a general public" and their audiences are very limited, even when they are promoted online. This is certainly in contrast to performance halls, movie theaters, and exhibitions that attract thousands of viewers.[104] While mindful of what goes on behind the walls of these educational platforms, the MCIG chooses not to intervene in their programs.

In tracing the sources of influence, including philosophical approaches and theoretical frameworks, I have tried to do justice to the goals of the artist rather than providing a distanced art-historical reading. By and large I have remained faithful to the artists' stories. In a few cases, if it seemed appropriate, I took the liberty of adding my own interpretations of particular scenarios. Some of the artists agreed with my "guesses," others remained indifferent; rarely did they reject them outright.

My research was frequently informed by social media feeds, in audio, visual, and textual forms. Many details were discovered in the unpredictable give-and-take of Telegram, WhatsApp, Skype, Instagram, and, more recently, Clubhouse posts and conversations. At times, my research progressed in a straightforward manner. At other times, it evolved more haphazardly and intuitively, the subversive weight of a given art project becoming clearer when I encountered interpretations of it on social media. Then, the seeming aimlessness and generally circular nature of my attempts to understand my subjects opened the door to something rarer—to what anthropologists Allaine Cerwonka and Liisa Malkki articulate as a "process of ethnographic improvisation."[105] This form of research "is not the steady, linear accumulation of more and more insight. Rather, it is characterized by rushes of and lulls in activity and understanding, and it requires constant revision of insights gained earlier," writes Cerwonka in *Improvising Theory: Process and Temporality in Ethnographic Fieldwork* (2007), which centers on her yearlong email correspondence with her mentor, Malkki, while she engaged in fieldwork in Australia.[106] As Cerwonka and Malkki see it, ethnographic work and its theorization are essentially *improvisatory* in nature: because ethnographic research is performed in real time, in invariably precarious circumstances, it involves both the objects of analysis and our ways of knowing and explaining them. Cerwonka's back-and-forth method of communications and revisions was mainly conducted via the email technology of the late 1990s. In my case, the social media and communication platforms that have proliferated since the start of this research in 2015 have necessitated ever greater improvisations. Like jazz improvisation, improvised research involves "a continual 'tacking back and forth' between the familiar and the unfamiliar . . . theoretical insights and surprising empirical discoveries."[107]

Such engagements and observations have fed into the structure of the book. With few exceptions, I have avoided organizing its various parts according to the conventional historic junctures in the political development of the Islamic Republic. Likewise, I have not relied on categorization based on artistic medium; for example, the seemingly unrelated fields of theatrical performances and design strategies are analyzed in the same thematic section. Throughout I have favored a more robust focus on common critical spatial practices and subtle interventionist tactics utilized by the artists, regardless of their areas of specialty.

Overarching Argument and Structure

Through four interconnected chapters that represent various modes of artistic involvement with spatial politics, *Alternative Iran* demonstrates that spatial constraints, political obstacles, and economic restrictions, far from leading to decay or forming a barrier to progress, are the source of the unique qualities of Iran's art scenes.

While the 1980s and 1990s provided opportunities for unconventional installations and performances, precisely because the partially covert spaces of alternative art practice were not regulated, the first two decades of the twenty-first century saw major transformations in regimes of control and art economics. As the case studies in this book show, in some instances the state and other powerful agents appropriate spatial techniques of *loose covertness* and bring aspects of the *alternative* into the limelight, either to better regulate the creative community or to challenge the system from within. Though fairly recent, such a paradigm shift has created a multitude of gray zones and push-and-pull games between the state authorities and the art community, culminating in instances of *tentative coalition* as opposed to *uncompromising resistance*. Hence, while primarily attending to nonconforming curatorial projects, independent guerrilla installations, escapist practices, and tacitly subversive performances, *Alternative Iran* also features case studies from *a house divided against itself* to counterbalance the long-held presumption of a deep divide between the progressive art community and the conservative, Islamist state.

Throughout the book, I identify the power of art to take a critical stance across semi-regulated and unregulated spaces, as well as regimes of appropriation and coalition. By bringing together the voices of like-minded artists, I hope to make visible a movement that goes unremarked in official art-historical narratives and even among those who practice art in Iran. This movement, as I will show, has formed around a series of often-obscure networks reflecting spatial, economic, and political discourses that are very specific to the circumstances of life in Iran. While I refer to "escapist sites," the vast majority of case studies are drawn from Tehran. Artistic activities in other cities go beyond the scope of this book, and undoubtedly deserve entire studies of their own.

The book is loosely structured in four thematic sections, each dealing with a particular aspect of alternative art and its relation to the partially *covert* sites in which it is produced. These four chapters are guided by critical spatial theory and by pertinent umbrella-theoretical frameworks emerging from their titles—invisibility, escapism, ephemerality, and improvisation.

Chapter 1, "Invisibility: Art in Concealed and Loosely Covert Spaces," unpacks the roots of regimes of invisibility and covertness, discussing mostly private and circumscribed alternative art scenes. After looking at the alternative cultural and art spaces created by nonconformist figures in the crucial years leading up to the 1979 revolution in Iran, I explore how the revolutionary regime's culture of control has led to self-censorship—to masking or modifying the intentions of the work, or to avoiding sensitive content altogether. Of interest to this study is an exploration of affect, or how these strategies have played out on the human body as well as spatially (i.e., through architecture and material objects).

Examining artistic and cultural resistance in tandem with a variety of spatial types—namely, the basement, the home, and derelict buildings—I explain how and why many forms of cultural and artistic defiance moved from the public to the private sphere in the 1980s and early 1990s. As the chapter evolves, I present examples of the gradual "institutionalization" of informal art projects. Paralleling the *aggressive mimicry* identified by art critic Gregory Sholette in the context of Western capitalism, Iranian authorities began in the late 1990s to grant permission—and even funds—for works of this kind.[108]

The desire to take refuge in concealed places is mirrored by the urge to go to remote spots outside the city. In Iran escapist sites have a long history. Under the Safavid Dynasty (1501–1736), the lives and activities of the Sufis, dervishes, literati, and other nonconforming figures of early modern Iran were centered around the then capital city, Isfahan, and in particular its coffeehouses. By the mid-seventeenth century, however, these coffeehouses had become contested spaces in the city, and they were shut down, one after the other, by the authorities.[109] Many dervishes and Sufis gradually withdrew from the city, and from society, and made their way to distant sanctuaries. Some built lodges atop mountains or in the wilderness, others took refuge in cemeteries or abandoned settlements.[110] The forms and functions of these sanctuaries and retreats then passed from one generation to the next. During the Cold War, for example, leftist groups such as the Iranian People's Fedai Guerrillas (*Chirik-e fadai-e khalgh*) took refuge in remote mountain areas.[111] There was a further displacement after the Islamic Revolution of 1979. Under renewed persecution, the *khaneghahs* of Shiraz—meeting places of the Iranian Sufi/dervish sect of the Zahabiya brotherhood—moved from their iconic locations to more unknown spots in the city.[112]

The role in art of this distinct and unbroken tradition of escapist sites is the focus of chapter 2, "Escapism: Critical Engagements with Remote Natural Sites." Because of the nature of these sites—mountains, deserts, caves, faraway forests, hidden gardens—my arguments are inevitably intertwined with Iran's environmental art and discourse. But rather than the environmental context, my emphasis is on the distance from the center that allows for a greater measure of personal freedom and independent thinking. Examining escapist sites chosen by musicians, visual artists, and performers, I look at the ways in which they create opportunities for performances and discussions that are not always possible or convenient in formal and official venues in major urban areas. This retreat to remote places—Michel de Certeau called it "escaping" the internal snares of a domineering culture "without leaving it"—was also a common practice among artists behind the Iron Curtain. Thus, this chapter draws on parallel examples from the former Soviet Union and the Eastern Bloc.

Toward the end of the chapter, in my own "escapist" digression, I argue that it is not just creative agents and dissidents who are interested in leaving the "center." Many people, including those inside the regime's political and economic system, escape to remote and desirable spots outside the capital to enjoy a luxurious life away from the observant eyes of others. These two categories of escapism—practiced not only by unconventional artists and marginal communities but also by the well connected—capture the essence of the built life of the two groups of Iranians under discussion in this chapter.

Chapter 3, "Ephemerality: Temporal Interjections in the City," reexamines the question of ownership of public space from a perspective that is unique to urban life in Iran and invites new ways of assessing the rhetoric of "openness" and "accessibility." In contrast to the spaces discussed in previous chapters, the case studies in this chapter are not necessarily concealed or out of reach. Performances and installations take place in plain sight, and in accessible spots around busy urban centers. However, due to their often subversive nature they are invariably short-lived, even if approved by the authorities.

In many ways, the postrevolutionary time-based urban art projects discussed in this chapter resonate, once again, with the practices that surfaced in the authoritarian public spaces of the Eastern Bloc. A prime example of this earlier tradition is *Aktual Walk—Demonstration for All Senses* by the Czech artist Milan Knížák in 1964. Through staged actions, such as a man lying in the street playing a double bass, Knížák set out to disrupt the everyday routine of his chance audience.[113] If not understood in the context of Cold War Prague, *Demonstration for All Senses* comes across as little more than a youthful prank. But Knížák's work strikes a chord with Iranian urban art. Both keep a low profile and can seem, on the surface, somewhat playful. Focused on theories of becoming and time, this chapter also looks at how the venues for these transitory expressive art forms accumulate positive and negative affective values, which are in turn transmitted to those who visit the sites. Unlike the enclosed spaces of chapter 1 or the escapist sites of chapter 2, these temporal art events in visible urban spots create opportunities for interaction with a wider public. Wherever possible, then, I reflect on the reactions of ordinary passersby. This chapter also offers myriad opportunities to discuss the state's implementation of regulatory apparatuses—a phenomenon I call *predatory aestheticization.*

Chapter 4, "Improvisation: Artful Curation and Spatial Reconfiguration in and out of Conventional Sites," focuses on unconventional curatorial practices in more conventional settings such as galleries and carefully designed architectural spaces. These activities, which are often sanctioned by the MCIG, could be seen as a quieter strand of the much larger activist movement that has redefined the ethics of global curating with innovative, often highly visible, projects on issues of feminism, race, sexuality, and exclusive affective responses to art.[114] Examples of these practices include Linda Nochlin's *Women Artists* at LACMA (1976–77), the first international exhibition of art by female artists at a time when the Feminist Art Movement was gaining momentum; Fred Wilson's *Mining the Museum* at the Maryland Historical Society (1992–93), which disrupted the institution's comfortably uncritical white, upper-class narrative by juxtaposing the permanent exhibition of silver repoussé vessels with slave shackles and whipping posts from the building's storage; Okwui Enwezor's acclaimed *In/Sight* at the 1997 Johannesburg Biennale, in which he demonstrated that the history of art was inevitably linked to the histories of peoples of color and their movements; and Jean-Hubert Martin's *Carambolages* at the Grand Palais in Paris (2016), where art and objects of all sorts were linked together by visual association, devoid of any canonical categorization and conventional chronology. In Iran, these radical and alternative curatorial practices appear in a more subdued form. Breaking with the usual strategies of covertness, they rely on a range of theoretical frameworks on improvisation and negotiation (e.g., Michel de Certeau). Thanks to these tactics, curation has become an art form in and of itself, engaging directly with the exhibition as a departure point for critical spatial practices. Curators, whether they are artists or professional gallery directors, have also radically transformed the space of the gallery through their choice of sites—often leftover spaces in the vicinity of the official art institution—and their careful choreographing of who is allowed to experience them. Toward the end of the chapter, I turn my attention to the ways in which architects and architecture enthusiasts "curate" the city and reconfigure common spatial organizations to open up new possibilities for how we live.

Finally, in the epilogue, "Alternative Iran: Allures and Aversions," I look at how alternative art is seen and judged in and outside of Iran. In its entirety, this book offers a window onto a complex terrain of critical spatial practices in contemporary art that have the capacity to take the imaged, the imagined, and the lived experience into alternative horizons.

1 Invisibility

Art in Concealed and Loosely Covert Spaces

IN MODERN IRAN engagement with covert spaces goes back to the late nineteenth century, a historical lineage that weighs heavily on the post-revolutionary culture of covertness and invisibility and elucidates the events of the present and recent past. During the nearly half-century rule of Naser al-din Shah (1848–1896), reformists, government officials, and members of the mercantile class and the religious-minded elites (*ulama*) formed a vast underground network of loosely defined associations or assemblies (*anjomans*).[1]

These assemblies played an important role in the Constitutional Revolution of 1906–9. To disseminate their ideas, assembly members distributed printed materials commonly known as *shabnamehs* (night letters), as they would be posted on the walls of buildings or slid under the doors of homes at night.[2] These political opposition sheets, leaflets, tracts, and pamphlets mostly expressed patriotic and democratic aspirations in simple prose. They were produced thanks to the popularity of hectographs (also referred to as gelatin duplicators, or jellygraphs), a nineteenth-century printing invention that involved the transfer of an original, prepared with special inks, to a pan of gelatin or a gelatin pad pulled tight on a metal frame.

This method of rapid printing did not require professional expertise, and it paved the way for the reproduction of a large number of *shabnamehs* in a short span of time.[3] The chemical materials for hectographic prints could be purchased from local drug stores on the pretense that they were being used for medical purposes.[4] Of particular interest to the spatial connotations of these stealthy acts, the *shabnamehs* were distributed around the city by attaching them to the walls of buildings along sidewalks, as well as to mosques, hotels, and embassies. There is not much information on the locations in which the hectographic *shabnamehs* were produced.[5] But newspaper reports and memoirs indicate that many defiant groups or individuals produced them in the privacy of their homes and specifically their kitchens. Because of this, it is not surprising that some were written by young women, including Banu Amirhajebi, the niece of the renowned Tabrizi clergyman, Sheikh Sagh al-Eslam.[6]

The distribution of night letters dwindled after the Constitutional Revolution of 1906, when rules of censorship and punishment of subversive political individuals were taken less seriously. This period of relative freedom of expression came to a halt, however, when Iran went through a dynastic shift with the beginning of Reza Shah Pahlavi's reign in 1925. In the following years, in response to restrictions on political groups imposed by the Mohammad Reza Shah's government, many Iranians went underground, notably the members of the Iranian pro-communist left, which included many subgroups, such as the *Tudeh* (the masses), that became instrumental in resisting the norms. They did so in their spaces of resistance, safe houses, otherwise known as team houses (*khanehay-e teemi*).

Following the CIA/MI6-sponsored 1953 coup that overthrew the democratically elected Iranian prime minister, Mohammad Mosaddeq, members of the Marxist-Leninist *Tudeh* party began to hold their meetings in rented modern houses and apartments, which also served as firearms storage depots as well as production venues for propaganda posters, journals, books, and pamphlets. Other communist artifacts, such as statues of Lenin and Stalin, could also be found in these dwellings. Covert underground leftist cells and members of other anti-Shah groups continued to use housing as a place of retreat during the 1960s and 1970s. The key to their persistent survival was that the public face they presented was one of typical families in typical homes.

During the even greater repression of leftist and antigovernment groups after the Islamic Revolution of 1979, team houses carried on, albeit with extreme caution. For example, a small group might gather at night under a blanket, or in the dim light of an oil lamp, to read books by Marx, Engels, and Lenin. "The *teemi* houses were everywhere," one former member of the leftist faction Fedai Guerrillas (*Chirik-e fadai-e khalgh*) recalls four decades after the revolution. "We needed to look as normal as possible, so party members joined us in the dark hours of the night . . . [in the] part of the home that was cleverly disguised. Two refrigerator doors were placed in front of low bookshelves that held books by Marx and Lenin, all in the kitchen. We sincerely believed that these books and documents could help us establish a new government."[7] These groups continued to use private homes as places of retreat. In his memoir, historian Behrooz Ghamari-Tabrizi—formerly a member of a small leftist group Fighters (*Razmandegan*), who was arrested in 1982 and served time as a political prisoner—reflects on how the *teemi* house, which he calls a "safe house," lost its identity as a normal family domicile and became unsafe:

> The safe houses were often mistaken for houses of debauchery. Migrant laborers were the only transient residents of Tehran's working-class neighborhoods. We raised suspicions because none of us resembled migrant workers. To make matters worse, in some cases, young women comrades frequented these houses, which added to the neighbors' suspicions. In their minds, how could women visiting young men in the middle of the night not be prostitutes? The dignity of the neighborhood was at stake. It had to be defended against the wickedness of youthful sinners. . . . I dreaded [the] meetings [that took place inside these homes].[8]

After the mid-1980s, fearful of being arrested and executed by the Revolutionary Guards, leftists and antirevolutionaries abandoned team houses and sought refuge in the homes of their relatives—especially the elderly, who drew less attention from the authorities. Sometimes a whole neighborhood collaborated to ensure that the leftist individuals and their belongings remained hidden. One anonymous former member of the Laborer's Path (*Rah-e kargar*) said that their leftist books and documents were hidden in the patio (*passio*) of his elderly mother's house. "The patio was full of flower boxes," he said. "It could not and did not provoke suspicion, even when a few members of the Revolutionary Guards stopped by to investigate my whereabouts. . . . Eventually I was arrested and served five years, but the books and documents remained intact."[9]

Indeed, the books and materials of the Left continued to circulate among the friends and extended family members of those who had been imprisoned, executed, or had fled the country. Nikolai Ostrovsky's *How the Steel Was Tempered* (1936) (*Chegooneh foolad abdideh shod*), a Soviet socialist realist propaganda novel, was among the many such books that I inherited from my uncle who abandoned a team house and fled Iran in disguise by crossing the Persian Gulf at night in a flimsy fishing boat. Ostrovsky's tale of struggle and sacrifice captivated my teenage imagination, inspiring me to copy the book's few drawings of the protagonist who joined the Red Army.

Later, I produced a few large-scale versions of these drawings and asked my parents to frame and place them on our living room walls. Having just watched the news of the breakup of Yugoslavia, which followed shortly after the fall of the Berlin Wall, my parents were less convinced of the imminent Soviet revolution. But they put up the drawings just the same. My story is one among many. In their homes, many artists of a generation who grew up after the revolution were exposed to such leftist materials, inherited from activist relatives. For instance, the painter Mehdi Farhadian (b. 1979) recalls his obsession with the illustrated books for Soviet children that had been purchased by his once-leftist father. Images by the prominent Soviet illustrator Alexei Fedorovich Pakhomov—who specialized in children's books—captured his imagination early on. Time and again, Farhadian faithfully copied Pakhomov's images, a practice that, by his own account, later influenced his visual idiom (see chapter 4).[10]

Another sign of the longevity of these kinds of political spaces in the art world is a site-specific project in a team house years after it was abandoned. In conjunction with a Tehran-based graffiti artist who goes by the pseudonym Black Hand, another anonymous graffiti artist, Ghalamdar, who now lives in England and goes by his own name, Parham Salimy or Parham Ghalamdar (b. 1994), showcased his calligraphic work in an historic house that was formerly registered as a cultural heritage site but later removed from the municipality's list. The owner of the house had scheduled its demolition but not before opening the venue to several Iranian street artists to display their work.[11] Presenting their works in dilapidated homes activated these sites for viewers. Between 2006 and 2014, Ghalamdar continued to appropriate abandoned homes in which to exhibit his art.

Perhaps the most intriguing and politically charged dilapidated structure that Ghalamdar used for creating his art was a *teemi* house that had been used by members of the Left during and in the aftermath of the Islamic Revolution of 1979.[12] By itself the *teemi* house, one of the most covert political spaces in Iran, does not elicit what French intellectual historian Pierre Nora has called "the will to remember." That is, without a deliberate act of remembrance, this historic politicized space remains little more than a passive component of the city. Nora suggests that without the *will* to remember, the place of memory "becomes indistinguishable from the place of history."[13] Ghalamdar hinted not only at remembering but also at forgetting.[14] By inscribing *siahmashgh* (a form of calligraphic practice consisting of overlapping diagonal words and letters used in combinations facing upward and downward, all devoid of meaning), he expressed his reaction to the building in what he called "anti-narrative" (*zedd-e ghesseh pardazi*).[15]

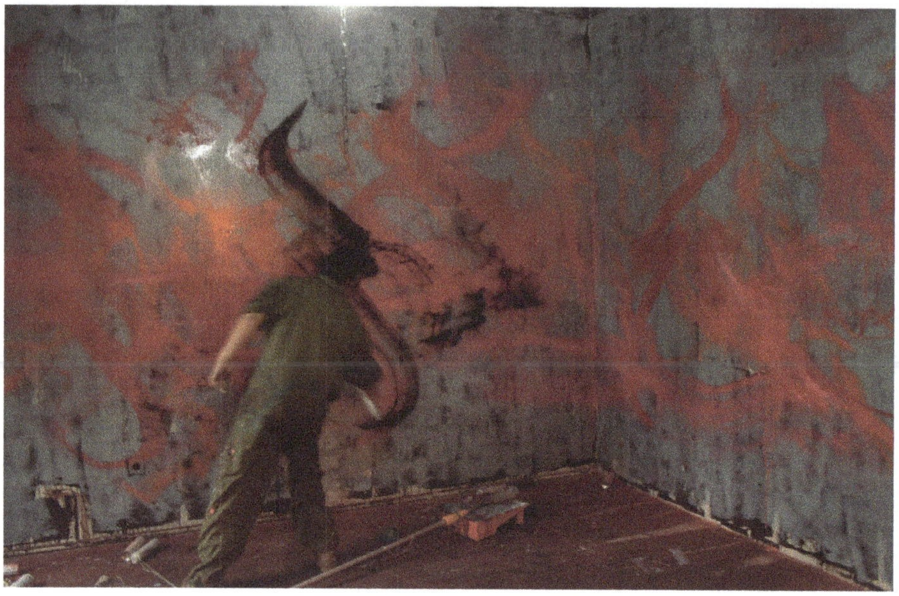

FIGURE 1.1A Parham Ghalamdar at work on a mural art project in an abandoned "safe home." 2012. Tehran. Courtesy of Parham Ghalamdar.

By his own account, Ghalamdar activated a traumatic moment in Iran's modern history, simultaneously implying how such moments had been obscured by authoritative mega-narratives. His performance was a way for him to "unlearn" the censored history of modern Iran told through school textbooks. As such, the artist's emotional views about censorship and suppression merged with the materiality of the walls within which political activists of the past had lived and breathed. Here the past is recovered from the perspective of the present. Past emotions of fear, seclusion, and hope worked to bind the building with the artist's body.[16] Embodying the past allowed Ghalamdar to participate in a process of remembering, identification, forgetting, and healing (figs. 1.1a/b).

Despite its significant site-specificity and aesthetic merits, Ghalamdar's *teemi* house project was conceived only for himself and a few of his graffiti artist friends. This was art as a liberating source in its utmost anti-institutionalized form.[17] Indeed, with its covert subversiveness and anti-institutional aura, the *teemi* house was an apt foray into the concealed art spaces of postrevolutionary Iran.

Two Kinds of Concealed Spaces

On February 22, 1979, Iran changed from a constitutional monarchy to a theocratic republic based on the *Sharia* or Islamic law. The previous regime, led by Mohammad Reza Shah Pahlavi, had used Iran's vast oil revenues to modernize the country by introducing Western principles, such as women's suffrage, and Western-style entertainment and cultural institutions. However, while such freedoms were generally granted to the Iranian people, force was used to silence dissident factions, such as anti-Western religious groups and leftist parties. These pressures applied by the Shah's regime created a divide in society and eventually led to the Islamic Revolution of 1979. At first, the new regime promised to rescind repressions of the past and to allow freedom of the press and the media, but shortly after the revolution, measures comparable to those imposed by the Shah were put in place to oppress unwanted voices. Unique to the newly established system of governance, which had constitutionally enshrined the nation's right to a democratically elected president and parliament, was the institution of the supreme leader (*velayat-e faqih*), who became responsible for establishing the boundaries of morality. The regime began to forbid ideas that were

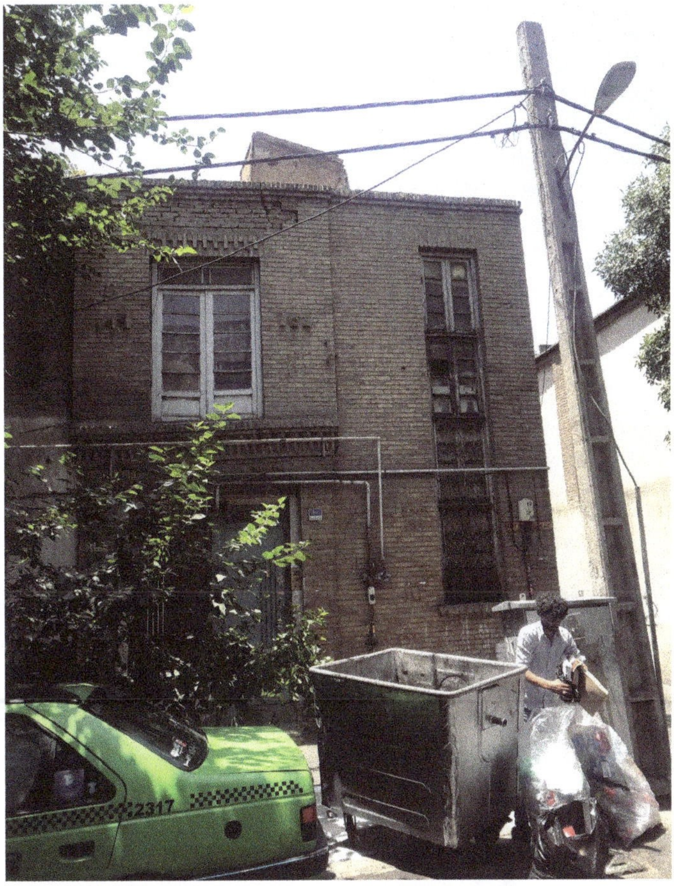

FIGURE 1.1B External view of the abandoned "safe home" in which Parham Ghalamdar and graffiti artist Blind executed their art projects. 2012. Tehran. Photograph by the graffiti artist Blind. Courtesy of Parham Ghalamdar.

"contrary to Islamic principles, or . . . detrimental to public rights."[18] In addition, anyone expressing condemnation of the supreme leader or advancing the views of dissidents would be considered guilty of a criminal offense.[19]

Before the rules and regulations regarding cultural and artistic activities were imposed, the fundamentalist Hezbollahs (the party of God) essentially functioned like a kind of police force, arresting and even surreptitiously executing opponents of the regime. Later, the same militants would form the *komiteh* (the Revolutionary Committee) and other Islamist groups.[20] On June 4, 1980, the newly established High Council of the Cultural Revolution (*Showra-ye ali-e enghelab-e farhangi*) ordered the closure of the universities, an edict that remained in place until 1983.

During this period, the task of defining authentic Islamic methodology in the humanities and the social sciences was assigned to the Center for Cooperation of Seminaries and Universities (*Daftar-e hamkari-ye howzeh va daneshgah*), supervised by Muhammad Taqi Mesbah Yazdi (1934–2020), a teacher at a seminary in the religious city of Qom. Working together, seminaries (*howzeh*) and universities integrated the religious and the university educational systems, dispensing with all unwanted and "un-Islamic" subjects and professors.[21] These developments were profoundly detrimental to Iran's culture and the arts. The goal was no less than to "Islamicize the universities," as Khomeini declared in a speech given to a group of students from universities in Tehran on April 26, 1980.[22]

During the Iranian Cultural Revolution, which extended beyond the closure of universities and is commonly believed to have lasted up to seven years (1980–87), artists and architects who had benefitted from the support of the Shah's regime and were sponsored explicitly through or with contributions from the Empress Farah's art and design initiatives went into exile. Prime examples of those who fled Iran during the revolution include Kamran Diba, the architect of many prominent buildings, such as the TMoCA, and political painter Nicky Nodjumi (b. 1942).[23] Some departed later, but their art was destroyed or confiscated by the regime. For instance, authorities raided the studio of Jaleh Pourhang-Ramezani (b. 1941), known for incorporating nude female bodies in her work, destroying close to a hundred of her works.[24] Meanwhile, many Iranian monuments were smashed, condemned as relics of "the age of idolatry."[25]

Shortly after the end of the closure of universities, in August 1984, the Supreme Council of the Cultural Revolution became the MCIG. The following

September, Tehran University's Department of Fine Arts began its work in a transformed environment. All "inappropriate" (i.e., nude or unveiled) figurative sculptures and paintings were covered. Several faculty members, including the prominent graphic designer and conceptual artist Morteza Momayez (1935–2005), were laid off (*bazkhareed*).[26] The regime's informants closely watched the activities of those who managed to maintain their positions.[27] Most forms of music, dancing, and sculpture were banned, not only from university curricula but also in all other venues, as they were deemed to be *taghooti*—pro-Shah, anti-Islamic.[28] Thousands of books were removed from libraries and university curricula, many due to representations of unveiled women or naked men. Those books that remained in the stacks were heavily censored, and art periodicals were among the three thousand publications from the previous regime that went out of print.[29]

Performance art and theater also became "socially, religiously and, above all, politically suspect."[30] In theater, women were no longer permitted to dance or sing solo on stage; any body movement that would provoke sexual thoughts was forbidden. Men and women were not allowed to touch on stage and scripts had to be submitted to a theater commission, which later grew into a branch of the MCIG[31] with a number of executive subdivisions, including the Department of Art Affairs (*Mo'avenat-e omoor-e honari*), the Performance Supervision Committee (*Komite-ye nezarat bar namayesh*), and, not least, the security department, or *herasat*, charged with observing "moral" behavior in art spaces.[32]

. . .

It was not only the books and periodicals that were subject to monitoring and censorship. Public spaces were also modified, and appropriated to accommodate the new regime's moral codes. As Iranian society became more gender-segregated, physical spaces were increasingly surveilled, not so much by CCTV as by the watchful "eyes" of God and the Islamic Revolutionary Guards. Only a few months after the revolution, mixed-gender swimming was banned on most accessible beaches along the Caspian coast, and later the shore and a portion of the sea were divided by tall, lengthy drapes. To contemporary Western eyes, this might have looked like an installation by Christo and Jeanne-Claude, but it was nothing short of an ideological intervention in nature.

In the Islamic Republic, disguise became a common characteristic of spatial practices. While revolutionaries had relied on it when protesting against un-Islamic ideas and mixed-gender spaces during the Shah's administration, antirevolutionaries and many laypeople embraced the secretive and the hidden to lead their lives as they wanted rather than following the ideals of the revolutionaries. Thus, two kinds of "concealed spaces" emerged: the conservative pro–Islamic Republic and the dissident, countering Islamic revolutionary precepts. A single story behind the May 1988 magazine cover of the popular women's publication *Zan-e rooz* (Women of Today) reveals the two kinds of concealed spaces that animated the lives of Iranian artists, particularly throughout the 1980s. When Farah Ossouli (b. 1953) was approached three months before the end of the Iran-Iraq war by the editors of *Zan-e rooz* to pose for the cover of the magazine, she was a young artist and mother and the partner of the prominent Iranian filmmaker Khosrow Sinai (1941–2020). As Ossouli recalls more than three decades later, the magazine decided to include a woman artist to encourage other Iranian women to think about innovative ways to entertain themselves at home.[33]

In those difficult months of the end of the war, Ossouli, who is otherwise known for her innovative interpretations of classical Persian miniature paintings, immersed herself in creating portraits of women from her immediate and extended family. Many of these realistic portraits and figurative oil paintings involved nudity and were meant for Ossouli's "own personal pleasure in artistic development, and not the least bit, for public viewing."[34] When the *Zan-e rooz* photographer entered Ossouli's home studio for the shoot, she was surprised by what she saw. The mounted large nude figure in progress portrayed a pregnant relative, trapped in an abusive marriage. Ossouli recalls that "the protagonist's life was a metaphor for that rigid dark space (*fazay-e dogm-e siah*) we were all trapped in."[35] Hence, a blocked window animated the backdrop of the protagonist. While the blocked window was a safe subject for the cover of the magazine, the nude figure was not. So, the photographer asked Ossouli to block the figure with her veiled body and did her best to capture the artist in profile, with not much of her face showing, as frontal portraits of women were strictly forbidden in the Iranian press. The subject of the painting alludes to people trapped in concealed private interiors, while the photograph of the painter at work implies the many layers of mandatory concealment in the public sphere. That the photograph was taken in a home studio is obviously of no significance here, because the image emerged in the public sphere. Above all, this cover image would appear as a silent image, as the editors of *Zan-e rooz* made the decision not to include the story of Ossouli's life and art.

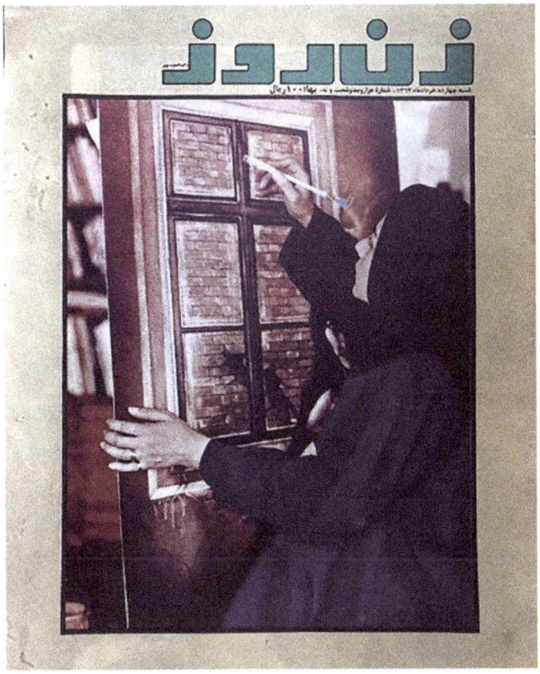

FIGURE 1.2.A Farah Ossouli at work, shown on the cover of *Zan-e rooz Magazine*. 1988. Tehran. Courtesy of Farah Ossouli.

On the face of it, Ossouli's voice is silenced and her ostensible compliance with the rules and regulations of the regime is honored. The editors followed the Islamic Republic's ethos by using images of women both to forge a new national identity and to emphasize women's proper place in society. The gloomy painting on which the artist had been working is perhaps a reminder of women's life behind the walls. The cover of the spring issue of *Zan-e rooz* was a microcosm of what transpired within professional art venues. As Ossouli herself remarks, "It was also telling of the future to come (*pishgooiy-e ayandeh*)," as the rules and regulations regarding women's choice of appearance in public spaces remained unchanged and the featured model lived on to face challenges in raising her child (figs. 1.2a/b).[36]

Like Ossouli's invisible nude and mostly hidden face, many Iranian art spaces dropped from public view. Iranian artists and activist intellectuals sought channels to disseminate ideas in the back alleyways of the marketplace of ideas, outside the approved territories defined by the government and the religious authorities. Throughout the 1980s, when art in public was heavily monitored, private life functioned for many Iranians as a valued space of alternative identity formation and latent dissent. Art exhibitions

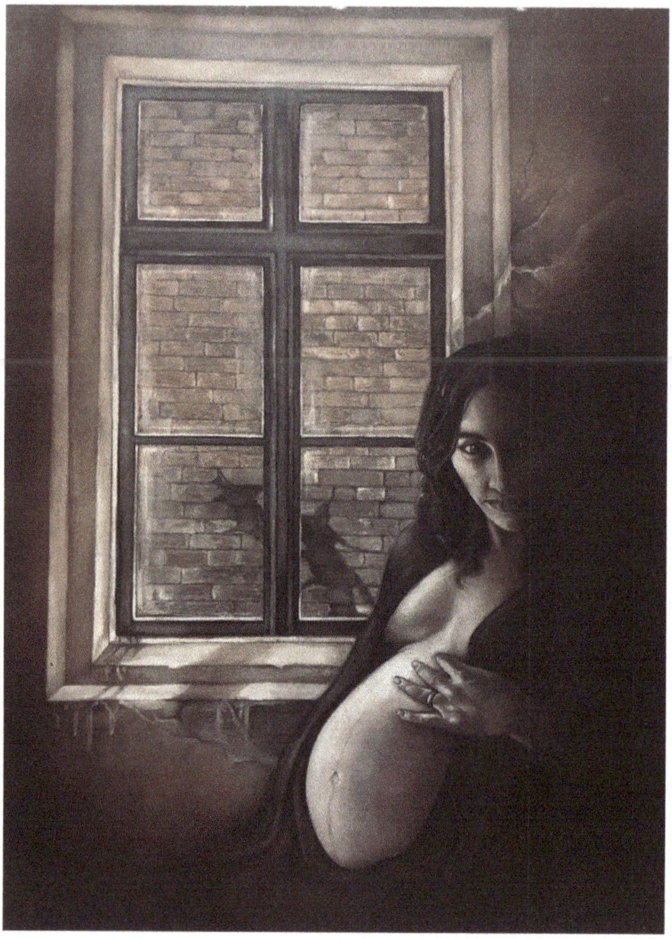

FIGURE 1.2B Original painting by Farah Ossouli, which was censored in *Zan-e rooz Magazine* cover photo. 1988. Tehran. Courtesy of Farah Ossouli.

took place inside homes or safe zones, such as public and private buildings that belonged to non-Muslim minorities, who were allowed more openness.

Minority Spaces as Safe Zones

Throughout history, ethnic minorities have filled significant gaps in Iranian society and in the economy and have assimilated into local and regional cultural and social contexts. However, while they enjoyed an exceptional period of high integration during the reign of the Pahlavis, after the Islamic Revolution, members of the Bahá'í faith were consistently subjected to discrimination and Jews were occasionally interrogated on account of suspected ties with Israel. On the other hand, Zoroastrians, Armenians, Mandaeans, Assyrians, and foreign communities associated with embassies and other diplomatic agencies were tolerated and could pursue their own cultural, art, and entertainment activities not only in their homes but in their own cultural and religious institutions.

Historically, minorities were known to have accommodated diverse people at times when Muslims did not show tolerance.[37] In the postrevolutionary atmosphere too, these communities shared their spaces with fellow Muslims. If not Iranian-born, non-Muslim groups were usually of Christian-European origin and had chosen to make Iran their home because they had diplomatic positions in embassies and other institutions with foreign ties. The homes and institutions of this minority population became places where Muslim Iranians showcased their art.

In 1985, Ossouli and her filmmaker partner, Khosrow Sinai, curated the first mixed-gender, Western-style art exhibition inside the home of the cultural attaché of the West German embassy. The exhibit included high-profile artists, actors, and writers, including the actress Susan Taslimi (b. 1950) and the writer Mahmoud Dowlatabadi (b. 1940). Ossouli recalls that the exhibition's opening and reception took place in a "Western style, complete with drinks and hors d'oeuvres and, of course, no obligation for women to wear the *hijab*."[38]

This was a unique opportunity, she said, "at the time when we had no idea what other artists were doing, as there were no opportunities for the public display of art unless it was related to revolutionary and war themes."[39] In an atmosphere in which even "using bright colors in a painting or a poster was deemed too Western and thus could very well be rejected in other public venues, this was truly a great opportunity to finally get to know what other professional artists in the field were up to."[40] These venues did not just accommodate socializing; they also created a market for the art, so that the artistic productions of high-profile and well-connected Iranian artists could be sold to collectors, many of whom were cultural attachés of European embassies (figs. 1.3a/b).

Subsequently, a church on Yakhchal Street—used mostly by German Protestants and one of approximately thirty churches of four different Christian denominations in Tehran—allowed Ossouli and Gizella Varga-Sinai (b. 1944), the Hungarian wife of filmmaker Khosrow Sinai, to convert one of the church's side rooms into a gallery space (fig. 1.4).[41] Ossouli and Varga-Sinai emptied the space, whitewashed the walls, and added professional lighting prior to their group exhibition, which also included works by Ossouli's painter sister, Shahrazad, and a West German artist affiliated with the embassy. As Ossouli recalled, the pastor was an art enthusiast and

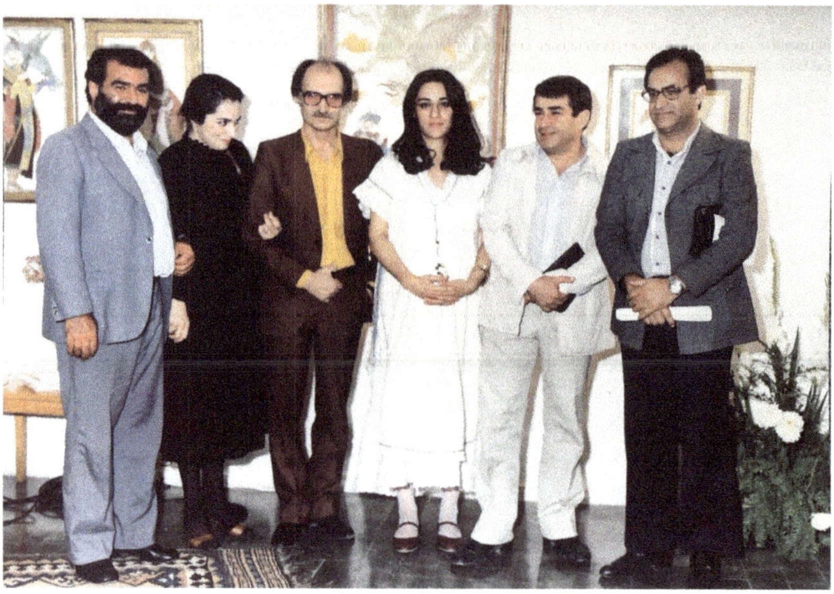

FIGURE 1.3A Artist Farah Ossouli (in white dress), shown with notable guests at her solo exhibition inside the home of the attaché of the West German Embassy. 1985. Tehran. Courtesy of Farah Ossouli.

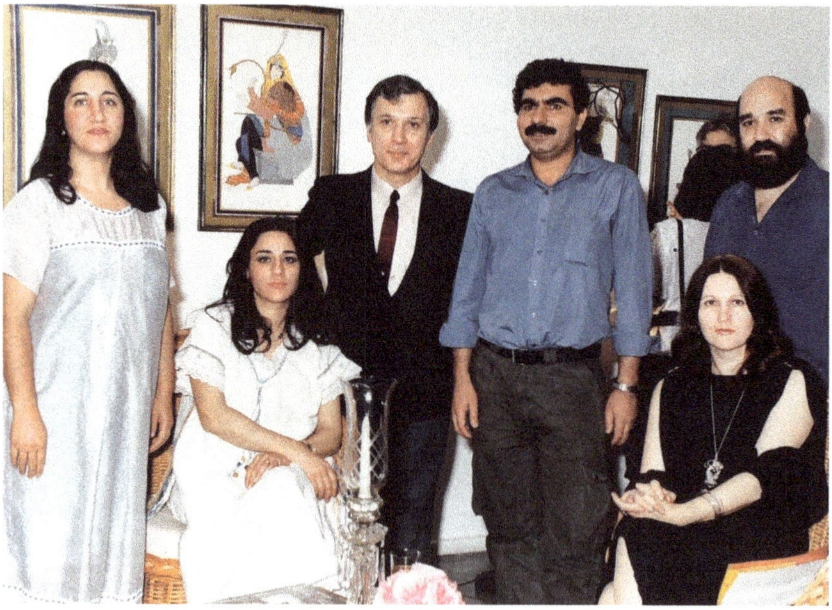

FIGURE 1.3B Artist Farah Ossouli (in white dress), shown with notable guests at her solo exhibition inside the home of the attaché of the West German Embassy. 1985. Tehran. Courtesy of Farah Ossouli.

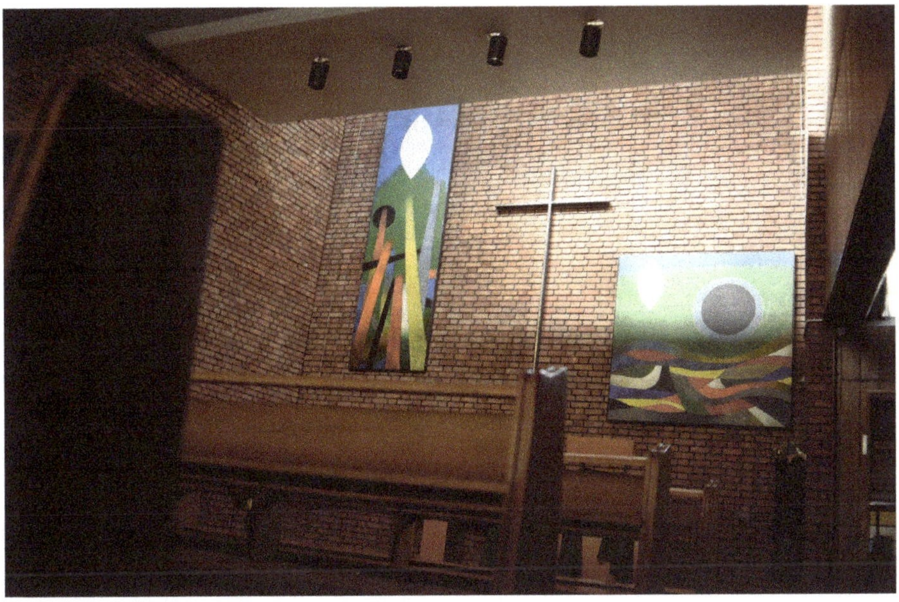

FIGURE 1.4 Community room at the Protestant German church used as an exhibition venue by Farah Ossouli and Gizella Varga-Sinai in the early 1990s. Tehran. Photograph by Mojtaba Fallahi.

even purchased several works by her and others.[42] The church on Yakhchal continued to serve Tehran artists in subsequent years. Yahya Alkhansa (born in 1981 to an Iranian mother and a Lebanese father), who later became the drummer for the music band 127, held his first rock concert inside this church, "thanks to the generosity and open-mindedness of the pastor and staff."[43]

Alkhansa recalled several other minority spaces that accommodated his performances. For example, one concert in 1998 took place on the second floor of the Society for Jewish Students (*Anjoman-e daneshjooyan-e yahoodi*) in the Yousefabad neighborhood, which had formerly been populated by a relatively large Jewish community.[44] Shahram Sharbaf (b. 1974), the lead singer and guitarist of O-Hum, attested to the role of the Armenian community in keeping music alive in the postrevolutionary period. "Without the Armenian community, music would have died," he recalled more than two decades after forming O-Hum in 1996.[45] He also pointed to the significance of music stores, all with Armenian names, in a neighborhood in central Tehran occupied by this minority community: "Rafik in Jomhoori Avenue was the only guitar and keyboard retailer in Tehran; the nearby Razmik was the only professional guitar repairer; Armik in Karimkhan Avenue had one of the rare private professional recording studios in the country and everyone

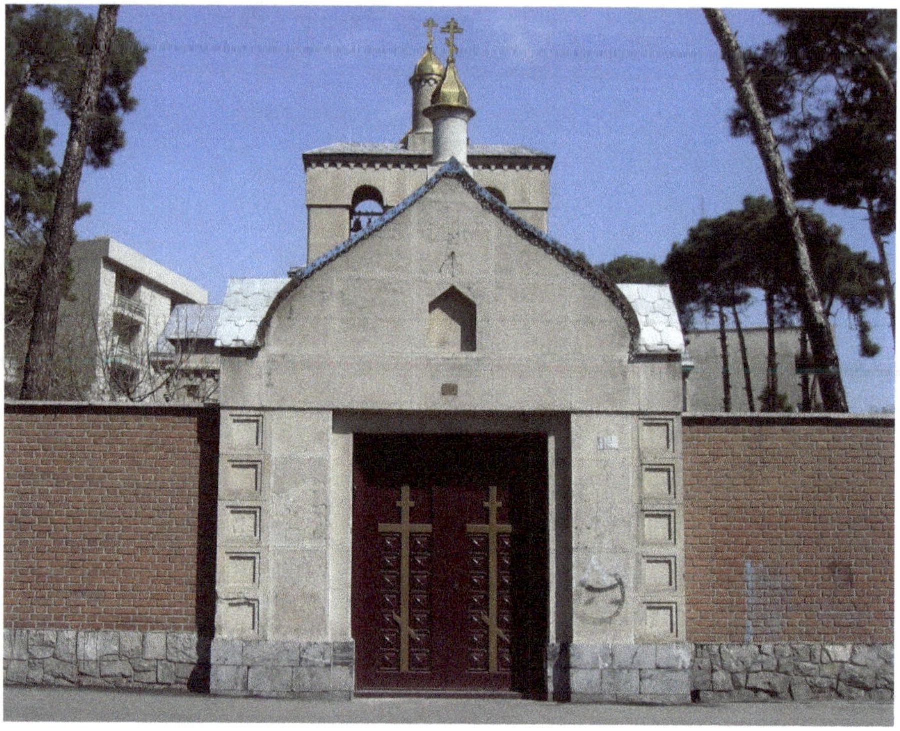

FIGURE 1.5A St. Nicholas Russian Orthodox Church. 2007. Tehran. Photograph by the author.

knew where to go if they needed guitar strings: Vartan."[46] "Often performed under the radar," what the Christian community did for Muslim-born musicians "was not free of risk."[47] O-Hum and other underground bands also performed in the community hall adjacent to the sanctuary of St. Nicholas Russian Orthodox Church. Designed in 1944 by Russian émigré architect Nikolai Markov, the church complex had been created for the Russian immigrants who came to Tehran after the Bolshevik Revolution and subsequently during World War II (fig. 1.5a) and was located within the precincts of the former American embassy (now a museum).

Arash Sobhani (b. 1971), an architect by training and the lead singer of Kiosk, described the band's experience within the walls of St. Nicholas:

> This church was probably our first performance venue beyond the home basements. Due to its location inside the peripheries of the big garden that surrounds the former American Embassy in Tehran, the church was perfectly suited to loud music rehearsals. Most importantly, the priest was a generous

man and a music lover who welcomed us to perform in his sacred space when there were no services or other religious functions.[48]

St. Nicholas's community hall also hosted O-Hum's first concert. In 2001, O-Hum accepted an invitation to participate in a fundraising campaign for repairing the church. Neither the church nor the band secured permission from the MCIG for the performance. The invitees were supposed to be members of the European embassies. However, the event's publicity mostly attracted the attention of Armenian youth. Planned for an audience of 150, the event instead drew more than three hundred Armenian kids, who came to dance to the music (fig. 1.5b). After a few hours, with the concert still going strong, the morality police arrived and shut it down. As punishment, the MCIG banned the group from recording or performing, and the band broke up, some members leaving the country. Sharbaf eventually regained permission to perform a decade later, but was barred from using the O-Hum name when producing music.

For rehearsals and recordings musicians used residential spaces. Kiosk rented a small place in the basement of a house in a predominantly Armenian neighborhood on Sohrevardi Street in central Tehran, where many Armenians were in the music industry and owned and managed Western music

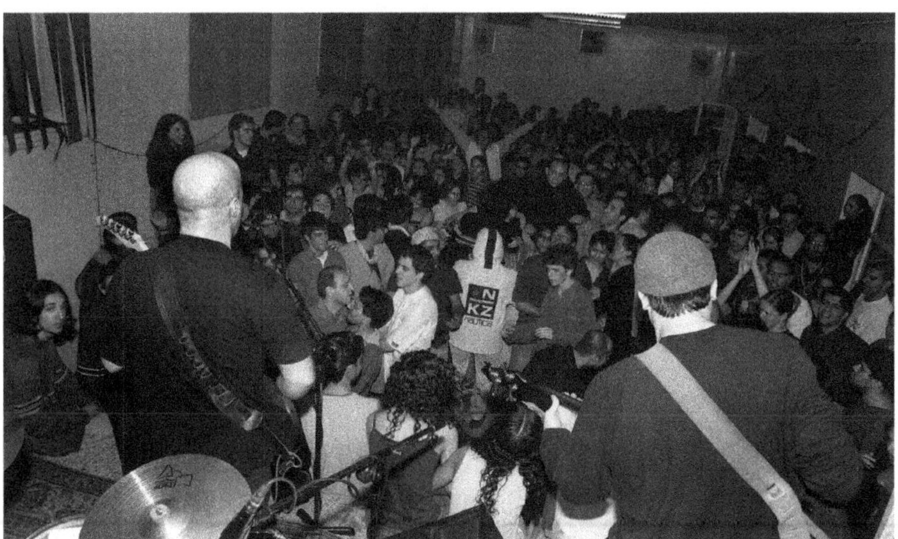

FIGURE 1.5B O-Hum rock band performing to a mixed-gender Armenian audience at the St. Nicholas Russian Orthodox Church. 2001. Tehran. Photograph by Ali Shahbazyar.

instrument and music score shops.[49] The basement was not soundproof, so Kiosk covered the walls with hundreds of egg cartons and windows with foam. "We needed a soundproof space to record. However, it was also necessary for our safety. Our music was loud, and we did not want the neighbors to report us to the police," said Kiosk's lead singer, Sobhani.[50] Over time, the making of such spaces became a business model and musicians could rent a makeshift studio and pay hourly for recording. "Often in the basements of residential units, these spaces were very hot and uncomfortable," O-Hum's Sharbaf recalled.[51] He also noted that these makeshift studios were often very short-lived. "It did not take too long for the studio owner to be reported to the morality police and for the business to be confiscated."[52]

Residential spaces played an important role in the survival of art and music among the minorities themselves, especially the Bahá'í, who were not allowed to attend college and thus relied on being educated at home. Classical guitar musician Saba Khozoie (b. 1966), niece of renowned Iranian filmmaker Bahram Beyzai (b. 1938) and composer of a few of his iconic film scores, including *Sag koshi* (*Killing Mad Dogs*, 2001), was among the first group of professors who taught music to Bahá'í learners in the underground Bahá'í Institute for Higher Education (BIHE).[53]

All classes took place informally and in professors' homes. This phenomenon of using homes as a venue to teach music was not just limited to the Bahá'í institute; indeed, as Khozoie noted, a vast hidden network of friends and colleagues kept certain kinds of taboo music alive in Tehran. Specifically, the guitar (both classical and electric) was banned by the regime. "If the morality police found you on the street walking with a guitar, they would smash it and probably arrest you too," recalled Khozoie of the early years of her career in 1980s Tehran. "My father had to accompany me everywhere when there was a private performance. There was absolutely no room to carry the guitar carelessly on the streets of Tehran. You had to carry it in a car and hide it in a box or wrap it in a blanket, so it would not attract attention."[54] Similarly, Sharbaf of O-Hum recalled an intense encounter with the morality police on the street, which led to the smashing of his band's guitars. "In the early 1990s it was very hard to find guitars in the black market of Tehran and this incident devastated us."[55] Thus all guitar classes, rehearsals, and performances were relegated to private homes. Indeed, it was not just the musicians or the Bahá'ís who had to confine their music performances to their homes. Many other artists appropriated residential spaces.

Art at Home

In 2000, the alternative rock band 127 rehearsed in an abandoned greenhouse near the tarmac of Mehrabad Airport, adjacent to Ekbatan, a chain of Brutalist-style apartment blocks on the outskirts of western Tehran. Designed under the Shah by a team of Iranian and South Korean architects, the Ekbatan complex consists of a double row of apartment buildings that are U-shaped in plan and step down toward a central spine. The block managers often control everything, including access to the roofs or other spaces that are hidden from plain sight.

Himself a resident of block no. 19, the one nearest the airport runway, 127 founder Yahya Alkhansa received permission from the managers to build double-brick walls around a greenhouse adjacent to the block with soundproof insulation sandwiched in between.[56] There the amplified rock music could be muffled by the drone of aircraft taking off.[57] Alkhansa, together with the other five members of 127, practiced there in the early evenings, after their day jobs and when the heat died down.[58] Although the group only allowed trusted audiences within the greenhouse, it soon attracted international media coverage, including articles in the press and documentaries in Sweden and the UK. This made it, in the eyes of the authorities, a center of corruption (*fesad*). Before long, according to Alkhansa, the paramilitary volunteer militia (*basijis*) destroyed the setup and confiscated all the musical equipment.[59] The greenhouse was just one among many other spaces that occupied different parts of residential areas.[60] For example, the group Barobax practiced in a soundproof space on top of a residential building in southern Tehran. The band Yellow Dogs (featured in Bahman Ghobadi's 2009 drama *No One Knows about Persian Cats / Kasi az gorbehay-e Irani khabar nadareh*) practiced in an unused pool in the basement of a multistory apartment.[61]

In smaller and especially more religious cities, ordinary people also confronted alternative artists. Abdi Behravanfar (b. 1975), a leading member of the underground music group in Mashhad, the Khorasan Blues, from which emerged the internationally known Mohsen Namjoo (b. 1976), recalled how his house was his "domain and turf," providing him and his fellow band members with a feeling of liberation "from all the difficulties and restrictions around [them]."[62] He further elaborated, "Sometimes we would not eat for two days . . . we would just jam and forget our hungry stomachs. . . . [It] was a way of distancing ourselves from the wretched surroundings in which we were struggling."[63]

On many occasions, Behravanfar was harassed by the authorities, who were presumably alerted by conservative neighbors: "The police, under the impression that we had established a subversive political cell, raided us. It took a while until I finally found a way to avoid the attention of the police."[64] In the following years, Behravanfar went after antagonistic neighbors "with a shovel and pickax" to force them to leave him alone. Many considered him to be "psychotic for holding on to that house," an accusation that later became the title of a piece of music Behravanfar coauthored with Namjoo, "Chronic Psychosis."[65]

. . .

In *Within Walls: Private Life in the German Democratic Republic* (2010), historian Paul Betts writes that amidst the scrutiny of social interactions, private life in the GDR operated for many citizens as a valued sphere of individuality, alternative identity formation, and latent dissent. Iranian artists of the 1980s and their counterparts in the Cold War Soviet Union and the Eastern Bloc faced both governmental censorship and a dearth of commercial galleries. More importantly, the living conditions of Iranians and those of socialist countries were in many ways analogous. Speaking of artists behind the Iron Curtain, Moscow-based art historian Ekaterina Degot writes:

> Living under no pressure in terms of housing (modest housing was provided by the state), career (theirs was nonexistent), and money (almost nonexistent), they had ample time to hang out indoors and outdoors (within Soviet borders, of course) in a kind of an endless and slightly Surrealist 'involuntary performance.' . . . the artists did not need to produce any work since they were constantly meeting and exchanging ideas.[66]

Because Iranians were experiencing a similar political atmosphere and socioeconomic conditions, it is not surprising that in the 1980s many private homes also became ideal platforms for Iranian artists, theater experts, and musicians. The government of the Islamic Republic extended welfare plans by, for example, distributing essential supplies through coupon rations and vouchers for buying consumer goods and producer goods at cooperative stores. As a result, creative agents and artists could spend more time developing ideas that benefitted their intellectual growth than on earning a living.

In the early 1980s, many professional art experts who were laid off from their university and museum posts held private art classes in their homes or rented apartments and taught subjects that could not be taught in schools and universities. The most popular of these educators was Aydin Aghdashloo (b. 1940), who saw it as his duty to "lift the veil (*bardashtan-e hijab*) from the knowledge of art and art history in those restrictive years."[67] There were also more informal gatherings for discussions about art. Having just graduated from Tehran's art high school (*honarestan*), at the time of the Cultural Revolution and consequent closure of the universities from 1981 to 1984, Rozita Sharafjahan (b. 1962) and her peers held small gatherings (*mahafel-e koochak*) inside an abandoned basement that had once been the site of a tailoring workshop belonging to Sharafjahan's parents. The space allowed them to continue their art practices, watch masterpieces of world cinema, and study art history.[68]

In the following years, when opportunities arose to show art in public, many artists still chose private homes, sometimes out of necessity. Even certain individuals affiliated with official institutions (yet less radicalized by the regime) knew that the privacy of their homes was the only place to show and sell their "unwanted" work. Painter Ghasem Hajizadeh (b. 1947) recalled an incident in the 1980s when his request to do a solo show at the Seyhoun Gallery—one of the very few privately run galleries in Tehran—was rejected by the MCIG. A resident of France who was known for his prerevolutionary homoerotic paintings, Hajizadeh was labeled by the ministry as "forbidden to display" (*mamnoo' al namayesh*): "When the show at [the] Seyhoun Gallery was cancelled, the director of the museum [the TMoCA] asked me to instead show my works in my apartment in Tehran. He also asked me not to make any publicity about it and only invite people by telephone."[69] Fereydoun Ave recalled how artists in the 1980s relied on rumor, gossip, and hearsay to get a sense of their status in the eyes of the regime. He believed that such unpredictable sources played an important role in pushing artists into their homes, sometimes for no more reason than that they were "delusional."[70] Indeed, "when private talk goes public, the results can be history making."[71] At the instigation of prominent directors like Mahmood Karimi-Hakak, theatrical rehearsals also took place in private homes. Karimi-Hakkak chose to rehearse and perform in his elderly mother's living room in Tehran, due to rumors, censorship, interrogation, and a host of other restrictions.[72] In theater a whole genre emerged that later came to be known as House Theater (*te'atr-e khaneh*) or Apartment Theater (*te'atr-e apartemani*).

. . .

Yet the very same private domestic spaces associated with unapproved acts gradually became public and authorized. For music it took longer (see the epilogue), and theater became privatized in 2009. The private spaces of the visual arts, however, surfaced into the public domain and secured permission as early as the late 1980s. A series of commercial home galleries with high standards came into being largely thanks to the efforts of women.[73] Translator Lili Golestan (b. 1944), a single mother of three, turned the garage adjacent to her family home first into a bookstore; then in 1987 she secured permission to convert the space into a gallery or *negar khaneh* (house of embellishments, a Persian term used by the MCIG). Subsequently, Golestan Gallery went on to become one of the most important privately run exhibition venues in Tehran.[74] As for the process of gaining permission to turn her garage into an official art space, Golestan recalled: "I went to the MCIG to get permission, and the man in charge asked me, 'Why do you come here every day? Where is your man?' I told him I don't have a man, and I'm pretty sure he felt sorry for me and issued the documents."[75]

Haft Samar Gallery, a basement in a family home, was set up in 1994 (fig. 1.6). The family's eldest daughter, Leyla Samari (b. 1950), previously a professor of tapestry and textile design at the Art University (*Daneshgah-e honar*), turned the basement into a registered gallery after a few private shows she held there in 1993 and 1994. Concerning the shortage of exhibition spaces in Tehran, Samari maintained, "The basement became a venue through which to showcase art by emerging artists who did not have opportunities elsewhere."[76] In 1999, Sharafjahan, along with her husband, Mohsen Nabizadeh (b. 1960), received permission from the MCIG to turn their subterranean family tailor shop into a gallery. The formation of these officially permitted home-based galleries coincided with the era after the Iran-Iraq war when many new cultural facilities were built by the regime, including the Bahman Cultural Center (*Farhang saray-e Bahman*). After a decade of self-imposed economic isolation when Ali Akbar Hashemi Rafsanjani was in office (1989–97), Iran sought technical assistance and credit authorization from the International Monetary Fund and the subsequent structural modifications led to "liberalization" of the economy.[77]

To solve the problem of the nation's "underdevelopment," the new administration aimed to build a state in which a development-oriented Islamic elite would modernize Iran without Westernizing it.[78] After a state visit to

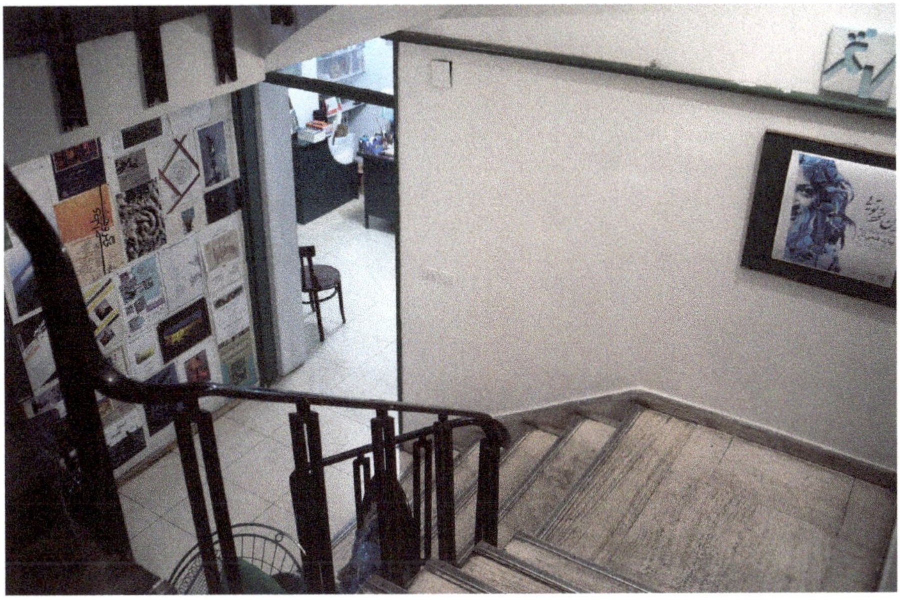

FIGURE 1.6 View into the basement gallery, Haft Samar. 2019. Tehran. Photograph by Mojtaba Fallahi.

Beijing, the government began to import aspects of the Chinese model of economic development. Consequently, some subsidies were cut, and labor laws were weakened to make factory ownership and private investment more profitable. Rules were eased on the importation of global consumer goods, and the use of commercial ads and advertisement billboards appeared to promote these goods.[79] Between 1989 and 2003, annual population growth fell and resources began to be more evenly distributed, benefitting a variety of areas, including art and cultural programs, urban renewal projects, and city park construction.[80] Appropriately, President Rafsanjani's time in office came to be known as the "reconstruction era" (*doran-e sazandegi*). The Tehran municipality collected fees and taxes from developers and investors in exchange for exemption from high-rise construction and zoning laws. This alliance between the municipality and speculators gave the municipality and the mayor unprecedented financial and political autonomy, which has continued to influence the trajectories of Tehran's urban development.[81] The construction tax law targeted those who wanted to build projects of more than two stories, including those from the upper classes who could afford to invest in high-rise construction. High-rises replaced the exquisite one- or two-story family villas built under the Pahlavis, especially in the northern parts of the city, where profit rates were higher and where most of Tehran's middle class wanted to live. And these old buildings, with their lofty rooms on the verge of disappearance, became ideal sites for Iranian alternative art practices of the early 1990s. Reminiscent of what the American artist and curator Jeffrey Lew calls "raw space," these vacated buildings offered opportunities for large-scale installations that would not have been viable in small home-based or commercial galleries.[82]

Creating Art in the "Raw" Spaces of the Reconstruction Era

In 1970, when Lew created 112 Workshop in an unrenovated Manhattan loft, he invited artists like Gordon Matta-Clark who were fascinated by the crude, unfinished, unprocessed, and rough nature of such spaces. Matta-Clark famously dug a hole in the basement floor and planted a cherry tree.[83] Such interest in "raw" spaces and artistic projects that matched the "raw" atmosphere of alternative exhibition spaces of the 1960s and 1970s New York stemmed from a desire to detach the arts from market-oriented institutions. But it was also rooted in an urge to dismantle the restrictive definitions of artmaking, "alluding to a frontier state where boundaries are negotiated and challenged and where space is explored and extended."[84] In Iran, artists wanted to push the boundaries of artmaking, but more importantly, they needed to create art spaces that were not constantly monitored. There was also a surge of nostalgic sentiment for the Pahlavi period with its perceived greater freedoms. To put it differently, Iran's fascination with raw spaces is based on a distinct model, one that relates to space as an emotionally, economically, and politically contested territory.

To clarify this point, let us start by looking at a single photograph. Photographer Gohar Dashti was born shortly after the 1979 Islamic Revolution and spent the first eight years of her life in wartime. She grew up in the border city of Ahvaz in southwestern Iran. With abundant oil resources and in close proximity to Iraq, Ahvaz became a major bombing target. As a child, Dashti endured many nights at the shelters.

After leaving Ahvaz, Dashti's life journey continued in the northwestern city of Mashhad, where she moved with her family and spent most of her teenage years before leaving to attend college in Tehran. The series *Home* is a testament to her brief yet formative time in Mashhad—a city far from war zones, packed with untouched remnants of the past, showcasing several

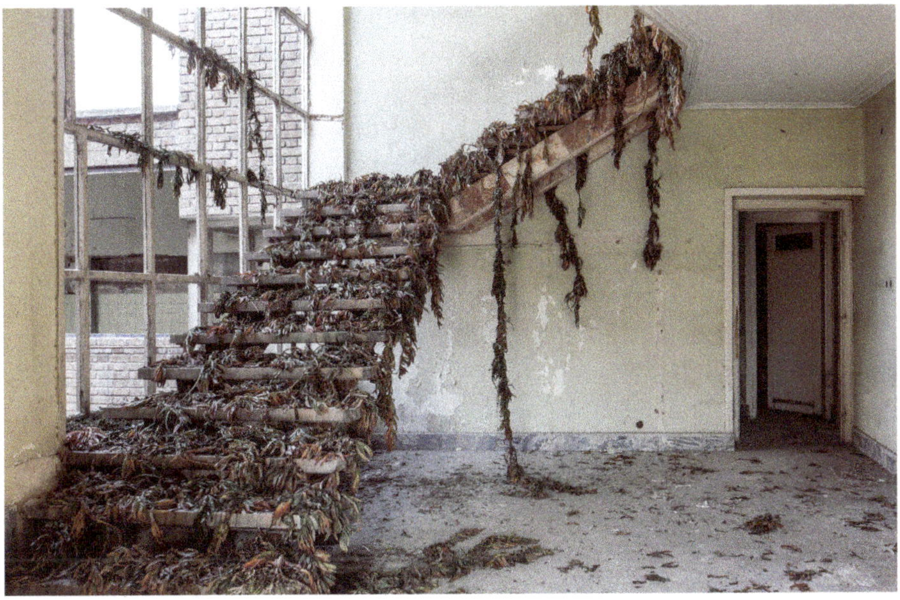

FIGURE 1.7 Gohar Dashti, *Untitled*, photograph from the *Home* series. 2017. Mashhad. Courtesy of Gohar Dashti.

dilapidated middle-class homes built during the era of the Shah (fig. 1.7). Like the era itself, the physical existence of these structures is now disappearing. Nonetheless, the material of Iran's modernism, which reached its peak during the Shah's reign—a period of avant-gardism and prosperity for a middle class that never reached maturity—remained in the collective imagination as the country went through a revolution, a regime change, and a ruthless war that destroyed many residential neighborhoods. But there is more to Dashti's *Home* series than just nostalgia for a long-gone period or a commentary on the war. The series also implies a desire for a room of one's own, alluding to oppression in terms of denied spaces, in Virginia Woolf's sense of the phrase. Since the 1990s, abandoned buildings of the Pahlavi era have become places of refuge for Iran's youth, who cannot freely express themselves in conventional urban spaces.

The history of postrevolutionary installations in abandoned and dilapidated buildings (known as *kolangi* in Iran) goes back to 1992, when a group of young painters took over a five-story residential complex built in the early 1970s on Koohestan Street, near posh Pasdaran Avenue in northern Tehran. The group included Mostafa Dashti (b. 1960), Sassan Nassiri (b. 1960), Farid Jahangir (b. 1957), calligrapher Yousef Rezaie (b. 1951), and the late actor, sculptor, and painter Shahrokh Ghiasi Farahani (1952–1996)—under the direction of coordinator Ali Dashti (1953–1999), who took care of all the logistics. There they produced original work for the three upper floors within the complex.[85] The house belonged to Jahangir's family and had been left vacant, waiting to be renovated into a higher-end residential complex. Having studied with Aydin Aghdashloo, the young group decided to turn their training into an opportunity to make art available to a broader public.

According to Nassiri, painters created a private artists' colony where they could use models, paint at night, and play music, enjoying an atmosphere detached from the rest of the city.[86] Titled *Independent Contemporary Art Workshop* (*Kargah-e azad-e honar-e mo'aser*): *Project 71/92*, the exhibition was conceptual and ephemeral in character. The works were created with the intention of being destroyed, and the group did not expect to make money from the show, resisting suggestions that pieces could be cut from the walls and taken into galleries and museums.[87]

Under the stair alcove and around the walls of the ground floor, Shahrokh Ghiasi created a group of Assyrian figures (*figurha-e asiri*, which in Persian could mean "figures in captivity"; also, *asiri*, in modern Persian literature, often refers to a young woman who is attractive and present but unattainable). Calligrapher Rezaie covered the whole surface of the floor with pseudo-calligraphic writings. Nassiri and Jahangir took over the second floor, where Jahangir painted a long *Last Supper* table that wrapped around the main living room. Some figures faced the room while others were rendered in silhouette with their backs to the viewer. Apparently, these were the friends of the artist who were included in this peculiar rendition of *The Last Supper*. Nassiri in turn placed cracked ceramics and "found" furniture around the kitchen and a few other rooms and encouraged the audience to break them. Having studied art in Madrid (1985–91), Nassiri had a keen interest in Spanish artists and decided to animate the wall with a projection of El Greco's *Burial of Count Orgaz* (1586), itself a reference to death and destruction.[88]

Among all the presentations, probably the most sensual was the work of Dashti, who had immersed himself in making J.M.W. Turner–style abstract paintings that hinted at oil products or vast landscapes tainted by fossil fuels, Dashti decided to turn the fifth floor of the exhibition into a dark room. The walls, animated by Dashti's paintings, were painted black, using powerful pumps and paintguns. To make his criticism of pollution in Tehran even more explicit, he installed a few "found" oil barrels in the middle of the rooms and before the opening asked a few friends to smoke cigarettes inside and had the whole space filled with fumes. The entire space was dark; even the windows were sullied. But a threshold of twenty-by-fifty centimeters on one window with a view toward the city below invited visitors to see Tehran and its polluted skyline.

During its display, the show also included a couple of private events, such as a dance session coordinated by filmmaker Bahman Farman Farma (b. 1942). A female dancer named Jeenous moved to the music of Bijan Bijani (b. 1963) from *Navaie* (a popular production at that time, inspired by spiritual music and the celebration of youth). Like a swirling dervish, the dancer performed on the calligraphically animated floor on the ground level. This performance piece was private and only open to a few "trusted" viewers.[89] The rest of the show was open to the public.

According to a required questionnaire at the door, more than two thousand visitors attended the show. Visitors, including both the general public and high-profile artists and filmmakers such as Lili Golestan and Abbas Kiarostami, were not required to pay an entrance fee, but they were encouraged to buy posters, which is how the group made a modest profit. Iranian film director Rakhshan Bani Etemad (b. 1954) made a short documentary about the event, which unfortunately was not seen by the public until 2019, when art historian Helia Darabi digitized the film and showcased it at the Iranshahr Gallery.[90] The group had not been successful in securing permission from the MCIG, and once the show received the attention of a few foreign journalists, someone from the ministry showed up and questioned the group, summoned and interrogated one of them, and then shut down the event. It was on display for only ten days. To appreciate how out of place these unusual installations might have appeared to the authorities, it is important to note that something as simple as installation art (*honar-e chideman*), as one prominent art history professor revealed to me, was considered Zionist in character (perhaps due to the prominence of installation art found in major Jewish museums around the world).[91]

. . .

In 1995, artist Houman Mortazavi (b. 1964) organized a solo show in a *kolangi* villa in northern Tehran titled *Life Accessories (Abzar-e zendegi)*. Like his companions at Project 92, Mortazavi had spent years in private painting classes with Aghdashloo.[92] Throughout the 1980s, Mortazavi and a few selected students immersed themselves in the world that Aghdashloo presented to them, not only through teaching them how to paint but also via art history lectures and film screenings. "I learned how to watch Federico Fellini films from Aghdashloo, who would play the film for us and then frequently pause to inform us about Fellini's cinematography and all other important cinematic features; as well, my first encounter with nontraditional artforms such as the forerunner of the assemblage technique, Joseph Cornell, was in one of Aghdashloo's art history lectures," Mortazavi recalled.[93]

As a graphic designer for film and theater projects, Mortazavi also was exposed to the unconventional theater practices of Atila Pesyani (b. 1957). "Pesyani used to work in small eccentric spaces; sometimes he would create a labor-intensive performance only to present [it] to less than a dozen audiences. It is astonishing how hard he worked for these small productions, many of which did not get approval from the MCIG to be displayed in more official spaces or to larger audiences," Mortazavi added.[94] Later, Aghdashloo would send Mortazavi to art archives to research materials for a TV series about the history of Iranian painting, *Beh sooy-e simorgh* (*Toward Phoenix*), which was scripted by Aghdashloo and directed by the renowned art documentary filmmaker Hamid Soheili (1948–2019) and broadcast for the first time in 1983. It was through considering such early encounters with the creative and cutting-edge thoughts of the generation before him that Mortazavi developed a keen interest in turning his 2D art into large-scale installations, particularly in unconventional spaces.

In 1995, Mortazavi was a young artist whose work was respected by the few existing galleries, 13 Vanak of Fereydoun Ave and Lili Golestan's Gallery. Both Ave and Golestan extended invitations to present Mortazavi's large-scale projects; however, due to limitations of space, it soon became evident that his project had to be displayed in a dilapidated home similar to those used by his cohorts back in 1992. Mortazavi managed to reserve a slot at the former home of Soleiman Behboudi (1896–1981), a high-ranking official in Reza Shah's court, with the help of Behboudi's granddaughter, Mehrnoush Behboudi (b. 1964), an art aficionado and more recently the cofounder of the Versus Visual Arts Foundation (2015–).

Located on Darband Street, the house had remained unoccupied since Behboudi's death.[95] By this time, Behboudi and his house and history had receded so far from public memory that Mortazavi did not even consider addressing the story of this once prominent figure in Reza Shah's time. In other words, the work was not site-specific (figs. 1.8a/b). Mehrnoush Behboudi says she made the home available to Mortazavi because she "had seen the excitement at the Project 71/92, through [her] husband Farid Jahangiri's

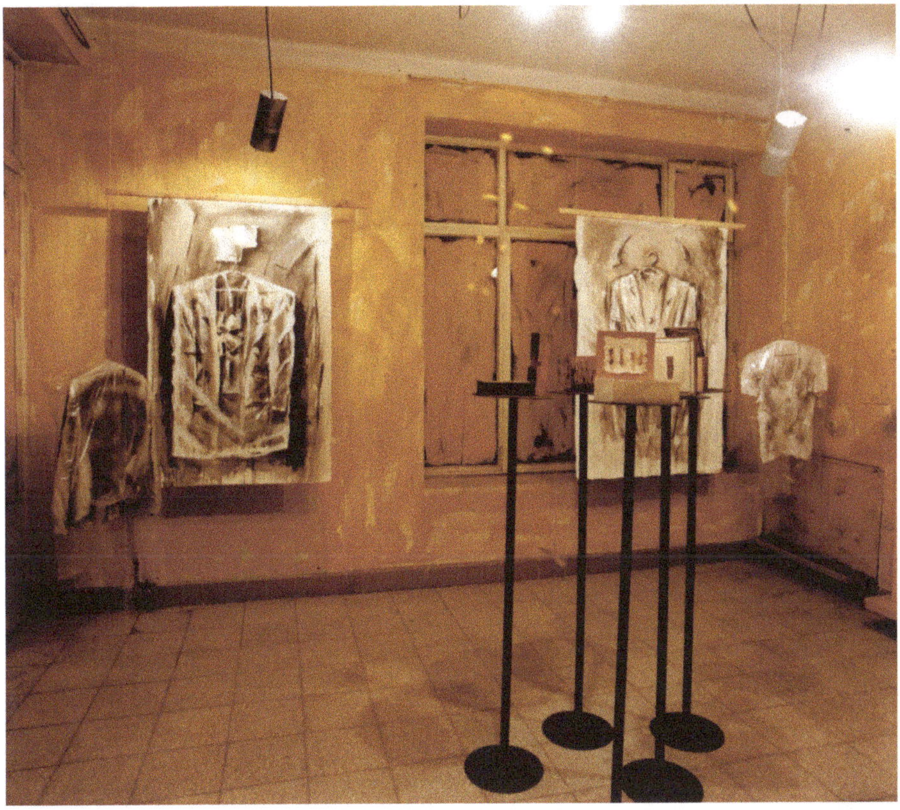

FIGURE. 1.8A Houman Mortazavi, *Life Accessories*. 1995. Tehran. Photograph by Mehrab Moghadasian. Courtesy of Houman Mortazavi.

work, and [she] wanted to reproduce it again."[96] Behboudi further recalls that the idea was to give Mortazavi room to express his artistic talent. There were, indeed, no direct political or historical references in the work, but as Behboudi aptly affirms, "The work was political by virtue of being alternative and due to lack of permission from the ministry."[97]

That the home of a high-ranking political figure and a confidant of Reza Shah became an art venue was for Mortazavi a mere coincidence in his view, and, as mentioned above, he did not make any effort to understand the history of the house, its political connotations, or the role of its occupant. Rather, his primary consideration was to find a large, private exhibition space:

> When I got there, I did whatever the hell I wanted! I tore the wallpapers, painted the windows. I even destroyed some sections of the interior; I could not possibly have done this anywhere else. This is what alternative sites offered

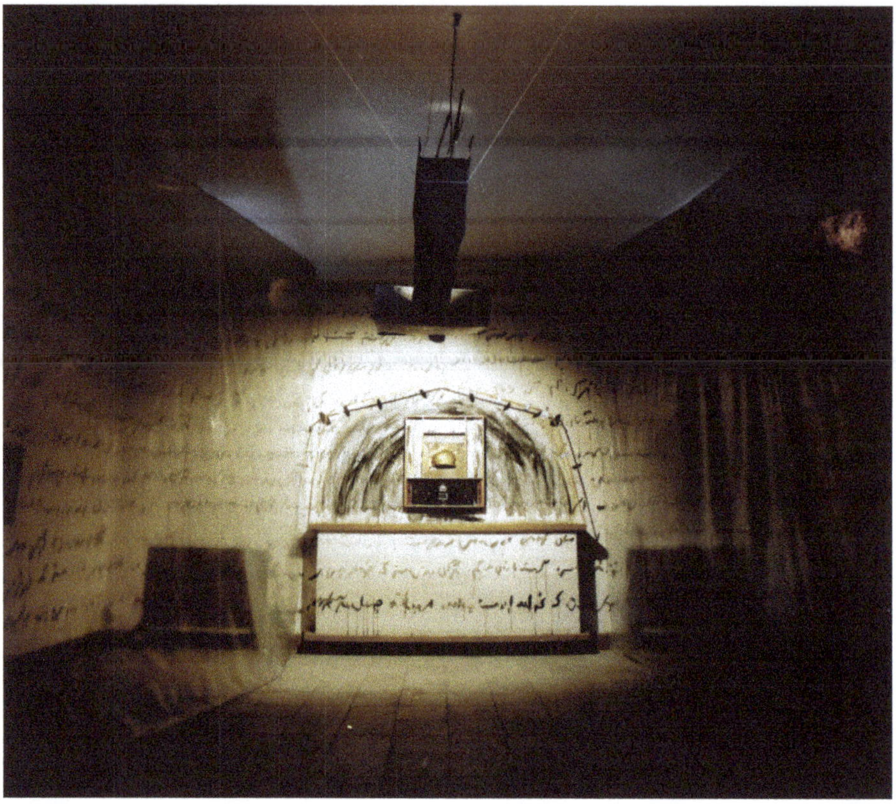

FIGURE 1.8B Houman Mortazavi, *Life Accessories*. 1995. Tehran. Photograph by Mehrab Moghadasian. Courtesy of Houman Mortazavi.

> us: they gave us freedom. Additionally, I wanted to go against the grain of finding an audience (*mokhatab*) for my work. At school or in public institutions of art learning, we were always told to create work for audiences and to make art with an audience in mind; however, I was interested in making art for myself and for "innocent," curious viewers. I certainly wanted to have random people look at my work. But I did not want to be responsible for the ways in which they made sense of it or drew conclusions. I just wanted to experience the freedom of artistic expression, something that was denied to us not only because of the social atmosphere of Iran but also due to the lack of exhibition spaces.[98]

Given Mortazavi's trajectory and the artistic circles to which he belonged, it is astonishing that a historical and politically charged space became a venue for a form of invisibility art. I ascribe the term *invisible* to this art project for multiple reasons. Despite his efforts, Mortazavi was unable to secure permission for the exhibition. In fact, he vividly recalled the ridicule and intimidation he encountered when he went to one of the officers at the MCIG.[99] Not only did they think such a form of art presentation was unnecessary, they had no barometer to gauge whether this form of art was suitable for public display. Indeed, their standards were defined within the limited categories of painting, sculpture, theater, and film and they had no way of measuring the quality of an installation project in an off-site location. The authorities and the morality police visited several times during the course of the show, demanding an explanation for the "nonsensical" project. Mortazavi cleverly denigrated his own art, describing it as "handmade" (*kardasti*, a term often applied to children's craftworks for school projects).[100] Nonetheless, he was forced to shut down the exhibition after ten days. One might associate this work with invisibility and covertness because of the ways in which the artist kept it apart from the outside world. As can be seen in the photographs (figs. 1.8a/b), all the windows were painted, and thus the house became further detached from the outside world.

The project was divided into thematic rooms: a women's room, a storage room, an everyday life room, a martyr's room, and the panic room. According to Mortazavi, this was just a way for him to summarize the themes of his daily life: the outfits, the headgear, the scarves, the propaganda, writings on the street walls, and so on. All of these were on display in the rooms.

To make the work more sensory, as his counterparts in the 1992 project had done, he worked with a variety of smells and sounds. In the everyday life room, for example, one could hear recorded sounds of Vanak Square. The martyr's room was suffused with petrichor, the earthy scent produced when warm rain falls on dry soil. While the project was probably the most unique of the solo shows after the Islamic Revolution, it did not attract the attention it deserved. Mortazavi documented it through photographs, but the press and other art critics remained largely uninterested.

. . .

To get a sense of how these early *kolangi* projects—semi-visible but lacking permission from the MCIG—operated, a comparison with an analogous example in the last years of the Soviet Union is revealing.[101] While most Iranian artists I spoke to were unaware of alternative art practices in apartments and dilapidated buildings in the Soviet Union, they could all relate to them when I brought them up. Between 1985 and 1987, a kindergarten for the children of members of the Communist Party closed, awaiting major renovations. The owner needed to guard the empty building at night. Four artists took on the job and at the same time formed an artistic collective, an initiative that was more opportunistic than planned. But over time the name Kindergarten came to be used by visitors and outsiders.[102] According to one founding member, Andrei Roiter, the project was an impulsive reaction to the system that made it difficult for artists to break into the official scenes. Additionally, as young artists they needed to make money to manage the expenses of daily life. Working as night watchmen seemed like a logical step. Because of the proximity of the building to the former KGB headquarters, a representative from the KGB was always aware that exhibitions took place, so by definition the space was not stealthy or underground like those that were more common in the Moscow of the 1960s.[103] The owner of the building, who was himself affiliated with the Communist Party, grew increasingly uncomfortable with the global attention the space attracted, including visiting art dealers from Deutsche Bank and a gallery in Chicago, as well as coverage of Kindergarten in a few international newspapers. Accordingly, the KGB proceeded to shut down the operation in 1987.[104] Like their Soviet counterparts, Iranian artists played a cat-and-mouse game with the morality police until a reformist era started, when artists were offered more opportunities for alternative projects.

. . .

In 1997, Hojjat al-Islam Sayyed Mohammad Khatami was elected president. Khatami was a prerevolutionary supervisor at an Iranian mosque in Hamburg, director of the National Library, and an open admirer of Enlightenment thinkers, who ran his campaign on the themes of expanding "civil society." Thanks to the freedoms given to artists by Khatami's government, a new wave of Iranian cinema flourished, and Iranian films won prizes at Cannes and Venice.

Khatami's reformist approach also led to a boom in the art market, both inside and outside Iran. By the time of Khatami's second term in 2001, galleries were steadily securing permission from the MCIG for artwork to be displayed on their walls. At that time, around fifty art galleries were already operating in Tehran, including the aforementioned Golestan, Haft Samar, and Azad, as well as 13 Vanak Street (in 1984 as a studio and in 2000 as an exhibition space), Arya (1992), Elahe (1999), Assar (1999), and Silk Road (2001), to name but a few.[105]

With the freedom that came with the privatization of the market, the art business expanded and eventually prepared the ground for the increasing availability of spaces for art production and pop-up art venues. In this context, another *kolangi* exhibition became more widely open to the public.

The artists who were involved grew more confident about documenting their projects and opening them up to wider audiences. The third *kolangi* visual art project—and the first one to be properly documented—would take place in 1998, when artists Farid Jahangir, Bita Fayyazi (b. 1962), Ata Hasheminejad (b. 1973), Khosrow Hassanzadeh (b. 1963), and Sassan Nassiri converted an abandoned home near the upscale Gholhak neighborhood into an art exhibition just before the site was to be razed to make way for a multistory building. The entire event, from inception to demolition, was recorded by filmmaker Maziar Bahari (b. 1967) in his documentary *Honar-e takhreeb* or *The Art of Demolition* (1998).[106] The film shows how the participating artists presented their collective project as a new phenomenon in the Tehran art scene. Artist Khosrow Hassanzadeh indicated that it was the first time in Iran, and especially since the revolution, that artists had joined forces to create a site-specific production, stating,

> It is against our norm; artists usually work by themselves and have a monologue rather than a dialogue. We have never had such group works in Iran, except for some artificial and formal exhibitions. But here, for the first time, a group of artists have come together and are able to observe the creative moments when a work of art comes to life. It is not important whether the work is good or bad. It is the spirit of the movement that is significant.[107]

In addition to working as a group, the collective engaged with the architectural elements of the building by chiseling its walls, forming thresholds, and linking one space to the next, so as to establish a dialogue between painted walls and featured installations. Jahangir allied his use of 2D and 3D media, such as protruding busts of humans, to the notion of a flexible space that would allow "human subjects to walk through its walls." Jahangir also alluded to the importance of spontaneity in art creation and his belief in the process rather than the final product: "Painting is a medium through which I think."[108]

Hassanzadeh and Jahangir spoke of engaging the space of the dilapidated house. Demolition, in and of itself, was not at the forefront of their artmaking process, but Nassiri alluded directly to demolition as a fact of life in Iran, the result of war or poor management in the aftermath of environmental disasters. Nassiri spoke of the rising level of the Caspian Sea (between 1994 and 1996), which not only decimated the habitats of rare species of aquatic vegetation but also destroyed homes and facilities on the waterfront, scattering debris and effluent that seemed likely to remain along the coastline for many years to come. As Nassiri described this source of inspiration, *The Art of Demolition* captured alternating footage of the demolished villas and trees by the Caspian and their reconstructed versions in one large room of the exhibition space.

As with Hassanzadeh and Jahangir, Nassiri's engagement with the notion of "destruction" was allusive and apolitical. Yet the artists, as well as the documentary film apparatus that accompanied the artists from beginning to end, referred to the destruction of physical environments as well as of human identities and hopes. The only female artist of the group, Bita Fayyazi, deliberately refused to speak to the cameraman about her art, but she is shown making countless papier-mâché crows that would first be scattered throughout the building, then scattered even further by the sledgehammers of the laborers tasked with destroying the building and the exhibit. More than ten thousand visitors, however, visited the exhibition before its scheduled demolition.

. . .

As mentioned above, the Iranian authorities denounced the first *kolangi* show in 1992 as "indecent" when rumors spread that it involved a dancer, and the second show was forced to close early, but the third show was looked on favorably by the MCIG, who called the artists to congratulate them and ask them to do more projects like it.[109] Instead of fighting the artists, the state thus gradually began to sponsor and authorize them, and with the state's support the artists were also able to secure funds from other organizations.

In January 2000, Hassanzadeh, Fayyazi, and Bahari joined photographer Sadegh Tirafkan (1965–2013) to create a multimedia show, *Blue Children, Black Sky* (*Koodakan-e abi, aseman-e siah*), which tackled the hot topic of the day: Tehran's pervasive air pollution and particularly its toxic effects on children. The venue was a three-story house on Nedjatollahi Avenue.[110] Once owned by a wealthy Zoroastrian businessman, the building had been abandoned since the revolution and was loaned to the artists for two months by the Tehran municipality.[111] One report of the exhibition in the Tehran-based *Golestaneh Magazine*, from the same year, revealed how the artists struggled to turn the building into an art exhibition. Reflecting on the artists' concerns about pollution, the author also alluded to the difficulty of creating a space for an "independent" (*mostaghel*) group: "Here, being independent is a sin. It means being subject to arrests and interrogations, lack of sponsorship and endorsement and even being subject to a never-ending silence."[112]

The author continued: "Exactly at a time when, much like the lives of small children in polluted Tehran all hopes were vanishing, the artists found a few friends."[113] The municipality of Tehran's sixth district had already made plans for the building and had dedicated all its spaces to administrative activities related to public art projects. When the artists turned to the head of the district, he agreed to clear one floor for the art exhibition. Rather than placing paintings and photographs on the corridor walls, these artists—like the *kolangi* artists before them—aimed for a *Gesamtkunstwerk* or "total work of art." They generated "a dark space, as a metaphor for the one seen and lived on the streets of Tehran."[114] Fayyazi made a series of white terracotta sculptures of a group of small children roped together, who stretched their arms toward the sky as if begging for oxygen. Paintings showcasing silhouettes of children playing under a heavy dark sky populated the walls. Other works were even grimmer in sentiment, much like the dilapidated home in which they were displayed.[115] In addition to the municipality, the publicity materials for *Blue Children, Black Sky* featured dozens of sponsors for the exhibition, acknowledging the National Iranian Gas Company and a whole host of private enterprises in a variety of trades, from food to art supplies and book publication.[116] The rooms in which these art forms emerged slowly began to be appropriated by the state as exhibition spaces. Indeed, a shift in ownership of venues and buildings paved the way for further consolidation of the state and other powerful agents.[117] Raw spaces were no longer only alternative venues for visual artists who did not want to distribute their works through official platforms; the state was also gaining a direct ownership stake in makeshift venues and abandoned buildings. In theater the story was slightly different. In addition to rehearsals and performances inside private homes, alternative "raw spaces" emerged adjacent to the official ones, but were somewhat out of sight.

. . .

Narges Siah (1996–2000), or Black Narcissus, was the first postrevolutionary theater group to choose an unconventional enclosed space on the grounds of a governmental institution. Tired of seeing the repetition of canonical and classical European plays, such as *Othello* and *Hamlet*, performed on official stages, in 1996 director Hamed Taheri (b. 1975) aimed for more experimental approaches.[118] An avid reader of Grotowski's works, Taheri believed in the creative adaptation of old plays as well as extreme body movements that engaged the viewer in an emotional way. Above all, he was influenced by Grotowski's notion of "poor theater," which came to stand for a performance style that rid itself of the excesses of theater, such

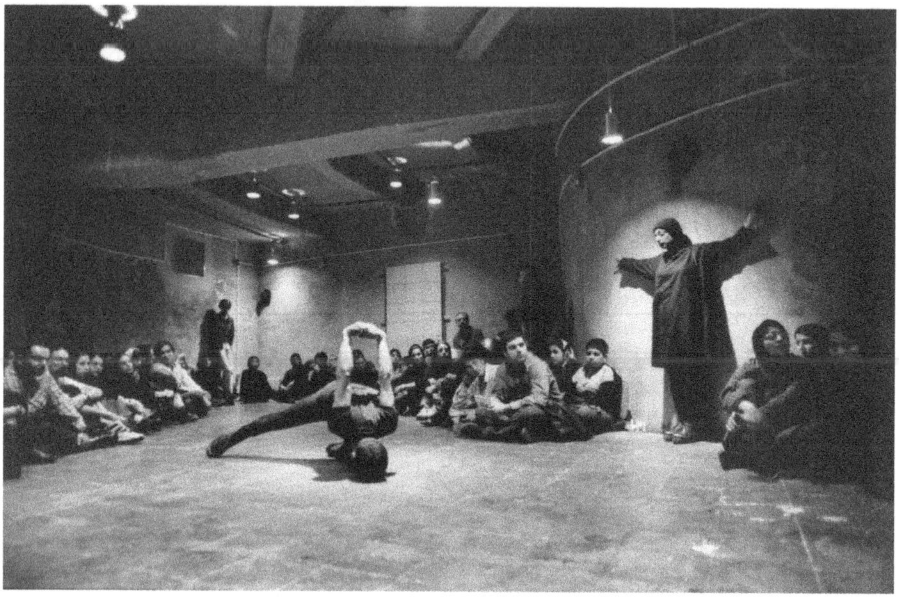

FIGURE 1.9 Black Narcissus Theatre Group, *The Blacks: A Clown Show* (*Les Nègres, clownerie*), adaptation of a 1958 play by the French dramatist Jean Genet, directed by Hamed Taheri. 2000. City Theater, Tehran. Photograph by Ali Shahbazyar.

as lavish costumes and detailed sets (hence "poor"). Regarding the concept, Grotowski writes, "No matter how much theatre expands and exploits its mechanical resources, it will remain technologically inferior to film and television. Consequently, I propose poverty in theatre. We have resigned from the stage-and-auditorium plant: for each production, a new space is designed for the actors and spectators."[119] Likewise, centered on the skills of the actors and performed with only a handful of props, Taheri's Poor Theater (*te'atr-e bichiz*) ventures necessitated alternative stages.[120] In 1996, the progressive director of the City Theater (*te'atr-e shahr*), Hossein Pakdel (b. 1959), gave the green light to Taheri and his young crew to practice in an underground hall adjacent to the furnace room of the City Theater (itself a six-hundred-seat structure built in 1972 under the auspices of Empress Farah by architect Ali Sardar Afkhami, 1929–2020). Over several months, Narges Siah prepared the room, washing off the diesel-stained bean-shaped floor, clearing the area of excess cement, and finally affixing hanging ducts, pipes, and cables.[121] There, they performed *The Blacks: A Clown Show* (*Les Nègres, clownerie*), a 1958 play by the French dramatist Jean Genet, which laid bare racial bias and stereotypes while also revealing aspects of black identity (fig. 1.9).[122]

Atefeh Tehrani (b. 1978), one of the lead players, recalled that over time, "the play attracted audiences who passed by the facilities."[123] The group then proceeded to sell tickets, and while at first, audiences casually squatted on the floor and near the actors, later they were provided with chairs. In the spirit of Grotowski's theater, Hamed Taheri's leaflet for the performance addressed participants with these words: "During the performance, you are free to create your own performance based on your encounters . . . and you are free to leave the hall anytime you like."[124] Once more, to comply with Grotowski's "poor" style, some performances were illuminated only by flashlight or candlelight, sometimes held by members of the audience.[125] Dubbed the Sun House, the space was incongruously dim and damp, with no openings to the outside. Even so, the Sun House was an apt reference to a verse in a poem by Ahmad Shamlou (1925–2000): "Our hearts are dark from pain, so where is the Sun's house?"[126] An actor from the group would recite this piece in this Iranian adaptation of *The Blacks*. Author Masoud Najafi Ardabili (b. 1976) writes, "When [we] bought . . . our tickets, [we] had to go behind the [theater] to enter The Sun House. . . . [W]e had to go down and . . . pass [through] a corridor to reach The Sun House . . . . [T]his corridor led [us] to a cold and wet basement with the . . . Sun House . . . at its end. Everywhere smelled wet. There was no window or sunlight. [We] waited there . . . until the doors . . . opened . . . . Entering this place felt like entering a forbidden area . . . to watch an underground activity."[127]

Photographer Ali Shahbazyar (b. 1970), who documented the play in its various iterations over multiple nights, communicated the intensity of his experience in these words: "The feelings the actors projected onto that dark, dingy space, were truly contagious."[128] He added, "For a while I could not imagine going about my everyday chores. I went on to shave my hair, just as the lead male actors had done. I kept thinking and even dreaming of the performance."[129] Regarding the ambience of the room, Shahbazyar added, "The subterranean space, which was otherwise cold and wet, could get boiling hot with all the energetic performers in action and the bodies of the audience packed against the walls. It made me sweat so much that I think I lost some weight there; however, I did not give up. I kept going back every night. It was like an alternative world unto itself."[130] Shahbazyar used the wide-angle lens at the hyperfocal distance to maximize the depth of field. Doing so, he could also capture the motion of the agile actors as they moved in and around the subterranean space. Pantea Panahiha (b. 1977) hung upside-down from the ducts. Like a professional contortionist and most probably conversant with Grotowski's "cat exercise," Majid Bahrami (1977–2014) bent his body in extreme poses. For the entirety of the play, another actress lay motionless in a casket with lab mice roaming around her face and body and Atefeh Tehrani turned and twisted her body into such strange and unnatural shapes that she wrenched her back and was unable to continue performing during the closing nights of the performance.

While the play required extreme body movements, a capella, and loud voices, it was still within the permitted framework of performance in the Islamic Republic. All female actors were dressed properly, and there was no illegal physical contact between men and women. The group had all the necessary paperwork in order, and the rules were largely adhered to, until one evening when some female actors allegedly took off their veils. Despite all the precautions, the performances were eventually halted by the authorities. In 2002, Taheri emigrated to Germany and Narges Siah was disbanded. Outside of private collections and some pictures at one official archive, not much remains of their unusual performances, bar a few videos that have only recently and minimally been available on the internet (partially due, perhaps, to self-censorship and partially, conceivably, as a legacy of Grotowski, who never allowed recordings of his theater as that would eradicate its "spiritual" essence). Despite the lack of textual and visual archives, the site itself remains alive in the minds of the younger generation, who still speak of the furnace room performances (*namayeshha y-e motorkhaneh te'atr-e shahr*). This resonates with similar situations experienced by Soviet artists. Regarding his installation of *Paradise* (a 1972 multistylistic installation in a Moscow apartment) for which there are only a handful of photographs, artist Vitaly Komar explains how this political art project, composed of a gigantic paper installation, "went straight into the garbage bin" following its brief exhibition.[131] Despite this, the legend remained—and continued to persistently manifest itself in the work of prominent artists such as Ilya Kabakov.[132]

Site-Specificity after the Reformist Era

After a period of freedom and flexibility during the early years of reformist president Khatami, all alternative intellectual activities (including art and literature) began to receive harsh criticism from conservative groups, culminating in a famous clash between riot police and students at Tehran University in July 1999, the most widespread and violent public protests since 1978–79. Several students were injured or killed, and many were jailed or went missing; more than eighty dissident intellectuals also went missing or were mysteriously murdered during an apparently organized operation that later became known as the Chain Murders of Iran (*ghatlhay-e zanjireh-ie*).[133]

The conservative-dominated judiciary soon instigated a new surge of censorship. For example, many films were given only short-duration screenings.[134] By 2005, when President Mahmoud Ahmadinejad took office, more than a dozen reformist newspapers had been closed and many more suspended, their editors fired or interrogated and punished. Satellite dishes that received Western TV broadcasts were banned. Although many people owned them, they were subject to search by the morality police (*komiteh* and *polis-e akhlaghi-e NAJA*).[135]

▪ ▪ ▪

According to artist and curator Amirali Ghasemi (b. 1980), as public venues became stricter and more selective, "artists became determined to [once again] showcase their art in unconventional spaces; thus, a kind of alternative space for art began to [reemerge]."[136] The new era gave artists the impetus to continue their creative occupation of old buildings but now in more deliberately radical ways. In this context, site-specificity became more relevant to alternative art practices. Attention to site, as art historian Miwon Kwon writes, is to "incorporate the physical conditions of a particular location as integral to the production, presentation, and reception of art."[137] Many works discussed so far in this chapter were site-oriented rather than site-referenced or site-specific, in the mold of Kwon's favored American sculptor Richard Serra's legendary *Tilted Arc* (1981–89), for example.

In other words, the shape of the site, the history of the site, and its socioeconomic conditions and sociopolitical connotations were less important than the fact that the location provided certain opportunities for freedom of expression that were not available in conventional art spaces. However, beginning in 2005, site-specificity slowly began to gain prominence.

In 2006, on the eve of Ahmadinejad's election as president of the Islamic Republic and the imposition of further restrictions on journalists, the abandoned headquarters of the most prominent state-run Iranian newspaper, *Ettela'at*, became a platform for a monumental installation by Farideh Shahsavarani (b. 1955), artist and professor of studio art and art history at the Faculty of Fine Arts at southern Tehran's Azad University.

In 2005, the *Ettela'at Newspaper* vacated the building near the historic Toopkhaneh Square that had served as its headquarters for more than fifty years. A private company planned to convert the empty building into a shopping mall. Shahsavarani learned about the site from her brother, who was a civil engineer and consultant for the developers. She spent nine months exploring different options for making an installation inside. She thought it was a perfect platform for a performance art project that would invite the participation of ordinary people from all walks of life in downtown Tehran, rather than aiming for a spot in one of the posh gallery spaces in the north of the city.[138] After drawing many sketches and fabricating storyboards, she finally came up with a plan for an installation entitled *I Wrote, You Read (Neveshtam, khandi).* In collaboration with ten laborers, Shahsavarani worked around the clock for twenty consecutive days to prepare the space before the opening of the one-week exhibition on November 20, 2006.

Shahsavarani's work was a commentary on government censorship of the news, which had reached its peak after eight years of relative freedom during the time of President Khatami. Visitors walked through the halls and interacted with newspapers. Some newspaper pages were trapped in barbed-wire stands; some simply covered the walls, windows, and ceiling; and others were shown in a series of original videos accompanied by the sounds of typewriters and sirens. The exhibition also dedicated a small room to the memory of journalists who had been arrested and detained by the state; this room stood out as it was the only space illuminated by warm light. The rest of the show was animated by blue light (fig. 1.10).

This *Gesamtkunstwerk* engaged multiple human senses, affirming a form of viewing art that, according to many cognitive psychologists, depends not only on our eyes but also on our bodies. As bodies moved through these repressive spaces, they became more agitated. Feelings of rage and unhappiness moved from architectural entities and objects to bodies, and from bodies to other bodies, and from bodies back to the objects themselves. According to cultural theorist Anna Gibbs, author of the widely cited article "Contagious Feelings," "Bodies can catch feelings as easily as catch fire: affect leaps from our bodies to another, evoking certain emotions."[139] Indeed, Shahsavarani's installation did create a sense of distress and rage. Some viewers reported a sense of discomfort. Some even wanted to look away from the writings on the wall. But this does not mean that they were uninterested. According to art critic Irit Rogoff, the viewer's decision to *look away* from a work of art may not be an intentional refusal. It can also be a choice to experience art with regard to the social spaces that enclose it. It can be a decision to *look around*.[140]

In Shahsavarani's exhibition, this embodied form of experiencing the art was manifested in other ways. One viewer was caught holding on to

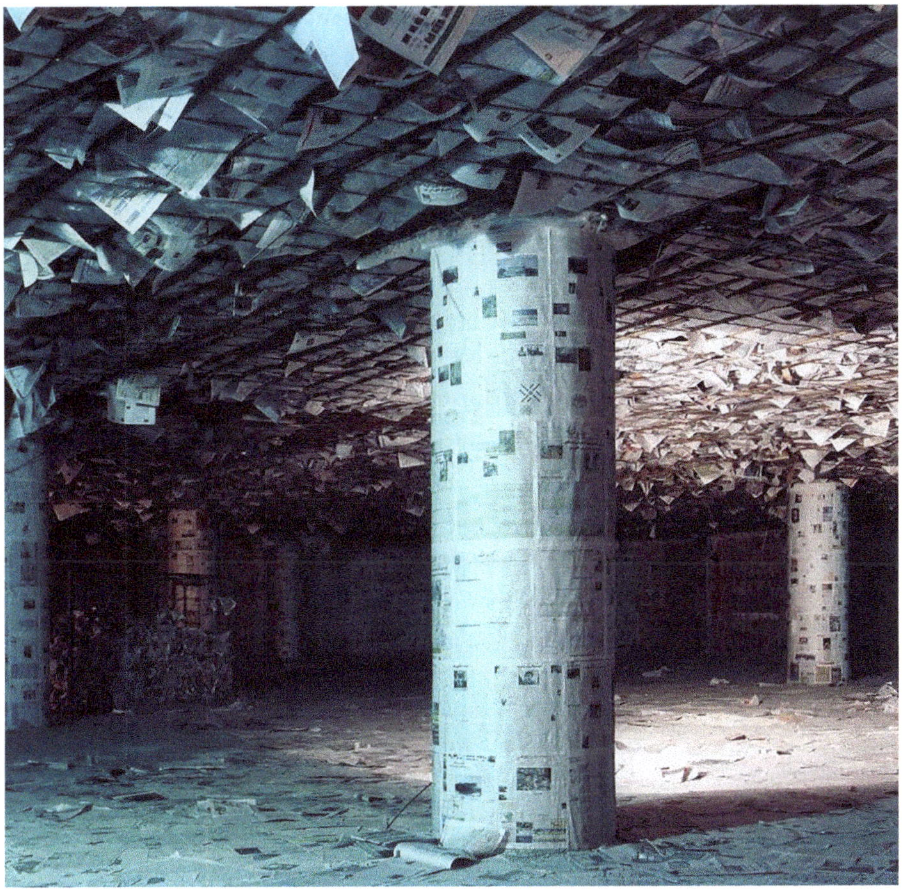

FIGURE 1.10 Farideh Shahsavarani, *I Wrote, You Read*. 2006. Former headquarters of the *Ettela'at Newspaper* in Tehran. Courtesy of Farideh Shahsavarani.

the newspaper-covered piers and crying. A few were discovered lying on the ground and mourning for their loved ones in the media industry who had been arrested and tortured by the government. Two university students brought a blindfolded friend to the installation and asked her to report on her feelings about the space, the sounds, and the overall tactile features of the ensemble. She reflected on her feelings in these words:

> I am blindfolded. There is a plethora of newspapers here. I am stepping on them. As I walk I hear the papers crush. The space around me feels abandoned. I hear the sirens. I hear the clock ticking, I hear war, fear, panic. I feel alienated. I am still walking. I am panicking as . . . I do not know where I am going. I bump into a column and touch it. It feels weary and neglected. This space is full of tension. . . . Then I open my eyes. Everywhere is white, but only at first glance. . . . Then I detect darkness. I am walking on the news that were written

> a while back. I have a feeling that some contain inaccurate reporting about individuals who were probably betrayed. Now they are all gone. I feel like I am stepping on these individuals. A space full of written texts, imbued with the sound of sirens. . . . In this freezing, abandoned space, I feel like I am awaiting a war, another war. I hear the typewriters too and with the sound of the typewriters I hear the voices of people who were written about until they disappeared into the pages of history. Black and white papers; black and white people. . . . The sound of the clock and a looming menace. . . . 'I wrote, you read.'[141]

The blindfolded student captured the overall mood of the show, as echoed by other visitors: a gloomy environment on display in one of the coldest Novembers Tehran had ever seen. Unhappiness was not, however, the endpoint of this show. To borrow from Sara Ahmed, unhappy effects give us an alternative set of imaginings that might count as a good or better life.[142] If this installation produced unhappy effects, it did so with the purpose of taking its viewers somewhere better. This novel installation by Shahsavarani marked a radical shift in engagement with the site. She widened the concept of site not only to foreground aesthetic merits but also to highlight the site's social and political connotations as well as the political conditions within which the artwork, the viewer, and the location were positioned.

Between Visibility and Invisibility in the Wake of the Green Movement

The 2009 (1388 in the Iranian calendar) Iranian Green Movement (*Jonbesh-e sabz*) might have been overshadowed by the Arab Spring, but in local collective memory, it is still considered a very important juncture in Iran's recent history, arising after the 2009 Iranian presidential election, in which protesters demanded the removal of Mahmoud Ahmadinejad from office. Green was initially used as the symbol of the campaign of Ahmadinejad's opponent, Mir Hossein Mousavi, but after the election it became the marker of antiregime sentiments. At first, those who protested the result of the election were largely nonviolent, but then conflicts broke out between police and protesters. These conflicts became increasingly fierce, and many people, most of whom were young and passionate Mousavi supporters, were injured, killed, or ended up in prison. When artists and curators speak of their projects, they often refer to pre- or post-1388 to signify the political atmosphere in which the artwork was produced. During this time, more restrictions were placed on art and artists. The MCIG became stricter when deciding whether to grant permission to gallery and museum exhibitions and outside galleries; any artistic practice was questioned. An example in this vein is a 2010 project in a dilapidated factory.

At 10 a.m. on March 2, 2010, five artists—Sonya Schönberger (from Germany), Mohammad Zahmatkesh (b. 1969), Amirali Ghasemi, Mohammad Khodashenas (b. 1975), and Ahmad Mirehsan (b. 1960)—displayed a series of artworks in an abandoned tea factory in the northern city of Lahijan near the Caspian Sea, once known for producing the finest black tea in Iran. Some were readymade displays, others were videos and installations (*chideman*), and a few paintings also animated the decaying walls of the factory. Previously owned by the renowned Lahijan tea merchants the Saffari family, it had closed, like most of the factories in the city, after the formation of a so-called tea mafia, which bought raw tea from local farmers at a low price and then shipped it to a more lucrative international market. A surfeit of articles and reports have lamented the loss of the industry and its impact on the local economy, as well as the decay of the century-old modernist factory buildings, many of which were built by German experts.[143] Given the dire situation, Khodashenas, who had previously collaborated with the renowned filmmaker Abbas Kiarostami on his Lahijan art workshops inside the vacant factories,[144] decided to invite a group of artists from Tehran to revive the spirit of the past and give new life to the decaying factory scene.[145] The show had secured permission from the Lahijan branch of the erstwhile Organization for Cultural Heritage. However, twenty minutes after its opening, men from the local branch of the MCIG shut down the show. The artists protested this embarrassing closure: Ahmad Mirehsan published a piece in *Etemad Daily* questioning the authorities' "wrongdoing" (*eghdamat-e ghalat*).[146]

Mirehsan, whose video *Lahijan with Bitter Tea* was included in the show, criticized the authorities for not even being willing to welcome a readymade work (*hazer o amadeh*), entirely created and coordinated through the artists' own budgets. Such repression, he noted, would lead to the self-destruction (*khodvirangari*) of Iran's history and heritage.[147] The exhibit was meant to be an ongoing project, with the aim of revitalizing more of Lahijan's decaying tea factories, but the closure put an abrupt end to that intention. For the next few years, at least, these abandoned factories would become venues for more political art forms, visible only to closed artistic circles (fig. 1.11).

A 2012 intervention in a Pahlavi-era kitchen utensil factory is a case in point. Along with Worm Brain and Elf Crew (whose members at the time were Ali F.J. One and Blind), Ghalamdar (mentioned earlier) occupied the factory and painted the walls. He combined the 2D paintings with found objects, most of which were remains of items produced by the factory. About the installation of the found objects (fig 1.12), Ghalamdar said: "The project wasn't about just painting graffiti. It was about transporting graffiti from a flat surface into a sculpted entity."[148] Worm Brain painted a mural consisting of his name repeated in stencil. The tableau was completed by a red found object at the factory site.

To the left and right of Worm Brain's composition are two "wild-style" graffiti by Blind (b. 1992); the one to the left reads *tajavoz*, a word connoting a variety of meanings ranging from rape to invasion and assault (fig 1.12). Blind explained his use of the word:

> Of course, *tajavoz* has a negative connotation, usually conveying the rape of a defenseless female. But my intention here was not to address this particular connotation of the word. Instead, I was alluding to the other commonly used meaning of the word, which is invasion or assault. The invasion of the factory was a form of *tajavoz*, but one that alludes to the invasion of spaces that are not afforded to us to fully express our artistic sentiments. . . . The style of writing

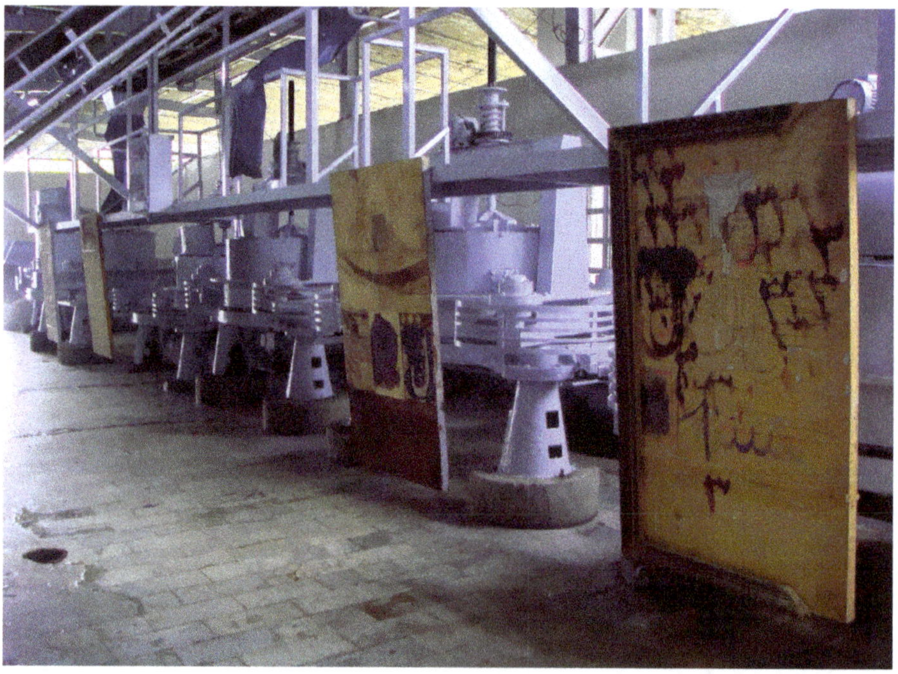

FIGURE 1.11 Abandoned tea factory in Lahijan appropriated for a group art exhibition, featuring calligraphic works by Mohammad Khodashenas. 2010. Lahijan. Courtesy of Mohammad Khodashenas.

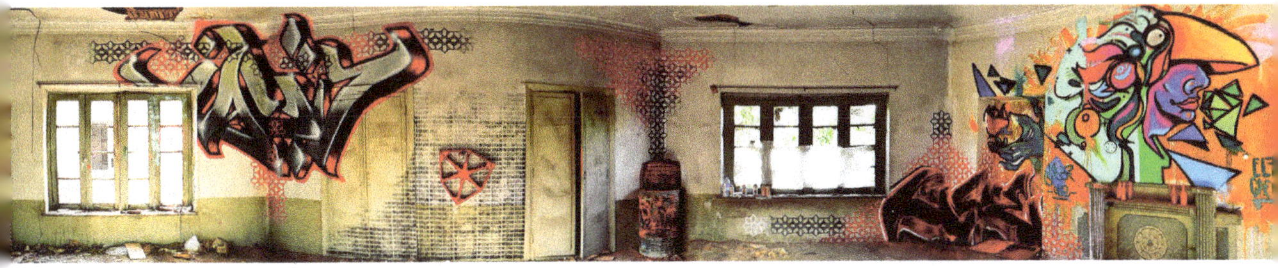

FIGURE 1.12 Worm Brain, Found object set against the stencil reproductions of the artist's name, all flanked by wild-style graffiti by Blind and Ali F.J. 2012. Abandoned kitchen utensil factory, Tehran. Courtesy of Parham Ghalamdar.

> alludes to the difficulty of day-to-day life in Iran. Otherwise known as "wild-style" graffiti—with interwoven and overlapping letters and shapes—this complicated and intricate form of writing is meant to be hard to read. We do not want to be read and understood by viewers. These are just artistic expressions that subtly tackle cultural and social issues in Iran.[149]

Indeed, although private space is meant to be a safe haven, there are many instances of the invasion of private events, a phenomenon captured in the 2009 drama *No One Knows about Persian Cats* by Bahman Ghobadi (b. 1969), in which underground musicians are busted and punished. The roughness of the dilapidated factory and the connotations of the words in the graffiti confirm, once again, that after the Green Movement those occupied rundown spaces projected a subtle political message, even if the art was short-lived and the audience was limited to the artists themselves and a few from their closed circles. Rather than celebrating the joy of practice in the "limitless" spaces of empty buildings, a mindset that enlivened the earlier *kolangi* projects, Ghalamdar and his friends used large, tucked-away, unoccupied, and decaying spaces to project the anxieties of their time.

. . .

After the 2009 Green Movement, alternative visual arts in abandoned buildings became available in sheltered spaces and amidst "trusted" audiences. Likewise, some theater experts took more extreme measures to ensure privacy. House Theater (*te'atr-e khaneh*) was one private venue that became prevalent during Ahmadinejad's time in office (2005–13). Before the Green Movement, Mohammad Rezaie Rad (b. 1966) was an established theater director, having produced an expansive portfolio of authorized scholarly and theater works. All of his plays were performed in official theater venues. Notable among his published works is his 2002 *Semiotics of Censorship and the Silence of Words* (*Neshaneh shenasi-e sansoor va sokoot-e sokhan*), in which he surveys the history of censorship in Iran through a semiotic lens. For example, he writes of how conservative magazines in the early 2000s attacked Khatami's progressive views by using the commonly employed sign "[. . .]," otherwise known as *momayyezi-e matn* (censorship of text) in Persian.[150] During the 2009 presidential election uprisings, Rezaie Rad was politically active. He joined a group of eight playwrights in condemning the election process, and wrote and directed a play about the unjust elections and the ensuing unrest in *Dream of Silent Saints* (*Ro'yay-e taheregan-e khamoosh*). He later staged the play twice in Paris.[151]

Upon his return to Iran, Rezaie Rad's official license with the MCIG was revoked, largely on account of his bold approach to theater and his scholarly publications.[152] This revocation continued until 2013. To avoid the despair caused by his lack of work, he formed the House Theater Group (*Gorooh-e te'atr-e khaneh*).[153] Plays in the House Theater Group were performed inside a private home, and audience members were selected from a group of artists and intellectuals who were close to Rad or the homeowner. None of these plays had secured permission from the authorities. Every time a play was hosted in a "friend's" house, the owner of the house would invite thirty to sixty friends and family, depending on the available space. Audiences were not obliged to buy tickets, but they were encouraged to donate money. Those friends may have brought their own friends, and so the audience was a "trusted public" whose female members could even remove their veils during the show. Female actors did not remove their veils, and there was no activity that exceeded the bounds of Islamic codes of conduct.[154]

Although lacking a public audience (*mokhatab-e omoomi*), the group continued their activities for some time. By Rezaie Rad's account, even two years after his license was reissued, he continued to conduct plays in private and inside people's homes. Without permission from the authorities, these performances fit into the underground art scene of Tehran, although Rezaie Rad himself does not necessarily agree with that designation. Like many of his peers, he believes that all forms of art can occupy a tenuous position between "underground" and "aboveground," depending on the circumstances.[155]

. . .

The genre of House Theater differed from another seemingly concealed genre known as Apartment Theater (*te'atr-e apartemani*). The latter was

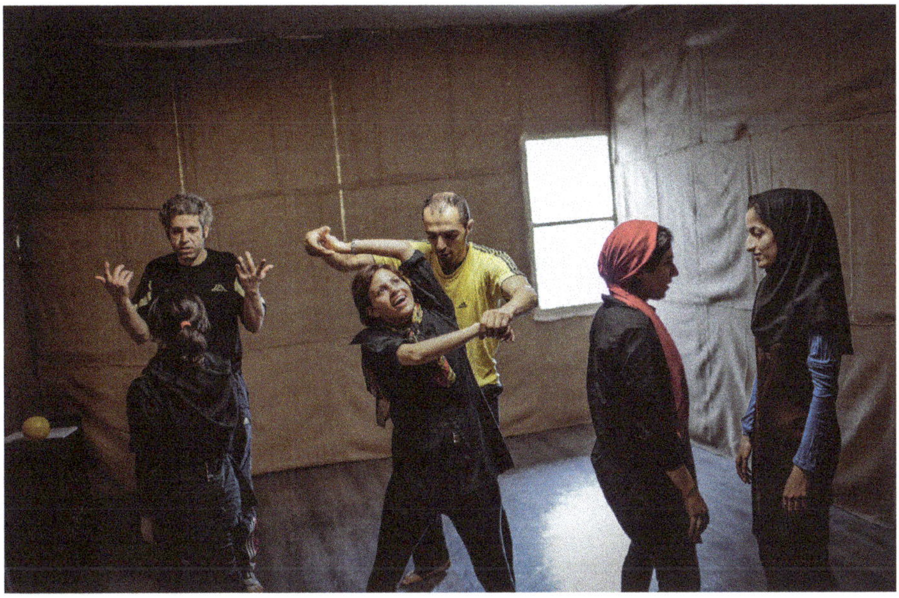

FIGURE 1.13 The Nyia Theater Group rehearsal in a rental apartment. 2014. Tehran. Photograph by Jeremy Suyker.

established primarily by theater majors at several universities who could not afford to perform in proscenium theaters; they congregated instead in apartments, especially at the Navvab residential complex in southern Tehran.[156] Inevitably, these private rehearsals provided opportunities for the kinds of engagements that were not feasible on stage. Over time these practices were also embraced by more professional groups. Nyia (an abbreviated form of *niyakan, ancestors*), an alternative theater group in Tehran whose principles are guided by the "ancestors"—ancient Greek theater and the Polish experimental theater of Gardzienice—is known to have rehearsed in rented apartments (fig. 1.13). Greek theater allowed Nyia to best capture the human feelings of rage, betrayal, revenge, and envy, while Gardzienice was their model for intense bodily interactions and greater engagement with the site.

The group calls these spaces *plateaus* (equivalent to the French *scène*). Typically, a side-room space in a major theater, plateaus have acquired a unique identity in Iran, as they mostly refer to private apartments.[157] The walls of such spaces must be soundproof, and the room must remain empty to eliminate distractions. In addition to being safe spaces (*fazay-e amn*) for the artistic development of the emerging actors, plateaus also provide room for what Niya director Pouya Pirouzram (b. 1975) calls corporal action (*konesh-e jesmani*).[158]

On actual official stages, if a play requires physical contact between men and women, the artists resort to little tricks like using a sheet or a sleeve as a shield.[159] Since women cannot make dramatic gestures on stage because such movements purportedly excite the senses of the men in the audience,[160] their movements become more restricted and subtle.[161] Niya's experience, as shown in figure 1.13, indicates how the apartment plateaus paved the way for men and women to have physical encounters, when and if needed.

. . .

In an ironic and unprecedented move, concurrent with the growth of home theaters and the rehearsals taking place in rented apartments, the government proceeded to privatize theater.[162] Between 2010 and 2017 at least twenty-four private theater companies, including Av (2010), Bazigah/Playground (2013), Mowjeh No/New Wave (2014), Mostaghel/Independent (2015), Konesh-e Mo'aser/Contemporary Interaction (2016), Emarat-e Rooberoo/Opposite Building (2016), and Shato/Chateau (2017), to name but a few, animated the capital. The background to the decision to privatize is itself a microcosm of the porous nature of the boundaries between public and private enterprise in Iran.[163] Discussions were held among a host of agents, from the parliament of the Islamic Republic and the municipality to private investors and theater experts. Each came in with a different agenda. In its third and fourth economic development plans of the early 2000s, the government hoped to relieve itself of the tremendous expense of cultural and entertainment initiatives and create the possibility of collecting taxes from the private cultural sector that would take over these ventures. Private investors and bankers saw an opportunity for profit. Theater experts hoped to elevate theatrical culture, replacing what they saw as ideological (*ideology zadeh*) government-sponsored performances, lowbrow presentations (*te'atr-e ammeh pasand*), and clandestine activities with works that were more experimental (*tajrobi*), sophisticated (*pishro*), and enriching (*fakher*). Privatization has had mixed results. Notably, many investors have gone bankrupt. It has also been suggested that the shift to privatization paved the way for corruption and the rise of what is referred to as the "art mafia" (*mafiya-ye honari*), signaling the activities of those involved in the *Khosoolati* economy.[164] Whether the government has benefitted financially from these activities is also debatable. Some theater experts believe that due to monetary concerns many private theaters dropped their earlier utopian goals (*ahdaf-e armani*) and instead organized themselves for monetary gain, as entertainers or marketers of luxury (*lagjery*), commercial (*bazari*), and even kitsch (*mobtazal*) theater.[165] With all its ups and downs, the privatization of theater, nonetheless, brought about some novel critical spatial practices.

Behind the walls of these MCIG-authorized private theater spaces, the use of techniques of invisibility lingered. The story of the first officially sanctioned private theater company in postrevolutionary Tehran, Av, underlines this point. Before Av, there had been public theatrical productions in Iran in unconventional public spaces such as the furnace room of the City Theater mentioned earlier. All these performances had some connection with official institutions, whether government-run theaters or those affiliated with universities.[166] Av, by contrast, did its best to remain as autonomous as possible.

Active since 2009 in natural and remote spaces (see chapter 2), the Av Theater Group settled in Tehran in 2012. Soheil Aarabi (b. 1982), co-organizer of Av, and Babak Mohri (b. 1977), theater director and co-founder, traveled to Poland to study experimental theater with the Gardzienice Theater Association, which was founded in 1977 in a tiny remote Polish village.[167]

Prior to this, Mohri had traveled to Poland to visit Gardzienice with other prominent theater figures, including Homayoun Ghanizadeh (b. 1980) and Payam Dehkordi (b. 1977). Upon their return, a small independent theater group, Mimic, which included Aarabi, Mohri, and other members, transformed itself into a new group, Av—a variant of *ab* (water) in the ancient Pahlavi language that refers to ancient water temples. In the spirit of Gardzienice, Av's performances took place without technology, for instance, in candlelight, and presented dramatic expressions of joy, anguish, prayer, and lamentation. These were coupled with strenuous physical and vocal training as well as anthropological fieldwork among marginalized communities. While on "stage" they engaged all senses of their audiences. For example, they served lime at the beginning of a play to generate alertness.

In October 2010 Av rented the basement of a midcentury two-story house on Khajeh Nasir Toosi Street near Sepah Square, complete with a kitchen and a small backyard that later became a café and gathering place. They turned the basement into a black box. Painted dark and rectangular in shape, black boxes create a neutral setting that allows for a wide array of design choices, a concept rooted in European avant-garde theater. Complete with a portable seating area, movable stage, and flexible lighting system, black boxes became popular during the explosion of experimental arts in the 1960s, particularly with Peter Brook. Storefronts, church basements, and even old trolley barns adopted the black box and became intimate performance venues.

Av's black box was a pronounced break from the elaborate proscenium stages found in most of Iran's Western-style theater houses. Khaneh Namayesh-e Av, or the Av Performance House, registered itself as an independent private organization with the MCIG. At that time, the ministry had not yet developed rules and regulations regarding private theater spaces, but they did outline a series of restrictions. For example, when Aarabi went to seek permission, the MCIG ordered the removal of Soheila Ghodstinat's (b. 1961) name from the company's brochures. Ghodstinat, a UK-based actor who has occasionally collaborated with Av, is the author of *A Journey to Starland* (2003), a bittersweet tale of how women in Iran must fight for their rights and freedom.

Furthermore, the MCIG did not allow tickets to be sold online, so the group had to secure the necessary funds (for rent, maintenance, and actors' fees) by selling brochures and photographic albums and booklets about each performance. Additionally, Av turned the kitchen into a café and at times sold food to their audience to make a little extra money. As Aarabi recalls, the MCIG officer was puzzled and said the group must be very naïve to put so much energy into an art project that did not generate a profit. "Luckily," Aarabi remarks, "in those days with my beard I looked like a *basiji* [a paramilitary volunteer militia], so they granted me permission and let me go, before warning me they would send someone to check on us periodically."[168]

Even when performing versions of classical Greek theater and adaptations of Middle Eastern folk tales, the group did not do so in the traditional ways that are the norm in official theater houses in Iran, but instead used movement and dialogue to encourage the participation of the audience—reminiscent of Gardzienice. This interactive quality was possible in part because of the black box created inside the old house. "The beauty of a black box theater," Aarabi explains, "is that you can have all kinds of interactions in a single space."[169]

In 2012, the owner of Av's rented house forced the group to leave, and later that year, the performers moved to an old subterranean thermal bath in central Tehran (fig. 1.14).[170] The bathhouse near Fatemi Square was cheap and designated for commercial use, but it was still too expensive for the group, so Av was offered the basement, which had been abandoned for many decades. The space required massive repair, including tiling the floors,

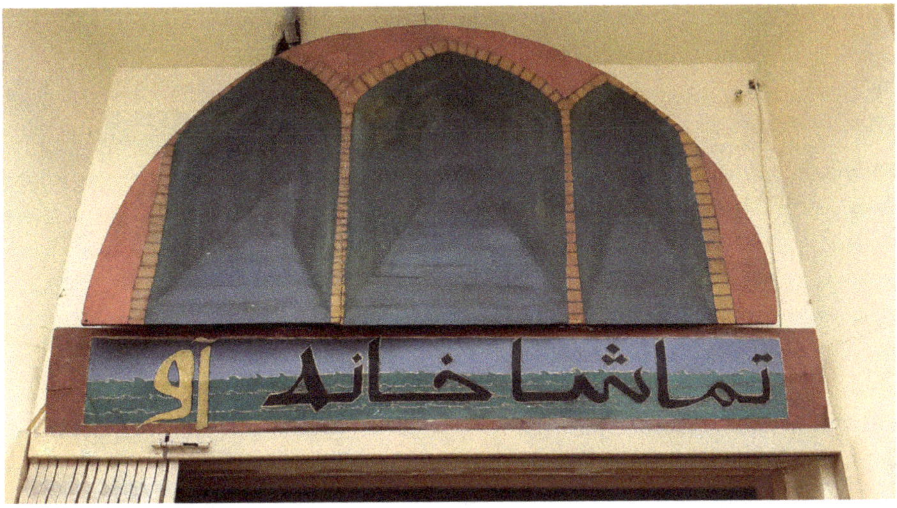

FIGURE 1.14 The main entrance to the AV Theater Group's official venue, a subterranean thermal bath in central Tehran, 2013. Courtesy of Soheil Aarabi.

dehumidifying the space, and removing mold from the walls. The building had not been used as a bathhouse for more than forty years, but the dampness and humidity were still present. Although the space was challenging to renovate and disinfect, they chose it because of its subterranean quality. Indeed, stepping into the hot and humid underground space was like entering another planet, according to Aarabi:

> We brought a few bags of beach sand to turn the floor into a natural-looking environment. Doing so, we accentuated the subterranean character of the space. We intended it to feel like a cave. The cell phones got no reception in there. That basement was timeless. We made food right there, and as the actors interacted with the viewers, we also fed them. Down there, everything turned into a performance. It was truly life as art or art as life. We went in early in the morning, and by the time we got out at night we were surprised by how much time had passed without us noticing.[171]

In addressing "life as art or art as life," Aarabi echoed sentiments expressed by Peter Brook, who had presented major site-specific performances at the Shiraz Arts Festival in *Persepolis*. Brook noted, "The theater is a search for an expression that is directly concerned with the quality of living."[172] Indeed, through "music, movement, dialogue and interactive participating of audiences," Av theater created a new form of life. This is the moment, in Brook's words, "when the actor . . . discovers himself . . .

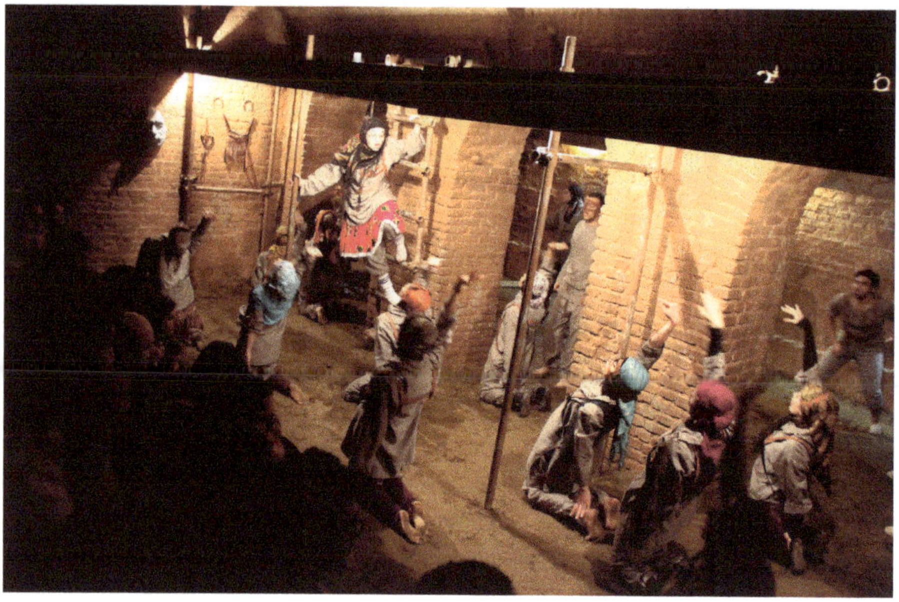

FIGURE 1.15 Av Theatre Group, *Melpomene*, directed by Babak Mohri. 2013. Old underground thermal bath, Tehran. Courtesy of Soheil Aarabi.

the actor, that is to say the human being, transcends the phase of incompleteness, to which we are condemned in everyday life."[173] The sentiment of "life as art or art as life" also calls to mind certain ideas of Jerzy Grotowski, who had likewise performed in Shiraz. Indeed, searching for answers to the question "how should one live?" was central to all of Grotowski's works.[174]

In 2013, Av embarked on a new performance project called *Gilgamesh*. Performed by fifty actors—men and women who were all born in the 1980s or early 1990s—the play took place in the new subterranean theater space. Organizers worked nonstop for forty days to make the space presentable. For the first time, Av also collaborated with an international team of directors from Florida, Amsterdam, and Berlin. The play was performed for sixty consecutive nights. Many theater specialists in Tehran came to see it, and all were astonished by the high quality of the performances. One of Iran's most respected pioneers in modern theater, Ali Rafii (b. 1938), for example, talked with admiration about the performances, confessing that he had been moved to tears for the first time in many years, in the presence of the kind of cutting-edge, compassionate theater that had become a rarity after the Islamic Revolution. In this sense, Av was a kind of therapeutic device, giving its audiences a sense of relief. This social therapy may be seen as a critical spatial practice. Without being too vocal about it, Av transformed the world of its participants through what Sara Ahmed calls an "affective economy" and anthropologist Kathleen Stewart terms "ordinary affects"—those connotations that work "not through 'meanings' per se, but rather in the way that . . . [meanings] move through bodies, dreams, [and] dramas . . . of all kinds" (fig. 1.15).[175]

The old subterranean thermal bath in Tehran is not the only venue to have made room for a wide range of emotional expressions. Many other art institutions have operated in a similar fashion. The creation of an alternative space, often involving its conversion from residential to commercial use, requires permission not only from the MCIG and the local municipality (*shahrdari*) but also the Public Property Bureau (*Edareh koll-e amaken*), which oversees legal matters as well as city traffic. While these art institutions are ostensibly sanctioned by the regime, the stories behind their buildings and naming preferences exude an air of invisibility and covertness.

What's in a Name?

Since the Islamic Revolution, the renaming of streets, buildings, housing complexes, neighborhoods, and institutions has become part of an enduring ideological practice. This is similar to what happened in Russia, when cities and streets were renamed in the aftermath of the Bolshevik Revolution, then again, three decades later, when Nikita Khrushchev adopted a de-Stalinization policy, and yet again, after the collapse of the Soviet Union and the fall from grace of its once-honored heroes.

After the Islamic Revolution, street names honoring the royal family and Western figures were erased from the map of Tehran. The renamed streets now commemorated martyrs of the Islamic Revolution and the subsequent war with Iraq as well as the new religious leaders. In Tehran, the Pahlavi Avenue became Vali Asr Avenue (a reference to the 12th Shiite Imam), Kennedy Square became Towhid Square (a reference to the oneness of God in Islam), Eisenhower Avenue (named after the American president who helped the Shah topple the democratically elected prime minister Mohammad Mossadeq) turned into Freedom Avenue, Elizabeth Boulevard (named after the Queen of England) was renamed Keshavarz Boulevard in honor of Iran's farmers, and the street adjacent to the British Embassy in Tehran, formerly known as Winston Churchill, was renamed after Bobby Sands, the renowned Irish Republican Army (IRA) martyr. The Shahyad Monument, commemorating the Shah, became Azadi (Freedom) Tower, while Farah Park became Laleh Park (to signify the tulip or *laleh*, the symbol of martyrdom in Iran). Similarly, Farah Pahlavi University, a women's college, was renamed Al Zahra University after the Prophet Muhammad's daughter. And the list goes on. The names of buildings and institutions are thus associated with political orientations. It is not necessary to know the history of an institution to guess what its agenda is. If the name has religious or revolutionary connotations, it is often pro-regime. If the name is less political, the institution is possibly more open. One needs to think of Tehran as more than just a generic metropolis with an infinite number of roads and buildings. Instead, it is an ideological construct, made out of a nexus of strategically positioned spaces with names layered with meanings.

By name and by architectural form, the aura of a culture of invisibility, covertness, and camouflage is alive in Iran. Curator Elham Puriya Mehr (b. 1979) noted that it is a challenge to locate a gallery in Tehran: "They are always hidden, somewhere in the basement or the back of a front room, etc.; one has to find one's way into the gallery through spatial exploration."[176] Even when permission is sought and legal processes concluded, there is a tendency to associate an art space with the bygone era of war and repression, sometimes nominally but often architecturally as well. Around Tehran one finds many art spaces with peculiar names. While the space itself is registered and public, the names associated with these establishments have exotic and mysterious connotations. Even when artists move out of Iran and establish their own art collectives, they still use vocabulary that is pertinent to the spirit of Iranian alternative art scenes. New York–based digital art platform Back Room (2010–14), co-organized by Iranian immigrant Ava Ansari (b. 1978), took its name from private rooms used by Iranian galleries to host meetings in relative freedom, meetings that were harder to convene in the more public front areas.[177] In what follows, I present a few of these institutions, many of which have been initiated in the past decade and amidst a major shift in real estate value and rapid privatization (*khosoosi sazi*) and gentrification (*a'yan sazi*). Coupled with an increase in purchasing or renting properties in northern neighborhoods, starting in the 2010s many artist communities have been drawn to central Tehran's gentrified areas, better known as the "Cultural Rectangle" (*morabba'-e farhangi*), which stretches from Enghelab Street (formerly Shahreza) in the south to Vali Asr (formerly Pahlavi) in the west, Iranshar Street in the east, and Karimkhan in the north.[178] Old houses in this area have been converted into cafes, bookstores, and performance and art spaces. Some owners independently rent or purchase a property and refurbish it. Others take advantage of tax breaks for "cultural institutions" and the loan programs initiated by the Ministry of Cultural Heritage, Tourism, and Handicraft, which has facilitated "public-private partnership," particularly for businesses that help restore the area's neglected historic homes.[179]

. . .

A Retreat in the Heart of Tehran. At 10 Yazdanniaz Alley on quiet Bahar Shomali Street, just off busy Taleghani Avenue, sits a modest two-story building dating back to the early Pahlavi period. The building is home to the Kooshk Art Residency. Established in mid-2014, the residency is a nonprofit space providing an exchange platform for artists, curators, researchers, writers, and filmmakers to encourage intercultural dialogue and art creation between Iran and other countries, predominantly from Asia and Europe. These exchange programs are often sponsored by European embassies inside Iran that work closely with EUNIC (European Union National Institutes for Culture). All these ties have been in flux due to the tightening of economic sanctions on Iran. But Kooshk continues its work, on and off.

The idea for the residency was developed by the ambitious director of the renowned Mohsen Gallery, Ehsan Rasoulof (b. 1979; see epilogue), in conjunction with an artist couple, Tooraj Khamenehzadeh (b. 1976) and Negin Mahzoon (b. 1984), who had already established the homeless project Rybon (*ry* meaning *nazar* or point of view, and *bon* meaning tree), in collaboration with documentary filmmaker Amirhossein Sanai (b. 1979). Because of the sanctions that were being imposed at the time of the initiative under President Ahmadinejad, Rybon was only supported in spirit (*hemayat-e ma'navi*) by the London-based alternative residency space Gasworks and by the Triangle Network and Res-Artis, global networks of artists and artist residencies that assist professional development and cultural exchange throughout the world. Through Rybon, Khamenehzadeh and Mahzoon invited international artists to their own private home in downtown Tehran. Interactions with international artists within the home opened the minds of Iranian artists to new ways of making art.

While at the home of Khamenehzadeh and Mahzoon, the Karachi-based conceptual artist Naiza Khan (see chapter 3) developed a series of projects by interacting with nearby sites. At first the couple arranged for invited artists, like Khan, to perform their works and present their art at the prestigious gallery, Arya. However, after a while it became clear that this

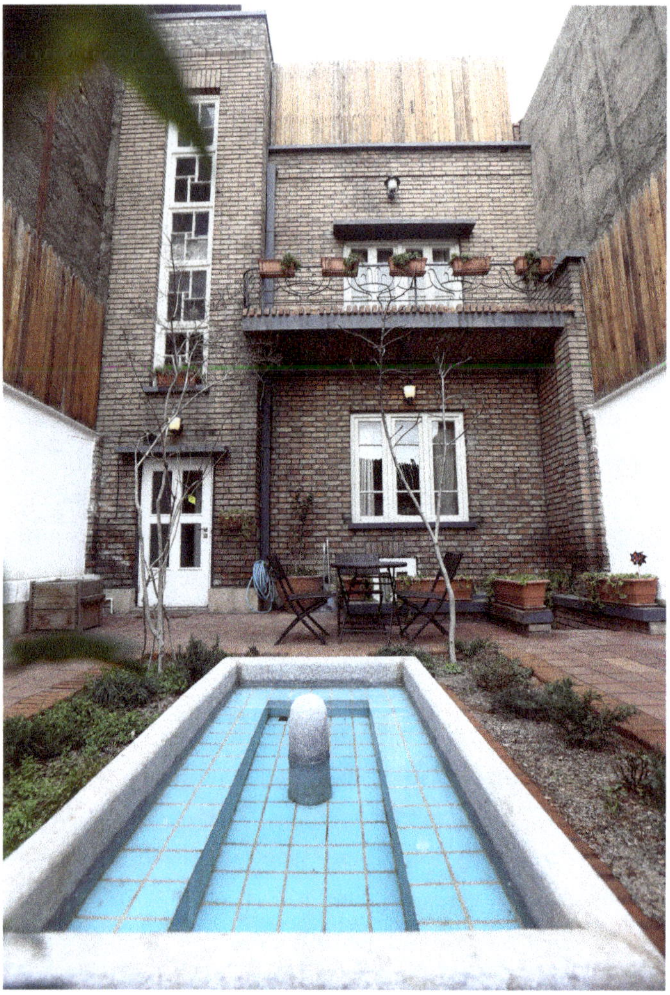

FIGURE 1.16 Kooshk (kiosk) Residency. 2018. Tehran. Photograph by Maryam Bagheri. Courtesy of the Kooshk Residency.

was not a sustainable model and that the project needed to be housed in a single independent space. So, Mahzoon and Khamenehzadeh approached Rasoulof for funding, space, and sponsorship.

Mahzoon and Khamenehzadeh started to look for a space that was deeply Iranian in character for what they called the "Exchange Program." It took months before they found a home from the mid-twentieth century on Bahar Shomali Street. At the time the house was rented, and in need of serious repair. The couple spent months renovating the space, and, in the process, they added more features, including midcentury furniture from an antique shop to enhance the historic character (fig. 1.16).

In addition, Mahzoon and Khamenehzadeh did their best to assure the neighbors, including a local supermarket, that not only would the residency not harm the neighborhood, it would actually make it safer and more prestigious. People welcomed the idea of foreign visitors to the neighborhood, and these negotiations provided opportunities for better hospitality and safety. Foreign artists often reported that they felt at home at the Kooshk Art Residency.[180]

Usually, the word *kooshk* refers to the freestanding pavilions of early modern Persia that sat amidst large gardens and were used predominantly as spaces of retreat and pleasure. Unlike the brick building of the Kooshk Art Residency, they were traditionally made from wood, raised on four or more pillars, and valued for their ability to provide shade.

These structures would become popular in the Ottoman Empire, as well as in many European countries, as summer retreats. Later, the word "kiosk" (a variant of *kooshk*) was borrowed to refer to freestanding wooden structures of varied functions,[181] a bandstand in a public park, a gazebo, or a summerhouse in a private garden. The name is also applied to newsstands and freestanding, solid cylindrical structures upon which advertisements are posted in European cities.

The Kooshk Art Residency does not capture any of the varied meanings and usages of that word. Nonetheless, when Rasoulof aimed for creating a venue for his ambitious dream of collaborating with Europe, he decided to call the venue Kooshk/Kiosk. Describing the establishment, he wrote, "we believe that to concentrate on [the] development of their artistic career, artists need to be able to distance themselves from their routine activities to focus on the creative process."[182] According to Maryam Bagheri (b. 1985), the executive manager of the residency, the word *kooshk* perfectly suits the atmosphere of the house.[183] Every day Bagheri thinks of her workspace as a small retreat in the heart of the chaotic capital. "One easily feels detached from the rest of Tehran when one enters this place," she said.[184] Animated by a terrace, a shallow pool (*howz*) reminiscent of those found in old retreats, and gardens, Bagheri added, Kooshk is a small haven in the heart of the capital.[185]

. . .

A Stair Alcove. In 2015, Houman Mortazavi, who, as mentioned earlier, created a major solo show in a *kolangi* home and also participated in guerrilla artmaking in public urban spaces (see chapter 3), began to contemplate creating an enclosed space in which young artists and those rejected by famous galleries would have the opportunity to present their works in an enclosed gallery space. In collaboration with the café and cultural institute UpArtMaan, Mortazavi created a space in the stair alcove (*zirpelleh*) of

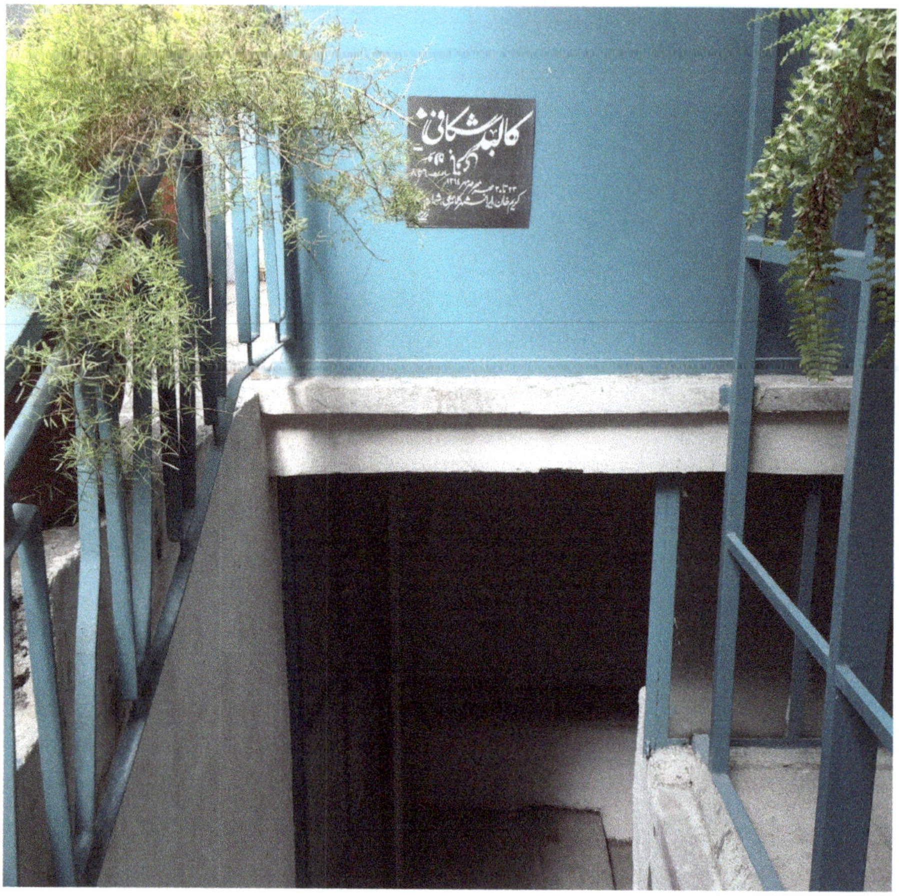

FIGURE 1.17 Zirpelleh (stair alcove) exhibition space. Entrance with signage for *Dissecting Cadaver* solo exhibition by artist Soodeh Bagheri. Photograph by Houman Mortazavi.

the institute—an early Pahlavi-era house on Iranshahr Avenue. Damp and dark, the three-by-four-meter space was "ideal for unconventional projects that were not commonly taken seriously or were censored due to sensitive content," Mortazavi remarked more than half a decade after Zirpelleh's creation (fig. 1.17).[186]

To be understood as a nongallery, Zirpelleh created a manifesto in which the collaborative artists expressed the goal of the space. These included "being a non-gallery; not indebted to anyone's history or heritage; avoiding clichés; encouraging thinking outside the box; inspiring artists to contemplate ways of making art public and interactive; reducing the fake sacredness (*ghedasat-e ja'li*) of art; depending on participatory budgeting; encouraging all visitors to purchase the signed artist work at low price, etc."[187] To borrow from Pouria Jahanshad, who believes that independent art enterprises should always take on a critical stance, instead of "blind[ly] follow[ing] the interests of the mainstream art market," Zirpelleh "establish[ed] an independent/alternative art market."[188]

Previously, the method of participatory budgeting used by Zirpelleh had rarely been implemented by other galleries. Before the revolution, many independent galleries, such as Ghandriz Hall (1964–78) and the Theater Workshop (*Kargah-e Namayesh*, 1969–79), benefitted from state subsidies for rent and limited administrative staffing.[189] Perhaps the closest comparable example to Zirpelleh is the 1960s nonprofit alternative art space, Rasht 29,[190] which was not only an exhibition space but also a restaurant, poetry-reading and music venue, and at times even a place to show films and slides.[191] Some artists would donate works as credit for free meals and drinks.[192] At the peak of its success, Rasht 29 hosted the first auction of modern art in Iran.[193] It was also a dress rehearsal for the activities of the Shiraz Arts Festival.[194] While there is no direct correlation between Rasht 29 and Zirpelleh, the similarities in how these places operated are noteworthy, once more affirming the parallel models that can be found in both pre- and postrevolutionary periods, each with distinct incentives specific to their times and contexts.

Notable among the projects featured at Zirpelleh during its short life of less than two years was a one-week exhibition in October 2015, *Dissecting Cadaver* (*Kalbod shekafi*). Emerging artist Soodeh Bagheri (b. 1985) hid some of her personal possessions inside molded plaster objects, which visitors were invited to break open to discover her secrets, such as items of her underwear and fragments of love letters to a boyfriend. Sharing "personal secrets" (*asrar-e khosoosi*) is not something women are supposed to do in public. The exhibition allowed Bagheri to express her hidden desires and riddles and thereby remained faithful to one of the tenets of Zirpelleh: bringing the private into the public domain. Not only did the name of the gallery suggest underground activities in a public place; it also intentionally accommodated art projects and practices that captured the same mysterious sentiments.

. . .

Counter to an Institution. The Rooberoo Building (*Emarat-e rooberoo*, literally the Opposite Edifice) is registered as a performance space, but it also presents artworks in the basement of an old, refurbished, midcentury Tehran home.[195] Located on Enghelab Avenue in downtown Tehran, the Rooberoo is just a block away from Vahdat Hall (formerly Rudaki), a prominent performance space built under the Pahlavis (figs. 1.18a/b). As if the small old house were a counterpart to the institution of Vahdat Hall, the name Rooberoo (front) suggests that confrontation. On the website of Rooberoo, the organizers have defined the purpose of the house in a short essay:

> The Rooberoo Building is a house, one that was built long before it assumed a new function as an art and cultural center in November 2016. This house is a manifestation of our dreams . . . . [W]e always wanted to have a multi-media space where we could get together and share our thoughts and ideas. The building is a manifestation of our individual voices . . . truly independent from all the preconceptions that are forced upon us. For a constructive future, we need to be independent thinkers. We want to play a part in all aspects of our society. . . . We need to put aside all those presuppositions that are imposed upon us by our culture. This requires much work and we have a complicated journey ahead of us. Creating a dialogue is essential; we need to become the change that we desire, and we need to define the contours of our culture and civilization. We expect to see our viewers as participants, and we aim for new media art and cutting-edge projects . . . in a safe space. We hope that others join us in this goal-oriented context and take action alongside us.[196]

In this manifesto, phrases like "safe space," "individual voice," "independent thinkers," and "viewers as participants" attest to the extent to which words matter as much as the architecture itself. Through these terms, Iranian artists define alternative art in critical and spatial ways.

. . .

Bomb Shelter as Art Space. Nabshi, another initiative of Ehsan Rasoulof, is a dynamic hub on a corner lot at the intersection of Khosrow Alley and Nejatollahi Avenue (formerly Villa). Nabshi thrives by promoting interdisciplinary perspectives in art, architecture, and design; it has adopted a collaborative approach to publishing books as well as holding exhibitions, workshops, panel discussions, and other cross-disciplinary events.[197] Of particular interest, in terms of the architectural form and function of the spaces, is the way in which Rasoulof, the sole mastermind behind the concept of Nabshi and its functions, associates the spaces within the house with the activities that take place inside them.

The most interesting of all is "Panahgah," a term associated with the large subterranean air raid shelter created beneath the front yard for the occupants of the house and their neighbors during the Iran-Iraq war (fig. 1.19). According to the institute's website, Panahgah "used to be a safe place . . . during wartime. Panahgah is a place for silence and observation."[198] Zav

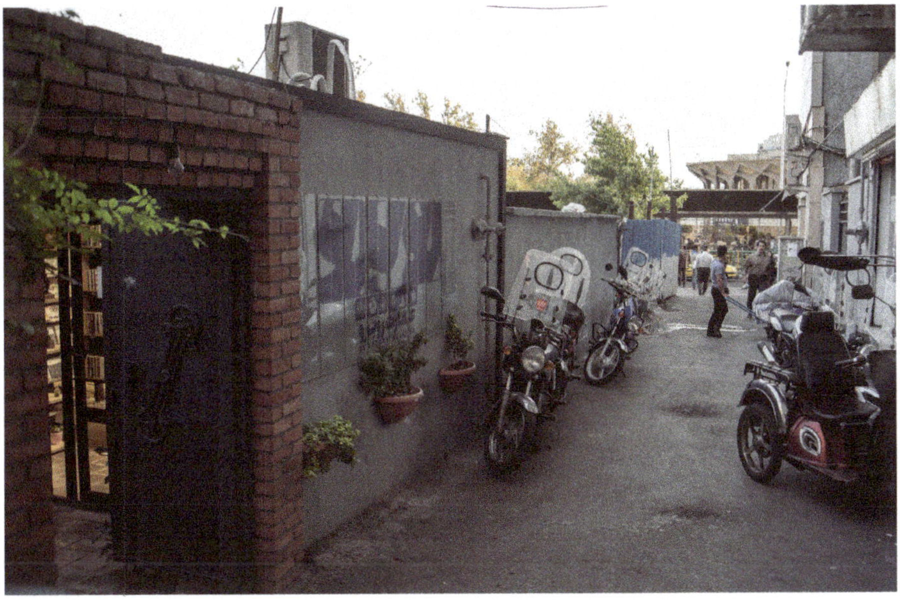

FIGURE 1.18A Exterior view of Emarat-e Rooberoo (the opposite building) with the City Theater visible at the end of the alley. 2018. Tehran. Photograph by Mojtaba Fallahi.

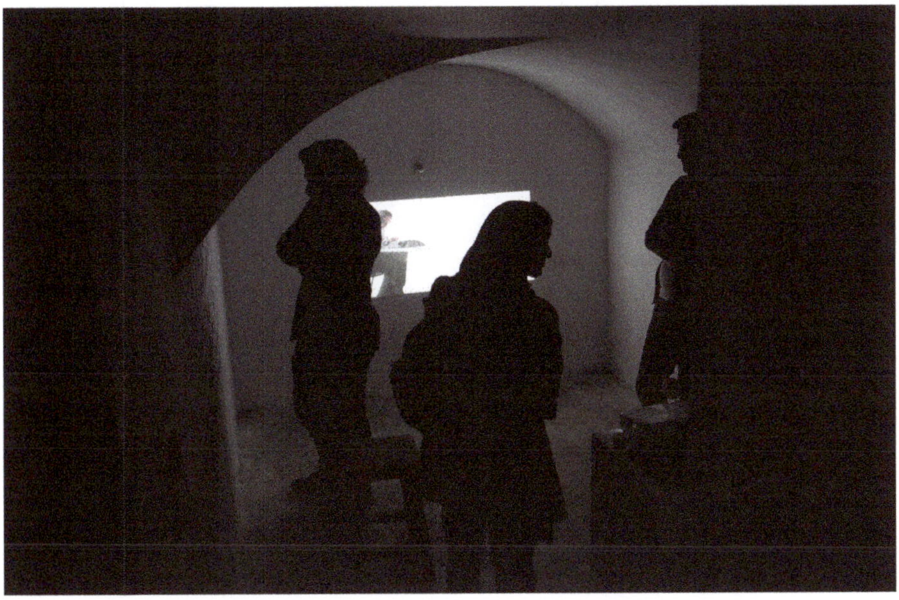

FIGURE 1.18B Exhibition space in the basement of Emarat-e Rooberoo. 2018. Tehran. Photograph by Mojtaba Fallahi.

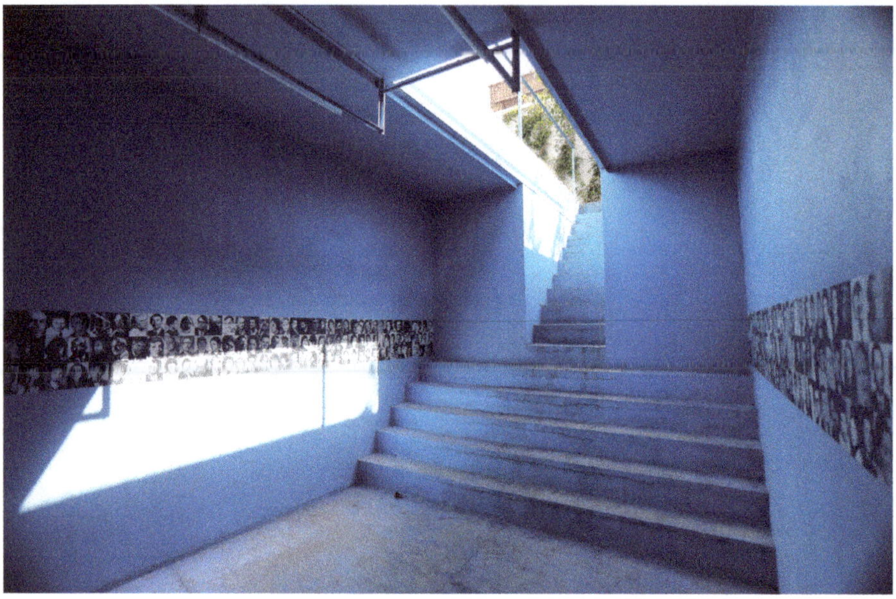

FIGURE 1.19 Snapshot from Nabshi's Panahgah (bomb shelter) Gallery. 2019. Tehran. Photograph courtesy of the Nabshi Center and Ehsan Rasoulof.

Architects, the firm responsible for materializing Rasoulof ideas by converting the old building into an art center, explained the significance of the bomb shelter: "[T]he building bears scars of the war era. . . . The bomb-shelter is the manifestation of a certain landscape of fear. The shelter, the very manifestation of spatial isolation and protectiveness, play[ed] a central role in this programmatic conversion, redefined as the start[ing] point [for] spatial continuity and fluidity."[199]

Nabshi sells (rare) art books in Pastoo—the name for storage in traditional courtyard homes, *anbar* in modern dialect. On their website, Nabshi describes the space in these words: "Pastoo is a place for reading and observation."[200] Pellekan, another arcane word referring to the stairwell of the old house, is described as "a place for encounters."[201] That Rasoulof and Zav highlight these spaces for their traditional functions, outdated names, secretive characteristics, and potentiality for covertness is an ingenious way to address how the privately run enterprise, Nabshi, recreates the underground culture while at the same time making it public.

. . .

An Underground Water Reservoir. Curator and director of the Abanbar Gallery in Tehran, Salman Matinfar (b. 1977) manages one of the most important commercial art spaces in the city from his base in London.[202] The gallery is housed in a former family compound built in the 1950s. Taking

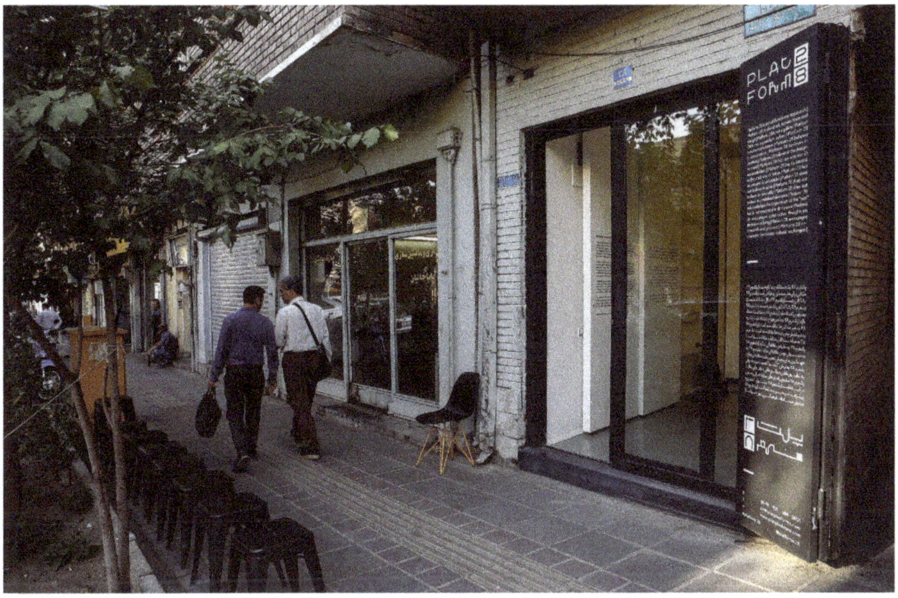

FIGURE 1.20A The storefront of Abanbar (water reservoir) and Platform 28. 2017. Tehran. Courtesy of Azadeh Zafarani.

a cue from his business partner, Sohrab Kashani (see chapter 4), Matinfar named the space based on the family's most valuable asset: the water storage space in the basement.[203] Before the introduction of domestic plumbing, subterranean cisterns—*abanbars*—were common in well-to-do family homes. If a house lacked such a private water storage space, residents had to rely on water sellers or walk long distances to use public cisterns. In tandem with its underground quality, the Abanbar Gallery is also perfectly camouflaged at its ground-level entrance, especially when seen in the context of the businesses surrounding it (figs. 1.20a/b). This is an intentional tactic of invisibility that has become a crucial aspect of survival for many art spaces in Tehran, especially in less prosperous neighborhoods.

After securing permission from the MCIG, Matinfar expanded the complex. His wife, Azadeh Zaferani (b. 1981), an architect by training, then dedicated the gallery's front space at entrance level (formerly a small welding shop, two by seven meters) as a room with movable walls for displaying architecture books and drawings and for hosting architecture-related workshops.[204] The purpose of the space, Platform 28, is to make "architectural thinking more accessible to the public" and to bridge the disparate circles of artists and architects.[205]

Not surprisingly, and appropriately, the conversations that take place in Platform 28 are related to historically significant critical spatial practices.

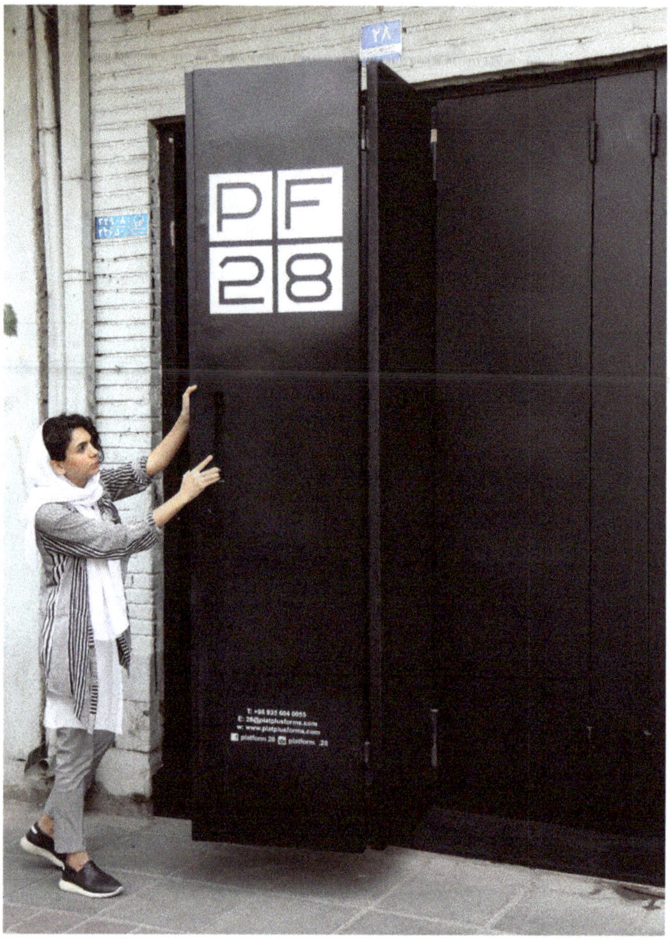

FIGURE 1.20B Platform 28. 2017. Tehran. Photograph by Salman Matinfar. Courtesy of Azadeh Zafarani.

For example, through the event series *The Recycling of Socialism* (2016), Platform 28 invited Eastern European architects to share their thoughts on political changes after the fall of the USSR as well as the design solutions that were emerging from their participation in the global marketplace. In its own words, Platform 28 seeks, "by drawing parallels," to continue to be creative despite the sanctions imposed on Iran.[206]

. . .

An Electric Room. The Dastan Basement (*Zirzamin-e Dastan*) gallery is located in the exclusive neighborhood of Elahiyyeh in northern Tehran. In this case, the choice of the word "basement," *zirzamini*, does not carry the usual connotations of underground art, according to Ashkan Zahraie (b. 1989), the lead curator. The original gallery registered with both the

MCIG and the Public Property Bureau was the engineering office set up by its founding director, Hormoz Hematian (b. 1983), on his return home after his civil engineering education in North America.[207]

In addition to gaining permission to operate as a general gallery, Dastan Basement also has to secure permission from the MCIG for each show. They document all the works on display and send a printed copy of the images to the ministry. If the ministry has objections, they send a representative to the venue to investigate; otherwise, no news is good news. While the gallery features the work of many high-profile artists, such as Fereydoun Ave, they also do pop-up displays in alternative spaces off-site. Notable is Electric Room, a small space that opened in June 2017 in downtown Tehran, within walking distance of the Faculty of Fine Arts at Tehran University as well as the Art University. Hematian chose to call the alternative site *Electric Room* (*Otagh-e bargh*) because the space was literally an electric control room, with independent access from the dead-end service alley (fig. 1.21). A double door provided access to and through the main building, which also included a café, a restaurant, and six floors of office space.

Before setting up Electric Room, Hematian had meticulously studied fig-1, a program of fifty weeklong projects in 2000 in a small space in

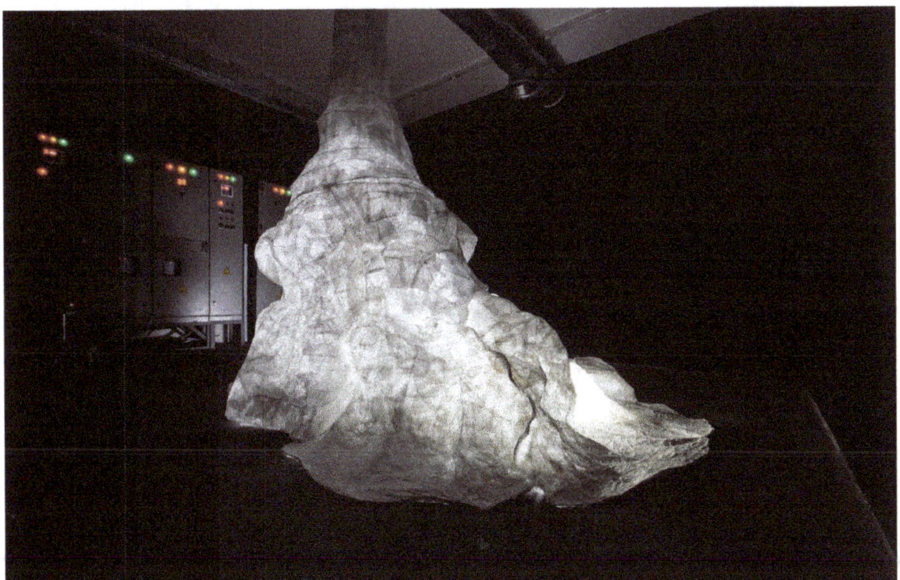

FIGURE 1.21 An exhibition of works by multimedia artist Shokoofeh Khoramroodi and performance artist Taba Fajrak at the Electric Room (project 19/50). Curated by Ashkan Zahraei and Alireza Fatehie Boroujeni. 2014. Tehran. Photograph courtesy of Ashkan Zahraei.

London's Soho district. The project, a collaboration between curator Mark Francis and White Cube gallerist Jay Jopling, showcased artists alongside architects, writers, designers, and musicians, and all events were programmed only a few weeks in advance in order to be as flexible as possible.

With this as inspiration, Hematian had been thinking about finding a space and running such a fast-paced program since 2013. In early 2016, as writer and consulting curator, he helped manage Abi Gallery, a small venue in the Dibaji neighborhood of Tehran that was a converted apartment parking garage with two spaces, one for a small office and the other for a pop-up gallery. The small scale of Abi Gallery made it a perfect choice for young and emerging artists as well as for more experimental projects. Modeled after Abi Gallery and fig-1, Electric Room also partners with a number of independent spaces, projects, and platforms, including Tehran's Mess Atelier, New Media Society, and Empty Space Studio.

"*Basement*" and "*electric room*" conjure up all kinds of associations with covert spaces and spaces of punishment. And yet, "Everyone abides by the rules here," asserts Zahraie.[208] According to him, there is a bit of undergroundness in every art space in Iran, but at the same time, they are all registered and they function within the framework of Iranian law. Thus, once again, the names and spatial conditions of these alternative gallery spaces are more curious than their operational attributes. These names inadvertently exude an air of criticality and defiance.

. . .

The main takeaway of the layered stories behind the making of these establishments is the imaginative way in which artists, against all odds, have appropriated unconventional spaces to maintain alternative artistic productions. Many of these appropriations are forms of micro-resistance that have escaped the visual threshold of the common spectacle of confrontation, such as object-oriented art with strong political themes. Above all, critical engagement with alternative sites has become a way of life and thought. Through their critical spatial practices, artists, performers, and musicians reveal the "tenuousness of maintaining illusory separations between art and life, theory and practice, work and the self, research and motivation."[209] These are the words of Lauren Fournier in *Autotheory as Feminist Practice in Art, Writing, and Criticism* (2020), in which she explores generating theory through artistic practice. Curiously, one source of inspiration for Fournier is the work of a 127 band member, Sohrab Mohebbi (b. 1982), whose career later shifted to curation and art criticism.[210] The point of reference is a small collection of essays edited by Mohebbi, *Hotel Theory Reader* (2016), in which the reader encounters writings by artists whose works aspire to push the boundaries of the theoretical discourse. One contributor to the volume is Tirdad Zolghadr (b. 1973), curator and a former member of Tehran's "underground" music scenes. Zolghadr discusses the significance of an early experience with Mohebbi in the space of an "underground band" in Tehran, describing how the unique spatial experience of those confined venues, the movement of the bodies and the playing with ideas, shaped the imaginations of artists.[211] Indeed, these testimonies imply how Iran's loosely covert spaces adhere to the Lefebvrian interpretation of space as that which is a continuous social dynamic.

The Gradual Disintegration of "Invisibility"

Throughout the 1960s and 1970s, the alternative art spaces that animated cities like New York had *visibility*, both physically and in terms of publicity and marketing. Indeed, visibility was at the forefront of alternative art spaces such as the A.I.R. Gallery, the first independent women's gallery founded in 1972 by a collective of feminist artists. Visibility allowed A.I.R. to enter a contested political arena, in which women could mimic "the conditions of the art market and thus . . . create an alternative *inside* the system."[212] Unique to the alternative art scenes in New York, this model did not (and still largely does not) work in Iran. As the examples in this chapter have demonstrated, alternative art sites have been produced in Iran out of necessity. To maintain their different character (that is, against the forms of art approved by the regime), many alternative art projects had to move to "invisible" places—and many still do. Homes, churches, basements, subterranean spaces, and dilapidated structures became the art spaces of the postrevolutionary period.

Taking creative activities into the "invisible" world of rundown buildings and homes was not always effortless and unchallenged, as we have seen. The 1990s *kolangi* projects each lasted only ten days due to conflicts with the authorities. Farideh Shahsavarani, who did not secure permission from MCIG for her site-specific project in the former headquarters of *Ettela'at Newspaper*, ended up taking down the show after just one week. Even though it was a monumental achievement, the project never received the attention it deserved. The Lahijan Tea factory exhibition was swiftly shut down after its opening and, following the 2009 Green Movement, many alternative art exhibitions in abandoned buildings as well as theatrical performances in private homes were delivered to "trusted" audiences only.

Then, within a couple of decades, all private projects moved from underground to aboveground, from invisibility to a loose covertness and some to total visibility. When theater became privatized in the early 2010s, the MCIG changed its permission policy. Previously, all plays seeking approval had to pass through two phases. First, the theater group was required to submit the text of the play or, if there was no dialogue, a proposal explaining what was to take place. Second, the group had to perform in front of a representative of the ministry to receive official approval for public presentation. After 2010, the first phase of approval was removed and directors were only required to obtain permission at the time the fully staged play could be viewed by an MCIG representative.[213] This procedure placed all of the responsibility on the private theater company owners, who did not wish to fund a play only to see it cancelled before it opened. Subsequently, funders such as businessmen and developers began to implement MCIG guidelines, to ensure that their money and efforts were not wasted. In this way, ordinary citizens were forced to police the theatrical realm.

The state thus began to regulate and control alternative art scenes because it could not eliminate them altogether. One means to do this was through *aggressive mimicry*, a strategy that involves the *predator* simply sitting and waiting for prey to come to it.[214] Adopting the ploy of "underground films," until recently the regime disseminated documentary-like films, with features that are ordinarily forbidden in Iranian cinema, such as displaying unveiled women. Distributed on street corners as exotic and contraband products—just like the exotic and illegal Western films that used to circulate back in the 1980s and 1990s—these are, according to anthropologist Narges Bajoghli, propaganda films designed to stigmatize those who advocate the overthrow of the leadership of the Islamic Republic of Iran, such as the People's Mujahedin Organization, or the *Mojahedin-e-Khalq*, an Iranian political-militant organization.[215] Further evidence of these efforts can be found in the launch, in February 2019, of the "*Asr-e Jadid* (New Age) Talent Competition," an imitation of *America's Got Talent*.[216] Indeed, according to a former staff member of the MCIG, Asr-e Jadid is simply "a strategy to prevent the youth from going underground, and an effective way to encourage them to bring their artistic talent above ground, under the supervision of the authorities."[217]

By managing alternative artists and funding them rather than suppressing them, the state slowly began to extend its power over alternative art sites. Loosely covert and privately funded establishments of alternative art were created, whose only affiliation with the underground, invisible, or covert culture was their preference for camouflage or tucking themselves away, or in the choice of the names for the establishment. Indeed, from 2000 on we see the rise of a slow regulatory regime—*a predatory aestheticization* strategy that gradually diluted the pure alternative nature of the independent art activities of the 1990s. It was in light of such early signs of state and corporate sponsorship that Iranian alternative art began to take on a more convoluted character. Strategies of escapism, ephemerality, and improvisation came to replace the old techniques of covertness and invisibility.

. . .

Most of the alternative art spaces described here had the capacity to descend along a vertical axis into the "underground." Alternative sites of art production have employed other spatial tactics, distancing themselves from the "official" centers of art production and growing, instead, across a horizontal axis. Hence, horizontality is taken up by other artists as a possibility for escapism—a spatial tactic used, for example, in the westward expansion of the United States.[218] The unique escapist choices in the context of the US are also applicable in Iran, due to somewhat similar environmental conditions. Two-thirds of Iran, a territory more than twice the size of Texas, is either desert or mountains. The Plateau of Iran, in the center of the country and extending eastward into Central Asia, encompasses two salt deserts that make up twenty-five percent of Iran's land area. These vast empty areas have long provided an opportunity for escape. By keeping their distance from the center and edging out toward the margins, artists and curators have attempted to create more opportunities for alternative and unconventional art, as we will see in chapter 2.

2 Escapism

Critical Engagements with Remote Natural Sites

FOR THE SHIRAZ ARTS FESTIVAL OF 1972, the Empress Farah invited the American performance artist Robert Wilson and his avant-garde theater group, the Byrd Hoffman School of Byrds, to showcase a seven-day nonstop performance across an entire mountain.[1] The event was meant to be "a kind of window into the world where ordinary and extraordinary events could be seen together. One could see the world at 8am, 3pm, or midnight, and the play would always be there, a twenty-four-hour clock composed of natural time interrupted by supernatural time."[2] In this way, Iranians were introduced to the idea of making conceptual art in remote natural environments and open fields, engaging with unusual places and time frames.[3]

Titled *KA MOUNTAIN AND GUARDenia TERRACE: A Story about a Family and Some People Changing*, the 168-hour performance became "a site-specific fantasia, a ritual and a pilgrimage across the seven hills of the arid rocky terrain of the Haft Tan Mountain, on the outskirts of Shiraz."[4] The site Wilson selected for his show—Haft Tan (Seven Bodies) Mountain—takes its name from the graves of seven Sufi poets who are entombed at its base. The action, which covered the seven biblical days of "Creation," was spread over the mountain (fig. 2.1).

The choice of location was a nod to Environmental Theater, a branch of the New Theater movement of the 1960s that had been pioneered by Richard Schechner, who was himself inspired by Polish director Jerzy Grotowski. In Shiraz, Wilson aimed to engage the audience by reducing the distance between them and the performers. His sets offered varied rooms in which the viewers could participate. Ossia Trilling writes in a 1973 issue of *Drama Review*, "The play combined the salient features [of] improvised playacting and action-painting with those of a planned 'Happening' [with a] fully involved audience."[5]

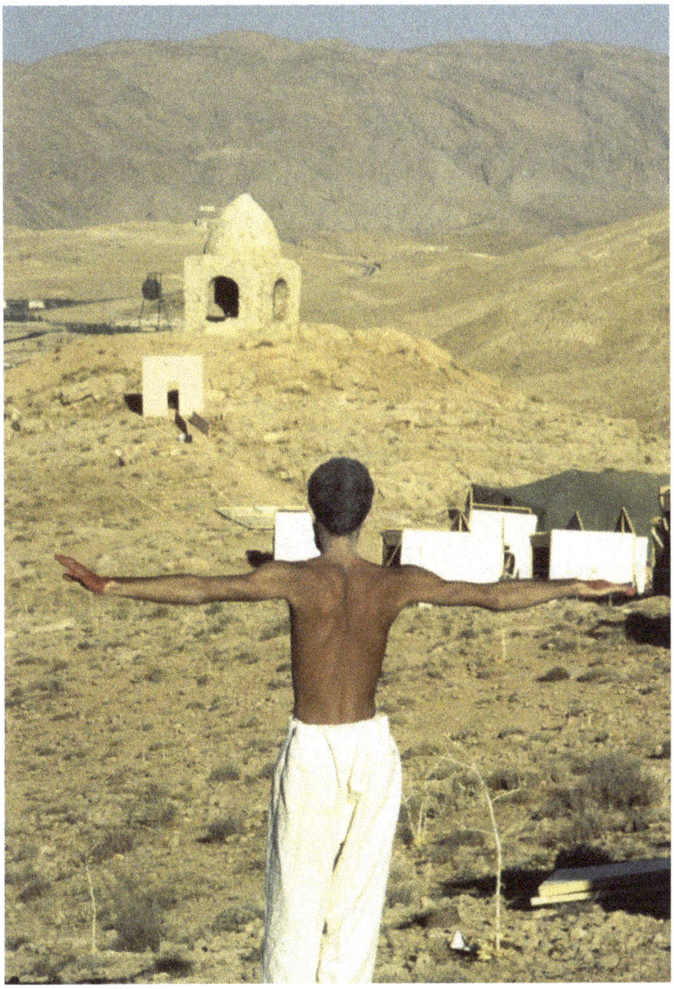

FIGURE 2.1
Robert Wilson, *KA MOUNTAIN AND GUARDenia TERRACE: A Story about a Family and Some People Changing.* 168-hour-long performance. 1972. Haft Tan Mountain, Shiraz. Photographers Bacil Langton and Bahman Jalali. Courtesy of the Robert Wilson Archives at the Byrd Hoffman Water Mill Foundation.

KA (a word common to Iranian, Egyptian, and Amerindian folklore) attempted to address the meaning of life in the troubled modern world. As an old man climbed up the mountain, a series of seemingly unrelated events took place concurrently on all seven foothills, alluding perhaps to the idea of the seven stages of human life. All kinds of people were involved in these activities, from an elderly storyteller from the bazaar to a New Jersey housewife.[6] They were joined by a similarly diverse nonhuman cast. Trilling comments that, from the foot of the mountain onward, "the audience was able to get a foretaste of some of what was to follow . . . they caught their first glimpse of the livestock Wilson had collected, some of them in uncomfortably small cages, including a bear, a lion, various horses, donkeys, poultry, deer, goats and an elephant."[7]

But it was the mountain that was the main protagonist. In the words of Wilson's biographer, Maria Shevtsova, "The mountain itself, with its searing heat during the day and intense cold at night, could be said to be the prime actor in this epic whose greatest significance probably lay in the personal inner journeys undergone by its makers."[8] The tops of the foothills were painted white, and the rest of the natural setting was dotted with cutouts of emblems such as Noah's Ark and the Acropolis, where performers and spectators paused and interacted with one another. Like cutouts in a surreal landscape painting, these marked the various stages in a seemingly disjointed pilgrimage that began down below with the menagerie of live animals, suggesting perhaps the passengers on the world's first sea voyage. The uphill journey then proceeded to the artificially snow-capped peak with its replica of the Manhattan skyline.[9]

Wilson had wanted to blow up the top of the mountain at the end of the seven-day pilgrimage, but the authorities, who otherwise had tried their best to give Wilson all that he needed and had avoided any form of censorship, refused his request, perhaps on environmental grounds. Instead, Wilson was permitted to set an emblematic cutout Chinese pagoda on fire. The landscape during this last scene became a fiery torch that burned throughout the night over quiet, sleeping Shiraz and, whether inadvertently or deliberately, came to evoke the fire-worship of the ancient religion of Iran, Zoroastrianism. Several commentators, including local critics as well as Shevtsova, have written that despite Wilson's efforts to understand the Iranian landscape, he saw it as akin to his hometown in Waco, Texas, and so the performance was not really site-specific. The work lacked direct cultural references to the site, which had been important to Sufis and other spiritually inclined people.[10] Even more awkward, throughout the play, as described by the reporters, the Bible was read instead of the Qur'an or Sufi texts or Persian poetry. However, Wilson himself has a slightly different take on how the play was perceived. Specifically, regarding the way it was seen by the locals, he told me:

> The play . . . was not understood by many people, most of all myself. It was exploring the idea that theater could always be happening, that one could go on a coffee break, one could go at midnight, one could go before going to the office or to work. It was never meant to be seen entirely by any one person. It was

> performed only once. Those witnessing the events of the play knew that they were seeing something special, something that would never happen again. In that way it was like a shooting star. . . . There were many Iranians participating in the performance: some students, some older people, . . . , people who lived in the foothills and who had never even been in Shiraz, people who had never heard a radio or seen TV and had no idea that Man had been to the moon. Some of the people in the foothills would sit and watch the play the same way that they would watch sheep cross a hill and clouds move in the sky. They were curious that it was happening in their backyard. In some ways, the Persian audience was more receptive than the audience would have been in New York City because of the pace and time of the work. It was close to nature and very different from the busy life of cities. Some audience members stayed all night and would sleep part of the time, as the play continued.[11]

Notwithstanding the criticisms, Wilson's own testimony helps to explain the enduring importance of the idea of a mountain as an art venue in the art scenes of Iran. In the following years, artists like Mohsen Vaziri Moghaddam (1924–2018), Marcos Grigorian (1925–2007), and Gholamhossein Nami (b. 1936) explored the arid landscapes on the outskirts of Tehran.[12] Grigorian was very keen to incorporate close-up views of the barren terrain in aerial perspectives of what appear to be plowed fields.[13] Gaining the moniker "the father of Iran's Earthworks," he favored a style that celebrated the visual vocabulary of parched earth (*kahgel*) and mud, which he also incorporated into his multimedia 2D works.[14]

In contrast to Wilson, Grigorian does not approach the natural environment as an exotic location in which a wide network of past and present stories, aspirations, and subjectivities overlap. Rather, he sees it as a place in which new realities might be envisioned and crystallized; indeed, within nature, Iranian art seems to have acquired a much more critical edge.

More polemical was an installation by a lay landowner, Darvish Khan, on the fringes of the eastern city of Sirjan in response to the Shah's land reforms launched in 1963. When Darvish Khan realized that the sanctuary of his garden was being violated, he roped large and small pieces of stones to its dried-up trees in a symbolic act of protest. The work came to the notice of the artistic community when it was reenacted in a pseudo-documentary film by Parviz Kimiavi, *Bagh-e sangi* or *The Garden of Stones* (1976). The film features the real Darvish Khan planting a dessicated tree and painstakingly hauling large blocks of stone from the desert to hang from its branches. At the same time and unbeknownst to him in the film, his family spreads rumors about the holiness of the garden of stone in the hope of drawing pilgrims. When their plot is eventually discredited, the villagers revolt against the garden. The film ends with an eerie sequence in which Darvish Khan learns that his installation has been stained white by a figure dressed and masked like an exterminator. This is the scene that precedes Darvish's cry of anguish;[15] in dismay, Darvish Khan ends up hanging himself by the foot from one of the trees, becoming the latest addition to his stone garden.[16] Elevated to the level of art by Kimiavi's film, *The Garden of Stones* holds a special place in the collective memory of Iranians. Indeed, a 2015 issue of *Mehr News* identifies Darvish Khan as "the progenitor of environmental art (*honar-e mohiti*)" in modern Iran.[17]

In other, nonperformative forms of art, such as painting, remote natural spots also took on a political dimension. During the revolutionary years, some leftist-minded artists were drawn to villages and remote areas, due to their sympathy with farmers, miners, and villagers. For his undergraduate capstone project, painter Hossein Maher (b. 1957) spent a great deal of time in remote villages to better capture the pain and daily labor of local coal miners.[18]

. . .

After the revolution, any creative engagement with the environment was put on hold for more than a decade. During the postrevolutionary era, Iranian artists were not allowed to discuss prerevolutionary interventions in nature—including the Shiraz Arts Festival projects—particularly not in university classrooms, at museum events, or at other official art-related gatherings. Artists and teachers nonetheless managed to inform their mentees and students through word of mouth. In my interviews with the generation of Iranian artists who began to implement their art in natural settings, many acknowledged the influence of the art forms that their mentors had described.[19] Above all, the Shiraz Arts Festival spurred new ways of thinking about displaying art other than in galleries and exploring how art might contribute to the expansion of what Lefebvre called "lived experiences."

Engagement with remote natural places is not just about environmental significance or the emotional and sensory feelings provoked by nature or the landscape. Conventional understandings of art in nature as something that must be situated outdoors or made of organic materials have given way to a wider range of meanings and media, particularly in the sociopolitical atmosphere of Iran. Spending long periods in remote natural environments involves actual physical engagement with areas outside the purview of the dominant power. It is, thus, a kind of "institutional critique" that stretches beyond the more usual practices of taking art out of museums and other official organizations in protest against their policies.

Escapism without Leaving

In his 2019 Frontline series, *Our Man in Tehran*, the Dutch director, reporter, and former Tehran bureau chief of the *New York Times*, Thomas Erdbrink, reveals a covert orchard in the suburbs of Tehran that served as a rehearsal venue for *Mandy*, a parody of the Los Angeles–based Iranian pop singer Andy. Here is how Erdbrink describes the space:

> It is . . . in a secret location, . . . far from Tehran. . . . Like starstruck teens, [the fans] . . . have driven for hours to be there. . . . These people have come together in secret because the nation's leaders have banned their favorite singer who sings innocent songs about love. The irony in all of this is that these activities take place in hidden spots, even though the whole country listens to the banned songs.[20]

Erdbrink's story captures the essence of a collective desire to escape, even if that escapism does not necessarily mean hiding or concealing something that is highly secretive, widely forbidden, or overtly political. The kind of escapism we see inside Iran is different from the experience of Iranians who have fled the country and live in the diaspora. In this case, people ostensibly adapt to the conventional frameworks while managing to remain in charge of their own destiny. This idealistic mentality is not unique to postrevolutionary Iran. Earlier, in the introduction, I outlined the historical roots of such forms of escapism inside Iran, but this is also often a universal action whose theoretical and philosophical foundations are globally entrenched. As early as 1903, in his essay "Metropolis and Mental Life," Georg Simmel writes about the "attempt of the individual to maintain the independence and individuality of its existence against the sovereign powers of society, against the weight of the historical heritage and the external culture and technique of life."[21]

Likewise, in her classic book *The Human Condition* (1958), Hannah Arendt writes: "It has always been a great temptation . . . [to] escape the haphazardness and moral irresponsibility"[22] in order to remain master of one's own actions from beginning to end.[23] Remaining master of one's own actions without abandoning the mainstream or openly breaking the dominant rules and regulations is also synonymous with what French literary and cultural theorist Michel de Certeau calls "escaping without leaving."

In *The Practice of Everyday Life*, de Certeau writes about the implications of "escaping" the internal snares of a domineering culture "without leaving it." Specifically, he addresses the concept in the context of the responses of the Aztecs and Mayans to the rituals and laws imposed by their Spanish subjugators. These "submissive Indians" disrupted the new ideas not by outwardly rejecting them but by performing them differently, and while "they lacked the means to challenge, they [nonetheless] escaped it without leaving it."[24]

De Certeau uses this historical example to prove that the dominant culture itself "tells us nothing about what it is for its users. We must first analyze its manipulation by users who are not its makers."[25] This "escapist" mindset can be taken literally and applied to the ways in which subversive groups physically leave a place to exercise their freedom elsewhere, but not necessarily outside the entire system. Nor do they want to break any rules or cross any lines in a clear-cut manner.

The countercultural activities of the 1960s and 1970s offer ample instances of such reactions to the prevailing culture by artists around the world. *Counterculture*, a term coined by Theodore Rozak in 1969,[26] is commonly associated with contexts in which protests against the existing order are led by groups that Herbert Marcuse deemed "the only viable social revolutionaries"—in other words, middle-class hippies.[27] Their simple premise was a culture that had values and norms substantially different from those of mainstream society.[28]

Consider Drop City, for example, a rural community in southern Colorado created in 1965 by a hippie artist group. For nearly eight years, Drop City helped youth to "drop out" of conventional life. A response to mainstream consumerist lifestyles and to the Vietnam War, what made Drop City stand out among all other informal hippie settlements scattered across the United States was its artistic quality. Using low-tech construction methods and the techniques of the pioneer of passive solar technology, Steve Baer, the group built homes that were essentially modified versions of Buckminster Fuller's geodesic domes, made out of car roofs reclaimed from junkyards. Beyond their escapist character, "such tactical refusals of dominant forms of life," as characterized by architectural historian Felicity Scott, are, historically speaking, among the most important critical spatial practices.[29]

Not only did members of the Drop City escape, they also engaged in alternative forms of spatial production.

The United States was not alone in encountering this culture of escapism in the decades that followed World War II. Recall that the sites of socialist escapes were often located in faraway places such as cabins in the woods, roadsides, campgrounds, and beaches. During much of the Cold War, physical escape from the Eastern Bloc was nearly impossible. There remained, however, possibilities for other forms of escapism—particularly, time spent away from party ideology and the strictures of everyday life. As such, "escaping without leaving" was for a long time the mindset of young people in socialist countries during the Cold War as they experienced new forms of control over their free time and leisure activities.[30]

In 1950s Poland, many took spirited hikes in the "wild west" of Bieszczady Mountains. In East Germany, pioneer camps in the countryside offered a brief respite from the surveilled mass housing projects, and from the late 1950s onward, the golden beaches of Bulgaria became safe havens for partying.[31] In the arts, the Soviet Collective Actions Group (*Kollektivnye Deistvia*) famously took their practices to faraway fields. In doing so, they did not set out to embrace the beauty of nature or create art that held environmental messages. As one member of the group, Sergei Sitar, noted, these faraway places were not chosen for their aesthetic merits "but simply as 'the lesser evil'—as a space that is the least occupied, the least appropriated by the dominant cultural discourse."[32] Another member, Igor Makarevich, described exploring the remote natural spots as an activity outside the social, while Georgy Kiesewalter maintained that in going to these areas, the aim was not to make "art" but to engage in "spiritual exercise" of a Buddhist kind.[33]

Before *perestroika* (an era associated with Soviet leader Mikhail Gorbachev and his *glasnost* policy reform), remote locations in nature were chosen primarily because the urban environment was viewed as corrupted by ideology.[34] Consequently, the motivations for escaping to nature were more existential than ideological. Alternative and underground artists in the Soviet Union and the Eastern Bloc pursued opportunities for fostering independent forms of living against an overbearing cultural system that constantly sought to regulate and homogenize. As art historian Claire Bishop argues, "Most artists wanted nothing to do with politics—and indeed even rejected the dissident position—by choosing to operate instead on an existential plane: making assertions of individual freedom, even in the slightest or most silent of forms."[35] These activities must be framed,

Bishop reminds us, as "*shared* privatized experiences."[36] The Slovakian artist Alex Mlynárčik, throughout the 1960s and 1970s, created a "total expression" of art as life "to fuse organically with life in the name of the totality of life, the totality of reality!"[37] Mlynárčik's works were sited in the countryside or in open natural spots in his hometown of Žilina in the north of Slovakia. He framed much of his work as "a celebration of life and joy, hope and love [and] a manifestation of . . . artistic creation and cooperation."[38]

. . .

Aligned with de Certeau's course of thought and the global examples sketched above, postrevolutionary Iranian art projects in remote natural spaces could be seen as a rehearsal for the creation of an alternative public sphere. In these faraway places, a communal culture of common interests took the place of policing and surveillance.

The deserts, mountains, caves, and remote spots in the deserts of Iran have long been chosen by postrevolutionary artists because they permit activities that are not possible in big city centers. For one thing, these remote areas allow artists to escape state-controlled urban surveillance, or the disciplinary mechanism Michel Foucault famously termed "panopticonism." This is not to say that art in remote natural settings necessarily involves forbidden (*makrooh*) activities such as obscenity or sexualized or outrageous performances. Rather, artists crave the opportunity for personal reflection or the kind of collective artistic spirit that is often perceived as a threat in urban centers—especially during election seasons, when the government limits gatherings of any kind in public places.

Case studies and associated stories of securing permission from the respective state authorities, however, show that the political undertones of all projects enacted in remote natural places are often indirect and subtle. The focus is on a personal desire to escape the obstacles of daily life, literally or metaphorically. At other times, the goal is to form a collective spirit. Because all art projects in open fields must have permission, none of the following examples should be seen as covert forms of resistance against the ideology of the Islamic Republic. Despite their subversive tones, they do not easily fit into the binary oppression/liberation paradigms defined by some scholars who have studied resistance movements in Iran.[39]

From Personal Soul-Searching to Galvanizing a Collaborative Spirit

In the late 1990s, self-described land artist Ahmad Nadalian (b. 1963) turned to nature to escape the polluted capital. In isolated riverbanks in the shadow of Mount Damavand and out-of-the-way islands in the Persian Gulf, he created ephemeral and perishable installations (*chideman*) made up of carved stones and small pebbles. In his mind, these remote natural locations were "utopian ideals" and "lost paradises" that would allow him to "escape" Tehran, which he considered "polluted in every way: environmentally, politically, and morally."[40]

In 2003, Nadalian was featured in a documentary by Mojtaba Mir Tahmasb (b. 1971). Titled *The River Still Has Fish* (*Roodkhaneh hanooz mahi darad*), the film shows the many ways in which Iran's natural environment is endangered by bad management and disruptive interventions, such as how Nadalian's own carved stones by the river were damaged by developers and their construction workers. Nadalian's escape to faraway natural spots, by his own account, was at first a self-indulgent practice.[41] The artist, however, eventually began to engage the local communities in his art. He organized art classes and invited others to participate in group projects. Nadalian also organized professional artist residencies and dozens of environmental festivals to encourage the younger generation of Iranian artists to travel to remote areas and to pay heed to environmental issues. Above all, the path he laid out proved an impetus for other artists who have left large cities to find solace in similarly secluded locations, where they may help organize field trips and collective art projects with, or without, environmentally themed messages.[42] As in Nadalian's case, the engagement of artists with isolated natural places is not uncritical and innocent, but comes with a subtle undercurrent of subversiveness and criticality.

For instance, after the devastating Bam earthquake in December 2003, which left at least 26,271 dead, up to 30,000 injured, and nearly leveled the historic twenty-hectare adobe citadel, many artists raised funds by creating site-specific art projects in Bam. However, sculptor Kourosh Golnari (b. 1964) chose instead to go to the top of Tochal Mountain and its ski resort just outside Tehran. On the twelve-kilometer-long ridge, and at the highest peak (3,964 meters), Golnari made a Stonehenge-like sculptural arrangement in honor of the dead, called *Dream of Bam* (*Khab-e Bam*) (fig. 2.2).

The difficulty of making the tall ice pillars in the cold winter wind on the ridge, coupled with the thin, oxygen-starved air, made Golnari feel closer to the pain of others. He associated this reaction to many parallel responses of Iranian artists and cultural activities to war, sociopolitical turmoil, economic uncertainties, and natural disasters.

Like the war itself, the earthquake deeply affected Iranians, as Golnari recalls nearly two decades after the event.[43] To paraphrase him, the ice

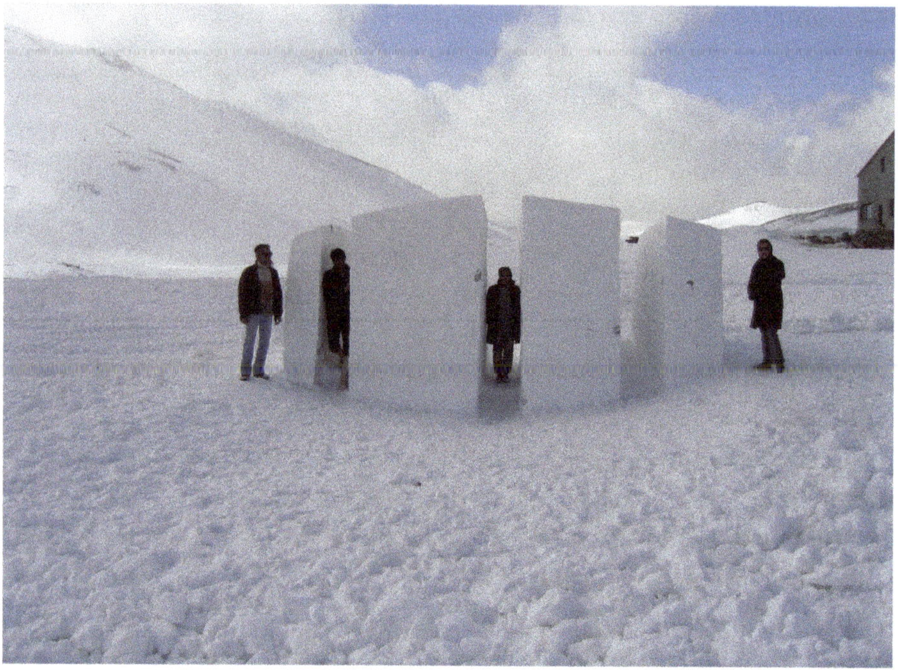

FIGURE 2.2 Kourosh Golnari, *In Memory of Bam*. 2004. Tochal Mountain, Tehran province. Courtesy of Kourosh Golnari.

sculpture was a response to a deeply traumatic event that resonated with him on a personal and intimate level, evoking memories of other misfortunes he had witnessed in the days before and since the Islamic Revolution.

Indescribable in common terms, trauma often appears to pass unregistered at a conscious level, and seemingly does not leave a trace.[44] Yet it survives as a repressed memory and, as Freud has shown, after a period of inactivity the repressed experience surfaces to disrupt and damage the possibility of experiencing the present or integrating it into a causal sequence. Ultimately, trauma remains as a living event that keeps coming to the surface.[45] This theory of trauma helps us comprehend Golnari's approach, which relentlessly revives not only the Bam earthquake but similar disasters. The remote location gave Golnari the ability to confront the pain as opposed to suppressing it.[46] His escape to nature speaks of personal soul-searching that does not directly produce subversive art proper because it does not seek to disseminate its message widely.

Artist Mahmoud Maktabi (b. 1985) has been more vocal in expressing his political position. In a catalog essay accompanying the 2016 *Nature-Art Variations* exhibition in Romania, which he helped curate, he writes:

"In Iranian environmental art the artists . . . accept the limitations and restrictions of not earning money and [of] lack of attention, in order to continue their works in freedom and beyond . . . governmental monitoring."[47] This statement displays his earlier critical engagement with remote natural spots. In 2008, while a senior undergraduate painting student at Shahed University, Maktabi received an invitation to participate in Nadalian's festival of environmental arts in Nowshahr, a city by the Caspian Sea.

The designated site was the lush Mashalak forest, often used at the time as an illegal dumping ground. Most of the participants were invited to recycle the waste and make art out of it. Maktabi, however, was motivated by the belief that art needs to be an expression of true feelings. Just a few years earlier he had formed the group Open Palm/Hand (*Panjeh baz*),[48] which consisted of a dozen artists, most of them women. As its name indicated, the group was open (hence the name Open Palm/Hand) to any artist who wished to explore remote natural locations.[49] "Sometimes, we spent days in remote areas. Away from the crowded city and the constrained university curricula that looked down upon any form of art that came after Picasso, we gained much freedom in expressing our artistic sentiments in any way we wanted," Maktabi recalls.[50]

More than a decade prior to the festival of environmental arts in Mashalak, the forest had gained notoriety as the site of the death of dissident Iranian novelist Ghazaleh Alizadeh (1947–1996). According to official sources, Alizadeh had hung herself from a tree, and shortly thereafter her family confirmed her suicide. Over time, however, a group of people in and outside of Iran came to believe that it was more likely to be a forerunner to the wave of killings by the authorities known as the Chain Murders of Iran (see chapter 1). The death was thus politicized. Maktabi's contribution to the festival—the upside-down hanging, shown in figure 2.3—can be interpreted as both an allusion to Alizadeh and a nod to Darvish Khan in *The Garden of Stones,* who used the same method of hanging in his garden. However, above all, it evokes an effective method of torture. When a body is suspended upside down, blood promptly flows to the head, bloody bubbles begin running from the nostrils, and, in some cases, eyes burst from the massive pressure.

To add to the drama, Maktabi embellished his surroundings with large, bloody camel bones, titling the piece, *I'm Not Political* (*Man siyasi nistam*). About the title, Maktabi told me: "In politicized (*siyasatzadeh*) places like Iran or elsewhere in the Middle East, people's lives are not valued. They die,

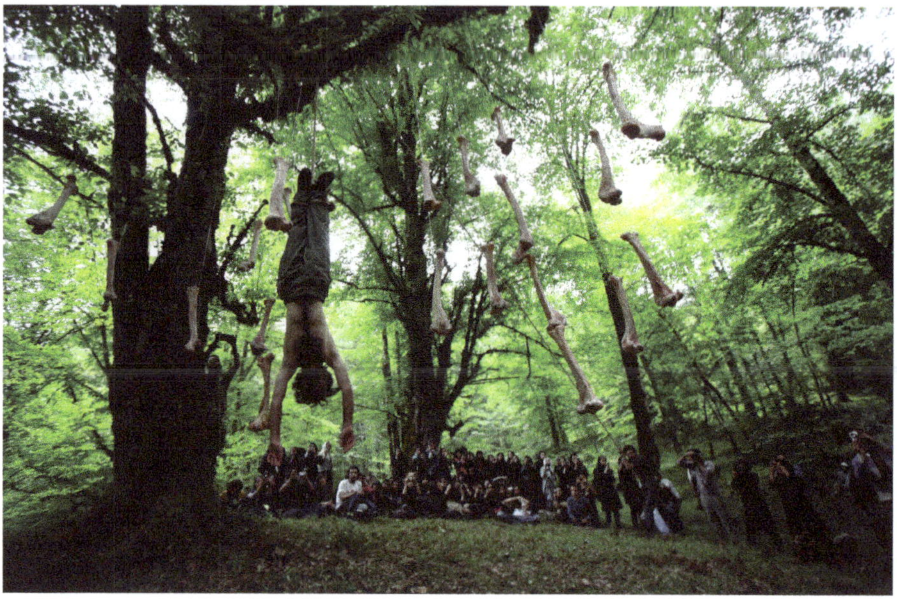

FIGURE 2.3 Mahmoud Maktabi, *I'm Not Political* performance. 2008. Mashalak Forest, Nowshahr, Mazandaran province. Courtesy of Mahmoud Maktabi.

they get killed, they disappear, and yet they are just another number on the long list of people who randomly lose their lives."[51]

He added, "Political or not, you are just another number on the long list of untimely deaths."[52] Until recently, none of these details could be found on Maktabi's personal artist website or other publications inside Iran. Nonetheless, the available picture of the performance itself, coupled with the ironic title, projects the defiant spirit of art in remote natural locations. Above all, Maktabi asserted, "The freedom granted by a remote natural setting is truly the essence of this work. Nowhere else in Iran can I take off my shirt. Nowhere in the city can I hang myself from a tree and expect to be appreciated as a performance artist. The forest of Mashalak granted me this freedom."[53] Similar to the Soviet artist Sergei Sitar, Maktabi's preference for faraway places, beyond solely aesthetic and environmental motivations, is a way to practice art in what Sitar referred to as "lesser-evil" sites.

If Maktabi's performance in Mashalak comes across as an escapist tactic, a parallel to Nadalian's early soul-searching interventions in faraway natural locations or Golnari's solo turn to nature as a strategy to cope with a traumatic event, more recent incursions into natural settings seem to be more focused on gaining greater freedom of expression and often occur in a collaborative form. While there have been many collaborative projects in natural places in Iran, not all of them have lasted. One successful sustained project, called Persbook, is a result of the efforts of one woman, an artist and curator who has worked tirelessly since the 1990s to create opportunities for artistic expression in remote areas among her circles of friends and colleagues in the visual arts.

Artist and curator Neda Darzi (b. 1971) was an avid skier during her years as a student at the Art University of Tehran in the 1990s, when she began to organize mixed-gender trips of artists and musicians to the ski resort of Shemshak, just sixty kilometers outside Tehran (figs. 2.4a/b). In a wooden chalet, one of the many lodges of this kind built during the last

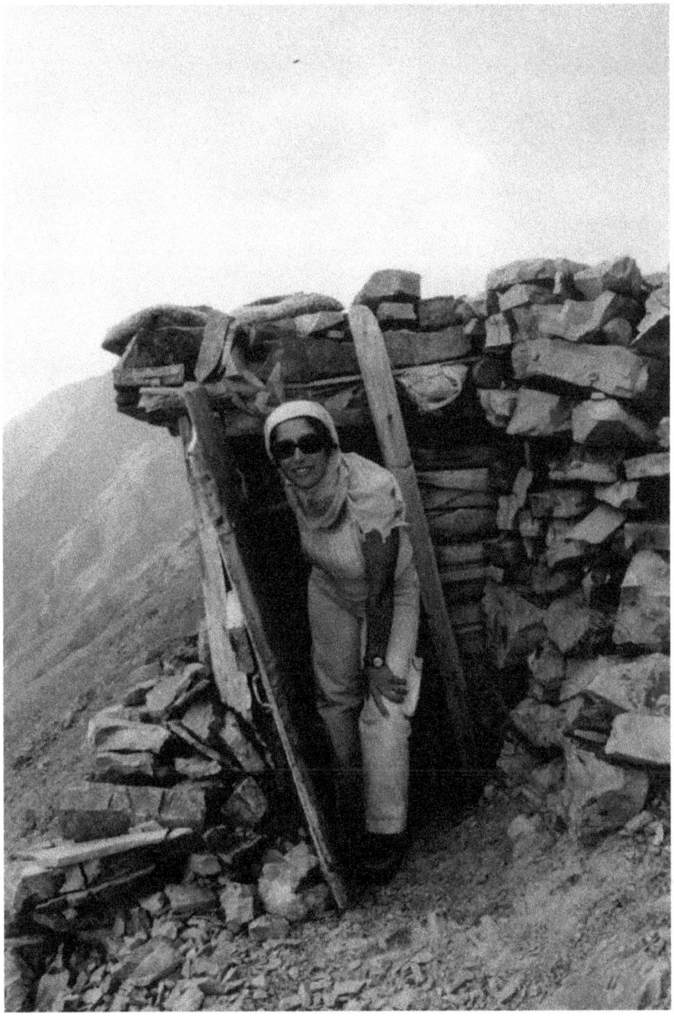

FIGURE 2.4A Neda Darzi at a mountain refuge. 2001. Shemshak, Tehran province. Courtesy of Neda Darzi.

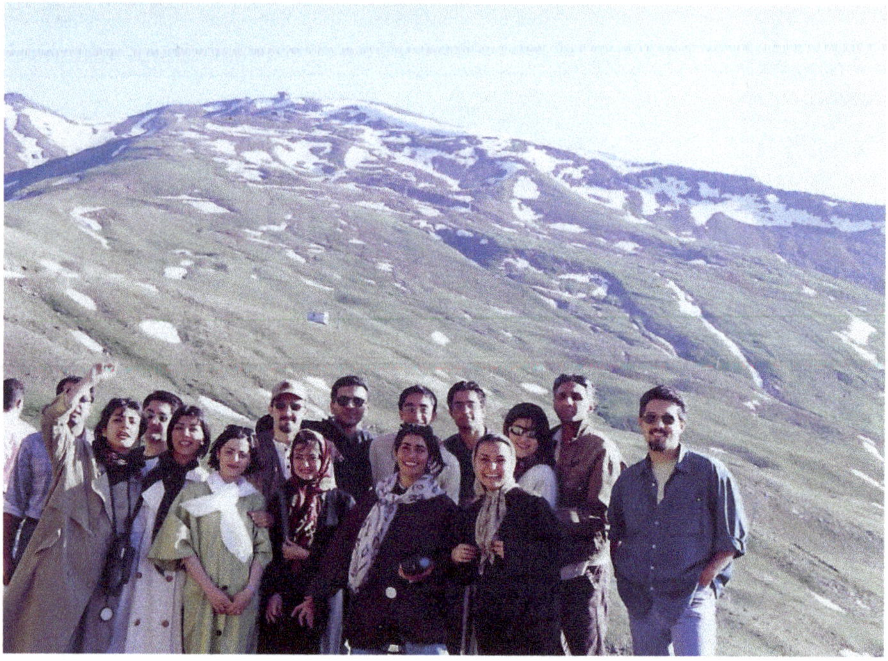

FIGURE 2.4B Neda Darzi and her artist friends. 1997. Shemshak, Tehran province. Courtesy of Neda Darzi.

years of the Shah, she accommodated artists overnight, hosted panel discussions about art, arranged improvised music performances, and guided skiing and hiking trips. Collaboration for Darzi was a way to "cope with the world around her."[54]

Above all, Darzi seems to have generated what Hannah Arendt called "the space of appearance."[55] That is, at a time when collective gatherings in open urban locations were viewed with suspicion, she created opportunities for artists and others to assemble and to act together as equals. Like her Slovakian equivalent, Alex Mlynárčik, Darzi seems to have created a "total expression" of art as life—a true celebration of artistic creation and cooperation.

In 2010, Darzi began to turn her efforts to official activities and established the nonprofit project Persbook. The name came from a combination of *pers* (an abbreviation of Persian) and *book*—a play on the social media platform Facebook, which had just gained popularity. Darzi's goal for using the platform, however, was more than just its trendiness. After the Green Movement, Darzi felt that Facebook was heavily used to showcase images of violence and that this needed to change. She said, "We needed to turn this highly utilized social media platform into a place where we could set in motion a collective spirit and use our skills to heal our communities through sharing more pleasant and optimistic images and ideas."[56] The initiative first appeared as a Facebook page and as an alternative to the more established biennials run by the TMoCA and other official organizations.

It was created in a collaborative and cooperative spirit, or what Sohrab Mahdavi (b. 1964), editor and founder of *Tehran Avenue*, a Tehran-based online art project that ran between 2001 and 2007, once described as unique to the postrevolutionary culture. In an interview with *Bidoun Magazine* in 2004, Mahdavi added, "It seems to me that such collaborative efforts are not few in the city of Tehran. During the war and shortages, people had to spend a great deal of time together, learning how to accept each other's ways and eccentricities."[57] To this I would add the spirit of collaboration that emerged because of the lack of state support for artistic practices. Instead of relying on sponsored projects, Darzi took it upon herself to push for more innovative art practices.

Between 2010 and 2016, all selected Persbook works were featured online and occasionally in a few galleries in Tehran, and since 2016, the artworks began to be presented in remote areas in the deserts of eastern Iran or the forests of the north. These site-specific installations frequently offer a conceptual lens through which to consider better solutions for collective living.

The collaborative performance piece *The Red Artery* (*Rag-e sorkh*), spearheaded in September 2017 by Nadia Sajjad (b. 1976) and Neda Darzi, showcased a procession of dozens of artists carrying a long red cloth in the desert of Khara, ninety kilometers outside Isfahan. The statement that accompanied the project highlighted the collaborative spirit of the project more than its environmental references, the stated intention being to literally and metaphorically bring together all the artists and invite them to "join in solidarity"[58] (fig. 2.5).

Like the artery that carries oxygen-rich blood from the heart to the rest of the body, the unbroken band of red organza signaled the infusion of life into the deserts of Iran. The project activated the site and brought men and women artists together in a single performance of team spirit. *The Red Artery* was only one of many performance projects that brought life to the desert. All kinds of places have served as venues for large-scale installations, from abandoned, disused adobe village settlements to the pigeon towers of Dorcheh, which are on the verge of collapse, their function as collectors of guano for natural fertilizers no longer in demand.

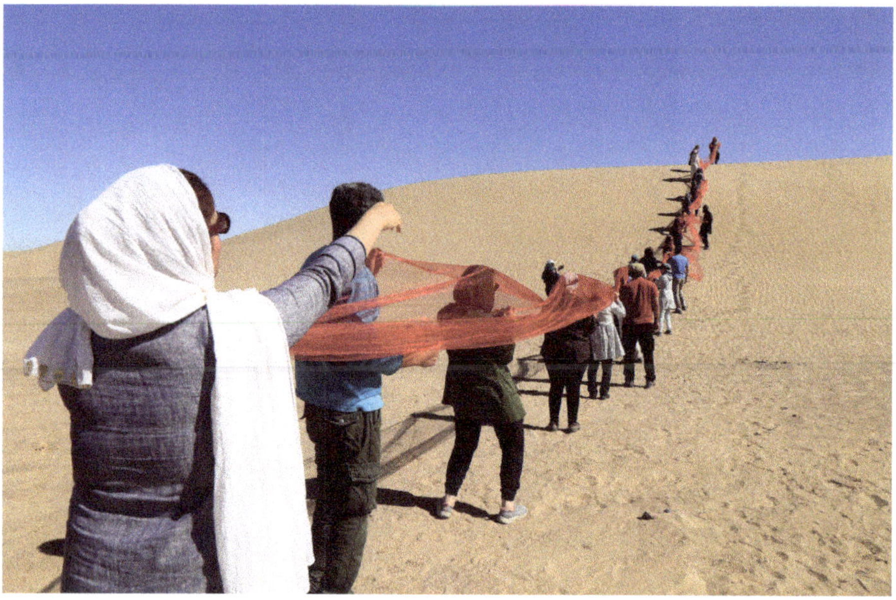

FIGURE 2.5 Neda Darzi and Nadia Sajjad, *The Artery* performance. 2016. Desert of Khara, Isfahan province. Photograph by Asghar Niazi. Courtesy of Neda Darzi.

In historic locations, artists must seek consent from multiple organizations. Consequently, for her projects, Darzi secured permission not only from the Isfahan branch of the MCIG but also from the erstwhile Organization for Cultural Heritage (*Sazman-e miras-e farhangi*). Despite the authorization issued by these bodies, the city council (*showray-e shahr*) of Dorcheh did not grant permission and delayed the projects for about a year. As a result, the seventh Persbook event took two years to organize instead of the usual one, and Darzi had to make numerous trips to Dorcheh to convince the authorities.

Most likely the religious character of the city made it difficult for artists to present their works. Obstacles like this, however, did not stop Darzi from taking artists to faraway natural spots. In her ninth Annual Persbook Contemporary Art event, she took artists and curators to the Hyrcanian mixed-forests ecoregion, a UNESCO Heritage site. This vast area of lush lowland and mountainous forests covering a massive region near the southern shores of the Caspian Sea provided art venues for dozens of installation artists whose works align with the activities of global eco-artists and community-engaged projects.

Darzi's Persbook events deliberately avoid overt social or political messages. In catalogs and brochures, in interviews and news statements, she has framed these efforts in terms of a benevolent discourse surrounding the celebration of community, the environment, and the decaying heritage in the desert.

. . .

Other artists, similarly, elevate the spirit of collaboration, albeit by other means. For example, they address existential questions. Such is the 2016 collaborative work between visual artist Mahdyar Jamshidi (b. 1982) and curator Elham Puriya Mehr (b. 1979), titled *I Am Here* (*Man inja hastam*). One evening in 2014, Jamshidi, a homesick graduate student in Sydney, Australia, typed the word "Iran" into Google Earth's search engine. Google swiftly identified the country by placing a red map pin in the center of the country. At first glance, the center seemed to be in the middle of nowhere in Iran's Central Desert (*Kaveer-e markazi*). Once back in Iran, Jamshidi made the ten-hour drive to find this place, which was a spot just outside the ancient, formerly Zoroastrian, town of Aghda near Ardakan in Yazd province. The home of many ancient adobe mosques, caravansaries, and houses, the city occasionally sees local visitors and tourists.

Jamshidi marked the location on the ground outside the village by digging a pit 150 cm deep and 250 cm in diameter. He placed a flat mirror at the bottom of the pit and installed red neon lighting around its perimeter, reflecting the color into the mirror, the sky, and the surrounding atmosphere (figs. 2.6a/b).

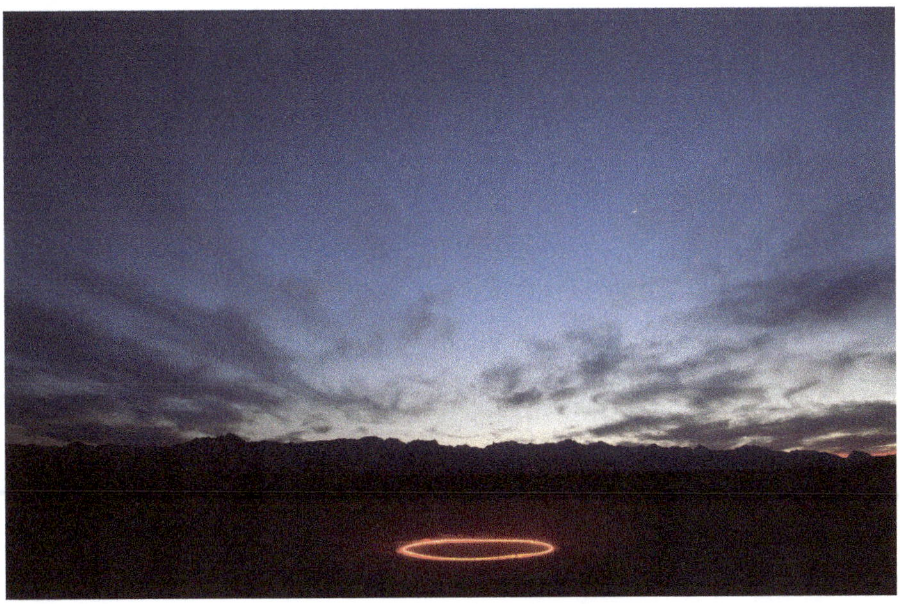

FIGURE 2.6A Mahdyar Jamshidi, *I Am Here*. 2016. Aghda, Yazd province. Courtesy of Elham Puriya Mehr.

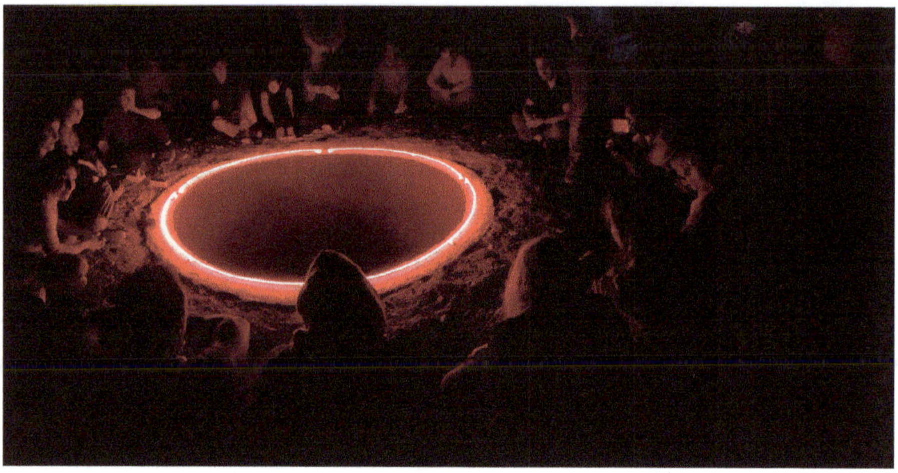

FIGURE 2.6B Mahdyar Jamshidi (in collaboration with Elham Puriya Mehr), *I Am Here*. 2016. Aghda, Yazd province. Courtesy of Mahdyar Jamshidi.

A review of *I Am Here* in an Iranian art journal linked Jamshidi's use of the mirror to the concept of heterotopia (*deegar makan,* literally "*other space*")—that is, the capacity of the "mirror" to project other possibilities for the lived experience.[59] Coined by Michel Foucault, heterotopia refers to spaces that are somehow "other" than the normative but that are by no means detached from the system in which they exist, like a brothel or a Turkish bath.[60] Even the mirror can be a heterotopia. Foucault writes of a "joint experience" between utopias and heterotopias, as if one mirrors the other. He adds,

> The mirror is, after all, a utopia since it is a placeless place. In the mirror, I see myself there where I am not, in an unreal, virtual space that opens up behind the surface; I am over there, there where I am not, a sort of shadow that gives my own visibility to myself, that enables me to see myself there where I am absent: such is the utopia of the mirror. But it is also a heterotopia in so far as the mirror does exist in reality, where it exerts a sort of counteraction on the position that I occupy.[61]

The mirror functions as a heterotopia because, according to Foucault, it makes a certain place "at once absolutely real, connected with all the space that surrounds it, and absolutely unreal, since in order to be perceived it has to pass through this virtual point which is over there."[62] This association reflects the ways in which Jamshidi's art engages critically with Iran's politics of spatial regulation.

Indeed, the project encompasses layered philosophical concepts and makes room for multiple readings. The simplicity of the illuminated circle was in line with Jamshidi's conviction that "the highest form of art is that which simplifies complicated issues."[63] Inspired by construal level theory in social psychology, which describes the relationship between psychological distance and the extent to which people's thinking (e.g., about objects and events) is abstract or concrete, Jamshidi decided to explore the notion of distance as defined in temporal, spatial (physical space), and social dimensions (interpersonal distances, such as the distance between two different groups or two dissimilar people). Distance to and from an object in the middle of the country seemed to be an interesting way to engage others in discussions about issues of identity formation.

A few weeks later, a tour of the site organized by curator and art historian Elham Puriya Mehr engaged participants, who came from a myriad of professional backgrounds—astrophysicists, art historians, and psychologists.[64] Out of this came an in-depth conversation and analysis around the concept of the center and the margin, with an emphasis on understanding and communicating from these various viewpoints. The existing footage from the project features the voices of several participants who sit around the pit at night, where the only source of light is the moon and the red neon glow from the rim of the ditch. Jamshidi maintains that *I Am Here* is simply an experimental exercise, an attempt to ask questions rather than provide answers.[65] Participating art historian Hamid Severi notes that while the pit is the center of Iran, its arrangement means that it incongruously tends to decentralize: indeed, because of its large size, what you see when you lean over the pit is not your own reflection, but the reflected images of others.[66] A cosmologist in attendance presents a brief history of the geocentric model.[67]

On the whole, the event promoted the decentralization of one's own position, a device to increase attentiveness to others, and provided a platform for the exchange of information and ideas. It aimed to create a thoughtful process of conversations without requiring a definitive and decisive conclusion. Puriya Mehr affirmed that this phase of the project created opportunities for participants to discuss issues of subject formation in the middle of nowhere, free from censorship or scanning by the state authorities.[68] In this respect, Puriya Mehr's thinking is aligned with that of the Swedish curator Anders Kreuger, who believes that the best critical spatial practices in curation are those that activate "thinking-togetherness." Bearing both ethical and aesthetic meanings, curation must be more than just "placing objects in rooms."[69]

While escaping into the desert was not necessarily a reaction to the more restrictive atmosphere of Tehran, it nonetheless created greater opportunities for contemplation and discussion than those afforded by more formal art venues. Art critics in Tehran saw it as a derivative imitation of land art from the 1960s and a belated discovery of this form of art.[70] However, as Jamshidi and Puriya Mehr have asserted, the project was a direct and timely response to debates about margin and center and issues of identity formation among the young generation of Iranian artists who, at that time, were increasingly traveling in and out of Iran. In addition, the project probed the ways that the desert, when taken as an embodiment of Iranian nature, can help detach us psychologically from the kinds of spatial conflicts experienced in city centers. Above all, the installation galvanized a collaborative spirit among artists in ways that were not feasible in busy art and conference venues back in Tehran.

Unlike other public art projects that remain undocumented, this one was carefully archived for its impact on social discourse in art within formal art spaces. In 2017, documents, video footage, and archives of the project were presented at Tehran's Ag Gallery. According to Jamshidi, the gallery installation was a kind of report (*gozaresh*) and was not meant to be understood as an artwork.[71] The setup was too sophisticated aesthetically, however, to be taken as mere documentation. Upon arrival, visitors found themselves at the center of a white cube. The neon cable that had animated the rim of the well in the desert was now installed horizontally halfway up the walls. Behind the cable hung drawings that, while resembling the contours of a desert landscape, were reproductions of the neural systems in the human brain and eyeball, reflecting the significance of human psychology in gauging physical distance. Two video screens suspended from the ceiling showcased the debates that had taken place around the illuminated circle a few months earlier, and a large table featured psychology books and other sources that addressed issues of distance and proximity. Lectures related to the concept of "center" and the "margin," as well as a catalog encompassing the project, accompanied the *I Am Here* exhibition (fig. 2.7).

These exercises of collective action in remote areas show how Iranian artists envision that the public sphere of democracy could become available through communal culture based on mutual aspirations. In theater, too, group ethos reigns in remote natural locations.

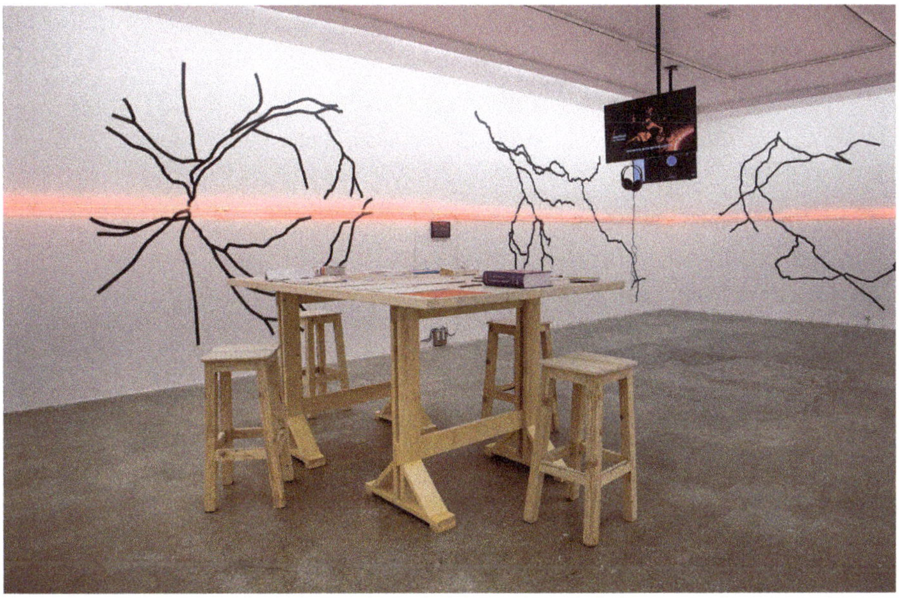

FIGURE 2.7 Mahdyar Jamshidi, *I Am Here*. Iteration at Ag Gallery. 2016. Tehran. Courtesy of Mahdyar Jamshidi.

Performing in Deserts, Caves, and Mountains

The choice of remote natural sites for contemporary performance is partially inspired by Jerzy Grotowski's concept of "paratheater."[72] Practiced between 1969 and 1976, when Grotowski and his crew openly withdrew from official venues, "paratheater" involved all kinds of alternative engagements with the site, including natural settings. Grotowski's group turned to the forests of Poland for what they called "nonperformance" events. In the same vein, at the 1976 Shiraz Arts Festival, Grotowski planned the *Desert Project*, which never materialized due to disagreements over the project's costs.[73] Contained within Grotowski's ideas was the significance of the location of the performance (in this case a desert caravanserai) and its connection to the theme of his play. Many Iranian experimental theater projects would be informed by this approach. For example, the play *Medea* (2006), performed by the college student experimental group Tantalos Theater (2005–9), took place in a desert outside Tehran. Grotowski's teachings had shaped the thinking of the Tantalos collective, particularly its director and choreographer Afshin Ghaffarian (b. 1986), who had closely studied Martha Graham and modern dance, Julian Beck and the Living Theater, Eugenio Barba and Odin Theater, as well as translated Thomas Richard's *At Work with Grotowski on Physical Actions* (1995) into Persian in 2009.[74] Ghaffarian conformed to the idea that the site of each performance should be exclusive and unrepeatable.[75] The Tantalos collective also included Mehdi Nassiri (b. 1980), who was formerly a traditional *ta'ziyeh* performer. An ancient Greek tragedy written by Euripides in 431 BCE, *Medea* might only remotely evoke the Shiite tragedy of the battle of Karbala for an Iranian audience. However, the location of Tantalos's adaptation of *Medea* was intended to conjure the spirit of the clash between Imam Hussein and his opponents in the desert of Karbala in Iraq.

Because it was a student capstone project, *Medea* did not have to secure permission from the MCIG. Instead, the Faculty of Theater at Tehran's Islamic Azad University—where Ghaffarian and his crew were enrolled—gave them the green light.[76] On the day of performance, the group invited a well-chosen audience, including their peers and college mentors. Next, they had them walk a distance in the desert before they came to the performance scene at the rear of a hill. The play involved dance moves and was largely devoid of dialogue. Female actors did not wear headscarves, but were conservatively clothed. Ghaffarian himself appeared only with loincloth. Male and female actors had occasional physical contact. On the whole, the existing footage of the play verifies that this performance could not have been staged publicly, at least not without heavy alterations.[77] Choosing a remote desert site and performing for a "trusted" audience guaranteed protection from the morality police. Undoubtedly, the location brought a sense of security and hence a feeling of liberation, not obtainable on the official theater stage. However, this and other performances in remote natural sites bolstered a sense of solidarity and collectiveness that was at the core of both Grotowski's and Tantalos Theater's practices. After *Medea* ended, the audience enjoyed a meal prepared for them by the performers, who mingled with them and happily answered their questions.[78] Indeed, the spirit of solidarity seems to be more significant than an assumed ethos of stealthiness portrayed in the highly sensationalized 2014 British film, *Desert Dancer.* Although loosely based on *Medea* and Ghaffarian's career—prior to his involvement with the Green Movement and asylum in Europe—the film's portrayal of alternative art in Iran is, regrettably, far from accurate.[79]

. . .

Another intriguing example of choosing far-flung venues for performance is the Av Theater Group, who became the first privatized theater company in Tehran in 2010 (see chapter 1). Prior to that, however, and before they secured a rented space in 2012 (see chapter 1), the Av performers began their practices in remote archeological sites and natural locations. Like the Gardzienice Theater Association, the Polish experimental theater that had originally inspired the founders of Av, their early work was rooted in nature. However, there were differences. Drawing on the teachings of Grotowsky, Gardzienice had turned to ethnic minorities in villages, and their performances were created from folk material gathered in these remote communities. This was the environment in which the group's early work, the "expedition" into the "culture of the earth," was born.[80] In Iran, by contrast, escapism to nature was not about exploring and documenting the different ethnic groups or local cultures around the country. Rather, it was about the freedom to bolster a collective spirit.

Av began their early outdoors rehearsals in 2007 in the Water and Fire Park (*Ab-o-atash*) in Tehran. Like their Polish counterparts, their dream was to be in nature and detached from the stage and official institutions.[81] The Av performers even dreamed about making a living from farming so they would not need to return to Tehran to earn money. The group soon realized this was unrealistic.[82] Instead, they embarked on performance journeys/expeditions, or what they referred to as *safar* (travel) theater.[83] When Av's performances became more refined, they began to invite audiences. Av called them participants because they wanted them to engage in the making of a performance rather than simply viewing it.

Even the actors' roles were not conventionally defined. According to Av's co-founder and theater director Babak Mohri (b. 1977), "There are no actors (*bazigar*) in [this] theater. There are only doers (*ejra' konandeh*)."[84] For their play *Ibrahim*, based on music, bodily movement, and natural elements, Av performers approached the MCIG in March 2010 to obtain permission for the journey that would include invitations to the German and Italian ambassadors. The MCIG denied it outright, since there were no defined regulations for performances in natural spots. One officer who felt some sympathy for Av was curious as to why they even bothered to seek permission. "You should not have come here. You should have done this surreptitiously. Now that you have reached us, we cannot grant you permission," he said, as one Av member recalled.[85] It is no surprise, then, that when refused by the MCIG, the Av performers turned the play into an ecotourist project, which was in vogue at that time.

Av turned to NGO environmentalists—specifically the renowned nature documentary filmmaker, journalist, and environmentalist Mohammad Ali

Inanlou (1948–2016), who had been running the Nature Institute (*Mo'asseseh Tabi'at*), offering ecotourism classes and tours, for more than a decade. At the height of his fame, Iranian media consistently referred to Inanlou as "the man of nature," claiming that he had traveled more than two million kilometers across Iran to learn more about the country's wildlife and plant species.[86] Involving Inanlou in the Av performance pieces in remote natural locations was a sound idea, so they would be seen as similar to Inanlou's own "harmless" educational tours.

With assistance from Inanlou and his colleague Fakhr al-Sadat Ghani (b. 1953), the Av performers presented their performance of *Ibrahim* in May 2010 in the form of an ecotourist project, having received the necessary approval from the local authorities to perform in the Varish Mountains, twenty kilometers outside Tehran.[87] Involving the Nature Institute proved essential, not only because AV lacked MCIG permission but also given the sensitivity of the region in which the mountain was located.

Known for their conservative culture, the nearby Varish villagers, who had observed the casual practices of certain members of the group for some time, objected to the play. According to Soheil Aarabi (b. 1982), just one day before the opening of the performance, the locals confronted the members of Av. The villagers condemned the mixed-gender group, their unusual activities and polyphony (i.e., several actors chatter loudly concurrently), and threatened to beat them up if they ever came back. The frightened performers initially wanted to cancel the show. Having sold the tickets, however, they eventually settled on an alternative approach, which was to extend the trip and literally circle the mountain to avoid the village. On the day of performance, Av and the Nature Institute organized buses to transport 250 people to their performance in Varish.[88] Performers engaged in energetic actions to relate to their audiences from a distance. For instance, they would scream and use dynamic and dramatic body movements.

Although Av sold tickets to attract audiences, they did not make any profit. In fact, they ended up out of pocket after they had covered the Nature Institute fees; bought props, costumes, and food for the audience; and paid for the buses from Azadi Square in western Tehran and back.

While Av performances functioned as tours or operated under the auspices of ecotourism, their projects did not degenerate into the monetary and attention economies of tourism. Delivering extraordinary performances, existing on the fringes of the art market, and frequently challenging the idea of being "touristic," Av tours became, instead, an effective means of

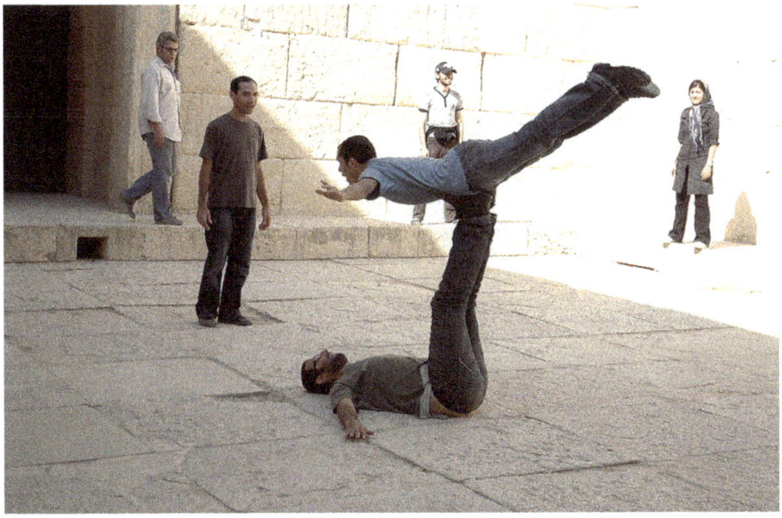

FIGURE 2.8 Av Theatre Group, *Ardvi Sura Anahita*, directed by Babak Mohri and Soheila Ghods-Tinat. 2010. Bishapour's Anahita/Water Temple. Ancient city of Bishapour, Fars province. Courtesy of Soheil Aarabi.

moving audiences into critical encounters with remote natural places. If conventional ecotourism tended to capture places through simple narratives, the critical tours offered by Av emphasized the site, in all its complicated specificity and in relation to much larger meanings and affective forces. As such, Av also avoided reproducing what the sociologist of tourism and mobility John Urry characterizes as "the tourist gaze"—one that generates a sense of getting a full picture of an attractive location without ever truly "seeing" and "feeling" it.[89]

. . .

Following the success of the Varish event, which received considerable attention and praise in both unofficial venues and the official press, the group embarked on a series of travel theaters (*safar te'atre*). These trips were not intended for audiences. Instead, the goal was to seek out experiences in natural and ancient sites and then bring those influences back to Tehran.

To avoid conflicts with the authorities or local people, Av selected isolated and often empty archeological sites. In line with its name, Av, meaning water, the group opted for places with remains of ancient water temples. One such destination was a remote historic site in the southern ancient city of Bishapour, 130 kilometers west of Shiraz.

Founded early in the first century CE in Sassanid Persia, Bishapour is on the ancient road between the Sassanid capitals of Estakhr (close to

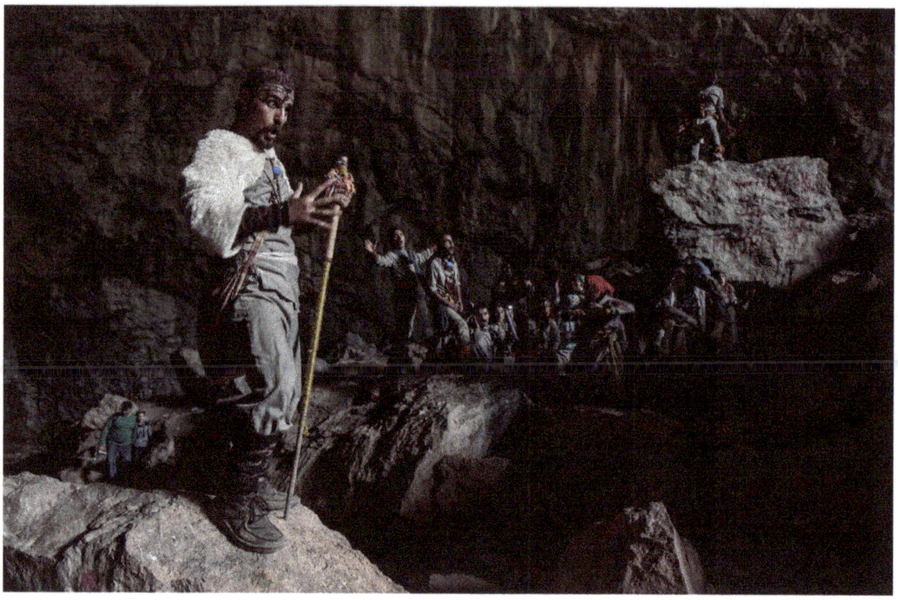

FIGURE 2.9 Av Theatre Group, *Melpomene*, directed by Babak Mohri. 2013. Rudafshan Cave outside the capital, Tehran province. Photograph by Jeremy Suyker.

Persepolis) and Ctesiphon. A water temple, widely interpreted as an Anahita temple, is probably the best-preserved structure within the vast archeological site. Dedicated to an Indo-Iranian goddess of water, it intimately appealed to Av. In *Ardvi Sura Anahita* the Av performers engaged with the architecture of the temple itself. After a series of abstract movements involving both male and female actors, the group met members of the local communities at the fringes of the archeological site (fig. 2.8).

A young girl from that rural community interacted with the group. She wrote letters to the actors, which were then read aloud back in Tehran when the play was performed. Her "pure" and "confident" voice was interpreted as the voice of Anahita herself, a true instance of art as life and life as art. A temple in a remote archeological site had provided the group with the freedom they needed to experiment with different modes of interaction with nature, architecture, and ordinary people. Such experiences eventually culminated in the last outdoor performance by Av in spring 2013 performance in the Rudafshan Cave outside of Tehran (fig. 2.9).

According to Aarabi, the group chose this cave because of its unusual vast space and wide threshold, as well as the possibility that a Sassanian water temple had once been there. "Practicing in such natural, wild spots,"

Aarabi recalled, "could improve our practices. We simply craved such challenging and difficult-to-navigate platforms for our performances."[90] Subsequently, Av members carefully designed the choreography within the uneven grounds of the cave and began to practice there. During these practice sessions, the male members of the group sometimes spent the night under the sky. Women slept in a small prayer room atop the mountain. These experiences would change the mood and affect the ways the group connected with nature. "The sky was our theater roof and the uneven contours of the cave our stage," Aarabi recollected.[91]

To secure permission for an official performance with audiences, Av turned to another agency responsible for exploration in nature, Zhivar Tours, which was able to help them with proper transportation but not with promoting the play or sorting out the logistics. At sunrise on May 17, 2013, 250 participants (both performers and viewers) left Tehran from a meeting place outside Av's official company, a thermal bath in central Tehran (see chapter 1). Each bus included a few actors who would gently prepare the audience for what they were about to see.

The monumental performance was titled *Melpomene*, a name derived from an ancient Greek word meaning to celebrate with dance and song. In the early days of her worship, Melpomene, the goddess of dance, was also the muse of choral singing. As time went by, she became the muse of tragedy, especially during the classical period of Ancient Greece. The actors had already begun to perform before the audience reached the cave, so the audience were already experiencing the play before they were close enough to see it. Different modes of body and visual engagement emerged. There was room for inventiveness as well as unexpected gestures toward the audience, acknowledging their presence. Some characters were designated as "jokers." They could roam freely and reroute a segment of the audience. Although partially improvised, everything went according to plan.

Coverage of the play in the Iranian press emphasized the significance of the location. A review of the performance in the May 2013 issue of *Cheragh Magazine* is animated by a photo taken by Mehdi Ashena (b. 1982) of an actor set against the walls of the cave and a bold headline that reads: "*Salonhatoon arzoonitoon*," which roughly translates as "We don't want your theater halls"[92] (fig. 2.10).

This open and public rejection of the Islamic Republic's formal art venues might have been interpreted by readers of the review as scandalous. However, the irony lies in the discrepancy between the title and the content

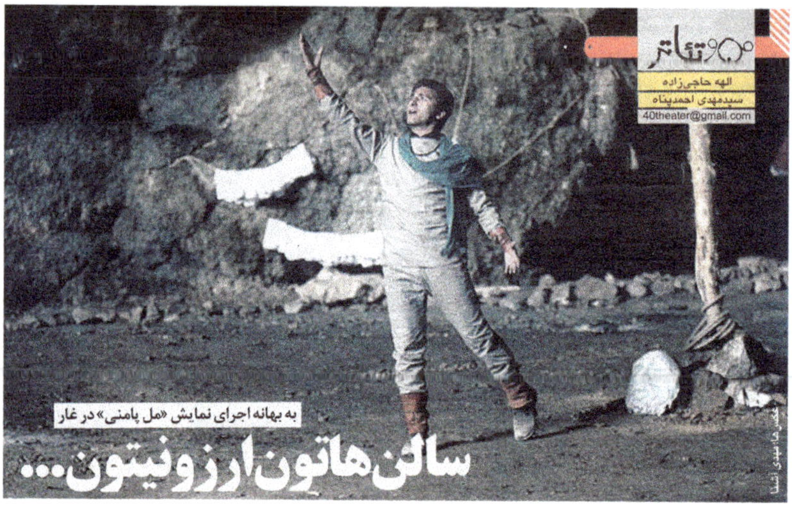

FIGURE 2.10 Snapshot of newspaper article. Elaheh Hajizadeh and Seyyed Mahdi Ahmad Panah, "Salonhatoon arzoonitoon" [We don't want your theater halls], *Cheragh Magazine* 11, no. 519 (4 Khordad 1392 [May 25, 2013]), 28. Courtesy of *Cheragh Magazine*.

of the article. The article explains that the play was different (*motefavet*), but then assures its readers that this "difference" (*tafavot*) was not intended simply for the sake of being different, or for the purpose of attracting mass audiences and media attention. Being different is valuable (*arzeshmand*) and memorable (*beyadmandani*)—the article asserts—only if the difference is justified and backed by reasons other than just being different.[93]

Such a difference, explains the director, Babak Mohri, in an addendum to the review, lay in the ways the audience was encouraged to interact with the actors and the environment. Rather than just employing their intellect, responding to didactic content, they were immersed in the play through all five senses (*havass-e panjganeh*).[94] The "lack of a coherent narrative and choreography" was the result of Mohri's emphasis on the tantalizing spontaneous body and language expressions of actors and audience alike.[95]

The review highlighted the spontaneity and natural progression of the play rather than discussing its lack of support, financial or otherwise, from more formal theater settings. Such discrepancies between bold titles and content are rife in press reviews, published critiques, and narratives of art performances in Iran. The reader is expected to "read" the bold title and the bold gesture of the actor in the accompanying photo just as he or she "reads" everything else in the Islamic Republic. Images do not necessarily show what they appear to show. Texts might sound at first as though they are questioning or challenging the state authorities, but eventually a kind of ambiguity sets in. Like the play itself, the message in the *Cheragh* review is open-ended, leaving the reader to interpret what has been written. Notwithstanding, the review's title indicates Av's unambiguous desire to distance themselves from the center.

. . .

In 2012, a new group, Nyia, branched off from Av and formed a separate group under the tutelage of director Pouya Pirouzram (b. 1975), who wrote his master's thesis at the Art University's College of Cinema and Theater on the spaces in which Gardzienice presented their plays. Following in the footsteps of Gardzienice and other Euro-American experimental groups, Nyia began its rehearsals in unconventional spaces outside the capital. Such places, according to Pirouzram, allowed them to be more experimental and to freely practice what he calls "corporal action" (*konesh-e jesmani*) in close intimacy with both men and women.

Such actions are not allowed on stage, and they are problematic in busy urban spaces, so in addition to rehearsing in covert apartments (see chapter 1), Nyia chose remote spots to avoid the watchful eyes of passersby and the morality police (fig. 2.11).[96] Partially planned and partially improvised, and set in remote natural environments, theatrical productions by Av and Nyia are positioned against the work of urban theater groups and companies, whether affiliated with the government or privatized. These alternative locations are artists' attempts to acquire their own agency in the arts in escapist venues.

Indeed, in some ways similar to what transpired in Eastern Europe, there has been a tendency to establish alternative spaces of creative action and joy along the horizontal axis and in less urban, less populated natural locations. While these theatrical performances could be seen as a form of resistance against sanctioned theater or a form of political intervention, they are often not framed as such. As the performances of Av show, the struggle to perform in remote regions is not limited to creative artists versus conservative authorities. Sometimes dealing with the public in rural areas can be more challenging than dealing with the MCIG or other government agencies that grant permission—as demonstrated by the villagers of Varnish. As in the case of the above-mentioned *Cheragh* review, the local interpretations of such plays can be complex and multilayered, rather than

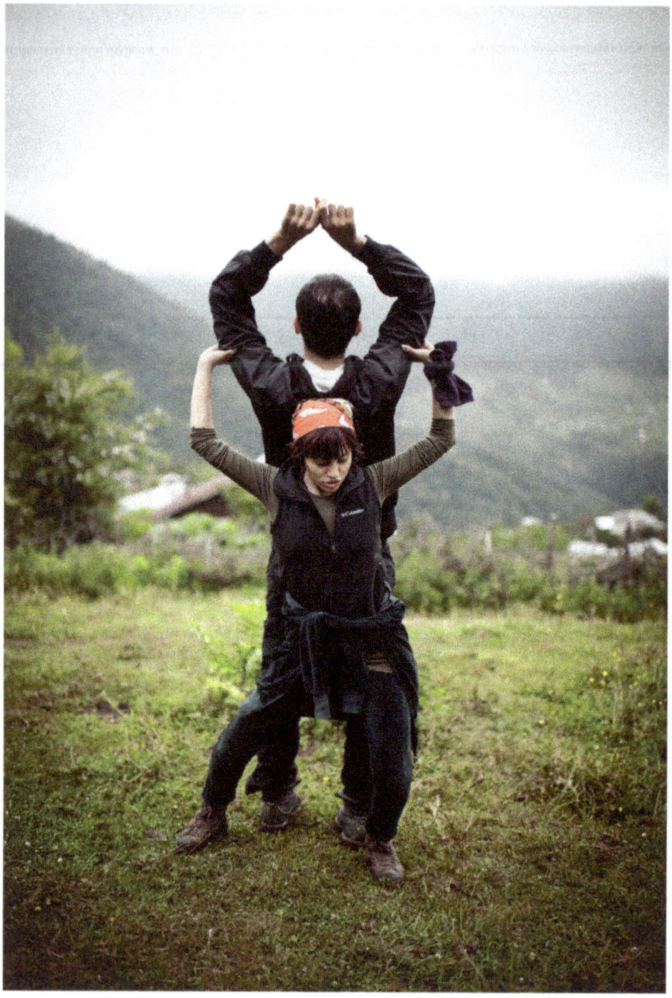

FIGURE 2.11 Nyia Theater Group rehearsing in the mountains. 2012. Mazandaran province. Photograph by Jeremy Suyker.

simply a form of resistance against the official theater sanctioned by the state. Even if there is a subversive dimension, it is allusive and indirect. Such is also the keynote of a countercultural movement in design.

A Countercultural Movement in Design

In the 1970s, the progressive director of the Department of Environment, Eskandar Firouz, brought together a team of Iranian and American architects to create *Pardisan: Plan for an Environmental Park in Tehran*, a monumental project intended to surpass all other parks of its type around the world. The revolution brought it to a halt.[97]

Against the backdrop of such grand national projects, there arose a countercultural movement in design. In the 1970s, architect Nader Khalili (1936–2008) abandoned his lucrative design business in Los Angeles and returned home for a five-year research odyssey in the desert and amid Iran's vernacular settlements. Soon afterward, Khalili embarked on a new design project. Using clay, water, and fire, he invented the Geltaftan system, a renewed approach to conventional methods of kiln firing. After extensive trial and error, he sought to improve the structural weaknesses of existing adobe buildings by enhancing their resistance to earthquakes in ways that were also inexpensive and ecologically responsible, and that were particularly suitable for the immediate and temporary accommodation of refugees and disaster victims.

In 1986, Khalili founded the Geltaftan Foundation and, in 1991, the California Institute of Earth Art and Architecture (Cal-Earth), where he taught his philosophy and earth architecture techniques.[98] The six books that he wrote while evolving these techniques—along with his general philosophy of architecture—had a significant impact on Iran-based architects, in particular his *Racing Alone* (*Tanha daveedan*), which was read by architecture students throughout the 1990s.[99]

One such student was Pouya Khazaeli-Parsa (b. 1974), who was intrigued by Khalili's building methods and design philosophy, especially after his visit to Cal-Earth in 2011. Following the completion of his education in Iran, Khazaeli-Parsa immersed himself in sustainable design projects including an innovative and low-cost, low-tech bamboo hut for a private client near a resort town by the Caspian Sea. Subsequently, he became involved in alternative environmental design through his experience abroad, first from 2004–6 at the office of the renowned environmentalist and refugee-shelter designer Shigeru Ban. Then, between 2012 and 2015, he attended workshops on modern earthen structures and sustainable architecture in Italy and Austria, including one organized by renowned environmentalist architects Anna Heringer and Martin Rauch.[100]

Following that, he joined the Pilosio Building Peace Organization and designed schools for Syrian refugees in Amman, Jordan. Along with architect Cameron Sinclair, the founder of Architecture for Humanity (1999) and a pioneer in socially responsive design, Khazaeli-Parsa used systems that allowed for the construction of durable temporary buildings using wall panels formed with scaffolding and grids, which are then assembled and filled with gravel, sand, or earth, creating well-insulated interiors at a low cost.

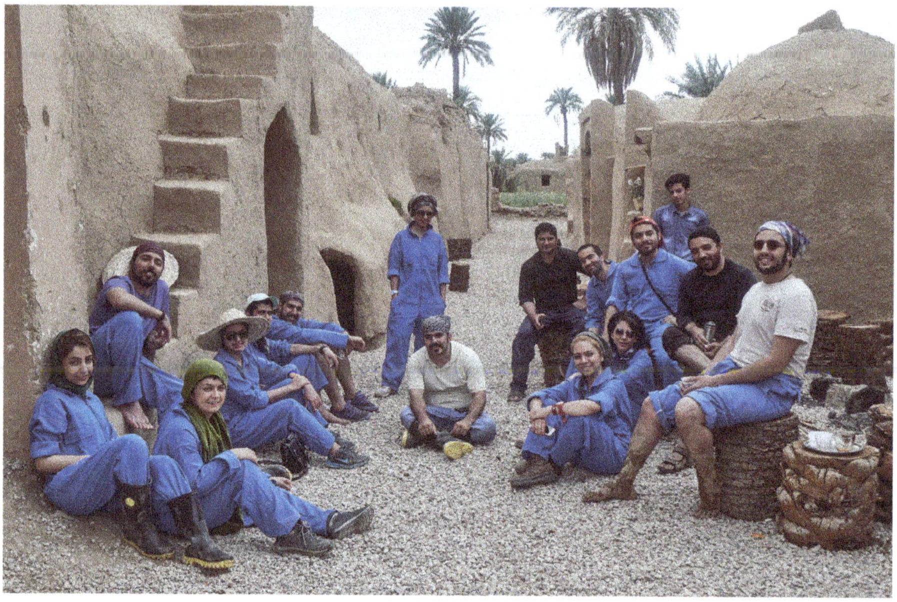

FIGURE 2.12 Pouya Khazaeli-Parsa (second from right) and students at an alternative architectural education workshop in a rural area. 2016. The Esfahk Mud Center, Mashahad province. Photograph by Davood Mohamadhasan. Courtesy of Pouya Khazaeli-Parsa.

Subsequently, Khazaeli-Parsa returned to Iran for good and began conducting field trips and engaging young volunteer students in experimental design projects in the remote deserts of Iran. At its core, the program remains faithful to a pedagogical trajectory initiated by Khalili. At his independent educational initiative, the Esfahk Mud Center in the village of Esfahk near the northwestern city of Tabas, Khazaeli-Parsa and his students advocate for traditional building techniques to generate environmentally friendly designs for the future (fig. 2.12).

Khazaeli-Parsa's goal is to learn from the last few remaining building masters, who have preserved the knowledge of sustainable design in the desert through word of mouth, and document these techniques before they are lost. Through student fees, the center manages to secure the required facilities and housing in old, renovated homes that are often offered at cheap prices. Esfahk Mud Center functions like an independent design residency. According to Khazaeli-Parsa, bureaucratic politics have meant the center has never become an official venue, despite his best efforts. However, perhaps due to its independence from architecture schools, the initiative attracts students from all artistic fields. Theater experts and stage designers, sculptors, young architects who want to enhance their knowledge of traditional building methods, and even hobbyists join the workshops.

One interesting aspect of the community is the surprisingly high proportion of female students, something that often astonishes local villagers, who rarely see women engaged in construction. According to Khazaeli-Parsa, while some villagers are critical of these activities, others see them as a positive step, boosting the tourist economy and encouraging women to be more present in public. At these settlements, as Khazaeli-Parsa pointed out, one can also encounter many Tehrani youths who have come to make their own colonies, like 1960s hippies. While many are attracted to these remote places due to the pollution and high cost of living in Tehran, others are in search of greater freedom.[101]

While the purpose of Esfahk Mud Center is to disseminate knowledge of traditional design methods, Khazaeli-Parsa admits that it perhaps inadvertently exudes an air of countercultural life—though its alternative quality is less like that of Drop City, and more in the spirit of the old dervish traditions of seeking refuge in faraway places. "Like the dervishes," Khazaeli-Parsa notes, "we move to faraway places and carve our own paths."[102]

Similar to the artist and theater counterparts featured earlier in this chapter, Khazaeli-Parsa's projects create humble opportunities for escapism and for gaining new architectural knowledge outside the confines of formal institutions. But escapism into remote areas is not always perceived positively. Remarkably, many design projects and more permanent interventions are seen as an extension of the state's problematic connection with nature.

The Battle over Engagement with Remote Sites

Iranian postrevolutionary environmentalism—often called "the protection of the lived environment" (*hefazat az mohit-e zist*)—came to the fore in the government's national planning during the 1990s. Rapid population growth, colossal traffic jams, and unplanned urban development that degraded the natural environment all demanded greater attention to the environment.[103] As anthropologist Satoshi Abe has argued, environmentalism connects in the first instance to a sense of national identity and pride.[104] In this discourse, Mount Damavand has a special place, as not only the highest mountain in Iran, and indeed the Middle East, but the richest in flora and fauna. Abol-Qasem Ferdowsi (940–1025 CE) depicted Damavand in the

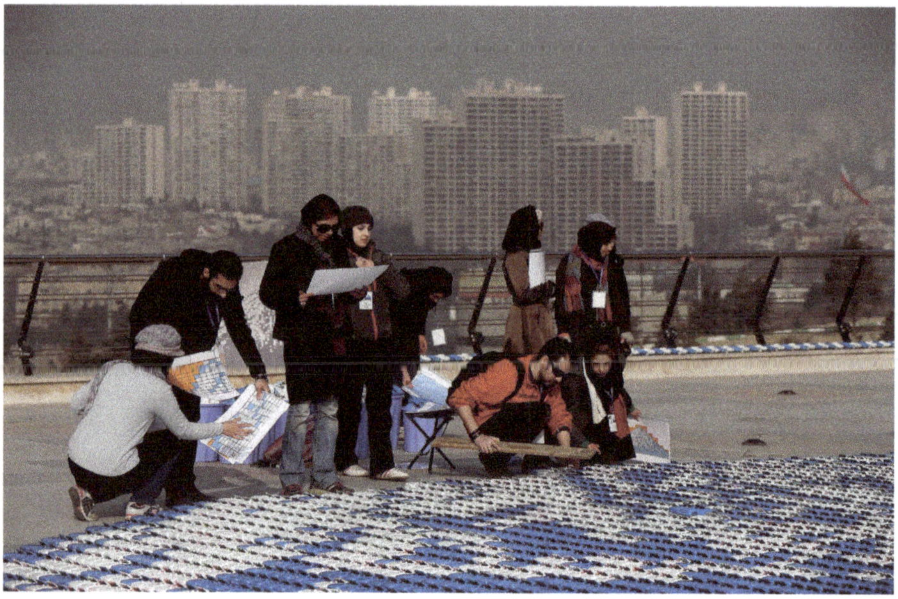

FIGURE 2.13 Hooman Mehdizadehjafari, *Little Airborne* installation, aerial view. 2014. Milad Tower, Tehran. Photograph by Mani Lotfizadeh and Khalil Emami. Courtesy of Houman Mehdizadehjafari.

epic poem *The Book of Kings* or *Shahnameh*, which most Iranians know. A national symbol, it is also frequently featured in posters and other visual culture that commemorate Iranian natural treasures or call for environmental protection.[105] Located north of the capital, the peak is almost always covered with snow, which would make it visible from every corner of the city, except that it is often obscured by a faintly acrid orange haze of smog from automobile exhaust.

It was no surprise, then, that on January 19, 2014, on Iran's national Clean Air Day (*Rooz-e havay-e pak*), a grand platform at Tehran's iconic Milad Tower came to life with a colossal image of Damavand. Hooman Mehdizadehjafari's (b. 1985) large, participatory (*mosharekati*) installation, *Little Airborne* (*Havadar-e koochak*), was composed of 5,200 "found" plastic toy cars painted in blue and white and arranged to depict the peak of Mount Damavand (fig. 2.13).[106]

. . .

Since the mid-2010s, environmentalism in Iran has become intertwined with political activism and protests against aggressive development projects by the government, which has erected scores of dams and laid hundreds of kilometers of highways across almost every river and habitat. The regime's response has been to detain protesters and remove conservationists from their posts.[107] In 2018, the government arrested Kavous Seyed Emami (1953–2018), founder of the Persian Wildlife Heritage Foundation, Iran's most prominent nongovernmental organization focused on the environment. Emami mysteriously died in prison a month after his detainment. A few months later, an Iranian revolutionary court accused a series of environmental experts of "collaborating with the enemy state of the United States" and sentenced them to prison terms ranging from four to ten years.[108]

Artists who work on environmental themes have been increasingly challenged (recall how, conversely, in early 2010s the Av Theater Group packaged their remote performance projects as ecotourism to be safe).[109] In this context, the earlier celebratory and sentimental approaches toward nature have become increasingly political in tone. When in July 2020 the news broke that the Iranian Vaqf Institute (*Sazman-e owghaf*, an Islamic charitable foundation that operates under the supervision of the supreme leader), claimed ownership of the lower parts of Mount Damavand, Iranian artist Ali Faramarzi (mentioned in the introduction) voiced his concern by linking the mountain to Iran's historical roots through a lament titled "A Scar on a Legend" (*Zakhmi bar ostooreh*), which then swiftly spread on social media and news platforms.[110] Implicit in Faramarzi's commentary are the phenomena known as mountain grabbing or mountain ingestion (*kooh khari*) and land grabbing or land ingestion (*zaminkhari*), which have accelerated in recent years. These developments in desirable (sometimes protected) areas are enabled by the government and are often tied to *Khosoolati* economics.[111] In this system, the wealthy are exempt from paying taxes and some buyers/developers remain undisclosed, both in terms of their identities and their financial records.[112]

. . .

In contrast to the visual and performing arts and theater and experimental design, the construction of buildings has a much more complicated relation to economics and politics. Because of the immense sums of money involved, such activity is inevitably tied to wealthy and powerful agents or even the state. As a result, major architectural projects in remote areas, even if conducted with extreme care and infused with creativity, are often targeted by Iran-based critics, and sometimes even by the very same people who may admire a performance project in the mountains. In highlighting the critical voices inside Iran, it is not my intention to take one side or the other. Rather, the aim is to present the kinds of discourse that emerge around design and its link to environmental and sociopolitical issues. The architects involved in the architectural projects I have chosen to introduce here are undoubtedly among the most gifted in the country. Respected in and outside Iran, they are committed to the demands of their clients and at the same time fully aware of cultural and environmental sensitivities. My interviews with dozens of top architects in Iran indicated how they genuinely do their best to take everything into consideration in their design process. Despite this, they are not immune from criticism, especially from local critics in both pro- and antiregime circles. These varied views show how spatial practice is discussed and debated among the experts and the literati as well as among laypeople.

. . .

In December 2020, *Dezeen*—a popular online architecture, interiors, and design magazine based primarily in London—featured yet another eye-catching and colorful architectural project from Iran. Located about eight kilometers from the main town on the Iranian island of Hormuz, the Majara Residence, fifteen interconnected holiday home complexes, later received Building of the Year honors in 2021 from *Archdaily,* "the world's most visited architecture website," according to its own tagline. The project description in *Dezeen* starts with a quote by the designers, Zav Architects, who call the complex of fifteen interconnected holiday homes a "cultural residence."[113]

As "a field of colonies that interlace in a fluid fabric similar to that of a neighborhood," the project is presented as an "alternative to standard high-rise holiday apartments."[114] Alluding to the surrounding natural environment and to local patterns of design, the *Dezeen* article goes on to say that "ZAV Architects arranged the domes closely together to create a sense of community and give the development a distinctive outline that was drawn from the island's natural forms."[115]

Architecture, here, is regarded as an agent, "a platform for changing the world" that can also help "increase the national and local GDP (gross domestic product)."[116] The article draws attention to both the environmental and cultural dimensions of the program. The inspiration for the bright colors of the domes is said to have come from the naturally colored sand beaches of the island, used historically by the locals for dying fabric and decorating the walls of their adobe homes.

The structures of the domes are reminiscent of Nader Khalili's adobe Sandbag Shelters in Ahvaz in 1995, all built of sand and not too far from

Hormuz. Like Khalili's design, the colorful domes of Zav are constructed using "a low-tech method with a structure made of stacked sandbags, which were filled with soil and sand."[117] The website of the group states: "The sandbags that create the spatial particles (aka domes) are filled with the dredging sand of the Hormuz dock, as if the earth has swollen to produce space for accommodation."[118] Emphasis is placed on the potential for "the low-tech construction method" to be "largely completed by [unskilled] people in the local community."[119] The project is further credited with attempting to reduce joblessness by providing opportunities to learn marketing and hospitality skills.

The website of Zav ascribes similar qualities to the project, ranging from "community empowerment" and "inclusion of local interest" to "the benefit of all" and "a proposal for internal governing alternatives."[120] Above all, Majara is presented as something that brings together, as partners in the project, "the owners of land from the neighboring port of Bandar Abbas who organize an annual land art event in Hormuz, the investors from the capital city Tehran, and the local people of Hormuz."[121]

Zav Architects then goes on to rationalize the economic dimensions of the project by linking it to the international sanctions imposed on Iran. In such a challenging environment, Zav claims, good design can generate "social change."[122] While the Western media and several local news outlets echo similar views, some Iranian critics have been less sympathetic. Notably, in an article from January 2021, the oppositional voice of Pouria Jahanshad (mentioned earlier) can be heard again.[123] The bold title of the article captures the essence of Jahanshad's sentiments: "A Place Where Hormuz Ends."[124]

To justify his opposition to the project, Jahanshad employs the same vocabulary that Zav used. He asks, "How can increasing the GDP lead to the equal distribution of wealth among the locals? Where exactly is the proof that an invitation was extended to the locals to participate in this project? Was there an organized effort, such as distributing surveys, to actively seek out the opinions of the local community?"[125] Jahanshad then concludes that the project would not lead to economic prosperity for the locals. Rather, it would pave the way for withdrawing the ownership of land and local resources from them.

Jahanshad writes that the vocabulary used by Zav Architects and other similar art and design entities was first defined by oppositional organizations, including his own: *Rokhdad-e tazeh mostanad* (New Documentary

Event), active on both physical and virtual platforms since June 2015. Among these newly introduced concepts are reinforcement of the right to the city (*ehya' haghgheh beh shahr*), participatory design (*tarrahi mosharekati*), empowerment of local communities (*tavanmand sazi jame'eh mahhali*), participatory production of knowledge (*toleed-e mosharekati danesh*), and expansion of political discourse (*tose'eh siyasi*).

As Jahanshad sees it, these terms have now been co-opted, becoming a tool in the hands of those who align themselves with the dominant economic system. Jahanshad's reaction to Zav's award-winning design might be seen as extreme by some. Indeed, many Iranians (architects included) have praised the Majara Residence. Some Iranian architects refer to it as the first built manifestation of Nader Khalili's method of sustainable design.[126] *Fars News Agency* regards it as a source of pride for Iran.[127] Despite Jahanshad's objections, the Hormuz example is generally viewed as not harmful to the environment and is, therefore, not contested, unlike other developments on the desirable fringes of the capital.

. . .

In recent years, the regime has itself co-opted strategies that helped disguise those opposing its surveillance apparatus. Many figures, including the super rich as well as those associated with the government—business tycoons or economic *basiji* (volunteer militia forces) and those who play key roles in industry, the legal system, and the military, as well as top officials including the families of important political and religious figures—have sought vacation spots that are hidden in plain sight.[128] The most sought-after locations are isolated areas that offer an escape from the traffic congestion and pollution of the big city, notably the precious natural environments outside Tehran, around Mount Damavand, and especially Lavasan, known to some as the Switzerland of Tehran.[129]

Drawing on the US experience for a comparison, consider the Survival Condo Project in Kansas, a series of subterranean luxury apartments that were recently built for the wealthiest people and their entourages as a refuge in the event of a major environmental or political catastrophe or nuclear war.[130] Located on the site of a former missile silo north of Wichita, the complex has a medical wing, a movie theater, amenities, a guns and ammunition room, a library, a classroom, and kitchen and living rooms and bedrooms. Although underground, the compound features pleasant rooms and seating areas that include windows with realistic-looking pictures of natural settings.

These interior spaces recall the United States' fallout shelters of the Cold War era. In tandem, wealthy communities in the Eastern Bloc not only protected themselves against possible nuclear attacks but also led leisurely lives away from the watchful eyes of the communist authorities. For example, throughout the 1950s in communist Romania, certain individuals, with close connections to the upper echelons of the Communist Party, had the freedom to move to remote villages along the Romanian-Bulgarian border and enjoy nudist holidays on the shores of the Black Sea.[131]

In Lavasan, since the 1990s, many well-to-do people—both independent and loosely tied to the government's wealth—have built luxury villas with walls as high as seven or eight meters. These developments are not in the interests of the locals, who wish to preserve their cultures and traditions and, above all, their natural resources. However, local discontent and ensuing complaints often remain unresolved or silenced by powerful agents.[132]

More recently, a few millionaires and their families, mostly the *nouveau riche* from different sectors of the government, formed a small, gated neighborhood of their own, *Basti Hills,* a play on Beverly Hills in Los Angeles County, home to many wealthy Hollywood stars. One of Lavasan's forty-seven settlements, Basti used to be farmland, but is now given over mostly to summer resorts. On the streets of this gated community, families can walk around freely and mingle without the mandatory *hijab,* and jog, cycle, and walk their dogs. Mixed-gender pool parties, alcohol consumption, and music performances all go unpunished by the morality police.

News and social media reports of life behind the walls of Basti Hills have provoked a scandalized reaction.[133] In August 2014, the local newspaper, *Lavasan News,* featured an extensive interview with journalist Hamid Reza Sadr (1956–2021), who was particularly critical of the phenomenon of "selling the mountain" (*padideh koohforooshi*). To resolve this problem, he says, it is necessary to investigate its root cause. Why are some people able to accumulate so much wealth that they can "move and buy a mountain"?[134]

Seventy-five percent of the Lavasan area is supposed to be a protected environment (*mahdoodeh tabi'i hefazat shodeh*), something equivalent to the protected areas of the United States that are managed by an array of different federal, state, tribal, and local authorities and that receive widely varying levels of protections.[135] The 2015 master plan of Lavasan prohibits any appropriation of natural resources. For example, it delineates areas with old trees that cannot be felled or encroached on by construction.[136] No property in Lavasan may exceed six hundred and fifty square meters, as stipulated by article 100 of the municipality commission.[137] However, there are properties with built areas of up to two thousand square meters. Normally, such properties would be subject to demolition, but here the building is allowed to remain, provided the owner pays the huge fines levied by the municipality for noncompliance. Indeed, in recent years, all of these rules have been bypassed by those who can afford to pay the substantial fines associated with breaking them.[138]

It is not only the so-called "un-Islamic" lifestyles of the occupants of Lavasan villas that are targeted by more traditional religious local critics, but also the architectural styles of the homes. For example, the Friday Prayer Imam (*imam jome'h*) of Lavasan, Seyyed Said Hojjat al-Islam Lavasani (b. 1961), has objected to the architectural styles of the villas, comparing them to the White House (*Kakh-e sefid*) and European cathedrals (*kelisa*), and wondering if these are appropriate models for the Muslim region.[139]

Some of the buildings are imitations of neoclassical and baroque styles reminiscent of those found in the work of Tehrani architects Farzad Daliri (b. 1954) and Ali Moosa Panah (b. 1970), known as the architects of branded buildings (*sakhtemanhay-e markdar*).[140] Others are designed by world-class architects such as New York–based Hariri & Hariri Architecture, directed by the Iran-born and Cornell-educated sisters Gisue (b. 1956) and Mojgan Hariri (b. 1955).

. . .

In 2016, Hariri & Hariri Architecture completed the Lavasan Villa on a challenging, steeply sloping plot, flanked by a series of older and not-so-well-received McMansions.[141] According to the architects, the design was guided by the client's desire for privacy, the "Islamic tradition of not being seen by public in the private quarters" (fig. 2.14).[142] Thus, part of the three-story, all-white structure is carved into the hillside, accessed by means of a staircase and an elevator. The upper portion of the house includes a pool and a roof garden with a view toward the adjacent Jajrood River basin, an important water source for metropolitan Tehran. Topped with a remarkable cantilevered living room with large glass panes, the elevated compound is angled in the direction of an undeveloped sloping site to its left, and is only moderately visible from the neighboring mansions or the street down below.

Given that the long, rich, and successful career of Hariri & Hariri Architecture has been guided by a philosophy of design rooted in cultural sensitivities, their dedication to creating privacy due to religious beliefs is genuine and honorable; however, religious concerns are not always the

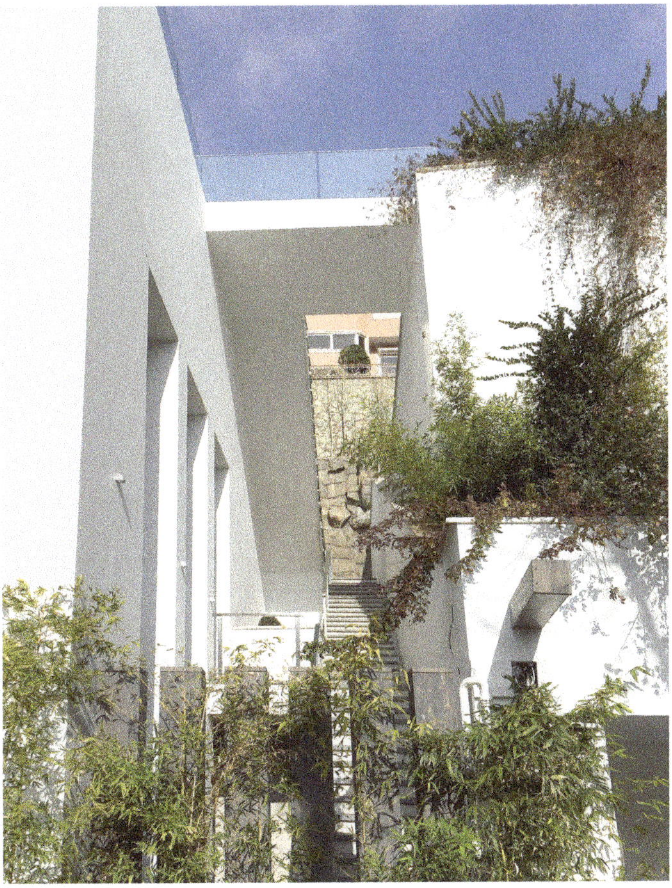

FIGURE 2.14 Hariri & Hariri Architecture. Lavasan Villa. 2016. Lavasan, Tehran province. Courtesy of Hariri & Hariri Architecture.

sole justification for Lavasan clients' excessive demands for privacy. While many villa owners are open to a "trusted" public, they do not want to be seen by the locals as their homes and lifestyles may violate the traditional norms of the area as well as the rules and regulations that limit the extent to which a residential building can spread its boundaries. Clients often refuse to openly speak about their properties. The owner and patron of the Lavasan Villa allegedly declined to be present for the site visit for the Building of the Year award, an honor the villa ultimately received. When journalists asked the reason for his absence, he simply said, "The building knows how to defend itself."[143]

. . .

On July 15, 2019, the Iranian right-wing national channel *Ofogh* featured an hour-long discussion between Hojjat al-Islam Lavasani and Milad Goodarzi, a young investigative journalist and chief editor of *Shahrdad*.[144]

Titled *Edalatkhahi-e omidbakhsh*, or "A Hopeful Quest for Justice," the discussion centered on the "problems" of Lavasan—from poor urban planning and the "inappropriate" behavior of villa owners to the lack of care for the environment. Lavasan was described as strange and exotic (*ajib o gharib*), rife with corruption (*sarriz az fesad*), and an environment that promotes royal culture (*farhang-e ashrafi*) that the Islamic Republic fought so hard to eliminate from Iranian values. The government knows what is going on, Hojjat al-Islam Lavasani asserted, and yet it refuses to address it, or to reveal the names of those responsible for creating and promoting such a corrupt system. Here we clearly see an instance of criticism that does not come from left-minded secular individuals but from those closer to the ideologies of the regime, who often refer to themselves as conservative justice seekers (*osoolgaray-e edalatkhah*). This resistance from within the system shows the "complex interworkings of historically changing structures of power."[145] Indeed, critical views from within the conservative and religious-minded system indicate the complexity of power relations and forms of resistance on the ground when it comes to art, design, and life in remote and inaccessible areas. As many experts have argued, Iran's environmental crisis is not so much due to economic sanctions or a lack of access to technology or technical expertise; rather, it is the result of poor governance and the involvement of too many stakeholders.[146] Water is mismanaged and land is overgrazed or disproportionately built upon. As environmental expert Kaveh Madani writes, "Actions are taken only after the problems have become so serious that they can hamper further development."[147] Likewise, in Lavasan, although the government has taken measures to address these complicated issues, many believe that some parts of the natural environment have become so damaged they can no longer be reclaimed and restored.

Above all, Lavasan seems to have become an escapist site that caters predominantly to the needs of the wealthy and the well-connected—one that, to borrow the words of art historian Celeste Olalquiaga, "creates an imaginary landscape through accumulation and camouflage, and . . . crystallize[s] the continued movement of life in the permeable disguise of fantasy."[148] It is an ideal place for exercising personal freedom (*azadi khosoosi*). And yet, as sociologist and Tehran University professor Yousef Abazari notes, "personal freedom" is not democracy; rather, "democracy is the training of people who can generate a debate."[149]

While remote natural places have served as refuges for artists and designers, allowing them to develop a greater freedom of expression and a spirit of solidarity and collaboration, they have also enabled the rise of another kind of culture, one in which many residents become essentially a detached community for exercising private and personal freedoms. As examples here have shown, *defiance* comes in different shades and has different motivations, and cannot be reduced to the common trope of "two opposing poles . . . [of] totalizing and repressive power of the state, and . . . heroic . . . social movements which lie outside the domain of power and resist the inroads of the state."[150] My purpose in this chapter has been to bring into dialogue a variety of approaches to *escapism* that underscore the complex ambitions and realities of artmaking and design production in Iran.

. . .

If engagements with private, semi-concealed, or remote spaces seems to be mainly focused on the interests of an individual artist or a select group of creative agents, critical engagement with urban spaces strives for a greater social impact. Indeed, many alternative art projects appear in central urban spaces and public places. The key to their survival, however, is that they are ephemeral or what is often referred to as "art that dies" (*honar-e mira*) or guerrilla art (*honar-e chiriki*), depending on the nature of the work. The mobility and ephemerality of the artwork and the artist within visible and accessible public spaces radically define the art-site relationship; for this reason, the following chapter underscores the *when* rather than the *where* of art.[151]

3 Ephemerality

Temporal Interjections in the City

ON WEDNESDAY, APRIL 4, 1979, just four days after the referendum in which some ninety-eight percent of the eligible electorate approved the creation of the Islamic Republic of Iran, at least according to the official results, a peculiar image featured in the popular *Ayandegan Newspaper* (fig. 3.1).[1] It showed a statue installed in 1976 outside the newly built *Te'atr-e Shahr* or City Theater, the work of Bahman Mohasses (1932–2010), an openly gay sculptor who had often been commissioned by the Pahlavi regime to create public art for Tehran. The midsection of the statue—a Minotaur-like figure playing a flute—had been covered up by the Islamic revolutionaries, because the figure's genitals were exposed, and a banner had been placed on the pedestal, seeking the opinion of the public on whether the sculpture should be removed or modified. No one knows where such an egalitarian approach might have led because the statue disappeared a few days after the banner went up. Nor did it take long for the new republic to give away to an authoritarian regime. Just like that statue, other forms of public art soon faced violation and censorship.

Instituted by the first supreme leader of Iran, the Organization for Islamic Propagation (*Sazman-e tablighat-e eslami*) would become the most prominent agency for disseminating agitprop. Its art branch, the Art Bureau of the Islamic Propagation (*Howzeh honari*), promoted propaganda-oriented mural arts, many of which were inspired by the social realist styles of communist and Latin American painting. During the Iran-Iraq war, these efforts were coupled with those of other parastatal organizations such as the Martyrs Foundation, the Ministry of Endowments and Charitable Works, and the local branches of the Organization for Mobilization of the Oppressed (*Basij-e mahalli*).[2]

After the Iran-Iraq war ended in 1988, the themes of murals in Tehran began to shift. Firoozeh Golmohammadi (b. 1959), a close relative of former prime minister Mir Hossein Mousavi, was appointed by several municipal

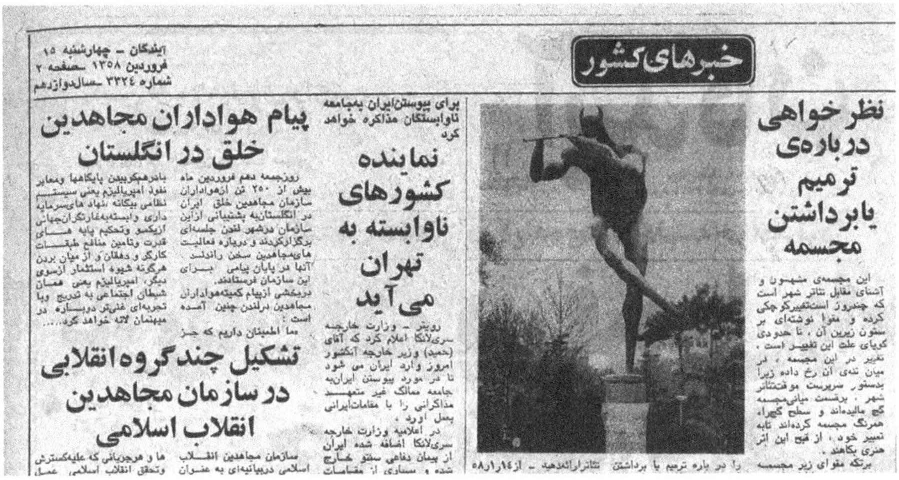
آیندگان - چهارشنبه ۱۵
فروردین ۱۳۵۸ - صفحه ۲
شماره ۳۳۲۴ - سال دوازدهم

خبرهای کشور

پیام هواداران مجاهدین خلق در انگلستان

نماینده کشورهای ناوابسته به تهران می‌آید

تشکیل چند گروه انقلابی در سازمان مجاهدین انقلاب اسلامی

نظرخواهی درباره‌ی ترمیم یا برداشتن مجسمه

FIGURE 3.1 "A Poll Concerning the Modification or Removal of a Sculpture." *Ayandegan Newspaper*, 3324/12 [April 4, 1979], 2. Newspaper excerpt from the personal collection of Homayoun Sirizi.

agencies in Tehran to propose new ideas for the walls of the capital.[3] Unlike propaganda murals that depicted realistic subjects in gloomy colors, Golmohammadi's murals involved abstract themes with mystical elements, all executed in lighthearted pastels.[4] Her unusual yet permitted move paved the way for similar public art projects.[5]

In late 1998, only six years after the Sculpture Department was revived at the College of Fine Arts at the University of Tehran and four years after the first postrevolutionary Tehran National Sculpture Biennial, the Office of the Expansion of Cultural Spaces of the Tehran municipality (*Sherkat-e tose'eh fazahay-e farhangi-e shahrdari-e Tehran*) began to commission temporary, three-dimensional artistic installations notably lacking in religious and propaganda iconography. The objective was to cheer up the city during the religious months, specifically the month of Ramadan which, unlike Muharram, is not associated with any ceremonies or public presentations. In Ramadan of 1998, sculptor Keivan Pournasr (b. 1970) and stage designer Siamak Ehsaii (b. 1957) were invited to "cultivate good vibes" (*ijad-e hesseh khoob*) at a busy intersection under the Parkway Bridge (fig. 3.2). Using temporary materials such as Plexiglas and fabric, the duo created a colorful abstract arrangement that elevated the artistic profile of the area, amid the heavy traffic of cars and pedestrians.

According to Pournasr, this was a challenging project because of the abstract (*enteza'ie*) quality of the work. Abstraction, which was devoid of

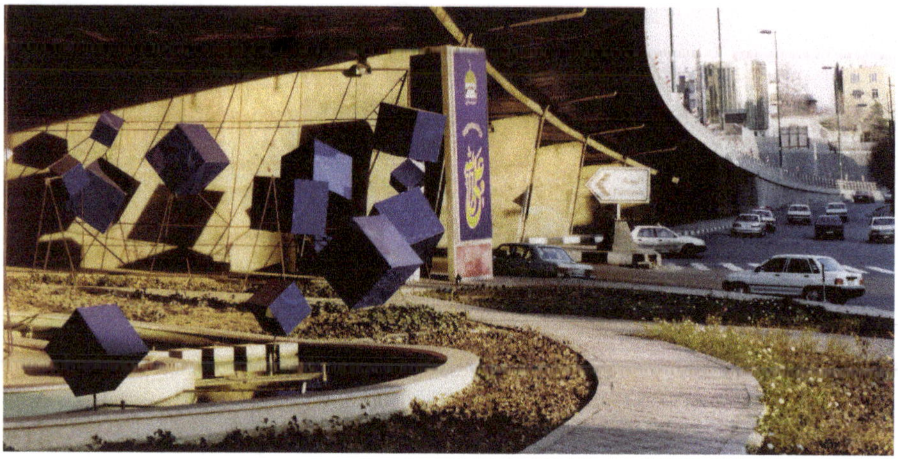

FIGURE 3.2 Installation by Keivan Pournasr and Syamak Ehsaie. 1998. Parkway Bridge, Tehran. Photograph by Keivan Pournasr.

references to traditional Islamic geometric patterns and did not play "a sublime (*vala*) role in the formation . . . of urban spaces and . . . the fulfillment of the . . . aesthetic needs . . . of Islamic Iran,"[6] was regarded as a Western import—as art without a committed mission. It therefore required a concerted effort to win over the MCIG as well as other municipal agents. Pournasr recalled, "I used to employ storytelling (*dastan saraie*) strategies to justify my abstract compositions. We needed to make sure that these geometric forms and random arrangements were not associated with the 'art for art's sake' discourse, but rather with something meaningful or spiritual within the Iranian culture."[7] Pournasr's method of negotiation marked a transformation in the perception of public art in Tehran.

In 2001, at the peak of President Khatami's call for an expansion of cultural activities and a "Dialogue of Civilizations," the Beautification Bureau of the City of Tehran became the main official sponsor of artistic murals. Even though Mohammad Bagher Ghalibaf—a conservative and Iran's former chief of police and commander of the Revolutionary Guards' Air Force—had been elected mayor of Tehran, the bureau continued to publish calls for mural competitions in major art magazines.

Among those selected for realization were bold and unusual works by Mehdi Ghadyanloo (b. 1981), who had grown up in a semirural suburb of Tehran. While Ghadyanloo took his cue from natural settings of his youth, he was also fascinated by Western artists such as David Hockney.[8] Somewhat surprisingly, the mayor would turn out to be a fan of his work, which is imbued with ironic messages. For instance, in his *Portrait of the Sky* (*Naghsh-e aseman*), we see a pedestrian bridge that leads nowhere, juxtaposed against the polluted sky of Tehran (fig. 3.3).

The Khatami-era appointment of a few progressive staff at the Tehran municipality allowed some pro-regime-sponsored public art to express subtle forms of resistance. Since that time, however, feeble imitations of Ghadyanloo's murals and debased versions of Pournaser's abstract monuments have spread across the walls and street corners of Tehran.[9] Known as "*plop art*" (translated by art critic Behzad Khosravi-Noori [1975] as *honar-e teleppi*), these are works that drop out of nowhere and "dump" in a place with little regard to site.[10] Some critics warn against the latent ideology that is "cleverly assimilated" into some of these seemingly innocent art and design developments, which are seen as short-term solutions, even temporary facelifts (*bazak*), to disguise larger urban problems. Some find that placing art in certain urban areas leads to the further displacement of the poor, the homeless, and the street musicians who would otherwise occupy these spots.[11]

Alongside the traditional *howzeh* and the more progressive Beautification Bureau, the House for the Artists of the Revolution (*Khaneh tarrahan-e*

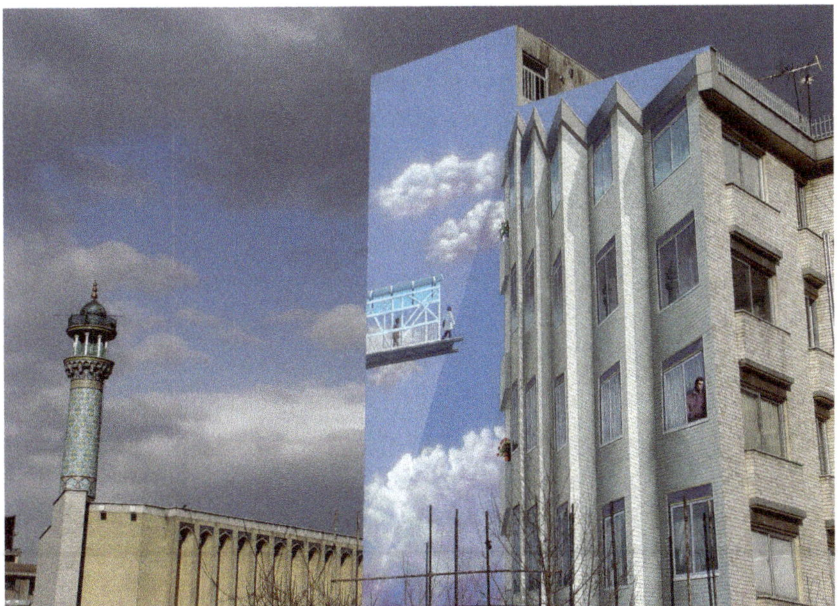

FIGURE 3.3 Mehdi Ghadyanloo, *Portrait of the Sky* mural. 2007. Tehran. Courtesy of Tehran Beautification Bureau.

enghelab) has been operating since 2012 under the aegis of the Owj Art and Communication Organization (*Sazman-e honari resaneh-ie Owj*), a private organization affiliated with the Islamic Revolutionary Guard Corps. Its role is to create large-scale digital billboards and eye-catching banners that promote the activities of the regime.

. . .

Given the dearth of official opportunities to participate in expanding public space, Iranian artists often turn to temporary and guerrilla-style performances. Tehran-based art historian Helia Darabi refers to this kind of intervention as "*manipulation* in urban spaces" (*dast kari dar fazahay-e shahri*).[12] The term *dast kari* is subtly political, as it refers to unexpected and unplanned activities. The phrase can even be construed to suggest vandalism. Indeed, by virtue of being unexpected and unplanned as well as being easily visible and accessible to the public and the state authorities, these forms of art are subversive, and one of the ways in which this so-called manipulation of urban space can sustain itself is by being temporal.

It is not easy to realize short-term projects and performance art in public places, and there are many instances of arrests and interrogations by the police. A map by graffiti artist Ghalamdar that documents his (and his collaborators') interventionist art in Tehran between 2010 and 2015 says it all.[13] The locations of Ghalamdar's public art are identified by a series of red splashes, reminiscent of bloodstains. These marks call to mind the violence of revolution and war over the past decades, but they also signify the civil freedoms that are constantly violated by the morality police and other authorities in Tehran. Some of the marks on Ghalamdar's map are casually labeled, indicating the neighborhoods or dilapidated buildings in which the graffiti art or covert art projects were created. Other stains are not labeled, and so the maps project the tentative nature of many public art activities in Tehran—their constant oscillation between legal and illegal, public and private, visible and invisible (fig. 3.4).

Indeed, artists have to be careful in navigating public spaces in Tehran. Opportunities are always there, but it is never easy to guess how the state authorities will respond. Although there are instances in which artists manage to secure permission from the state authorities, more often than not spontaneous projects are swiftly shut down. Rules and regulations also change depending on which president, mayor, or local city council committee is in power. Periods of heightened political tension add further obstacles to executing the work. For example, the 2009 Green Movement, the 2019

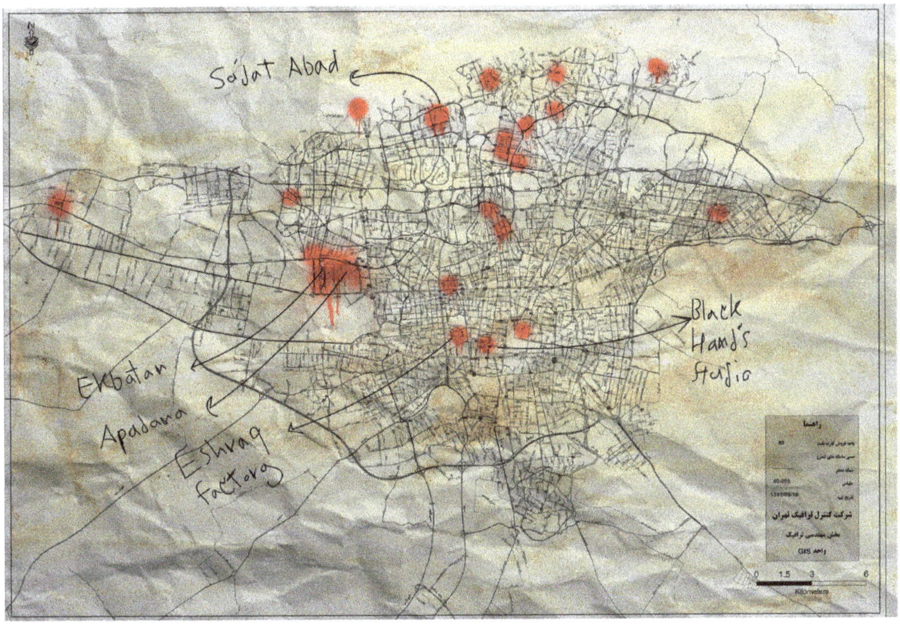

FIGURE 3.4 Parham Ghalamdar, map of the interventionist art projects spearheaded by Ghalamdar and his colleagues in various locations of the capital. 2015. Tehran. Sketch by Parham Ghalamdar.

November student uprisings, and the assassination of Qasem Soleimani all intensified surveillance around Tehran and other Iranian cities. During these periods, many urban art projects were short-lived. Some never got beyond the level of sketches and proposals.

Despite their differences, the interventionist public art projects animating urban spaces of Tehran have one thing in common: whether art performance or theatrical projects or graffiti and object-oriented art, they are all temporary and event-based. Sometimes they appear for a brief period in temporary spaces or spaces that are in transition. Some only go on for a few hours; others may last for days. In almost all these projects, art intersects with space and gives it new meanings, whether through explicit partnership or role changing. Urban interventionist artists in Iran engage with what Lefebvre calls "rythmanalyse" (*rhythmanalysis* in English; *zarbahangkavi* in Persian), a necessary sensory and time-based tactic for interrupting the "proper" domain of power. Attuned to the lived, sensed, and perceived rhythms that orchestrate everyday lives and mobilities, the "rhythmanalyst" "not only observe[s] human activities he also hears . . . (in the double sense of the word: noticing and understanding) the temporalities in which these activities unfold."[14] In this way, "without claiming to *change life*, but by fully reinstating the sensible in consciousnesses and in *thought*," the rhythmanalyst manages to "accomplish a tiny part of the *revolutionary* transformation of this world and this society in decline." And they do this, Lefebvre argues, "without any declared political position."[15] Engaging with the unfolding rhythms of everyday life, the rhythmanalyst disrupts functions or "malfunctions of rhythm" in the city and all it contains: roads, cars, architecture, people, etc. Following the lead of Lefebvre, like rhythmanalysts, Iranian artists create moments of rupture in the everyday life of open urban spaces, without declaring an overt political position.

"Guerrilla Style" Performances and Installations

The artistic lineage of "guerrilla style" interventions in public urban spaces in Iran goes back to the late 1970s. Although many renowned Iranian visual artists and leading theater experts took their inspiration from street performances and their routine walks in the bazaar and explorations in other traditional urban areas (e.g., the Saqqakhaneh group addressed later in this chapter), they rarely made art that was exclusively for short-term presentation in busy urban centers. One exception is the work of Gholamhossein Nami (b. 1936). Although largely forgotten, the work and stories associated with his work provide a perfect introduction to the ephemeral interventionist arts of the postrevolutionary period.

In 1977, during the difficult period before the Islamic Revolution, Nami made a giant Styrofoam knot, three meters in length and one and half meters in height. The work was executed in Nami's studio on Villa Street,[16] then taken outside to "interrupt traffic." Capturing the randomness and unpredictability of an *event*, this unusual presentation could be seen as an appeal for a new order of things on the eve of the revolution (fig. 3.5).

Nami photographed this moment as a significant time in the life of the *Knot* (*Gereh*). When the *Knot* went on display at the second Azad Group art exhibition, Nami says that some people interpreted it as a "symptom of political problems of the time."[17] The work was shipped out of Iran for a show in Washington, DC, and on its return was placed in a storage facility in downtown Tehran. It went missing during the revolutionary uprisings, and has never been recovered, assuming it still exists.[18] The story of the *Knot*, from its inception to its disrupting traffic to its disappearance in 1979, was a microcosm of things to come. If guerrilla art projects did not necessarily register a polemical message before the Islamic Revolution, they certainly did after it.

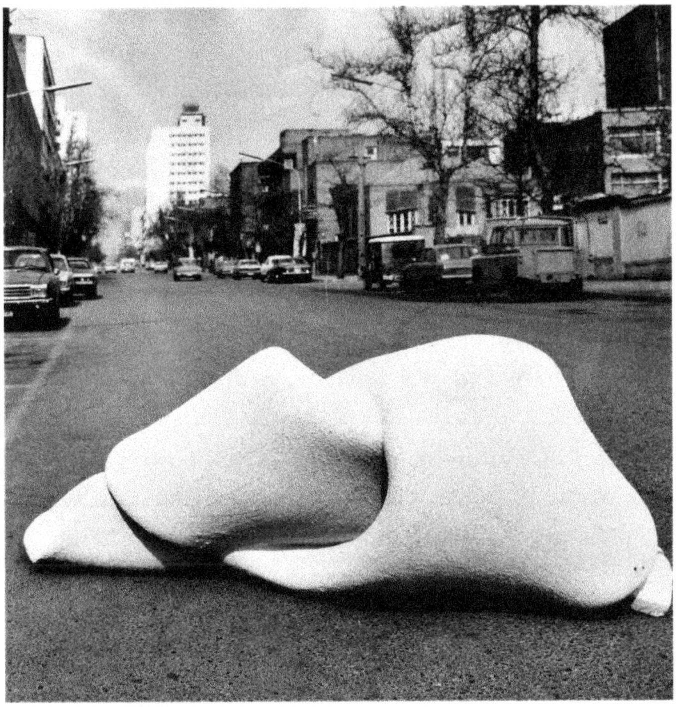

FIGURE 3.5 Gholamhossein Nami, *Knot*. 1978. On display in the middle of Villa Street, Tehran. Courtesy of Gholamhossein Nami.

In 1997, Bita Fayyazi (b. 1962) and Mostafa Dashti (b. 1960)—two artists who had been involved in the earlier *kolangi* projects (see chapter 1)—took their art into open urban space. Their installation, *Roadkill* (*Tasadof-e jaddeh-ie*), consisted of terracotta dogs that looked as though they had been crushed.[19] The dogs' subsequent burial in a mass grave, on the site of a soon to be constructed high-rise, was a statement about the politics of rapid urban development in Tehran.

Indirectly, the project was a metaphor for the government's disregard for life, human or animal (as exemplified by the gruesome killing of stray dogs, including puppies, some years later). In retrospect, in its use of terracotta and papier-mâché, the project calls to mind the politically radical Bread & Puppet theater of Peter Schumann in the 1960s. Schumann's puppets, which were also presented in Iran during the fourth Shiraz Arts Festival, may have had more political weight, particularly in terms of their anti-Vietnam war messages, but the terracotta dogs' significance is also undeniable.[20] They may not have attracted the attention of passing cars, and ordinary people may not have engaged with them in a meaningful and sustained way, but the powerful photographs of the installation continued to live on in the imagination of Iranian art circles. In an interview with *Bidoun Magazine* in 2004, Alireza Sami-Azar (b. 1961), the former director of the TMoCA, pointed out that "[these projects] proved that art can remarkably contribute to the quest of our people for social reforms and civil society."[21]

Roadside performances would later become widespread among art circles. In 2005, Houman Mortazavi (1964), who was also involved in the earlier installations inside vacated homes, created the *Parallel* (*Movazi*) project. The work was based on the principle of participatory budgeting, through which Mortazavi and his colleagues invited a group of artists to fund an installation and realize it within a designated period. At first the group contemplated creating elaborate sculptures out of recycled materials on the busy sidewalks of Tehran, but it soon became clear that the project had to be "quick," or else they would be hassled by the police.[22] Mortazavi recalls that they had to mount them guerrilla style (*nasb-e chiriki*) and then leave the scene right away.[23] The unauthorized works may have appeared shoddily put together, but they were thought-provoking.

Notable among them was an installation spearheaded by Mortazavi himself, which recreated the roadside stands typically used by fruit, ice, and vegetable vendors. But in place of the usual signage, describing the produce and its price, Mortazavi wrote words such as trust, stability, silence, calm, and security—words that by his own account are absent from the urban life of Tehran (fig. 3.6).[24] To be visible, albeit for a brief period, was central to Mortazavi's project.

In this sense, visibility prevails over the direct political language of art. Art gains political purchase when it becomes *mahsoos* or, in French, *sensible* (in English, "felt"), a term art critics borrow from the French philosopher Jacques Rancière, whose work also holds a special allure in Iran.[25] According to Rancière, "artistic practices are 'ways of doing and making' that intervene in the general distribution of these ways of doing and making as well as in the relationships they maintain to models of being and forms of visibility."[26] In the same vein, the artistic practice of Mortazavi expands the realm of the perceptible, allowing us to see and hear those who are often invisible and whose demands are often denigrated as "noise." Mortazavi's guerrilla style and quick engagement with the roadside did not cause any conflicts with the authorities, but other artists have faced obstacles.

Artist Jinoos Taghizadeh (b. 1971) recalls an instance in 2002 when she shared her art proposal with the staff of Kashan's historic Fin Garden.[27] The garden is known as the place where Amir Kabir, the celebrated chief

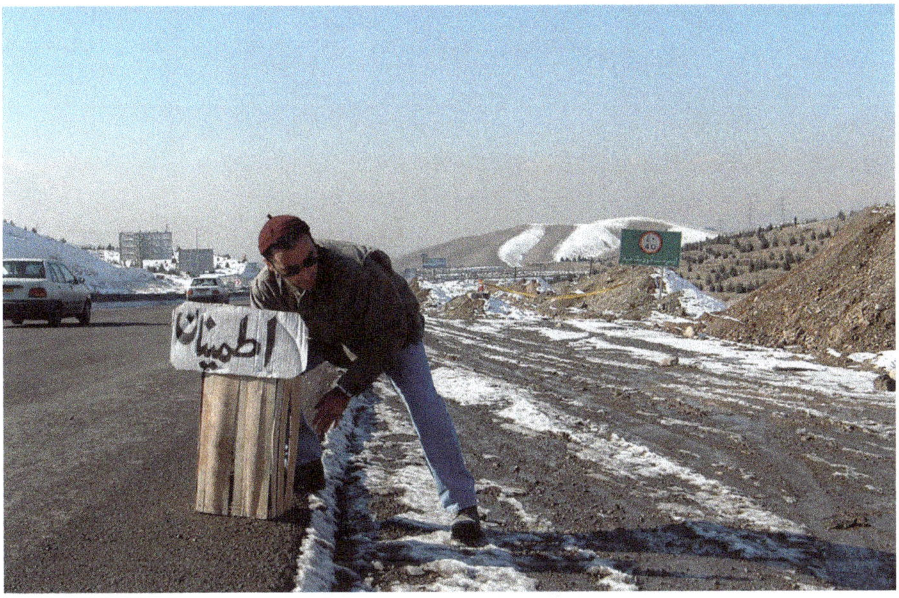

FIGURE 3.6 Houman Mortazavi during his performance on a roadside. The sign reads "Trust." 2006. Tehran. Courtesy of Houman Mortazavi.

minister to Naser al-Din Shah Qajar, was assassinated in 1852 at the age of forty-five by the shah's powerful circle of courtiers. During his time in office, Amir Kabir was responsible for many progressive projects. In today's Iran, Amir Kabir is so revered in folk memory that his oppression of the religious minority group the Babis (later Bahá'ís), and his refusal to listen to powerful voices among women, are completely overlooked. Amir Kabir was especially instrumental in subjugating the Baha'i Qurrat al-'Ayn (1817–1852), an influential female poet, women's rights advocate, and activist against forced veiling. Taghizadeh's proposal envisioned a reenactment of a challenging discussion between Amir Kabir and Qurrat al-'Ayn. The reference to Qurrat al-'Ayn was enough for the staff to spot a problem and reject her proposal out of hand.[28]

The following September, Taghizadeh installed her work *Oblation* (*Nazr*) in front of Isfahan's historic Sheikh Lotf Allah Mosque. She had not obtained permission from the authorities, however, and was asked to remove it only an hour after it was launched. The installation consisted of a ten-meter-long tarpaulin sheet on which hundreds of pears were placed. Passersby were invited to pick up the pears free of charge, just as they would in a typical religious offering. The choice of the mosque (which was designed

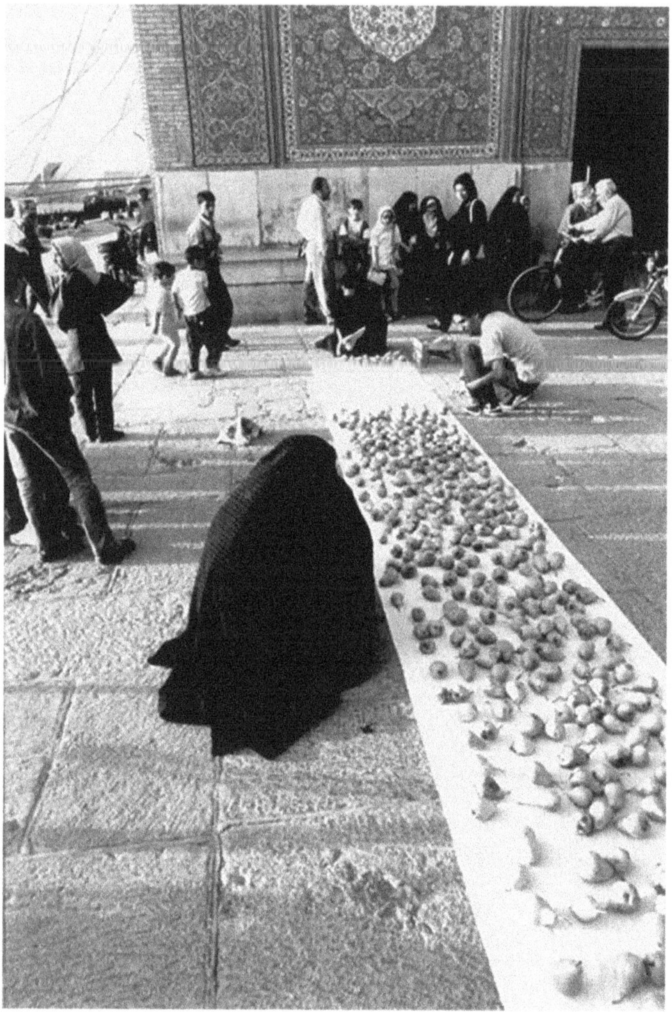

FIGURE 3.7
Jinoos Taghizadeh, *Oblation*. 2003. Naghsh-e Jahan Square, Isfahan. Courtesy of Jinoos Taghizadeh.

for the women of the royal Safavid court) and pears (which resemble the curves of the female body) were intended to serve as a reminder of the lack of women's voices in public spaces and especially at religious sites.[29] But the intentions remained unexpressed, even when the authorities questioned the project because pears are not offered in oblation (traditionally it would be stew or dates or saffron-rice-pudding). On her website, Taghizadeh writes: "According to the custom, one should never speak of the reasons for which the pledge or oblation or *nazr* is done."[30] The work thus had an ironic twist. While it was presented as a religious act, it also had an interventionist character that questioned the very idea of what a religious ritual could mean and do (fig. 3.7).

Oblation also encapsulated Taghizadeh's conviction that rather than "the final result" (*natijeh nahayi*), the focus should be on the "action" (*amal*) itself.[31] In anticipating the short life of the installation, Taghizadeh also remained faithful to the ontology of time-based art, whose "only life is in the present" so as to avoid contamination with "the economy of reproduction" and market-oriented aesthetics.[32]

. . .

That timing is crucial to such acts of public intervention is better expressed by a prominent outsider artist, Naiza Khan of Pakistan (mentioned in chapter 1), who had to "make critical decisions on the spur of the moment."[33] Khan made a video based on the movement and interactions of people in the incongruously titled metro station, Metro Beheshti (Heavenly Metro; also the title of Khan's video).The station is named after the martyr Ayatollah Mohammad Beheshti, but what was more significant for Khan was the daily life of people. While the video steered clear of any problematic or politically sensitive topic, filming inside the metro was considered "crossing the red line," as Khan recalled.[34]

Accompanied by an Iranian friend artist, Khan sought permission from the station manager. After lengthy negotiations purely about the aesthetic merits of the video, the manager acquiesced, saying he "would turn the other way." The artist accompanying Khan "acted as camouflage and [they] pretended to be talking amongst [themselves] casually. [Khan] would stand there . . . camera wrapped in fabric, chatting, eating chips, and drinking Coke, acting as if [they] were waiting for the metro. Then [Khan] would position [her] camera and start recording."[35]

Each recording lasted about ten minutes, before they changed location, and each time the Iranian artist friend would deflect attention away from Khan while she recorded another scene. In retrospect, Khan said, it was "extremely courageous" of her hosts to allow her to "take such a risk."[36] Indeed, actions that might cause trouble for an Iranian artist can cause even greater problems for a foreign guest. Soon after this, Khan proposed to stage a provocative performance at the end of a cul-de-sac outside the Arya Gallery, where she would sit at a dressing table applying eyeliner and lipstick, then take off her scarf and brush her hair.

Her request was rejected outright and she was told it would not be discussed further. Khan was "baffled by all the negotiations" but then agreed to take the performance inside.[37] The gallery delayed the performance, asked ordinary visitors to leave, and then permitted thirty-odd "trusted" people to see the show. As Khan has stated elsewhere, she always tries to

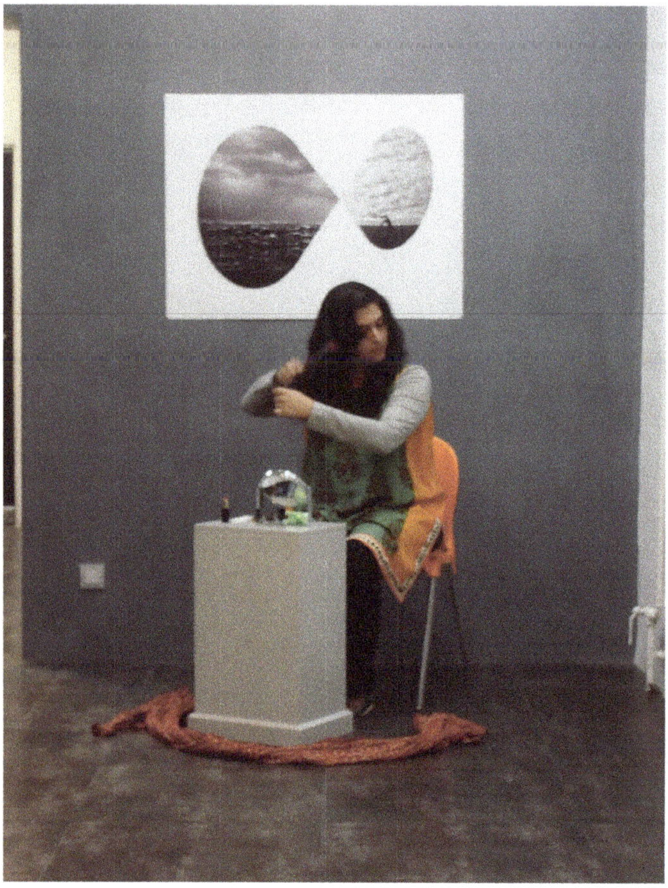

FIGURE 3.8
Naiza H. Khan, *Who Makes the Boundary?* 2012. Arya Gallery, Tehran. Photograph by Mehdi Vosoughian. Courtesy of Naiza H. Khan.

"find strategies of accessing . . . space," and in doing so, she negotiates "on terms that she cannot completely control."[38] The time of the performance, *Who Makes the Boundary?* (*Cheh kasi marzha ra ta'een mikonad?*), was delayed, but the place of the performance remained open and active (fig. 3.8).

If the sensitive art of Khan was carefully timed and even delayed, another art project became a site of political intervention in bright light, albeit in a single pincer-movement-like act (*ejra'-e shebh-e gazanbori*), a term I borrow from Tehran-based art critic Mohammad Bagher Ziyayi (b. 1969).[39] While enrolled in an architecture program at the Faculty of Fine Arts at Tehran University, Homayoun Sirizi (b. 1981) became fascinated with Foucault's writings on the insane, criminals, and sexual deviants, as well as his analysis of the panopticon. Sirizi conceived the idea of a collective building bringing together Tehran's deviants and outliers. The proposal was rejected outright by a committee of "traditional-minded professors" and Sirizi was threatened with expulsion from the university. Undeterred, Sirizi proposed instead to use a prison, and this time the project was approved on the condition that he would not politicize it.[40] Sirizi's capacity to stir up interesting debates around abstract concepts attracted the attention of a part-time drawing faculty member, who was none other than Alireza Sami-Azar, the progressive director of the TMoCA.

With support from Sami-Azar, Sirizi found his way into the world of conceptual art. In fact, he would become the youngest artist of the postrevolutionary generation to be granted a solo show at the prestigious Niavaran Cultural Center (*Farhangsaray-e Niavaran*). Sirizi's projects are mostly interventionist, and have a spatial character informed by his background in architectural design and his interest in the ways in which outliers and cutting-edge thinkers are often marginalized through spatial devices. One of his missions was to "gate-crash government-sponsored exhibitions," Sirizi recalls, "because I felt I had no voice to convince our colleagues and gallery directors to stop collaborating with the regime."[41]

One prime example of the kind of collaboration that Sirizi railed against was a major show on the fortieth anniversary of the Islamic Revolution in 2018. The exhibition venue was the former Qasr Prison—the notorious political prison where the Shah's enemies were tortured and executed—which had been converted into a museum in 2007 to jog visitors' memory of the brutality of the previous regime. The show received substantial support from a renowned curator and pioneer in creating high-end commercial galleries, and was organized as part of the MCIG-run Fajr Visual Arts Festival, which is held on the anniversary of the Islamic Revolution every February since 2008. Even if the artworks on display did not necessarily allude to revolutionary themes, or actively celebrate the fortieth anniversary, many regarded the whole enterprise as a form of collaboration with the regime and its propaganda apparatus.

Seeing the immense efforts of the regime to glorify the fortieth anniversary, Sirizi called on all gallerists to boycott the Fajr Festival. Many initially supported him, but word soon got out that their permit to operate could be revoked if they did not collaborate. Sirizi then asked independent gallerists and artists to "hack official celebrations" by issuing statements calling for the MCIG to stop censoring artists.[42] This time, Sirizi's appeal was largely ignored. As he recalls, he found the whole atmosphere nauseating.

Sirizi took it upon himself to singlehandedly gate-crash the opening attended by ministers and journalists. His *chiriki* (guerrilla style) move was to distribute four hundred airplane-issue vomit bags, containing safety cards with instructions on how to deal with the sickening atmosphere of the art scenes in Tehran and the revolting idea of appropriating quotations from political prisoners who had been confined in Qasr (figs. 3.9a/b).

While one side of the bag read "for vomit," the other had the words "for reconciliation," urging those behind the events to reconcile with the opposition and seek forgiveness. There were also instructions on how to shake off motion sickness after looking at the artworks and how to exit the space in case of "emotional emergency." The idea of distributing information on mock Air France information cards and motion sickness bags alluded to the iconic image of the revolution: Ayatollah Khomeini descending from the stairs of a chartered Air France Boeing 747 on his arrival in Iran on February 1, 1979, as three million Iranians waited on the streets of Tehran to salute him.

The work was titled *Total Monument* (*Mojassameh kamel*). The main title was taken from a phrase used by Bozorg Alavi (1904–1997) in his autobiographical book, *Fifty-Three Persons* (*Panjah o seh nafar*, 1942). An influential Iranian writer, novelist, and a founding member of the communist *Tudeh* Party, Alavi spent most of his life in exile in East Germany. In his book, he writes of his experience as a prisoner in Qasr Prison during the Pahlavi era. The Qasr Prison, he says, could be read as a "total monument" to the Iranian people, embodying their existence under surveillance and dictatorship. Designed in 1929 by the Russian émigré architect Nikolai Markov, the prison is laid out as interlocking quadrangles, ensuring the constant surveillance of the inmates at the intersection of each straight corridor of tiny cells. The figure on the mock safety cards is modeled after Mohammad Dargahi, who also allegedly became its first inmate, imprisoned for two days after making the mistake of inviting Reza Shah to enter a prison cell at its inauguration. By alluding to Dargahi, Sirizi reflected on the danger of liaising with the authorities: there is no promise of security and a friend might soon turn into an enemy, depending on the political atmosphere.[43]

Because of his interventionist activities, by his own account, Sirizi has been "forbidden to work" (*mamnoo' al kar*). So, he has made the street and public space his gallery. While guerilla art projects and unexpected interventions often seem to emerge out of nowhere, without securing a permit, more lasting engagements in visible urban locations invariably require permits and are, unsurprisingly, less shocking and more predictable, once again validating the multiplicity of interventionist art. In parallel with the

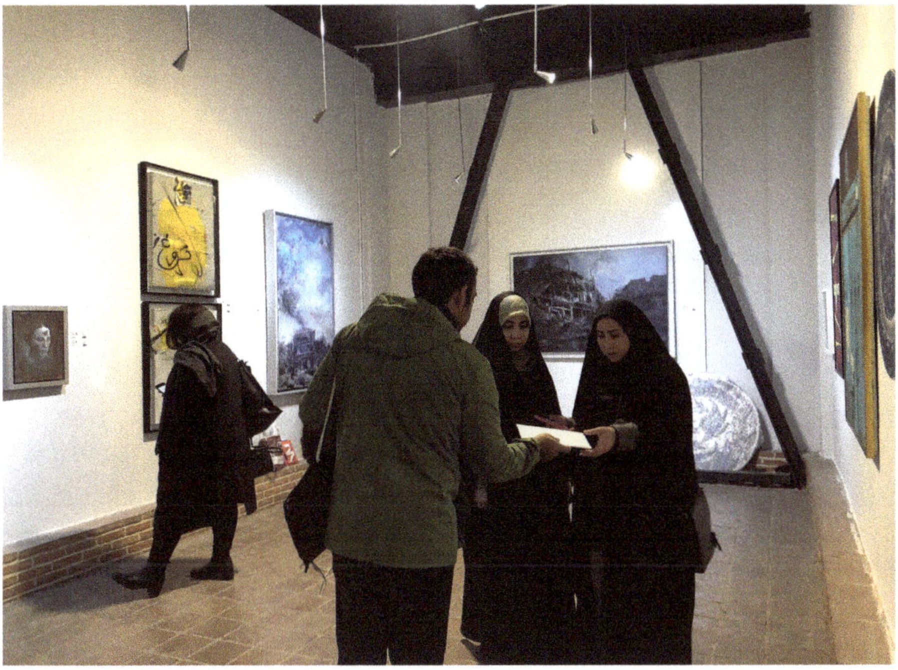

FIGURE 3.9A Homayoun Sirizi, *Total Monument.* 2018. Qasr (Prison) Museum, Tehran. Photograph by Mohammad Ghazzali. Courtesy of Homayoun Sirizi.

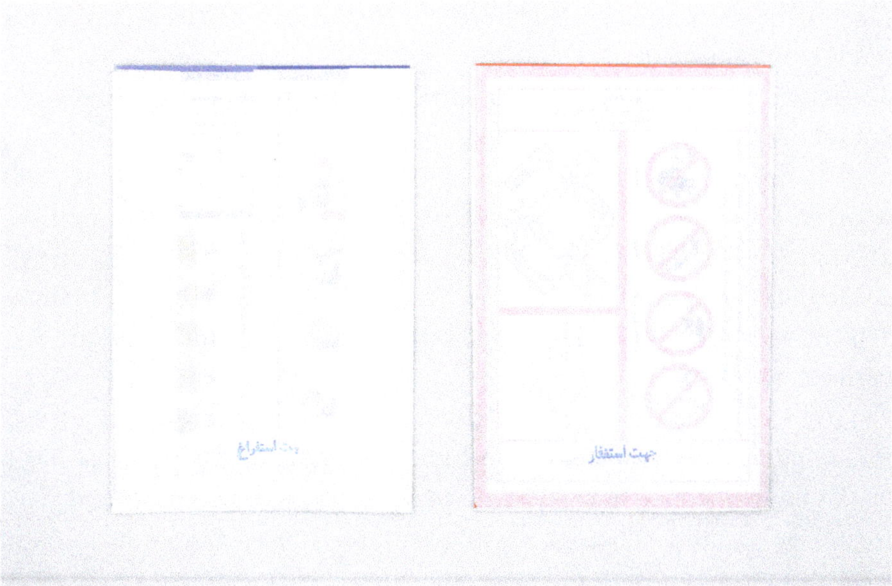

FIGURE 3.9B Homayoun Sirizi, Components from the performance, *Total Monument.* 2018. Tehran. Photograph by Mohammad Ghazzali. Courtesy of Homayoun Sirizi.

rise of *kolangi* art projects, discussed in chapter 1, alternative art projects emerged in leftover urban spaces and buildings under construction.

Art in Leftover Urban Spaces

Since the early 2000s, in addition to taking over derelict homes and factories (see chapter 1), artists in Tehran have occupied what I call public leftover spaces—vacant lots, suspended construction sites, unused underpasses, and empty water canals. At first glance, artists' occupations of these spaces bear a resemblance to activities in other metropolitan areas. Recall how since the 1980s, creative agents have utilized the leftover urban spaces of deindustrialized America, otherwise known as the Rust Belt. A prime example in this vein is Tyree Guyton's Heidelberg Project in Detroit, especially his DOTS (Dancin' on the Street) festival that encouraged the crowds to dance down the abandoned streets of the city to Michael Jackson's *Thriller*. Detroit is one of the once great, now humbled cities, declining in both population and opportunity, that is welcoming artist colonies who can help boost microeconomic developments.[44] Such initiatives, widespread in all postindustrial urban areas, have also been executed elsewhere in the developing world. In Tehran, however, the leftover urban spaces are not the result of infrastructure decline, withdrawal of industries, or depopulation; on the contrary, they are the byproducts of rapid development. From 1990 to 1998, through a municipality-sanctioned trend called "sale of density" (*foroosh-e tarakom*), developers began to split plots of land and built high-rises well above the official norm, in explicit violation of established zoning laws.[45] Since 1992, there has been a surge of new multilane highways, stack interchanges, and underpasses, each of which generates leftover space during construction. The artists who work in these leftover spaces are rarely invested in microeconomic developments; rather, they opt for these sites for the freedom of artistic expression they offer, outside the regulated institutions of art and performance.

. . .

Buildings under construction, steel and glass baubles, stretches of beige brick and gray concrete facades, newly built stack interchanges and freeways, heavy traffic, pollution, peeling war and propaganda murals—these were the images that captured the imagination of Neda Razavipour (b. 1969), on her return to Iran in 1999 after more than a decade of residing in Paris, during which she was trained as a conceptual artist at the Département des

Arts Plastiques at the University Paris I Panthéon–Sorbonne and as a stage/space designer at the École des Arts Décoratifs.

During her studies, Razavipour became increasingly interested in the work of land artists such as Christo and Jeanne-Claude.[46] She was also involved in conceptual practices that demanded engagement with the city. For example, for one studio assignment, Razavipour collected some dirt from the Montparnasse Cemetery in Paris and turned it into a series of paintings in the abstract expressionist style.[47]

Razavipour's conceptual education, bridging different disciplines, allowed her to see her home city in a new light. In the early 2000s, Iran was at the peak of an economic boom that had been gradually gaining momentum since the end of the Iran-Iraq war in 1988. Old buildings were being torn down to make way for new developments. Massive urban development projects from the previous regime, which had stalled due to the revolution and the war with Iraq, were once again activated.

Citizens of Tehran had little input in any of these projects. As mere onlookers, they could only marvel as entire skylines rose from out of nowhere. Artists, however, saw something else. In 2003, driving around the city with her architect and multimedia artist colleague Shahab Fotouhi (b. 1980), Razavipour noticed the "abstract splendor" of the concrete towers under construction.[48] These were "cubical gray structures dotted with rows of dark, square-shaped frames marked by large-scale numbers written in bold red, indicating the floor level to which each row fitted," she recalled.[49]

One such construction was Ati Saz, a gigantic housing complex in northwestern Tehran. Begun in 1976 under the Pahlavis, with the involvement of a number of international firms, the complex was only partially built at the time of the revolution. In the mid-1980s, a decision was made to restart the stalled construction, but it took decades to realize the entire complex. In the meantime, many of the towers remained empty and unfinished. One of those towers, a half-built high-rise off the busy Chamran expressway, would be the site of a 2003 project by Razavipour and Fotouhi. After securing permission from multiple organizations—including the MCIG, the Beautification Bureau, the Tehran traffic police, and the Ati Saz management chief of staff—the artists filled the windows of the high-rise with seventy back-lit portraits of unidentified Tehranis, taken by photojournalist Abbas Kowsari (b. 1969), which randomly lit up and faded away. Titled *Census*, the work was a play on the equivalent of the term "counting heads" (*sar shomari*).

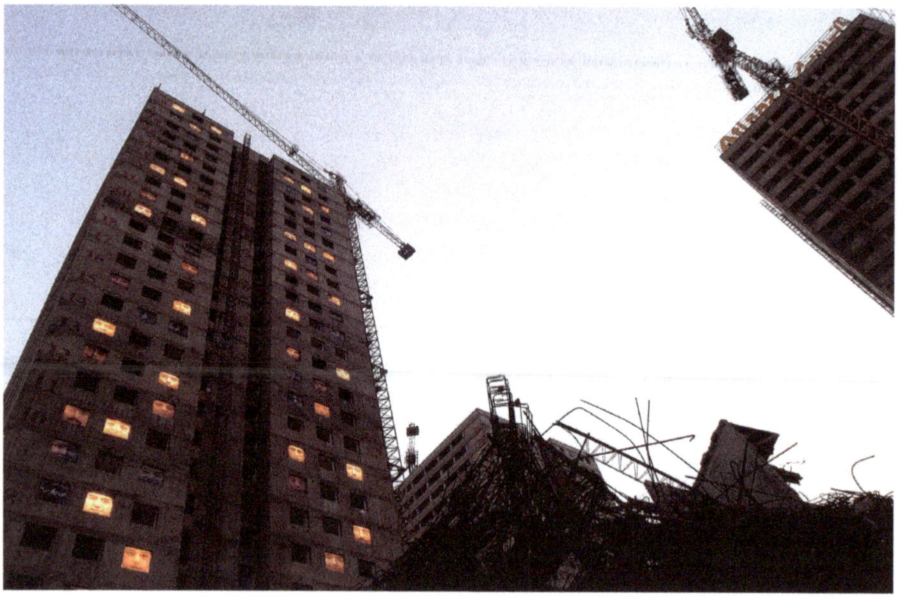

FIGURE 3.10 Neda Razavipour (in collaboration with Shahab Fotouhi), *Census*. 2003. Ati Saz, Tehran. Photograph by Abbas Kowsari. Courtesy of Neda Razavipour.

This choice conceptually related to headshots and the bold numbers that flanked them (fig. 3.10).

Above all, the project was created for its impact on the ground.[50] In a brief documentary accompanying the project, we hear the repetitive sounds of cement mixers and concrete being poured, perhaps alluding to the unending expansion of Tehran. At times, the repetitions are interrupted by a jackhammer that sounds like a firing squad.[51] Most importantly, the video also features passersby commenting on what they see from below. While some perceived it as an unnecessary waste of money, others indicated they had at first seen the faces as the regime's propaganda portraits and walked away without paying them any further attention. Another passerby interpreted them as photographs of imprisoned people, a metaphor perhaps for the restrictions that apartment life places on the people of Tehran.[52] Other commentators assumed that the project was a prank. A few Afghani construction workers on site admired the artistic quality of the work.

Despite the subdued contemporary reception, in retrospect the project can be seen to have had a lasting significance for many Iranian artists and art aficionados. Razavipour still receives comments and accolades from a younger generation of artists who remember how it fired their imagination when they saw it as a child.[53]

Coinciding with *Census* at Ati Saz, seven of these portraits, with the same dimensions and lighting techniques, were exhibited at the 13 Vanak art space. One of the portraits was installed in the space's display window while the others were featured inside. One wall of the space was covered with the scores of letters that had to be written to get the necessary permits for the unusual display of art in buildings under construction. Through their supplications to a labor-intensive bureaucracy, Razavipour and Fotouhi gained the space to experiment with novel concepts.

Two years later, in 2005, the end of the Khatami era, Razavipour and Fotouhi proposed *Orange on Gray: Homage to Mark Rothko* (*Narenji rooy-e khakestari*). The orange referred to the fluorescent uniforms of hundreds of sanitary workers, the gray to the slabs of concrete on which the artists wanted them to stand, in rows, for a few hours. This site was again a building under construction, the Tehran International Tower. Located north of Yusef Abad and Amir Abad districts and visible from Kordestan and Resalat expressways, the fifty-six-story residential building in Tehran was, at the time, the tallest of its kind and the only one to meet the definition of a skyscraper.

The nod to Rothko was a way for Razavipour and Fotouhi to express universal human emotions, as they sincerely hoped to generate an art of awe-inspiring intensity. But there was more to this project than just a formalistic approach to colors and forms. Just as Rothko's canvases inspired the reverence traditionally associated with monumental religious paintings, Razavipour and Fotouhi sought a celebration of pure color on a large scale that would lead them to engage Tehran's architecture in a violent clash of opposites—vertical versus horizontal, hot color versus cold—summoning the existential clash between the neoliberal revamping of Tehran and its religious and conservative attributes.[54]

The submission of the proposal coincided with Ahmadinejad's coming to power as mayor of Tehran. The proposal was rejected by the Tehran municipality. It was also turned down by the management team at the Tehran International Tower Complex, who were not keen for one of the most exclusive residential building in the capital to be associated with low-ranking sanity workers. While the Ahmadinejad team of evaluators probably rejected the work based on what they saw as an abstract concept that had little to do with Iranian art or values, the tower's management team recognized it as a leftist criticism of luxury developments in Tehran.[55] Whether materialized or not, by incorporating aspects of Tehran's built environment,

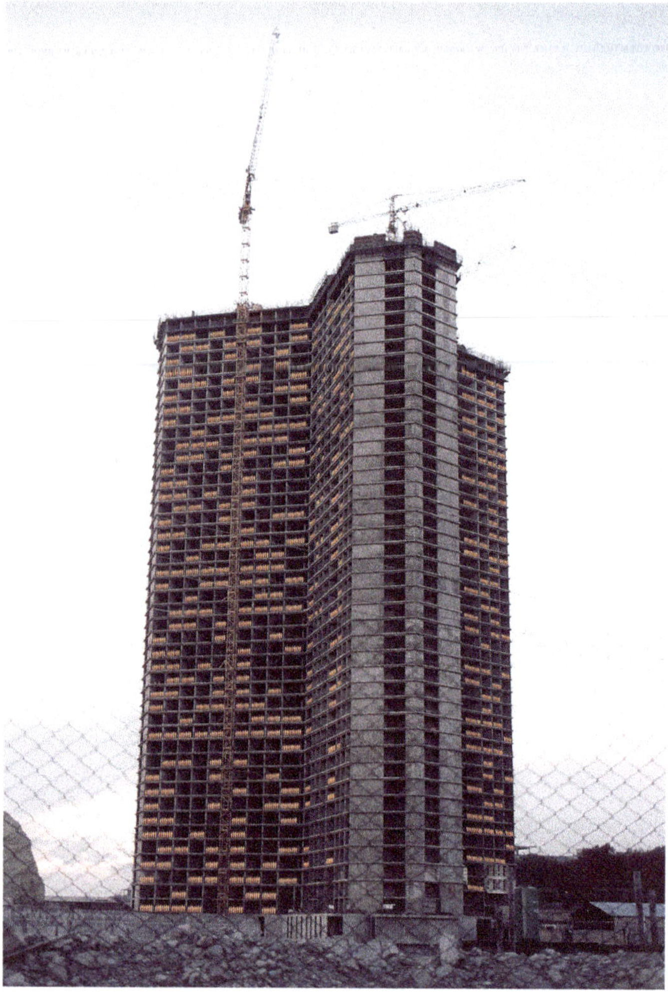

FIGURE 3.11 Neda Razavipour and Shahab Fotouhi, *Orange on Gray: Homage to Mark Rothko*. 2005. Photograph of the proposed project in the form of a model, Tehran. Courtesy of Neda Razavipour.

which is always a work in progress, the art of Neda Razavipour, along with her collaborator Shahab Fotouhi, tackles issues of urban life in an innovative way (fig. 3.11).

. . .

Although the difficulties of securing permission from the authorities prevented Razavipour and her colleague from continuing large-scale installations in buildings under construction, other leftover urban spaces enthused the minds of experimental theater experts. Established in 2006 by Hadi Kamali-Moghaddam (b. 1973) and Mina Bozorgmehr (b. 1980), the Tehran-based Noir Art Group (*Gorooh-e honari-e noir*) is known for its site-oriented urban performances. The couple bring complementary areas of expertise to their multidisciplinary group. While Kamali-Moghaddam is a trained theater performer who turned to experimental (*tajrobi*) and improvisational (*bedah-e*) theater after working in conventional theater for a decade, Bozorgmehr comes from a background in architectural design and scenography.[56]

Noir's improvisational techniques are mainly inspired by Happenings and by Jerzy Grotowski's experimental theater and other major theater genres that are extensions of Grotowski's ideas, namely Richard Schechner's Environmental Theater (*te'atr-e mohiti*), Eugenio Barba's Odin Teatret (*te'atr-e Odin*), and Augusto Boal's Forum Theater (*te'atr-e showraie*).[57] Following in the footsteps of these masters, Noir is interested in spectators influencing and engaging with the performance. Because of their improvised nature, the plays change with every performance, providing opportunities for growth and discovery, or what Kamali-Moghaddam calls "gratuitous repetitions that seize the soul of the performance (*jan-e ejra'*)."[58]

By taking the performance to unconventional urban locations, Noir escapes the rigid form (*shekl-e monjamed*) of conventional theater and avoids impenetrable (*ghofl o bast dar*) dialogue and mise-en-scène.[59] They inhabit what Peter Brook famously called the "bare stage," an empty space that can effortlessly host the encounter between viewer and performer—that "is all that is needed for an act of theater to be engaged."[60] According to Bozorgmehr, who combined her architectural studies with theater at Paris's École Internationale de Théâtre Jacques Lecoq, it is through experience, movement, and use that architecture becomes meaningful. For this reason, Noir integrates what Bozorgmehr calls the narrative of the soul of a place (*revayat-e rouh-e makan*).

For Bozorgmehr, space is intertwined with narratives—she refers, for example, to the way the built environment in Iran is in constant flux, shifting in line with the political landscape. Spatial change, then, speaks of political and social change.[61] She points to the same intertwining of space and narrative in theater, which she describes as spatial poetry (*she'r-e fazaie*).[62] Influenced by the Stalker—a collective of architects and researchers connected to the Roma Tre University who came together in the mid-1990s—Bozorgmehr engages in participatory actions to create "situations" and to construct a "collective imaginary" for ignored places.[63] Appropriating Stalker's method of collective walking, mapping, and listening in the "indeterminate" or "void spaces" of the city, Bozorgmehr brings to light disregarded or problematic urban spots.

. . .

Noir Art Group's move into unconventional urban locations—they had previously mainly performed in unconventional private spaces—followed a refusal of permission to perform in a formal venue. Rejected by the MCIG-run Annual Fajr Theater Festival committee in February 2010, Noir chose the open arena outside of Tehran's City Theater (where the festival's approved performances took place) to perform *This Is Not an Apple* (*In yek seeb neest*), a play written by Kamali-Moghaddam that went on for nine consecutive nights and involved references to ancient Iranian and Western mythologies.[64]

Every night, a total of twenty performers held containers of the four natural elements (water, wind, earth, and fire), which are considered sacred in ancient Iranian mythology. While keeping themselves busy with these elements—for example, by sweeping the dust on the ground—the actors took turns narrating myths and legends, from Adam and Eve to the Arash Kamangir, the legendary figure who gave his life to preserve the territorial integrity of Iran.[65] As they performed their parts, the actors sometimes congregated in one spot, and at other times walked around the circular periphery of the City Theater, seen as the birthplace of modern Iranian theater. In this way, they indirectly and subtly questioned the legitimacy of formal theater spaces (fig. 3.12).[66]

Noir's next major production, *Horses at the Window* (*Paykoobi-e Asbha posht-e panjareh*), by the internationally celebrated Romanian playwright Matei Vişniec, was performed over the course of two months in the winter of 2011, in a portion of the parking lot and junkyard of Vahdat (formerly Rudaki) Hall, constructed by the Shah as the national stage for opera and ballet. An antiwar play—an absurdist journey through three centuries of war and destruction—the performance also evokes the work of Samuel Beckett and carries the political edge found in Kafka's novels. Vişniec studied philosophy at Bucharest University and was an active member of the so-called Eighties Generation. Through his insistence on the capacity of art and literature to resist totalitarianism, he left a clear stamp on the anti-socialist-realism movements in his native Romania.[67] Exiled in France since the 1980s, his work has also had a lasting influence on the French performance art circles that Bozorgmehr got to know during her studies in Paris. The temporary stage was later removed when the new directorship of the Vahdat Hall declined permission for the continued use of the junkyard (fig. 3.13). After its termination at the Vahdat Hall, *Horses at the Window* was transferred to the

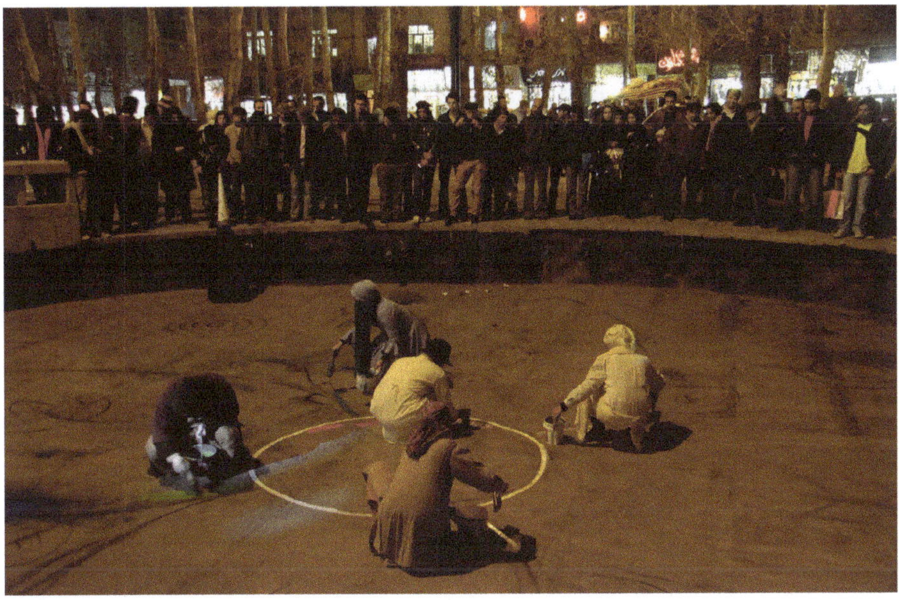

FIGURE 3.12 Noir Theater Group, *This Is Not an Apple*, directed by Hadi Kamali-Moghaddam and written by Hadi Kamali-Moghaddam and Mina Bozorgmehr. 2010. Performance outside City Theater, Tehran. Photograph by Shahin Amirshahpari and Babak Mehrbakhsh. Courtesy of Mina Bozorgmehr.

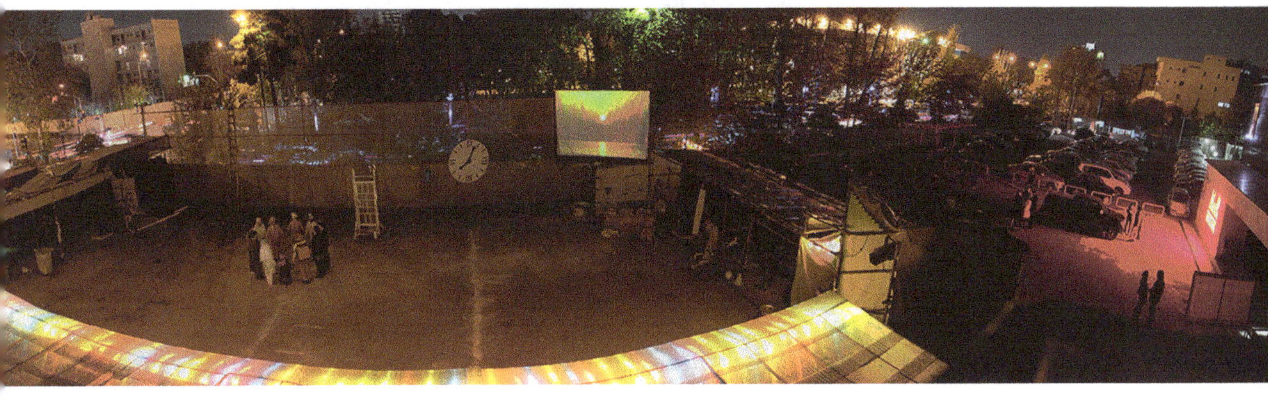

FIGURE 3.13 Noir Theater Group, *Horses at the Window*, directed by Hadi Kamali-Moghaddam and written by Hadi Kamali-Moghaddam and Mina Bozorgmehr. 2011. Performance in the parking lot of Rudaki/Vahdat Theater, Tehran. Photograph by Siamak Mohebalian. Courtesy of Mina Bozorgmehr.

Azadi Tower. On the days of the performance, Noir "activated" what they refer to as the "dusty" and "sleepy" corridors (*dalanha-ye khak khordeh va khamoodeh*) of the interior of the Azadi tower complex.

Built by architect Hossein Amanat in 1971, the forty-five-meter tower is an imposing form that resembles a gigantic upside-down letter "Y" in the cityscape of Tehran.[68] Before the Islamic Revolution, the tower was called *Shahyad* or "memorial to the Shah" and was a symbol of the Shah. After 1979, the new regime renamed it *Azadi* ("freedom" in Persian) and made it an icon of the Islamic Revolution's victory and the country's liberation from 2,500 years of monarchic rule.

Once used for pro-Shah parades, the vast fifty-thousand square meters of open space that wrap around the tower, forming an oval traffic circle known as *Meydan-e azadi* (Freedom Square), has always been a political space. Once used for pro-Shah parades, it would later become a focus for demonstrations against the Shah's regime in the lead-up to the Islamic Revolution. A sensitive site, it is always tightly controlled—particularly during annual celebrations and other pro-government rallies. However, the citizens of Tehran have also appropriated it for their own political gatherings, including the massive antiregime demonstrations that took place in the aftermath of the 2009 presidential elections. Against this politically charged backdrop, Noir's choice to "activate" the Azadi tower complex through art was a brave move (fig. 3.14).

According to Noir, their intervention paved the way for other artists to use the Azadi premises for alternative art practices (see, for example, the work of Negar Farajiani and Nastaran Safaie, described later in this chapter). By shifting their "stage" from leftover urban spaces to an openly accessible and politically charged arena—the "dusty" interiors of the Azadi Tower, as well as the open area around it—Noir gave their critical engagement with space a "blatant visibility," to borrow from London-based art critic Suhail Malik. Evocatively, Malik describes, such acts of occupation of unconventional public spaces as not being situated "liminally, in between, or to the side of power, but in its teeth."[69] But activating politically charged spaces is not without risks. As Kamali-Moghaddam notes, years of systematic censorship (*momayyezi*) reduced Iran's formal and official theater to a state of fear (*vahshat*) and stagnation (*rekhvat*), and artists have to be brave to fight these limitations.[70] The prominent theater critic Fariborz Daraie (b. 1974) explicitly linked Noir with the concept of "*brave theater*" in the spring of

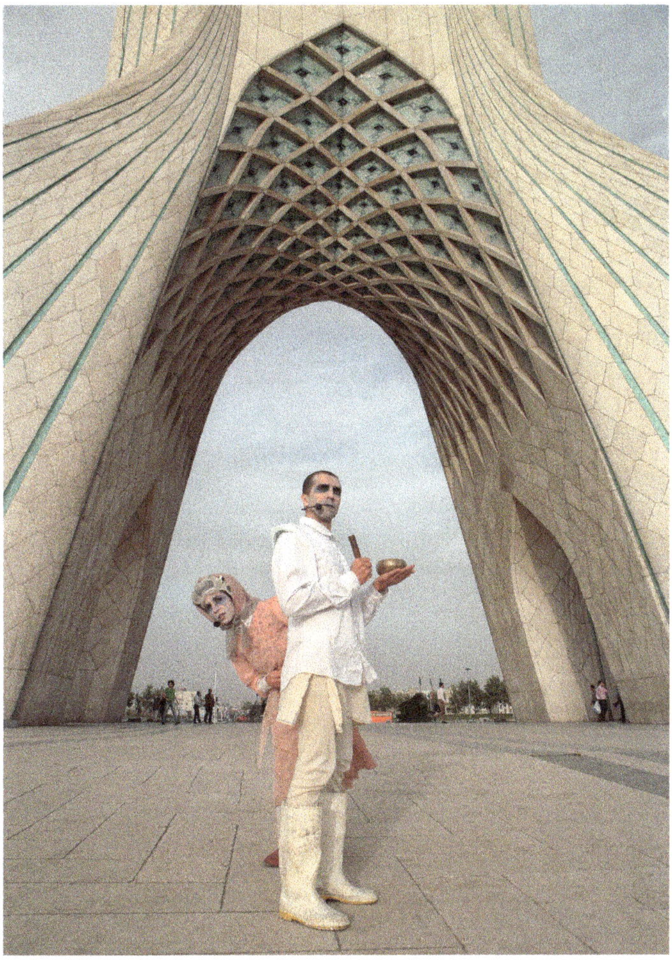

FIGURE 3.14
Noir Theater Group, *Horses at the Window*, directed by Hadi Kamali-Moghaddam and written by Hadi Kamali-Moghaddam and Mina Bozorgmehr. 2013. On the premises of the Azadi Complex, Tehran. Photograph by Siamak Mohebalian. Courtesy of Mina Bozorgmehr.

2020, when he gave his extensive interview with Kamali-Moghaddam and Bozorgmehr the bold title: "Theater Needs Brave People."[71]

Urban Interventionist Art on the Move

Moving art involves displacement, a transition from one location to the next. In the process, art inevitably encounters and interacts with complex structures: the street, the traffic, the passersby, the police, buildings, and a whole host of other agents. In facilitating a wide range of perspectives, moving art helps extend its meaning. Often making art mobile is a preemptive decision by the artist, and there are a variety of tactical interventions that are factored into this process.

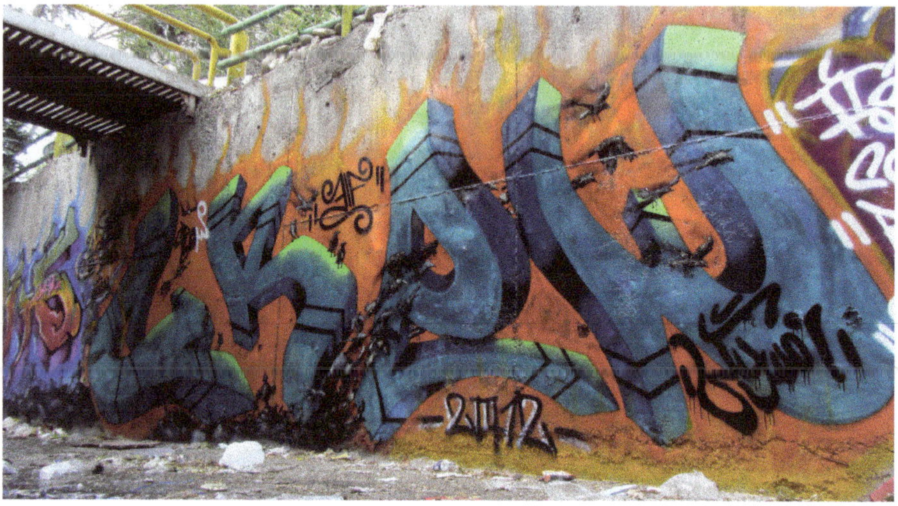

FIGURE 3.15A Ghalamdar, ELF Crew, and Blind, wild-style graffiti on the walls of an abandoned water canal. 2013. Tehran. Photograph by Blind. Courtesy of Parham Ghalamdar.

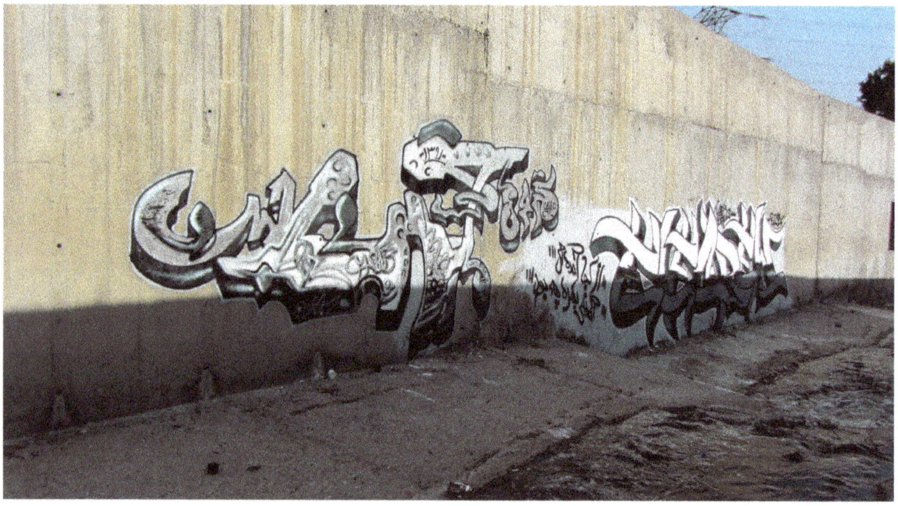

FIGURE 3.15B Ghalamdar, ELF Crew, and Blind, wild-style graffiti on the walls of an abandoned water canal. 2013. Tehran. Photograph by Blind. Courtesy of Parham Ghalamdar.

In 2013, along with the ELF Crew (which includes Blind, mentioned in chapter 1), Ghalamdar appropriated canals in the western suburbs of Tehran (figs. 3.15a/b). The performers scrawled over approximately two hundred meters of the canal walls. Although at first glance the images evoke interwoven and overlapping Latin letters used in Western wild-style graffiti, a closer look reveals many Persian words, including one for "depression" (*afsordegi*) followed by a quote in English: "It's like a cold story, repeated over and over again." Another wall presents a passage from one of Rumi's poems: "Where is this place? What is the purpose of my existence?"

Although Iranian municipal authorities continue to erase the work of independent street artists, more and more venues have been dedicated to presenting graffiti to new audiences. Ghalamdar's projects were often executed very quickly; the action was more important than the outcome. Out of principle, Ghalamdar and his colleagues did not run when the police arrived on the scene.

> We were not committing vandalism; we were not destroying public property; we were just making art for the public. So, we did not see ourselves as wrongdoers and as a result we did not feel the need to flee the scene. We were prepared to negotiate with whoever questioned us. Sometimes I would improvise. For example, if the authority was unhappy with the meaning he understood from the work, the next day I would add to the composition something of interest to him, such as the flag of the Islamic Republic. This was a game we played in order to stay safe.[72]

Ghalamdar added, "When someone gets caught doing graffiti in New York, the police arrest them or fine them [for vandalism]. But in Iran, our 'crimes' were [defined in more convoluted ways]; the authorities did not know what to accuse us of. You could be accused of revolting against the government or disturbing the public, basically whatever [the state authorities] wanted."[73]

Despite all their precautions, Ghalamdar and his friends were arrested while working on their murals in the western neighborhoods of Tehran. Among the many accusations were promoting Satanism or worshiping Satan (*sheytan parasti*) and spreading anti-establishment (*zedd-e nezam*) sentiments.[74] Worshiping Satan was a particularly dangerous accusation, with a lineage that goes back to 2007, when the rock bands Dativ and Font were tortured by the morality police and received long jail sentences following a concert at a garden party outside Tehran. The concert was performed in front of a large mixed-gender audience, but what attracted the accusations of Satan worship were the Goth-inspired images on the invitation cards.[75]

Blind's response to threats of this kind was to make his art mobile, raising the graffiti to a "three-dimensional and portable level, so that the artist can always implement, remove and replace it as he wishes."[76] Blind, who is known for his bold, calligraphic, wild-style graffiti in leftover urban spaces and dilapidated homes, now creates the letters in three-dimensional plaster objects and places them amidst the ruins of historic neighborhoods that are being razed to make away for more profitable developments. In figures 3.16a/b, the letter *zad* stands for the word *zolm* (cruelty) toward historic neighborhoods and cultural heritage. This unconventional execution of graffiti art in and around architectural spaces in the city is a novel way to protect graffiti from being removed. To borrow from the New York–based anarchist theorist Hakim Bey (aka Peter Lamborn Wilson), Blind sought to identify "temporary autonomous zones" without obliterating the grids that constituted them.[77]

. . .

Creating mobile art is not the only way in which Iranian artists navigate urban space. The body of the artist, too, is engaged in mobile interventions. Wandering, drifting, and walking in the city are important parts of artistic interjections in the city. These activities evoke those of the Situationist International group, which has been of immense interest to Iranian artists, critics, and bloggers alike.[78]

The Situationists were a group of avant-garde artists in Paris who came together in 1957. Led by the Marxist cultural critic and philosopher Guy Debord, they sought a life outside the bounds of the capitalist system, which they targeted through their political and artistic enterprises. For example, by wandering, by letting oneself float or drift (*dériver* is the French word used), each person could discover his or her own unique way into the city. Moreover, instead of following rational paths, the Situationists incorporated emotional strategies into their walks; for instance, when they navigated within a given site, they sought to be aware of how buildings and objects drew their attention toward the past.

Contemporary with the activities of the Situationist International in Paris, artists like Charles Hossein Zenderoudi (b. 1937) of the Saqqakhaneh group (a midcentury artistic movement inspired by coffeehouse paintings and religious paraphernalia) explored the capital to understand the contrasts between its more traditional southern parts and the modern and upscale northern neighborhoods.[79]

Surveying the Tehran bazaar, Zenderoudi became fascinated with cheap printed posters depicting Shiite religious scenes, talismanic seals, and other traditional raw materials. In 1962, he made a watercolor-and-ink piece on glossy paper that showcased a portion of the map of central Tehran. Framed by a string of cartouches bearing the words "map of Tehran," the map featured blocks animated by talismanic forms with dense numbers. These blocks were overlaid by a series of intersecting bands identified by street and

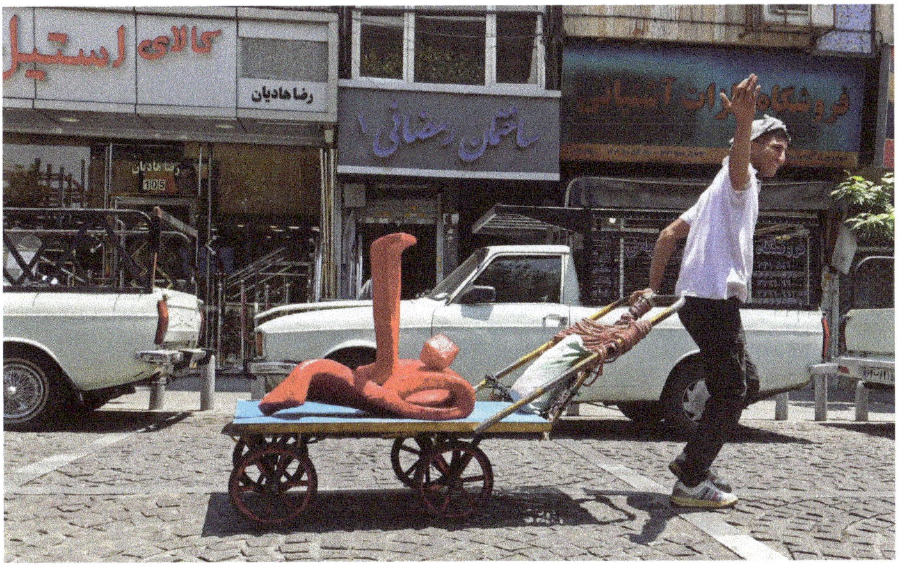

FIGURE 3.16A Blind transporting his three-dimensional graffiti to vanishing cultural heritage sites. 2019. Tehran. Courtesy of Blind.

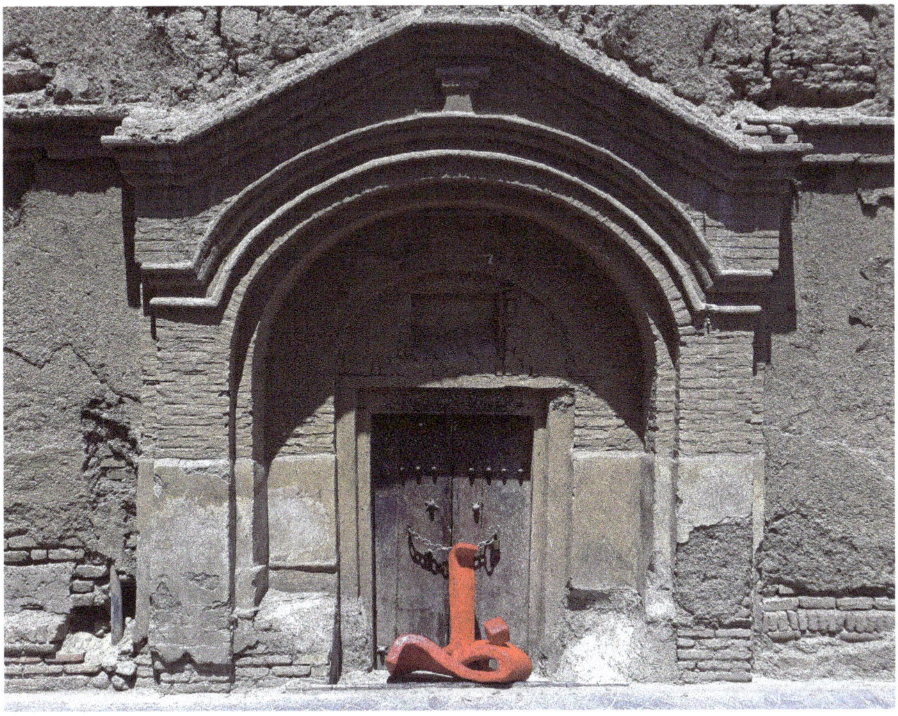

FIGURE 3.16B Blind's portable graffiti. 2019. Tehran. Photograph by Blind. Courtesy of Blind.

alley names that were all written in large calligraphic scripts. Art historian Clare Davies asserts that "at first glance these ink grids filled with numerals and . . . letters suggest a scientific or administrative demarcation of space; a bird's eye view characteristic of modern map making; an omniscient and disembodied perspective central to modern forms of colonialism as well as an image of the city privileged by the Iranian state."[80] But this seemingly modern map is animated by items from traditional visual and material culture, signifying the artist's grappling with the rapidly changing spirit of his culture. Indeed, the whole ensemble stood for the more traditional culture of southern Tehran as seen through the eyes of the modern artist during his routine wanderings.

Influenced by traditions of both the Saqqakhaneh and the Situationist International detours (*détournements*), Iranian artists of all media wander perpetually around the city. As one anonymous graffiti artist told me, he would walk around Tehran day and night, sometimes dozens of kilometers, to discover all the hidden places in the Tehran bazaar and many other neighborhoods, places nobody was aware of.[81] In these expeditions, he found "street people, homeless poets, and poor prophets of dead-end alleys."[82] As to how these kinds of discoveries help generate art, Rebecca Solnit aptly asserts that "walking allows us to be in our bodies and in the world without being made busy by them. It leaves us free to think without being wholly lost in our thoughts."[83]

Mohammad Khodashenas (b. 1975, also mentioned in chapter 1) refers to this phenomenon of endless walking in the city, so rooted in Iran's modernist artistic traditions, as "meandering in the city" (*parseh zani dar shahr*). What Khodashenas has discovered over years of meandering in the cities of Iran are overlapping histories.[84] He thinks the walls of Iran have a lot to say about the ways in which power operates and how people manage their emotional responses to events and sociopolitical developments. "On one wall you can find an homage to the leftist pre-revolutionary group *Chirik-e fadaie khalgh*, Iran-Iraq war propaganda, and commercial advertisements," he revealed during one of our conversations.[85] Leftist politics, religious ideology, and commercialism all live on one wall, in one space, within one city, and this is what Khodashenas discovers on his daily meanderings and reproduces in what he calls *padideh siahmashghi* (the *siahmashgh* phenomenon, referring to the traditional practice of superimposing calligraphic scripts; see the earlier fig. 1.11).

Khodashenas's meandering in the city is possible because he is a man; there are obstacles for women when it comes to activities like this. Women artists rarely use *parseh zani* as a tactic for interrupting daily life, either literally or metaphorically. If women wander in the streets with no destination or goal in mind, they become subject to harassment, especially later in the day, whether artists or not. Reporting on her inconvenient nocturnal navigation of streets on foot, one female architect student proclaimed, "Tehran hurts at night (*Tehran shabha dard mikonad*)."[86] This and other similar testimonies by women about the difficulties of exploring the city likely explain why most wanderer artists are men.

The works of Nastaran Safaie (b. 1984) in Enghelab (Revolution) and Vali Asr (Restorer of faith) address this issue. Enghelab and Vali Asr are two main old thoroughfares in Tehran. Enghelab is traditionally known as the axis of state parades and demonstrations. Vali Asr, however, is more associated with shopping, strolling, and commercial and entertainment activities. The reason women artists are not so keen on walking, according to Safaie, is that "Tehran is not a walkable city, definitely not for women, and most certainly not for women in high heels."[87]

Her video piece *High Heels* (in Persian the title is *Revayathay-e kaf-e khiaban* or *Pavement Narratives*) (2017) has her walking the full length of Vali Asr (eighteen kilometers)—in five hours in her high heels. She filmed her walk with a hidden GoPro camera from 10:30 a.m. to 5:30 p.m. and captured a great number of staring and puzzled or furious looks, mostly from women toward the high heels, as well as thirty-six sexually explicit pickup lines and verbal harassments from men, half of which were about the shoes. In addition to capturing the pain of being a wandering woman in Tehran, the six blisters she got stood for the harm that gentrification of Vali Asr has done to its historic buildings and entities. Safaie's work thus has a double meaning; while it is subtly feminist, it is also a criticism of urban planning strategies employed by the state.[88]

Safaie's tactical interventions in Tehran's two major thoroughfares resonate with the nineteenth-century phenomenon of the *flâneur*, a person with enough freedom and leisure and money to stroll around the city at his own convenience. The figure is always a man who is both part of, and separate from, the urban spectacle; present and yet predominantly a passive observer. As Anne Friedberg writes, a female equivalent, *flâneuse*, also began to appear on the streets of industrial cities; evidence of women's increased mobility is found in panoramas, dioramas, photography, and motion pictures.[89] But the *flâneuse* experienced a different kind of freedom than the male *flâneur*—one strictly circumscribed by the activity of window-shopping that accompanied the rise of the department store.

Safaie is aware of the connotations of the figure of the *flâneur*.[90] Her intention is not to attempt to shoehorn a woman into a masculine concept of a wanderer, but to redefine the concept itself. In doing so, her work calls to mind the counter-traditions of the *flâneuse*, performed in the work of the French conceptual artist Sophie Calle, who began to secretly follow random people on the streets of Paris, documenting her experience through photographs and notes.[91] The main sources of inspiration for Safaie's tactical urban interventions, however, are local ones, notably the writings of Dariush Shaygan (1935–2018), and in particular, his *Afsoon-e zendegi-e jadid: Hoveyyat-e chel tekkeh va tafakkor-e sayyar* (*The chaos of modern life: Fragmented identity and roaming thoughts*, 2018) and *Dar jostejooy-e fazay-e gomshodeh* (*In search of the lost space*, 2017). Both books allude to the deterioration of identity and a search for truth in Tehran. Shaygan wrote of the importance of paying attention to layers of identity and history and to the slow contemplation of things and places that enfold them, rather than living a fast-paced life. This message appeals to artists of Safaie's generation, who have grown up in a city whose past is being constantly eroded by politics (removal of signs of the past regime) and economic choices (neoliberal urbanism or gentrification).[92]

Walking along the second street, Enghelab, provided the artist with the opportunity for a *dérive* (playful drifting) that called for the real meaning of the city's main political axis. In *Enghelab-Azadi / Revolution-Freedom* (2018), Safaie walked ten kilometers, from Enghelab Square to Azadi Square and back, serving seventeen boxes of dates on trays to pedestrians along the way. Dates are customarily served at Iranian funerals. In Safaie's account, this act was a subtle commentary on the "demise of the revolution, the downfall of freedom."[93]

In her video *In Tehran* (2017–18), Safaie did what she was not supposed to do and wandered aimlessly, like her male counterparts. She printed nude self-portraits on stickers and put them up across the city, immediately censoring each of them with a black marker. Safaie reflected on her desire to explore the city: "I long for the freedom to go out alone late at night; this is why I envy men"[94] (figs. 3.17a–c).

More restrained perhaps, but much more radical in its message, is the street wandering by another female artist, Jinoos Taghizadeh (also mentioned earlier in this chapter). In 2015, Taghizadeh secretly mounted a Go-Pro camera on her forehead—secretly, because making videos in public spaces is not allowed without official permission—and roamed around a

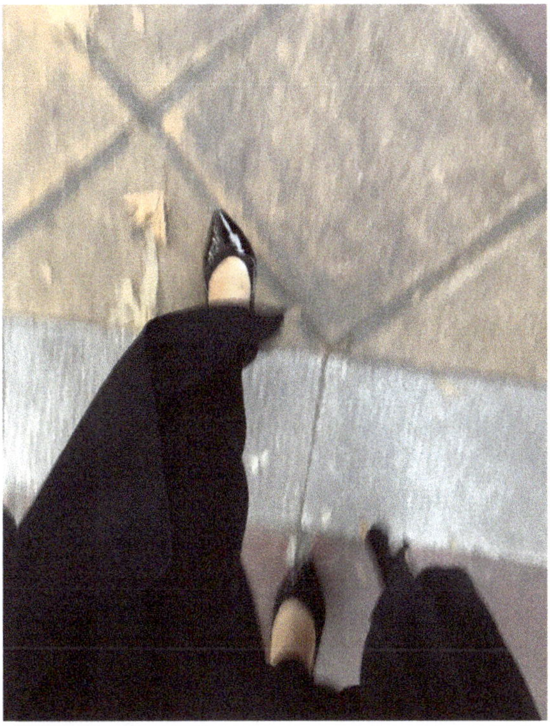

FIGURE 3.17A Nastaran Safaie, snapshot from *High Heels*. 2017. Tehran. Video capture by Nastaran Safaie.

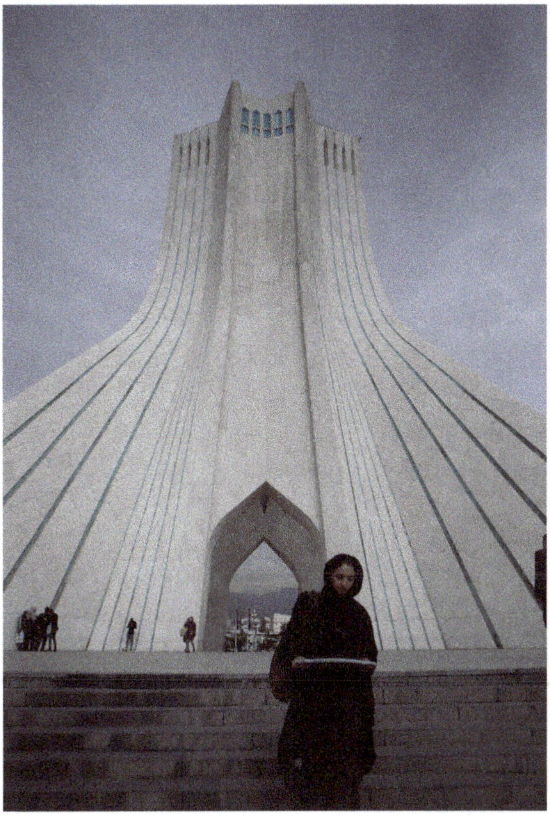

FIGURE 3.17B Nastaran Safaie, snapshot from *Enghelab-Azadi / Revolution-Freedom*. 2018. Tehran. Video capture by Nastaran Safaie.

series of politically charged sites in Tehran. The result is an almost three-hour-long video inspired by William Shakespeare's most violent work, *Titus Andronicus*. The tragedy, one of Shakespeare's first and lesser-known plays, captures massacre and bloody revenge around five locations in ancient Rome.

For each of the five acts in *Titus Andronicus*, Taghizadeh visited five significant venues in Tehran, each a setting for acts of violence, physical or legal, toward citizens. At each location, Taghizadeh shifted the camera, lowering her head to show portions of Shakespeare's text, then raising her head for quick captures of the specified buildings or locations, such as the unmarked mass burial grounds of political activists in Tehran's Behesht-e Zahra Cemetery, the Islamic Republic Parliament, and the infamous political prison, Evin (fig. 3.18).[95]

Taghizadeh's presence in this 160-minute video is registered not through her physical presence but through her voice. Rather than becoming a subject of the spectators' gaze, she makes herself an observer of both the street and her own film. Assuming a voyeuristic position in both her actual walks and the film, she also identifies these effective engagements as

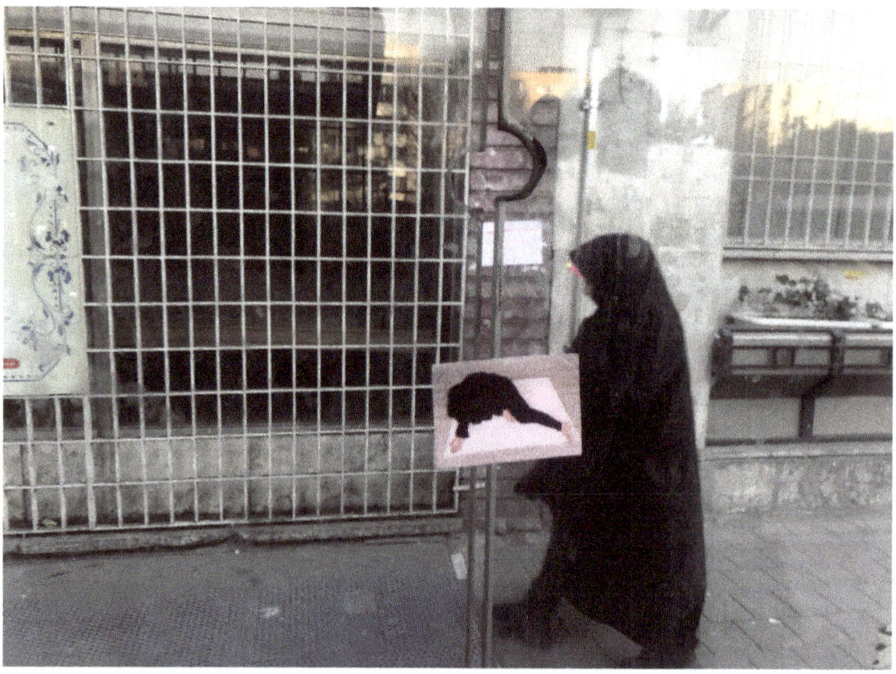

FIGURE 3.17C Nastaran Safaie, snapshot from *In Tehran*. 2017–18. Tehran. Video capture by Nastaran Safaie.

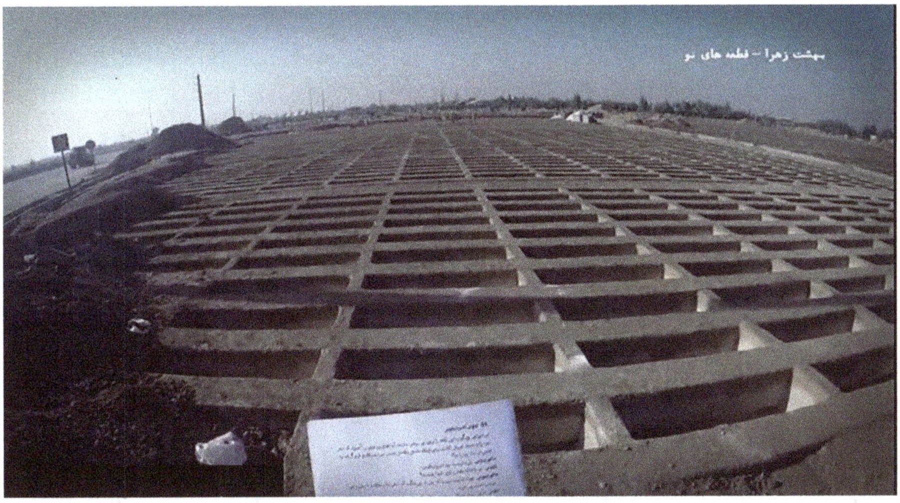

FIGURE 3.18 Jinoos Taghizadeh, *Titus Andronicus*. 2015. Snapshot from reading and walking in Behesht Zahra Cemetery. Tehran. Video capture by Jinoos Taghizadeh.

mental mapping (*naghsheh zehni*).[96] Like the Situationist counter-maps of Paris that challenged the centralized, institutional logic of urban development and prompted impulsive routes,[97] this kind of mapping alters the experience of everyday life and exposes a flux that vastly exceeds the boundaries set by state officials.

While avoiding personal risk, the impromptu walks of women artists in the city interrupt the everyday flow of street life. In doing so, they reclaim the street, a form of critical engagement with space that is only possible through alternative acts of reclaiming. As artist Martha Rosler has aptly put it, "[The] street is the space most feared by the rulers and must be reclaimed, even if only periodically, tactically."[98]

. . .

In addition to providing freedom for artists to create risky interventionist art in public, movement allows a plurality of viewpoints. Those who are familiar with Kiarostami's *Ten* (2002) and Jafar Panahi's *Taxi* (2015) know that the taxi in Tehran is not just a vehicle for moving from one location to the next. Sometimes the taxicab can be a place in which passengers can listen to banned music. However, most of the time the taxi provides a safe haven to discuss all kinds of disappointments, cynicism, or conspiracy theories.[99] At times discussions get so intense that the driver is keen to drive for longer without increasing the fee, just to have a few more minutes to carry on the conversation.[100] And just as *Ten* and *Taxi* were filmed entirely in taxicabs, so the taxi became a venue for a series of performances by the theater director and Tehran University professor Azadeh Ganjeh (b. 1983).

Ganjeh is primarily known as an expert in Shakespearean theater, having written a dissertation on performances of *Hamlet* in Iran between 1900 and 2012.[101] However, she is also extraordinarily innovative in delivering the classical plays. Drawing on her extensive knowledge of Forum Theater (*te'atr-e showraie*), Ganjeh uses theater as a tool for exploring and rehearsing actions that Iranian citizens could take to transform their everyday spaces.[102] Her plays aim to conjure collective memories, erased histories, and intense feelings related to national events such as revolutions, uprisings, war, and trauma.[103] And an essential component of these plays, according to Ganjeh, is the choice of realistic loci. In fact, it is through city icons, major streets, and historically significant public squares that the viewer gets a chance to experience what has been "removed from collective memory."[104] As such, Ganjeh gives Tehran the sense of a living stage with ongoing dramas on every unseen corner.[105] This is rooted in her firm belief that theater is a vehicle for promoting democracy. She writes:

> The Greeks invented both democracy and theater, together with a political theory, which retrospectively is called 'theatrocracy,' to conceptualize relations between the other two. Plato's interlocking critiques of democracy and drama formulated a general intuition, according to which theater played a central role in the political life of the democratic city.[106]

In a personal interview, Ganjeh revealed to me that in 2006, when she first began to present her work in public, the supervising authorities were baffled by her proposal to stage a performance in random public spaces with no particular invited audiences in mind and no plan to sell tickets or collect money.[107] At that time, and indeed, up until 2010, public theater performances or Street Theater (*te'atr-e khiabani*) were often propagandist, government-initiated events relating to the holy war (i.e., the Iran-Iraq war, or in Persian, *defa'-e moghaddas*).[108] Following the privatization of theater in the early 2010s (see chapter 1), Ganjeh's plays were often supported by the NGO-oriented Urban Art House (*Khaneh honarha-ye shahri*) in Tehran, and so required securing permission from the MCIG's committee of Theater Supervision.[109] By carefully balancing a diplomatic approach to the authorities with a virtuoso artistic choice—the construction of a spontaneous audience—Ganjeh was able to realize *Unpermitted Whispers (Najvahay-e biejazeh)*, a play set inside a taxicab in 2012 (fig. 3.19).[110]

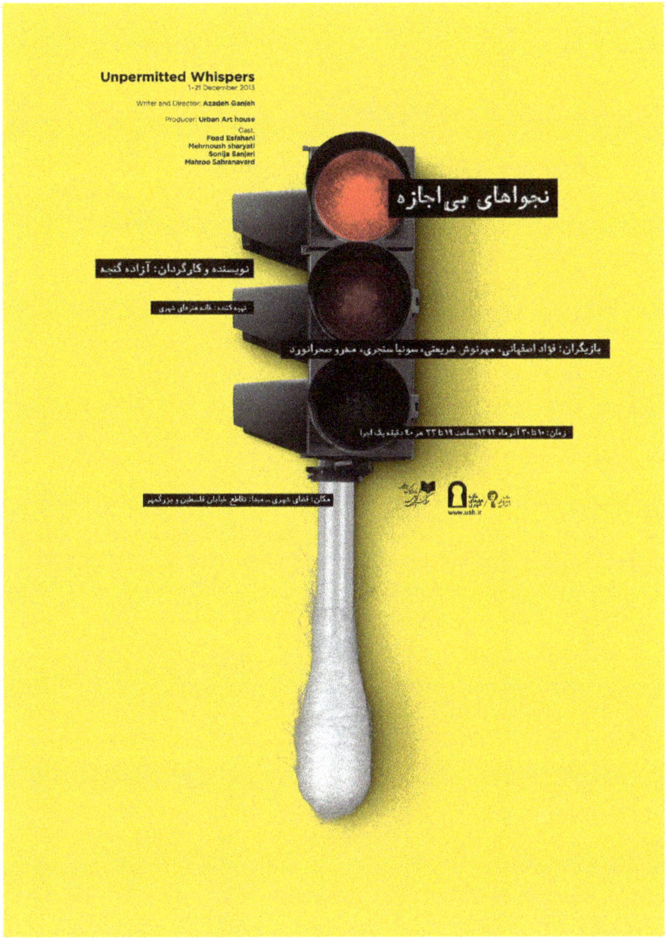

FIGURE 3.19 Azadeh Ganjeh, *Unpermitted Whispers* (poster). 2013. Tehran. Poster designed by Pedram Harbi. Courtesy of Azadeh Ganjeh.

The thirty-five-minute performance was staged four times a night using ordinary Tehran taxis, which navigate the capital along fixed and often straight-line routes. A taxi would pull up in front of a café to pick up three passengers wanting to see the play. Before the taxi pulled away, a young woman would throw herself into the front seat, alongside the driver, and the play would begin.[111] For each performance, three actors were picked up and dropped off in sequence. The characters in the performance were three women in Shakespeare's plays: Ophelia from *Hamlet*, Desdemona from *Othello*, and Katherine from *The Taming of the Shrew.*

The choice of Shakespearean characters might sound a bit out of place for Tehran, but the intention was not to recreate them as they exist in the play but rather to capture the mood and emotions of the characters. For example, Ophelia's intense love, madness, and despair were personified in the character of a woman from Tehran looking for a couple of individuals lost during the 2009 Green Movement, and the ensuing conflicts between ordinary people and the police forces and the Revolutionary Guards.[112] Thus, while they were from a different historic and geographic era, the three Shakespearean characters responded to their surroundings in Tehran.[113] To add to the drama, the taxi driver made abrupt turns that unsettled the passengers. In one especially sharp turn, the female actor jumped out of the car, shocking the passengers, or audience of the play.

In *The Practice of Everyday Life* Michel de Certeau writes of "tactics" or "hit-and-run" acts of random engagement that ordinary citizens use to appropriate the dominant systems of power. De Certeau's tactics are subtle forms of negotiation of space and infrastructure.[114] Specifically, they apply to the ways in which ordinary people "walk in the city" while also managing to avoid the fences, bridges, passageways, and regulated crossings that rational planning imposes on the modern city. Routes for cars and buses are typically more planned and governed than those for pedestrians. But through Ganjeh's work, we see that car drivers too can choose their own routes and itineraries through unexpected U-turns, lane swapping, breaking speed limits, and driving over curbs; in such ways, the actor/driver of Ganjeh's play resists the hegemony of planned and policed routes.[115]

Ganjeh added, "The taxi in Iran is a place where all kinds of human feelings are shared, from the sense of touch, to hearing, seeing, and smelling. Specifically, it is a place where all of the cab's occupants see their bodies and thoughts having close encounters."[116] So, while *Unpermitted Whispers* resembles the everyday therapy that goes on in Tehran's regular taxis, it also creates a space for affective encounters—a space to express one's feelings, of course, in this case through the guise of Shakespearean characters.[117] In traffic-congested Tehran, taxi drivers listen without being judgmental: "No one has their ears closer to the beat of the city than the taxi drivers."[118] Likewise, by not passing judgment, the play's "driver" (Ganjeh's husband, Foad Isfahan, b. 1987) allowed both the actors and the viewers to feel safe, to be intimate, and to be reminded of a place that is so central to their daily lives (fig 3.20).[119]

Whereas the taxi provided a safe stage for Ganjeh's Shakespearean play, the bus became an alternative art venue for Elham Puriya Mehr (b. 1979; also mentioned in chapter 2). Taxis are mixed-gender, but Iran's buses are gender-segregated: men sit in the front and women occupy the rear section

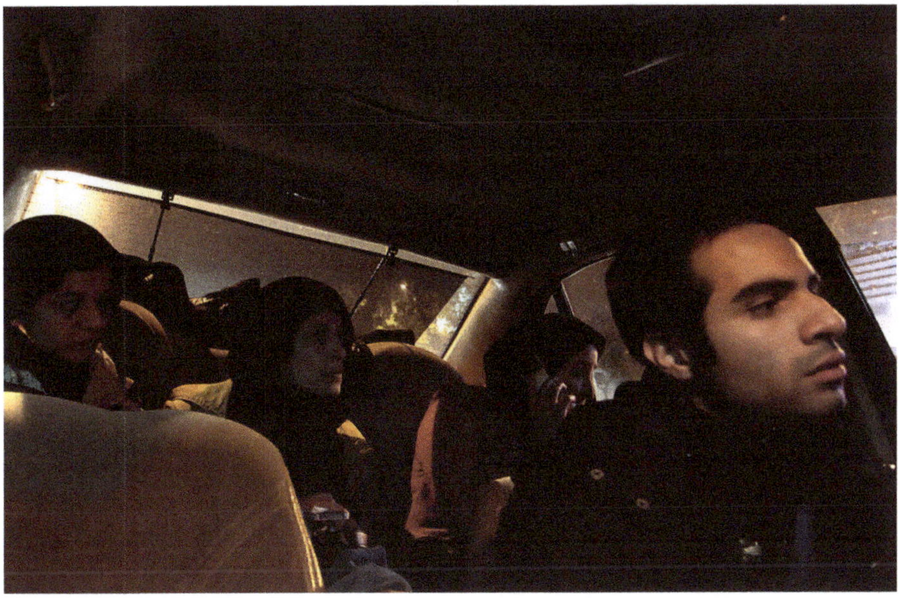

FIGURE 3.20 Azadeh Ganjeh, *Unpermitted Whispers*. 2013. Tehran. Photograph by Nooshin Jafari. Courtesy of Azadeh Ganjeh.

with a metal bar separating the two. On rare occasions, women have been known to move to the men's section if seats are available, but in general men do not move to the back. The bus, according to Puriya Mehr, "provides a space for reflection; one can sit back and observe others talking about politics, and the most astonishing part about it is that when a passenger leaves a given conversation at a particular bus stop, another new passenger takes over. It all looks like an uninterrupted theater played right in front of your eyes."[120] To be on a city bus in Tehran, Puriya Mehr asserted, "is to become an audience for the unending story of the role of politics in Iranians' daily lives."[121] A city bus, then, was an apt venue for an exhibition focusing on the boundaries that separate men and women, public and private, oppressive and democratic atmospheres, and so on. The exhibition, *My Own Privacy Policy (Siyasat-e harim-e shakhsi-e man)*, was planned to run for three days, starting from November 19, 2013, but due to a lack of coordination with the bus company, the show only lasted for a three-hour slot on a single day.

A decade earlier, sculptor and performance artist Bita Fayyazi had exhibited her sculptures in a mobile van with stops every forty-five minutes, in an attempt to reach viewers outside the elite circle who frequent art exhibitions. Fayyazi described how the "[the] sculptures were experienced by passersby,

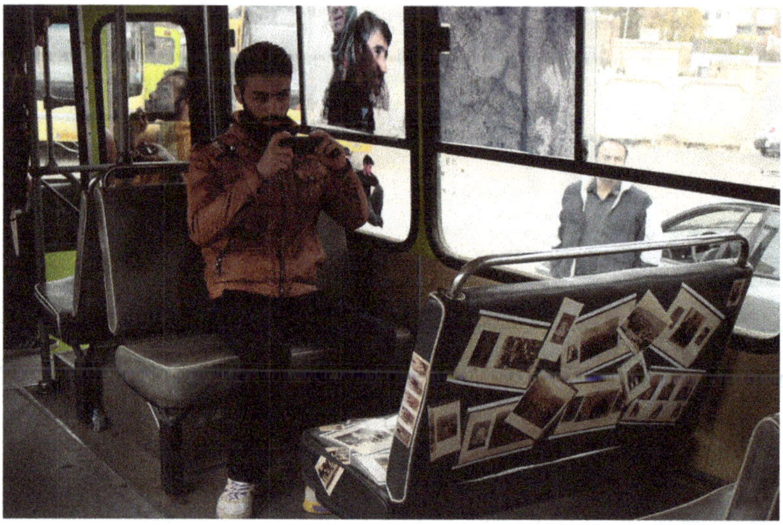

FIGURE 3.21 Elham Puriya Mehr et al., *My Own Privacy Policy*. 2013. Sanandaj, Kurdistan province. Photograph by Elham Puriya Mehr.

school children, drivers, shopkeepers, road-sweepers, tramps—a cross-section of Tehran society."[122] While Puriya Mehr's project struck a similar chord, it had a larger aim than bringing art to disadvantaged citizens.

Puriya Mehr's converted bus, a city transportation vehicle from Sanandaj in the Kurdistan province of Iran, was scheduled to follow its afternoon routine, picking up and dropping off passengers at every stop (fig. 3.21).[123] Customized inside and out, the bus was animated by artworks created by the A3 art project group: Negar Farajiani (b. 1977), Babak Kazemi (b. 1983), Sohrab Kashani (b. 1989), Maryam Khosroshahi (b. 1982), and Khadije Mohammadi-Nameghi (b. 1976).

The artworks varied in medium, ranging from a large display of facsimiles of old images of the people of Kurdistan (from the album of photographs by Ali Khan Vali that Qajar prepared between 1879 and 1896), a mock shadow play, a soft sculptural piece, and a video. Some of the art on display was plainly political in tone. For example, one artwork was titled "Evin," which means *love* in Kurdish but, as mentioned earlier, is also the name of the most notorious political prison in Iran. Hoping that her "audiences" would interact with the mobile exhibition in their own unrehearsed way, Puriya Mehr did not publicize the show widely in advance.

Puriya Mehr aimed to confront private sentiments in public places, saying, "The question I [wanted] to ask with this project was, what is the privacy policy exactly?" Too often, Iranians' privacy is violated by powerful agents such as the morality police or even by ordinary passersby who, for example, persist in chiding a young person about how to behave properly in public. Older religious women are particularly prone to offering advice to young girls on how to conduct themselves in public. In "Public Spaces in Captivity" (*Fazahay-e omoomi dar hesar*), Tehran-based sociologist Maserrat Amir-Ebrahimi writes that while public spaces might sometimes offer anonymity and freedom, at other times they become like *andaruni*, the private spaces of the traditional extended households. Thus, people—especially women—have to change their behavior depending on *when* they appear in public, otherwise the structure of the public space will be tarnished.[124] Similarly, German filmmaker Daniel Kötter, who made an art film about residential spaces of Tehran, attests to the "confusing dividing lines" between public/private, noting that the confusion opens up unexpected opportunities to dismantle these divisions: "In [Iran] the dividing line between inside and outside . . . is codified [ambiguously]. . . . There is no one rule that you can learn from . . . *Lonely Planet*. . . . It is something that can even change during the day. It can be a little bit different today or tomorrow."[125] Equally, Puriya Mehr understands the notion of privacy as a porous and tentative concept. Having spent a good portion of her youth commuting on Tehran's public buses, Puriya Mehr believes that the bus in Iran is a place where strangers can share private thoughts, where women can talk to other women about all kinds of things, from their feelings to the latest news.

Reenacting these social dynamics, the Sanandaj bus passengers were expected to discuss the art with one another, a form of interaction that is much less controlled and regulated than in an official museum context or a formal art gallery. Regarding her role as a curator, Puriya Mehr writes: "Curators . . . are [only] mediators. . . . accepting the role of [a] mediator, I . . . examine how relations are altered and transformed during the [curatorial] process."[126] On entering the bus, some passengers took pictures of the artworks while others discussed them with their fellow passengers. Meanwhile, the curator on board took pictures of passengers interacting with the artworks, and a videocam livestreamed the show for audiences back in Tehran. Thus, the curator "invaded" the passengers' privacy and passengers were in turn given the opportunity to do the same. Indeed, in the absence of regulations defined by institutions of art, everyone was uniformly set free to invent their "own policies" regarding the concept of privacy. Thus, politics were laid bare in a public and mobile exhibition space where people were treated as players on a stage set, invited to reflect and discuss, and encouraged to break the boundaries. Puriya Mehr's thoughts on public and private life were informed by Hannah Arendt in her book *The Human Condition* (available in Persian as *Vaz'e bashar*).[127] Of particular interest is Arendt's account of the close correlation between public and private space for an engaged and productive life.[128]

Under ordinary circumstances, having one's privacy "invaded" on public buses may not be a pleasant experience; in Puriya Mehr's work, the invasion of privacy is meant as a tool to generate public debate about freedom of expression, freedom to interact with art, and freedom to break the existing rigid boundaries between curators, artists, and audiences. Above all, *My Own Privacy Policy* offered a unique opportunity to celebrate and initiate a dialogue with the often-marginalized Kurdish people of Iran. Puriya Mehr writes, "By going into dialogue with the Kurdish people, we actually heard the voices of Kurdish people instead of just hearing about them in the media."[129]

Fragile Presences in Public

In this chapter I have addressed public art in the form of guerilla performances with direct intent to disrupt and condemn the existing order. I have also featured projects that are sanctioned by the MCIG and can thus recur or enjoy a certain permanency. But what of those artworks that are more fragile, less long lived? Many public art projects, regardless of whether they are sanctioned by the MCIG, are vulnerable to a whole host of forces, including not only the (morality) police but also ordinary passersby. What makes an artwork legitimate in the public eye? Who else, beyond the government, defines the parameters of art's validity? Who takes note of public art and who ignores it? Is ignoring art unintentional, or is something else implied? Ashkan Zahraie (b. 1989), the curator of Dastan Gallery, asserts that the religious *ta'ziyeh* passion plays are the only forms of "art" in Iran that have enough legitimacy to be fully performed in public.[130] Like the *Tasu'a* and *Ashura* ceremonies, all of which take place during the lunar month of Muharram, in which Imam Hussein was killed in the battle of Karbala in 680 CE, *ta'ziyeh* passion plays have surfaced continuously in urban public spaces, apart from a brief period during the modernizing reign of Reza Shah, when the performances were moved to designated rural spots outside city centers.[131] Today there are many versions of the *ta'ziyeh*, from amateur Muharram *ta'ziyeh* to professional *ta'ziyeh* drama companies. Like

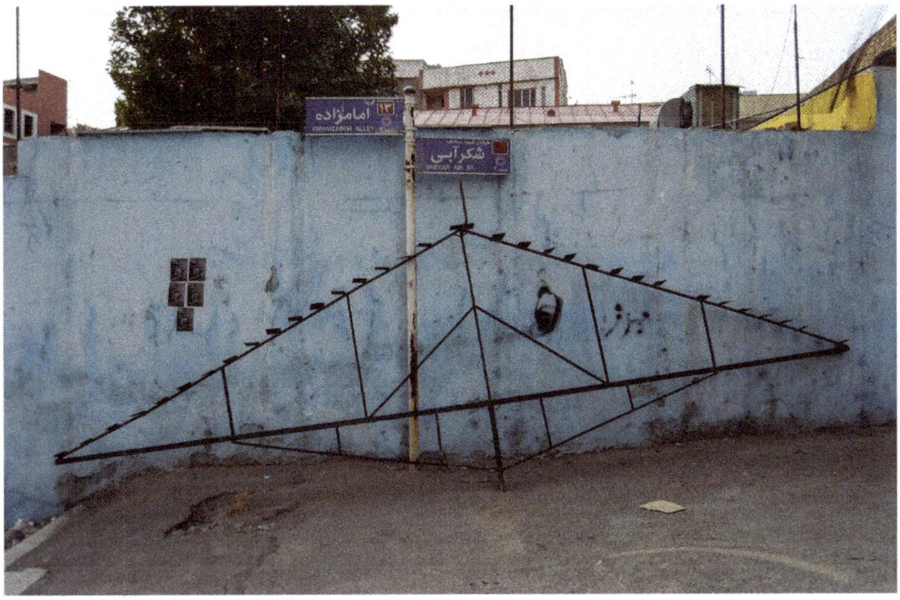

FIGURE 3.22 Ehsan Barati, *Untitled*, from the *Ashura* series. 2009. Tehran. Photograph by Ehsan Barati.

Zahraie, Tehrani artist and photographer Ehsan Barati (b. 1982) also sees these ceremonies as performances of the state, leaving no room for personal expression.

Instead of capturing the performances in action or with what is known in postrevolutionary Iran as "ritual photography" (*akkasi-e a'yini*), Barati shoots in the very short period between the end of the ceremonies and the arrival of the city's cleaning crew to collect and dispose of the remnants of props and other installation objects. Barati's photographs capture abandoned banners and signage (*alams*), showcasing the iconic elements of hanging fabric with names of imams and martyrs stitched into them (fig. 3.22).

Stripped of their decorative elements, devoid of any human presence, these remnants become the "skeletons" of a state-sponsored ceremony. Placed against bare walls, the photographs of these objects reflect the ways in which a new generation of artists in Tehran regard the most common public performance in the capital: the religious and state propaganda elements that are tangibly present and yet remain largely unseen.

While Barati brings a sense of eeriness to the ubiquitous religious performances, filmmaker and performance artist Mohammad Hosseini (b. 1977) reflects on other "visible unseens" related to bygone eras—events, individuals, and ideas—that have been banished into the realm of an enforced collective amnesia due to their association with the Shah's era.

. . .

On a late afternoon in July 2011, people on the busy sidewalks of the northeastern side of Tehran's Ferdowsi Square saw seventy-four women dressed in red, standing motionless and mostly silent (fig. 3.23). Curated by Mohammad Hosseini (b. 1978) the performance was repeated daily for nearly three months (July to September), and each time the women appeared at the same spot for an hour between 5 and 6 in the evening. They were there to commemorate the Lady in Red, who symbolized love in the popular imagination of Tehran from the 1960s until her sudden disappearance in 1983. The legendary "Yaqut" (meaning "ruby") was "a woman with a bony, weathered face, who always wore makeup, [who] stood in Ferdowsi Square from dawn to dusk."[132] Everything she wore was in red, including her bag, her shoes, her stockings, and her skirt. She often carried a red rose. After the revolution, she appeared with a red scarf to conform to the new rules of public appearance for women. Because of her expression, people believed she was waiting for someone whom she expected to show up at any minute—her beloved—but he never showed up.

Rumors abounded: some said Yaqut was the daughter of a Russian émigré who had moved to Tehran shortly after the Bolshevik Revolution. Her legend appeared in a few memoirs and in poetry and prose.[133] The closing shots of Khosrow Sinai's documentary *Tehran Today* (1977) are animated by Yaqut, showing her walking away from the camera and disappearing into the thick traffic around Ferdowsi Square, perhaps a metaphor for Tehran itself on the eve of a revolution.[134]

Although Yaqut was often featured in prerevolutionary media, she was forgotten in the postrevolutionary years. Reenacting her presence in a public space was an unprecedented and particularly bold move in a city still traumatized by the aftermath of the Green Movement of 2009. The *Shargh Newspaper* was quick to report that Hosseini's *Women in Red* (*Banooy-e sorkhpoosh*) event was not a performance piece but a film shoot that had been sanctioned by the state authorities. Some also claimed that it was a rehearsal for a project at the forthcoming Fajr Theater Festival. Hosseini later declined the invitation to submit the work for this festival, reasoning that "it was not street theater, but performance art."[135] The event eventually went on to be recorded and presented as a short documentary at a private festival held in Aaran Gallery.[136]

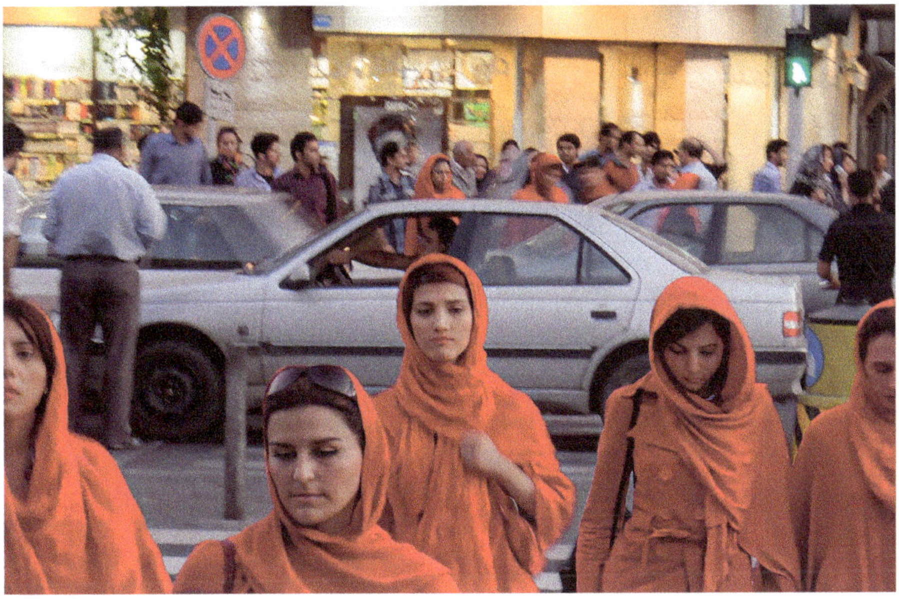

FIGURE 3.23 *Women in Red* performance, curated by Mohammad Hosseini. 2011. Ferdowsi Square, Tehran. Photograph by Saeed Kiaee.

At the time of its execution, Hosseini promoted the performance on Facebook under the title "Lady in Red, Pre-performance," and invited interested women to join.[137] To his surprise, within five days more than eighty women had volunteered. One of them, a young college student in Tehran, described her involvement with the performance in these words:

> I first heard the story a long time ago, probably from my mom. . . . My dad had also told me that he always saw her on his way to school. Some say she was last seen around 1981 or 1982. I had almost forgotten about this story until I heard about this performance. A friend called me and asked if she could borrow my red shoes. She performed the *Lady in Red* for one day. Looking through the event's Facebook page, I realized that many of my friends, mostly theater students, had participated in the *Lady in Red*, too. Some stood silent, others spoke to people, and some even handed out red roses . . . The *Lady in Red* is a symbol of love in Tehran, and these days, people think about all sorts of things when they think of Tehran—but not love. So, I think this performance was a great idea.[138]

She went on to say that they were interrupted several times by uniformed men, including the police. Another volunteer agreed, saying, "Many people came up to ask if we had been given authorization. Many people were very curious, even intimidated. Some filmed us and took photos of us. The residents congratulated us for bringing a familiar story back to life. Still many others, men mostly, did not seem to appreciate it much."[139]

Fragmented footage of the performance, recorded by Hosseini, echoes parallel difficulties. In one instance, a performer is questioned about whether they were associated with a satanic cult.[140] On another occasion, a man persists in his attempt to get a performer's phone number, despite her repeated refusal. One girl is criticized by an older woman in full *hijab* (*chador*) for sitting in an allegedly disgraceful (*zesht*) cross-legged position.[141] Another female passerby tells a performer that she is demeaning not only herself but women in society in general.[142] Reviewing the performance, as a whole, art historian Bavand Behpoor (b. 1980) describes it as a fragile statue (*mojassameh-e shekanandeh*)—one that can only stand fleetingly in Tehran, as the city does not permit displays of sentimentality.[143] Photographer Saeed Kiaee (b. 1983), who meticulously documented these women at Ferdowsi Square, reflected on the irony of the whole event: "Similar to real life the women were in utter silence, despite their bold and visible presences."[144] It seems like the effects of visibility for women in this performance operated as a "double-edged sword . . . a source of both empowerment and disempowerment."[145]

Underlining the "love story," of course, is the conspicuous presence of women. Though women today can get away with more colorful attire, back in the early 2000s, as fashion historian Alexandru Balaşescu points out, they would have been better off "dressing down, in faded colors, or in conformity with the Islamic moral rules."[146] That way, they would avoid "impolite comments from passers-by, or the risk of being stopped and questioned."[147]

Amir-Ebrahimi writes about the "absent presence" of women in urban public spaces of Iran.[148] As she describes it (in 2006), women are always active and present in public spaces of the city, but at the same time they exercise strategies to appear or feel absent.[149] For women, being seen is often synonymous with "being subjected to judgment by others, attracting danger, and increasing their feeling of insecurity."[150] Being in public feels like "being subjected to constant control by others (morality police, neighbors, community, at work, at university and so forth)."[151] It is no surprise, then, that many female Iranian artists who take their physical art into public urban spaces do so in subtle ways, using found objects and readily available materials from the locations where they operate. Unlike men, they do not have the luxury of spending ample time outdoors, being "present" and "visible," contemplating their process and their final product.

. . .

In 2009 six young women created an urban art collective, which three years later became Tehran Carnival. Ayda Alizadeh, Mahtabeh Alizade, Elnaz Ezzati, Elmira Yousefi, Elmira Mahnia, and Sepideh Zamani—were all born in the early 1980s, and their intention with the collective was to "have fun."[152] Yousefi articulated the purpose of the collective in these terms: "The Carnival gives us pure joy (*sarkhoshi*). We did all those projects so that we would feel better (*halemoon khoob sheh*)."[153] For one of these projects, titled *Private Ocean (Oghiyanoos-e khosoosi*, 2013), the collective could have chosen an entire building in mid-construction, but decided instead to use just the basement to display their large papier-mâché shark inside a plastic cube. For Yousefi, "There was something liberating about creating a subterranean world, something detached from the rest of the society. We just wanted to create a private joyful space for ourselves; it was not our intention to toot our horns and attract viewers."[154] The installation was not an imitation of a Western artwork; the collective only became aware of the similarity to Damien Hirst's *The Physical Impossibility of Death in the Mind of Someone Living* (1991) when other artists pointed it out on social media. Nor was going underground a political statement about the lack of opportunities in ownership of public space, especially for women; rather it was simply motivated, as mentioned above, by the desire to "feel better."

According to one of the collective's founders, Sepideh Zamani, the fact that all the members are women was the result of practical, rather than ideological, considerations. "[It] was just easier . . . to form an all-female group, but if the opportunity had arisen to collaborate with a man, we would have done so. It is not at all our intention to be a feminist collective."[155] Likewise, the timing of the group's formation right after the Green Movement of 2009 was, according to Zamani and Yousefi, not a political decision.

In 2014, when the group was invited to exhibit at the Mohsen Gallery, one of the most prominent venues in Tehran, they created an installation—a yellow cardboard Peykan (the first Iranian-made car produced by Iran Khodro, between 1967 and 2005)—for the sidewalk outside the gallery, rather than the gallery space itself. The intention here was not to attract a larger public, but to express an anti-institutional idea. The size of their audience was not important to Tehran Carnival. Indeed, some of their projects have been in such remote urban locations that they have had no audience at all.[156]

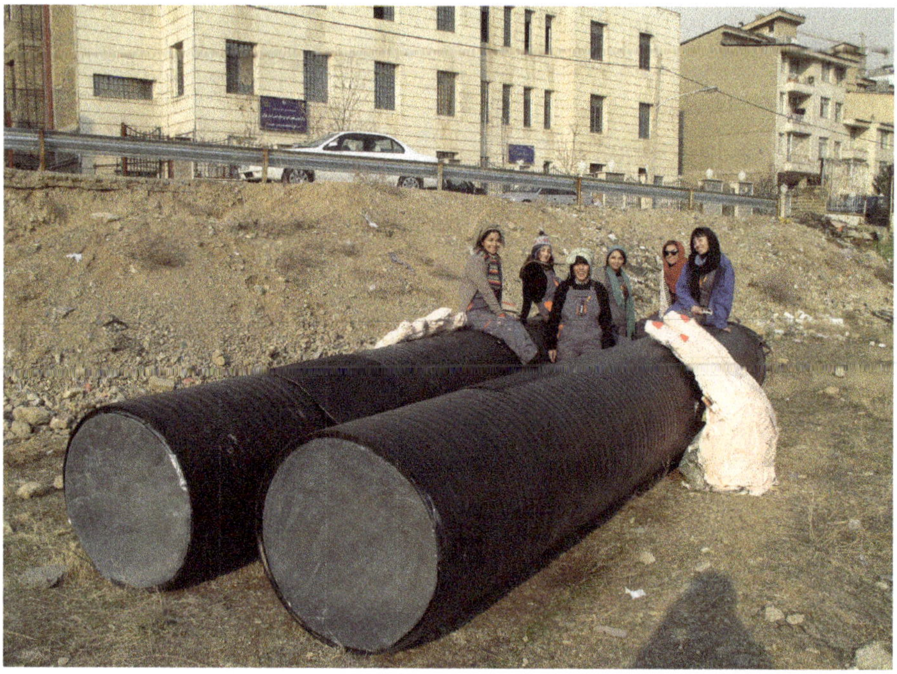

FIGURE 3.24 Tehran Carnival, *Binoculars*. 2014. Velenjak, Tehran. Courtesy of Tehran Carnival.

Another project from 2014, *Binoculars* (*Doorbeen*), was constructed out of two gigantic sewage pipes found in an abandoned site in Velenjak. The binoculars were held by two gigantic papier-mâché (female) hands with red nail polish. "It felt like we were spying on the city," said Yousefi (fig. 3.24).[157]Again, in the absence of an audience, the women simply got a kick out of "looking into the city" from a distance.

Gendered spectatorship finds its most important early articulation in "Visual Pleasure and Narrative Cinema," a 1975 essay by filmmaker and theorist Laura Mulvey.[158] Mulvey showed how classical Hollywood cinema situates male viewers in an active position of dominant looking, reducing women to passive objects of that gaze. To explain this asymmetrical dynamic, Mulvey used psychoanalytic terms such as *scopophilia* (pleasure in looking), *exhibitionism* (pleasure in being looked at), and *voyeurism* (pleasure in looking at what is not supposed to be seen, often without being seen). One can perhaps apply these forms of looking to the gendered spectatorship at work in public urban spaces in Tehran, where the political system grants men a spectator position of power and keeps women in invisibility, presumably to undo women's perceived "exhibitionism."

In the oversized binoculars, we can see a subtle sense of humor at work. To follow the humor theorist Simon Critchley, "the extraordinary thing about humor is that it returns us to common sense; by distancing us from it, humor familiarizes us with a common world through its . . . strategies of defamiliarization."[159] The group's choice of name, Carnival, recalls Mikhail Bakhtin's notion of the carnivalesque, a literary device that subverts the assumptions of the dominant atmosphere of society through humor and chaos. The primary act of carnival is the mock coronation and subsequent de-crowning of a carnival king, a "dualistic ambivalent ritual" that typifies the upside-down world of carnival and the "joyful relativity of all structure and order."[160] The carnival sense of the world "is opposed to that one-sided and gloomy official seriousness, which is dogmatic and hostile to evolution and change."[161] The spirit of carnival grows out of a "culture of laughter" and is inherently anti-elitist. Bakhtin's interpretations could also be said to apply to Tehran Carnival, an art collective that is anti-elitist, that delights in exercising a subtle sense of humor, and that incorporates nonsensical forms such as larger-than-life binoculars and papier-mâché animals. Resembling an A-frame circus tent, the group's logo is the tapering Azadi Tower animated by red and white stripes. Is Tehran Carnival meant to be a circus? Is it meant to be a joke? The logo definitely blurs the line between two very different events: the traveling circus, with its clowns, always moving from one place to the next; and the carnival, an annual celebration of a particular religious, historical, or cultural event.

If Tehran Carnival is meant to merge the meanings of the two, what role, we might ask, do joy, joke, and humor play in Iranian public art? In the Middle East in recent years, humor has been used as a creative weapon against political targets in times of oppression. One notable example is the subtle opposition movement, "the laughing revolution" (*al-thawra al-dahika*).[162] Algerians have likewise been using humor to bolster their sense of political agency since at least 2014, in their own "smiling revolution." Demonstration placards, graffiti art, memes, political jokes, prank calls, send-ups of official speeches on social media platforms—all offer outlets for laughing in the face of adversity. These efforts, in the words of journalist Hiyem Cheurfa, "highlight the strategic function of humor and its relationship to dynamics of power and democracy in the contemporary Arab region. The use of humor to communicate and address authority is instrumental in setting a carnivalesque mood of dissidence."[163] Cheurfa further adds, "This dissident laughter nurtures the protesters' sense of collectivity through subverting socio-political orders, challenging hierarchies, bridging social differences among protesters and providing a collective comic relief."[164]

Such activities are less prevalent in Iranian art scenes; whereas laughter and jokes are common in private and on social media, they only rarely appear in public art, especially when they touch on political issues. Even before the Islamic Revolution, humor in art was uncommon, and for good reason. Among others, the satirical artist Ardeshir Mohasses relocated to New York in 1976, following warnings from the Shah's dreaded secret police.[165] After the Islamic Revolution, the government tried its best to cultivate a collective sense of gravitas. Even children's programs and publications were serious. Political humor was essentially censored. Amid such restrictions, the appearance in the 1990 of *Golagha* (*Flower Man*), an Iranian version of Alfred E. Newman, came as a great surprise. The satirical magazine swiftly became the largest-selling periodical in the country, featuring a weekly dose of humorous jabs at ministers, parliament members, and foreign politicians. Many more satirical publications ensued in the 1990s, and a few spoof films were even made. One of these, from 2004, was *Marmoolak* (*The Lizard*), which openly satirized the clergy and lasted three whole weeks in the cinemas before it was taken down.[166] From 2000 to 2006, many satirists were interrogated and arrested, and a large number of cartoonists had to find new jobs in other areas.[167]

The lack of focus on humor in Iranian art is not simply the result of political restrictions; there is also a cultural element at work. Anthropologist Michael Fischer points out a connection between ethical wisdom and religious teachings that have long discouraged humor: "Two-character types are often contrasted: *adam-e sangin* (the weighty or serious person) who rarely laughs . . . [and] *adam-e sabok*, who laughs and jokes and is lightweight, a fool."[168] Humor is not just looked down on in everyday human behavior in Iran; humorous gestures are considered cheap and low class in Iranian dance, as historian Ida Meftahi reminds us.[169] In art, too, humor is arguably not considered a sophisticated way of communicating. Even when Iranian artists inject humor into their work, it is at best dark humor. Consider, for example, Ahmad Aali's iconic *Self-Portrait (Khodnegareh,* 1964, reconstructed in 2010), in which the artist appears to be suffocating, choked by the fumes of the stove pipe protruding from his mouth, calling to mind a term used in everyday Iranian dialect, *khafekhoon* (or suffocation), which also implies political clampdown, repression, and censorship.

Returning to Tehran Carnival, photographs of the collective show them posing joyfully next to their colorful installations. Often dressed in blue overalls (which are admittedly only partially visible through their unbuttoned trench coats, a mandatory street *hijab* in Iran), they evoke the iconic Rosie the Riveter. But while they project the image of carefree, strong artists, they nonetheless have a darker side, as Tehran-based art critic Ali Gholipour (b. 1979) has observed:

> Tehran is . . . a city without carnivals. The streets on which our generation strolls . . . have not witnessed the bright . . . carnival colors. . . . Tehran has not seen any carnivals and, in turn, carnivals are [un]familiar with Tehran. [Yet] by digging [into the] hidden layers of the city, Tehran Carnival . . . reminds [us] of something that could have happened before. Indeed, since Tehran has a weak memory and confused mind, [someone] must activate [these] conceivable pasts. If we were to give a [single title] to Tehran Carnival projects, we ought to have called them 'Artificial Memories in Short-Term Memory of the City.' . . . [The] process of making the [papier-mâché objects] and the presence of their creators are hidden from [plain] sight. The viewers arrive when everyone is gone and the 'carnival' has 'ended.' But there remains a massive . . . pig in [the] ruins, a [giant] hanging cardboard air-freshener in a wrecked factory, a dangling horse on the front porch of a dilapidated home! The audience might ask . . . there must have been people here before me; But who? The [artists] would have probably responded 'we were here.' . . . [A] few girls who go to ruined sites, unfinished buildings, [deserted] places in the suburbs, all culturally forbidden for women to go to. . . . Let us say these are all 'dead spaces.' . . . The objects that remain in them . . . seem bruised, beaten up, rough and unfinished. [Indeed], these objects, too, are dead. There is no one around. . . . The creators are gone; silence has swallowed everything, but one can still see a huge colorful mass stuck in its throat. These remaining objects pop out and [indicate] that 'someone was here.' . . . But even these lasting parts, these [indexical] signs, would be gone too . . . the wind and the rain and city's [polluted] air would destroy them all. The busy capital would soon forget the carnival, as it always has.[170]

This dark side, so strongly emphasized by Gholipour, does not instantly resonate with the viewers of Tehran Carnival's artworks. Indeed, instead of falling into the binary oppositions of provocative and decorative, artistically sophisticated or plop, political or nonpolitical, Tehran Carnival opened up possibilities for a place between those extremes with their nonserious, nonchalant, and gently humorous projects that exposed slippages between critical remarks and inert indecisiveness. Yet even the subtle, seemingly joyful intervention could be constructed as a vandalism if set in the wrong context. *The Urban Greenhouse* (*Golkhaneh shahri*, 2011), consisting of dozens of large-scale red roses made from rice bags, was installed on a green island between the Hemmat and Sheikh Fazlollah Noori thoroughfares, on land purportedly owned by the Islamic Revolutionary Guard Corps (IRGC). The authorities promptly disposed of the massive flowers, either because they deemed them "exhibitionist," or saw them as an attempt to "manipulate" (*dastkari*) an official urban space—or possibly simply because they disapproved of their lightheartedness.

A display of childlike innocence, as opposed to pointed humor, has proved a more successful strategy for art interventions in urban spots claimed by the state—and indeed for nonconformist art in general. For example, since the Islamic Revolution of 1979, many Iranian filmmakers have focused on the perspective of children as a safe and concealed way of expressing sensitive sociopolitical commentary (e.g., Abbas Kiarostami's 1987 landmark *Where Is the Friend's Home?*). The juvenile characters acted in lieu of adult protagonists who could not freely express their political stances either in real life or in the fictive world of cinema. According to film historian Hamid Naficy, by focusing on the worldviews of children, these directors have explored "the nature of repressive authority through the eyes of youngsters who prove to be adept at deconstructing the world of the adults who say one thing and do another."[171]

Playfulness also comes to the rescue of interventionist art in public spaces. In 2014, the vast area beneath the monumental Azadi Tower was the setting for *Made in China* (*Sakht-e Chin*), by Tehran-based participatory and social-practice artist Negar Farajiani (b. 1977). Passersby were invited to interact with a giant custom-made Chinese beach ball tethered to the foot of the tower (fig. 3.25).

The beach ball had been previously displayed in other unlikely places, including an abandoned factory in Yazd. Regarding this project, Farajiani said:

> The idea is to observe how people interact with this ball. Tehran is a gloomy city. People are not used to acting in unusual ways. Play, any form of play, is seen as inappropriate or forbidden. Dance is prohibited, and even recreational activities

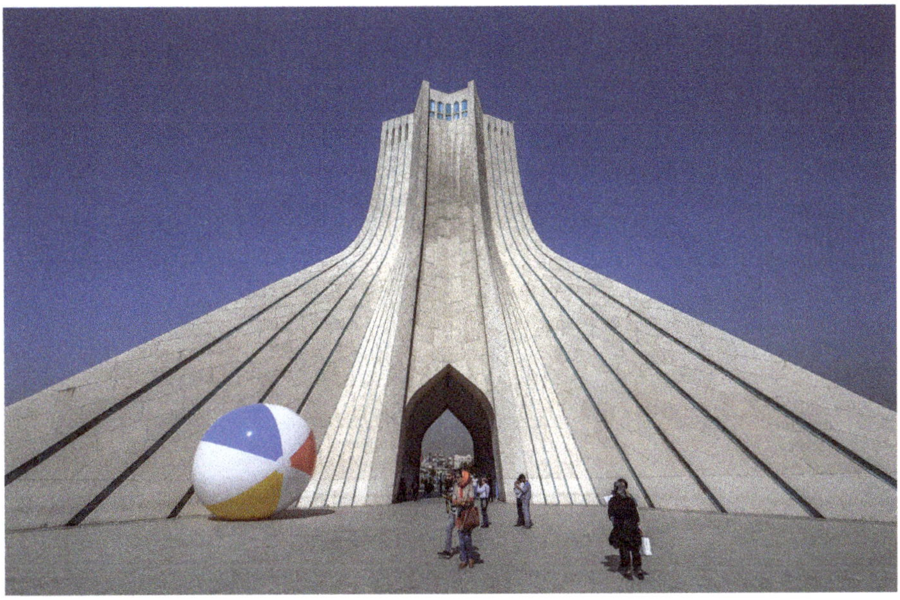

FIGURE 3.25 Negar Farajiani, *Made in China*. 2014. Azadi Square, Tehran. Photograph by Hoofar Haghighi. Courtesy of Negar Farajiani.

> such as jogging are deemed unusual for men and unsuitable for women. Considering this seriousness, I decided to create an atmosphere of play. For ten days in a row, I observed people walking by the beach ball. Some paid attention, but only as the backdrop for a selfie. Others ignored it. I noticed only small children and street vendors were comfortable with the ball. Adult street vendors played with the ball and had fun. However, the more conventional types, the middle and upper classes, ignored the ball. I had taken the ball to other cities around the world, and nowhere did I witness the uneasiness I saw in Tehran.[172]

In comparing the Iranian response with the concept of play in other such public spaces around the world, Farajiani reflected on how fear and repression prevent Iranians from playing and having fun in visible urban spaces.

If expressing joy and playfulness is difficult in the visible public spaces of Tehran, these concepts have proved easier to materialize for artists outside the capital and in less visible urban spots. It is impossible to separate "the space of art from the space of fun," said Fatemeh Sadat Fazael Ardakani (b. 1996), whose *White Cubes* (*Moka'bha-ye sefid*, 2018) brought to life the rooftops of the historic adobe homes in her hometown city of Ardakan.[173] During the performance, people were given a short time slot to enter the cubes and perform their favorite activity. Those on the outside could see what was going on, as the cubes were made of white mosquito nets. Inside the cubes, Ardakani explained, "one person prayed, two people kissed each other, a child played, two people rested, each time the concept of the work . . . changed from [one] installation to an[other] interactive artwork according to the public and the atmosphere they created" through their preferred activities.[174]

As several scholars have shown, rooftops in Iran traditionally created conditions not only for seclusion, escapism, and visual unavailability from the street but also, and more crucially, for participating in the daily life of the city, albeit in unconventional ways, for example by tuning into the soundscape of the city.[175] Seclusion and escapism are often rooted in the traditional function of roofs as sleeping places at night, especially in warmer and arid climates. In addition to sleeping, nocturnal rooftop life evokes the romantic acts of lovemaking, sleepover conversations, stargazing, and coming-of-age fantasies associated with desirable bodies sleeping in proximity—staples of nostalgic memories and fiction, harking back to the pleasures of everyday life in pre-industrialized Iran. But the same rooftops also allowed the political left to safely watch and gain knowledge of the events unfolding in the streets below.[176] Indeed, participation in urban life from the rooftops involves a multitude of activities that transcend its use for nighttime sleep in a bygone era. For example, in various Iranian cities, in the 1950s and 1960s, the rooftops of houses near open-air cinemas were used as places to watch films free of charge.[177] During the Green Movement many cried out from their rooftops the name of their defeated presidential candidate, Mousavi, or shouted "death to the dictator!" and "God is great." Doing so in the late hours of the night guaranteed anonymity, while at the same time reassuring others they were not alone in feeling mistreated, a gesture harking back to the months ahead of the Islamic Revolution when people also shouted under cover of darkness.[178] Rooftops are also prime sites for an illegal satellite dish or the kind of "vulgar" activities that attract the attention of the morality and cyber police.[179] For example, some young men and women were arrested in 2014 after they posted a YouTube recording of their rooftop dance to Pharrell Williams's song "*Happy*." In 2020, Alireza Japalaghy (b. 1992), a popular Iranian rooftop parkour athlete, and his stunt accomplice were arrested by Tehran's cyber police after photos of the pair kissing in extreme poses on rooftop edges went viral on social media.[180]

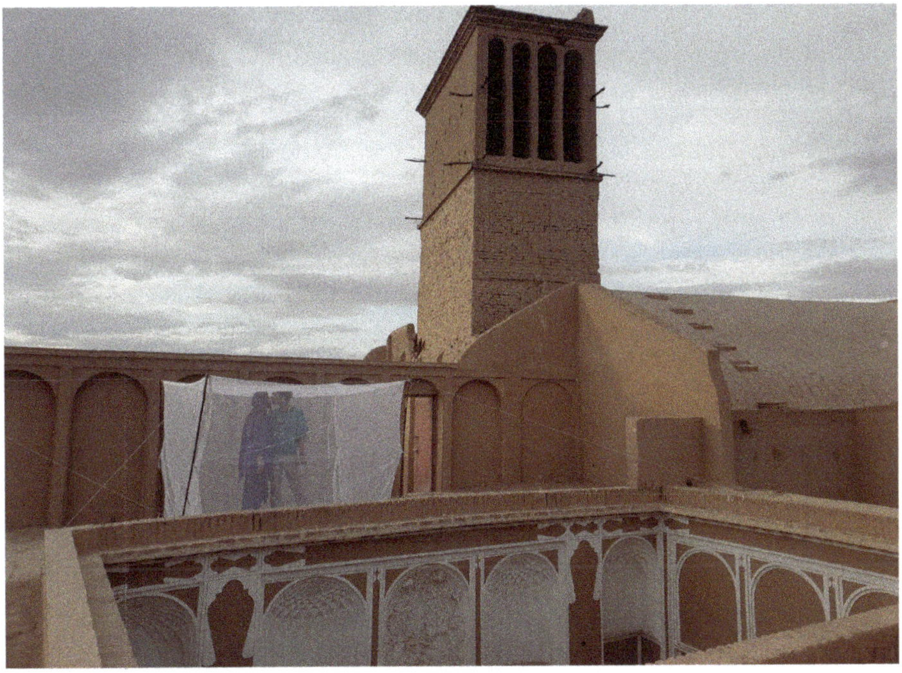

FIGURE 3.26 Fatemeh Sadat Fazael Ardakani, *White Cubes*. 2018. Ardakan, Yazd province. Photograph by Amirhossein Dehghan. Courtesy of Fatemeh Sadat Fazael Ardakani.

For Ardakani, the simple most important aspect of the *White Cubes* was the reenacting of old habits (*zohoor mojaddad-e adathay-e ghadim*) on the rooftops of old adobe homes. However, as the audience got more involved, the art went on to encompass all sorts of connotations entrenched in Iranian rooftops: from nostalgic and romantic actions to subversive deeds. The art allowed the participants to exercise their freedom in a public space and in the presence of others. Kissing on the lips in public is a taboo in Iran, but inside a mosquito net on an old rooftop, it suddenly became permissible (fig 3.26). The art seemingly allowed the public to "play" and "reenact" the past, to imagine themselves in another time while remaining in the same space. The engagement with the past here is not a romantic one; neither it is of a kind famously criticized by Linda Nochlin in her studies of nineteenth-century Orientalist paintings, notably those of Jean-Léon Gérôme. As Nochlin observes, these paintings tended to depict the culture of the Middle East as stagnant, deprived of mobility and progress.[181]

By contrast, Ardakani's art activates alternative presents and sets in motion potentials for less restrictive lifestyles in the future. The events inside the nets were not pre-planned with the participants, but came to life through spontaneity and chance, or through what Elizabeth Grosz, in her book *Becomings: Explorations in Time, Memory and Futures* (1999), describes as "an essence of a time that is not regulated by causality and determination but unfolds with its own rhythm and logic . . . [by] that which signals the openness of the future, its relative connection to but also relative freedom from the past, the possibilities of paths of development, temporal trajectories uncontained by the present."[182] That Ardakani's work facilitated an element of chance or risk does not indicate "*indetermination*, as the absence of a cause . . . ; rather, it is the *excess*, superfluity, of causes, the profusion of causes, which no longer produces singular . . . effects but generates events."[183] As such, Ardakani's participatory project was a tactical intervention (recall de Certeau's notions of tactic as fleeting, as mobile, as "everyday")—an artistic scene organized around negotiations and adaptations to different situations instead of forceful resentment against the official codes of conduct in public.[184] Akin to Tehran Carnival, the installation and its surrounding events may even be interpreted in the light of Bakhtin's description of the carnival—as that which disrupts a carefully ordered and strategized "official" culture, with its fixed rules, timetables, and monuments (recall de Certeau's notions of strategy as bounded, fixed, "proper"). Official modes of behavior in public are strategized, complete, and eternal, while the carnivalesque is tactical, transitory, incomplete, active, and ever-changing.[185]

Despite its open subversiveness, Ardakani's short-term project did not cause any conflicts with state authorities. Its afterlife, however, has proved more challenging, with Ardakani describing the documentation and presentation of the project as a curious case of censorship and self-censorship. But if the afterlife of Ardakani's "kiss" has affected the artist only marginally, the "afterlife" of another public art project caused national concern and international angst.

. . .

On July 19, 2020, the *Etemad Daily* featured an extensive report on the sudden overnight removal of a larger-than-life concrete sculpture. The piece, an L-shaped assembly of letters—M and A in Persian—might at first sight have evoked Robert Indiana's renowned Pop image *Love* (1967). Those two letters, however, spelled out the Persian word *Ma* (or "us" in English). Rather than love, what they proclaimed was an air of collectivity and community.[186]

Who Are We? (*Ma keesteem?*), hereafter *Ma*, was designed by sculptor Shahin Seyghali (b. 1982). Selected for Tehran's Seventh Biennial of

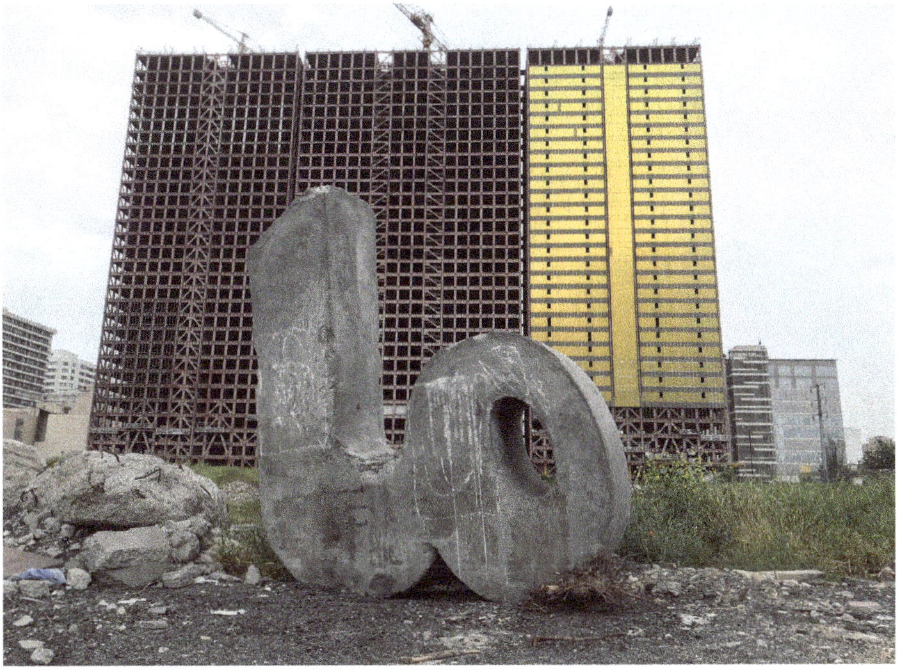

FIGURE 3.27 Shahin Seyghali, *Who Are We?* (aka *Ma*) statue at the waste disposal site of the Tehran municipality. 2020. Tehran. Photograph by Shahin Seyghali.

Sculpture, it stood to the left of the entrance to the TMoCA from September to October of 2017. The impetus for *Ma*, by Seighali's account, came from his fascination with the writings of Jorge Luis Borges,[187] and specifically Borges's notion of memory as expressed in the short story "Funes the Memorious."[188] Reading Borges made Seyghali wonder what would happen if we had an unlimited capacity to remember:

> In Tehran everything is subject to forgetfulness; buildings get demolished without being documented; people's ideas and contributions become suppressed every time a new regime or an administration takes over; all the signs and signals from the past are constantly removed and forgotten. What if we could create art that could remain forever; what if art could be repaired and rejuvenated at all times? My *Ma* was an effort to address the topic of forgetting of "us" and everything else that makes us.[189]

To make the cast concrete sculpture, Seyghali enlisted the formwork techniques he had learned in industrial design. The piece weighed nearly four tons, but its edges were weak and crumbling as he wanted it to show wear and tear over time, and thus the need for constant repair. Instead of being "rejuvenated at all times," however, it would come in for a different kind of treatment.

When the biennial was over, *Ma* was moved to Laleh Park adjacent to TMoCA (itself known for a remarkable collection of outdoor sculptures assembled shortly before the 1979 revolution, including René Magritte's *The Healer* and Alberto Giacometti's *Standing Woman* and *Walking Man*). Then one summer's day in 2021, Seyghali received a message from a friend who had happened upon *Ma* at the edge of a municipal waste ground (fig. 3.27).

When Seyghali approached the Tehran municipality, which assumed responsibility for transferring the artwork to their waste disposal site, he was told the sculpture exuded an air of protest (*bar-e e'terazi*) and was thereby subject to removal. Thus "Us" became subject to disposal, the artist lamented. He told me that when the sculpture had been placed at the park, many had asked him, "What do you mean by *Ma*?" He said it had been hard for him to explain the complex connotations it carried, but that the manner of its displacement ironically revealed exactly what he had meant by *Ma*.[190]

In the days following the *Etemad Daily* report, the removal of *Ma* became more controversial by the hour, featuring on international news websites, including *Deutsche Welle Persian* and the *BBC*, and in thousands of social media posts. One widely shared tweet, critical of the regime, came from Len Khodorkovsky, senior advisor for Global Affairs in the US State Department in the Trump administration, and a force behind abandoning the "Iran Deal."

For many, the removal of *Ma* stood for broader political problems, laying bare the divide between the people of Iran (us) and the authorities (them). In just a few hours, *Ma* was presented on social media as a victim hung on gallows or as a bloody entity against a wall, as if it had been executed by a firing squad. These illustrations were coupled with captions such as "They remove 'Us' one by one," or "Don't execute 'Us'" (fig. 3.28).

When international responses escalated, the Iranian authorities transported the piece back to its original location. A tweet from the deputy minister of public relations for the Tehran municipality, Seyyed Mojtaba Taghavi Nejad, also offered a new justification for why it had been moved in the first place: it was just that it needed repairs, and nothing more than that. *Etemad Daily* was quick to report the artist's view that repairing minor damage hardly required its removal to a dump. It could easily have been fixed in situ and in consultation with the artist himself.[191] The municipality eventually took the sculpture back to Laleh Park, but this time placed it near a security kiosk to make sure that no one would attack it.[192]

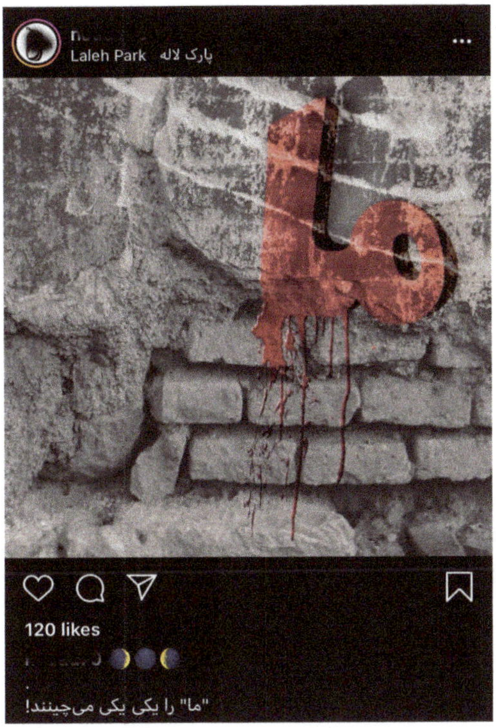

FIGURE 3.28 Snapshot from an iteration of *Ma* on Twitter. July 20–21, 2020. Courtesy of Shahin Seyghali.

As the story of *Ma* continued to unfold over social media platforms, the authorities responded through a series of performative acts, perhaps none more unusual than that of the Museum of Contemporary Art in Isfahan. Shortly after *Ma* was brought back to the park, the museum director approached Seyghali and ordered fifty small *Ma*'s. These sixteen-centimeter-tall objects were then offered as commemorative tokens at a ceremony that celebrated the heads of Isfahan-based NGOs (fig. 3.29).

At the ceremony one prominent official figure is said to have delivered a long lecture about the importance of the word "ma" in the Qur'an, which means "what?" in Arabic. All the commotion surrounding *Ma* was exactly "what art should do in Iran or elsewhere in the world; art must push the power system (*system-e ghodrat*) to respond to people's queries," said Seyghali during a phone call with me.[193] A self-described disciple of the German artist Frank Uwe Laysiepen, better known as Ulay, Seyghali indicates the extent to which his own views about the power of art were shaped by Ulay's brave 1976 performance, during which he stole Hitler's favorite painting—Carl Spitzweg's 1837 *The Poor Poet*—from Berlin's national museum and hung it in the home of a Turkish immigrant family in Kreuzberg "to bring this whole issue of discriminated Turkish foreign workers into

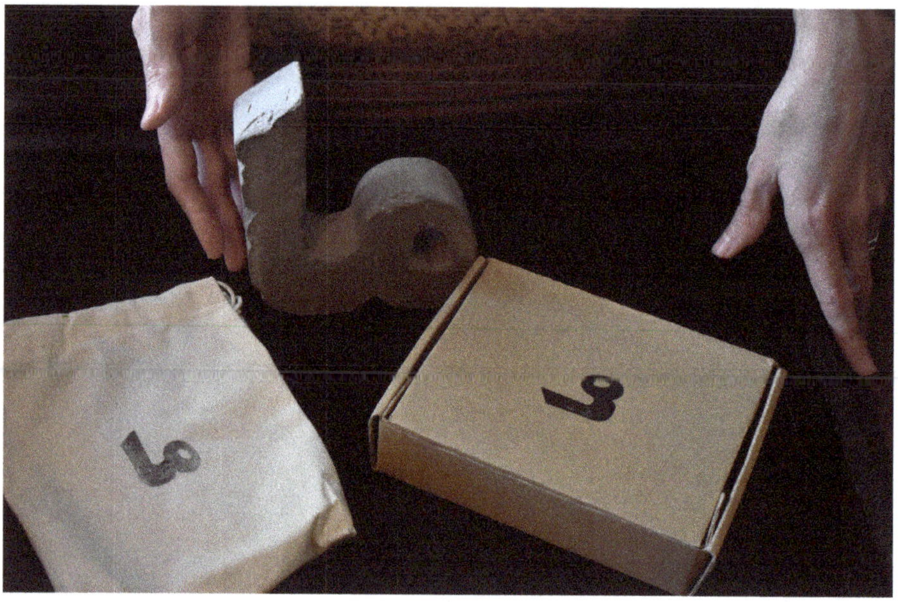

FIGURE 3.29 *Ma* trophy by Shahin Seyghali. Photograph by the author. Courtesy of Shahin Seyghali.

the discussion."[194] Like Ulay's art, Seyghali's *Ma* went on to become an influential work, with power and agency to exert a force on the world around it and to transform one's thinking about the right to the city as well as the ways in which the regime in Iran appropriates alternative art to serve its own purposes.

Ma's convoluted trajectory—from Tehran sculpture biennial, to anti-regime political object, to its final reincarnation as a piece evoking religious sentiment—is indicative of the many forces that have turned public art in Iran into a battleground. The debates surrounding art are particularly heated when creative aesthetic approaches become entangled with the regime's *predatory aestheticization* strategies.

From Interventionism to Integrationism

This chapter opened with the story of a challenging public sculpture outside the Tehran City Theater on the eve of the revolution of 1979. It is perhaps apt to conclude with a story concerning recent debates about art and design projects in the area surrounding that iconic modernist building, which was commissioned by the Shah in the 1970s. The City Theater stands at an important intersection that has seen many popular demonstrations, both for and against the regime. It is also within walking distance of the Student/

Daneshjoo Park and AmirKabir and Tehran universities. The area has become a site of contestation since the completion of an adjacent controversial and modern-looking mosque in 2018 by the Fluid Motion architectural firm, led by Reza Daneshmir (b. 1965) and Catherine Spiridonoff (b. 1968). Deemed by Daneshmir as an "open structure" and an "event space," the building evokes Snøhetta's Oslo Opera House completed in 2008, whose marble-clad roofscape forms a large walkable space in the city and the neighboring fjord. For Daneshmir, however, the "openness" of the structure has to do with the specific circumstances of public urban spaces in Iran. Guided by architect Adolph Loos's theory of *raumplan*, in which walls are broken and all spaces and annexes are seamlessly connected, and architect Bernard Tschumi's principles of reciprocity, Daneshmir hopes to "break the boundaries."[195] Through a cautious language, he publicly defines his mission as one that can "not only remove the physical walls but also help eliminate the mental walls."[196] In this way, the mosque generates conditions for people to move, interact, and meet, just as Daneshmir's favorite designer Tschumi would have done. Recall how in the Parc de la Villette in Paris, a park created between 1984 and 1987 with insights from Jacques Derrida's deconstruction theory, Tschumi based his design on a pattern of points and lines that, among other things, directed the movement of the visitors. The park, as human geographer Tim Creswell sees it, "is not there to tell you what to do, but to provide an opportunity to move and, in doing so, make things happen."[197] Furthermore, echoing *Rancière's* notion of dissensus, it seems like the Fluid Motion Architects wanted to "open up a territory to allow different identities to coexist and be choreographed so that they [could] play out their differences in a conflictual, but non-violent way."[198]

Inspired by the concept of the traditional mosque as first and foremost a gathering space, the Vali Asr Mosque invites people to explore the site in its entirety, even to clamber up its sloping roof.[199] Despite the architects' extensive efforts to justify the design, criticisms ensued, primarily from two factions. Secular-minded intellectuals call it an *anti-progressive* design, as evinced in an *Etemad Daily* article with the blunt headline: "Contemporary or Reactionary?" And in the opposite corner, a *Tasnim News* article titled "A Look at the Anti-Islamic Architecture of the Vali Asr Mosque" puts forward the case of religious-minded clerics, who accuse the architects of creating a sacrilegious environment by omitting the traditional minarets and domes, essential components of Iranian mosques, and allowing passersby to climb atop a sacred space.[200]

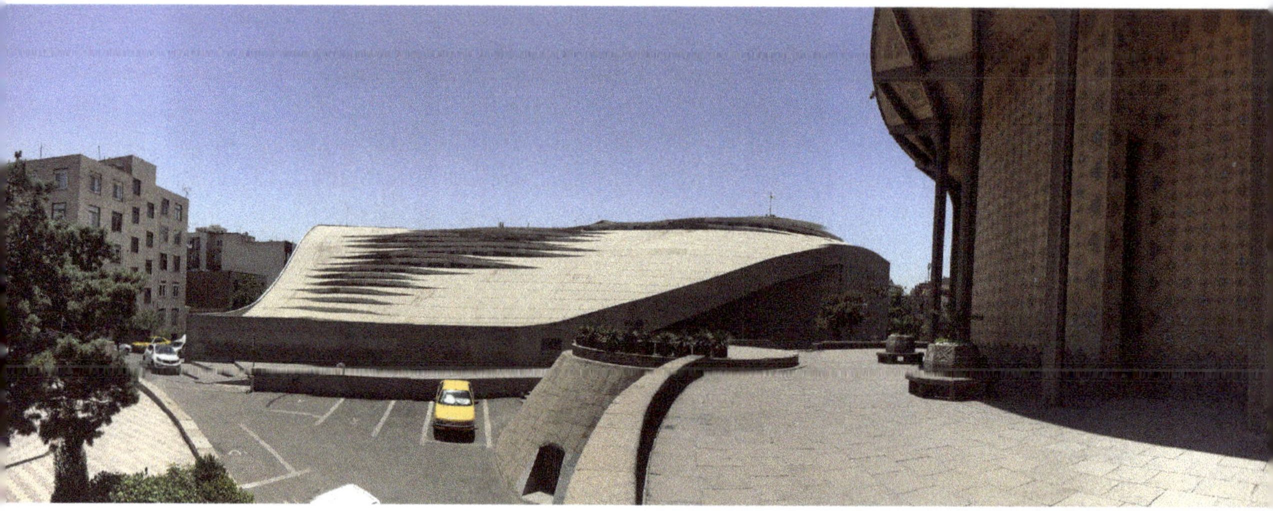

FIGURE 3.30 City Theater and Vali Asr Mosque Plaza. 2021. Tehran. Photograph by Mojtaba Fallahi.

The Tehran municipality attempted to avoid further tensions by barricading the precincts of the roof. They also restricted the use of this space, the so-called art plaza, to sanctioned public art or ceremonial events.[201] Their excuses for doing so were tracked in various debates over social media and particularly on Clubhouse. At one point, the government line was that they simply wanted to "protect the sanctity of art" (*hefazat az ghedasat-e honar*). Other times, the imposition of restrictions was framed as a device to prevent addicts and offenders from congregating in these culturally significant areas (fig. 3.30).[202] Thus, despite Fluid Motion's efforts to generate a space of sociability, the function of the space would eventually become a visual field governed by the principle of surveillance.

. . .

The area adjacent to the City Theater is just one example of the "plaza fever" (*tab-e plaza*) that has gripped the capital since the 2010s. While the regime often heralds creation of open pedestrian public spaces as the "advancement of civic solidarity" (*ertegha'-e hess hambastegi-e madani*),[203] many of these so-called plazas are created for state-sponsored demonstrations and religious ceremonies. A prime example in this vein is the Beautification Bureau's recent revamping and pedestrian-izing of the formerly traffic-choked Imam Hossein Square.

Designed in 2012 by Karl Schlamminger (1935–2017), German artist and prerevolutionary sculpture professor at Tehran University, who is best known for his designs in Kufic script and his collaboration with the Aga Khan Foundation, the mounting towers and walls around the plaza are punctuated by intricate Islamic design. The pro-regime press describes the gigantic Imam Hossein Plaza as imparting a "feeling of soaring" (*hess-e bala raftan*) (fig. 3.31).[204] Still, the colossal ensemble frames the plaza and as such removes it from becoming integrated into the nearby businesses, thus allowing for easier surveillance of the area. The tall, ornate metal walls and towers also can be used to hang banners and facilitate religious and political installations.

Schlamminger was an apt choice for the Tehran municipality to showcase its worldliness. However, perhaps because of his advanced age, the project was executed by a team of Iranian designers, appointed by the municipality. Inside Iran, it is primarily this team, rather than Schlamminger himself, who are given due credit for this design.

The example of the City Theater Plaza shows how what was previously seen as "interventionist" art has become "integrationist" art. Art historian Miwon Kwon has written on a similar transformation in the United States in the 1960s, when an increased emphasis on social responsibility and racial integration–among art experts as well as the National Endowment for the Arts (NEA)—encouraged site-specificity and cultural relevance for all public art projects.[205]

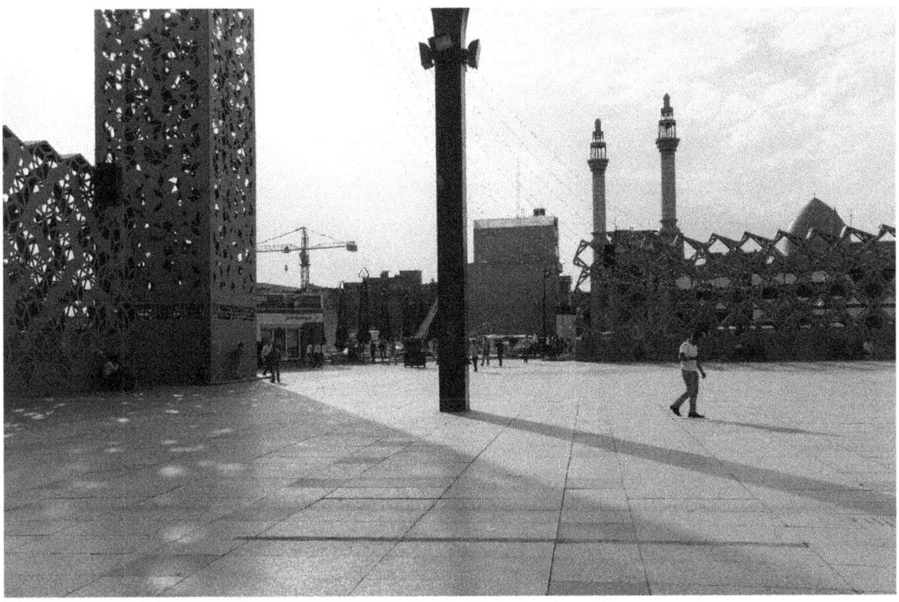

FIGURE 3.31 Imam Hossein Plaza. 2019. Tehran. Photograph by Farhad Mantegh.

Spatial practices, however, are more susceptible to being co-opted by institutional and market forces. Now, in the neoliberal economies of the US and elsewhere, the corporatization of "interventionist" art is often an adjunct to profitable investments in urban development projects. In Iran investment in urban development projects has not only brought financial benefits for those who control from above: it has also, and especially, according to the voice of the opposition, helped nourish the state surveillance apparatus.

Yet against all odds, interventionist projects continue to materialize in the city and in debates about the use of public space. A look at the publications of the Tehran municipality's Beautification Bureau indicates the extent to which interventionist agents are present next to integrationist forces. For example, in 2015 the bureau's bulletin dedicated a special issue to nocturnal life in the public urban spaces of Tehran. One article by Isa Alizadeh (then the bureau's chief director) emphasizes the need to carefully design, light, and maintain public urban spaces to "lessen anomalous behaviors" (*kahesh-e raftarhay-e anomik*) at night. Another piece in the same volume is penned by the young architect Kourosh Asef Vaziri, who occasionally receives commissions from the municipality.[206]

In contrast to Alizadeh, Asef Vaziri highlights the need to recognize the spaces that ordinary citizens have invented for themselves (*fazahay-e khod angikhteh*).[207] In this context, the case of the City Theater, along with more recent debates in government publications, suggests a clear shift from the earlier policies outlined in the opening pages of this chapter. Rather than the black-and-white division of independent interventionist artists versus state-run ideological public art projects, there is a new wave of correlation, intersection, and overlap in the spatial practices of the two.

Careful urban management by the authorities, which once again evokes the *predatory aesthetization* phenomenon, is not an end in itself. Perhaps inadvertently, while regulating artists and architects, the state seems to have granted them the possibility of resisting the system, validating my point about the ebb and flow of power. To interpret this whole convoluted enterprise in an even more optimistic light, the restoration of free public space requires more than just a shift in policy-making, and this is precisely why art and design practices, which help undo these *predatory regimes*, are integral to this process.

In this chapter I opened a place between art and urban space that allowed the two to be explored in relation to one another, thus generating an interdisciplinary discussion about important critical spatial practices. But interventionist spatial practices conducted in bright daylight are not limited to ephemeral guerilla practices, "fragile" presences, and temporary events. Through their clever curatorial strategies, artists, gallerists, and designers have managed to create alternative modes of thinking, artmaking, and living in the precincts of official museums, galleries, art institutions, and even amidst the more challenging large-scale architectural projects. These practices, which often deploy "improvisational" tactics, animate the pages of the following chapter.

4 Improvisation

Artful Curation and Spatial Reconfiguration in and out of Conventional Sites

UNTIL THE 1950s, curation in Iran mostly involved looking after collections of invaluable artifacts in a museum, managing new acquisitions to enlarge the collection, and planning and overseeing displays. Work like this took place in a range of collections and museums, from the royal collection of Naser al-Din Shah of the Qajar Dynasty to the Museum of Ancient Iran.[1] Slowly, however, the concept of curation began to shift with the emergence in Tehran of noncommercial or alternative galleries like Apadana. Apadana was set up in 1949 by artists Mahmoud Javadipour (1921–2012), Hossein Kazemi (1924–1996), and architect Houshang Ajoudani (1921–2010). The galley consisted of five rented storefronts and was easily accessible from the street. It focused on modern painting, and also functioned like a salon—a hub for discussions of art and art history, with lectures and slide presentations, accompanied by music, refreshments, and drinks.[2]

Around the same time, traditional modes of representation began to be challenged. Up to the late 1960s, public monuments mostly served to reinforce the nationalistic ideals of the governing elite, and typically took the form of a figure—invariably a great man—standing on a pedestal (e.g., the iconic Ferdowsi statue by Abolhassan Sadighi, 1894–1995). It was against this backdrop that Parviz Tanavoli (b. 1936) created *Farhad and the Deer* (*Farhad o Ahoo*) (ca. 1960). Made of metal scraps found in a junkyard, the sculpture shows the distorted figures of a man and an animal, reminiscent of the relief of Darius fighting a lion, found in the west entrance to the Palace of Darius the Great (522–486 BCE). The authorities dismissed the work—the references to Iran's cultural heritage were apparently not enough to compensate for the usual approach to form—so, *Farhad and the Deer* got its only public showing on the balcony of Tanavoli's studio, which nonetheless faced busy Pahlavi (now Vali Asr) Avenue. Tanavoli's interventionist tactic was daring for its time.[3]

In 1966 Tanavoli began to collaborate with architect Kamran Diba and artist Roxana Saba (b. 1942) in the Rasht 29 Art Club, which developed unconventional curatorial practices (see chapter 1). In the years that followed, the Azad (independent) Association of Iranian Artists—composed of Gholamhossein Nami (b. 1936), Masoud Arabshahi (1935–2019), Faramarz Pilaram (1937–1982), Abdolreza Daryabeigi (b. 1931), and Morteza Momayez (1935–2005)[4]—also made and curated unusual, conceptual, and interactive art projects.[5]

Alongside these alternative modes of display, unconventional curatorial strategies also surfaced in more official state-sponsored exhibitions such as the Tehran biennials (1958–76) and the Shiraz Arts Festival (1967–77). For example, the 1977 Shiraz Festival featured *Pig! Child! Fire!*, a play by the radical Hungarian theater troupe Squat that evoked Dostoevsky, Breton, and Artaud while deploying graphic nudity, an animal carcass, and acts of extreme sexual violence.

Squat's antics had gotten them expelled from a number of European cities, and they had been stripped of their Hungarian citizenship. Their appearance in a display window of a shop on a busy street in Shiraz felt like their greatest provocation to date. From exile, Khomeini denounced such "indecent" acts and displays. He did not have to issue further statements of this kind: 1977 was to be the final Shiraz Festival, and Khomeini himself would be returning to Iran soon enough.[6]

. . .

After the revolution and until the end of the Iran-Iraq war in 1988, curatorial activities in official museums were primarily centered on revolutionary (*enghelabi*) and committed (*mote'ahhed*) art. Curation took on a *ceremonial* character, although it was vastly different from the conceptual, interactive, and performative styles that had recently gained a firm foothold in the second half of the 1970s.

Instead of allowing audiences to make—or even play with—their own interpretations of art objects, museums became places for ritualistic displays that promoted the ideology of the regime. Young students went on school trips to the palaces of the Shah, where their guides would continually denounce everything that was on display—from conformity to Western imperialism and cultural aggression (*tahajom-e farhangi*), to the expenditure of national funds on unnecessary artworks and decorative elements.

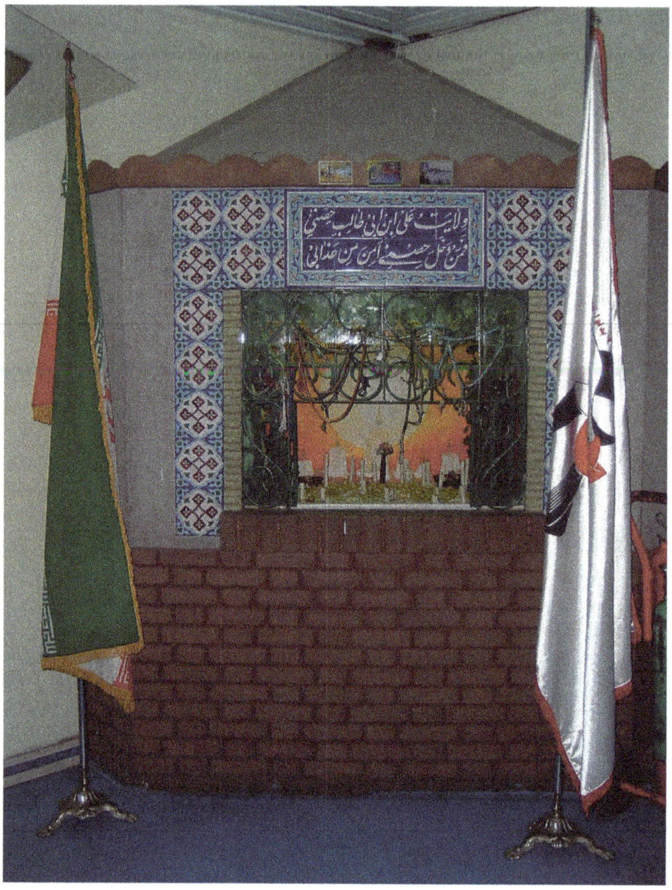

FIGURE 4.1 Saqqakhaneh flanked with the flags of Iran and the *Bonyad-e shahid* (Foundation of Martyrs). 2007. Second gallery on ground floor, Martyrs' Museum. Tehran. Photograph by Christine Gruber.

During the Iran-Iraq war, governmental agitprop institutions were set up to display the visual and material cultures of the war and martyrdom. War murals appeared on the walls of every city. The Central Martyrs' Museum in Tehran, founded in 1980 to commemorate martyrs of the Islamic Revolution, expanded twice in 1966 and 2006, to accommodate the swollen ranks of martyrs of the Iran-Iraq war.[7]

The Martyrs' Museum would become the venue for the most ideological form of curation, where the viewers were expected to engage in communal acts of mourning after encountering the ritualistic display of personal items and art relating to those who had lost their lives in the Islamic Revolution and the Iran-Iraq war. As art historian Christiane Gruber argues, the museum institutionalized and aestheticized war and violence, and "became a ceremonial setting that prompts ritual activity" (fig. 4.1).[8] The Sacred Defense Garden and Museum, launched in 2012 by the office of Mayor

Mohammad Bagher Ghalibaf, similarly adopted what Narges Bajoghli calls a "*narration-based*" curatorial tactic, delivering the story of the Islamic Republic's success in safeguarding the nation's self-esteem and pride, against the failed examples of Iran's previous leaders and governments.[9]

Art museums were likewise affected by propagandist curatorial strategies. In the 1980s, TMoCA would occasionally show a scatter of items from its collection of Western modern art, such as a few landscape paintings in the Impressionist and Expressionist styles by artists like Claude Monet. But it mainly focused on agitprop themes such as photographs of the Mexican revolutionary murals, ideological graffiti, Palestinian resistance movement, political cartoons, and art by war veterans.[10] These exhibitions were also limited in media, appearing mostly as painting, photography, and graphic design.[11] The reconstruction (*sazandegi*) period of President Rafsanjani partially overlapped with future reformist president Mohammad Khatami's tenure as minister of culture and Islamic guidance. Under the supervision of the Institute for the Development of Plastic Arts (*Mo'asseseh tose'eh honarha-ye tajassomi*), a subdivision of MCIG, TMoCA began to launch biennials and triennials that were also more inclusive in terms of preferences for art media, such as photography (beginning in 1987) and painting and graphic design (beginning in 1991).[12]

The cultural and artistic freedoms granted during the tenure of President Khatami (1997–2005) gave rise to a renewed interest in curation at TMoCA, under the directorship of Alireza Sami-Azar (also 1997–2005). In collaboration with the Association of Iranian Artists, formed in 1997, Sami-Azar invited bold proposals from performance, conceptual, and new media artists. A case in point is a 2002 project by filmmaker, theater expert, and university professor Sadegh Safaie (1961–2021). Safaie was an avid theater fan; while in senior high, he attended a performance in Mashhad's *Mehraban Hall*, a work with a religious theme, albeit with the soundtrack of Carl Orff's *Carmina Burana*, that would probably best fit into the postrevolutionary category of rhythmic movements (*harakat-e mowzoon*). What intrigued Safaie was the use of bodily movements and the lack of narrative. In 1988, Safaie directed and produced *And Now Women!* (*Va inak zan!*), possibly one of the first instances of performance art in postrevolutionary Iran. Presented only twice, at Tehran's Sooreh and Mehrab Halls, it included a scene with a couple on the opposite sides of a seesaw. The movement of the seesaw suggested sexual interaction, and after a few minutes the woman pulled out a few dolls from underneath her dress. This was enough for the authorities to shut down the show, leaving Safaie with an enormous debt.[13] Safaie did not give up on performance art as a powerful medium. On October 1, 2002, at the invitation of Sami-Azar, and along with producer Mehran Houshyar (b. 1970), he created *The Road Is Under Construction (Jaddeh dar dast-e ta'meer ast).* The live performance, which took place on a single day over the course of an hour and a half, presented three scenarios. The first involved eight men and women (all Sadeghi's art students at Sooreh University) dressed in black, military-style overalls and stocking masks and holding paper batons, who marched into the museum demanded that all attendees show their invitation cards to the ongoing *New Media Art* exhibition.[14]

In the second scenario, members of the crew, now joined by a man dressed as a chef, assembled behind barbed wire in front of the main museum entrance, asking the audience to choose between crimpers or stocking masks and batons emblazoned with the phrase, "We thank you for your cooperation." Those who took the crimpers could cut their way through the barbed wire and enter the museum amid a series of moving frames. Those who chose the stocking masks and batons would join the crew to interrogate the others; anyone with the temerity to disobey would be tied to the metal frames just outside the museum. Meanwhile, a second group of crew members stood still, holding placards that read: "The road is under construction or you are free to say what you want to say." According to Safaie, after a few European visitors who were familiar with performance art picked the crimpers, others followed their lead. No one joined the militant-looking crew. And only one young woman protested the whole process and insisted that she should be allowed to enter the museum without having to choose any of these restrictive methods (later, in a public lecture, art historian Helia Darabi revealed that she was that young woman).[15] This, according to Safaie, was a reminder of the ways in which Iranians in real life conform to or contest the rules of authority. The reenacting of a real-life situation encouraged the audience to think about notions of freedom of expression in society.[16]

Despite its provocative spirit, the performance unfolded without any problems. As Safaie noted, the MCIG showed flexibility at the time; even the progressive minister, Ahmad Masjed Jame'i, participated in the performance.[17] After *The Road Is Under Construction*, TMoCA became even more courageous, exhibiting works by world-class contemporary artists such as Gerhard Richter, Damien Hirst, and Mona Hatoum and mounting cutting-edge exhibitions of conceptual art by emerging artists.[18]

The last year of President Khatami's time in office, 2005, would see several new initiatives. For example, the Tehran municipality launched the sculpture biennial, part of which took place on the grounds of the TMoCA. But everything changed in August of that year, when hardliner Mahmoud Ahmadinejad gained the presidency.[19] The new conservative approach affected the direction of many newly established art centers such as The Home of the Artists (*Khaneh honarmandan*), which had also opened its doors in 2005. After that, directorship of museums altered—all of the programs that had been permitted were suspended and replaced by more conservative exhibitions. TMoCA was one museum that responded swiftly to the shift, with a 2006 exhibition dedicated to criticizing Israel's policies. The show was a reaction to the controversial cartoons of the Prophet Mohammed in a 2005 issue of the Danish newspaper *Jyllands-Posten*, and was planned in the form of a cartoon contest.[20] Earlier that year, the popular newspaper *Hamshahri* announced that the twelve best contributions would receive a bullion gold coin each—later increased to $5,000–12,000 prizes for the top three cartoons, with twelve runners-up receiving the rest of the bullion gold coins. *Hamshahri* published an English introduction to the contest, as well as preliminary rules for entries. The newspaper denounced Western hypocrisy regarding freedom of speech, alleging, "It is impossible in the West to joke upon or even discuss certain topics related to Judaism, such as the Holocaust, and the pretexts for the creation of Israel."[21] Out of 1,200 submissions from around the world, the museum awarded first prize to the Moroccan cartoonist Abdellah Derkaoui, whose drawing featured an Israeli crane constructing a wall around Jerusalem's Dome of the Rock.

. . .

From 2008 to 2012, TMoCA's new conservative director, religious scholar Mahmoud Shaloui (b. 1966), tightened administrative control over all curatorial aspects of the museum. Meanwhile, the International Fajr Annual Festival—the MCIG initiative that had been active in the areas of film and theater since 1982—added the visual arts to its programs in 2008. After the 2009 Green Movement, many artists boycotted collaboration with state institutions, including TMoCA, which pressed on, regardless, with its programs, mostly in conjunction with the Fajr Festival.[22]

Set against this background, artists had no choice but to turn to alternative modes of curation in both official galleries and alternative spaces such as homes, abandoned sites, and rented spaces. Under Ahmadinejad, unconventional curation of art became increasingly political. To remain safe, those involved were obliged to use strategies to justify their projects. Under difficult circumstances, *improvisation* rather than overt *activism* became key to many of the alternative curatorial practices.

Curation evolved into something more than simply acts of selecting and arranging, gradually coming to encompass a whole host of activities, from acts of improvisation, to negotiations across words and images, to the spatial configuration of the conventional gallery and the careful shuffling of people around art, design, and performance. Curation, in this broad sense, is powerful and deeply relevant to critical spatial practices. It has allowed space to emerge as a site of contestation.

Curation, choreography, and reconfiguration facilitate the conversion of place (*lieu*) into space (*espace*), to borrow from de Certeau. Whereas "place is . . . an instantaneous configuration of positions . . . space occurs as the effect produced by the operations that orient it, situate it, temporalize it, and make it function in a polyvalent unity of conflictual programs or contractual proximities."[23] Focused mainly on official places and sanctioned projects, this chapter foregrounds how artists, designers, and performers manage to turn "place" into "space," while also showing how they operate within a challenging sociopolitical environment. Most of the works discusses in the following pages are subversive in nature, dating from 2005 onward, after the conservative president Ahmadinejad came into power.

Improvisation and Negotiation through Words and Images

In *Thinking in Jazz: The Infinite Art of Improvisation* (1994), Paul Berliner refutes the common assumption that jazz musicians just stand up and play "out of their heads," without any preparation.[24] Far from making "something out of nothing," Berliner writes, "[t]here is, in fact, a lifetime of preparation and knowledge behind every idea that an improviser performs."[25]

Over the past four decades, Iranian alternative artists, like jazz musicians, have perfected their skills in their own ways. Improvisation (*bedah-e), as* a style of performance, has spread beyond music and into the arts. As mentioned previously, performance artists and experimental theater directors often openly refer to themselves as improvisation or *bedah-e* artists. Alternative visual artists use the term less often, but in many ways they employ improvisational techniques—especially in their interactions with the MCIG and other authoritative agents such as the morality police, the municipality, or even security guards.

In chapter 1, I described how Houman Mortazavi presented his work as *kardasti* (children's craftwork) to the authorities. Such packaging of professional work as immature educational material was also common among musicians. For example, in late 1990s, the band 127 secured permission for several performances inside educational institutions by rebranding them as "experimental student projects." The president of the Art University gave the band the green light to perform on campus: anything under the rubric of *ejra'-e pajooheshi* (experimental performance) was permitted.[26]

Other, more complicated bureaucratic forms of negotiation play an essential part in legitimizing a work of art. As shown in chapter 3, in negotiating his abstract style of public art in 1998, Keivan Pournasr employed storytelling (*dastan saraie*) strategies, with points of reference that were imaginative and indirect. Similarly, when talking in public about his destruction series, which shows precious historic artifacts from ancient Iran blown to pieces, Aydin Aghdashloo often refers to his fascination with the vision of total destruction in the final scenes of Michelangelo Antonioni's *Zabriskie Point* (1970). Only on rare occasions does he reveal that these paintings are also allusions to the ways in which revolution, war, and internal policies have harmed Iran's cultural heritage.[27] Obscuration (*iham*) likewise saved the day for Kourosh Golnari (b. 1964) during his exhibition at Aun Gallery in 2011. The state authorities identified one of his *Salatin* (Sultans) series—a bust of a turbaned male figure covered entirely with gold coins—as a political statement associating the ruling clergy with affluence and the material life. When questioned, Golnari denied the accusations and remained elusive about the true meaning of the work. The figure had nothing to do with Iran's current leaders, he argued—the turban/*ammameh* was not the same kind they wore. Rather, it depicted a medieval sultan wearing the "*dastar*"—an archaic word for *ammameh*, which is not in use in colloquial Persian.

Alternative curatorial activities are, of course, more prone to be questioned. In a 2012 *Al Jazeera* interview, Nazila Noebashari (b. 1970), founder and manager of Tehran's Aaran Gallery, asserted: "There are, of course, sensitivities in [Iran]. The government [draws] boundaries. But, fortunately, most of our artists have grown up with these limitations and so they find a way to pass on their messages [regardless]."[28] "Finding a way" is a form of negotiation and improvisation. In a private conversation, Noebashari reiterated a similar sentiment, telling me that Iran's art scenes blow hot and cold (*ba das pas mizanan, ba pa pish mikeshan*). To illustrate what she meant, she described two episodes that had required her to negotiate her way through a confrontation with the authorities.

In 2013, President Mahmoud Ahmadinejad's last year in office, Noebashari curated a solo show by artist Mehran Saber (b. 1972), known for his surrealist figurative paintings, which at times reveal human body parts, including those of women.[29] The MCIG granted permission, but on the condition that Noebashari removed five of the nine works on display. In protest, Noebashari canceled the show. In some of the exhibitions that followed, Noebashari avoided the cumbersome permission process altogether. When exhibiting without permission, you sometimes get lucky, Noebashari asserted. Other times, "all it takes for an exhibition to be terminated or a curator or artist to get into trouble is someone reporting it."[30]

In early 2019, Noebashari curated an exhibition based on the work of Nastaran Safaie (b. 1984). It included a five-hour video of Safaie walking the entire length of the Vali Asr Avenue (eighteen kilometers), showing how she was assailed with pickup lines and other kinds of verbal abuse (see chapter 3). A woman in full *hijab* (*chador*) turned up to examine it; presumably, she had been sent by the authorities, who had not granted permission for the show. After a long conversation, Noebashari managed to convince her that the purpose of the art was to protect women's rights in the city, where they are always being harassed by men, whatever grade of *hijab* they wear.[31] The inspector could not have agreed more with Noebashari and left the gallery without further dispute.

These two episodes are microcosms of the kinds of improvisation employed by Tehran gallerists. They show how curation might be inflected through interpretative markers and verbal contextualization, invoking different emotions and debates. But this improvisation does not always have to be enacted in verbal form. Sometimes such negotiations are communicated through more visceral acts of curation and via images.

In 2009, in the aftermath of the Green Movement, Behnam Kamrani (b. 1968) and Rozita Sharafjahan planned an exhibition, *School* (*Madreseh*), as a critique of the government's treatment of Iranian youth and a nod to Pink Floyd's dark projection of the suppressed life of a young generation in their legendary album *The Wall*. Soon, however, they had to accept that it was unrealistic to expect the authorities to grant permission for the show. Working with other prominent artists, they then took a curious turn, looking to the "safe" subject of the socialist realist kitsch produced under Stalin.[32] As Kamrani recalled, "Our sarcastic response was to produce something that would not raise any flag and would make everyone, including the MCIG, happy." The cohort of sixteen artists produced sixteen almost identical and intentionally shabby replicas of a rose and nightingale (*gol-o-bolbol*) painting by the old-style miniature artist Ali Akbar Tajvidi (1927–2017),

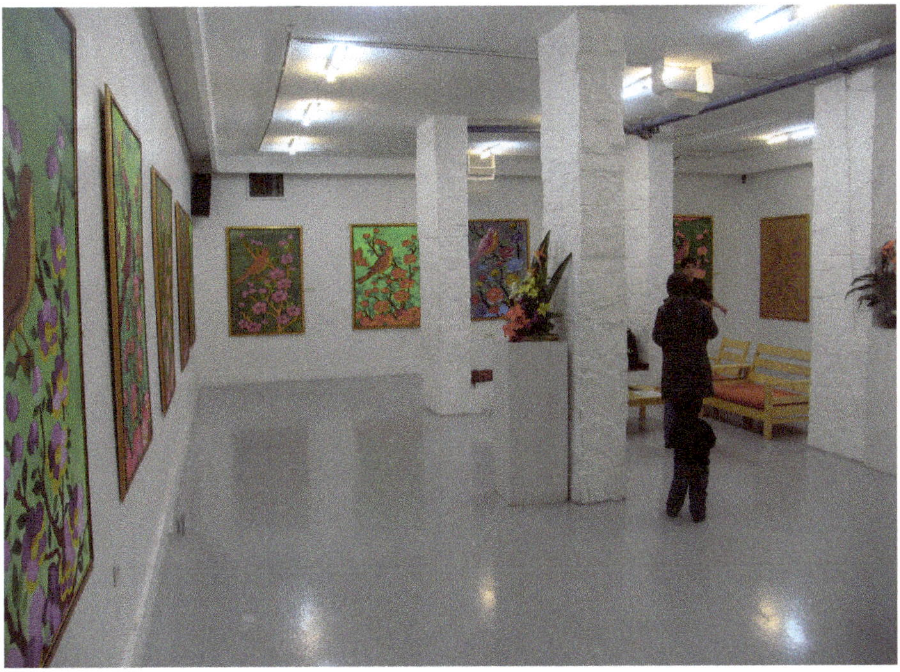

FIGURE 4.2 *Rose-and-Nightingale* exhibition, curated by Behnam Kamrani and Rozita Sharafjahan. 2009. Azad Art Gallery, Tehran. Photograph by Behnam Kamrani.

which appeared *en masse* on the covers of the government-sanctioned *Divan of Hafez* (a fourteenth-century collection of mystical poems).[33] To make the exhibition even more cynical, the artists framed their rather hideous looking *gol-o-bol-bols* with cheap and gaudy gilded frames (fig. 4.2).

According to Kamrani, turning to kitsch in Iran is a kind of survival tactic. He remembers how "in the restrictive atmosphere of the 1980s, the Dadashi Gallery was one of the few existing commercial art galleries that openly sold Western-looking art. The government apparently did not see any problem with replicas of the eighteenth-century and colonial-style romantic oil paintings adorned with gilded frames that packed the Dadashi shop walls and display windows, and could be seen from one of the busiest intersections on Vali Asr (formerly Pahalavi) Avenue"[34] (fig. 4.3).

If Kamrani and his colleagues poked fun at Soviet-era kitsch by putting together a one-off exhibition, artist Mahmoud Bakhshi (b. 1977) takes the concept a step further by making this cynical approach his signature-style artistic mission. His art appropriates all manner of Islamic Republic kitsch products. He told me:

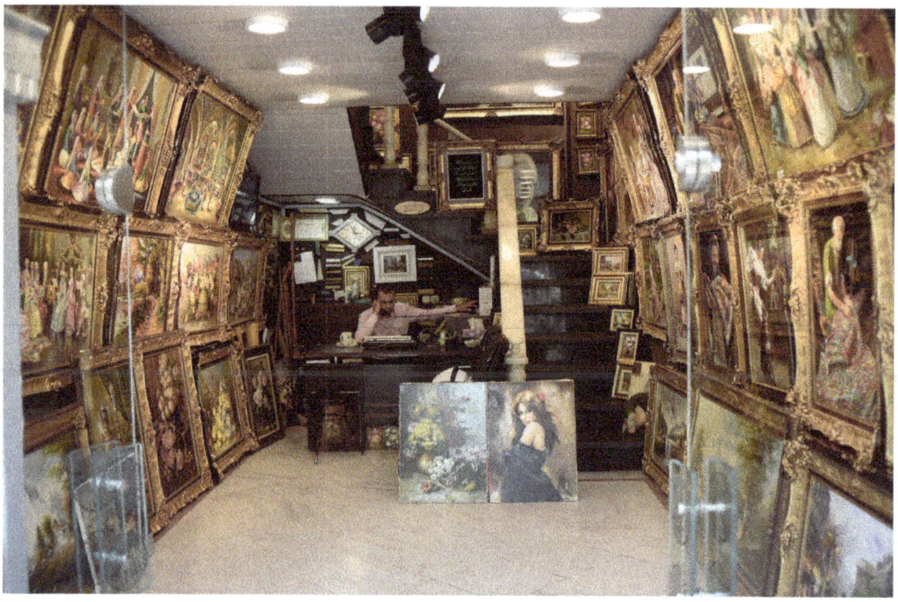

FIGURE 4.3 Interior view of the Dadashi Gallery. 2018. Tehran. Photograph by Mojtaba Fallahi.

> There is something inherently Soviet about this culture; we cannot escape it. We cannot ignore the fact that years of living in this society have inured us to the Soviet-style propaganda promoted by the regime. So, in my art I adopt the same styles and strategies. Sometimes anti-regime audiences get frustrated with me for employing the exact same visual language used in agitprop. They simply assume that this is an attempt to perpetuate and promote the regime's propaganda. At the opening of one of my exhibitions, in the presence of other people, a man called me fatuous (*bi-sho'ur*). But the regime's visual language is what most of the society has become; this is part of our identity and we cannot escape this visual culture. My art possesses a degree of truth and sarcasm at the same time.[35]

Even the notion of "committed art" (*honar-e mote'ahhed*) is of interest to Bakhshi. Committed art was promoted by both the Soviets and the Islamic Republic regime as a counterforce to what they saw as "art for art's sake" of the previous regimes. Bakhshi maintained, "I became exactly what the regime wanted us to be: I am a fully 'committed' artist; I am not a formalist; instead, I try to communicate something meaningful through my art, something that might have an impact on society; something that serves society, something that is abundantly committed."[36] Beyond verbal and visual negotiation strategies in curatorial practices, another effective survival tactic for gallerists is to alter the space of the gallery.

Spatial Reconfiguration of Exhibition Space

Adaptability (*ene'taf paziri*) and slow transformation (*degardisi*) are two of the improvisation tactics that were applied to the physical spaces of the Azad Art Gallery in Tehran to merge the public and the private and to create the potential for more cutting-edge productions. In a lecture given at Tehran's Art University on November 19, 2018, Behnam Kamrani described in detail the transformation of Azad in the twenty years since its founding in 1999.[37]

He spoke of how the gallery, which started out with a focus on conventional paintings, had gradually turned into the most progressive space for radical exhibitions, including the highly influential 2007 exhibition *Ethnic Marketing* (*Bazaryabi-e ghowmi*) by Tirdad Zolghadr (b. 1973), which made use of the gallery's kitchen, among other alternative curatorial strategies, in an attempt to undo the "curatorial clichés."[38]

All of these unconventional art displays, Kamrani noted, involved a process of altering the gallery space, converting its kitchen into exhibition space, adding walls, and even removing its built-in brick benches and stripping brick from the I-beam steel columns. Shrinking the gallery's architectural mass created more room for alternative art practices. Using the revamping of the Azad Art Gallery as a microcosm of the wider Iranian art scene, Kamrani demonstrated how *adaptability* (*ene'taf paziri*) in the alteration of space (*makan*) and thinking in spatial terms (*andisheh-e makan-mehvar*) have led to the transformation (*degardisi*) and progress (*pishraft*) of art practices in Iran.

A similar transformation took place at the increasingly experimental art space, Parkingallery. Subsequent to Lili Golestan turning her home garage into a commercial gallery (see chapter 1), Parkingallery started out in the garage of the family home of media artist, graphic designer, and curator Amirali Ghasemi, located in the Shahrak-e Gharb neighborhood. After graduating from university, Ghasemi was continually rejected by established galleries. There were limited opportunities at the art colleges, and, according to Ghasemi, the discourse surrounding art was largely outdated.[39] Distressed that he could not find a readymade audience for his art, Ghasemi took matters into his own hands (fig. 4.4).[40]

In the summer of 1998, with the equivalent of just fifty dollars, Ghasemi launched Parkingallery as a self-governing, makeshift art space. The gallery

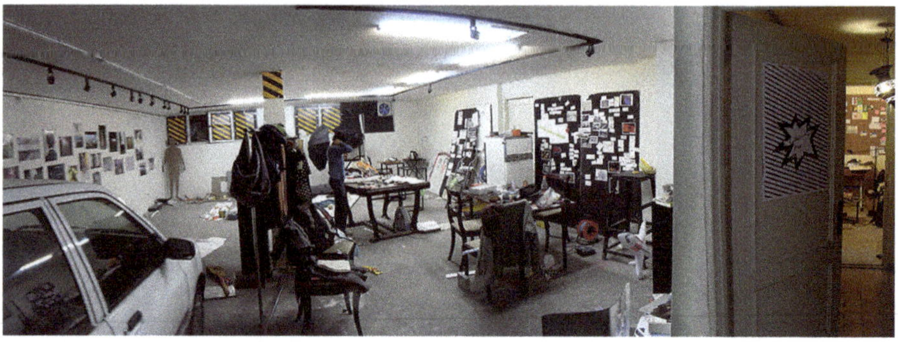

FIGURE 4.4 Panoramic view of the two-part space in the Parkingallery. 2012. Tehran. Photograph by Amirali Ghasemi.

sold works to raise funds for events and exhibitions, and to support young and emerging artists. It was also instrumental in bringing European art experts to Iran, and in organizing exhibitions of Iranian media arts in Europe. Between 2007 and 2011, for example, Ghasemi curated The Limited Access Festival (*Jashnvareh dastresi-e mahdood*): works by several German and Polish artists based in Berlin were showcased at the Azad Art Gallery, and in return, artworks by fifteen Iranians were shown in Berlin.

In terms of its spatial configuration, Parkingallery adopted a "strategy that utilizes intense fluidity between the private and the public, so as to maintain a longer and more productive work period."[41] Gatherings inside Parkingallery were held in a two-part space: a garage and a studio. Ghasemi's family parked their car in the garage, but over time that space evolved into a noncommercial gallery space (to commemorate its former function as a garage, one of the early exhibitions included car parts). The other space was a twenty-two-square-meter room, on the ground floor of the three-story family house. This was designated as Ghasemi's personal studio, but it was used periodically as a screening room or conference space. Sometimes events spread into the front yard of the complex or up to the first floor. In an interview delivered in 2010, Ghasemi asserted that the intention of the gallery was to move beyond what are commonly perceived outside Iran as "stealthy freedoms":

> Underground musicians must deal with such governmental institutions as *vezarat-e ershad* [Ministry of Culture and Islamic Guidance] and *seda va sima* [Islamic Republic of Iran Broadcasting]. We, however, are not so concerned about distributing the artwork via official channels. Our meetings are informal,

and the exhibitions navigate quietly between underground and overground venues.[42]

Ghasemi added that there are multiple publics and "multiple islands in Iran"—echoing the social theorist Michael Warner, who defines a public—not *the* public, but one of many—as a collectivity "that comes into being only in relation to texts and their circulation," that is, "by virtue of being addressed."[43] Ghasemi's audience, then, was a "particular public," a phenomenon also referred to as "trusted" audiences.

In a lecture on "Independent and Artist-Run Initiatives in Tehran" at the 2009 Global Art Forum in Dubai, Ghasemi described a fashion show staged at the gallery in the summer of 2005. The story of the show, together with the peculiar style of its presentation, illustrates the extent to which Parkingallery operated in the liminal space between public and private, between real and representational spaces. Ghasemi showed a slide of a drawing evoking a Pac-Man-like environment (the 1980s maze arcade game was widely popular in Iran, thanks to the travelers who came from abroad, especially Mecca) (fig. 4.5, right slide).[44]

The dots in the main space of the garage indicated the arrangement of chairs for the fashion show and catwalks. The four red dots in the corner of the garage space represented works showcased by multimedia conceptual artist Shahab Fotouhi and Rozita Sharafjahan (the founding curator of Azad Art Gallery). The remaining two red dots stood for works by photographers Shirin Aliabadi (1973–2018) and Solmaz Shahbazi (b. 1971). The smaller room to the right of the garage, Ghasemi's studio, now doubled as a changing room for the models. The gray dot in front of the stairwell indicated Ghasemi's position during the show—to block any attempt by the morality police to interrupt the event—while the yellow dot outside the front yard indicated the position of his father, who played the same role. In another slide, Ghasemi alluded to "four encounters with the [morality] police" at one of his curated exhibitions in Azad Art Gallery (fig. 4.5, left slide).

In addition to the dots indicating people and artworks, a gray Pac-Man figure represented a "surprise guest" performance by Shahab Fotouhi, who came into the gallery with his face covered by a gas mask to present a history of Tehran through the works of Iranian photographer Bahman Jalali (1944–2010).[45]

This method of concealing persons and events reflects Ghasemi's tactical approach to discussing the difficulties of exhibiting art in Iran. One

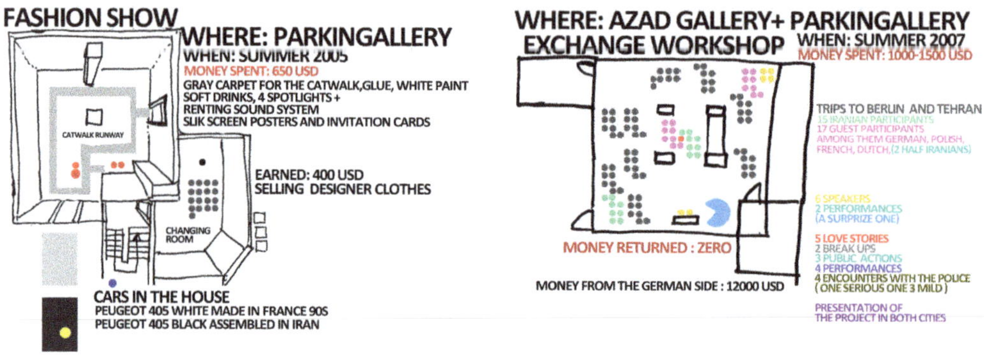

FIGURE 4.5 Left: Axonometric projection of Parkingallery during a fashion show. 2005. Parkingallery, Tehran. Right: Floor plan of Azad Art Gallery during an exhibition with Pac-Man's titular character in blue. 2007. Azad Art Gallery, Tehran. Drawings by Amirali Ghasemi.

can assume that he positions himself as the player who controls the character Pac-Man, with the dots representing the "power pellets," monsters, and ghosts. The titular character must eat all the other characters inside an enclosed maze while avoiding four ghosts. The backdrop music of the video game sounds a bit like the repetitive sounds of police sirens. Pac-Man's maze-like environment is full of obstacles as well as opportunities, requiring a state of heightened awareness to avoid obstacles and seize opportunities. Indeed, the Pac-Man environment is an apt metaphor for the challenges of curating across public and private spaces.

. . .

A good curator, according to a widely cited article by Craig Burnett, is one who has the capacity to become invisible, allowing artists and audiences to engage with each other without being aware of the presence of a mediator.[46] Perhaps Mahmoud Bakhshi (b. 1977) had this so-called invisibility in mind when he dared to conduct an unusual curation that gave new meaning to the concept of an exhibition space. As mentioned earlier in this chapter, Bakhshi is known primarily for his artistic appropriation (*azan-e khod sazi*) of the Islamic Republic's propaganda materials such as flags and insignias (e.g., *Tulips Rise from the Blood of the Nation's Youth* or *Az khoon-e javanan-e vatan laleh damideh*, 2008), In the summer of 2007, however, he turned Fereydoun Ave's alternative art space, 13 Vanak Street, into a solitary confinement cell.

The project was inspired by the clampdown on the Iranian journalists by President Mahmoud Ahmadinejad's government. Titled *Solo Show*

(*Namayeshgah-e enferadi*), the work mocked the surge of imprisonments, using a safe word that means both a solo show and solitary confinement (*zendan-e enferadi*), the shorthand for both being *enferadi*.[47] For one full week, the artist locked himself inside the gallery, surviving on bottled water and starvation rations. During this time, he had no contact with the outside world.[48] No audiences were invited in, and the only clue an exhibition was in progress was a poster in the display window of the gallery. Artist Arash Hanaie (b. 1978) photographed the display for the whole seven days Mahmoud was locked inside.[49] This is the only document indicating the "confinement" of the artist. Bakhshi said:

> No one could believe it. Everyone thought I was faking the whole thing. But in truth I was in there for all those days. At first, I thought of projecting my daily confinement via a live video camera on a screen at the gallery's display window, so passersby could see me in there; but this would not have done justice to the nature of solitary confinement in Iran. When journalists, artists, and intellectuals end up in these cells, no one hears about them. There are no pictures or footages. In truth, the inmates disappear from the face of the earth, provoking rumors about their possible death.[50]

In capturing the true essence of solitary confinement, Bakhshi was also inspired by Franz Kafka's "A Hunger Artist" ("Ein Hungerkünstler," translated in Iran as *Honarmand-e gorosnegi* or "The Artist of Hunger").[51] The short story begins by describing a "hunger artist," who performs in a cage for spectators, attended by a team of watchers to make sure that he does not cheat. Despite these precautions, and to the annoyance of the artist, some still suspect him of eating in secret.

The artist is also infuriated by the forty-day limit imposed by his producer, which prevents him from fasting for an indefinite period. In the end, not even the artist himself keeps count of the days of his fast. Completely ignored, he starves to death. In interpreting this tale, critic Maud Ellmann argues: "It is the public gaze that keeps him visible, however ruthlessly he wills his flesh to disappear, and it is only when he is deprived of this surveillance that he dies. The moral seems to be that it is not by food that we survive but by the gaze of others; and it is impossible to live by hunger unless we can be seen or represented doing so."[52]

Similarly, Bakhshi reveals strange and undeniable affinities between the labor of starvation and the birth of art, between perceptibility and indiscernibility. Regarding the visibility of the art and the artist, Bakhshi remarked,

"I spent most of the early stage of my career in my studio, which was the basement of my parents' house. Having my first solo show in a formal art gallery seemed like walking naked in public; it even felt a bit flashy."[53]

While Bakhshi's *Solo Show* was a way for him to subtly criticize the politics of President Ahmadinejad's government toward writers, journalists, and artists, it was also an exercise in questioning regimes of visibility and invisibility in Iran. Through his *Solo Show*, Bakhshi seemed to ask important questions about the place of art in Iranian society: "What is more detrimental to an artist in Iran, visibility or invisibility? Starvation or financial fulfillment?"[54] These questions mark the power of *artful curation* in and out of conventional spaces. They also highlight the significance of an alternative art space that not only accommodated artworks with a subversive theme but also allowed the artist to challenge the very essence of the gallery as a space for exhibiting art.

Bakhshi's *Solo Show* helped set the tone for other artist-led curatorial practices that became highly political as the country entered a tumultuous period. Recall that the 2009 Iranian Green Movement reached a climax with the civil unrest that followed the Iranian presidential election. As protesters demanded Mahmoud Ahmadinejad's removal from office, his challenger, Mir Hossein Mousavi, was placed under house arrest, and many of his supporters were silenced, among them artists who had been involved in his campaign.

Just as 13 Vanak was turned into a solitary confinement cell, another alternative art space, Azad Art Gallery, became the site of an "invisible theater"—its boldest exhibition to date, though there is no record of it on the gallery website. Conceptual artist and architect Shahab Fotouhi, in collaboration with graphic designer Farhad Fozouni (b. 1980), created a performance art project titled *By the Horses Who Run Panting* (*Ghasam beh asbani keh nafashayeshan beh shomareh oftadeh*, 2009, a reference to chapter 100 of the Qur'an, *al-Adiyat* or "The War Horses That Run Swiftly," in which there is a warning about the unveiling of one's secret thoughts on Judgment Day) that was shown from June 6–10, 2009, in the week before the troubled election.[55] The performance was a direct engagement with Mousavi's campaign managers. Mousavi's long career as an artist and architect, coupled with his more open-minded and democratic views, made him a favorite among artistic communities across the country.[56] For this performance, Fotouhi and Fozouni covered the gallery with posters and banners, but these were not typical campaign materials, in that they had no textual

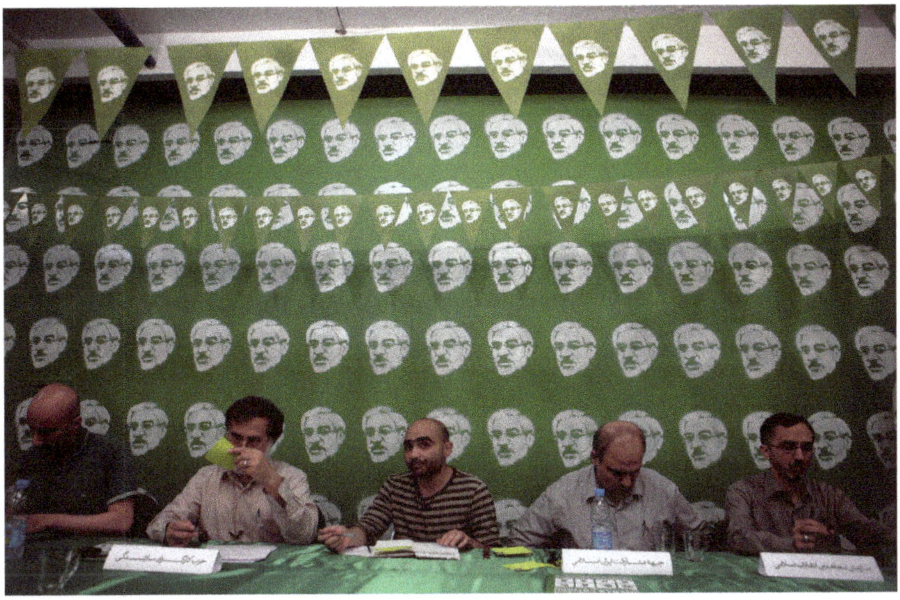

FIGURE 4.6A Shahab Fotouhi in collaboration with Farhad Fozouni, *By the Horses Who Run Panting* performance. 2009. Azad Art Gallery, Tehran. Photograph by Newsha Tavakkolian. Courtesy of Shahab Fotouhi.

substance or propaganda value. A small selection of paintings by Mousavi himself animated other walls of the gallery. To bypass the regulations that prevented art institutions from intervening in political affairs, Azad exploited a new piece of legislation that allowed private businesses to use their premises for political campaigns. The art gallery closed its doors temporarily and reopened as an actual campaign headquarters for Mousavi.[57] Transforming its function overnight, it became a space of intense political debate. The morality police turned up on the day of the opening to make sure that all the authorizations were in order and the "show" went ahead as scheduled.

On the first day of the show, Fotouhi moderated a discussion involving key figures from Mousavi's main campaign headquarters (*setad-e markazi*). Four of these were prominent politicians, including Mohammad Atrianfar from the Party of Executives of Construction of Iran or PECI (*Hezb-e kargozaran-e sazadegi-e Iran*), Hamid Reza Jalaiepour from the National Participation Front (*Jebheh mosharekat-e melli*), Abdollah Naser from the Islamic Revolution Fighters (*Mojahedin-e enghelab-e eslami*), and Shahab Tabatabaie from the Youth Organization of the Presidential Elections Headquarters for Mir Hossein Mousavi (*Setad-e javanan-e 88*) (fig. 4.6a).[58]

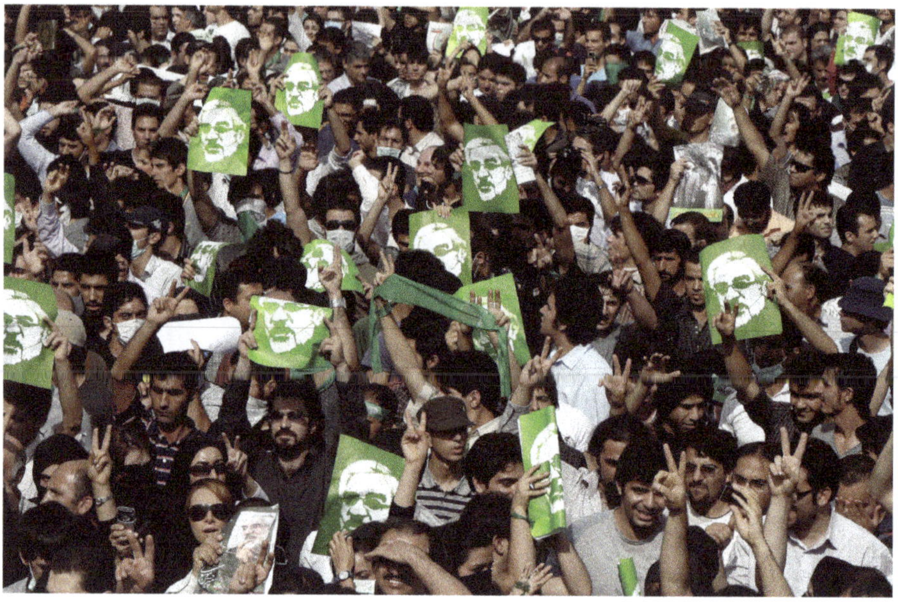

FIGURE 4.6B Pro-Mousavi rally, Monday, June 15, 2009. Tehran. Rally posters designed by Farhad Fozouni. Photograph by Abedin Taherkenareh. Courtesy of Shahab Fotouhi.

Just two days after the end of the show, all hopes for Mousavi's election would be shattered.

During the spontaneous demonstrations that followed the election, Fotouhi handed out some two thousand extra copies of the posters made originally for the show to random people on the street. The distribution of these posters—basically stenciled images of Mousavi in green—was extensively photographed by journalists who documented the pro-Mousavi rallies around Tehran. In this way, posters for an art exhibition lived on to become iconic images of one of the most important political events in the modern history of Iran (fig. 4.6b).

We may posit that this performance was a form of "invisible theater," to borrow again from the Brazilian theater expert Augusto Boal, who often enacted theatrical performances in a place where people would not normally expect to see one, such as in the street or a shopping center. In Boal's projects, performers disguised the fact that it was a performance, thus leading spectators to view it as a real, unstaged event. Here Fotouhi reversed the working of the invisible theater by turning a gallery into a mundane place and by bringing nonartistic actions into an art space.

One year after the presidential election, Fotouhi and Mahmoud Bakhshi performed a mock version of a debate (*monazereh*) between Ahmadinejad and Mousavi, held again at Azad Art Gallery. Fotouhi and Bakhshi each sat on a chair with a toaster between them to time the speech of each "candidate." They read from a printed version of the actual presidential debate. The reproduction of this debate was confusing, the timing of the presentations deliberately awkward. It was never clear who was talking, "Mousavi" would read "Ahmadinejad's" words, and vice versa. Fotouhi confirms that a conscious decision was made not to document the mock debate. The artists even warned viewers not to take any photographs.

According to Fotouhi, the idea of the mock debate was influenced by the Brechtian distancing effect (*faseleh gozari-e brechti*), also called strangeness in Jacques Rancière's characterization of effective political art.[59] More commonly known as the alienation or estrangement effect (*Verfremdungseffekt*), the distancing effect is a performance concept indicating "playing in such a way that the audience was hindered from simply identifying itself with the characters in the play. Acceptance or rejection of their actions and utterances was meant to take place on a conscious plane, instead of, as hitherto, in the audience's subconscious."[60] Brecht conceived of the distancing effect not only as an aesthetic technique but also as the political responsibility of theater. By compelling his viewers to ask questions about the artificial environment and how each individual element correlated with real-life events, Brecht gave them an active role in the production of the play. In doing so, he hoped that viewers would be able to "distance" themselves emotionally from issues that necessitated an intellectual engagement. Similarly, in enacting the presidential debates, Fotouhi pushed his audience to intellectually understand the dilemmas of the presidential candidates, and he wanted the wrongdoing that produced these predicaments to be exposed in his mock plot. By being "distanced" emotionally from the characters and the action on stage, Fotouhi wanted the audience to reach a level of intellectual empathy. In theory, while alienated emotionally from the action and the characters, they would then be empowered on an intellectual level both to analyze and perhaps even to try to change their world—Brecht's social and political goal as a playwright. By producing what Rancière calls "a sensory form of 'strangeness,'" developing "an awareness of the reason for that strangeness," and mobilizing "individuals as a result of that awareness," Fotouhi's projects about the 2009 election and the Green Movement evoke Rancière's definition of "critical art," as that which "aims to produce a new perception of the world, and therefore to create a commitment to its transformation."[61] Indeed, many onlookers and critics, notably art critic Daria Kirsanova, saw Fotouhi's Green Movement projects as a prime example of politics as art and art as politics, noting, "Fotouhi reconfigured the fabric of the sensory experience of a gallery goer," and as such, "despite the failure of the demonstration to produce a dramatic change in the Iranian political system and its ideological direction, the Green Movement still managed [to] re-configure . . . the perception of the political texture of society."[62]

. . .

As shown by the examples of Fotouhi's performances, Azad Art Gallery granted artists ample freedom to change the meaning and function of an official gallery. According to art critic Mohammad Bagher Ziyayi (b. 1949), Azad Art Gallery avoided imposed challenges (*chaleshhay-e tahmili*) in favor of more provocative engagements with space.[63]

In 2010, in *Come Caress Me* (*Bia navazesham kon*) artist Amir Mobed (b. 1974) turned Azad into a shooting range, with the shielded body of the artist placed in front of the shooters/viewers who targeted him with a pneumatic rifle, from three suggested firing lines marked on the floor as *Hate you*, *Like you*, and *Love you*, respectively, where hatred was the farthest from and love the closest to the target.[64] That same year, conceptual artist Neda Razavipour (b. 1969) turned the gallery into a streetscape, inviting professional graffiti artists and viewers to paint graffiti art on the gallery walls. Razavipour addressed the oppressive atmosphere of the post–2009 Green Movement, when the color green was purged from city walls, along with personal expressions. Titled *Alice in the City* (referencing *Alice's Adventures in Wonderland*), Razavipour reflected on the political underpinning of the work: "Spring 2010, more than ever, I thought that I was living in a . . . wonderland. Green painting was replaced by black or white color on the city walls. Slogans and political graffiti that were forbidden, and [at] high risk, covered walls and facades. *Alice in the City* was like one week of therapy, with graffiti artists and visitors invited to express themselves, over and over, layer by layer" (fig. 4.7).[65]

The post–Green Movement period coincided with curatorial strategies that reflected a desire to give a home to sensitive subjects that could not be displayed publicly, even if this entailed a challenge to the function of the gallery or a transformation of its physical space. There was also a renewed interest in granting artists the right to mourn. In May 2020, just a few months after the events of the Green Movement, Kourosh Golnari was invited to participate in the *Second Imagination* (*Khallaghiyyat-e dovvom*) group sculpture show at the Farvahar Gallery on Tehran's posh Jordan Street. Better known for his sculptures and commitment to national traumas, Golnari

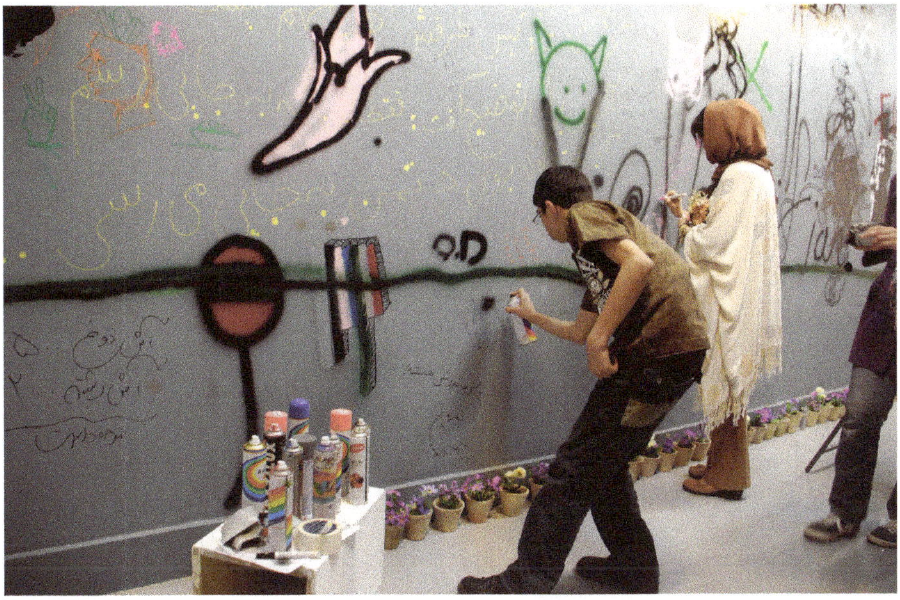

FIGURE 4.7 Neda Razavipour, *Alice in the City*. 2010. Azad Art Gallery, Tehran. Photograph by Azad Art Gallery staff. Courtesy of Neda Razavipour.

engaged here with critical spatial practice. Not content with the layout of the gallery itself, he sought other possibilities on the grounds of the property.

At the back of the gallery, he found a small basement storage space, 2.5 by 6 square meters, that had not been used for decades. It was windowless, damp, dark, and filled with spider webs, as Golnari recalled a decade later.[66] After installing metal bars along two sides of the dark space, to give it the feel of a prison, he placed two rows of six burning candles behind the bars, along with small plates of salt, and books of philosophy and accounts of historic persecution, such as Shahrokh Maskoob's *Mourning for Siavash* (*Soog-e siavash*, 1971), a modern take on the unjust killing of a heroic figure from Ferdowsi's tenth-century epic, *Shahnameh*. These objects were placed on the floor, as though in the presence of six political prisoners, who themselves were absent from the installation. The arrangement was coupled with the sound of dripping water, evoking water torture.

The space was tomb-like, and so tight only one person could enter at a time. Uncomfortable to experience, it heightened the anxieties and frustrations that characterized the mood of the times. Mockingly titled *Feast* (*Ziyafat*), the work commemorated all those who were harmed during the Green Movement (fig. 4.8).[67]

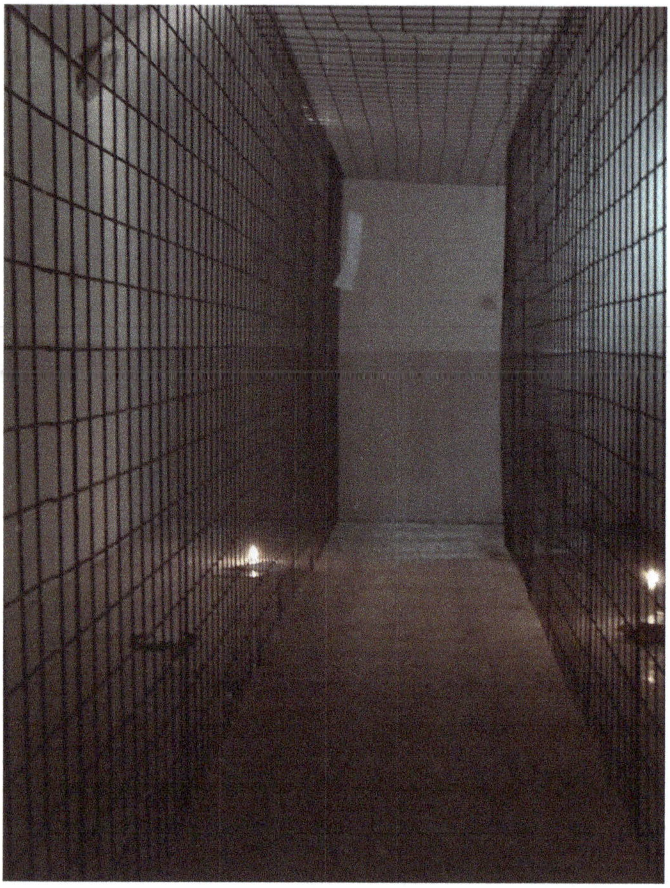

FIGURE 4.8
Kourosh Golnari, *Feast* installation. 2010. Farvahar Gallery, Tehran. Photograph by Kourosh Golnari.

Once again, similar to the *kolangi* projects featured in chapter 1, the artist and the gallerist were obliged to cut short the display because of its unconventional space and undercurrent of political references. Also akin to the *kolangi* projects, the site of this project was not directly related to the artwork made by Golnari. The primary concern of the artwork was to assert the right to mourn a collective traumatic event. To do this, Golnari subverted the conventional gallery as institution. Not finding the formal precincts of the gallery a legitimate setting for a particular form of artistic expression, he turned to more covert spaces. This kind of sentiment was particularly widespread after the Green Movement. It is no surprise that, at this juncture, showrooms with "trusted" audiences came to play an important role in ensuring time and space for such curatorial activities.

. . .

For many, the term *showroom* suggests an aura of a commercial art space for a select audience of wealthy connoisseurs and art dealers. In Tehran, however, this category also encompasses daring and highly intellectual examples. One of them is the Igreg Art Studio (or Y Art Studio), known among the artist community as a showroom and one of the few places that has shown and sold partial-nude works, such as the 2009 *Resurrected Series* (in Persian, *sansoor*/censorship series) by Katayoun Karami (b. 1967). Once again, invitations for these shows go to a limited, "trusted" audience.[68] All are marketed as private (*khosoosi*) events (fig. 4.9).

Posters and invitation cards for these private art events feature an axonometric of the gallery space—an indication of the significance of the spatial agency of the venue. The founder and director of the Igreg Art Studio, Ayda (Lili) Vakilian (b. 1974), launched the gallery on posh Gandi Street in 2010.[69] From early on, it sought to provide a space for artists to present artworks that could not be shown in conventional galleries and museums, due

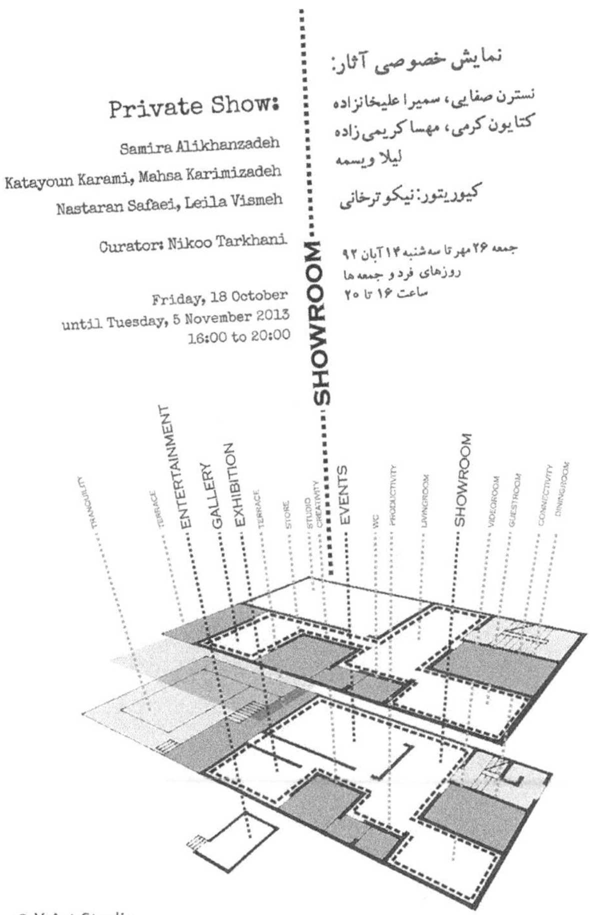

FIGURE 4.9
Private invitation card. 2013. Igreg (Y) Art Studio, Tehran. Design by Y Art Studio. Courtesy of Ayda Vakilian.

to government censorship. Vakilian notes that many artists in Iran are habitual self-censors. They produce art in a society and culture that does not appreciate directness, and "even if we put the regulations of the government aside, there are still social norms that prevent the artists from fully expressing themselves and being open about certain subject matters such as the nude or half-nude human body, transgender people, girls with provocative hairdos, and presentations of mixed-gender get-togethers."[70]

Igreg was set up to operate like a private assembly, and although Vakilian secured permission from MCIG, she did so under her own name rather than the Igreg (Y) Art Studio, in part because Igreg is French and the MCIG automatically rejects galleries with foreign names. More importantly, registering under her own name allowed Vakilian to be more flexible with the space. Like a nomad curator, she could move the space of the gallery if she deemed it appropriate—and, indeed, it was later moved to a downtown location. Private gatherings were restricted to "trusted" and select invited audiences, and as a result no one bothered Vakilian during the decade she successfully ran the gallery.

Rather than viewing her activities as political, Vakilian sees them as a kind of ethnographic examination of Iranian society. This is not the kind of "ethnographic turn" criticized by art historian Hal Foster, who coined the term. For some, the whole process of examining a community is a "self-fashioning" endeavor that makes "the artist [a] cultural authority" and "remakes the other in neo-primitivist guise,"[71] reminiscent of colonial-era white male ethnographers.[72] Neither is it of the kind art critic Grant Kester calls "abusive appropriation of the community for the consolidation and advancement of the artist's personal agenda."[73] Instead, it is an exercise in understanding the limits of censorship and self-censorship. These projects frequently offer fruitful content for subsequent discussions among artists, curators, and even ordinary members of the community.

Shielded by the "private" circumstances that granted her relative freedom, in 2011 Vakilian curated *Irma*, which was perhaps one of the most provocative group exhibitions of recent times. When asked about the significance of the choice of the name Irma, Vakilian shrugged it off as inconsequential. However, it did not take long for me to make a connection with the widely celebrated film *Irma khoshkeleh* (Pretty Irma), the dubbed version of *Irma la Douce,* a 1963 American romantic comedy starring Jack Lemmon and Shirley MacLaine, directed by Billy Wilder. Lemmon is the honest police officer, Nestor, and MacLaine is Irma, the most popular hooker in a

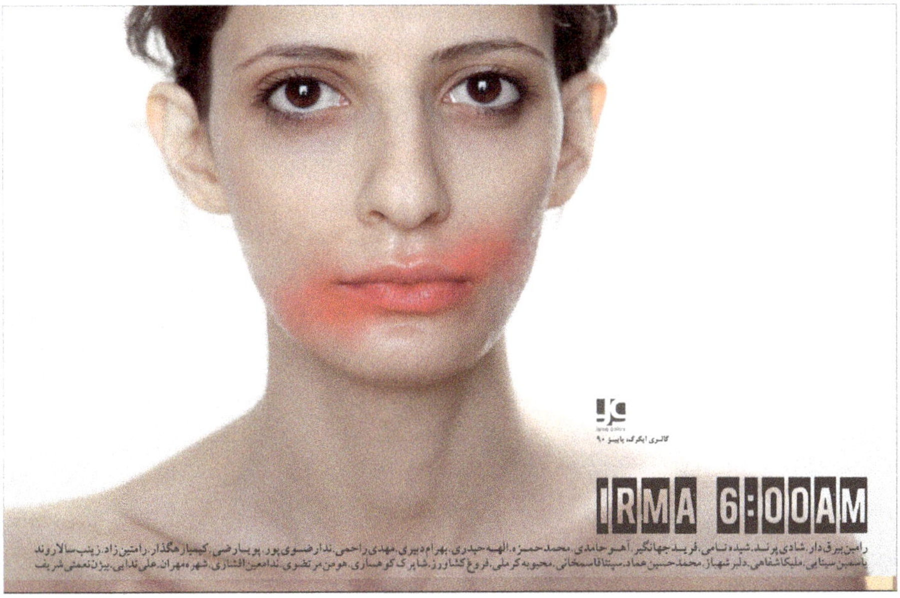

FIGURE 4.10 Poster of *Irma* exhibition. 2011. Igreg (Y) Art Studio, Tehran. Design by Y Art Studio. Courtesy of Ayda Vakilian.

street of prostitutes. The story revolves around the many ways Irma's sex labor defines the fate of not only Nestor but other men in the area around the central fresh food market of Paris, Les Halles.

Tacitly conjuring the story of *Irma la Douce*, Vakilian picked a female model of her choice and sent her to thirty selected male and female artists (fig. 4.10). Vakilian asked them to make art based on her, and they were all given the freedom "to do whatever type of work they envisaged." The model was described by Vakilian as a *zan-e asiri* (*asiri* woman; a word in *modern Persian literature* that often refers to a young woman who is attractive and present but unattainable).[74] Vakilian's curatorial statement for the participating artists summarized the project in these words:

> Irma is a phenomenon. Irma emerges and then turns into an artwork. At 6 o'clock in the morning, on an ordinary day, your doorbell rings; a silent, gorgeous, tall girl enters the room holding a note with your name and the date of that day on it. You have a day to create an artwork . . . which may be different from all your previous works. Due to . . . cultural restrictions, the travels of Irma must be pre-planned. Although I had hoped for unexpected encounters between you and Irma, I had to inform you of the exact time she would show up at your doorstep. We are not a nation of [spontaneity]; instead, we want

> everything pre-planned. . . . To create the artwork, you will need your own tools and materials. . . . Irma is a raw material. . . . You'll have Irma to yourself. . . . She will be with you for a while. Some weeks later . . . Irma will be reproduced multiple times. We will then examine the reproductions of the Irma phenomenon![75]

In this way, Irma is introduced as a "nomadic subject," in feminist philosopher Rosi Braidotti's sense of the term, as that which allows "mov[ing] across established categories and levels of experience: blurring boundaries without burning bridges."[76]

Additionally, like Billy Wilder's *Irma*, Vakilian's Irma functions as an agent, defining the fate of every artist whose home she visits. They may get caught by the morality police; they may become wealthy because of the sale of their Irma-inspired art; they may find true love in Irma. A woman, as such, determines the economic and moral underpinnings of a society. The choice of the character, coupled with the curatorial strategy, also calls to mind Marina Abramović's *Rhythm 0* (1974)—a six-hour performance in Studio Morra, Naples, in which Abramović stood still while the audience was invited to do to her whatever they wished, using objects such as scissors, a scalpel, nails, a metal bar, and a loaded gun.

The purpose of Abramović's piece was to find out how far the public would go: "What is the public about and what are they going to do in this kind of situation?"[77] Similarly, Vakilian tested her artists: "I wanted to know how far they could go with the concept, and ironically none of them did anything provocative. As I had predicted, they all remained within the confined boundaries of artistic expression in Iran; no one had a bold (*jasooraneh*) approach; they all respected the boundaries; no one portrayed Irma nude or did anything out of the ordinary."[78] Vakilian concluded that this was proof of the simple fact that we "reflect" (*baztab*) what the regime and the traditional culture wants us to reflect. In other words, the society has seemingly been numbed by the laws and regulations, and most people are unable or unwilling to break the boundaries. Cautiousness (*mohafezeh kari*), according to Vakilian, is a fact of life in Iran.

Vakilian's showroom, Igreg, prudently expanded its boundaries, beyond its address on Gandhi Street. While the making of *Irma* took place in multiple covert locations (i.e., artists' private homes), the outcome was brought back to Igreg. We may thus conclude that Vakilian's private curatorial practices, described by her as *mahfel-e khosoosi* or private assembly, are probably among the boldest undertaken by curators in Iran; although confidential and clandestine, Vakilian's curation extends the definition of a private showroom with "trusted" audiences.

. . .

Parallel to the private assembly, there are daring curatorial strategies that call for public assembly or *patogh*. These public gatherings, too, often focus on sensitive topics, albeit in a subtler form. Since the beginning of the twentieth century, Iranian cafés have played an important role in fostering artistic cultures. Notably, Café Ferdowsi, across from the British Embassy, was a hot spot for leftist intellectuals. It was frequented by well-known poets, and although it was often male-dominated (the poets allegedly did not even allow their wives to accompany them), it constituted a sort of public cultural sphere. This café culture, otherwise known as *patogh* (hangout) culture, would persist into later periods, defining the ambience of many alternative art institutions. According to Tehran-based art historian Mohammad Reza Moridi (b. 1978), "most cutting-edge and alternative art movements in Iran were generated by artists who were *patogh-neshin* (hangout spot occupants)."[79]

Performance artist and curator Ali Ettehad (b. 1983) and his frequent collaborator, performance artist Nikoo Tarkhani (b. 1983), set up the Anahita Art Studio in 2009. Here they created a performance art series that was subtly critical of the apparent trend in Iranian visual arts toward making object-oriented work for sale in the commercial markets of Iran, the Gulf, and Western countries. By contrast, Anahita Art Studio sought to have a more lasting impact on audiences and ordinary people on the ground. Ali Ettehad, who is critical of the commodification of Iranian art in contemporary global art markets, turned to performance art to express the richness of Iranian art culture and the profound experience of living (*tajrobeh zisti*) in Iran, as opposed to shallow images that he more specifically refers to as "touristic encounters" or "pleasing to others" (*barkhord-e touristi va digar pasand*).[80]

In 2013, the Anahita Art Studio produced *1,001 Afternoons* (*Hezar-o yek asr*), "open projects for performing arts," conceived for public spaces. The events built on the tales of *One Thousand and One Nights*. In that classic work, the protagonist Shahrazad manages to delay her death by telling only a portion of a long series of enticing tales to the king, who, after discovering that his first wife had been unfaithful to him, decides to marry a new wife every day and then execute her the following morning before she has a chance to betray him. During the storytelling nights, the king falls in love with Shahrazad, marries her, and finally abandons his vengeful scheme. In a similar vein, *1,001 Afternoons* was designed to make the authorities "fall in love" with performance art.[81]

The location for the project was the Café Markof in the garden of the Qasr Museum (*Bagh-e moozeh Qasr*; see chapter 3), whose permanent collection Ettehad helped curate. The café (named after its designer, the Russian architect Nikolay Markov) had the potential to also serve as a gallery space for more experimental presentations. After securing permission from the authorities, the Anahita Art Studio invited ten artists to perform their pieces—a different one each Friday afternoon. The projects were wide-ranging, involving everything from pseudo-musical performances that remained merely at the level of tuning instruments to interactive painting. Notable among these was "Direct Negotiation" (*Mozakereh mostagheem*), an interactive painting project conceived by sculptor and art educator Mohsen Gorji (b. 1983).

The title was an allusion to the nuclear negotiations between Iran and the P5+1, and principally the United States, which were then still two years away from the historic deal of July 2015. Gorji invited ordinary café-goers to join in as spectators of a collaborative painting project performed by two well-known visual artists. The reference to Iran's nuclear negotiations remained unspoken throughout the show, and even stayed unspecified in the reviews of the event published in prominent local newspapers such as *Hamshahri* and *Honar va resaneh*.[82] Ettehad, the lead curator, was careful not to specifically mention the Iran-US situation. He told the media that while the project was playful in nature, it was also an indirect commentary on how attempts to open up new channels of constructive dialogue in the Iranian art world (indeed, in Iranian society as a whole) often ended unresolved and opaque.[83]

Aspects of the project, however, highlighted the difficult nature of the nuclear negotiations. The two artists had vastly different styles—like the polarized ideologies of Iran and the United States. While Saeed Ravanbakhsh (b. 1970) used traditional Iranian motifs, his counterpart Abdolhamid Pazooki (b. 1955) was known for his abstract expressionist paintings (fig. 4.11). The duo was asked to paint on a medium-sized upright pane of glass that divided the square table in front of them. Each was required to add layers of paint to their side of the glass to the point where they were unable to see each other at all, signaling the absence of understanding between Iran and the US. Moreover, the resulting thick and colorful glass canvas was dark

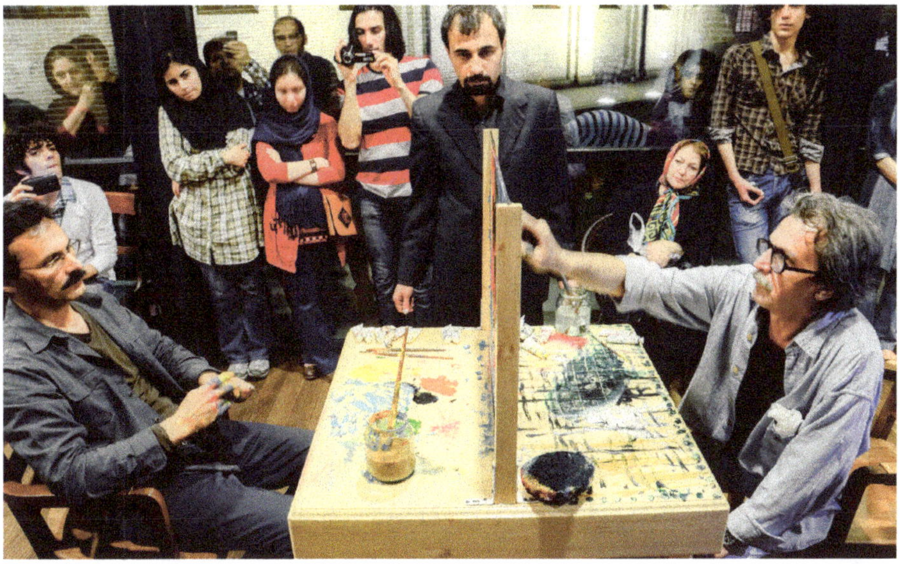

FIGURE 4.11 Mohsen Gorji, *Direct Negotiations* performance. Curated by Ali Ettehad on behalf of Anahita Art Studio. 2013. Cafe Markof, Qasr Museum Garden, Tehran. Photograph by Shauheen Daneshfar. Courtesy of Mohsen Gorji.

enough to create a mirror effect, leaving each painter with only a reflection of himself, as opposed to realizing the other. The square table also made it difficult for onlookers to gain proper visual access to the art as it unfolded in front of them. Indeed, this was nothing like the well-known Round Table Talks, a series of negotiations that took place in several countries of the Eastern Bloc between communists and the opposition that culminated in the downfall of the communist regimes and their transition to democracy.

Throughout, Gorji administered the performance by standing between the artists, offering tubes of acrylic paint and directly observing the process. While he may have seemed like a pit boss or a referee, he was actually there "to embody the people of Iran who are mere observers in such negotiations and have no role in decision-making processes. . . . They hang on passively," he noted, "to see their fate unfold in front of them, because they have no agency in all of these decision-making processes."[84]

After holding ten consecutive events there, security forces showed up and put a stop to the public performance, most likely because of the international media attention it received. *1,001 Afternoons* would not have been halted had it not been featured in *Deutsche Welle Farsi News*, and especially in the purportedly anti–Iranian regime GEM TV, which is a Persian-language entertainment satellite channel administered from Turkey. Though in theory the performances could have continued in the private homes of artists and friends, for Ettehad, what gave these projects their power was the fact that they were enacted in a privately funded space with authorization from the government. Consequently, the Anahita performances were put on hold.

In general, it proved difficult to sustain bold curatorial projects in public cafés. Thus, artists turned once more to official galleries, but this time relying on a curatorial tactic that helped generate subversive thoughts in subtle yet innovative ways.

Choreography as Critical Curation

By carefully directing, mobilizing, and rerouting the movement of the viewer across the exhibition space, alternative curation has helped establish not only new modes of viewing art but also innovative ways of interacting with space as well as generating dialogues about art and sociopolitical issues. Recall how through alternative practices of moving the body in space—*dérive* (playful drifting) and *détournement* (rerouting)—Situationist International members as well as their Iranian counterparts (described in chapter 3) aimed to enhance the alternative ways in which urban space could be seen, lived, and produced. In using the word choreography, I borrow a term from dance, aligning myself with theorists who have used the "dance metaphor" to show how just as in dance particular corporal movements may be characterized as either correct or improper, so too "mobile practices are policed, codified and choreographed at the same time as they can be mobilized as means of expression, improvisation and creativity."[85] Using the dance metaphor of choreography can also help us engage with curatorial practices beyond their final representational outcome. We can study curation in the time-space of the gallery and as it evolves and unfolds. In his book *Non-Representational Theory* (2007), geographer Nigel Thrift writes that "dance can sensitize us to the bodily sensorium of a culture, to touch, force, tension, weight, shape, tempo, phrasing, intercalation, even coalescence, to the serial mimesis of not quite a copy through which we are reconstituted moment by moment."[86] To Thrift, "The body is not just written upon. It writes as well."[87] Along the same lines, choreography, with itineraries of discipline and creativity, improvisation and implicit routines, focuses on the process of becoming. Choreography figures strongly in the ways in which artists and gallerists curate movement within the exhibition space.

. . .

Choreography in art was introduced to Iranian art circles during the Shiraz Arts Festival in 1972, when the Merce Cunningham Dance Company performed on the grounds of the ancient palace of Persepolis. The experience made a strong impression on both Iranians and the Cunningham dance troupe.[88] But choreography need not be limited to the professional dance movements; it is also central to the work of contemporary performance artists (e.g., Tania Bruguera, Tino Sehgal, and Jérôme Bel, to name but a few). The keynote here is navigation of audiences. In Iran after the revolution, any form of navigation of humans across space is usually associated with state ideology. Shuffling masses of people along the major streets in large cities is a quintessential image of the Islamic Republic's propaganda apparatus.

In state-sponsored demonstrations and political parades, people are carefully choreographed along main thoroughfares and around important monuments, notably the Azadi Tower, and these carefully choreographed arrangements are often designed for the media and the camera. The photographs of the shuffling masses continuously testify to the Iranian people's support of the state ideology. In these presentations, individuals seem to lose their agency, to paraphrase the German critic Sigfried Kracauer, who famously revealed the contradictions that were inherent in carefully choreographed presentations, including the conforming crowds in *The Triumph of the Will* (1935), a Nazi propaganda film by Leni Riefenstahl.[89]

The Islamic state's interest in choreographing swarms of people is deeply rooted in the Shiite processions that take place during Muharram—part of a set of rituals that also encompass the *ta'ziyeh* passion plays. These processions are highly celebrated by the Islamic Republic regime, but the connection between the Muharram commemoration rituals and the design of Iran's urban space goes back much further to the Safavid period, when wide streets or squares were made with niches in the walls facing them, allowing spectators to observe the events from a higher vantage point. As if the spectacle of the crowd was not enough, its image was mirrored through the looking glasses of the *nakhl*—a huge structure supposedly carried in procession by the miraculous agency of Prophet Mohammad's daughter, Fatima (in reality, of course, it was carried by the crowd) (fig. 4.12).[90] Since the Islamic Revolution, these ritualistic processions have become increasingly political. As anthropologist David Thurfjell has rightly argued, the

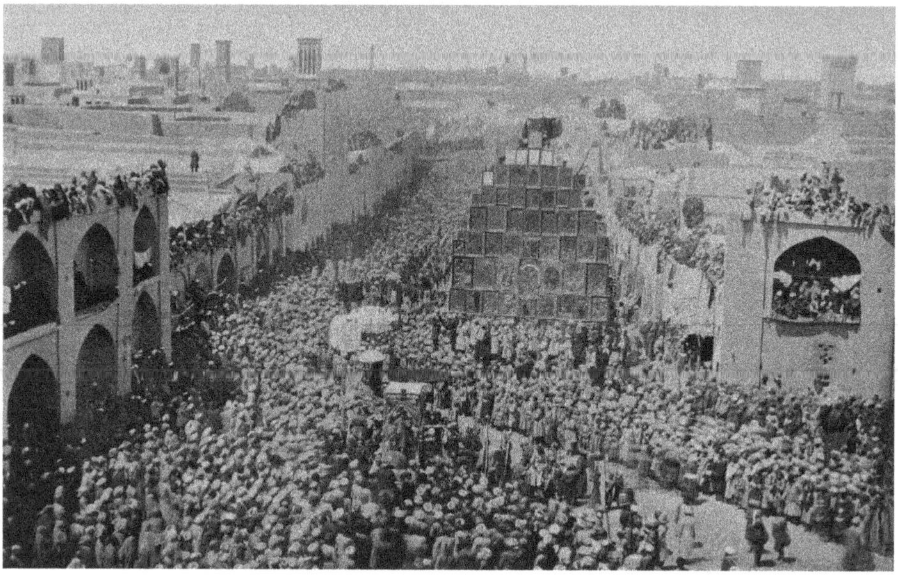

FIGURE 4.12 Nakhl with looking glasses surrounded by mourners in a square in Yazd. From Napier Malcolm, *Five Years in a Persian Town* (London: John Murray, 1905), 135. Photograph by Napier Malcolm. Courtesy The Newbury Library, Chicago.

sorrowful Shiite rituals "have become expressions of loyalty to the regime. And, hence, have become directly linked to the preservation of the present state of affairs and for the maintained authority" of the ruling elites.[91] As shown by the example of the Imam Hossein Square renewal project (see chapter 3), the Iranian state made a determined effort to configure Tehran's public spaces to accommodate Muharram ceremonies. And it is not only the actual physical space, but the whole timetable of urban activities that is organized around these religious rituals. In 2009, the MCIG initiated the "Adhan to Adhan" (*az azan ta azan*) program in the month of Ramadan. Movie theaters and food stands stay open all night, allowing the citizens to enjoy a complete nocturnal life, while also paying homage to the state-sponsored Ramadan religious rites. During the other months of the year, however, night life is much less vibrant, undermined by safety issues (particularly for women), a lack of well-lit streets or places for youth to gather, and scarcity of diverse entertainment venues.[92]

With this sociopolitical context in mind, the recent urge among artists to deliberately choreograph the movements of visitors to Tehran's upmarket galleries seems like an ironic take on the ways in which the state controls the movement of the body in public space. Weighing up regimes of subordination (*enghiad*) against authoritative agents, Iranian artists use choreographed performance to draw attention to these problematic relationships. Akin to Cuban artist Tania Bruguera's iconic performance work *Tatlin's Whisper #5* (2008), when she patrolled the space of the Tate Modern and controlled the audience's movement with two mounted policemen in uniform, the artists presented in the following pages use choreography to reflect on and challenge the ways in which people are organized, surveilled, emotionally mobilized, and made to fear.

. . .

On the evening of Friday, September 23, 2011, nearly five decades after the Shiraz Arts Festival choreographic performances, Iranians came to see a choreographed performance at Tehran's Aaran Gallery. Developed by Iraqi-American artist Wafaa Bilal at the invitation of the gallery director, Nazila Noebashari, *A Call* (*Baang*) commemorated the thirtieth anniversary of the start of the Iran-Iraq war. Although Bilal was denied a visa to Iran, Noebashari collaborated with prominent experimental theater director Hamid Pourazari (b. 1969) to realize his vision.

Eighty young male and female theater performers, dressed all in black or all in white, entered the basement gallery from an upper staircase while the Bomrani ensemble (formerly an underground music band) played marching music. Those dressed in white slowly made their way to a grave-like space, a deep, empty swimming pool in the backyard of the gallery, while those in black seemingly mourned them at the edge of the pool (fig. 4.13).[93] They did so in a gallery packed with an audience, and against walls hung with photographs by the Iranian photojournalist Jassem Ghasbanpour (b. 1963), who meticulously documented the war-torn southern city of Khorramshahr between 1981 and 1985.[94] Noebashari described the emotional engagement of the audiences:

> The way viewers stared at the silent performers, and how the performers, with their motionless gazes, forced the viewers to similarly stand still and quiet was . . . extremely somber. Remembering the effects and the costs of a senseless war led many to . . . watch with tears in their eyes. The borders of the artistic work were blurred, and art was physically and emotionally absorbed into life—viewers could identify with the performance and felt they were part of it. As one viewer later told me, this was probably the first time that people genuinely honored the innocent lives lost to war—a simple, yet extremely effective performance.[95]

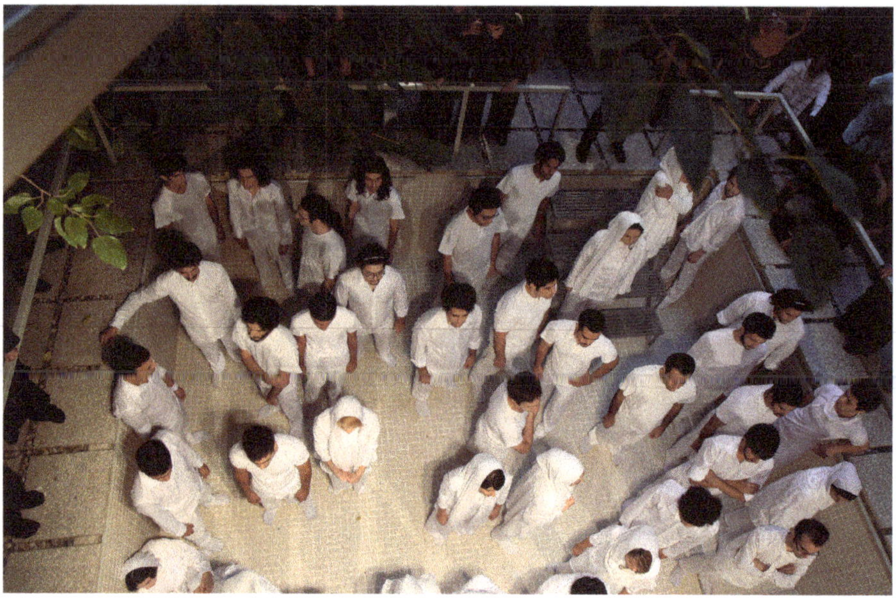

FIGURE 4.13 Wafaa Bilal et al., *The Call* performance. 2011. Aaran Gallery, Tehran. Photograph by Aliyar Rasti and Sassan Abri. Courtesy of Nazila Noebashari.

Noebashari revealed that this performance is probably the only commemoration of the Iran-Iraq war victims that was not initiated by the government. "We have all been affected by this war to varying degrees," she added, "but because the Islamic Republic has used this war to justify its existence, people tend to pay no heed to it."[96]

Bilal participated in the performance remotely, from a parallel opening at White Box in New York City, where the video of the choreography was streamed live. The mediated performance, according to Bilal, "enacted the dislocations, delays, and ruptures that war breeds."[97] The thirty-minute performance, presented for three days in a row, transformed the space of a visual art gallery into a mobile stage set. The actors moved, and the spectators moved along with them.

Above all, as both Noebashari and Bilal anticipated, the performance helped *de-politicize* the Iran-Iraq war not only in the minds of those who saw the performance but also among the artist community more generally. Entirely disregarding Iran's own culpability, the regime consistently characterizes the conflict as a "holy defense" (*defa'-e moghaddas*) and an "imposed war" (*jang-e tahmili*). At every opportunity the regime deploys this "victim narrative" to contextualize the hostilities of "foreign aggressors":

the United States, Israel, and other neighboring countries with opposing policies.[98] The war is also often used to justify internal policies that have no bearing on it at all. For example, the morality police have targeted women with loose *hijabs* on the grounds that they disrespect the thousands of martyrs who sacrificed their lives for them (and for the ideals of the Islamic Republic). The war is so caught up in the regime's propaganda apparatus, the right to mourn in a fitting manner, in public, seems to have been taken away from ordinary citizens.

The carefully choreographed performance at Aaran "called" for a different model of parading in public. Neither militaristic nor ritualistic, this performative march was silent. The marchers made no symbolic gestures, they only walked in sheer grief. The event culminated in a visually arresting gathering at the bottom of the empty swimming pool. By going underground, the performance evoked the bodies of the fallen soldiers wrapped in white cotton in mass graves below ground level. But they also conjured up the air raids when the bodies of Tehran's citizens were jammed into underground bomb shelters. Rather than promoting a public message about the war, the performance thus "called" the onlookers to remember their personal experiences, to connect with the victims on a personal and intimate level. Here, curators, performers, and all other involved parties came together to find a new way of commemorating the war—one in sharp counterpoint to the flamboyant military parades held during Sacred Defense Week (*Hafte defa'-e moqaddas*) in the last days of September every year.

A few months later, on December 21, 2012, another performance work at Shirin Art Gallery incorporated choreography as part of its curatorial tactic. This time, however, it was not the performers but the audiences who were carefully choreographed. Conceptualized and curated by the media artist, stage designer, filmmaker, and author Mohammad Parvizi (b. 1972), *Come Closer, Closer, Closer Than This? (Nazdiktar bia, nazdiktar, nazdiktar az in?)* featured multiple talking-head videos of Iranian actress Pegah Ahangarani (b. 1984) in a carefully designed series of temporary structures and scaffoldings. Along with a team of fifty designers and artists, Parvizi spent a month refurbishing the interior of the Shirin Gallery, which is an old Qajar house in the upscale Velenjak neighborhood in northern Tehran. The walls were covered with panels and decorative elements were plastered over to erase all visible signs of the old house. According to Parvizi, this was to reference a thought process: there were to be no distractions, no ornamentation, no signs of Iran's oriental past.[99]

Upon arrival, audiences were invited to take a series of built-in stairs that led to a mezzanine constructed of metal scaffolding, four meters above the gallery floor.[100] From there they saw two ultra-wide LED screens laid on the floor, projecting Ahangarani's talking head. The screens flanked a suspended cubical structure with a glass bottom, on which sat a disguised cello player (Athena Eshteiaqee, b. 1989), who for three hours a day played the 1890 *Élégie* by the French composer Gabriel Fauré. At certain junctures Ahangarani's words were literally reversed. When the LED screens froze, the music stopped too. The whole performance was constantly interrupted by such unexpected gestures.[101] After viewing the performance, the audience slowly found their way from the mezzanine into darker nooks, still hearing the voice of Ahangarani talking to herself.

Although it was not possible to fully make out Ahangarani's thoughts, her anxiety as a woman living in Iran was clear. The previous year, in July 2011, she had been arrested and interrogated by the law enforcement arm of the Islamic Republic of Iran (also known as the *NAJA* Police), and imprisoned for several months. A few days before her arrest Ahangarani had been scheduled to attend an event in Berlin, but she was denied permission to leave the country because of her participation in the 2009 Berlin Film Festival, where she had shared her thoughts on "social problems of the young generation" of Iranians with *Deutsche Welle*.[102] In the performance, Ahangarani spoke of unpleasant encounters with individuals who seemed like potentially abusive boyfriends, law enforcement interrogators, and other such threatening characters. These stories overlapped and intermingled as the viewer walked through the corridors carefully choreographed by the artist (fig. 4.14).

According to Parvizi, the whole purpose of the exhibition was for the viewer to get a taste of the political atmosphere *(fazay-e siyasi)* of Iran.[103] This disjointed and enmeshed narrative was inspired by the "stream of consciousness," a literary style used by authors such as Marcel Proust and Virginia Woolf, in which a character's thoughts, feelings, and reactions are depicted in a continuous flow, uninterrupted by objective description or conventional dialogue.[104] In designing his self-defined "labyrinth," Parvizi also consulted with Dr. Abdol Rahman Najl-Raheem (b. 1946), the renowned Iranian neurologist and translator of Paul Ricoeur and Jean Pierre Changeux's *What Makes Us Think? A Neuroscientist and a Philosopher Argue about Ethics, Human Nature, and the Brain* (2002). Najl-Raheem offered insights into how the brain functions when it encounters repeated content

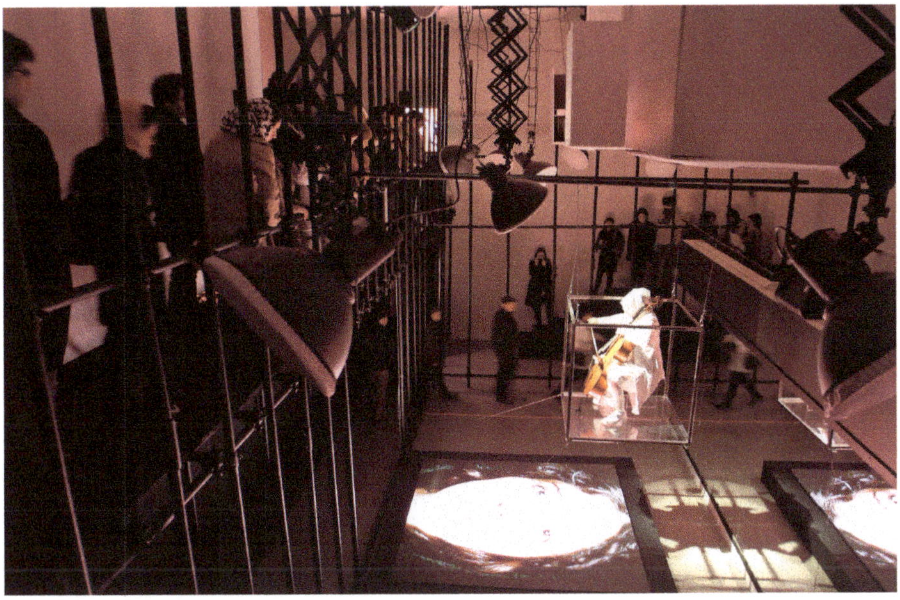

FIGURE 4.14 Mohammad Parvizi, *Come Closer, Closer, Closer Than This?* 2012. Shirin Gallery, Tehran. Photograph by Tahmineh Monzavi. Courtesy of Mohammad Parvizi.

or when it senses that it is trapped in a loop of narratives that overlap, replicate, and continue with no particular sense of closure.

By passing through Parvizi's labyrinth, the audience moved closer and closer to the Ahangarani's thoughts and feelings in a continuous excursion. Instead of following their own thoughts and conclusions, they were ensnared in the voice and thoughts of a female character.[105] The experience was visceral and intense. Both Ahangarani and Eshteiaqee reported anxiety, and on one occasion, Eshteiaqee had to be taken to the emergency room. Audiences also reported discomfort: some left soon after visiting, and others later reported that the show was one of the most difficult experiences of the Tehran art scene.[106]

Susan Sontag's *Regarding the Pain of Others* (2003) has been translated by a number of authors and published in Iran under the titles such as *Tamashay-e ranj-e digaran* (Viewing the pain of others) and *Nazar beh dard-e digaran* (Looking at the pain of others). Both of the translated titles suggest a connection between the economy of pain and modes of looking—themes of interest to Iranian artists, including Parvizi.[107] Parvizi echoed Sontag's sentiments when he asserted that his exhibition was "meant to be an open wound, an unfinished story."[108]

But in his attempt to establish a dialogue between the pain of the protagonist of his art and the viewers, he went beyond the realm of vision. He also generated an affective economy. By focusing on the facial features of Ahangarani, Parvizi shifted the attention from the realm of vision to the realm of touch. Parvizi accentuated the feelings that are not constrained by language but that are, in feminist philosopher Teresa Brennan words, "material, physical things" with "an energetic dimension" that can move nonverbally.[109] Thus, rather than communicating verbally, Parvizi takes us to the realm of the feel-able, carefully choreographing the bodies of his audiences to highlight tactile sensations, where emotions are registered at the surface of the monitors and by the bodies of the viewers.

Identifying with a woman's pain or frustrated life and thoughts in the Islamic Republic was the central theme of the exhibition, but this message surfaced in such an abstract way that it took the media and authorities a while to grasp its political connotations. During a phone conversation, Parvizi told me, "The life of my mind is none other than an underground existence (*zist-e zirzamini*)."[110] Instead of going underground in a physical sense, he "thinks" and "creates" in the underground and then finds ways to translate those thoughts into a form that is passable aboveground. Parvizi's desire for ambiguity is plausible. As art critic Nato Thompson writes, the quest for ambiguity is, essentially, the quest for individual freedom and thus "[a]ny discussion of political . . . art must begin with an acknowledgment of this basic instinct, which resides in the hearts of many artists and must be respected."[111]

Neither Parvizi nor the director of the gallery, Shirin Partovi (b. 1970), had secured permission for this exhibition from the MCIG. The performance was scheduled for twenty-five days, but in the face of threats from the authorities they decided to bring it to a close on the twenty-second day.[112]

. . .

Curation as a strategy to invoke critical encounters with space as well as to communicate sociopolitical issues through bodily engagements continues to live on in other exhibition spaces. A few months after Parvizi's exhibition at Shirin Gallery, on August 5, 2013, President Mahmoud Ahmadinejad was sworn in for a second term. Outside parliament, the police attacked crowds who had gathered to protest the inauguration, arresting many people. Against the backdrop of this chaos, Ahmadinejad called for national unity and repeated phrases from article 121 of the Iranian constitution, promising to dedicate himself "to serving the people and . . . [to]

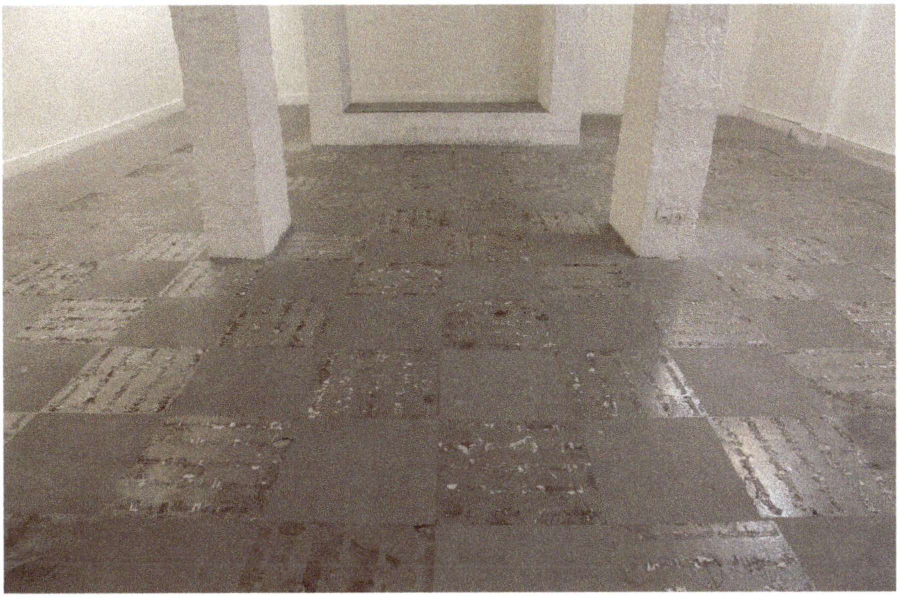

FIGURE 4.15 Katayoun Karami, *Good Thoughts, Good Words, Good Deeds*. 2013. Azad Art Gallery, Tehran. Courtesy of Katayoun Karami.

spreading justice and refraining from any dictatorship." Artist Katayoun Karami (b. 1967), who took part in the protest, was angered by the president's deceitful proclamations.

The thought of that dark day remained with Karami. Four years later, for the next election day, she created an installation based on article 121 in alliance with curator Rozita Sharafjahan at Tehran's Azad Gallery. Titled *Good Thoughts, Good Words, Good Deeds* (*Pendar-e neek, goftar-e neek, kerdar-e neek*), an ancient Zoroastrian threefold motto that sums up that religion's worldview, the project sarcastically "trapped" the visitors as they walked around the gallery. An architect by training, Karami had laser-cut the words of article 121 from mats coated on both sides with extremely sticky adhesive to trap rodents. The mats formed a checkerboard pattern that covered the entire gallery floor (fig. 4.15).

Whether "you walked on the empty modules or the ones filled with words, you could not escape the sticky mess of the floor; this was a metaphor for always being caught in the political predicaments," Karami told me, nearly eight years after the installation.[113] The idea, she said, "was to demonstrate the irony of the seemingly positive phrases that nonetheless led to devastation and death."[114] Indeed, beautiful presentation of shimmering Persian words on the floor had the incongruous power to irritate both in terms of their meanings as well as in the ways they "trapped" the viewer's feet. The words were hardly visible to the visitors at first; however, after many visits, the sticky pads became dark and more decipherable. The visitors, in turn, reluctantly carried home some of the sticky materials on their shoes, and by the end of the show the gallery's floor was completely damaged.

Karami, who is from a generation who has seen it all (i.e., the revolution, the Iran-Iraq war, the Green Movement, etc.), believes that engaging the body of the visitors in this way conveyed the collective discontent with Iran's political system. As Mehran Mohajer (b. 1964) writes in his review of the exhibition:

> This installation is not about seeing (*deedan*) but rather about *walking (rah raftan)*, the repetitive and mundane act of walking . . . with every step the walker doubts the next step; walking after a while becomes increasingly troublesome . . . in this way, walking, the most routine act of everyday life, becomes a conscious effort. . . . The installation carries a strong political message and the way the artist conveys this message is very subtle; it transpires through our own actions. . . . These sticky floors do not let us leave the space peacefully; perhaps this whole experience is a reminder that we need to take our deeds, thoughts, and words more seriously.[115]

The material space of the gallery (the floor) and the physical bodies of the viewers (their feet) meet and clash in this work, restructuring one another, and it is this restructuring, rather than a simple encounter between body and space, that makes the curated choreography of Karami so exceptional. Despite its political theme, the low-key installation did not cause any trouble for the artist or the gallery, but years later Iranian artists still remember it as one of the strongest politically themed shows in the aftermath of the Green Movement and Ahmadinejad's unpopular presidency. Indeed, like Parvizi, Karami capitalized on the power of subtlety in communicating dissent. Whereas these two artists used choreography to manage their audiences, Alireza Amirhajebi (b. 1970) choreographed his own body across the gallery.

The third annual festival of *30 Performances, 30 Artists, 30 Days* (*Si performance, si honarmand, si rooz*), was initiated by curator and theater expert Mohammad Rezaie Rad (b. 1966) and hosted by Taraneh Khosroshahi (b. 1974), director of the East Art Gallery (eventually shut down in 2017 due, allegedly, to its occasionally daring approaches).[116] The inaugural piece, on

September 26, 2013, was a forty-minute performance work, *Euphoria* (*Sarkhoshi*), by Alireza Amirhajebi (b. 1970), conceptual artist, musician, and translator of the works of the American Art Workers' Coalition (AWC) into Persian.[117] Amirhajebi, who studied at the Institut de Recherche et Coordination Acoustique/Musique, appropriately sees himself as a sound artist who produces avant-garde electro-acoustical art music, with a focus on the architectural characteristics of the venue in which he performs.

Here, Amirhajebi marked out with tape a six-square-meter area. Onlookers stood outside the tape, watching as Amirhajebi hauled his body over the delineated space, licking the floor—and sometimes an onlooker's shoe—and occasionally breaking for a cigarette.[118] The performance was accompanied by a piece from *Persian Surgery Dervishes* (1972) by Terry Riley, which is supposed to have evolved from Riley's lasting fascination with Rumi and Sufi devotional music. Riley's notable, innovative use of repetition provided the impetus for Amirhajebi's repetitive intervention on the gallery's floor. However, there is more to the tongue-wiping than just the repetitive act of cleaning the floor. The artist's own statement frames the work as a critique of the "putrid space" (*fazay-e mote'affen*) of art in Iran—a choice of words directly derived from the American conceptual artist Dan Graham.[119] Although Graham is best known for his two-way mirror pavilions that signify commercial store windows and consumer culture, it was his involvement with the AWC and his "open hearing" testimony on museum reform that captured Amirhajebi's imagination.[120]

The same concerns that surfaced in the work of American artists in the 1960s are evident among conceptual Iranian artists today, who are critical of the market-driven art atmosphere of Iran. Recall, for instance, the iconic 1973 "maintenance art" performances at the Wadsworth Atheneum in Hartford, Connecticut, by Mierle Laderman Ukeles, who washed and scrubbed the steps, entry plaza, and the floors inside the exhibition galleries. In this way, Ukeles elevated the tedious house chores associated with women to the level of art, and indirectly criticized the hierarchical system of labor and gendered relations in elite institutions of art.

Like many among her generation, Ukeles called for the deaestheticization and dematerialization of artwork as well as a critique of the art market. Similar messages regarding labor and the art market animated the performance by Amirhajebi. It is no surprise, then, that Amirhajebi finished his performance by saying to the audience: "Welcome to the art space of Iran. It's now clean!" The performance was meant to be seen as a preparatory act for the remaining twenty-nine performances that were scheduled at the East Art Gallery. The gallery was to be cleansed of its marketing-oriented grounds to make room for conceptual and thought-provoking art. Some onlookers interpreted it as a lovemaking gesture. As art historian Staci Gem Scheiwiller writes:

> The performance conveyed a facet of sensuality as the artist's tongue wiped the floor in strokes as if licking a human body, and then he dragged his own body all over the demarcated galley space. The mere act itself elicits visceral attraction and repulsion in any context, but probably even more so in Iran, where the public space is seen as so incredibly filthy that one would not even dare put his face near the floor in a public gallery, let alone use his tongue to clean it in an almost lovemaking gesture.[121]

Amirhajebi rejects any personal inclination toward presenting the taboo act of kissing and lovemaking in a public gallery. In an interview with me, he spoke of the difficulty of the work. Several times, the taste and the smell of the parquet wax nauseated him, but he resisted the urge to run for the bathroom.[122] Nonetheless, Amirhajebi appreciates the possible sensual reading by certain members of the audience (including Scheiwiller).[123] Indeed, licking, like kissing, evokes sensual connotations (fig. 4.16). Feminist philosopher Luce Irigaray described how the kiss alters the perception of the "kisser" through its capacity to make the "world grow so large that the horizon itself disappears."[124] While painful, the performance gave Amirhajebi an opportunity to "escape," to see the horizon expand, and to become one and the same with a space that he both detests and loves because of its potential for transformation from a market-oriented mentality to one that pushes us to think about the labor of intellectual art, tackling issues of the art market. Amirhajebi's horizon disappeared, and so he experienced what he calls "euphoria."[125]

In *Kissing Architecture* (2011), Sylvia Lavin develops the concept of "kissing" to describe "mutual attraction" between architecture and contemporary art—particularly multimedia installations. Examining works that embrace the viewer in powerful affects and visual sensory atmospheres, Levin explains that "a kiss is the coming together of two similar but not identical surfaces, surfaces that . . . deform when in contact, . . . a union of bedazzling convergence and identification during which separation is inconceivable."[126]

Amirhajebi's licking/kissing is likewise a statement about two surfaces coming together in a "a union of . . . convergence." In making affective

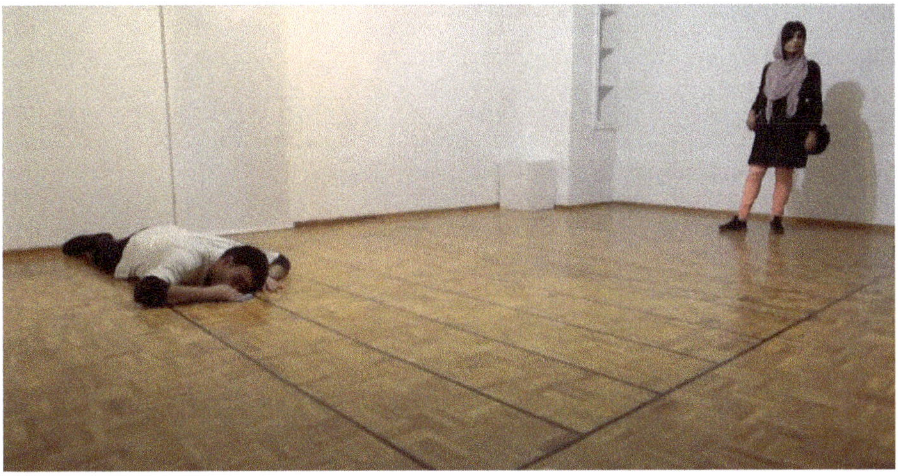

FIGURE 4.16 Alireza Amirhajebi, *Euphoria*. 2013. East Art Gallery, Tehran. Video capture by East Art Gallery staff. Courtesy of Alireza Amirhajebi.

gestures toward architecture, Amirhajebi's actions suggest to the viewer the lack of expression of human feelings in the public spaces of Iran. The work not only overlays itself onto architecture but also offers a way to understand the power of architecture as an artistic and intellectual medium, a process that has also captured the imagination of other artists who continue to transform the space of the gallery through choreography.

. . .

If moving the artist's body gave Amirhajebi a different perspective, a particular choreographic strategy of moving the viewers' bodies allowed another artist to shape the thoughts and feelings of his viewers. This approach to curation was taken up in 2016 by Peyman Shafieezadeh (b. 1983) in his solo exhibition *Negative Positive Space* (*Fazay-e manfi mosbat*) at the Etemad Art Gallery. The artist controlled his viewers' movements through scaffolding installed both inside and outside the gallery space. The poles were etched with calligraphy of revolutionary and Shiite slogans. The artist's choice of choreography to control the movement of his audiences allowed him to manage the ways in which the viewers saw his anamorphic drawings of prominent social and political figures in Iran, such as Ayatollah Khomeini and former presidents Ahmadinejad and Khatami, among others.

Anamorphic drawing is a technique that many viewers would have known through the iconic image of a distorted skull in Hans Holbein's *The Ambassadors* (1533). Rendered in anamorphic perspective, the skull is a visual puzzle as the viewer must approach the painting from high on the right side, or low on the left side, to see the form as an accurate rendering of a human skull. The skull was intended as a *vanitas* or *memento mori*, and the painting was supposed to hang in a stairwell, so that persons walking up the stairs and passing the painting on their left would be startled by the skull. Shafieezadeh's initial point of reference was not Holbein's iconic painting and the role that the skull and space play in understanding it. In fact, he was inspired by his daily encounters with two large portraits of Ayatollahs Khomeini and Khamenei hung at the entrance of the Grand Mosalla mosque of Tehran (The Imam Khomeini Mosalla). He said, "As I drove away, the portraits seemed distorted, as if they transformed into some abstract concept rather than signifying the powerful agents in the Islamic Republic. I thought of it as an allegory for the daily perception of the ideological underpinnings of the Islamic Republic itself, something between reality and imagination, between being and not being (*boodan va naboodan*)."[127]

Shafieezadeh's assessment of propaganda images is applicable to a whole host of sociopolitical underpinnings of everyday life in the Islamic Republic. The choice of scaffolding and the seemingly shoddy look of the exhibition captured what the artist describes as the *hey'ati*, "rushed style," a kind of temporary architecture inspired by traditional Shiite religious ceremonies. While associated with the ephemeral structures erected in conjunction with the annual mourning of the death of Hussein during the month of Muharram, the *heya'ti* style has become a defining characteristic of all rushed and temporary structures built by the Islamic Republic, especially for propaganda purposes during times of sudden turmoil. Consider, for example, the massive scale of the funeral ceremonies for General Qassem Soleimani in January 2020, and the speed with which they were put together, following his assassination in a drone strike authorized by the Trump administration.[128]

In a more abstract sense, Shafieezadeh's exhibition reflected on the ways in which people in Iran react to the propaganda of the regime. They abide by the rules, but they also ignore them. They give their consent to the regime's powerful agents by not reacting against their propaganda, but at the same time they deny any affiliation with the ideologies that keep these dominant figures in power. Indeed, life in Iran is a life in between "negative" and "positive" spaces. Commenting on the images of the Occupy Movement and the Arab Spring, art critic W. J. T. Mitchell writes, "Images can only come alive against a background. Every figure requires a ground, a landscape, or an environment in which it can appear and move."[129] So rather than images occupying the space of the media, the empty space, or the *negative space*

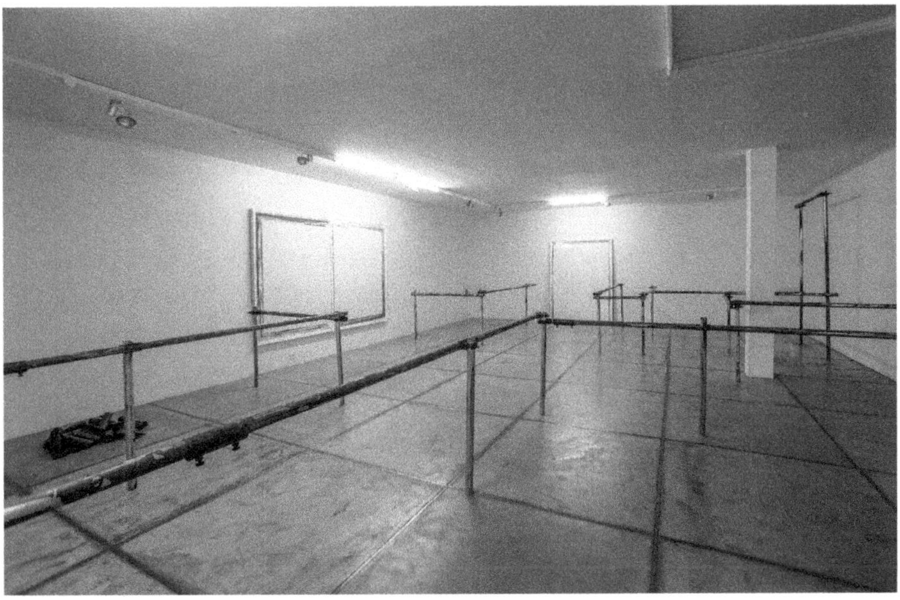

FIGURE 4.17 Peyman Shafieezadeh, engraving on aluminum pipes and distorted drawings at *Negative Positive Space* exhibition. 2016. Etemad Art Gallery, Tehran. Photograph by Etemad Art Gallery staff. Courtesy of Peyman Shafieezadeh.

of the background (e.g., Tahrir Square), was "the appropriate monument to the movement."[130]

Similarly, through careful choreography Shafieezadeh encouraged his viewers to contemplate the "background" or the "negative space" against which the propaganda drama of the Islamic Republic is rehearsed and "comes to life." Through controlled walking in the "background," the visitors both saw and did not see the political figures; at times they only encountered their own reflections in the glass covering blank canvases, whose very protagonists were compressed to the sides through anamorphic perspective (notice the white pictures on the gallery walls in fig. 4.17). By turning the gallery into a negative or background space, the artist transformed a commercial gallery into a space of contemplation and subtle political action. The minimalist and abstract character of the installation, combined with its apparent *heya'ti* style, meant that the exhibition did not raise a flag with authorities, who missed its political content.

. . .

This "activation" of the architectural space—as it is occupied in more sophisticated ways, engaged with ever more critically—is also evident in the work of theater experts. Hossein Tavazoni Zadeh (b. 1991), the founder of

Kariz Theater Group (*Gorooh-e te'atr-e kariz*), is a civil engineer by training, an architectural enthusiast, and a filmmaker.[131] Between 2015 and 2019, prior to his departure from Iran, he developed experimental theatrical projects that engage with architecture and urban space, inspired and guided by his professors, Azadeh Ganjeh (b. 1983) and Hamid Pourazari (b. 1968), both of whom experiment with unconventional performance spaces. Pourazari has directed plays in the storage rooms of the Bahman Cultural Center (*Farhangsaray-e Bahman*), while Ganjeh, as addressed in chapter 3, has performed mobile plays around Tehran public spaces, as well as on various floors of The House of the Artists (*Khaneh honarmandan*) and the TMoCA.[132]

When Tavazoni Zadeh's group performed for the Fajr Festival of University Theater Students, the spaces they engaged with were not the official performance sites or open-ended urban spaces, but rather dilapidated residential buildings from the early Pahlavi period. Tavazoni Zadeh himself grew up in one of the best-known of the early-Pahlavi housing projects, Chaharsad Dasgaah.[133]

Architectural historians inside Iran frame the architectural style of the early Pahlavi era as "suspended architecture," or *me'mari-e ta'lighi*. Tavazoni Zadeh is fascinated by how much this style speaks to his age group, otherwise known as *daheh shastiha* (roughly defined as a generation born in and around the 1980s).[134] Tavazoni Zadeh told me, "Like my generation, the suspended architecture of the Pahlavi era is somewhere between modernity and tradition; being Iranian and being European; being conservative and open, all at the same time."[135]

According to Tavazoni Zadeh, his generation has a peculiar relationship with space. Public and private are always separated; public life is restricted, while private life is not.[136] The generation that is torn between freedom and restriction, religiosity and secularism, thus finds a home in the early Pahlavi context, when these dichotomies began to be challenged by the modernization of the country. Indeed, as mentioned in chapter 1, many middle-class young people who have lived all their lives under the Islamic Republic feel a particular nostalgia for this "glorious past." Iran's early Pahlavi era is central to many publications, films, and TV series, including the popular drama *Shahrzad* (broadcast between 2015 and 2017).[137] Dozens of Instagram and Facebook pages are dedicated to recording Tehran's Pahlavi buildings before they completely disappear in the ever-changing landscape of development in contemporary Tehran.[138] But Tavazoni Zadeh's work was different from these rather sentimental engagements. Instead of picturing the past, he reinvented the mood of the spaces of the Pahlavi era.[139]

The difference between Tavazoni Zadeh's occupation of old buildings and earlier *kolangi* projects (see chapter 1) is highlighted by the fact that he did not only secure permission but he also deliberately selected locations in buildings that possess *shenasnameh* (literally, personal identification; a reference to buildings that have some historical significance, even if they are not listed in the official records of Tehran's cultural heritage).[140] While these dilapidated spaces were not the plateaus of the so-called Apartment Theater (*te'atr-e apartemani,* addressed in chapter 1), they nonetheless provided a novel opportunity to establish a more engaged dialogue with viewers and architecture, according to Tavazoni Zadeh.[141]

Theatrical engagements with domestic residential spaces are also rooted in the practices of Jerzy Grotowski at the 1970 Shiraz Arts Festival. For his play *The Constant Prince*, Grotowski chose the free-standing mansion, or *Kooshk*, within the historic Delgosha Garden. The recommendation came from Bijan Saffari (1933–2019), an architect and the chief director of Iran's first experimental theater, Theater Workshop (*Kargah-e Namayesh*). At the Delgosha mansion, the audience could watch, or in Grotowski's own words, "witness," the performance from the upper-floor verandas around the central courtyard that housed the main stage. They could also sit on the staircase opposite the stage.[142] Following in the footsteps of Grotowski's successful experimentation, Theater Workshop took their own play, *Suddenly* (*Nagahan*), to the same mansion. At the 1972 Shiraz Arts Festival, instead of limiting themselves to one location in the mansion, the actors appeared and disappeared in abrupt and "sudden" ways, in and out of the mansion's rooms, while staying in close proximity to their audiences.[143] The architecture itself seemed to become a protagonist in the play; the charming Qajar-era arches and intricate wall adornments "suddenly" appeared as significant as the actors moved in and out of these architectural elements.

Even under current rules and regulations, this unconventional form of theater creates situations in which the actors may have bodily contact with each other, or even with the viewer. According to Tavazoni Zadeh, however, they were never given a hard time by those who come to preview the play before its performance.

Tavazoni Zadeh's two-hour play *Narges* (Narcissus; first performed in May 2017) concerned the relationship between a man and a young woman, the eponymous Narges, who had been forced to marry as a minor, from their childhood up to the present day. The audience, limited to four people, were invited to enter the setting, an old, derelict house, and were given blue uniforms to distinguish them from the actors. The actors first seated them in a row of chairs, then took them with them as moved to different rooms and floors of the building.

In one scene, the female actor engaged a male member of the audience in a face-to-face interaction across a coffee table. She asked him about his interests; he admitted he loved poetry, so she asked him to read a poem, which he did from his social media page. When she asked him to write the poem, he wrote it on a wooden door in the corner of the room. In another scene, as the audience were led to the second floor, they passed a room in which a man was gently playing a traditional Iranian musical instrument. Instead of engaging with him, they only had caught a quick glimpse as they moved on. In addition to an intimate theatrical experience, the audience was also engaged in a cinematic sequence, all carefully choreographed around walls, staircases, windows, and doors.

Tavazoni Zadeh has studied how film directors such as Andrei Tarkovsky and Alexander Sokurov used architecture and space to convey meanings and establish a relationship with the audience. Translating this into his own work, he thinks of the viewer as a camera, following actors in the corridors, in the hallways, and even into small spaces like the bathroom. Before each of his plays in Tehran, Tavazoni Zadeh envisioned how they would record each scene. Sometimes he provided an opportunity for a wide shot, other times for a close-up, or for angled and lopsided views from above or below the staircase or the rooftop. According to Tavazoni Zadeh, many spectators described their experience as watching a film while they were physically moving.[144]

Before each play, Tavazoni Zadeh carefully examined the house and its possibilities for all kinds of mobile viewing. His way of looking at space from a spectator's point of view was inspired by the paintings of Edward Hopper. A particular source of inspiration is Hopper's 1939 *New York Movie*, in which viewers, due to their positioning at the back of the theater, at once see the screen, the backs of the audience, as well as a mysterious woman waiting in the hallway near the door of the auditorium. Because of her fancy shoes, Tavazoni Zadeh did not see her as an usherette, but says, "Lit by the lamp under which she stands, the seemingly bored woman suddenly becomes the centerpiece of the canvas."[145] Indeed, the loneliness and melancholy of the woman, in a theater that could sit hundreds, invites the viewer to identify with the piece on an intimate level. In a similar way, Tavazoni

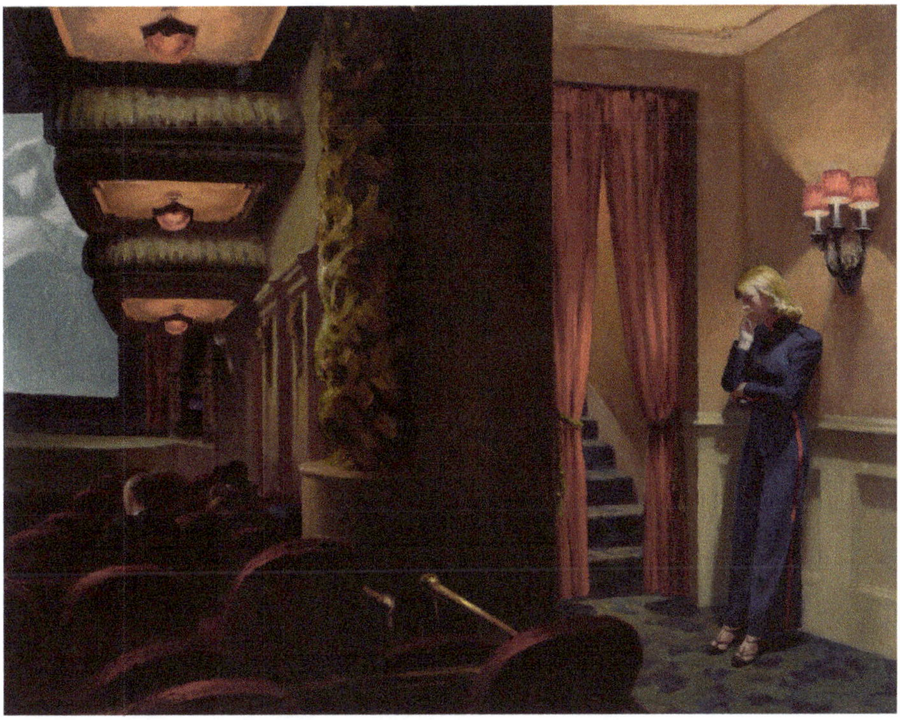

FIGURE 4.18A Edward Hopper, *New York Movie*. 1939. Museum of Modern Art, New York. Courtesy of Artists Right Society.

Zadeh aimed to place his viewers in between spaces, giving them visual access not just to the main protagonists but to what lied on the other side. In a scene in the 2016 play, *Amsterdam*, for example, the viewer encountered a scene with multiple characters and a door that signals the passage from one physical space into another, or even from one temporal realm to another. However, instead of crossing the threshold, the viewer's gaze became fixated on the inescapable presence of a deeply pensive woman who sat to the right of the doorway (figs. 4.18a/b). They saw the space anew.

While Tavazoni Zadeh was impressed by the earlier experimental theater of his mentors and at the Shiraz Arts Festival, he wanted a more direct engagement with architecture. When *Narges* was submitted, approved, and performed in a different house during the 36th International Fajr Theater Festival, the play was modified to accommodate the new location, architecture, and other details.[146] The narrative was directly tied to the architectural characteristics of an Iranian house from the early Pahlavi era: Narges moved in and out of the house, recalling memories of the interior and the backyard during the early years of her marriage, as if telling the architectural history of a bygone era.

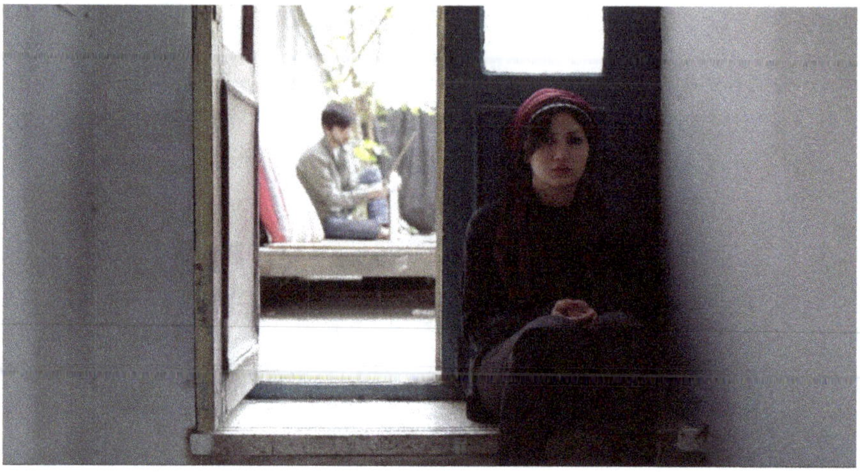

FIGURE 4.18B Kariz Theater Group, snapshot from the play *Amsterdam*, directed by Hossein Tavazoni Zadeh. 2016. Performed in an old house in the Jamalzadeh neighborhood in downtown Tehran. Photograph by Amir Hossein Haji Arab. Courtesy of Hossein Tavazoni Zadeh.

Tavazoni Zadeh began most of his projects by understanding the architecture of the place and its history, and all rehearsals took place inside these spaces. His intention was to create an "atmosphere" and a "unique hour" for the viewer, turning the space, its smell, and its feeling into a symphony for all the senses, from sight and hearing to smell and touch. Inspired by architects such as Johani Pallasmaa and Peter Zumthor, Tavazoni Zadeh saw the historic house and objects within it in terms of phenomenology; in other words, as structures of experience. Consider how Pallasmaa in *The Eyes of the Skin* (1996) calls on architects to contemplate ways of engaging of all five senses rather than the single sense of sight; also note how in *Thinking Architecture* (1998) Zumthor expresses his enthusiasm for designing buildings that have an emotional connection and possess a powerful and unmistakable presence and personality. Tavazoni Zadeh invited both the actors and the viewers to "see, feel, and hear the house."[147] The house was not just a platform; it became part of the play. All objects and all spaces had agency and influenced the actors as well as the viewers. If someone knocked on the door or a cat strolled in, the actor reacted and incorporated it into the play.

Before each project, Tavazoni Zadeh and his crew cleaned up the chosen location and also contributed to preserving the old architecture. In short, what Tavazoni Zadeh did was to activate a bygone era through what he called "intimate interaction with its architecture" (*ta'amol kardan ba me'mari*) (fig. 4.19). However, the main concern of these projects—the main focus of the interaction—is not to preserve or reconstruct, but rather to engage with space in a symbolic manner. In what ways then can these projects be considered critical spatial practice? One way, perhaps, is their attempt to learn from the past through its tangible remains. Tavazoni Zadeh brought to light a cluster of overlapping contexts—historical and spatial—for contemplating the "particular intimacy" between textures and emotions that feminist scholar Eve Sedgwick has so remarkably named "touching feeling," that expressive instance in which "the same double meaning, tactile plus emotional," inhabits both terms.[148] Another means of critical engagement with space could be seen in the way the buildings are occupied by the parties involved in these performance projects. Fully sanctioned by the regime, in contrast to the *kolangi* installations or interventionist projects of the past, Tavazoni Zadeh's plays may seem to lack a defiant dimension. And yet, they have a subtle subversive quality, in that the course of the narrative, as well as the perception of events, can be altered both by the audience and by the building itself.

Such an approach in artmaking evokes socialist writer Raymond Williams's sentiments in "Structures of Feeling": these performances find their subversive meanings in the way that they pick up density and texture as

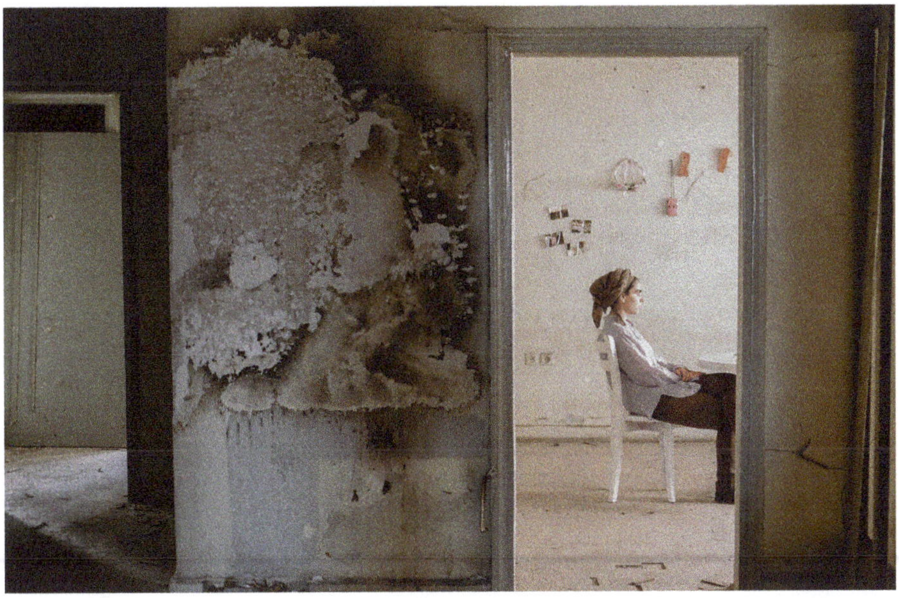

FIGURE 4.19 Kariz Theater Group, still from *Narges*, directed by Hossein Tavazoni Zadeh. 2017. Performance in an abandoned historic home in Vesal Shirazi neighborhood in downtown Tehran. Photograph by Ali Ahmadian. Courtesy of Hossein Tavazoni Zadeh.

they move through bodies and architecture.[149] The subtle modes of swapping roles and allocation of agency not just to a single protagonist but a variety of them (whether actor, audience, or stage set) allow us to better understand how regimes of subversiveness function in Iranian art and how audiences are carefully "curated," "steered," and "choreographed" not to mirror the state's techniques of homogenization of the masses but to practice individuality and to rehearse possibilities for freedom of choice. We must not always expect to "read" the political weight of a work of art as if it is a "text." Rather, as Williams instructs us, we must grasp art's meaning in its totality, in the layered and intricate set of registers that give shape to it.

Tavazoni Zadeh's sentiments toward the powers of curation and choreography and their roles in activating both the architecture of a bygone era and the often-absent freedom of choice in public everyday life lead me to another important creative group in this enterprise of artful choreographic and curatorial negotiations across space. This latter group consists of architects who have exercised their right to subtly exceed the usual boundaries and confines of building codes and regulations of the Islamic Republic—to operate, in Jane Rendall's words, between theory and practice, public and private, art and architecture.

. . .

Like their treasured Bernard Tschumi, innovative architects in Iran create possibilities for spatial challenges and interactions (*chalesh/konesh*), event (*rooydad*), and becoming (*shodan*).[150] Architecture, to Tschumi, is "an organism passively engaged in constant intercourse with users, whose bodies rush against the carefully established rules of architectural thought."[151] Rather than starting from plans and sections, Tschumi draws on the metaphor of choreography in dance and starts from the movements of bodies. "The logic of movement notation," he writes, "suggests real corridors of space, as if the dancer has been 'carving space out of a pliable substance'; or the reverse, shaping continuous volumes, as if a whole movement has been literally solidified, 'frozen' into a permanent and massive vector."[152] The significance of Tschumi's work is not about the final built product. Rather, it is about his design method as his architectural apparatus, which consists of "sequence, open series, narrativity, the cinematic, dramaturgy, [and] choreography."[153] Similarly, the Iranian architects featured below design predominantly around the movement of bodies in space and engage in critical spatial practices by carefully caring for the ideas and ideals of their users.

As architectural historian Reinhold Martin states, "architectural thinking can contribute something invaluable" to critical spatial practice "by offering tangible models of possible worlds, possible forms of shelter, and possible ways of living together, to be debated in general assemblies both real and virtual."[154] Similarly, we can argue that the role of architects, in building long-lasting unconventional spaces, is increasingly crucial to the making of an alternative Iran. For this reason, the last pages of this chapter are dedicated to curation and reconfiguration of space by architects and architectural enthusiasts.

Designing the Alternative, Building the Critical

On June 9, 2021, the Tehran-based Clubhouse group "Architecture Discussions" generated debates around "censorship of space" and "underground architecture." One commentator asked: "We have underground music, but why don't we have underground architecture? Where do architects cross the line? In space activism what is the agency of the architect, as opposed to the user of architecture? Instead of just being a part of the lexicon of larger socio-political events, can architecture in and of itself *enact* political ideologies?"[155] These are also the questions that have occupied me since I started writing this book. Of course, the fact that architecture is always closely tied to economic conditions and urban regulations (the remit of the municipalities) means it is difficult, if not nearly impossible, to identify architects who "cross the line." There are no traces of such modes of thinking in architectural books and journals published in Iran. However, through in-person interviews, one can uncover the ways in which architects manage, against all odds, to fulfill the needs of clients who seek alternative forms of displaying art, or even of living daily life.

In all these improvisations, the architect takes on the role of a curator rather than a builder. Just as Lefebvre saw space as more than just a vacant entity with a shell, many Iranian architects consider space as a collection of objects, with people being part of the design process. In this way of "producing space," to borrow again from Lefebvre, these architects mobilize spatial elements, including resources (materials) and tools (matériel) in a rational manner so that they can organize "a sequence of actions with a certain 'objective' (i.e., the object to be produced) in view."[156] Through their creative interventions and invitations to engage critically with space, Iranian architects disclose unexpected aspects of space and novel ways of

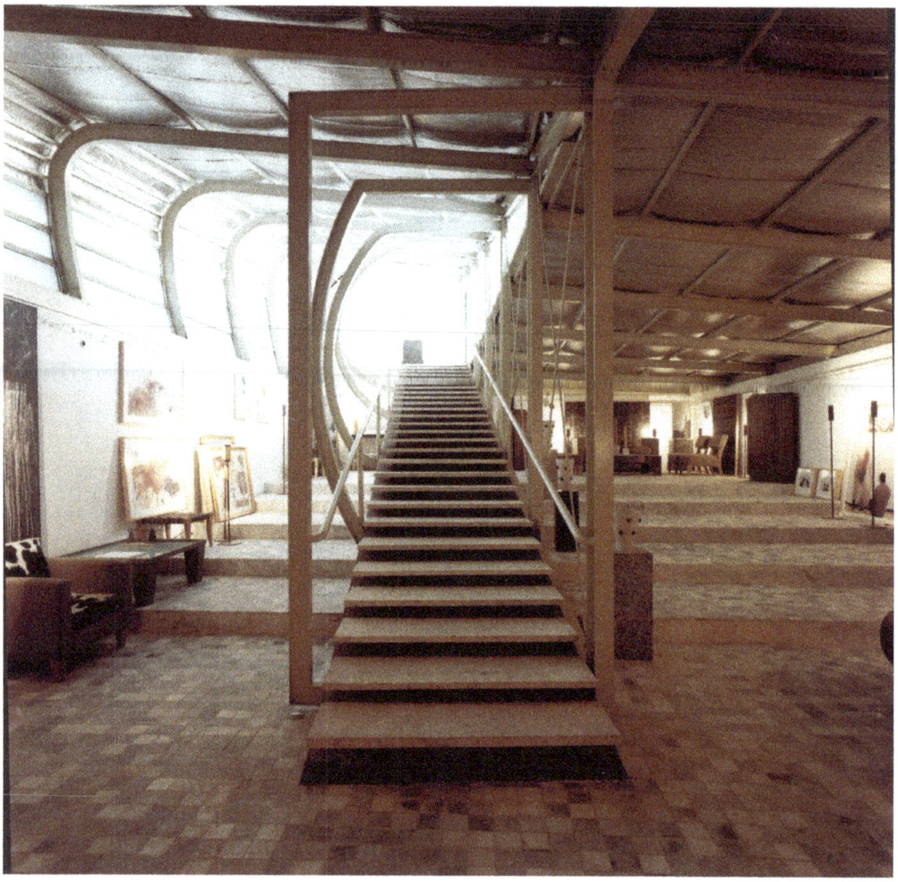

FIGURE 4.20 Reza Daneshmir in collaboration with Catherine Spiridonoff, Ave Gallery and Showroom. 2001. Fluid Motion Architects archive, Tehran. Photograph by Fluid Motion Architects. Courtesy of Reza Daneshmir.

seeing and inhabiting it. The careful, considered arrangement and curation of space can be seen as a form of design thinking that opens possibilities for an alternative life.

In a book about alternative art scenes, it is especially appropriate to look at an example of a subterranean art gallery. The work is a showroom belonging to Fereydoun Ave (also owner of 13 Vanak), who in 2001 commissioned acclaimed Tehran-based architects Reza Daneshmir and Catherine Spiridonoff to convert the Olympic-size swimming pool of his private home into a showroom (fig. 4.20). Completed in 2004, the empty space of the pool was roofed over, using simple, low-cost materials, and made accessible by a long staircase penetrating the subterranean space of the pool.[157]

Daneshmir was one of Ave's protégés; his friendship with Ave goes back to the mid-1980s, when Daneshmir, as an architecture student, attended the private painting classes of Parvaneh Etemadi (b. 1948). Once a week, he had a unique opportunity to explore large-scale imaginative drawings, rather than the usual practice of producing still painting. In February 1988, there was a group exhibition of the work of Etemadi's students at Tehran's prominent Seyhoun Gallery. There Daneshmir met Ave, who purchased some of his drawings, and their friendship began.

Daneshmir was eventually invited to Ave's home, an old three-story house the curator shared with his sister and mother.[158] As Daneshmir described it, the whole building—from the staircase to the rooms and hallways—was filled with an extensive collection of antique objects and artworks. It looked into a vast garden of a thousand square meters. Over time, new high-rise constructions encroached on the privacy of the garden. During a visit in spring 2000, Ave told Daneshmir that the pool had essentially become useless and asked him to convert it into a low-cost building, a sanctuary to house all the art objects and antique items but also a place to meet with artists and clients.

Animated by historic stone statues and carefully arranged lush plants, "the garden was too beautiful to be tarnished by a shed," Daneshmir recalled nearly two decades after he undertook the project.[159] After much trial-and-error, Daneshmir and Spiridonoff finally came up with a low-cost scheme that did not look like a cheap industrial shed. An oblique "cut" (*boresh*) in a large piece of insulated metal sheeting raised above the span of the pool accommodated a staircase that plunged into a flexible open plan space (interrupted only by a few exposed I-beam pillars) able to house all kinds of art displays or gatherings for Ave's favored artist friends. The slope of the shed roof brought light into the space and made room for people to socialize. The bottom of the pool was covered with recycled stone from a nearby storehouse.

How the space operated was determined by the chaotic bureaucratic system of art organizations in Iran. Ave claimed that "when a society becomes shattered the way it did with the revolution, the bits and pieces that are left get themselves together in a funny way, in an improvised way."[160] Though the showroom did not cross the line, it catered solely to its own limited and "trusted" audiences and accepted visitors only by invitation.[161] There was never an opening or closing event, or invitation cards, or even fixed

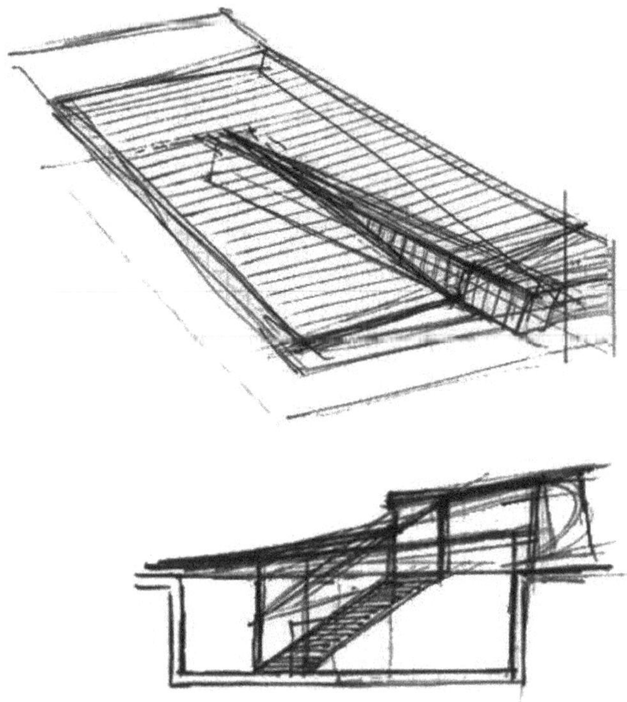

FIGURE 4.21 Reza Daneshmir, Ave Gallery and Showroom preliminary sketches. 2001. Fluid Motion Architects archive, Tehran. Sketches by Reza Daneshmir.

working hours. The obscure form of the showroom, coupled with "private" invitations and an opaque operation, created an air of undergroundness.[162]

Understandably, given that he continues to live and work in Tehran, Daneshmir did not address the cultural and political issues underlying the design of this subterranean space. But if words fall short, the drawings allude to the architects' mode of thinking. The preliminary sketches of the showroom are not mere "illustrations, but pure expressions of architectural thinking."[163] The necessity of descent, and the making of bold "cuts" into an ordinary shape, project a desire for finding alternative paths, of a kind explored by the architects of the deconstructivism movement (fig. 4.21).

The cuts call to mind Daneshmir's favorite building, the Wexner Center for the Arts on the campus of Ohio State University.[164] Just as the iconic diagonal gridwork cuts across Peter Eisenman's building to create a rupture in the common "order of things" and generate a state of "undecidability," the "cut" in Daneshmir's project questions the status quo. In an interview with the social media platform *Memarikahneh* (The house of architecture),

Daneshmir asserted: "It is not through its form, but through its responsiveness to the socio-political issues of its time that architecture gains its outmost significance."[165]

. . .

If Daneshmir's alternative path was to create a rupture in the routine of daily life and to "cut" the surface of the earth to offer the opportunity to go down into a flexible open interior, Alireza Taghaboni (b. 1977) took the notion of malleability one step further by actively engaging the inhabitants of the space in its transformation.

One example of this is his 2013 design for the Sharifi-Ha house—a multistory building, three floors of which are animated by revolving wooden volumes. While carefully separated from the public, the private life of the inhabitants can be made visible to passersby if the mutable façade is altered. For example, the guest room can literally rotate with the push of a button, thanks to imported small-scale German marine anchor and mooring winches.[166] With systems like this, Taghaboni created opportunities to tame the harsh daylight. At the same time, he allowed the residents to either conceal the interiors or reveal them to the outsider's gaze, giving them agency over their private lives and (perhaps unintentionally) also defying all-encompassing spatial regulations of the regime.

Rather than blind habits that are repetitions of traditional ways of life, Taghaboni and his crew at the Next Office created a *habitus*, in Pierre Bourdieu's sense of the term: one that resists as much as it adapts and improvises.[167] All of these design decisions were inspired by conversations with the client, who wanted a house that had the capacity to be flexible, that could create opacity and transparency at the same time (fig. 4.22).

Some critics have suggested that Taghaboni's design is out of place for Iran, or too luxurious for Tehran.[168] The 2017 *Architectural Review* article "Behind the Veil" states: "Next Office principal Alireza Taghaboni caused a stir when he claimed the project was 'grounded in need rather than luxury'; while it may respond to elite needs for conspicuous display, it certainly has little grounding in the Tehranian context and would be equally at home in California."[169] This assessment is precarious in two ways: on the one hand, it indirectly conveys that such a display of wealth and taste is the sole preserve of Euro-Americans, and on the other, it seems to disregard the designer's actual engagement with the cultural atmosphere of Iran.

Taghaboni is not alone in his critical engagement with the façade. Since 2005, there has been a proliferation of facades covered by a variety

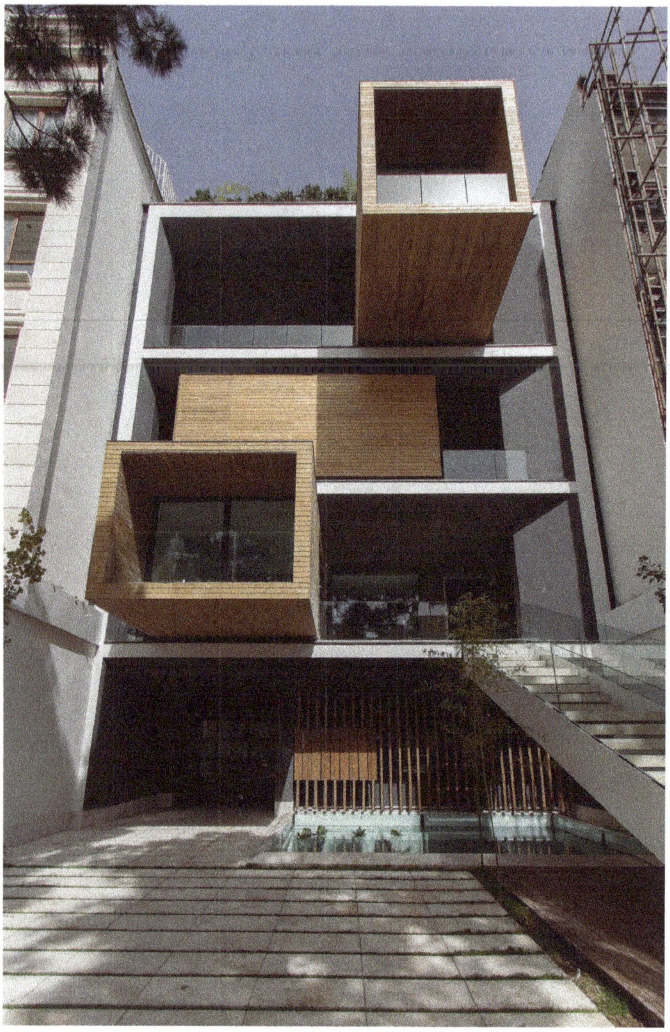

FIGURE 4.22
Next Office and Alireza Taghaboni, Sharifi-Ha House. 2013. Tehran. Photograph by Parham Taghiof. Courtesy of Next Office and Alireza Taghaboni.

of materials, from bricks to slabs of stone and from woven wood splints to wooden beams. These facades, which are often designed using the parametric software Grasshopper and are otherwise known as *namay-e porker* (heavily labored or richly adorned facades), create privacy and break the harsh midday light; however, the reasons for their allure go beyond issues of climate control, "veiling," visibility, and invisibility.[170] In Tehran, residential buildings must not exceed five floors, unless they are built within a large plot of green space. In the latter case, the architects and the clients can get permission for the construction of what is called a residential tower plus garden (*borj o bagh*).[171]

The only way to change the rigid box form is to subtract volume from the allocated square meters—a move incompatible with every client's desire to create as much living space as possible within the boundary lines of their property. In recent years, architects have also been obliged to conform to certain standard facades defined and delineated by the façade committee (*komiteh nama*) of the local municipality. According to architect Atefeh Karbasi (b. 1979) of Ayeneh Office, one defined "standard" calls for symmetry of the building's volume. Any design that lacks symmetry is automatically rejected.[172] It is possible to bypass the laws by paying bribes (*reshveh*), which in official language translates into fines (*jarimeh*). Although many of the owners of uptown voluminous and curvaceous neo-Baroque buildings can easily pay these additional costs, for most clients they are unaffordable, so the architect has to produce a clever design that satisfies privacy and aesthetic needs without violating the standards set by the municipality.

Rather than *Architectural Review*'s "conspicuous display," a better way to describe the creative desire in this context is "defensible space," a term coined by architect and city planner Oscar Newman in the 1970s amidst a surge of massive urban development and gentrification projects as well as an increase in policing in the United States.[173]

A look at Taghaboni's sketches and architect's blueprints—his trial-and-error and other performative means—indicates how much he engaged in a dialogue with local issues. Just like Daneshmir's sketches, these drawings and blueprints display a crucial knowledge of architecture that is not generic and universal but specific to the conditions of life in Iran, while also evoking Tschumi's technique of "movement notation."

Rather than being inspired by the slick projects featured in glossy architecture magazines, these designs are culturally specific. In one drawing (fig. 4.23), Taghaboni tinkers with conceptions of opacity and transparency. To what extent can the skin of a building allow for a better life inside an Iranian home, given all the sensitivities toward visibility and invisibility? Where is the limit, and what is the best strategy for creating a "defensible space"?

Daneshmir and Taghaboni generate "defensible space" as an alternate to a variety of mechanisms—real and symbolic barriers, strongly defined areas of influence, and improved opportunities for surveillance—that combine to bring an environment under the control of its occupants.[174] They cleverly curate the sequences of engagement with space and generate opportunities for alternative forms of living that make room for privacy while

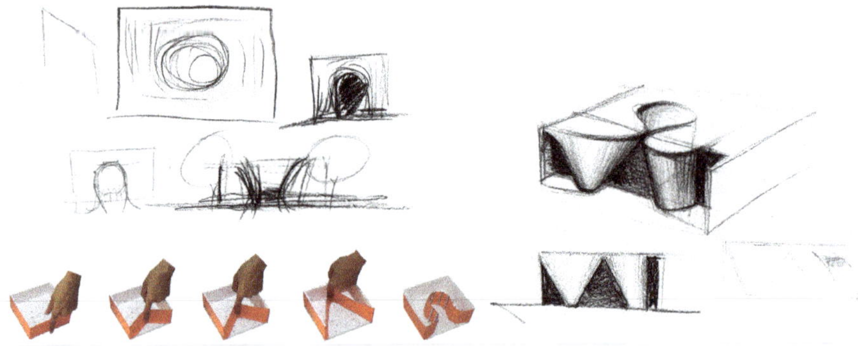

FIGURE 4.23 Sketch by Alireza Taghaboni, lead designer and founder of Next Office. 2014. Tehran. Courtesy of Alireza Taghaboni.

offering agency to occupants of the space and opening up possibilities for a more subtle, yet deliberately subversive life.

. . .

Design strategies of this kind are not limited to private spaces. In public spaces too, architects have afforded room for alternative living. While curating alternative spaces within the private realm may be considered an exclusive job for a privileged few, curating space across metropolitan scales can accommodate more people and contribute to the formation of practices by which space can become gradually democratized.

Indeed, design on an urban scale is an ideal medium for curating as it realizes its "potential as caring-for, constructing and consuming/consummating of the dialectic entity that is the city."[175] A case in point is the internationally celebrated Tabi'at Pedestrian Bridge (known in Iran as *Pol-e Tabi'at*), completed in 2014 by architect Leila Araghian (b. 1983) in collaboration with a team of experts at Diba Tensile Architecture and the Italian engineering firm Massimo Maffies.[176] After four years of hard work, finding ways around the obstacles thrown up by the economic sanctions on Iran, the bridge was inaugurated by former Tehran mayor Mohammad Bagher Ghalibaf, who had overseen a significant increase in Tehran's municipal budget.[177]

The bridge comprises three separate platforms, including a lower level for cafés, a mid-level platform for walking, running, and biking, and a third on top for viewing the highway and its wide green median strips below, or enjoying the towering Alborz Mountains on a clear day. Approached from the west through the Ab-o-Atash (Water and Fire) Park, the bridge's extensive entrance is animated by flower gardens; then come the multiple paths created from "a hundred percent recyclable composite wood" that lead the visitor to the different levels. While the structure itself is made of steel and concrete, it sits well within the adjacent parks thanks to its tree-like columns and curvilinear mass.

One might think that the bridge was inspired by the High Line in Manhattan (2009–14); however, through one-on-one discussions with Araghian I came to realize that what she and her team had in mind was consistent with the urban atmosphere of Tehran. Araghian recalls a late afternoon stroll in the capital with her friend and later collaborator Alireza Behzadi (b. 1980); when they passed a bridge along Zafar Street, the view of the river underneath and the surrounding trees made them want to pause and spend some time there, but there was nothing to lean on and nowhere to sit. A few meters away from the bridge they came across a discarded large leather sofa, which they dragged onto the small bridge, one of the many hovering over the creeks of northern Tehran. As they sat there watching the water flow by, they dreamed of designing a bridge that was not just a crossing point, but a place where the inhabitants of the city could relax.[178] When a competition was announced for a project to connect two parks separated by a highway in northern Tehran, they seized their chance.

All their personal preferences and approaches were incorporated into their competition-winning design. "Usually, bridges are designed in a straight line. And that straight line will produce a one-point perspective that will tell you to just go. But we want to keep people on the bridge. The bridge is not just a structure to connect from one point to another, but also a place to stay and enjoy," Araghian asserted.[179] This idea chimes with the character of the historic bridges in Iran, notably two spectacular seventeenth-century examples—Khaju and Siosepol—in Isfahan, capital of the Safavid Persia. These historic bridges linked neighborhoods on either side of the Zayandeh River. Flanked by coffeehouses and resting spots, they were also places of pause and shelter.

On the other hand, the form of the Tabi'at Pedestrian Bridge also responds to the restrictions imposed upon citizens, and especially the youth, in the public urban spaces of Tehran. To create a space where people could see and be seen—a place they could freely relax in public without fear of being harassed by the morality police—the bridge was designed so that "when you are walking on it, you don't really see where you are heading, adding to the mystery, as if you are walking on a path" (fig. 4.24).[180]

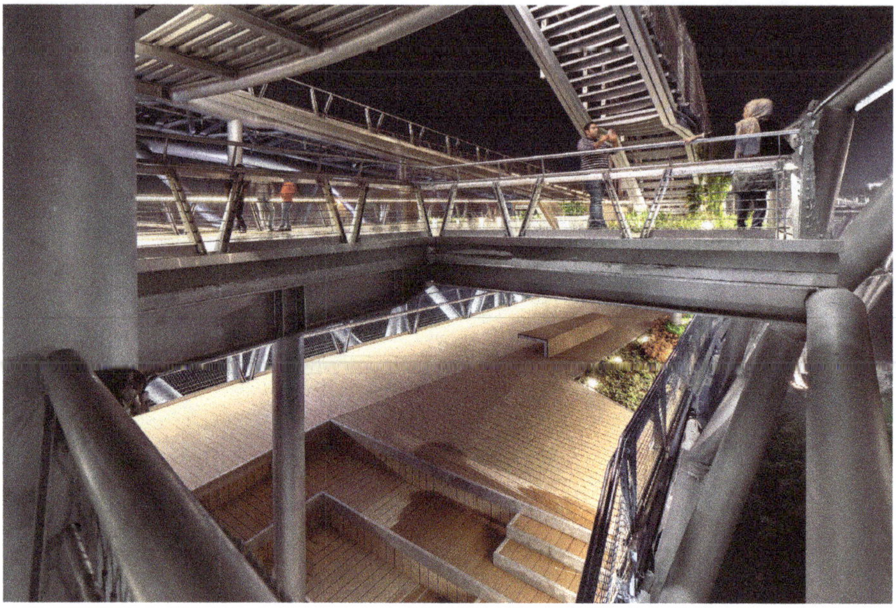

FIGURE 4.24 Leila Araghian et al., Tabi'at Bridge. 2015. Tehran. Photograph by Mohammad Hassan Ettefagh.

For a thesis project at the University of British Columbia, Araghian had studied the works of Adolf Loos in depth, drawn to the ways in which his interiors were full of mystery and surprise.[181] In the Moller house (Vienna, 1928), Araghian saw a host of design strategies—raised sitting areas, uneven floors, and walls randomly punctuated by openings—that simultaneously instill a sense of (in)security and curiosity in occupants and visitors alike. There is also a sense of theatricality in Loos's interiors. When stationed at a particular spot, architectural historian Beatriz Colomina tells us, one could get the impression "that someone was just about to enter the room [and] that a piece of domestic drama [was] about to be enacted."[182] Such a theatrical (or cinematic) dimension in design is similar to Araghian's cinematic spaces on the bridge, which are inspired not only by Loos's interiors but also by postrevolutionary Iranian cinema (and recall, once more, Tschumi's architectural apparatus, the cinematic). Araghian is intrigued by various cinematic strategies, especially the "moments of visual surprise."[183]

These influences shape the ways in which she choreographs movement in space (once again, conjuring Tschumi's "logic of movement notation").[184] Over the past forty years, Iranian filmmakers found innovative ways to overcome restrictions on taboo subjects such as romantic relations between men and women; famously, Driush Mehrjui's (b. 1939) *Leila* (1997) incorporated a long scene of interaction between a young couple in the privacy of their bedroom. While the audiences could hear the dialogue, the screen remained in utter darkness. Araghian's many nooks, niches, and recessed alcoves—in which visitors to the bridge can socialize without fear of being harassed by the morality police—signify such an influence.[185]

Araghian's interest in cinema is related to its potential to be more subversive than architecture, as it is arguably less regulated, and not subject to the same heavy economic pressures. That she borrows from film and theater to create opportunities for dissent within a public structure commissioned by the state is further testament to the agency of architects in crossing boundaries that are even more unyielding than those facing the visual artists. The examples of architectural design I have introduced thus far center on making alternative spaces and building critical spaces from scratch. Other projects have focused on rescuing censored and suppressed places, or on securing the longevity of alternative spaces by reassembling and reactivating their physical remains.

(Re)collecting and Curating Alternative Spaces

How should one envision architectural spaces and monuments that are barely visited? Is it possible to reconstruct a space in its entirety through scattered archival information, written anecdotes, and hearsay? Instead of a simple answer in the affirmative, painter and architectural enthusiast Mehdi Farhadian offers a response that reflects on the role humans play in the gaping space between a site and its real or imagined history. Through a concerted effort to activate histories of forgotten places and destroyed monuments of bygone eras in Tehran, Farhadian lures his viewers into a world they may never have visited, known, or remembered, but nonetheless have longed for subconsciously.

Born just one year after the revolution of 1979, the youngest child in a family of six, Farhadian missed out on the experience of living during the Shah's era. He says he often felt resentful that he had never seen the so-called "good spaces," or the glamorous events, where men and women mingled easily. In the strict postrevolutionary years, when many texts were censored, Farhadian turned to the colorful prerevolutionary books in his parents' home. Time and again he faithfully copied the images in them, even though he believed he was committing a crime when he did so.

The young artist had been so brainwashed by the ideological school system that he thought of his imitation of the banned images as *dozdi-e tasviri*, or image theft. But over time, the act of "stealing" images shaped his imagination. Upon enrolling in the University of Tehran's Faculty of Fine Arts, Farhadian was once again frustrated by the scarcity of visual resources. All art history books were heavily censored: images were blackened, cut, or retouched, and accompanying texts were redacted. But the library had a "forbidden" section with an abundant collection of colorful Western art books and Shah-era journals assembled in the 1960s and 1970s.

Farhadian befriended one of the librarians and was able to borrow some of the banned items, one at a time. Years later, when he became a lecturer at the same school and pursued more ambitious archival research, another friendly librarian at the Golestan Palace Library gave him access to a collection of thousands of "forbidden" Qajar images, for three hours at a time. Farhadian described the experience as intense: "My heart would start beating faster and faster as I got closer to the end of my permitted slot."[186] Having grown up in a stricter phase of the Islamic Republic, the fear of censorship remains deeply ingrained in his psyche.

Farhadian's preoccupation with censored content from Iran's modern history weighs so heavily that he often dreams about those untold and unseen histories. A frequent location in his dreams is the Amin-al-Doleh Park in Tehran, named after a nineteenth-century minister and wealthy entrepreneur. The house Farhadian has been living in since childhood shares a wall with the Amin-al-Doleh complex, but since the complex was converted into an all-girls school after the revolution, Farhadian has never had permission to enter.

What did the park look like in the nineteenth century, and how did it cater to the leisurely lives of Qajar aristocrats? In an art history book, Farhadian finally came across an old black-and-white image of the gardens, featuring an elaborate kiosk and a boat floating on the lake next to it.[187] The grainy photograph was a revelation—a scene straight out of his dreams, animated by descriptions he had read years earlier. The scene also reminded him of the romantic rural scenes painted by John Constable, at the beginning of the Industrial Revolution, capturing the artist's desire to preserve the authentic essence of a landscape that was being rapidly transformed by factories and railways. In the same spirit, Farhadian's obsession with the green spaces of premodern Tehran indicates his yearning to preserve the remains of a bygone era (figs. 4.25a/b). Farhadian helps us "remember" and envision censored architectural spaces. But these kinds of "forbidden" spaces are not only activated by Farhadian's paintings, they are also reconfigured and even remade by Iranian architects.

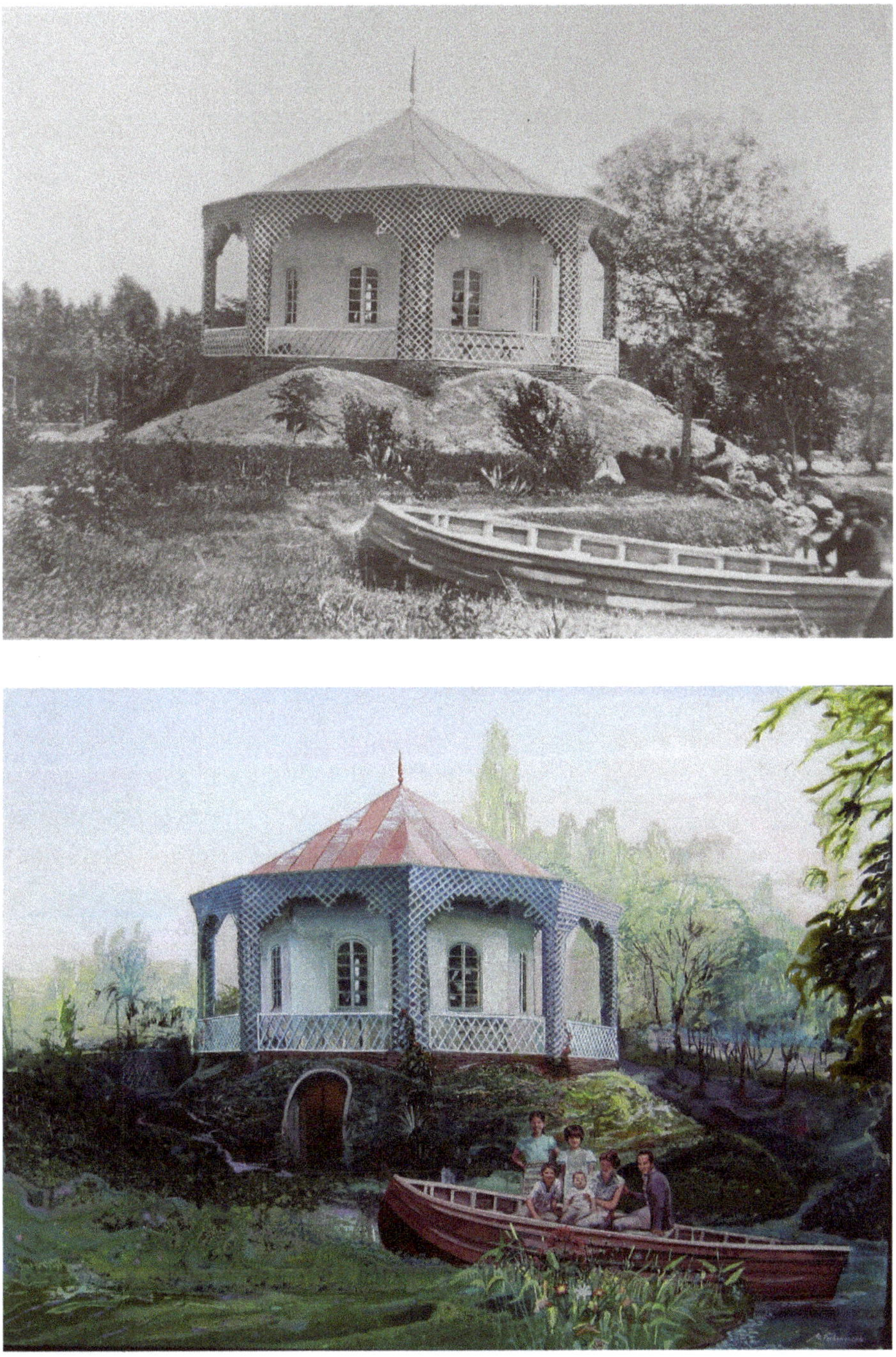

FIGURE 4.25 Mehdi Farhadian, *Amin-al-Doleh Park in Tehran*. 2018. Painting and its original source. Painting by Mehdi Farhadian; black-and-white photograph courtesy of Yahya Zoka, *Tarikh akkasi dar Iran* [History of photography in Iran] (Tehran: Elmi va Farhangi, 1376 [1997]). Composite courtesy of Mehdi Farhadian.

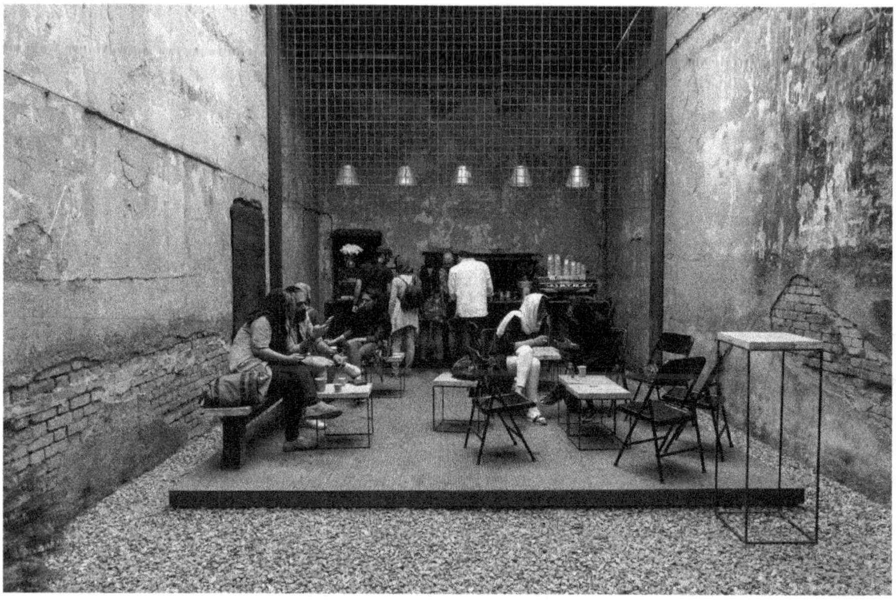

FIGURE 4.26A Ali Shakeri Shemirani, The Pejman Foundation, et al. Argo Factory, renovated interior with exhibition space and cafe. 2015. Tehran. Courtesy of Ali Shakeri Shemirani and the Pejman Foundation.

When the revolution broke out, many liquor stores and spirits factories were vandalized.[188] Any facilities that survived were converted into other spaces, erasing from the public consciousness all the places in which alcoholic beverages were made, sold, or consumed. Thirty some years after the revolution, a single beer factory in central Tehran (a few blocks from the historic Ferdowsi Square to the north of Lalehzar Avenue, a theater and entertainment district in the Shah's era) remained completely intact, although of course not in production. Argo Factory had been a major beverage producer in Iran in the decades before the revolution. Dating back to the early 1920s, it was one of the first factories constructed in Iran and had unique architectural features like high smokestacks as well as a strategic geographical location in the heart of the city.

Stripped of its original function and taken into state ownership, Argo Factory survived revolutionary vandalism simply because it had already been abandoned a few years before the revolution. The factory's neighbors had managed to shut down the operation sometime in the mid-1970s; it was polluting,[189] and for a few years before the revolution the place served as a refuge for heroin addicts.[190] In 2015, however, after almost four decades of neglect, the Pejman Foundation for the Arts purchased the tumbledown building from local authorities, then renovated and converted it into a nonprofit space (figs. 4.26a/b).[191]

Set up by entrepreneur Hamidreza Pejman (b. 1979), the foundation hosts a collection of contemporary Iranian and international art; it also organizes workshops, lectures, and panel discussions, initiates exchange programs, and finances art publications.[192] This wide range of activities are housed in a physical space heavily redolent of nostalgia. Architect Ali Shakeri Shemirani (b. 1982), who was involved in the earlier phases of Argo's renovation, insists that because of all the history associated with that space, his first idea was to retain as much of the original as possible. In fact, he associated this first impression with stories (*ghesseha*) of the building, as well

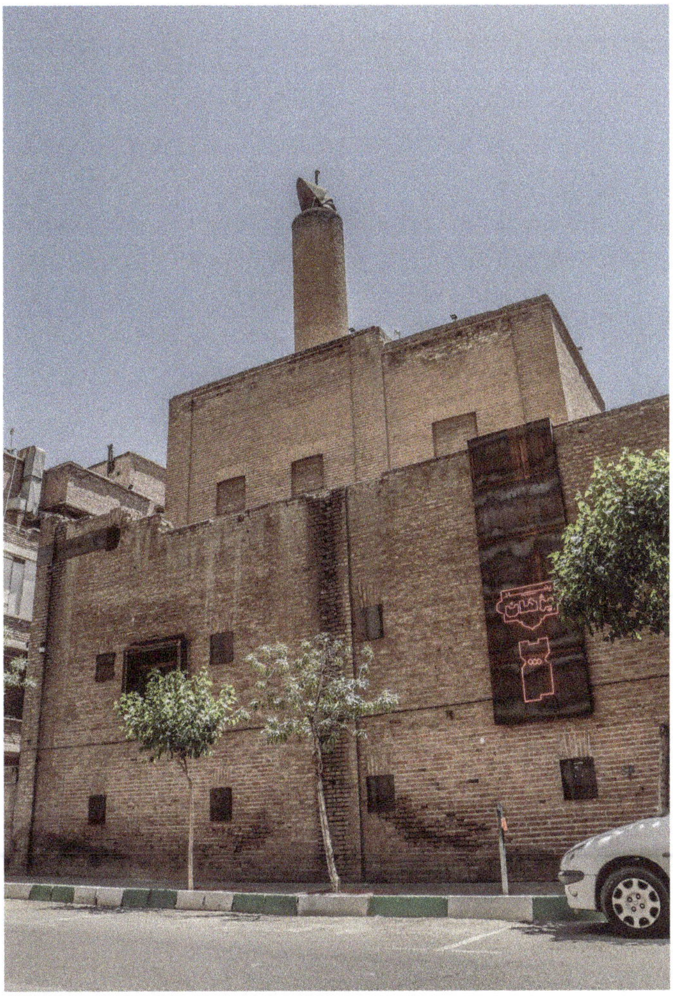

FIGURE 4.26B Argo Factory, renovated exterior. 2015. Tehran. Courtesy of Ali Shakeri Shemirani and the Pejman Foundation.

as the "feelings that move around the space" (*hesse jari dar bana*), emphasizing the crumbling textures of the walls and how these textures provide entry points into the past.[193]

Shakeri Shemirani even went as far as anthropomorphizing the building by personifying it as an old man who had witnessed tumultuous decades in Iranian history: "I did not rebuild the Argo; I initiated a dialogue with it."[194] This way of thinking about architecture, to borrow from the authors of *Spatial Agency: Other Ways of Doing Architecture* (2011), "shifts the focus of spatial attention away from the static objects of display that constitute the foreground of so much architectural production, and moves it onto the continuous cycle of spatial production, and to all the people and processes that go into it."[195]

Ahmadreza Schricker Architecture–North, a New York–based practice with a satellite office in Tehran, spearheaded major portions of Argo's renovations at a later stage. The team lessened the costs through creative usage of cheaper materials (e.g., concrete paneling in lieu of brass cladding), amidst Iran's weakened currency due to further sanctions. It also expanded the structure from two levels to three—all of which are climate-controlled and seamlessly connected via a monumental spiral staircase.[196] Completed in January 2020, the Argo Factory maintains its historic look, and the renovations seem to have done justice to the different lives of the building. Some new elements were added, while major parts of the building were carefully preserved; some brick walls maintain their original Flemish look, while others are visibly altered to differentiate between the old and the new.[197] On its ground floor, the building contains a café that serves nonalcoholic draft beer; its basement holds an "archive" where objects such as old Argo beer bottles are kept.[198] In this way, Hamidreza Pejman, together with his team of engineers and design specialists, helped turn a former brewery, with its "shabby" (recall the *kolangi* homes of the early 1990s) ambiance, into a new aesthetic of art and curation for Tehran.

The renovation of the Argo Factory is exemplary among the many other such projects that deal with "forbidden spaces" from a bygone era, such as nightclubs and cinemas in the famed Pahlavi-era entertainment district, Lalehzar Avenue. Ali Shakeri Shemirani also participated in Tehran municipality's renovation of Lalehzar Avenue's Nasr Theater. Named after the renowned prerevolution director and playwright Seyyed Ali Nasr (1894–1962), the theater was abandoned in 2002. In April 2019, as part of its long-delayed renovation, the Tehran municipality organized a one-week event at the theater that included an exhibition of documents, news clippings, photographs, and posters of Pahlavi-era events at the venue, as well as a sound performance with hundreds of visitors. Several celebrated actors, including Parviz Parastooie (b. 1955) and Golab Adineh (b. 1953), read and recorded parts of a long text relating to the history of the Lalehzar district. Shakeri Shemirani has a personal collection of photographs of the event.[199] Akin to the celebrated photographer Thomas Struth, who took photographs of contemplating art in museums, Shakeri Shemirani's collection captures the wide range of emotional responses among the hundreds of viewers, from looking intently, to expressing joy, to crying. These affective responses can be seen in light of the ways in which built history has been sealed off by the regime over the past four decades. The modalities of creativity entrenched in contemporary preservation practices in Tehran help unite architecture with social purpose.[200] While many archival materials from the Pahlavi period were destroyed or censored, the remaining built environment of that era is ever-present in everyday lived experience. By removing decades of dust to reveal the original brick and mortar, a long-suppressed history is allowed to resurface. Even if only temporarily and sentimentally, Shakeri Shemirani's creative preservation activities are forms of critical spatial practice. This approach also animates the work of architecture enthusiasts who collect, archive, and curate the remains of the fast-disappearing pioneer "alternative" spaces of art.

. . .

The much-loved "nonexistent," "under the radar," and "noncommercial" space belonging to Fereydoun Ave, 13 Vanak, had "a display window [*vitrine*]," Homayoun Sirizi recalled, "which was unique in Tehran gallery scenes; it was the only venue for me to engage with the urban environment through my art."[201] Indeed, as most galleries in Tehran are obscured behind the walls of formerly domestic spaces and basements, 13 Vanak did seem like an outlier (fig. 4.27). The space's "storefront worked as a camouflage mechanism, to be seen [by] the audience who would spot it, and invisible to the normal passerby. The trajectory applied to the space was also a translation of the architectural space; a small shop, an extension of a private artist studio, which move[d] in between legal and illegal, between the street and the studio."[202] Akin to its modest display window, 13 Vanak was discreet in its methods of publicizing shows: no opening or closing events were scheduled, no invitations were sent, and gallery opening hours fluctuated during the week.[203] The "white cube" interior perfectly accommodated

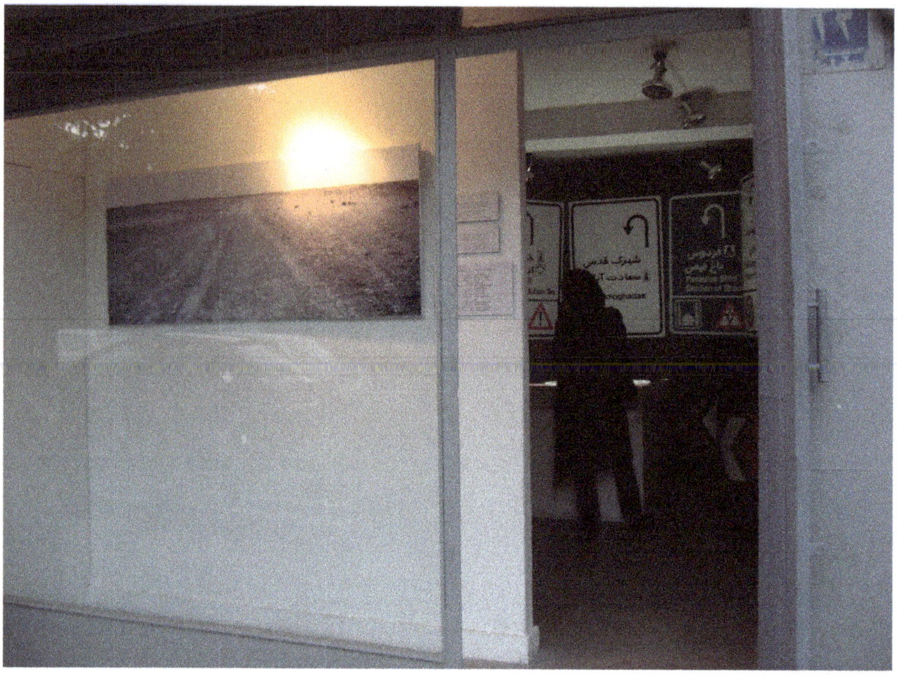

FIGURE 4.27 Homayoun Sirizi, *U-Turn*. 2007. Luminescent horseshoe and traffic signs installation, seen from the street facing 13 Vanak storefront. Tehran. Photograph by Homayoun Sirizi.

all kinds of projects—artists who exhibited there were often disappointed by other house/gallery spaces with walls interrupted by radiators, fireplaces, light fixtures, and exposed plumbing.[204]

Despite its popularity among artists, 13 Vanak quietly closed its doors on December 11, 2008, after eight years of productive operation. It did so because of multiple issues that had attracted the attention of the authorities. Some believe the main cause was an unusual performance, in which a female artist lay like a corpse in 13 Vanak's storefront, enshrouded in a white sheet topped by flowers; attracting an audience of thousands, the work interrupted traffic on busy Vanak Street. Others put the blame on a widely distributed controversial poster, depicting an art form inspired by architecture, but allegedly read as a phallic form with the name "Ave Gallery" attached to it. Regardless of the trigger, Ave, who did not wish to have any form of engagement with the authorities, closed the gallery before legal notices were served.

Thus, 13 Vanak ended in a quiet and "organic" manner; in Ave's own words, "It was created organically, and it died organically."[205] For the next decade the legendary 13 Vanak remained vacated, until it was finally demolished in March of 2019 to make way for a new building. Throughout its entire life, first as a studio in the 1980s and 1990s and then as a public alternative art space, 13 Vanak ran without securing permission from the MCIG. Yet at the same time it was officially declared a confiscated property by the Executive Headquarters of Imam's Directive, or simply *Setad*, a parastatal organization under direct control of the supreme leader of Iran.[206] In truth, 13 Vanak was just a kiosk, formerly a place where the security to the parking lot of a mini-golf course establishment belonging to the Ave family operated; it was the larger plot of land of the then "forbidden" business of mini-golf that was seized by the *Setad* but otherwise remained untouched. For the following three decades, Ave, who held the keys to the kiosk, continued to use it first as a private studio, then as a gathering place, and finally as an open alternative gallery. The curious birth, life, and death of 13 Vanak is a microcosm of the complicated character of alternative art spaces in Iran. They are simultaneously sanctioned and not; they have not been specifically granted permission to exist and yet may be affiliated with the strongest governmental institutions. The past forty years have shown that while these spaces may operate without any conflicts with the authorities during certain time spans, at other times they can simply turn into a nuisance. As Fereydoun Ave aptly put it, Iranian art like its politics is "an ever-changing scene," such as how green, once a color of Shiite Islam, became an anti-regime symbol after the Green Movement of 2009.[207]

Many artists who worked with Ave used the space, especially its small display window, to project their alternative thoughts in public space. The closure was devastating for some who did not see a similar potential in any other gallery around Tehran. One such artist (and architect by training) is Homayoun Sirizi, who regularly exhibited his architectural and urban conceptual projects at 13 Vanak. When in 2007, Sirizi presented his *U-Turn* (*Dorbargardan*) at 13 Vanak (see fig. 3.13), he showcased a luminescent horseshoe encircled by traffic signs from seven major Tehran U-turn sites. The signs were placed into blue barrels, an urban addition that appeared during the time when soon-to-be-president Mahmoud Ahmadinejad was the mayor of Tehran. The traffic signs looked original, except for modified translations; for example, Nobonyad Square, which simply translates as Newly Founded Square, became Neo-Fundamentalism Square.[208]

In a personal interview, Sirizi explained, "Similar to an untitled artwork, 13 Vanak was an untitled space, an untitled architecture and I, too,

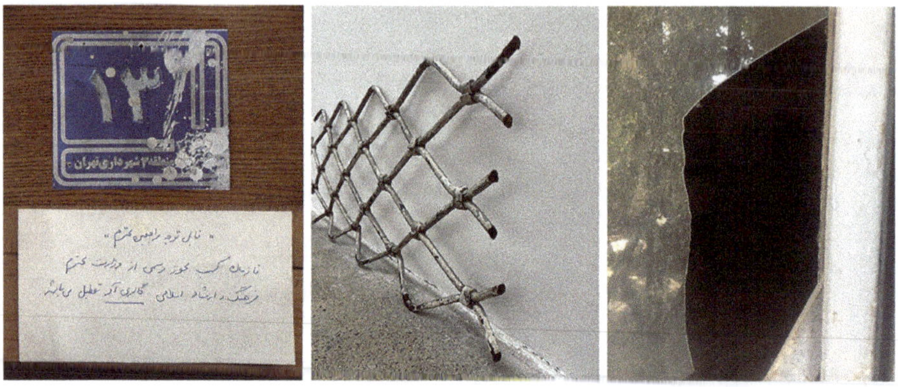

FIGURE 4.28 Relics of 13 Vanak. 2020. Tehran. Composite by Homayoun Sirizi.

was an untitled artist. At Ave, I . . . presented my ideas, rather than my art."[209] To show his commitment to the idea of 13 Vanak as a nongallery, following its closure in December 2008, Sirizi resisted presenting his work at any other gallery for the next thirteen years.[210] Just a few days before its demolition, Sirizi rushed to collect the remains of the space. He grabbed the plaque (*pelak*) 13, photographed the broken display window, and picked up part of the rolling security bar as well as a note left on the door by Ave's assistant Kaveh Najmabadi (1960–2021), which incongruously reads: "Until securing permission from the respected Ministry of Culture and Islamic Guidance, the Ave Gallery will be closed." At the time of its closure, Sirizi recalls, 13 Vanak finally became Ave Gallery, a designation always disavowed by Ave (fig. 4.28).

Sirizi collected these fragments because he strongly believes that Iranians do not appreciate such alternative spaces. He became aware of the significance of such losses when Aun Gallery was suddenly closed by the authorities in 2016. Subsequently, a court in Tehran sentenced the Zoroastrian director, Karan Vafadari, to a sentence of twenty-seven years in prison, 124 lashes, a fine of $243,000, and confiscation of all his assets. His co-director and wife, Afarin Neyssari, an architect, was sentenced to sixteen years in prison.[211] At this point, Sirizi remarked, "I realized how much we showed lack of appreciation for such spaces. So, I began to collect the relics of the most important of alternative spaces in postrevolutionary Iran."[212] The relics of 13 Vanak are testimonies to the efforts of a people during the nation's three formative decades of push and pull, improvisation, and endless negotiations. They also designate a desire for constructing a social memory against the censored official history. Given his consistent effort to collect other such tangible remains—for example, the surviving molds of sculptures that were neglected, damaged, or disappeared during tumultuous times or a few original concrete blocks discarded following the controversial 2018–20 renovations of the TMoCA—Sirizi hopes, through his open-ended collecting, to construct a model of historical memory and continuity of alternative experience.[213] His collection of architectural remains is an "anomic archive," to borrow from Benjamin Buchloh, who attributed the term to Gerhard Richter's monumental *Atlas* (1964–). An open-ended compendium of photographic panels and tableaux, the *Atlas* originated at the time of the Frankfurt Auschwitz trials between 1963 and 1965 and was initiated by the artist as a reflection on the relationship between the photographic and historiographic. Contrasting the rigid principles of collecting in official museums and archives, Richter amassed an alternative collection, just as Sirizi has done (albeit with no knowledge of Richter's *Atlas*).[214] While Sirizi's tangible items still largely stay within the privacy of the artist's own collection, other alternative spaces find their way into the virtual world through the efforts of those who manage to leave Iran. Indeed, it is perhaps fitting for the last case study of this chapter to take us back to the aura of earlier examples from chapter 1: the shielded domestic space that became the hub of artistic activities.

Initially an open studio in 2008, Sazmanab was reconfigured a year later as a nonprofit "social studio"[215] by Sohrab Kashani (b. 1989),[216] the son of a scriptwriter, an aspiring hacker in high school, and an interdisciplinary artist and independent curator based in Tehran.[217] The original venue—owned by Kashani's grandmother—was on the ground floor of an apartment complex in Sadeghiyyeh, a neighborhood in western Tehran. It took its name from the building opposite, the city's Department of Water (*Sazmanab*). Regarding the significance of the name, Kashani remarked, "I liked the idea of a department that oversees a fluid that is constantly on the move. It is a great metaphor for the creation of an art space that wants to defy simple definition or location, allowing for the most artistic freedom. My desire was to [create] . . . a space whose identity could change and evolve over time."[218]

In early 2014, Sazmanab moved to a new location, an old building on Khaghani Street near Darvazeh Dolat in downtown Tehran. The place soon became Kashani's home, his studio, and his art event space where he hosted multimedia performances, concerts, workshops, residencies, and artist talks. Windows were covered to avoid attracting attention from the outside and the space often served multiple purposes at once. For example, at night Kashani would hold parties for his friends, when the kitchen counter was used as both a performance stage as well as a place to serve food.[219]

Writing of New York's forerunner alternative spaces—112 Workshop / 112 Green Street (1970–78) and artist-run restaurant Food (1971–74)—art critic Martin Beck explains how these spaces "offered a viable alternative to the presentational apparatus and support systems of the traditional world . . . and became, at least for those actively involved, a means of production."[220] He argues that the manifestation of these spaces coincided with Lefebvre's notion of space as a field and basis of action, because they were not just venues for presenting of artist's works but also sites that "artists manipulated, penetrated, and attacked in the process of producing artworks. The physical space thus became an integral condition for the artworks to emerge."[221]

In *The Production of Space* (1974) Lefebvre argues that humans as social beings not only produce social relations and use values (in a Marxian sense) but also produce social space: "Each living body *is* space and *has* its space: it produces itself in space and it also produces that space."[222] On the other hand, space itself is not a thing, not a container and a means of production.[223] Space is a "social reality" and "a set of relations and forms."[224] It subsumes products and their interrelations.[225]

There is a dialectic of social space and human action: "Itself the outcome of past actions, social space is what permits fresh actions to occur, while suggesting others and prohibiting yet others."[226] Space is part of the process of production: "Space is at once result and cause, product and producer."[227] The integration of physical space and social experience at Sazmanab produced a spatial alternative that conceived of space as "neither a mere 'frame'. . . . nor a form of container of a virtually neutral kind, designed simply to receive whatever is poured into it."[228] The kitchen at Sazmanab, in this sense, could be seen as what Lefebvre refers to as something that is "simultaneously, both a *field of action* (offering its extension to the deployment of projects and practical intentions) and a *basis of action* (a place whence energies derive and whither energies are directed)."[229] With all its domestic features and functions, Sazmanab perfectly exemplified the spirit of alternative art spaces in Iran—not only a place for presenting the work by artists but also a venue for discussing the process of art production (fig. 4.29). Like the covert homes of the left described in chapter 1, in which political activists lived their lives, made food, produced propaganda, and studied together, the home as an art space becomes a "field of action."

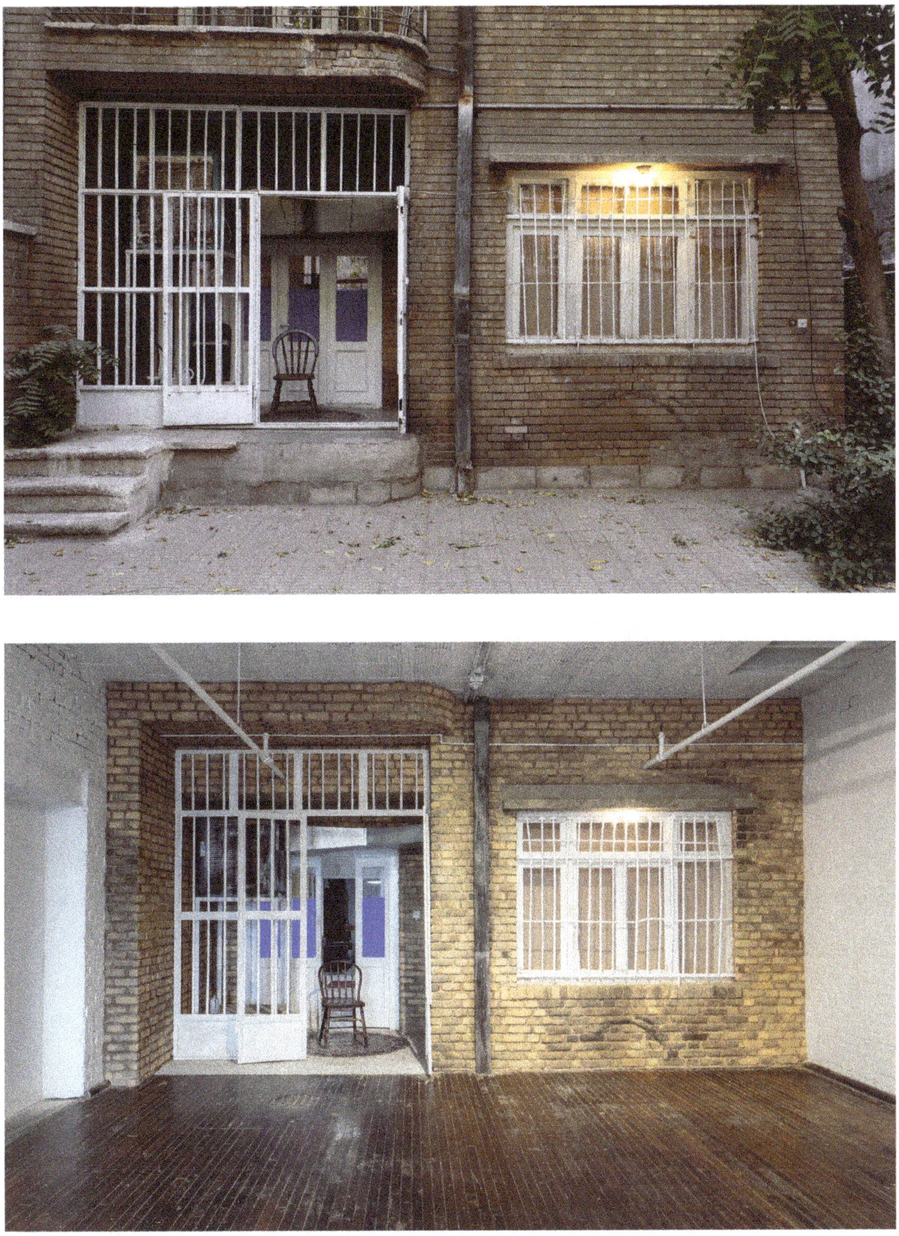

FIGURE 4.29 Jon Rubin and Sohrab Kashani, *The Other Apartment*, exterior view. Fall 2019–Spring 2020, Tehran and Pittsburgh, PA. Photographs by Sohrab Kashani and Tom Little, respectively. Courtesy of Sohrab Kashani.

The image of the home as the "basis" and "field" of action, which occupies such a strong place in the minds of Iranian artists, came into play even more forcefully in a 2019 project in which Kashani made the experience of his home/gallery/art space/studio available to American audiences. At the Mattress Factory Museum in Pittsburgh, viewers could walk into a duplicate of Kashani's apartment in Tehran, and touch and hold exact replicas of all its contents, from book shelves to bathroom tiles, which had been created by a team of fabricators, sometimes by hand, other times using 3D printing. Titled *The Other Apartment*, the project was a collaboration with Jon Rubin, an American artist, Carnegie Mellon professor, and co-creator of the *Conflict Kitchen*, a restaurant/art project/nonprofit that served cuisine from countries with which the United States is in conflict, including Iran.

The Other Apartment was accompanied by a program of art ventures, exhibitions, and events—with each object, video, or performance that happened in one space being meticulously duplicated in the other. For those familiar with these types of museum arrangements, the work might evoke Russian artist Ilya Kabakov's "total installations" at Western museums. Similar to Kabakov's reproductions of his lived spaces back in the Soviet Union (including part of his own *kommunalka* apartment unit), the replica of Kashani's apartment was "not based on a model of a picture, but on the world as a picture."[230] Kabakov's experience was one of "engulfment," where visitors "are not just surrounded by a physical scenario but are 'submerged' by the work; [they] 'dive' into it, and are 'engrossed,' as when reading a book, watching a film, or dreaming."[231] All of these characteristics were also present at the Pittsburgh mock apartment, where the visitors could walk into the installation and inhabit a "picture," which offered them a "total" experience. Of her experience at the Mattress Factory, University of Pittsburgh art history graduate student Golnar Yarmohammad Touski writes, "My heart skipped a beat. I was thrown back to the sea of blue, rusty coolers on roofs, their humming noise a soothing sound on hot summer nights in Tehran. Seeing such an object in the American Midwest sparks a moment of dissonance."[232]

The effort involved in reproducing the replica of an alternative art space in Iran is a further indication of the desire to keep such spaces alive. These acts of collection, replication, and curation of alternative spaces must also be seen as critical spatial practice. Being critical entails, among other things, the creation of conditions for the spread and continuity of alternative life practices. Kashani states: "*The Other Apartment* functions as a series of theoretical and practical questions within the sad absurdity of our current political condition: What if there was more than one absolute reality; can you build a reality that functions as a loophole around national borders and economic sanctions; and what gets lost and gained in the act of that duplication?"[233]

This comment leads into the next and final chapter of this book, which takes into consideration the ways in which *alternative Iran* is assessed by Iranian critics as well as on a global stage.

EPILOGUE

Alternative Iran

Allures and Aversions

DO ALTERNATIVE ART PROJECTS and critical spatial practices live up to their ambitions? Can they be read as forms of resistance against the established art market or the apparatus of the state? What are the differences in the way the work is perceived inside and outside of Iran? Is the aspiration of these art forms to enact social change recognized and celebrated—or conversely challenged? What is the relation between the early covert examples featured in this book and the contemporary unconventional art projects that are openly sponsored by powerful individuals? With each case study in the book, these are the questions that I have tried to address. Here, by way of conclusion, I would like to bring these topics into sharper focus.

In researching this book I talked to artists, curators, theater experts, urban visionaries, and designers. Several times during interviews, I was challenged on my use of terms such as "underground" and "political art." Even a phrase like "fighting for civil rights" raised concerns—and justifiably so, as many Iranians have found themselves in trouble for using these terms in writing about their work outside Iran. As the first draft of this book neared completion, Iranian filmmaker Mohammad Rasoulof (b. 1972) was put on trial, in large part because the Western press had interpreted his "controversial" films, *Manuscripts Don't Burn* (2017) and *Lerd* (aka *A Man of Integrity*, 2017), as critiques of the Islamic Republic's social and economic policies. A correspondent for the *Hollywood Reporter* wrote that Rasoulof's *Manuscripts Don't Burn* was a banned story about censorship under the Islamic regime.[1] Another news agency discussed *A Man of Integrity* as a tense, engaging drama about corruption, injustice, and corporate oppression in Iran, noting its strong prospects for international distribution despite the inevitable domestic ban.[2] Oddly, the charges against Rasoulof were constructed using similar language. Indeed, what shocked many Iranian artists was not so much the accusations on the themes of the works but that the court presented these journalistic reviews as evidence of Rasoulof's desire to disrupt the system.

Yet anxiety about the external perception of the work goes beyond a fear of attracting the label of "dissident" and, with it, the attention of the authorities. Iranian literati and artists are fully cognizant of the Western discourse of "otherness," and are particularly well versed in Edward Said's *Orientalism*—a book on the cultural discourse that the powerful construct about the powerless in order to control them. In Western art institutions, one enduring aspect of this self-reflective process of "sanctioned ignorance" was the presumption of the superiority of Eurocentric artistic templates.[3] For many years after the Islamic Revolution of 1979, the Iranian art covered in Western media and academic books was mostly limited to object-oriented art on old-school poetic, religious, or spiritual themes. There was a profitable market and audience for an orientalized image of Iran.

Neda Razavipour (b. 1969), whose large-scale installations in buildings under construction are discussed in chapter 3, recalls that during her studies at the University of Paris in the 1990s she received more accolades and higher grades if her art captured aspects of traditional Iranian culture such as calligraphy, veiled women, or Persian poetry. For one assignment she filled an entire corridor of the school with the poems of the legendary medieval poet Omar Khayyam. "I just made this installation and at the final reviews was too shy to say anything about it, so I remained silent," Razavipour recalled, adding that this clichéd image of the "shy, voiceless Muslim woman mixed with Persian poetry and calligraphy" somehow brought her recognition, making her an overnight star among her cohort.[4] For better or worse, the incident put her on a different path. Since then, Razavipour has been careful not to become that clichéd image. Rather than producing images that appeal to the global Iranian art market, she has immersed herself in urban installations and participatory art practices in Tehran.

Rozita Sharafjahan, the founding director and curator of Azad Art Gallery, observed that "the global art market is generally interested in promoting and buying art with codes and conventions that are easily readable."[5] Examples of this kind of art based on familiar Iranian signs and symbols include the fully veiled women from Shirin Neshat's (b. 1958) *Women of Allah*, or Shadi Ghadirian's (b. 1974) *Qajar* series depicting nineteenth-century harem girls juxtaposed with modern elements such as Pepsi cans. Rather than the conceptual works, which are harder for Westerners to grasp, these are the art forms that are systematically exhibited and acquired by prominent art museums and collectors. Indeed, as Iranian-American art critic Negar Azimi has put it in the context of reductive visual materials that circulate on mainstream media, such images are "convenient and, in their own ways, extremely effective in confirming certain stock ideas and narratives about Iran as a place."[6]

There is also what Azimi calls a "poornographic" realm of art, "that is the circulation of images and ideas that tend to perpetuate the image of the [poor], victimized [Iranian] people," portraying Iran as "a sealed vacuum of repression."[7] Taking a similar approach, historian Siamak Delzendeh (b. 1973) notes, "Many of those who travel to Iran find a country very different from what they had known through the media."[8] Of course, the relative lack of attention to Iran's vibrant ephemeral art scenes is largely the result of the obstacles to travel encountered by Iranian artists (as well as their foreign audiences), in the form of economic sanctions and visa issues.

Alongside these practical difficulties, there seems to be a covert model of censorship in place—a version of the "market censorship" of liberal democracies, whereby the manipulation of economic opportunities limits the theoretically endless expression of opinions and interests and marginalizes certain views.[9] In Iran, this model encourages the propagation of the dominant ideology while marginalizing unconventional practices—among them, making art in loosely covert dilapidated spaces—that are interpreted as signs of resistance to the conservative, Islamist state.

In 2015, *Ocula Magazine* ran a feature on "underground art" in Tehran, describing a two-day foray to the city's major galleries by a small number of European gallerists and art experts.[10] "In a country . . . where religion dictates such a marked difference between public and private spaces," the visitors reported, "these spaces feel tucked away and private."[11] While such interpretations are not necessarily wide of the mark, they do not begin to take into account the many complex ways in which Iranians themselves engage with and sustain these spaces.

Anthropologist Zuzanna Olszewska and music scholars Laudan Nooshin and Theresa Parvin Steward have written on how Western literature on Iranian urban youth culture tends to "fetishize resistance" (Nooshin's phrase) and thus "feed into wider regimes of orientalist representation."[12] Regardless of their actual intentions, alternative art and cultural activities are invested with the status of a rebellion against the political establishment. Iranian "underground music," in particular, is seen as a bastion of opposition to the Islamic regime, populated by advocates for political change. Nooshin mentions a 2001 *Washington Post* article titled "Roll Over, Khomeini! Iran Cultivates a Local Rock Scene, within Limits,"[13] while Steward provides a larger sample of the fetishizing headlines: "A Rock Band from a Country That Arrests Rock Bands," "Rage against the Regime," "Iran's Illegal Rappers Want Cultural Revolution," "Life as an Illegal Rock Star in Iran's Islamic State."[14] Such examples are symptomatic of the "reductive dichotomies"—e.g., between tradition and modernity, or between religion and secularism—that infuse tabloid rhetoric surrounding Iran, distorting the complexity of alternative art and life on the ground.[15]

Olszewska further argues that the problem with dramatizing resistance lies "not so much with the idea of studying cultures of resistance or defiance in themselves, but with the failure to seriously consider their boundaries."[16] Focusing on underprivileged Iranians and Afghan immigrants (rather than the upper-class youth who star in other studies of resistance),[17] Olszewska observes that subjectivity in Iran is "shaped by both the opportunities and the instances of coercion that arise not only from top-down state initiatives but also from broader social factors."[18] She gives the example of a young girl from a poor neighborhood in Tehran who joined the 2009 Green Movement simply because it offered the opportunity to mix with more affluent north Tehranis.[19]

No one could deny that the Iranian regime has enacted restrictive policies, or that artists have in turn resisted these pressures through mechanisms such as invisibility, escapism, ephemerality, and improvisation. Thus, it is not incorrect to underscore artistic opposition to the state; however, as the case studies in this book have shown, the means of resistance and opposition are not always so forceful and clear-cut. More importantly, within Iran there are varied interpretations of alternative art scenes, and not all of them praise this form of art or see it as a heroic act intended to liberate society against all odds. Rather poignantly, they critique it for a perceived lack of social responsibility.

Alternative Art Economies and Social Responsibility

Disconnected from the global art economy, a career in today's alternative art scenes frequently involves a multitude of very mixed projects that are not object-based but more attuned to interactions with people, sites, and other intellectual fields. Practices such as countermapping, with its subtle underpinning of political messages, or the brave interventionist presence of women in "unwalkable" urban areas, or the quickfire execution of political graffiti art, are rarely rewarded financially.[20] When projects of this kind are presented at a gallery or a museum, the costs of documenting them or cleaning up afterward usually fall on the artists themselves.

While these ephemeral performances might not generate any profit for Iran's alternative artists, the critical engagement with space can offer them a sense of satisfaction and autonomy, and, above all, greater *hope* for a more democratic Iran. In the productive framework theorized by the Marxist philosopher Ernst Bloch, this "hope" gives Iran's artistic labor an agency, making its mark on society in the long run.

Similarly, the longevity of these movements arises from what anthropologist Hirokazu Miyazaki has called acts of "repetition and replication."[21] Repetition, as Derrida insists, "carries with it an unlimited power of perversion and subversion," even if it were "to change neither thing nor sign."[22] Shahram Khosravi has described how ordinary Iranians claim "their right to potentialities that make prospects for a better future possible" through their constant petitioning for change within certain infrastructures.[23] In the same way, artists who repeatedly dedicate their time and energy to the unpaid or undercompensated labor of ephemeral artmaking are exercising their right to claim a better society for themselves and others.

For the female graffiti artist known only by her tag, "Ada" (b. 1988), creating public artworks (while disguised in men's clothes) not only gives her joy and the freedom to explore urban space but also brings together micro-communities with a shared interest in transforming dilapidated spaces or disrupting the walls and limits of the city.[24] When approached by a top-notch Tehran gallery that wanted to display her graffiti art (applied to portable, and therefore sellable, rocks), she refused. Likewise, when she was accidentally discovered by a municipal authority, she turned down his request to revamp a dilapidated area in the southern city of Bandar Abbas, where she spent three years with her spouse. Since beginning her career as a graffiti artist in 2012, Ada has consistently prioritized her privacy and anonymity over fame and the sale of her art, relying on other ways of earning a living.[25] Ada's decision could perhaps be attributed to the nature of her art—all over the world, graffiti artists prefer to remain independent from government or corporate sponsorship. However, all too often, the labor of Iranian artists is offered free of charge.

An artist with tenure at a major Tehran university told me, in a private conversation, that he could greatly boost his income if he accepted invitations from government institutions keen to benefit from his expertise and showcase his art. While there are no restrictions on this kind of activity, he refuses to "participate in or collaborate with the Fajr Festival of Visual Arts" because of his "own principles."[26] Fajr is a long-standing festival initiated by the minister of culture and Islamic guidance. Many artists see it as heavily censored and designed to promote government agendas. The professor said that when his paintings were displayed in an associated exhibition without his permission, he demanded their immediate removal.[27] But at the same time, he conforms to the rules of the governmental organizations that coordinate art competitions and festivals promoting art from regions outside Tehran. For him, these state-run events give artists who do not have access to the art resources of the capital a rare opportunity to showcase their work and hone their skills.[28]

Occasionally, artists benefit from the sponsorship of wealthy private gallerists but use this money to promote a higher cause. One such artist—an activist for the rights of Iranian labor unions—told me that "instead of seizing the opportunity for personal gain, I take the cash and turn it into a common good."[29] Eric Hobsbawm in 1969 called this phenomenon "social banditry," referring to men who gained a Robin Hood reputation by championing the interests of the masses against elite oppression. What they got in return was popular adulation: peasants admired, protected, and aided them.[30] In Iran such a partnership is regarded as *ayyari*—a concept rooted in a classically macho mode of conduct where the ends are always seen to justify the means. Like an *ayyar* (or Robin Hood), the artist exploits the *Khosoolati* economy to open up better opportunities for other artists, for example by helping to curate a group exhibition with an important social or political message, or by initiating collective projects intended to benefit the community.[31]

All these cases attest to the fact that artists do not simply belong to one tribe or another and that the boundaries between private and public and correlated economies are more porous than is usually assumed. Despite this, critics continue to see alternative art projects as a top-down enterprise tending toward intellectual elitism and obscurantism. In keeping with the Lefebvrian models of spatial production mentioned in the introduction, Aidin Torkameh (b. 1987) refers to "opaque artistic practices" culminating in "conjectural spaces" (*fazahay-e enteza'ie*) that are unable to establish a meaningful connection with society at large.[32] For such critics, this is highbrow art that appeals only to a limited audience. Rather than artists, they look to guerrilla gardeners, social activists, and advocacy groups as the sources of an authentic and transformative community-engaged art.[33]

To illustrate such concerns, it helps to tell the story of a failed entry to the prestigious annual competition organized by a prominent gallery in Tehran. In 2017 artist Mahmoud Maktabi (b. 1985) proposed a sustainable system for collecting and storing clean drinking water during the monsoon season in Sistan and Baluchistan provinces. Impoverished villages in this arid region currently lack the proper equipment to do this, and instead collect the water in badly made ditches, where it quickly becomes infected, spreading disease; to ease the pain, the villagers turn to illegally imported opium from neighboring Afghanistan and Pakistan. Maktabi's proposal, informed by months of research and fieldwork, seemed like a perfect prototype to inspire other design strategies. Yet it was harshly criticized by the competition jury, who deemed it "charity work" (*kare- kheiriyyeh*) rather than art.[34] According to Maktabi, one member of the jury went so far as to say that even if the work had some conceptual or aesthetic qualities, it did not cater to the right audience.[35] "Art," the juror opined, "must be presented to gallery-goers who understand art; the villagers may not be able to appreciate the value of art."[36] Perhaps Maktabi's project would have been rejected in another country or context due to its affinity with industrial design and architecture (rather than conceptual art). But in this instance, the jury's criticism reveals the disdain for the art-in-public-interest model among certain elite artistic circles of Iran. It is this same milieu that offers the most vocal opposition to alternative art in Iran.

. . .

Many art critics remain unconvinced of the socially transformative potential of conceptual art. In relation to the *Women in Red* performance piece discussed in chapter 3, for example, Tehran-based critic Pouria Jahanshad (b. 1974) acknowledges the significance of invoking the taboo topic of women and the expression of love in public places, but questions whether the work had a wider impact. For Jahanshad, such performances are simply a continuation of studio practices and can only speak to a select audience versed in art. In his way of thinking, real change can only come from within: "Ordinary people are capable of public interventions that are much more impactful."[37]

The significant role played by ordinary people is highlighted in the works of several sociologists, and most famously by Asef Bayat.[38] In his *Life as Politics: How Ordinary People Change the Middle East* (2013), Bayat describes the "tactics of informality" that allow government regulations to be adroitly sidestepped. Rather than attempting to dismantle the system or demand radical change through militant acts, ordinary people slowly appropriate commonplace situations for a distinctive mode of citizenship focused on what Bayat calls the "art of presence" in everyday public life.[39] Instances of this "art of presence" include informal occupations by the underprivileged, such as squatting, or the use of sidewalks for commerce; women's collective involvement in public activities conventionally dominated by men, such as establishing NGOs; and the determination of the urban youth to express themselves through distinctive hairstyles, outfits, and corporal behaviors.

Jahanshad, who admires these approaches, highlights the action of a young woman who defied Iran's morality police by taking off her headscarf on Tehran's busy Enghelab (Revolution) Street in December 2017. To make sure she was seen, she stood on a utility box on the sidewalk, waving her headscarf—now attached to a stick—like a flag. The woman was arrested on the spot, but others reenacted her protest, and posted images that swiftly went viral on social media platforms. Collectively, the "Girls (or Daughters) of Revolution Street" became a symbol of Iranian women's resistance to the imposition of the *hijab*. Back in Tehran no detail of this event has been too small for the authorities. The utility box has since been given a pitched roof to prevent people from standing on it.

Jahanshad sees the Enghelab "performance," which was widely reported in both the local and the international press, as a perfect example of what he calls true "informal art," a more elevated and effective form of alternative practices in public space. When asked whether it is appropriate to refer to political protest as art, Jahanshad responded by referring to Boris Groys's assertion that a community built on artistic projects "is not necessarily a transformative community—a community that can truly change the world."[40] Jahanshad and Groys both reflect Guy Debord's earlier line of argument—allegedly stirred up by a dialogue with Lefebvre—that the use of art for political action is ultimately self-defeating, as aestheticization and spectacularization divert attention from the practical goals of the protest.[41] In Jahanshad's view, even well-intentioned, ephemeral art goes on to become a commodity as its images are endlessly circulated on the web and social media platforms.

Jahanshad is not alone in thinking that artistic interventions in public spaces are of less significance than public interventions spearheaded by nonartists and vanguards of change.[42] Architects Kaveh Rashidzadeh

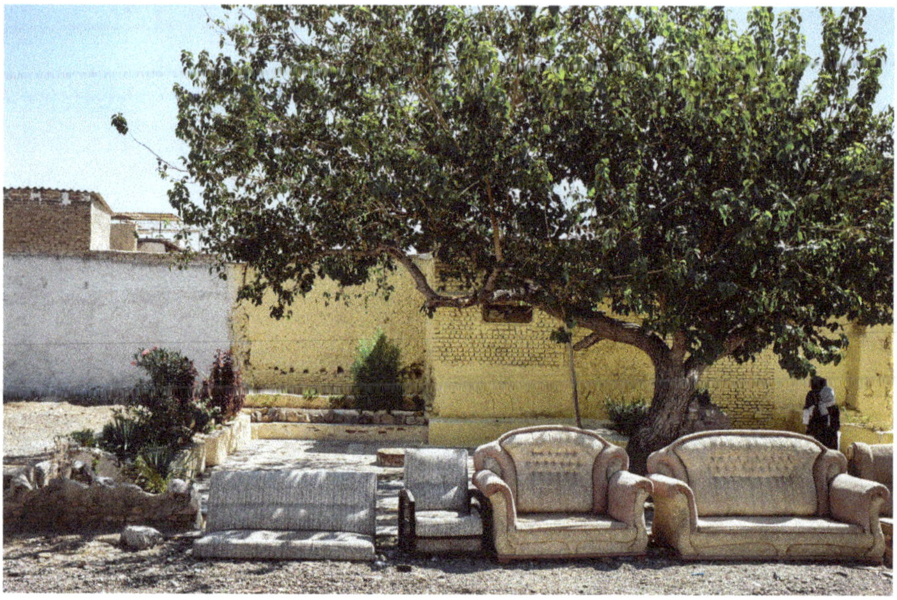

FIGURE E.1 Outdoor living room created by members of a local community, circa 2015. Nafar Abad, southern Tehran. Photograph by Hamed Alaie.

(b. 1981) and Niloofar Niksar (b. 1977) have highlighted the work of ordinary citizens in the historic neighborhood of Nafar Abad in their respective talks and publications. While the government was systematically destroying the neighborhood to make way for newer and more profitable housing, the local community created an outdoor "living room" on the site of a demolished courtyard house. Though warned off many times by the authorities, they continued to use the place as a venue for neighborhood gatherings and grassroots activities. The project brings to mind the works of contemporary American social practice artist Matthew Mazzotta, who collaborates with local laborers, community members, and activists to create participatory public interventions. However, the Nafar Abad living room was organized by the community for the community, and in that sense, it does not fit into the category of art. Because of its bottom-up nature, it is of interest to Iranian critics who find public art inadequate (fig. E.1). The value of the work, according to these critics, lies in its ethical and real engagement with the community, its connection with their cultural and political histories. Rather than a symbolic gesture, it is an active critique of neoliberal urban development and a riposte to the market-driven spirit of art creation.

Alternative Iran against Alternative Iran?

Thomas Erdbrink, former Tehran bureau chief of the *New York Times,* describes Ehsan Rasoulof (b. 1979) as the "son of a wealthy banker" who "looks like a typical aspiring Iranian artist, wearing . . . ripped jeans" and riding a taxi instead of driving a Maserati.[43] Rasoulof (cousin of the filmmaker Mohammad Rasoulof) is arguably one of the most powerful voices in contemporary art in Tehran. Perhaps best known as the owner and director of the Mohsen Gallery, established on Mirdamad Street in 2010, Rasoulof is also behind the creation of several of the alternative art institutions and residencies that have energized the capital's art scenes since 2012.

If the financial kickstart for the Rasoulof art enterprise came from Rasoulof's father, Jalal—former minister of agriculture and current head of Ayandeh Bank, a private bank operating under the supervision of the Central Bank of the Islamic Republic of Iran (*Bank-e markazi*)—Eshan Rasoulof is its undisputed creative leader, guided by a singular vision of "malleable hardware expansion" (*tose'eh sakht afsari-e narm*). By "hardware," Rasoulof means architecture in its *brick-and-mortar form* or *physical appearance* (*sakht-e fiziki*) as an instrument for expanding civil society.[44]

Akin to Jonas Staal, the contemporary Dutch artist who shows how art and space can shape civil action, Rasoulof believes in the power of an actual physical space to give a structure to the performance of free speech and the democratic process, especially in Middle East societies where people are accustomed to congregating in social settings.[45] This process, he asserts, must be materialized physically, situated in the world, and put into words. For him, it is precisely this conjunction of physical appearances that creates an opportunity for Iranian society to transform.[46] In this he also evokes the Lefebvrian outlook that space expresses social relations but, in turn, reacts to and is conditioned by those relations.[47]

In Iran, where official public space is not a space for the free exchange of ideas, creating spaces of interaction and discussion is more important than having a gallery that caters to a limited audience. Rasoulof emphasizes the collective impact of art over its aesthetic, monetary, publicity, or propaganda value.[48] Rather than being driven by profit, these alternative art spaces have other functions. For example, the Kooshk Residency (described in chapter 1) has been collaborating with European embassies since 2014 to bring in international artists to work with communities in central and southern Tehran.

Nabshi (also discussed in chapter 1) was set up in 2018 in an old house on Villa Street known for its handicraft shops, a favorite with foreign tourists. The center quickly became what Rasoulof calls an alternative museum space, hosting exhibitions and discussion panels on historical and cultural topics, some of them previously considered taboo (one example being the 2020 exhibition *Red Paper (Kaghaz-e sorkh)* on the Soviet Union's agitprop visual culture).[49]

The transformation of the otherwise conventional space of the Mohsen Gallery is an even more provocative critical spatial practice. A self-confessed architecture enthusiast, Rasoulof saw the potential of the "leftover" spaces of the gallery, which (like many other galleries in Tehran) occupies a former single-family home on the exclusive Zafar Street. Here, I refer to these "leftover" spaces as "abstract" spaces, after Henri Lefebvre.

The space of the Mohsen Gallery dates from the far-reaching Pahlavi modernization campaign, which began in the early 1960s. Throughout Iran, cities were transformed by urban planning projects that promoted a globally standardized model over regional ways of life. Traditional houses were replaced with modern spaces that seemed alienating to those who occupied them. Modern architects and urban planners, both homegrown and foreign, produced diagrams to show the processes of urban evolution and developed generic grids for deindustrialized metropolises. Not only did these new spaces seem abstract on paper, having emerged from an amalgam of datasets, codes, and diagrams, they also gave the same impression in their built forms. Above all, they were abstract regarding their processes of production, which rendered obsolete the aspects of social life that were formerly marked by distinctions between center and periphery, or between industry and agriculture. Labor-saving technology had the effect of deskilling workers, transforming people into mere appendages of the all-pervasive machinery.[50]

Lefebvre asserted how, in the name of efficiency and profitability, modern architecture led to a *separation* between people and activity, triggering the passage from the *production of things in space* to the *production of space itself*.[51] The modular and carefully coordinated spaces of modernity became imbricated within a global market, fueling the gradual disappearance of the historical Iranian city. From the mid-1960s in Iran—as in much of the rest of the developing world—a mass of row houses, apartments, and large-scale housing complexes, all built to the same modernist template, began to encroach on the old urban centers.

Space began to look not only more methodical but also, in a Lefebvrian sense, more abstract, more indifferent. In lower-income neighborhoods, new constructions peripheralized the core of the house and its purpose, to the detriment of private life within the home. All two-story houses followed the same floor plan: they were constructed in rows, the property line marked by a low wall between adjoining courtyards. All the windows were the same size, regardless of whether they faced north or south. The large glass windows and second-floor balconies looked directly onto the courtyards—and even parts of the interior—of neighboring homes.

Many single-story units lacking a courtyard incorporated a small glass-enclosed *passio* (a variant of a patio) that housed plants, presumably to replicate the aura of the garden in the traditional courtyard house. With its glass ceiling, the *passio* was often the only means of bringing natural light and air into the living room. However, rain would often accumulate on its surface, causing mold to grow. So much for the efficiencies of modernist "abstraction."

The spread of modernism in Iran had two main consequences. As the new typologies flouted traditional Muslim taboos against mixing public and private areas, many families began to conform to the dictates of public life in the "private" spaces of their houses: for example, women in more traditional households wore the veil all day, even at home. At the same time, to gain more privacy, many inhabitants altered modernist regimes of transparency, blocking balconies or dividing shared entrance thresholds.[52]

The "abstract" spaces of one such modernist home would become exhibition venues for the Mohsen Gallery. Spaces that had been underutilized when the building was lived in would realize their full potential as platforms for artistic presentations when Rasoulof created *Mohsen Projects* (*Projeha-ye Mohsen*) in the roof (*bam*), patio/greenhouse (*passio*), and yard (*hayat*) in 2015, five years into the gallery's operation. A challenge to "the conventional white cube of art exhibitions," Rasoulof's intervention is also designed to encourage multimedia and installation artists.[53] The gallery issues open calls inviting young and emerging artists to apply for grants to hone their skills with alternative methods of presentation.

Notable among the recent crop of *Mohsen Projects* are three site-specific works, each of which establishes new forms of communication with the "abstract" space. In his 2018 installation, artist and filmmaker Aliyar Rasti (b. 1988) made an artificial green space inside the *passio*, which is normally used for plants. Like his counterparts in the environmental art discourse,

Rasti connects nature to broader sociopolitical issues: "*Passio* is a spot that exists on the thin line between possibility and impossibility."[54]

In 2019 Armenian-Iranian artist Sanahin Babajanians (b. 1992) used the rooftop space to showcase the deep historical conflicts, and affinities, between the nations of Iran and Armenia. Through her placement of architectural elements taken from Armenian churches and Islamic mosques, she represented the impossibility of oneness between the two cultures.

In his 2018 project for the front yard, the graffiti artist Black Hand offered an oblique criticism of the government's blocking of internet sites and the lack of playfulness in the city. Channeling the spirit of the pixelated T-Rex that shows up on Google Chrome when a computer is not connected to the internet, *Offline* turned the yard into a playground. In this way, Black Hand brought a portion of the city into the domestic space of the Mohsen Gallery and established a dialogue between public and private—between forbidden and permitted, visible and invisible. In the artist's own words, "This artwork is a tribute to the citizens and children who live in the city and are surrounded by rough and rigid buildings, where there is no space left for playfulness."[55] As the structure suggests, the games that the people of Iran are obliged to "play" in daily life are not fun but rather disruptive, whether they involve finding ways to access restricted websites, or simply apply to the endless game of politics (fig. E.2).

In addition to its creative approach to spatial organization, Mohsen Gallery has a long track record of presenting highly political art. Many art experts in Tehran credit the gallery with groundbreaking exhibitions on taboo subjects, among them *Kitchen* (*Ashpazkhaneh*, 2010), where many of the works embodied strong feminist themes.[56] Some of the artists endorsed by Rasoulof also make work that is highly political in tone. Among them is Amir Mobed (b. 1974), whose daring performance at Siin Gallery is addressed in the introduction. Mobed is also known for inflicting harm on his own body during performances. By his own account, this behavior is triggered in part by childhood abuse.[57] But more importantly, it is a consequence of the violence that Mobed and his generation have observed and endured since the Islamic Revolution. By reenacting near-actual circumstances, Mobed's performances are meant to shake the audience out of the passivity that is the standard response to state violence. In some projects (e.g., the *Opening* in the introduction, or *Come Caress Me* in chapter 4), he has even pushed the onlookers to harm him—to reproduce the acts of violence that in his view characterize daily life in Iran. In another piece, *The*

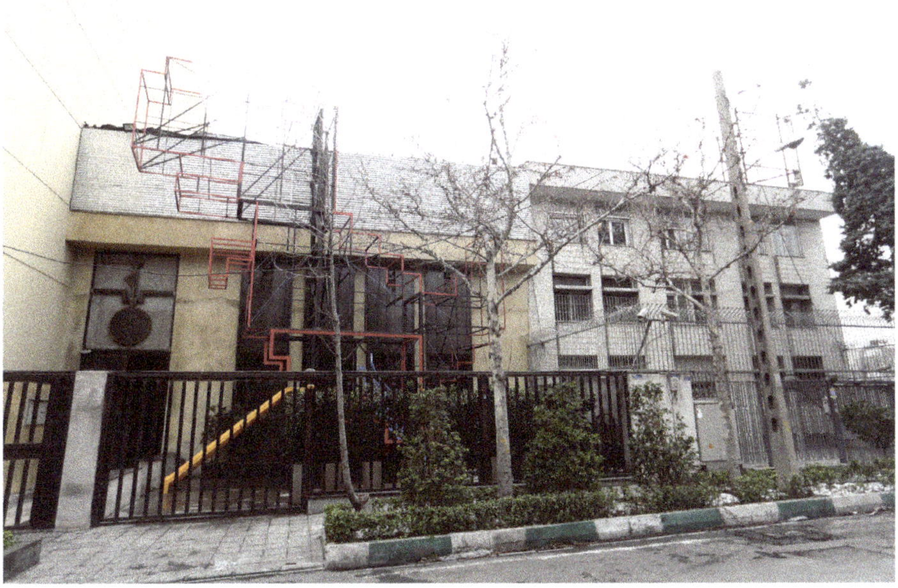

FIGURE E.2 Black Hand, *Offline*. 2018. Mohsen Gallery's front yard, Tehran. Photograph by Mohsen Gallery staff. Courtesy of Ehsan Rasoulof.

Killing (in Persian, *Keshtzar or the field)*, performed in 2011 in the whitewashed backyard of the Mohsen Gallery, Mobed stood cordoned off from the audience, beneath a white scaffolding that resembled the typical gallows used in Iran to hang political activists (and criminals alike). He had a white noose around his neck, and balanced on a white stool, on top of a melting block of ice that dripped with blood-like liquid (fig. E.3).

The presence of an ambulance outside the gallery entrance made the audience worry that they might be witnessing a suicide or, at the very least, an intentional act of self-harm. As time went on, people began to react, with some trying to turn off the hot-air blower that was accelerating the melting of the ice block, bringing the artist's suspension and death ever closer. The frustration of the audience escalated as a few men who appeared to be security guards prevented them from doing so. Mobed insists that no part of his performance was coordinated with the audience in advance, and that he and Rasoulof made sure that onlookers were offered no guidance on how to react.[58] From the available footage of the performance, however, it seems that the highly professional art practitioners among the audience, such as Jinoos Taghizadeh and Barbad Golshiri, participated with intent. These sophisticated viewers seem to have been influenced by the erstwhile president of the former Czechoslovakia, Vaclav Havel—particularly his 1979 essay "The Power of the Powerless," in which he proposes that overlooking the actions of an authoritative system will grant it more power and that the oppressed always have the power within themselves to overcome their own powerlessness.[59] Specifically, after the 2009 Green Movement, when the Iranian government accused many activists, artists, intellectuals, and students of intending to unleash a Czechoslovakian-style Velvet Revolution (*Enghelab-e makhmali*), more attention was given to Havel and his ideas. Notably, the journal *Mehrnameh* published an extensive interview with Havel just before his passing in 2011.[60] As if taking a lead from Havel, regarding his emotional reaction, Golshiri recalls that for most of the performance he stood still, did nothing; just as most Iranians habitually do nothing in the face of state-sponsored violence. But then, Golshiri said, "I rebelled (*tamarrod kardam*), I confronted the 'security' head on, when they pushed me away."[61] After this, there was total chaos as the rest of the viewers broke through the cordon and rushed to save the artist. Amid the confusion, Mobed finally removed the noose.

The state-sponsored execution of political prisoners was brought into sharp focus during the course of five months in 1988, when thousands of

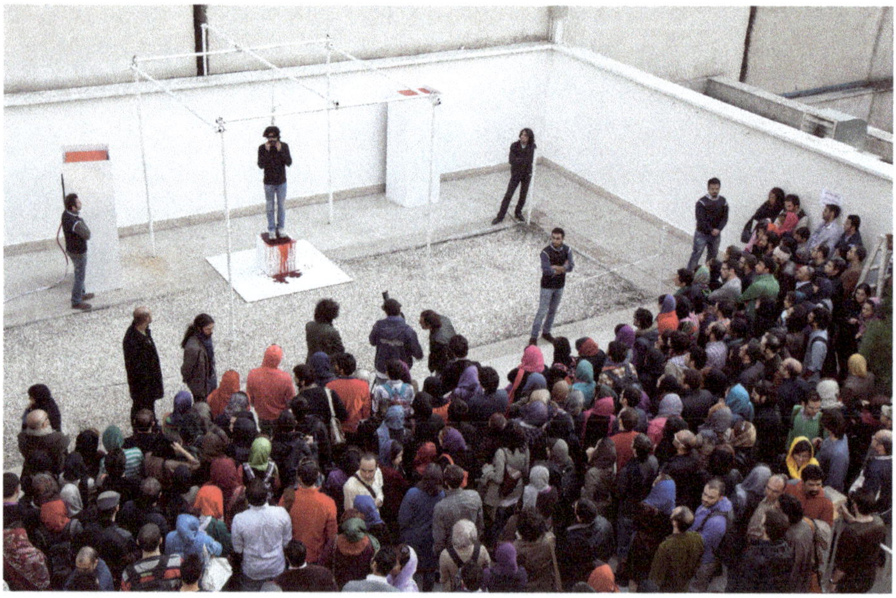

FIGURE E.3 Amir Mobed, *The Killing* (aka *Field*). 2011. Mohsen Gallery's backyard, Tehran. Photograph by Zarvan Rouhbakhshan and Omid Mehdizadeh. Courtesy of Amir Mobed.

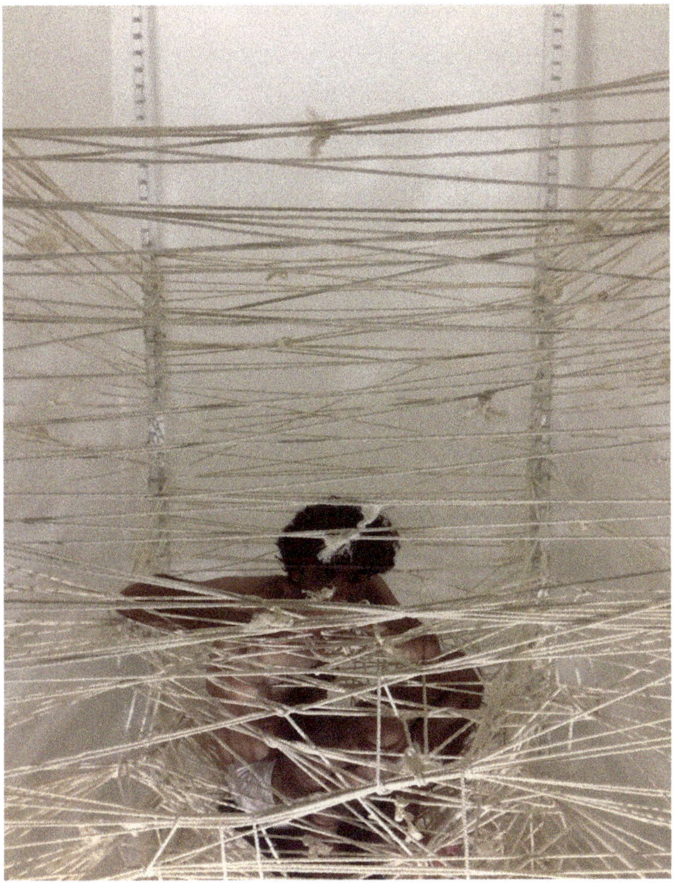

FIGURE E.4 Amir Mobed, *Disformission*. 2018. Mohsen Gallery's patio space, Tehran. Photograph by Siamak Ebrahimi, Mehrdad Motejalli, and Hamed Khosravi. Courtesy of Amir Mobed.

leftist members of the Iranian People's Fedai Guerrillas (*Chirik-e fadai-e khalgh*) and the *Tudeh* (Communist) Party of Iran were put to death by hanging. The reenactment, as art, of one of the most violent episodes in the life of the Islamic Republic owed much to Rasoulof's boldness as a gallerist.

Mobed would return to the alternative spaces of the Mohsen Gallery in 2018, this time using the *passio* for a lengthy performance, *Disformission* (or *Kajidan*; literally, weaving together) (fig. E.4). From 10 a.m. on October 11 to midnight on October 13, Mobed remained trapped inside the whitewashed *passio* in a projected act of self-inflicted torture. For sixty hours, without interruption or eating, he used balls of yarn to weave a spiderlike web around his body. As he wove, he climbed further up the web of his own making, becoming more trapped, more hidden. Careful not to directly highlight the political significance of the work, the Mohsen Gallery ingeniously describes the project in these words:

> In [this] performance . . . Mobed weaves a narrative in which he will get caught later; this narrative, he believes, is a naked representation of reality. However, the patience and perseverance in the performance of "Disformission" results from long hours of focusing on actions and controlling emotions: it is not the result of a shift in processes that the artist had earlier adopted in the nakedness of his concepts and performances. It is like the calm before the storm. The beginning and the end of this process-based performance do not really matter. [I]t is about Mobed's narration and the audience viewing it in passivity, like we are used to do for years now. If Amir Mobed had depicted this suffering in a straightforward fashion in his earlier works, he is now presenting the process of pain in a symbolic manner. If he painted a personal portrait of the state of suffering, now he is sketching out a collective misery: weaving a tangled web all around himself.[62]

In a personal interview, Mobed spoke of how he saw the *passio*, an often dysfunctional part of a modern house in Iran, as an apt venue in which to symbolically "reproduce the absurdity of the repeated acts of struggle in the everyday life of Iranians (*roozmarregi-e tekrar shavandeh abas*)."[63] The various openings on the *passio* allowed viewers to witness the performance from different angles—from below, the second floor, or the roof. With *Disformission*—at first glance seemingly only the tale of a trapped body—Mobed made them feel the painful history of modern Iran, moving along with them, and through them, as they moved up and down the building.

In addition to sponsoring art with provocative themes, Mohsen Gallery endorses artists who tackle gentrification—paradoxically a phenomenon that Rasoulof and his ilk are occasionally criticized for enabling. *Displacement* (*Jabejaie*) was a participatory performance installation created in 2017 by multimedia artist Golrokh Nafisi (b. 1981), in collaboration with curator Helia Hamedani (b. 1981). The artists invited a group of Tehrani participants to help make a sewn map of numerous movements between their rented places in different neighborhoods to show an urban landscape constantly reshaped by three decades of rapid development and gentrification.

Although interrupted by multiple pandemic lockdowns since the summer of 2020, a new Mohsen Gallery initiative, the Pelak Project (*pelak* refers to the street number of a house or business), has been created by Rasoulof in collaboration with media artist and filmmaker Mohammad Parvizi (b. 1972, also discussed in chapter 4). Parvizi suggested that visual arts exhibitions could be approached in the same way that a film crew scouts for locations. The aim is to promote work that is more site-specific, that "engages and interacts with the city on a larger scale, with an approach that alters each time around."[64]

The inaugural Pelak exhibition, *Friends and Enemies* (*Doost o doshman*), showcasing the work of Mahmoud Bakhshi, was held in a dilapidated (*kolangi*) building in central Tehran. In this respect, Pelak is not only a nod to the early 1990s *kolangi* projects described in chapter 1 but also a way of continuing to engage artists in discussions about gentrification and the destruction of Tehran's old buildings. Presented covertly thirty years ago, *kolangi* projects have now found a powerful sponsor.

Artists that Rasoulof has supported respect him for a variety of reasons. Amir Mobed confesses that the Mohsen Gallery is the only one to have honored his performances financially; in all other cases, his performances have been unpaid "cultural activities" (*fa'aliyat-e farhangi*) funded by the sale of his sculptures.[65] For Tooraj Khamenehzadeh and Negin Mahzoon (mentioned in chapter 1), Rasoulof combines very high artistic standards with a knowledge of the operation of different networks, a vital asset in their collaborative project to create international art residencies in Tehran. If a foreign artist arrives at the wrong moment—an unpredictable risk, given Iran's political instability—there is a chance that the slightest misstep will lead to their interrogation by the morality police. But Rasoulof knows how to negotiate and has "a good sense of what to do and when to do it."[66] He is also adept at securing additional sponsorship from private donors or cultural agencies within the European embassies, and at teaming up with other private enterprises to get special deals from local publishers, restaurants (e.g., Café 78), and hotels (e.g., Mashhad Hotel). As Khamenehzadeh and Mahzoon make clear, the inner workings of the alternative art scene remain shrouded in mystery: "It's like a James Bond film; no one knows how hard one should try to negotiate one's way through the complicated project of a privately sponsored foreign artist residency."[67]

. . .

In the "private" world of the art economy, there are of course other ways to sponsor art. Following, perhaps, the lead of the participatory budgeting movement, initially an antipoverty measure, started in Porto Alegre, Brazil in 1989, many liberal art experts become involved in nonprofit organizations or participatory budgeting projects, which in theory give members of the community a real say over how their money is spent. In practice, because the Iranian economy and currency are constantly in flux—mainly as a result of trade sanctions—these nonprofits and participatory budgeting projects (such as the Zirpelleh initiative described in chapter 1) tend to be short-lived. Rasoulof cites the fragile nature of these initiatives as the reason for his choice of the alternative route: the privatization of art venues by affluent agents. "For improving democratic spaces in Iran, we need longevity," he asserted.[68] But the difficulty of knitting together a sustained art economy outside of market forces is not limited to Iran. As we see from the experience of the United States and other places in the developed world, guerilla activities, pop-up projects, collaborative art, and short-term land leases may be cost-effective, but their impact is usually ephemeral.[69]

To explain the role played by privatization in opening up new opportunities for art, Rasoulof reminded me of how a major cut in state funding for theater under Ahmadinejad led to the emergence of a whole host of private theater companies, most of them nurtured through the efforts of a single donor or collective private sponsorship (see chapter 1).[70] For Rasoulof, privatization is the only means to create "democratic spaces for the exchange of ideas."[71] Coupled with his "malleable hardware expansion," it makes it possible to bring to light events that were previously underground and invisible. His initiative *Scaffolding* (*Darbast*)—a black box in the backyard of the Mohsen Gallery—was one of the earliest aboveground venues for formerly underground music bands.[72] Among others, it has hosted the fusion/alternative band Pallett, who presented their first "safe" and uncensored public performances there from May 30 to June 1, 2012.[73]

. . .

Visionary approaches by private galleries and foundations are not immune from criticism. Leftist in their views, some critics believe that the greatest threat to genuine artistic expression is not the restrictions imposed by the government of Islamic Republic but rather the politics of the art market, a kind of regulatory regime that art critic and curator Sandy Narine called the "institutionalization of dissent" in the early 2000s and amidst the rapidly declining alternative art scenes in Europe and America.[74]

The logic of the Islamic Republic's opposition to alternative art practices resonates in some ways with the apparent fate of such practices in a very different social and economic context—the United States. An early instance in this vein is the fate of Drop City (addressed in chapter 2). When Buckminster Fuller acknowledged the commune's appropriation of his design techniques and awarded them his first Dymaxion award in 1966, he inadvertently, perhaps, attracted mass media attention to the otherwise remote community.[75] In utter contrast to the invisibility and seclusion that the original creators of Drop City had pursued, the media attention invited a large crowd of young people and tourists. Unable to turn them away due to its open-door policy, the commune began to lose its unique identity and atmosphere. By 1969 all original members had left, and Drop City became somewhat of the degenerate joke that it had been viewed as from the beginning by its uncompromising critics.[76] Subsequently, urban alternative spaces too lost their original appeal or disappeared altogether. Starting in 1978, the National Endowment for the Arts (NEA) established a grant for "artist's spaces" and alternative venues. In the 1980s, right-wing politicians and religious groups began to condemn the NEA for sponsoring alternative art practices that they deemed inappropriate (referring specifically to provocative themes and homosexual art). Subsequently, NEA withdrew federal funds from many alternative spaces, including Franklin Furnace in New York.[77] During the Reagan administration, NEA-funded consultants assisted artist-run alternative spaces to turn themselves into profitable businesses. As such, "NEA effectively neutralized dissent by instilling a self-regulating standard of professionalization" in administrating and financing artist-run spaces.[78] Thus, "formerly autonomous artists were required . . . to see themselves as part of a professional class."[79] Eventually, as curator Brian Wallis writes, through the "NEA's patronage of alternative spaces, social control supplanted censorship" of earlier Cold War years, noticeably during the Nixon administration.[80]

With the 2008 economic crisis and the ensuing Occupy Movement, once again a new surge of independent artist-run spaces and alternative initiatives emerged. Specifically, artists began to get involved in economically declining neighborhoods and cities. This time, too, independent and grassroots efforts largely fell prey to powerful corporations. Many US scholars and economists have criticized Richard Florida's theory that the creative class could play a major role in regenerating economically declining urban zones, as articulated in his 2002 book, *The Rise of the Creative Class*.[81] Attempts by cities to implement Florida's ideas have ostensibly failed. Urban experts have shown how traditional theories of economic development greatly outperform the microeconomic changes brought about by the so-called creative class, and at least one analysis suggests there is no correlation at all between microeconomic changes and economic expansion.[82]

And yet the role of critical spatial practice in art cannot be reduced to this economic aspect. Commenting on the fate of activist art in the face of the staggering power of neoliberalism, Gregory Sholette writes that when creative energy "refuses to be productive for the market, it remains linked, however diffusely and ambiguously, to an archive of resistant practices."[83] Similarly, Stephen Duncombe insists that "where the activity of cultural creation (or observation) ends, the work of political organization begins."[84] In the same vein, in varying degrees of resistance and coalition, alternative art in Iran continues to grow in opposition to the mainstream. It remains in flux, sometimes improvising on, sometimes challenging the very foundations on which it was built. Its goal, however, remains constant: to create a better society.

Closing Remarks

In bringing this book to a close, I would like to add a few personal notes on my involvement as a historian with this project. I left Iran in the immediate aftermath of the Iranian Student Protests of July 1999 (also known as the Kuye Daneshgah Disaster; *Fajaye' kooy-e daneshgah*). At the time, this was the most significant grassroots protest movement since the Islamic Revolution. Sparked by the closure of the reformist newspaper *Salam*, the demonstrations began with demands for freedom of expression. Peaceful at first, they turned violent when the police got involved and arrested and injured many students, killing a number of them. As I was preparing to leave Iran for the United States, I steered clear of all political engagement, although I felt guilty for turning a blind eye to what was going on less than three kilometers from my home in Tehran. In the US, in the years that followed, I immersed myself in a new culture and a new language, in my new home. My education in both architectural history and comparative cultural and literary studies made me aware of the activist movements in art that had helped shape a more progressive civil society, from France's Situationist International to America's countercultural artistic movements and Moscow's conceptualism. Back then, I was unaware that similar activities were being pursued widely and systematically in Iran throughout the 1980s and 1990s. In part, this lack of knowledge was due to the mostly concealed nature of the events, which received little coverage, even in instances when they were open to the public.

Following the 2009 Iranian election protests, otherwise known as the Green Movement, there was a resurgence of activist art in Iran, very much in the spirit of the canonical countercultural movements. The intellectual scope of the work became apparent to me as early as 2015, as I immersed myself in conversations with Iranian artists. Meanwhile, I also led a collaborative curatorial project that tackled issues related to the Black Lives Matter movement that are important to the community on the south coast of Massachusetts where I live and teach.

The project took me out of my comfort zone, but it also opened my eyes to a host of connections between art and critical spatial practice, and between material culture and subtle forms of resistance. Over the next five years I had many encounters with Iranian artists, all of whom were extremely generous in discussing their projects and I am immensely grateful to them for enlightening me. I came to this project to study them, but soon it became clear that they too were studying me, challenging me, and questioning me on many fronts. As a result, I feel I am a more fulfilled scholar and person.

While my version of these events cannot redress the difficulties of the past four decades, I hope that it helps keep the artists' stories alive for current and future generations of Iranian artists and activists. During the writing of this book, the tightening of sanctions by the Trump administration caused extreme economic and political turmoil in Iran. The atmosphere in the arts darkened, as connections with the international art and design world were severed and the weakening currency created endless financial problems for artists and designers. But to my astonishment, alternative artists did not give up. They continued their efforts on the ground, and even if some of them left the country, they continued to contribute to the artistic intellectual discourse through social media.

The final revisions to this book were made during the COVID-19 lockdown. Here, again, Iranian artists displayed astonishing resilience. Initial feelings of despair and hopelessness quickly gave way to an intellectual discourse promoted via social media platforms, particularly Instagram and Clubhouse, with a high degree of savviness—many art experts are fully aware of the ways social media is exploited by powerful governments and corporations.

Some of these sessions focused on the writings of Hannah Arendt and Yuval Noah Harari concerning public and private, the right to civil society, and surveillance capitalism. Specific to the context of Iran, some condemned slacktivism (*koneshgari-e zir lahafi*; literally, under the blanket activism), and instead called for tangible engagement with important social issues. Notwithstanding, the usage of social media platform accelerated during the pandemic, so much so that in June 2021 the Iranian government revived its controversial legislation, the "internet restriction bill" (*tarh-e si-anat az fazay-e majazi*; literally "protecting users in cyberspace"), which had been in the making for some years. Intended to criminalize the use of blocked services by transferring internet control to the armed forces, the bill was immediately suspended by the parliament due to massive grievances.[85] Nonetheless, many social media conversations were subsequently organized around the subject, including by the architecture community, in which one middle-aged participant called for an alternative "underground" solution, if the bill were to be enacted. Speaking on the Clubhouse platform, he reminded his (architect) listeners of the vast network of Paris sewers. Built between 1853 to 1880 under the direction of Georges-Eugène "Baron" Haussmann and Eugène Belgrand for Emperor Napoleon III, these were significant means of escape for the "revolutionaries," as envisaged in Victor Hugo's *Les Miserables*. Hugo famously saw the sewers of Paris as the "conscience of the city," a place where there were no secrets. "What if," the Iranian architect asked, "we organize ourselves through more tangible solutions, like the way Hugo projected for Paris or how we ourselves used to do in the good old days of the pre-internet era?"[86] Although overly sentimental (as some listeners remarked), the statement is indicative of how the desire to find concrete solutions and going "underground" is still alive among a certain generation of creative agents.

Meanwhile, others became increasingly more pessimistic and took a more radical approach. Coupled with the unsatisfactory outcome of the 2021 presidential election, heated debates were renewed around engagement with the regime. Several artists took to social media to announce their intention to boycott any project that required permission from the authorities or necessitated close collaboration with the government. Oppositional voices escalated in a number of Clubhouse discussion platforms, particularly in August 2021 when Mohammad Mehdi Esmaili (b. 1975), the newly appointed minister of culture and Islamic guidance under President Ebrahim Raisi, issued a new "program" (*barnameh*) for revamping MCIG's existing rubrics to further "Islamicize" the arts.[87] Every single faction of the arts community, from filmmakers and theater experts to graphic designers and painters, published open statements addressing the newly appointed minister, scrutinizing and disapproving almost every single phrase within the new "program."

On his Instagram page, one prominent artist wrote: "So far, we have shown elasticity (*en'etaf*) as much as we could. But now it is time for disobedience (*sarpichi*). . . . From now on I would not participate in any art project or art publication that requires permission from the MCIG. . . . There are other ways for appearance (*hozoor*) in the realm of the arts and the domain of thoughts (*howzeh honar va andisheh*). The path to thinking (*rah-e tafakkor*) can never be blocked."[88]

Alternative Iran has attempted to capture and contemplate these issues. While the necessarily limited scope of the book has meant that many artists have been left out, I hope that Iranian art historians will expand on the contents of this book. Much of the work presented here is desperately awaiting documentation, presentation, and theorization.

In addition to exploring art, this study has also been an argument for the creation of spaces and practices that produce novel ways of seeing the world and new modes of thinking. The alternative spaces and informal collective environments discussed in this book are vital not only for producing innovative art but also for challenging the ideological and economic system of the Islamic Republic of Iran. My hope is that readers will take from this book an appreciation for all the creative agents who are perpetually transforming Iran's culture from "below" and against all odds. The extraordinary efforts of the art community in Iran will not be in vain. As Margaret Mead reminds us: "Never doubt that a small group of thoughtful, committed people can change the world. Indeed, it is the only thing that ever has."[89]

Acknowledgments

The topic of the current book became the main focus of my research in 2015 thanks to a sabbatical semester generously supported by an Iran Heritage Foundation Fellowship at the School of Oriental and African Studies at the University of London. I am grateful to Hassan Hakimian for supporting me during my time there. London itself brought a whole host of amazing scholars to my world, including Nelida Fuccaro, Haleh Anvari, and Hamid Keshmirshekan, from whom I learned a lot. I am particularly grateful to my dear friend and esteemed colleague Orkideh Behrouzan, who spent many hours discussing important issues related to the theme of this book and beyond. In the following years, she continued to encourage me to pursue this topic and even read an entire first draft of the book with much needed feedback. Sussan Babaie warmly welcomed me to her outstanding scholarly circle at the Courtauld and in conjunction with Robin Schuldenfrei invited me to give a talk based on the book's topic, and I am grateful for the responses that helped sharpen my focus.

In Massachusetts I am indebted to Houchang Chehabi. Always generous toward me since my graduate studies at MIT, he provided thoughtful suggestions for this work. Alice Friedman invited me to present a portion of this project at the prestigious McNeil Seminar at Wellesley College, where I was given input by top scholars in the field, including Daniel Abrahmson and Sibel Bozdogan. At MIT Nasser Rabbat could not have been more considerate when he sponsored my second sabbatical semester there. There I also learned from Caroline Jones, whose own scholarship I endlessly admire. Elmar Seibel and Azita Bina welcomed me to their precious collection of Iranian art. The scholarships of Elaheh Kheirandish and Afsaneh Najmabadi have been inspiring and I value their mentorship. In New Bedford, my journalist neighbor Ralph Hickok broadened my perspective by frequently leaving all kinds of helpful books and articles at my door.

Additional endorsement was provided by Iftikhar Dadi and Esra Akcan, who invited me to speak at Cornell in their respective departments and made many fruitful suggestions. Abbas Milani and Ala Ebtekar at Stanford University recognized this project and invited me to speak there. At Stanford I benefited from discussions with curator Hanna Regev and artist Joelle Benvenuto. At Yale, I gained valuable insights from faculty and graduate students at the School of Architecture who kindly hosted a seminar based on the topic of this book. Fatemeh (Shahrzad) Shams kindly accommodated me at UPenn, where I presented chapters from this book twice. I mostly profited from comments generously given by Mikhal Dekel and Firoozeh Kashani-Sabet. Other conferences and scholarly venues afforded opportunities to discuss Iranian art with Nahid Siamdoust, Ladan Nooshin, Marjan Moosavi, Laila Diba, Shiva Balaghi, Naghmeh Sohrabi, Staci Scheiwiller, Talinn Grigor, Siamak Delzendeh, Kaveh Ehsani, Norma Moruzzi, Pedram Khosrownejad, Kamran Talattof, Min Kyung Lee, Blake Atwood, and Azam Khatam, and I am thankful to all of them.

I am particularly privileged to be in dialogue with Negar Mottahedeh, whose work I have the utmost respect for and whose friendship I cherish. Behrooz Ghamari-Tabrizi and Shahram Khosravi, whose own excellent works have helped shape my thinking, provided words of support and encouragement throughout the entire writing process and I am immensely indebted to them. Colleagues Lori Handelman and Pamela Johnston read earlier versions of the chapters of this book and offered invaluable suggestions.

I have incurred a great debt to my colleagues in two fabulous research collaboratives to which I luckily belong. Working with my peers in the Aggregate Architectural History Collaborative Group—Arindam Dutta, Jonathan Massey, Daniel Abramson, Meredith TenHoor, Michael Osman, Lucia Allais, Timothy Hyde, Charles Davis, Lauren Jacobi, Zeynep Celik Alexander, Laila Seewang, and Ayala Levin—prompted many occasions to think outside the box. I want to especially acknowledge Daniel Abramson, who has been a great mentor to me over the years. For the compassionate reception of new approaches and for their endless intellectual curiosity, I have found the collegiate atmosphere of the Association of Modern and Contemporary Art of the Arab World, Iran, and Turkey (AMCA) unmatched. I benefited immensely from conversations with Sarah Rogers, Elizabeth Rauh, Anneka Lenssen, and most especially Jessica Gerschultz and Nada Shabout. Gerschultz provided rich commentary on this manuscript and

Shabout invited me to her community at the University of North Texas, where she offered laser-sharp remarks.

Colleagues and affiliates at my home institution, UMass Dartmouth, have been generous in similarly valued ways. It is my pleasure to acknowledge Lawrence Jenkens, Gloria De Sa, Don Burton, Merri Cyr, Jennifer McGrory, Anna Dempsey, Memory Holloway, Michael Swartz, Staci Ladd-Savage, Rebecca Hutchinson, Brian Williams, Thomas Stubblefield, John Buck, and Rebecca Uchill, who were supportive of this project from its inception. Rebecca Uchill, in particular, was a keen listener. Her enthusiasm for art inspires me and her collegial spirit sustains me. I am doubly grateful to Dean Jenkens, Chairperson Dempsey, and the Office of Faculty Development and the Provost Office for providing a subsidy to help pay for the book's colored pictures. The images in this book could not have been produced in this animated way without the additional financial support from the Millard Meiss Publication Fund of the College Art Association and the Graham Foundation for Advanced Studies in the Fine Arts. I am indebted to all those who voted in favor of celebrating the hard work of Iranian artists, which would have remained fragmentary otherwise.

At Stanford University Press, it has been my pleasure to develop this project under the expert guidance of Kate Wahl. I cannot thank her enough for her belief in this project from our very first discussion. Caroline McKusick and Susan Karani kindly helped facilitate logistical issues. I would also like to recognize the careful editorial attention paid to my text by Paul Tyler. Above all, my deepest gratitude goes to all the creative agents in Iran who generously shared their stories with me. Many of the interviews are cited properly in this study. A few were taken out due to word limitation. I cannot possibly list all the names here. But I want to take this opportunity to express my sincere gratitude. At the height of the COVID pandemic, when Iran struggled more than many other nations, the artists, architects, critics, and theater experts welcomed me into their communities, and I am most grateful for their willingness to present their world to me in the most generous way imaginable. Beyond our interactions at academic and scholarly levels, I also found new friendships in this brilliant community and I learn from them every day. I continue to follow these amazing artistic minds on social media, particularly Clubhouse and Instagram Live, and I cannot express how proud I am to belong to these precious virtual circles. With their willingness to use art to ameliorate social and political issues in Iran, art experts from across three generations inspire me every day. I am humbled by their determination and perseverance.

Although I am unable to list all of the Iran-based experts who have helped to shape my thinking, I want to use this platform to thank a few Iranian scholars who took time out of their busy schedule to discuss important issues with me. Theater, in particular, is a field out of my comfort zone, and I cannot be more grateful to Masoud Najafi Ardabili, who opened my eyes to salient details, particularly regarding his own scholarship and monograph on Jerzy Grotowski in Iran.

Additional conversations and email exchanges with Behnam Kamrani, Pouria Jahanshad, Hamid Severi, Masserat Amir-Ebrahimi, Azadeh Ganjeh, Homayoun Sirizi, Houman Mortazavi, Surena Parham, Jinoos Taghizadeh, Farah Ossouli, Aidin Torkameh, Kianoosh Motaghedi, Alireza Amirhajebi, Parham Ghalamdar, Ehsan Rasoulof, Rashin Ghorbi, Tooraj Khamenehzadeh, Farideh Shahsavarani, Negin Mahzoon, Saba Madani, Samar Saremi, Mehdi Farhadian, Amirali Ghasemi, Siamak Filizadeh, Azadeh Akhlaghi, Behzad Khosravi Noori, Negar Farajiani, Shahin Seyghali, Elham Puriya Mehr, Mahmoud Maktabi, Sohrab Kashani, Alireza Amirhajebi, Ali Shahbazyar, Mohammad Parvizi, Kourosh Golnari, Gholamhossein Nami, Parastoo Forouhar, Kamran Diba, Robert Wilson, Shahram Mohaddes, and Ali Shakeri Shemirani were particularly instructive. Mojtaba Fallahi kindly photographed several important sites for me and enabled interviews with a few galleries, and Saba Madani capably assisted with locating important archival documents in Tehran.

My scholarly collaboration with Tehran-based art experts also expanded beyond the scope of this book. I have had the good fortune to collaborate on several curatorial projects, symposia, virtual panels, and Persian publications and in the process have been privileged to partner with Pouria Jahanshad, Homayoun Sirizi, Kianoosh Motaghedi, Gohar Dashti, Mehdi Farhadian, Mehdi Ghadyanloo, Hafez Aslani, Behnam Kamrani, Bavand Behpoor, Hadi Fardanesh, Niloofar Rasooli, Neda Darzi, Hamed Noori, Shiva Biravand, and Amin Shahed.

Sadly, a couple of the artists discussed here passed away due to COVID or other health-related issues that could have been resolved had there been ease of access to health facilities. Sadegh Safaie walked me through the early days of performance art in Iran. He was genuinely enthusiastic about this book and was looking forward to seeing it in print. Alas, this will not happen. But I hope that future generation of artists find his unique story inspiring and follow in his footsteps.

Svetlana Boym's *Another Freedom: The Alternative History of an Idea* instantly captured my imagination when it was first published in 2010. Although set in the context of the former Soviet Union, the stories told by Boym struck a chord with me. Subsequently, I became more curious in comparative studies of Iran and the former Soviet Union and the Eastern Bloc. I am particularly thankful to Moscow-based artists German Vinogradov and Andrei Roiter, who returned my calls and opened my mind to the world of alternative art scenes in the 1980s Soviet Union. I am indebted to Alla Vronskaya for facilitating these connections.

The love and companionship of family was dear to me, especially during the difficult time of the pandemic and life in isolation. I want to offer my deepest appreciation to my parents, who have endlessly supported me since my academic journey began many years ago. Their youthful spirit and positive outlook never cease to astonish me. With her own enthusiasm for history, my mother encouraged me to write with passion. My father, on the other hand, reminded me to take time off from the screen and jog when and where possible. My sister, Pantea, was a great follower and admirer of this project. Her own artistic mind and life has inspired me over the years, and I thank her for communicating with me the stories of her artistic trajectory as a young college student in Tehran's alternative art scenes. With his deep affection for Iran, my brother Parham pointed me to the right sources on- and off-line and I cannot be more appreciative for his wisdom and deep knowledge of Persian sources. My youngest sibling, Pedram, spent valued time to discuss the concerns of his own generation, which would have been ambiguous otherwise. Two wonderful practicing architects based in Toronto, Parham and Pedram also presented all kinds of feedback related to things "spatial." My brother-in-law, Hamid, offered endless support when I needed it. My admiration and respect for his humanity and intellectual curiosity is boundless.

Finally, I want to single out my wonderful husband, Robert Fisher, who believed in this project and encouraged me to stay with it every day. Robert's affectionate understanding sustained me during our unconventional pandemic life, when I spent most of my time with *Alternative Iran*.

Notes

Introduction

1. Jeremy Suyker, "Iran's Underground Art Scene," *Maptia*, 2015, https://maptia.com/jeremysuyker/stories/iran-s-underground-art-scene (accessed February 10, 2015).

2. The Iranian artist community is diverse and spans a variety of age groups with different experiences of Iran's modern art scenes since the 1960s. For this reason, important art and cultural experts who have primarily lived and worked inside Iran appear with their birth dates. Providing these dates will allow readers to have a better sense of what generation the featured experts belong to and how they might have been influenced by the sociopolitical events and art movements that unfolded during their respective life spans. I have avoided such designations in cases where the expert is based outside Iran and is internationally known. Lastly, in these notes and the following bibliography for publications from Iran I have used both the Persian solar and the Gregorian calendars.

3. Ibid.

4. Ibid.

5. I have adopted a modified version of the transliteration system of *Encyclopedia Iranica* for Persian words, without diacritics except for ʻ (*ʻyn*) and ʼ (*hamzeh*). Unless otherwise indicated, all translations and transliterations are mine. To introduce the significance of the varied connotations of technical terms in the fields of art, architecture, (urban) design, and visual culture, I have provided transliterated Persian equivalents of titles of art projects and art publications as well as key English-language art historical concepts. I have highlighted the latter to help shed light on the efforts of Iranian artists, architects, and art historians in translating or (re)inventing technical terms in their respective fields. Doing so, I hope to open up possibilities for a deeper appreciation and culturally specific comprehension of the arts of Iran, while also diminishing the dominance of the Western canon.

6. Roland Barthes, *Camera Lucida: Reflections on Photography*, trans. Richard Howard (New York: Hill and Wang, 1981), 81.

7. In these terms, Suyker's photograph is what the cultural historian Marianne Hirsch describes as "a point of intersection between past and present, memory and

post-memory, personal remembrance and cultural recall." See Marianne Hirsch, *The Generation of Postmemory: Writing and Visual Culture after the Holocaust* (New York: Columbia University Press, 2012), 61–63.

8. Spaces of entertainment and consumption of forbidden alchoholic beverages are also highlighted in mainstream media as underground cafes and speakeasies. In this book I only address spaces of art and cultural activities. For an example of reports on Iran's speakeasies, see Gandom Khatib, "Tehran's Underground Speakeasies," *Daily Beast*, July 15, 2014, https://www.thedailybeast.com/tehrans-underground-speakeasies (accessed July 10, 2018).

9. Blake Atwood in conversation with Beeta Baghoolizadeh, "Blake Atwood on the Secret Life of Video Cassettes in Iran," *Ajam Media Collective*, November 29, 2017, https://ajammc.com/2017/11/29/video-cassettes-in-iran/ (accessed April 2, 2019).

10. Personal interview with California-based artist Pantea Karimi, July 12, 2020.

11. Atwood, "Blake Atwood on the Secret Life."

12. In this assertation I am indebted to my conversations with many Tehran-based theater experts, particularly Warsaw-based Grotowski historian Masoud Najafi Ardabili.

13. Nahid Siamdoust, *Soundtrack of the Revolution: The Politics of Music in Iran* (Stanford: Stanford University Press, 2017), 224.

14. Personal interview with Rozita Sharafjahan, January 10, 2019.

15. Personal interview with Homayoun Sirizi, April 7, 2021.

16. Fereydoun Ave in conversation with AB Gallery in Lucerne, Switzerland, "Fereydoun Ave at AB Gallery," 2010, https://www.youtube.com/watch?v=2v1IP9CIPAE (accessed March 2, 2021). I am grateful to architect Reza Daneshmir for bringing this recording to my attention.

17. Hamidreza Sheshjavani, "*Honar dar zamaneh hokmrani-e pool*" [Art in the age of the rule of money], *Giyumeh*, January 21, 2019, http://guillemetcircle.com/1397/10/19/ (accessed May 10, 2020).

18. In choosing the term *loose covertness*, I draw from a collection of essays, titled *Loose Space*, in which the contributors provide a variety of case studies from around the world where ordinary people appropriate sidewalks and plazas or vacant buildings to protest or celebrate and to experiment with alternative modes of living and meet their individual needs and desires. See Karen A. Franck and Quentin Stevens, eds., *Loose Space: Possibility and Diversity in Urban Life* (New York: Routledge, 2006).

19. Victor Tupitsyn, *The Museological Unconscious* (Cambridge, MA: MIT Press, 2009), 33–121.

20. Volker Diehl, Maria Popova, Matt Watkins, and Nina Mial, eds., *Glasnost: Soviet Non-Conformist Art from the 1980s* (London: Haunch of Venison in

collaboration with Galerie Volker Diehl, 2010), 14–17. Also see artist Vitaly Komar and Sasha Obukhova in conversation at the Garage Museum of Contemporary Art, which restores the archives of alternative and underground art in Russia, available at https://www.youtube.com/watch?v=z5yN2LsVNBg (accessed May 10, 2017).

21. David Morris, "Introduction: Anti-Shows," in *Anti Shows: APTART 1982–84*, ed. Margarita Tupitsyn and Victor Tupitsyn (London: Koeing Books for Afterall, 2017), 8–21.

22. See also David Morris, "Anti-Shows," in *e-flux* 81 (April 2017).

23. On these topics see, for example, Thomas Crow, *The Rise of the Sixties* (New Haven, CT: Yale University Press, 1996); Julie Ault, ed., *Alternative Art, New York, 1965–1985* (Minneapolis: University of Minnesota Press, 2002); Christopher Dunn, *Contracultura: Alternative Arts and Social Transformation in Authoritarian Brazil* (Chapel Hill: University of North Carolina Press, 2016).

24. Personal interviews with Jinoos Taghizadeh, July 3, 2020, and Houman Mortazavi, June 27, 2020.

25. See Talinn Grigor, *Contemporary Iranian Art: From the Street to the Studio* (London: Reaktion, 2014); Hamid Keshmirshekan, *Contemporary Iranian Art: New Perspectives* (Los Angeles: Saqi Press, 2014); Abbas Daneshvari, *Amazingly Original: Contemporary Iranian Art at Crossroads* (Los Angeles: Mazda, 2014); Shiva Balaghi, "Against the Market: The Art of Shirin Neshat," *Ibraaz: Contemporary Visual Culture in North Africa and the Middle East* (2016), https://www.ibraaz.org/essays/164 (accessed July 10, 2018); Fereshteh Daftari, *Persia Reframed: Iranian Visions of Modern and Contemporary Art* (London: I.B. Tauris, 2019). It is noteworthy that there are also important, albeit less disseminated and recognized, discussions about the relationship between art and art sites, including in articles published and talks given by Darabi (mostly in Persian). The relationship between art and urban cultures is also partially explored in Seyed Hossein Iradj Moeini, Mehran Arefian, Bahador Kashani, and Golnar Abbasi, *Urban Culture in Tehran: Urban Processes in Unofficial Cultural Spaces, Urban Book Series* (Cham, Switz.: Springer International, 2018); Annabelle Sreberny and Massoumeh Torfeh, eds., *Cultural Revolution in Iran: Contemporary Popular Culture in the Islamic Republic* (London: I.B. Tauris, 2013).

26. While I do not rely on this term in this book, I am influenced by the literature that exists on activist art forms and I am indebted to the scholars who have discussed them in their respective works. For example, Nina Felshin, Nato Thompson, Grant Kester, and Gregory Sholette, among others.

27. Interview with Sharafjahan. Also see the conversation between Rozita Sharafjahan and Saba Mousavi, "*Nasl-e roozhay-e sakht boodeem va zendeh mandeem*" [We were the generation of difficult days and we survived], in *Mo'asseseh farhangi, matboo'ati-e Iran: Iran Newspaper*, n.d., http://www.iran-newspaper.com/newspaper/BlockPrint/157782 (accessed May 10, 2019; site discontinued).

28. Interview with Sharafjahan.

29. Ave, "Fereydoun Ave at AB Gallery."

30. David Adjaye, "Building Critical Space," in *What Is Critical Spatial Practice?*, ed. Nikolaus Hirsch and Markus Miessen (Berlin: Sternberg Press, 2012), 9–10.

31. Claire Bishop, *Artificial Hells: Participatory Art and the Politics of Spectatorship* (New York: Verso, 2012), 1.

32. Examples of such alternative spaces are documented by Julie Ault in *Alternative Art, New York*, 17–76.

33. Lucy Lippard, *Six Years: The Dematerialization of the Art Object, 1966–1972* (New York: Praeger, 1973). Also see Mark Rosenthal, Sean Rainbird, and Claudia Schmuckli, eds., *Joseph Beuys: Actions, Vitrines, Environments* (New Haven, CT: Yale University Press, 2004); Paulo Freire, *Pedagogy of the Oppressed*, trans. Myra Bergman Ramos (London: Continuum Press, 1993).

34. Personal interview with Ashkan Zahraie, July 20, 2019.

35. Hamid Dabashi, *Shi'ism: A Religion of Protest* (Cambridge, MA: Belknap Press in conjunction with Harvard University Press, 2011), 220.

36. These performances are seen as entertainment and often looked down on. Street musicians are sometimes regarded as beggars. See Gay. J. Breyley, "Between the Cracks: Street Music in Iran," *Journal of Musicological Research* 35, no. 2 (2016): 72–81.

37. See also Masoud Najafi Ardabili, *Grotowski in Iran* (Berlin: Peter Lang, 2019). For the history of the Shiraz Arts Festival, see Mahasti Afshar, *Shiraz Festival of Arts: Shiraz, Persepolis*, updated and illustrated version of a paper originally commissioned by the Asia Society for "*The Shiraz Arts Festival: A Global Vision Revisited*" symposium (New York, Asia Society: 2013), https://asiasociety.org/files/uploads/126files/Festival%20of%20Arts%2C%20Shiraz-Persepolis%201967-77.pdf; Robert Gluck,"The Shiraz Arts Festival: Western Avant-Garde Arts in 1970s Iran," *Leonardo* 40, no. 1 (2007): 20–28.

38. Daniel Gerould, "Jerzy Grotowski's Theatre and Parenthetical Activities as Cosmic Drama," *World Literature Today* 54, no. 3 (Summer 1980): 382.

39. Margaret Croyden, "Peter Brook Learns to Speak Orghast," *New York Times*, October 3, 1971.

40. Grotowski was available for four consecutive days on the set of one of Naser Taghvai's (b. 1941) documentary films, *Arbaeen*, about the Shiite rituals in 1971.

41. Gerould, "Jerzy Grotowski's Theatre."

42. For example, one member of the Tantalos Theater (2005–9) was Mehdi Nassiri (b. 1980), formerly a traditional *ta'ziyeh* performer. He encouraged the rest of the group to include elements from these ritualistic passion plays in their otherwise nonreligious plays. See Najafi Ardabili, *Grotowski in Iran*, 126.

43. Dabashi, *Shi'ism*, 86–87. Hashim Mohd Nasir and Farideh Alizadeh, "A Comparative Study: The Principles of the Distancing Effect in Brechtian Theater

and Ta'ziyeh," *Cogent: Arts and Humanities* 7, no. 1 (2020), https://www.tandfonline.com/doi/full/10.1080/23311983.2020.1790195 (accessed July 10, 2020); Peter Chelkowski, "Ta'ziyeh: Indigenous Avant-Garde Theatre of Iran," in *Ta'ziyeh Ritual and Drama in Iran,* ed. Peter Chelkowski (New York: New York University Press, 1979).

44. Diba's interest in the Neo-Dadaists was also noted by Karim Emami. See Houra Yavari, ed., *Karim Emami on Modern Iranian Culture, Literature, and Art* (New York: Eisenbrauns, 2014), 211. Cited in Staci Gem Scheiwiller, "Disrupting Bodies, Negotiating Spaces: Performance Art in Tehran," in *Performing Iran: Cultural Identity and Theatrical Performance*, ed. Babak Rahimi (London: I.B. Tauris, 2021), 113–27, at 113. I am grateful to Scheiwiller for generously offering an earlier draft of this article. The Dada influence was also confirmed by Diba himself in a personal interview in July 2020.

45. Personal interview with Kamran Diba, July 20, 2020.

46. Hannah Crawforth, "About Kamran Diba," in *Kamran Diba: Good News, Bad News, No News*, ed. Negar Diba (Dubai: Gallery Etemad, 2012): 8–11; photographs of the art appear on page 11.

47. Hamid Keshmirshekan, ed., *Koorosh Shishegaran: The Art of Altruism* (Los Angeles: Saqi Books, 2017). On Eastern European mail art, see Kornelia Röder, "Ray Johnson and the Mail Art Scene in Eastern Europe," in *Mythmaking Eastern Europe: Art in Response*, 2014, *kunsttex-te.de/ostblick* 3, ed. Mateusz Kapustka, www.kunsttex-te.de/ostblick (accessed May 10, 2020); Geza Perneczky, "In the Underground between East and West," in *Promote, Tolerate, Ban: Art and Culture in Cold War Hungary*, ed. Cristina Cuevas-Wolf and Isotta Poggi (Los Angeles: Getty Research Institute, 2018), 95–109.

48. For more information on the accepted form of dance after the revolution, or *harekat-e mowzoon*, see Ida Meftahi, *Gender and Dance in Iran: Biopolitics on Stage* (London: Routledge, 2017), chap. 7: "*Harekat-e Mozun*: The Post-Revolutionary Theatrical Dance." According to Meftahi, the genre also was referred to as "structured movements" (*harekat-e formi*), "expressive movements" (*harekat-e bayani*), and "ritual movements" (*harekat-e a'yini*).

49. Personal interview with Saba Khozoie, June 17, 2019.

50. For examples of artworks and exhibitions, see Helia Darabi, "*Fazahay-e Jaygozin*" [Makeshift spaces], *Hamshahri*'s *Alef Magazine* 89, special issue, Art and Books (Bahman and Esfand [January and February], 1390 [2012]), 112–17.

51. Saba Sebti, Zahra Rahbar Niya, and Mehdi Khabbazi Kenari, "*Mafaheem-e Merleau-Ponty: Bastari baray-e tahleel-e honar-e ta'amoli*" [Merleau-Ponty's views: A context for understanding interactive art], *Kimia-ye honar* 5, no. 19 (1395 [2016]): 43–52.

52. Personal interview with Nazila Noebashari, June 17, 2020.

53. This divide is often mentioned in artist debates about the overlap of art and politics in Iran. For example, in a roundtable discussion about art and politics,

artist Barbad Golshiri reminds his artist audiences of the need to pay homage to the significance of the political effects of graffiti art in Iran. See Iman Afsarian, "*Nesbat-e mas'aleh dar-e honar va syasat dar honar siyasi-e Iran*" [The problem of the relationship between art and politics in Iranian political art], *Herfeh honarmand* 60 (Summer 2016): 64–77, at 71.

54. Farshid Rahimi, "*Goshayeshi bar honar-e modakheleh gar*" [An introduction to interventionist art], https://amirmobed.com/fa/publication/ (accessed May 12, 2020).

55. Helia Darabi, "*Rokgooyi behtarin rah nist*" [Directness is not the best solution], *Aseman Magazine* 93 (1390 [2011]), n.p.

56. Interview with Taghizadeh.

57. Sara Kamalvand, "MesoCity Tehran Workshop, Art, Ecology & the City," *Tavoos Art Magazine*, 2020, http://www.tavoosonline.com/Articles/ArticleDetailEn.aspx?src=163&Page=1 (accessed July 11, 2020); emphasis mine. Also see Daniela Terrile, "Tehran's Ecological Corridors," *Domus*, February 14, 2010, https://www.domusweb.it/en/news/2010/02/14/tehran-s-ecological-corridors.html (accessed May 10, 2018).

58. Terrile, "Tehran's Ecological."

59. Kamalvand, "MesoCity"; emphasis mine.

60. Ibid.

61. These categories are also mentioned in Mohammad Reza Moridi, *Honar-e ejtema'yi: Maghalati dar jame'eh shenasi-e honar mo'aser-e Iran* [*Social art: Essays on the sociology of contemporary art in Iran*] (Tehran: Aban Press in conjunction with Art University, 1397 [2018]), 78–83.

62. Samila Amir-Ebrahimi, "*Ma ba haman: Seyri dar honar-e siyasi ejtema'yi-e Iran-e mo'aser*" [Us and the Same: A look at the sociopolitical art of Iran], *Herfeh honarmand* 60 (Summer 2016): 2–26, at 10.

63. Afsarian, "*Nesbat-e mas'aleh*," 73.

64. Ibid., 72.

65. In this I am inspired by the work of Lucy Lippard on artist *David Wojnarowicz*. See Lippard, "Out of the Safety Zone," *Art in America* 78 (1990): 130–39. Also see Jennifer Doyle, *Hold It against Me: Difficulty and Emotion in Contemporary Art* (Durham, NC: Duke University Press, 2013), 8.

66. Ali Alizadeh (@Ali-Alizadeh), "Ali Alizadeh in Conversation with Habib Rahimpour Azghadi," Instagram, Thursday, April 22, 2020, available on YouTube at https://www.youtube.com/watch?v=sdcwH7HgngQ (accessed April 24, 2021). Azghadi has an insider's perspective. Before being dismissed for his open approach to sensitive issues, he was the director of *Zavieh*, a program on the Islamic Republic's official Channel 4.

67. Amir-Ebrahimi, "*Ma ba haman*," 12.

68. William Reddy, *The Navigation of Feeling: A Framework for the History of Emotions* (Cambridge: Cambridge University Press, 2001), 335.

69. Sara Ahmed, "Affective Economies," *Social Text* 79/22, no. 2 (Summer 2004): 117–39.

70. Ibid., 119.

71. Darabi, "*Fazahay-e jaygozin*."

72. On the possibilities of rethinking these spatial relations, see Jane Rendell, *Art and Architecture* (London: I.B. Tauris, 2006). It is noteworthy that in contrast to proponents of informal art, she also honors the activities of professionally trained artists who create unconventional forms of art such as interactive and temporary installations or ephemeral performances. On informal art practices in Iran, see Pouria Jahanshad, "*Honar-e gheyr-e rasmi va gheyr-e rasmi sazi-e honar*" [Informal art and making art informal], in *Bazkhani-e shahr: Hokmrani-e shahr* [*Rethinking the city: Urban governance*] (Tehran: Ruzbahan Press, 2022), n.p. I thank Jahanshad for sending me the article in advance of its publication.

73. Hans Ulrich Obrist and Karen Marta, eds., *Monir Shahroudy Farmanfarmaian: Cosmic Geometry* (Bologna, Italy: Damiani; Dubai, UAE: Third Line, 2011), 19.

74. Seyyed Hossein Nasr, *The Garden of Truth: The Vision and Promise of Sufism, Islam's Mystical Tradition* (New York: HarperCollins, 2007), 24. Cited in Sophia Rose Shafi, "Glass Palaces: The Role of *Aineh-Kari* in Shi'a Pilgrimage," *Shia Studies* no. 2 (July–September 2011): 6–9.

75. Ibid.

76. Personal interview with Pooya Aryanpour, June 28, 2020.

77. Ibid.

78. For more information about this exhibition, see https://faryarjavaherian.com/# (accessed June 28, 2020).

79. Interview with Aryanpour.

80. Rosalyn Deutsche, *Evictions: Art and Spatial Politics* (Cambridge, MA: MIT Press, 1996); Michel de Certeau, *The Practice of Everyday Life*, trans. Steven Rendall (Berkeley: University of California Press, 1984); Henri Lefebvre, *The Production of Space*, trans. Donald Nicholson-Smith (Oxford: Blackwell, 1991).

81. Rendell, *Art and Architecture*.

82. On these authors see, for example, Edward Soja, *Seeking Spatial Justice* (Minneapolis: University of Minnesota Press, 2020); David Harvey, *Spaces of Hope* (Berkeley: University of California Press, 2000); Liz Bondi et al., *Subjectivities, Knowledges, and Feminist Geographies: The Subjects and Ethics of Social Research* (Lanham, MD: Rowman & Littlefield, 2002); Doreen Massey, *Space, Place and Gender* (Cambridge, UK: Polity Press, 1994); Linda McDowell, *Gender, Identity and Place: Understanding Feminist Geographies* (Minneapolis: University of

Minnesota Press, 1999); Gillian Rose, *Feminism and Geography: The Limits of Geographical Knowledge* (Minneapolis: University of Minnesota Press, 1993).

83. See, in particular, the first in the series, Nikolaus Hirsch and Markus Miessen, eds., *What Is Critical Spatial Practice?* (Berlin: Sternberg Press, 2012). Also see http://criticalspatialpractice.org/ (accessed July 2, 2019).

84. Markus Miessen, "(Critical) Spatial Practice?" in Miessen, *Crossbenching: Toward Participation as Critical Spatial Practice* (Berlin: Sternberg Press, 2016), 31–65, at 37, 38.

85. Asef Bayat, *Street Politics: Poor People's Movements in Iran* (New York: Columbia University Press, 1997); Shahram Khosravi, *Young and Defiant in Tehran* (Philadelphia: University of Pennsylvania Press, 2008); Abbas Kazemi, *Parsehzani va zendegi-e roozmarreh Irani* [*Iranian strolling and everyday life*] (Tehran: Nashr-e Farhang-e Javid, 1388 [2009]). Also see Haleh Ladjevardi, *Zendegi roozmarreh dar Iran* [*Everyday life in Iran*] (Tehran: Nashr-e Sales, 1388 [2009]); Asef Bayat, *Life as Politics: How Ordinary People Change the Middle East* (Stanford: Stanford University Press, 2010); Shahram Khosravi, *Precarious Lives: Waiting and Hope in Iran* (Philadelphia: University of Pennsylvania Press, 2017); Nazanin Shahrokni, *Women in Place: The Politics of Gender Segregation in Iran* (Berkeley: University of California Press, 2019); Pedram Dibazar, *Urban and Visual Culture in Contemporary Iran: Nonvisibility and the Politics of Everyday Presence* (London: Bloomsbury Press, 2020).

86. Dell Upton, "Architecture in Everyday Life," *New Literary History* 33, no. 4 (Autumn 2002): 707–23.

87. Esra Akcan, *Architecture in Translation: Germany, Turkey, and the Modern House* (Durham, NC: Duke University Press, 2012), 19.

88. Personal interview with Aidin Torkameh, March 8, 2021. This important aspect of translation has been highlighted by other authors on Iranian subjects. For example, the Iranian American journalist Hooman Majd has written that, in order to understand Iran's foreign policy, one needs to learn at least some Farsi or Persian. He justifies this by claiming that certain words are not fully translatable to English, and as a result, miscommunication between the United States and Iran is rampant, especially in the sensitive context of the nuclear deal. See Hooman Majd, "Pride and Prejudice in Tehran: To Understand Iran's Foreign Policy, You Need to Learn a Little Farsi," *Foreign Policy* 229 (July 16, 2018): 8–9. Similarly, Omid Tofighian (b. 1975), the translator of Behrouz Boochani's celebrated prison memoir, writes that in the process of translating the work, it was "crucial to interpret the [words] as rooted and imbedded in lived experience, lived endurance and active resistance." For example, he writes of the challenge of translating Boochani's often-used term *system-e hakem*, connoting the spirit of Australia's ubiquitous detention center. The term could be simply converted into "oppressive system" or "ruling system." Instead, Tofighian opted for "kyriarchal system," a term stemming from the work of Elisabeth Schüssler Fiorenza that implies interconnected

systems of domination and submission. Rooted in feminist theory, the term transcends the implication of patriarchy to recognize that there are overlapping, complicated power strata that subjugate women. See Omid Tofighian, "Translator's Tale: A Window to the Mountains," in Behrouz Boochani, *No Friend but the Mountains: Writing from Manus Prison* (London: Picador, 2018), 4–27; Kwok Pui-lan, "Elisabeth Schüssler Fiorenza and Postcolonial Studies," *Journal of Feminist Studies in Religion* 25, no. 1 (2009): 191–97.

89. Henri Lefebvre, *Le droit a la ville* (Paris: Anthropos, 1968); David Harvey, "The Right to the City," *New Left Review* 53 (September–October 2008): 23–40; Anna Plyushteva, "The Right to the City and the Struggles over Public Citizenship: Exploring the Links," *Urban Reinventors* 3 (November 2009), http://www.urbanreinventors.net/paper.php?issue=3&author=plyushteva (accessed May 9, 2017).

90. Pouria Jahanshad, "*Toleed-e Tehran*" [The production of Tehran], unpublished paper and topic of a series of presentations on the eighth Tehran National Sculpture Biennial in December 2020. I am grateful to Jahanshad for providing the recordings of these presentations.

91. Ananya Roy and Aihwa Ong, *Worlding Cities: Asian Experiments and the Art of Being Global* (New York: John Wiley and Sons, 2011), 16. Neoliberalism in its global sense cannot be applied to Iran. After the renewed and more severe US-imposed sanctions under President Donald Trump (2016–20), the country fell virtually outside the global free market.

92. For more than three decades, the welfare programs of the 1980s, such as for higher education and health, have been increasingly removed from the public sector. According to Tehran-based sociologists Yousof Abazari and Arman Zakeri, this withdrawal is surprisingly even more extensive than in some European countries. See Yousof Abazari and Arman Zakeri, "*Se daheh hamneshini-e deen va Neoliberalism dar Iran*" [Three decades of the entanglement of religion and neoliberalism in Iran], *Naghd-e eghtesad-e siyasi*, February 2019, https://pecritique.com/2019/02/24/ (accessed August 1, 2019), 36.

93. Ali Ghadimi, "*Sherkat-e khosoolati chist va chera Rouhani ba an mokhalef ast?*" [What is the *khosoolati* agent and why is Rouhani against it?], *BBC Persian*, May 24, 2017, http://www.bbc.com/persian/iran-features-39993711 (accessed August 8, 2018).

94. Abazari and Zakeri, "*Se daheh hamneshini-e deen va Neoliberalism dar Iran*," 38.

95. Ibid.

96. Shahrokni, *Women in Place*.

97. Ibid.

98. Quoted from Jane Rendell's Critical Spatial Practice website, www.criticalspatialpractice.co.uk (accessed May 9, 2020).

99. Nicholas Mirzoeff, "Empty the Museum, Decolonize the Curriculum, Open Theory," *Nordic Journal of Aesthetics* 53 (2017): 6–22.

100. Michel Foucault, "Panopticism," in *Discipline and Punish: The Birth of the Prison*, trans. Alan Sheridan (New York: Vintage, 1979), 195–228.

101. *Rybon International Artists Workshop,* October 10–23, 2012, exhibition catalog (Tehran: Mohsen Gallery, n.d), 97.

102. See also Richard Penn's personal website. Content regarding Penn's Tehran residency is available at http://richardpennart.com/the-rybon-international-artists-workshop-tehran/ (accessed May 10, 2021).

103. Paul Stoller, *Sensuous Scholarship* (Philadelphia: University of Pennsylvania Press. 1997), xv.

104. Personal interview with Hamid Severi, September 10, 2019.

105. Allaine Cerwonka and Liisa H. Malkki, *Improvising Theory: Process and Temporality in Ethnographic Fieldwork* (Chicago: University of Chicago Press, 2007), 6.

106. Ibid., 5.

107. Ibid., 183.

108. Gregory Sholette, *Delirium and Resistance: Activist Art and the Crisis of Capitalism* (London: Pluto Press, 2017); "Aggressive Mimicry," *Wikipedia article*, https://en.wikipedia.org/wiki/Aggressive_mimicry (accessed May 8, 2019).

109. Farshid Emami, "Coffeehouses, Urban Spaces, and the Formation of a Public Sphere in Safavid Isfahan," *Muqarnas* 33, no. 1 (2016): 177–220, at 208.

110. The literature on the architectural character of Iranian dervish lodges is scarce. For a parallel study, see Heghnar Watenpaugh, "Deviant Dervishes: Space, Gender and the Construction of Antinomian Piety in Ottoman Aleppo," *International Journal of Middle East Studies* 37, no. 4 (November 2005): 535–65.

111. Numerous memoirs by members of the Fedai Guerrillas refer to group readings of the works of Marx in their mountain refuge. See, for example, Fatemeh Saidi Shaygan, "*Sokhanrani rafeegh madar dar marasem-e yade-yaran yad bad*" [The speech of a comrade mother in memory of her fallen son], *Payam-e fadayi* 84 (Ordibehesht 1385 [May 2006]): 2–4, http://www.siahkal.com/index/right%20col/payam84-Sokhan-raniy_Madar.htm (accessed November 10, 2018). A modified version is also available at https://www.siahkal.com/payam/Payam-Fadaee-84.pdf (accessed November 10, 2018).

112. Setrag Manoukian, *City of Knowledge in Twentieth Century Iran: Shiraz, History and Poetry* (London: Routledge, 2012), 119–22. For the recent persecution of Iranian Sufi sects by the Islamic Republic, see Loes Witschge, "Iran's Gonabadi Dervishes: A 'Long History' of Persecution—Clashes between Members of Iranian Sufi Order and Police Follow More than a Decade of Increasing Tension," *Al Jazeera*, February 28, 2018, https://www.aljazeera.com/indepth/features/iran-gonabadi-dervishes-long-history-persecution-180227193000395.html (accessed March 2, 2018).

113. A full description of the work is included in Allan Kaprow's anthology, *Assemblage, Environments & Happenings* (New York: Harry N. Abrams, 1966), 305.

114. See Maura Reilly and Lucy Lippard, *Curatorial Activism: Towards an Ethics of Curating* (London: Thames and Hudson, 2018).

Chapter 1

1. Mongol Bayat, Hamid Algar, and W. L. Hanaway, Jr., "*Anjoman*" [Organization]," *Encyclopedia Iranica,* vol. 2, 77–83, http://www.iranicaonline.org/articles/anjoman-gathering-association-society-general-designation-of-many-private-and-public-associations (accessed on December 30, 2018).

2. Mehdi Malekzadeh, *Tarikh-e enqelab-e mashrootiyat-e Iran* [*The history of the constitutional revolution in Iran*] (Tehran: Sokhan Press, 1387 [2008]), 73–79. Also see Gael Cohen, *Tarikh-e sansur dar matboo'at-e Iran* [History of censorship in Iran's periodicals] (Tehran: Agah Press, 1360–62 [1981–83]).

3. Naser-al-din Parveen, *Tarikh-e rooznameh negari Iranian va deegar Parsi neveesan* [*The history of Iranian and Persian language newspapers*], vo1. 1 (Tehran: Markaz nashr-e Daneshgahi, 1377 [1999]), 23.

4. Ibid.

5. Shahla Eyvas Zadeh, "*Shabnameh: Resaneh janeshin-e asr-e mashrootiyyat*" [Night letters: Alternative publications in the era of the constitutional revolution], *Ganjeeneh asnad* 16, no. 2 (Summer 1385 [2006]): 208, 214. For examples of two *shabnamehs,* see the same publication; for evidence regarding the lack of information on the whereabouts of the production spaces of the *shabnamehs,* see Mansoureh Ettehadiyeh, "*Tarikh-e naneveshteh-ha: Barresi elamiyeh-ha va shabnameh-hay-e enghelab-e mashrooteh*" [Unwritten history: Exploring the night letters of the constitutional revolution], *Shargh Newspaper,* 6 Shahrivar 1383 [August 27, 2004], http://asre-nou.net/1383/shahrivar/6/m-mashroute1.html (accessed May 2, 2019).

6. Banu Amirhajebi, "*Avvalin shabnameh-ie keh dar Tabriz montasher shod*" [The first *shabnameh* that was published in Tabriz], *Tehran Musavvar* 397 (1329 [1950]): 10, 19; Pari Sheikh al-Eslami, *Zanan-e rooznameh negar va andishmand-e Iran* [*Iranian women journalists*] (Tehran: Zarrin Press, 1351 [1972]).

7. Personal interview with an independent member of the leftist group *Rah-e kargar,* who wishes to remain anonymous, August 10, 2019.

8. Behrooz Ghamari-Tabrizi, *Remembering Akbar: Inside the Iranian Revolution* (New York: OR Books, 2016), 83–84.

9. Personal interview with a member of the leftist group *Rah-e kargar,* who wishes to remain anonymous, September 12, 2018.

10. Personal interview with Mehdi Farhadian, September 10, 2018.

11. Ibid.

12. Personal interview with a former *Tudeh* Party member, who wishes to remain anonymous, April 10, 2015.

13. Pierre Nora, "Between Memory and History," *Representations* 26, special issue, Memory and Counter-Memory (Spring 1989): 19.

14. Personal interview with Parham Ghalamdar, June 29, 2020.

15. Ibid. In doing so, Ghalamdar was inspired by renowned Iranian graphic designer Reza Abedini (b. 1967) and the Saqqakhaneh movement/group (1962–79), a movement in which artists looked to calligraphy and other elements of folk and local vernacular culture for inspiration.

16. In reference to Ahmed, "Affective Economies," 119.

17. In the years leading up to and in the immediate aftermath of the revolution of 1979, art magazines such as *Labor and Art* (*Kar va honar*) promoted Marxist ideas. Albeit short-lived, existing for only two issues, *Labor and Art* had a print run of between two and three thousand copies, was distributed by hand, and was produced by the most active forces among leftist Iranian art students. Labor exploitation and class struggle, with either a Soviet or a Maoist inflection, was of interest to artists such as Amir Esbati (b. 1956), a member of the 57 Group that took its title, retrospectively, from the revolution's year in the Iranian calendar (1357 [1979]). Esbati penned an insightful piece about the 1968 European leftist student movement and its impact on fine arts students, in which he asserts that Marxist ideas were open to interpretation and appropriation by Iranians, as they had to share spaces with religious groups and others. The writings of such prominent Marxist art historians as Arnold Hauser in his book, *The Social History of Art (1951)*, were presented in the weekly magazine *Ketab-e jom'eh* [*The book of friday*], vol. 1 (1358 [1979]), 96–105, edited by renowned poet Ahmad Shamlou (1925–2000), and published in 1979 and 1980. Also see Morad Montazami, "Introduction to Amir Esbati, 'The Student Movement of May 1968 and the Fine Art Students,'" *ARTmargins* 6, no. 6 (October 2017): 111–21; Amir Esbati, "*Jonbesh-e daneshjooy-e May 1968 va daneshjooyan-e honarhay-e ziba*" [The student movement of May 1968 and the fine arts students], *Kar va honar* (1358 [1979]): 6–9. For a relevant reflection on this matter by Esbati, see *Gallery Online*, "*Jay-e posterhay-e enghelabi dar resaneh ma khalist*" [We miss the revolutionary posters], editorial, February 6, 2016, http://onlineartgallery.ir/graphic/?m_id=8&id=5822 (accessed May 10, 2018).

18. Jonathan Green and Nicholas Karolides, *Encyclopedia of Censorship* (New York: Facts on File Inc. Press, 2005), 290. Also see Agnes Callamard, Bethan Grillo, and Sophie Redmond, eds., *Article 19: Global Campaign for Free Expression: Unveiled, Art and Censorship in Iran*, 2006, https://www.article19.org/data/files/pdfs/publications/iran-art-censorship.pdf (accessed July 10, 2017).

19. Ibid.

20. Ibid.

21. Sohrab Behdad, "Islamization of Economics in Iranian Universities," *International Journal of Middle East Studies* 27, no. 2 (May 1995): 193–217.

22. Published in *Kayhan-e hava'i* (1359 [April 30, 1980]). Reproduced in Ruhollah Khomeini, *Islam and the Revolution: Writings and Declarations of Imam Khomeini*, trans. Hamid Algar (Berkeley: Mizan Press, 1981), 295–99.

23. Grigor, *Contemporary Iranian Art*, 105.

24. Azadeh Karimi, "Iranian Painter Whose Artworks Were Destroyed in the Revolution Has Berlin Show," *Kayhan Life*, November 30, 2018, https://kayhan life.com/culture/art/iranian-painter-whose-artworks-were-destroyed-in-the -revolution-has-berlin-show/ (accessed December 10, 2018).

25. Talinn Grigor, *Building Iran: Modernism, Architecture, and National Heritage under the Pahlavi Monarchs* (New York: Periscope, 2009).

26. Grigor, *Contemporary Iranian Art*, 106.

27. Talinn Grigor in an interview with Alireza Sami-Azar (former director of TMoCA, June 14, 2009). Cited in Grigor, *Contemporary Iranian Art*, 106. Also see my references to Parvaneh Etemadi's work in *Domesticity and Consumer Culture: Interior Revolutions of the Modern Era* (London: Routledge, 2013), 165. On this topic, I also interviewed artists who went to art school immediately after the end of the Cultural Revolution. Examples include Surena Parham (b. 1968), who was a photography major at the University of Tehran's Faculty of Fine Arts from 1984–88.

28. Ahmad Karimi-Hakkak, "Censorship," *Encyclopedia Iranica* 5, fasc. 2 (December 15, 1990): 135–42. On the censorship of dance see Meftahi, *Gender and Dance*. On the censorship of music see Siamdoust, *Soundtrack of the Revolution*.

29. See also Glenn Harcourt, Pamela Joseph, and Francis M. Naumann, *The Artist, the Censor, and the Nude: A Tale of Morality and Appropriation* (New York: DoppelHouse Press, 2017).

30. Willem Floor, *The History of Theater in Iran* (Washington, DC: Mage, 2005).

31. Liliane Anjo, "Contemporary Iranian Theatre: The Emergence of an Autonomous Space," in *Cultural Revolution in Iran: Contemporary Popular Culture in the Islamic Republic*, ed. Annabelle Sreberny and Massoumeh Torfeh, 81–94 (London: I.B. Tauris, 2013).

32. Don Rubin, ed., *World Encyclopedia of Contemporary Theatre*, vol. 5, Asia/Pacific (London: Routledge, 1998), 253. Also see Babak Rahimi, "Censorship and the Islamic Republic: Two Modes of Regulatory Measures for Media in Iran," *Middle East Journal* 69, no. 3 (July 2015): 358–78. For film and music performances, besides MCIG, two other governmental bodies are responsible: Iranian Radio and Television (*Seda va sima*) and the Arts Foundation (*Howzeh honari*).

33. Personal interview with Farah Ossouli, March 17, 2021.

34. Ibid.

35. Ibid.

36. Ibid.

37. A case in point is Sapir Hospital, the only Jewish philanthropic health institution in Tehran, whose main agenda was famously to "treat all patients, without regard to their ethnic or religious orientation." Also see Lior B. Sternfeld, *Between Iran and Zion: Jewish Histories of Twentieth Century Iran* (Stanford: Stanford University Press, Kindle Edition, 2018), 576–80; Houman Sarshar, "Judeo-Persian

Communities xi. Music (1)," *Encyclopædia Iranica*, vol. 15/2 (2012): 160–63, http://www.iranicaonline.org/articles/judeo-persian-xi-1-a-general-survey-of-persian-jewish-music (accessed May 10, 2018).

38. Personal interview with Farah Ossouli, June 4, 2015.

39. Ibid.

40. Ibid. Ossouli adds that it was only in 1994, after Maryam Zandi, the renowned Iranian portrait photographer, published a book on portraits of contemporary Iranian painting masters that the works of these masters were publicly accessible. See Maryam Zandi, *Seemayi az naghashan-e mo'aser-e Iran* [*Portraits of contemporary Iranian painters*] (Tehran: Nashr-e Mo'allef, 1373 [1994]).

41. For more information on churches in Tehran, see Andranik Hovian, *Kelisahay-e maseehiyan dar Iran zamin* [*Churches of Christians in Iran*] (Tehran: Entesharat-e Moavenat-e Farhangi, 1383 [2004]).

42. Interview with Ossouli.

43. Personal interview with Yahya Alkhansa, July 24, 2019.

44. Ibid.

45. Personal interview with Shahram Sharbaf, August 14, 2021.

46. Ibid.

47. Ibid.

48. Personal interview with Arash Sobhani, March 24, 2015. After the Bolshevik Revolution, the Russian Civil War ensued, which lasted from 1918 to 1922. It forced out many who could not find a place under the new regime. More than one million emigrants went looking for a new home in Europe, the United States, and, to a lesser degree, Iran. For more information on St. Nicholas, see *Russian TV (RT)*, "Fleeing 1917 Revolution: Orthodox Church in Tehran Maintained by Russian Émigré Descendant," *RT News* editorial, November 5, 2017, https://www.rt.com/news/408825-russia-revolution-1917-iran-church/ (accessed May 2, 2018).

49. On Eskandarian, Tehran's most important music store in the 1980s, see *Shargh Daily*, "*Kasi nist keh Ketabforooshi ra Bekharad*" [There is no one to purchase this bookstore], editorial, no. 1348, September 20, 2011, http://old.sharghdaily.ir/news/90/06/29/33455.html (accessed November 10, 2016).

50. Interview with Sobhani.

51. Interview with Sharbaf.

52. Ibid.

53. The Bahá'í Institute for Higher Education (BIHE) was established in 1987 in response to the Iranian government's ongoing campaign to suppress Iranian Bahá'ís and their access to higher education. The BIHE offers thirty-eight university-level programs across five faculties and continues to enhance and deliver academic programs in the sciences, engineering, business and management, humanities, music, and social sciences. See http://bihe.org/ (accessed June 10, 2019).

54. Personal interview with Khozoie, June 17, 2019.

55. Interview with Sharbaf.

56. Interview with Alkhansa.

57. For more information on Iranian underground music, see Heather Rastovac, "Contending with Censorship: The Underground Music Scene in Urban Iran," *Intersections* 10, no. 2 (2009); Laudan Nooshin, "Underground, Overground: Rock Music and Youth Discourses in Iran," *Iranian Studies* 38, no. 3 (2005): 463–94; Siamdoust, *Soundtrack of the Revolution.*

58. The members were Sohrab Mohebbi, vocals; Sardar Sarmast, guitar; Slamak Khaledi, trombone; Alireza Pourassad, bass; Yahya Alkhansa, drums; and Shervin Shahamipour, sitar. Cary Darling, "Iran's 127 Uses Net to Beat Repression," *Fort Worth Star-Telegram*, March 16, 2006, E1; Evan Osnos, "Rockin' Hard, Rockin' Risky; A Hot Band in Iran Has to Be Furtive, in Part Because It's Fun, Members of the Underground 127 Tell Correspondent Evan Osnos," *Chicago Tribune*, June 20, 2005, 1.4.

59. Interview with Alkhansa. The greenhouse is now a commercial space belonging to a hairstylist.

60. Personal interview with Sohrab Mohebbi, July 20, 2019.

61. Interview with Alkhansa.

62. Fatemeh Shams and Eskandar Sadeghi-Boroujerdi, "Q&A: Head to Head with Abdi Behravanfar, Khorasan Blues Pioneer," *Tehran Bureau, Frontline, PBS*, January 12, 2012, https://www.pbs.org/wgbh/pages/frontline/tehranbureau/2012/01/qa-head-to-head-with-abdi-behravanfar-pioneer-of-the-khorasan-blues.html (accessed July 20, 2020). I am grateful to Fatemeh Shams for bringing this source to my attention.

63. Ibid.

64. Ibid.

65. Ibid.

66. Ekaterina Degot, "Performing Objects, Narrating Installations: Moscow Conceptualism and the Rediscovery of the Art Object," *E-Flux Journal* 19, November 2011, https://www.e-flux.com/journal/29/68067/performing-objects-narrating-installations-moscow-conceptualism-and-the-rediscovery-of-the-art-object/ (accessed May 2, 2017).

67. Homa Art Gallery (@homaartgallery), "Interview with Aydin Aghdashloo," July 7, 2020, https://www.instagram.com/homaartgallery (accessed July 8, 2020). As mentioned in the introduction regarding Faramarzi's classes, there were also more open, unofficial venues inside business complexes. Prominent Iranian photographer Mehran Mohajer (b. 1964) owes his knowledge and skills to the teachings of Yahya Dehghanpour. Mohajer and a few other University of Tehran classmates gathered in Dehghanpour's photography studio in the basement of a business building near Tehran University, where Dehghanpour also offered official courses on photography but was constantly monitored in terms of what he could

and could not teach. While many of these alternative art spaces followed the moral guidelines set by the Islamic Republic—for example, holding gender-segregating teaching sessions—they all became entirely or partially invisible. The parameters by which we determine what is or is not incorporated within the realm of the "visual" and the "official" are themselves a matter open to dispute. I am indebted to discussions with Mehran Mohajer and Surena Parham on various dates in 2021.

68. Rozita Sharafjahan in conversation with *Arte: Tarikh-e shafahi-e farhang va honar-e Iran* [Arte: Oral history of Iran's contemporary culture and art], Summer 2017, https://www.youtube.com/watch?v=n3UZb8uKtVo (accessed May 10, 2019).

69. Azadeh Jafarian, "*Bad az chehel sal rahat khabidam*" [I slept well after forty years]," *Shargh Newspaper* 9, no. 1542, 10 Khordad 1391 [May 30, 2012].

70. Ave in conversation with AB Gallery.

71. Kathleen A. Feeley and Jennifer Frost, eds., *When Private Talk Goes Public: Gossip in American History* (New York: Palgrave McMillan, 2014).

72. Mahmood Karimi-Hakak, "Exiled to Freedom: A Memoir of Censorship in Iran," *TDR: The Drama Review* 47, no. 4 (Winter 2003): 17–50, at 27.

73. Once the permit was issued for a gallery by the MCIG, it had to be renewed annually based on the owner's records of negative testing for drug use and on the absence of criminal activity. Depending on the political atmosphere and the MCIG leadership, the bureaucratic procedures were susceptible to change. For example, between 1997 and 2005, many of the procedures were altered as the ministry stopped requesting authorization for each individual show and for pictures of exhibition contents. Instead, each gallery was required to submit an annual report of their activities. However, the ministry continued to keep an eye on all shows. Grigor, *Contemporary Iranian Art*, 137–42. Also based on a personal interview with gallery director Behzad Nejadghanbar, July 2, 2020.

74. In the visual arts the history of the usage of private homes as art venues can be traced to the early Pahlavi period, when many Iranian artists were trained by private tutors. In 1957, Jazeh Tabatabai (1931–2008) opened the Modern Art Gallery (*Honar-e jadid*) in his home on Takht-e Jamshid (now Taleghani) Street. There were also informal salon-like gatherings in the homes of high-profile artists like Monir Shahroudy Farmanfarmaian (1922–2019). Unlike the postrevolutionary cases, these were only an extension of the official art venues. Some functioned as counter-exhibitions for works that were rejected for display in more limited official venues (a situation that also led to domestic-space *salons des refuses* in other parts of the Middle East). On these topics, see Media Farzin, "A Short History of Art Exhibitions in Iran, 1946–78," in *Iran Modern*, ed. Layla S. Diba and Fereshteh Daftari (New Haven, CT: Yale University Press, 2014), 67–72; Obrist and Marta, eds., *Monir Shahroudy Farmanfarmaian*, 29. On a parallel situation elsewhere in the Middle East, see Amin Alsaden, "Alternative Salons: Cultivating Art

and Architecture in the Domestic Spaces of Post-WWII Baghdad," in *The Art Salon in the Arab Region: Politics of Taste Making*, ed. Nadia Von Maltzahn and Monique Bellan (Beirut: Bergon Verlang Wurzburg in Kommission, 2018), 168–208.

75. Lili Golestan's TEDx Talk in Tehran, https://www.youtube.com/watch?v=lp2N2--nVtA (accessed October 2018).

76. Personal interview with Leyla Samari, June 20, 2019.

77. Kaveh Ehsani, "'Tilt but Don't Spill': Iran's Development and Reconstruction Dilemma," *Middle East Report* 191 (1994): 16–21.

78. Farhang Rajaee, *Islamism and Modernism: The Changing Discourse in Iran* (Austin: University of Texas Press, 2007).

79. Ervand Abrahamian, *A History of Modern Iran* (Princeton, NJ: Princeton University Press, 2008), 187–88.

80. Ibid., 187–88.

81. Kaveh Ehsani, "Survival through Dispossession: Privatization of Public Goods in the Islamic Republic," *Middle East Report* 250 (Spring 2009): 26–33, at 29.

82. Ault, *Alternative Art, New York*, 30.

83. Martin Beck, "Alternative: Space," in Ault, *Alternative Art, New York*, 249–79.

84. Ibid., 254–55.

85. Antonia Carver, "Dead Dogs: A Decade of Public Art Experiments in Tehran," *Bidoun: Art and Culture from the Middle East* 1 (Summer 2004), https://www.bidoun.org/articles/dead-dogs (accessed August 10, 2018).

86. Personal interview with Sassan Nassiri, June 23, 2020.

87. Personal interview with Mostafa Dashti, June 21, 2020.

88. Interview with Nassiri.

89. Ibid.

90. An audio recording of this event is available on the official website of the Iranshahr Gallery: https://iranshahrartgallery.com/fa/podcast/ (accessed June 23, 2020).

91. Based on Behnam Kamrani's presentation at "*Hamayesh-e porsesh az honar-e mo'aser-e Iran*" [A panel on contemporary Iranian art], Farabi Hall, Art University, Tehran (November 19, 2018), audio recording. I am grateful to Kamrani for kindly sharing this material with me.

92. These classes were available from 1982–2016.

93. Personal interview with Houman Mortazavi, June 22, 2020.

94. Ibid.

95. More information about Behboudi can be found in Gholamhossein Mirza Saleh, *Reza Shah: Khaterat-e Soleiman Behboudi, Shams Pahlavi and Ali Yazdi* [*Reza Shah: According to the memoirs of Soleiman Behboudi, Shams Pahlavi and Ali Yazdi*] (Tehran: Tarh-e Now, 1372 [1993]).

96. Ibid.

97. Personal interview with Mehrnoush Behboudi, June 23, 2020.

98. Interview with Mortazavi.

99. Ibid.

100. Ibid.

101. Diehl et al., *Glasnost*, 33. The artist-founders of Kindergarten were Andrei Roiter, Garik (aka German) Vinogradov, Nikolay Filatov, and Alexander Ivanov.

102. Personal interview with New York-based Russian artist Andrei Roiter, July 31, 2019.

103. Ibid.

104. Personal interview with Moscow-based artist German Vinogradov, June 26, 2019.

105. For a complete list of galleries, see Minoo Iranpoor, "*Padideh-ie taht-e onvan-e gallery*" [A phenomenon called the gallery] (master's thesis, Art University, Tehran, 1381 [2002]).

106. Negar Azimi, "Don't Cry for Me, America," in *My Sister, Guard Your Veil; My Brother, Guard Your Eyes: Uncensored Iranian Voices*, ed. Lila Azam Zanganeh (Boston: Beacon Press, 2006), 104–12, at 108. I am indebted to Norma Claire Moruzi for bringing this essay to my attention. Also see Negar Azimi, art critic and senior editor of *Bidoun Magazine*, who asks: "What is the difference between representing politics and enacting it?"; in Azimi, "Good Intentions: Art Has a Long History of Engagement with Politics; Does Recent So-Called Socially Engaged or Political Art Effect Change?" *Frieze* 137 (March 1, 2011), https://frieze.com/article/good-intentions (accessed May 28, 2018). Also cited in Kareem Estefan, Carin Kuoni, and Laura Raicovich, eds., *Assuming Boycott: Resistance, Agency, and Cultural Production* (New York: OR Books in partnership with Counterpoint Press, 2017), 11–12.

107. *The Art of Demolition* (1998). I am grateful to Maziar Bahari for offering a copy of this recording to be studied for this volume.

108. Ibid.

109. Mentions of these shows can be found in the writings of art critic Negar Azimi and in Nato Thompson, *Living as Form: Socially Engaged Art from 1991–2011* (Cambridge, MA: MIT Press 2012), 152–53. Thompson only highlights the first *kolangi* project; unfortunately, here the project is attributed to the wrong artists. More recent are the lectures and writings of Tehran-based art historian Helia Darabi back in Iran. Also see Carver, "Dead Dogs"; Azimi, "Good Intentions."

110. In 1998, the Iranian media began a massive campaign that warned against the dangers of Tehran's pollution to human health. The media highlighted that many schoolchildren who spent most of their days outside in schoolyards and on the street were particularly at risk. A quick glance at popular newspapers, such as *Abrar* and *Ettela'at*, from 1988 to 2000 reveals the urgent level of concern over

Tehran's polluted air. Many articles are animated by images of children with face-masks, featured against the backdrop of vehicles with diesel *exhaust*. Some school-children are shown holding placards with environmental messages. See, for example, Ali Valizadeh, "*Yadeh aseman-e abi Tehran bekheir*" [Farewell Tehran's blue sky], *Abrar Newspaper* 2960, 28 Dey 1377 [January 18, 1999], 1.

111. Carver, "Dead Dogs."

112. Zohreh Soleimani, "*Gozareshi az yek namayeshgah-e veejeh dar Tehran: Koodakan-e abi, aseman-e siah*" [A report on a special exhibition in Tehran: Blue children, black sky], *Golestaneh* 12 (Dey 1378 [January 2000]): 91–94, at 91.

113. Ibid.

114. Ibid.

115. Carver, "Dead Dogs."

116. Behnam Kamrani and Setareh Hosseini, "*Honar-e mo'aser-e Iran va asar-e zist mohiti*" [Contemporary Iranian art and environmental works]," in *Haftomin salaneh honar-e mo'aser-e Persbook, honar-e zist mohiti-e Iran* [*Persbook: The seventh annual festival of contemporary art (Iranian eco art)*] (Tehran: Nashr-e Bongah, 1396 [2018]), 84–95, at 91–92.

117. On legal and political debates about ownership of public buildings during this period, see Kaveh Ehsani, "The Politics of Property in the Islamic Republic of Iran," in *The Rule of Law, Islam, and Constitutional Politics in Egypt and Iran*, ed. Said Amir Arjomand and Nathan J. Brown (Albany: SUNY Press, 2013), 153–78, at 154.

118. Personal interview with Narges Siah's lead actor, Atefeh Tehrani, June 22, 2019. Regarding this play, also see Roxanne Varzi, *Last Scene Underground: An Ethnographic Novel of Iran* (Stanford: Stanford University Press, 2015), xv–xvi.

119. Jerzy Grotowski, *Towards a Poor Theatre* (New York, Routledge, 1968), 19.

120. Grotowski's *Towards a Poor Theatre* (1968) was translated into Persian in 1970 by Hasan Marandi under the title *Be sooy-e te'atr-e bichiz*.

121. Grotowski, *Towards a Poor Theatre*, 116.

122. Associated with the Theatre of the Absurd, Genet had a contentious past as a homosexual petty thief. As an outsider to society, he could relate to the pain of marginalized groups and underdogs. Also see Elisa Bray, "'The Blacks': Genet's Contentious Play Returns," *The Guardian*, October 18, 2007, https://www.independent.co.uk/arts-entertainment/theatre-dance/features/the-blacks-genets-contentious-play-returns-394981.html (accessed May 10, 2018).

123. Ibid.

124. Cited in Najafi Ardabili, *Grotowski in Iran*, 123.

125. Tehrani recalls that lay audiences did not appreciate it as much. Some saw it as absurd, others as too loud and incoherent. Theatergoers at the time were not accustomed to creative adaptations of old plays. All they wanted to see was a

"linear narrative," Tehrani recalled. And some asked for their money back. Regardless, the performances astonished artists and theater experts, and the performances were sold out for the entirety of the run.

126. A verse in Shamlou's 1979 poem "*The Story of the Daughters of the Mother of the Sea*." Interview with Tehrani.

127. Najafi Ardabili, *Grotowski in Iran*, 118.

128. Personal interview with Ali Shahbazyar, August 3, 2021.

129. Ibid.

130. Ibid.

131. Komar and Obukhova, conversation, Garage Museum. For more information about paradise, see Matthew Jesse Jackson, *The Experimental Group: Ilya Kabakov, Moscow Conceptualism, Soviet Avant-Gardes* (Chicago: University of Chicago Press, 2010), 221.

132. Komar and Obukhova, conversation, Garage Museum.

133. Also known as the Serial Murders, this series of murders and disappearances from 1988 to 1998 were allegedly carried out by Iranian government operatives against Iranian dissident intellectuals who had been critical of the Islamic Republic. To this day, the specific motives and persons behind these murders remain unresolved.

134. See Said Amir Arjomand, *The Turban for the Crown: The Islamic Revolution in Iran* (New York: Oxford University Press, 1988); Shaul Bakhash, *The Reign of the Ayatollah: Iran and the Islamic Revolution* (New York: Basic Books, 1984).

135. On this topic, see Rudabeh Pakravan, "Territory Jam: Tehran—The Rise of Illegal Satellite TV Has Made the Private Home the True Public Realm," *Places*, July 2012, https://placesjournal.org/article/territory-jam-tehran/ (accessed May 10, 2019).

136. Amirali Ghasemi, "Iran: Making Room for New Media," lecture given at Center for Contemporary Art, Ujazdowski Castle, Warsaw, Poland, 2014, https://vimeo.com/105141219/514d13d046? (accessed August 10, 2020).

137. Miwon Kwon, *One Place after Another: Site-Specific Art and Locational Identity* (Cambridge, MA: MIT Press, 2002), 1.

138. Personal interview with Farideh Shahsavarani, June 13, 2020.

139. Anna Gibbs, "Contagious Feelings: Pauline Hanson and the Epidemiology of Affect," *Australian Humanities Review*, December 1, 2001, http://australianhumanitiesreview.org/2001/12/01/contagious-feelings-pauline-hanson-and-the-epidemiology-of-affect/ (accessed May 2, 2019).

140. Irit Rogoff, "Looking Away: Participations in Visual Culture," in *After Criticism: New Responses to Art and Performance*, ed. Gavin Butt (London: Blackwell, 2005), 117–34.

141. Text derived from a recorded audio made by artist Farideh Shahsavarani. Also based on the personal interview with Shahsavarani cited above.

142. Sara Ahmed, "Happy Objects," in *The Affect Theory Reader*, ed. Melissa Gregg and Gregory J. Seigworth (Durham, NC: Duke University Press, 2010), 29–51, at 50.

143. Mehri Shirmohammadi and Maedeh Esfandmaz, "*Ru siyahi bar bozorgtarin karkhaneh chay Lahijan*" [A stain on the biggest tea factory in Lahijan], *Paygah-e khabari va tahleeli farhang va honar* [*Culture and art news agency*], 2 *Mehr* 1392 [September 24, 2013], http://gilmehr.com/ (accessed May 10, 2018).

144. For more information on this event see https://guilanian.wordpress.com/2008/01/01/ (accessed May 10, 2019).

145. Personal interview with Mohammad Khodashenas, July 15, 2019.

146. Ahmad Mirehsan, "*In yek hazer amadeh ast*" [This is a readymade], *Etemad Newspaper* 8, no. 2170, Bahman 1388 [February 6, 2010]), 16, http://www.magiran.com/npview.asp?ID=2038346 (accessed May 30, 2019).

147. Ibid.

148. Interview with Ghalamdar.

149. Email correspondence with Blind, May 11, 2019.

150. Mohammad Rezaie Rad, *Neshaneh shenasi-e sansoor va sokoot-e sokhan* [*Semiotics of censorship and the silence of words*] (Tehran: Tarh-e Now, 1381 [2002]), 71.

151. Personal interview with Mohammad Rezaie Rad, July 24, 2019.

152. *ISNA (Iranian Students' News Agency)*, "*Bazgasht-e yek kargardan-e te'atr-e mamnoo' al kar beh sahneh*" [The return of a banned theater director], editorial, 31 Khodad 1393 [June 21, 2014], https://www.isna.ir/news/93033116744/ (accessed May 10, 2018).

153. Ibid.

154. Ibid.

155. Siamdoust, *Soundtrack of the Revolution*, 224.

156. Personal interview with Azadeh Ganjeh, February 22, 2019.

157. Vahid Khaneh-Saz, "*Shoghl-e jadid-e plateau dari*" [The new business of the plateaus], *IscaNews*, 28 Mordad 1393 [August 19, 2014], http://www.iscanews.ir/news/29260/ (accessed June 28, 2019).

158. Personal interview with Pouya Pirouzram, June 28, 2019.

159. Pauline Eiferman, "Creative Disobedience: Q&A with Jeremy Suyker," *Roads and Kingdoms*, February 26, 2015, https://maptia.com/jeremysuyker/stories/iran-s-underground-art-scene (accessed May 21, 2019).

160. Ibid.

161. Ibid.

162. Mohammad Roozkhosh and Fereshteh Sadeghi, "*Te'atr-e khosoosi Iran az manzar-e fa'alan-e arseh namayesh*" [Private theater in Iran from the experts' points of view]," *Motale'at-e farhang va ertebatat* 77 (1398 [2019]): 57–83.

163. Ibid., 66–67.

164. Ibid., 74.

165. Ibid., 75–81.

166. Personal interview with Soheil Aarabi, March 15, 2019.

167. The influence of Eastern European, and particularly Polish, art, theater, and cinema on Iran is substantial, even if it is not always acknowledged. In popular culture, memories of the Polish refugees living in Iran during World War II still linger. Documentaries have been made about them, both inside Iran (by Khosrow Sianie) and by foreign Persian networks such as *BBC Persian*. In the 1960s, many Iranian artists were influenced by major Eastern European performers and unconventional artists. After the revolution, while pro-government graphic designers and illustrators were inspired by Soviet-style agitprop, the opposition took its cue from Polish underground poster designers. The translation and original authorship of several key Eastern Bloc and Soviet film books became available thanks to the efforts of film historian and critic Ahmad Zabeti Jahromi (b. 1951), who authored more than a dozen titles published between 1976 and 1993 on classic Soviet and Hungarian films from directors Sergei Eisenstein, Esfir Shub, István Szabó, András Kovács, and more. Shortly after its publication in 1984, Milan Kundera's *L'Insoutenable légèreté de l'être* (*The Unbearable Lightness of Being*) was translated into Persian by Parviz Homayunpour (1939–2011) and found a huge audience. In the 1980s and 1990s, Iranian filmmakers were influenced by Eastern Bloc filmmakers such as Krzysztof Kieślowski and Andrei Tarkovsky, in part owing to the large group of leftist activists and artists in Iran who had already introduced these films to the Iranian audience through such venues as the Youth Palace (*Kakh-e javanan*).

168. Personal interview with Soheil Aarabi, March 21, 2021.

169. Ibid. Also see Maryam Jafari Hesarloo, "*Honarmand dar roozmarregi mimirad*" [Mundane Life Kills the Artist], *Iran Newspaper* 5557, no. 19, 23 Day 1399 [January 12, 2021], 8.

170. Suyker, "Iran's Underground Art Scene."

171. Interview with Aarabi.

172. Peter Brook in Margaret Croyden, *The Centre: A Narrative* (Paris: CICT, 1980), 1

173. Peter Brook in Anthony Charles H. Smith, *Orghast at Persepolis* (New York: Eyre Methuen, 1973), 52.

174. See Zbigniew Osinski, ed., *Grotowski and His Laboratory*, trans. Lillian Vale and Robert Findlay (New York: PAJ, 1986), 130.

175. Kathleen Stewart, *Ordinary Affects* (Durham, NC: Duke University Press, 2007), 3.

176. Elham Puriya Mehr in conversation with Vista Art Gallery, June 10, 2020. Audio recording made available through Vista Art Gallery.

177. "The Back Room in conversation with Media Farzin," in *New Museum Six Degrees Blog*, April 9, 2014, https://www.newmuseum.org/blog/view/the-back-room-in-conversation-with-media-farzin (accessed April 2, 2018).

178. Personal interviews with artist Golrokh Nafisi and urban sociologist Azam Khatam, August 28, 2018.

179. These rules fluctuate depending on leadership and the availability of funds. There are scores of complaints by owners and tenants who cannot resolve their legal and financial issues. See, for example, Fatima Karimi, "*Heech organi mojavvez fa'aliyat beh kafeh khaneh-ha nemidahad*" [No organization issues permission for café-homes], *Mehr News*, August 23, 2019, https://www.mehrnews.com/news/4716713/ (accessed May 10, 2020).

180. Personal interview with Tooraj Khamenehzadeh and Negin Mahzoon, February 21, 2021.

181. Sussan Babaie, *Isfahan and Its Palaces: Statecraft, Shi'ism and Architecture of Conviviality in Early Modern Iran* (Edinburgh: University of Edinburgh Press, 2008), 178–79. For the history of the kiosk outside Iran, see Nebahat Avcioğlu, "A Palace of One's Own: Stanislas I's Kiosks and the Idea of Self-Representation," *Art Bulletin* 85, no. 4 (December 2003): 662–84.

182. Ehsan Rasoulof, "Director's Note," *2016 Koosh Residency,* exhibition catalog (Tehran: Kooshk Residency, 2017), 13.

183. Personal interview with Maryam Bagheri, July 27, 2019.

184. Ibid.

185. Ibid.

186. Interview with Mortazavi.

187. Information sheet of the UpArtMaan Cultural Institute and Zirpelleh. Made available through the personal collection of Houman Mortazavi.

188. Pouria Jahanshad, "Cross-Cultural Interactions: Trend, Deception, or Reality?" in *2017 Kooshk Residency*, exhibition catalog (Tehran: Kooshk Residency, 2017), 25–29, at 29.

189. Ruin Pakbaz and Hassan Mourizi Nejad, *Talar-e Ghandriz: Tajrobehyi dar arseh ejtema'yi honar* [*Ghandriz Hall: An experiment on the impact of art on society*] (Tehran: Herfeh Honarman, 1395 [2018]), 39; *BBC Persian (*Tamasha Program), "Tamasha: Kargah-e Namayesh, a Conversation with Arbi Avansian," editorial, March 27, 2014, https://www.dailymotion.com/video/x571042 (accessed May 10, 2018); Aria Kasaie, Studio Kargah, and the AB Projects, *Graphic Design Archive of Kargah-e Namayesh Theatre Workshop* (Tehran: Pejman Foundation Press, 2017).

190. Media Farzin, "A Short History of Art Exhibitions," 69.

191. Interview with Diba.

192. Sohrab Mohebbi, "Rasht 29 Revisited," in *Into the Night: Cabarets and Clubs in Modern Art,* ed. Florence Ostende and Lotte Johnson (London: Prestel, and Barbican Art Gallery, 2019), 290–97, at 290.

193. Ibid.

194. Ibid.

195. Visit the website of the institute, http://rooberoomansion.com/ (accessed June 18, 2018).

196. Ibid.

197. Visit the website of the institute, http://www.nabshi.center/about/ (accessed March 1, 2018).

198. Ibid.

199. Information from the official website of Zav Architects, https://zav architects.com/works/nabshi-gallery (accessed April 4, 2021).

200. Ibid.

201. Ibid.

202. Personal interview with Salman Matinfar, June 1, 2019.

203. Matinfar and Kashani had wanted to run this initiative together, but they could not reach an agreement on dividing the space into nonprofit and commercial, so they separated (on Kashani's projects see chapter 4 of this book).

204. Personal interview with Azadeh Zaferani, June 10, 2019. Also see https://www.disegnodaily.com/article/azadeh-zaferani-platform-28-art-architecture-tehran (accessed May 10, 2019).

205. Interview with Zaferani.

206. Interview with Ashkan Zahraie.

207. Ibid.

208. Ibid.

209. Lauren Fournier, *Autotheory as Feminist Practice in Art, Writing, and Criticism* (Cambridge, MA: MIT Press, 2020), 13.

210. Sohrab Mohebbi, ed., *Hotel Theory Reader* (Vancouver: Fillip Editions, 2016).

211. Tirdad Zolghadr, "The Biotechnical Haruspex," in Mohebbi, *Hotel Theory Reader*, 141–52.

212. Beck, "Alternative: Space," 267.

213. I am grateful to Masoud Najafi Ardabili for explaining to me this post-2010 permission process. Based on a personal interview with Najafi Ardabili, August 14, 2021.

214. Sholette, *Delirium and Resistance*; "Aggressive Mimicry," *Wikipedia article*, https://en.wikipedia.org/wiki/Aggressive_mimicry.

215 Narges Bajoghli, *Iran Reframed: Anxieties of Power in the Islamic Republic* (Stanford: Stanford University Press, 2019), 91–93.

216. Ibid.

217. Personal interview with a former staff member of the MCIG, who wishes to remain anonymous, June 28, 2020.

218. Sina Najafi, "Underworld: An Interview with Rosalind Williams," *Cabinet* 30 (Summer 2008), http://www.cabinetmagazine.org/issues/30/najafi.php (accessed September 10, 2019).

Chapter 2

1. Rubin, *World Encyclopedia of Contemporary Theatre*, 253. The decorative elements were by designers Ann Wilson (no relation to Robert), Melvin Andringa, and Saito Kikuo.

2. Robert Wilson, "KA MOUNTAIN AND GUARDenia TERRACE: A Story about a Family and Some People Changing," in Daftari and Diba, *Iran Modern*, 93–95, at 93.

3. Ibid. Also based on the personal interview with Diba cited earlier.

4. Maria Shevtsova, *Robert Wilson* (London: Routledge Performance Practitioners, 2019), 10–12.

5. Ibid., 34.

6. Wilson, "KA MOUNTAIN," 95. There were a few others from Latin America, Europe, and the Far East, according to Wilson. Personal interview with Robert Wilson, August 10, 2021.

7. Ossia Trilling, "Robert Wilson's 'Ka Mountain and Guardenia Terrace,'" *TDR: The Drama Review* 17, no. 2 (June 1973): 33–47, at 36.

8. Shevtsova, *Robert Wilson*, 10.

9. Trilling, "Robert Wilson's 'Ka Mountain," 36.

10. Shevtsova, *Robert Wilson*, 12.

11. Personal email communication with Robert (Bob) Wilson, August 23, 2021. I am grateful to Christoph Schletz for facilitating the interview.

12. Personal email correspondence with Gholamhossein Nami, June 10, 2020.

13. Most engagements with the environment in the MENA region took place from the late 1970s onward and rarely earlier. For the movement in the Arab context, see the initiative of Moroccan artist Mohammed Melehi in 1978 that entailed a public works program of cleaning and restoring nature while also inviting artists to create art. See Anneka Lenssen, Sarah Rogers, and Nada Shabout, eds., *Modern Art in the Arab World: Primary Documents* (Durham, NC: Duke University Press, 2018), 419–24.

14. Maryam Ekhtiar and Marika Sardar, "Modern and Contemporary Art in Iran," in *Heilbrunn Timeline of Art History*, Metropolitan Museum of Art, New York, October 2004, http://www.metmuseum.org/toah/hd/ciran/hd_ciran.htm (accessed May 10, 2018); also see Fereshteh Daftari, *Marcos Grigorian Earthworks*, exhibition catalog (New York: Leila Heller Gallery, September 27–October 29, 2011).

15. Ramin S. Khanjani, "Fact, Fiction and Eccentricity in Parviz Kimiavi's Images from 'The Garden of Stones,'" *Offscreen* 19, no. 6 (June 2015), https://offscreen.com/view/garden-of-stones (accessed July 10, 2018).

16. Ibid.; Hamid Naficy, *A Social History of Iranian Cinema: The Industrializing Years, 1941–1978*, vol. 2 (Durham, NC: Duke University Press, 2011), 393.

17. Asma Mahmoodi, "*Baghi keh mivehayash sang shod*" [A garden whose fruits turned to stone], *Mehr News* 9, no. 39 (23 Esfand 1393 [March 14, 2015], https://www.mehrnews.com/news/2512814/ (accessed March 18, 2016).

18. Moridi, *Honar-e Ejtema'yi*, 61.

19. This was mentioned repeatedly during the course of my interviews with experts in theater and cinema. Also see testimony to this influence by other artists in Ali Ettehad and Joobin Bekhrad, "Street Fighting Man," *Reorient Magazine*, June 2, 2015, http://www.reorientmag.com/2015/06/performance-art-iran/ (accessed August 29, 2019).

20. *Our Man in Tehran* (Part Two), season 36, episode 15, https://www.pbs.org/video/our-man-in-tehran-part-two-7elm5x/ (accessed June 12, 2019). Officials in Iran's Foreign Ministry have repeatedly assured *The Times* that Mr. Erdbrink's credential would soon be restored, but have offered no explanation for the delays, or for why it was revoked.

21. Georg Simmel, "Metropolis and Mental Life," in *Rethinking Architecture*, ed. Neil Leach (London: Routledge, 1997), 67.

22. Hannah Arendt, *The Human Condition* (Chicago: University of Chicago Press, 1998), 220.

23. Ibid., 222.

24. De Certeau, *The Practice of Everyday Life*, xiii.

25. Ibid.

26. It is noteworthy that the term was actually first used to mean "subculture" by sociologist J. Yinger Milton in 1960. It was then popularized by Rozak, and hence often attributed to him. See, J. Milton Yinger, "Contraculture and Subculture," *American Sociological Review* 25, no. 5 (1960): 625-35; Theodore Rozak, *The Making of a Counterculture* (Berkeley: University of California Press, 1995).

27. Herbert Marcuse, *One-Dimensional Man: Studies in the Ideology of Advanced Industrial Society* (Boston: Beacon Press, 1964).

28. These involved such activities as communal living, neopaganism, and the Rainbow Gatherings. On these topics see, for example, Ronald Fraser, *1968: A Student Generation in Revolt* (London: Chatto & Windus, 1987); Todd Gitlin, *The Sixties: Years of Hope, Days of Rage* (Toronto: Bantam, 1988); David Pepper, *Communes and the Green Vision: Counterculture, Lifestyle and the New Age* (London: Merlin, 1991).

29. Felicity Scott, "A Swerve," in *What Is Critical Spatial Practice?*, 121–23, at 121.

30. Cathleen M. Giustino, Catherine J. Plum, and Alexander Vari, eds., *Socialist Escapes: Breaking Away from Ideology and Everyday Routine in Eastern Europe, 1945–1989* (Oxford: Berghahn Press, 2013).

31. Ibid.

32. Sergei Sitar, "Four Slogans of 'Collective Actions,'" *Third Text* 17, no. 4 (2003): 363–68, at 364. Cited in Bishop, *Artificial Hells*, 160.

33. Jackson, *The Experimental Group*, 188.

34. Ibid.

35. Bishop, *Artificial Hells*, 137.

36. Ibid., 129.

37. Ibid., 141–47.

38. From Pierre Restany, *Ailleurs: Alex Mlynárčik* (Paris: Galerie Lara Vincy; Bratislava: Galerie Nationale Slovaque, 1994), 123. Cited in Bishop, *Artificial Hells*, 146.

39. See, for example, Pardis Mahdavi, *Passionate Uprisings: Iran's Sexual Revolution* (Stanford: Stanford University Press, 2009).

40. John K. Grande, "Nadalian: River Art," in Grande, *Dialogues in Diversity: Art from Marginal to Mainstream* (Italy: Pari, 2007), 39–48.

41. Ahmad Nadalian in conversation with Behnam Kamrani, August 19, 2020. Audio recording at Vista Gallery. I am grateful to Behnam Kamrani for providing the recording.

42. Later, Nadalian went on to create multiple land art residencies, including in Tehran, Polur in Mazandaran province, and the island of Hormuz in the Persian Gulf.

43. For the traumatic effects of the war on a single generation of Iranians (known commonly as *Daheh Shastiha* or those who were born in the 1360s/1980s), see Orkideh Behrouzan, *Prozak Diaries: Psychiatry and Generational Memory in Iran* (Stanford: Stanford University Press, 2017).

44. See Sigmund Freud, "Mourning and Melancholia," in *Standard Edition of the Complete Psychological Works*, vol. 12 (London: Hogarth Press and Institute of Psychoanalysis, 1953), 243–58.

45. Cathy Caruth, *Unclaimed Experience: Trauma, Narrative, and History* (Baltimore: Johns Hopkins University Press, 1996).

46. Personal interview with Kourosh Golnari, July 7, 2020.

47. Mahmoud Maktabi, "Eco Avant-Garde Exhibition," in *Nature-Art Variations* (Budapest: Musarnok/Kunsthalle, Institution of the Hungarian Academy of Arts, 2016), 206–15, at 206.

48. Other founding members of the group were Atefeh Khas, Minoosh Zomorodinia, Sarah Gudarzi, Zahra Shafiabadi, and Shahrnaz Zarkesh, all of whom are women born in the mid-1980s.

49. The group was formed at Shahed University's Painting Department and it is noteworthy that, at the time, most art majors in this program were women.

50. Personal interview with Mahmoud Maktabi, August 15, 2020.

51. Ibid.

52. Ibid.

53. Ibid.

54. Personal interview with Neda Darzi, June 10, 2021.

55. Arendt, *The Human Condition*, 178.

56. Interview with Darzi.

57. Sohrab Mahdavi, cited in Carver, "Dead Dogs."

58. Kamrani and Hosseini, "*Honar mo'aser*," 72.

59. *Tazarv*, "*Bazshenasi mafhoom-e 'heterotopia' dar honar-e shahr*" [Reconsidering the meaning of "heterotopia" in urban art], editorial, *Tazarv* 1, no. 1 (Summer 2016): 48–64.

60. Email correspondence with a graffiti artist who does not wish to be named in this book.

61. Michel Foucault, "Of Other Spaces," *Diacritics* 16 (Spring 1986): 22–27.

62. Ibid.

63. Mahdyar Jamshidi, "*Sadeh kardan-e pichidegiha bozorgtarin honar ast*" [The highest form of art is that which simplifies complicated issues], *Setareh sobh* 7, no. 180 (10 Dey 1394 [December 31, 2015]): 9.

64. Personal interview with Elham Puriya Mehr, January 17, 2019.

65. Footage from May 2016, courtesy of the Cooler Gallery. I am grateful to Mahdyar Jamshidi for providing a copy of this footage.

66. Ibid.

67. Ibid.

68. Interview with Puriya Mehr.

69. Andres Kreuger, "Thinking-Together Spaces," in Hirsch and Miessen, eds., *What Is Critical Spatial Practice?*, 73–77, at 73.

70. Personal interview with Mahdyar Jamshidi, June 30, 2019.

71. Ibid.

72. Najafi Ardabili, *Grotowski in Iran*, 134.

73. Ibid., 51.

74. Ibid., 126.

75. Ibid., 132.

76. Interview with Najafi Ardabili.

77. I am grateful to Masoud Najafi Ardabili for generously sharing the footage for this performance.

78. Najafi Ardabili, *Grotowski in Iran*, 136.

79. After he was granted asylum in France following the 2009 Green Movement, Afshin Ghaffarian's practice in the Iranian desert became an inspiration for the 2014 British drama *Desert Dancer*, directed by Richard Raymond.

80. See http://gardzienice.org/ (accessed May 2, 2019).

81. Personal interview with Soheil Aarabi, March 15, 2019.

82. Ibid.

83. Ibid.

84. Babak Mohri, "*Te'atre baray-e hameh mardom deegar sho'ar nist*" [Theater

for all is no longer just a slogan], *Cheragh Magazine* 11, no. 519 (4 *Khordad* 1392 [May 25, 2013]), 29.

85. Interview with Aarabi.

86. *The Iran Project*, "Iranian Environmentalist Inanlou Dies at 68," editorial, January 3, 2016, https://theiranproject.com/blog/2016/01/03/iranian-environmentalist-inanlou-dies-at-68/ (accessed May 12, 2017).

87. Ibid.

88. Also see Suyker, "Iran's Underground."

89. John Urry, *The Tourist Gaze* (London: Sage, 2002), 13. Also see Sarah Kanouse, "Critical Day Trips: Tourism and Land-Based Practice," in *Critical Landscapes: Art, Space, Politics*, ed. Emily Eliza Scott and Kirsten Swenson (Berkeley: University of California Press, 2015), 43–56.

90. Personal interview with Soheil Aarabi, March 21, 2021.

91. Ibid.

92. Similarly, other reviews of Av's plays are more intrigued by the novelty of the venue than the meaning of the play itself.

93. Elaheh Hajizadeh and Seyyed Mahdi Ahmad Panah, "*Salonhatoon arzoonitoon*" [We don't want your theater halls], *Cheragh Magazine* 11, no. 519 (4 Khordad 1392 [May 25, 2013]): 27–28, at 28.

94. Ibid., 29.

95. Ibid.

96. Interview with Pirouzram.

97. Kathleen John-Alder, "Paradise Reconsidered: The Early Design History of Pardisan Park in Tehran," in *Contemporary Urban Landscapes of the Middle East*, ed. Mohammad Gharipour (London: Routledge, 2016), 120–48.

98. For more information on Khalili's work and the CalEarth Institute see https://www.calearth.org/our-founder (accessed May 10, 2020).

99. Khalili's *Racing Alone* was translated (*Tanha daveedan*) and taught in several undergraduate programs. Khalili's other books include *Ceramic Houses and Earth Architecture: How to Build Your Own*; *Sidewalks on the Moon*; and *Emergency Sandbag Shelter and Eco-Village: How to Build Your Own*, which include information about the building techniques Khalili researched and developed at Cal-Earth.

100. Personal interview with Pouya Khazaeli-Parsa, June 11, 2020.

101. Ibid.

102. Ibid.

103. Ali Madanipour, "Urban Planning and Development in Tehran," *Cities* 23, no. 6 (2006): 433–38.

104. Satoshi Abe, "Conceptions of Nature in Iran: Science, Nationalism, and Heteroglossia," *Journal of Anthropological Research* 69, no. 2 (Summer 2013): 201–23.

105. Satoshi Abe, "Iranian Environmentalism: Nationhood, Alternative Natures, and the Materiality of Objects," *Nature and Culture* 7, no. 3 (Winter 2012): 259–84.

106. Personal interview with Hooman Mehdizadehjafari, June 18, 2020.

107. Peter Schwartzstein, "How Iran Is Destroying Its Once Thriving Environmental Movement," *National Geographic*, November 20, 2020, https://www.nationalgeographic.com/environment/article/how-iran-destroying-once-thriving-environmental-movement (accessed July 10, 2020).

108. *Human Rights Watch News*, "Iran: Environmentalists Sentenced Unfair Trial; Continued Due Process Violations," editorial, November 19, 2019, https://www.hrw.org/news/2019/11/22/iran-environmentalists-sentenced (accessed July 2, 2020).

109. For example, on January 19, 2016, on the occasion of another national Clean Air Day (*Rooz-e havay-e pak*), artist Jinoos Taghizadeh rallied a few artists. In underground trains they all began to read manifestos about protecting the environment and citizens' rights to changes in the city. They moved from car to car to address as many people as possible. After three rounds they sensed that they were being chased by the metro police, so they halted the project altogether.

110. Fatemeh Khalili, "*Dar naleh ha-ye Damavand cheh razi nahofteh ast?*" [What are the secrets behind Damavand cries for help?], *Iranian Students' News Agency* (*ISNA*), July 28, 2020, https://www.isna.ir/news/99050704584/ (accessed July 29, 2020).

111. See, for example, *Mashregh News*, "*Gasht o gozari dar Lavasan: Jazireh amn-e luxury neshinha*" [A stroll in Lavasan: The safe island of luxury tenants], editorial, January 2019, https://www.mashreghnews.ir/news/930512 (accessed March 10, 2019).

112. Ghadimi, "*Sherkat-e khosoolati chist va chera Rouhani ba an mokhalef ast?*"

113. Tom Ravenscroft, "ZAV Architects Creates Colourful Domed Cultural Retreat on Iranian Island of Hormuz," *Dezeen Magazine*, December 15, 2020, https://www.dezeen.com/2020/12/15/zav-architects-holiday-accommodation-hormuz-iran/ (accessed April 20, 2021).

114. Ibid.

115. Ibid.

116. Ibid.

117. Ibid.

118. Ibid.

119. Ibid.

120. See https://zavarchitects.com/works/PRESENCE-IN-HORMOZ-02 (accessed July 10, 2021).

121. Ibid.

122. Ibid.

123. *Sobh-e Sahel*, "In conversation with Pourya Jahanshad: A Place Where Hormoz Ends: Art, a Stage for Disavowing Ownership," editorial, *Sobh-e sahel* 36, no. 4238 (January 20, 2021): 8–9. An extensive version of the article appears at *Meidaan*, https://meidaan.com/archive/76237 (accessed April 1, 2021).

124. Ibid.

125. Ibid.

126. Personal interview with Tehran-based architect Hadi Fardanesh, April 10, 2021.

127. *Fars News Agency*, "*Hormoz-e Iran, negin bargozideh jahan*" [Iran's Hormuz, the jewel of the world], editorial, July 31, 2021, https://www.farsnews.ir/news/14000507000039/ (accessed August 10, 2021).

128. For more information about Rafsanjani's property in Lavasan and its allegedly unlawful proximity to the Latian Dam, see *Entekhab*, "*Ayatollah midanest keh dar rabeteh ba khatereh sad-e latian janjal khahad shod*" [The Ayatollah knew that the memoir of the Latian Dam would create a scandal], editorial, 7 Ordibehesht 1395 [April 26, 2016], https://www.entekhab.ir/fa/news/265292/ (accessed May 10, 2019); also see *Mashregh News*, "*Safarhay-e tafrihi-e Hashemi Rafsanjani va Khanevadehash dar daheh Moharram*," editorial, 12 Mehr 1395 [October 3, 2016], https://www.mashreghnews.ir/news/638612/ (accessed August 1, 2019).

129. *Homing.ir*, "*Zendegi dar mahalleh Swiss-e Tehran*" [Life in the Swiss neighborhood of Tehran], 2 Azar 1397 [November 23, 2018], https://homing.ir/mag/area/lavasan-area/ (accessed August 1, 2019; site discontinued).

130. Evan Osnos, "Doomsday Prep for the Super-Rich: Some of the Wealthiest People in America—in Silicon Valley, New York, and Beyond—Are Getting Ready for the Crack-up of Civilization," *New Yorker*, January 22, 2017, https://www.newyorker.com/magazine/2017/01/30/doomsday-prep-for-the-super-rich (accessed May 10 2017).

131. Giustino, Plum, and Vari, *Socialist Escapes*.

132. See *Mashregh News*, "*Basti Hills kojast? Shahri keh vorood beh an baray mardom mamnoo' bood*" [Where is Basti Hills? A city that forbids the public from entering it], editorial, 19 Tir 1398 [July 10, 2019], https://www.mashreghnews.ir/news/973945 (accessed August 1, 2019).

133. *Marshregh News*, "*Gasht o gozari dar Lavasan*."

134. *Lavasan News*, "Exploring a New Master Plan." Additionally, the YouTube channels *Koocheh* and *AvantTV*, which cover issues of significant social importance in the same fashion as *Vice YouTube*, have consistently broadcasted detailed stories of Basti Hills with a negative, critical tone. See, for example, *AparatTV*, "*Kodam Vazir-e mohem az dastgiri mofsedin-e eghtesadi narahat shod*?"

[Which important minister was upset about the arrest of the corrupt businessmen?], https://www.aparat.com/v/BzfD6 (accessed July 30, 2019).

135. Ibid.

136. Hamkar Parsboom Consulting Engineers for *Vezarat-e rah va shahr sazi* [Ministry of Roads and Urban Planning], *Tarh-e jame' shar-e Lavasan* [*Lavasan's master plan*], vols. 1–3, Winter 1995. For more information about ameliorations to the master plan, see *Lavasan News*, "*Barresi tarh-e jadid-e jame' Lavasan dar gorooh karshenasi*" [Exploring a new master plan for Lavasan with the experts], editorial, no. 9 (1394 [2015]): 12, http://www.lavasan.ir/_DouranPortal/documents/No%2009.pdf (accessed August 10, 2018); also see *Donyay-e Eghtesadi*, "*Hadaf az tarh-e jame' Lavasan chist*?" [What is the goal of the Lavasan master plan?], editorial, August 30, 2015, https://donya-e-eqtesad.com/بخش-سایت-خوان-62/2965526-از-هدف- چیست-لواسان-جامع-طرح-تصویب- (accessed May 10, 2019).

137. Ibid.

138. See *Koocheh* Channel, "*Lavasan: Jazireh amn-e kakh neshinan ya zakhmi bar zakhmhay-e Iran?*" [Lavasan: A safe haven for the super rich or another scar on Iran?], YouTube video, May 30, 2019, https://www.youtube.com/watch?v=mHjWAHEPCfE (accessed July 10, 2019).

139. *Ofogh TV*, "*Edalatkhahi-e omid bakhsh*" [A hopeful quest for justice], https://www.youtube.com/watch?v=cVVf2mRujgg (accessed July 10, 2019).

140. For more on Farzad Daliri, see the last chapter in my book, *Domesticity and Consumer Culture in Iran: Interior Revolutions of the Modern Era* (London: Routledge, 2013). For more on the work of Ali Moosa Panah, see *Memari TV*, "*Goftegooy-e sareeh ba mohandes Ali Moosapanah, me'mar-e classic kar*" [An honest interview with architect Ali Musapanah, a classicist architect], editorial, 1399 [August 22, 2020], http://memaritv.com (accessed December 1, 2021).

141. For more information about the project, see the official website of Hariri & Hariri Architecture, http://www.haririandhariri.com/projects#/lavasan-villa/ (accessed July 30, 2019).

142. Ibid.

143. *Daneshnameh Honar-e Memari*, "*Villa Lavasan asari az khaharan-e Hariri*" [Villa Lavasan: A work by the Hariri sisters], editorial, 2016, https://aoapedia.ir/ (accessed July 2, 2019).

144. *Ofogh TV*, "*Edalatkhahi-e omid bakhsh.*"

145. Leila Abu-Lughod, "The Romance of Resistance: Tracing Transformations of Power through Bedouin Women," *American Ethnologist* 17, no. 1 (February 1990): 53.

146. Kaveh Madani, "Iran's Looming Water Crisis," *Middle East in London Magazine* 11, no. 2 (February–March 2015): 9–10.

147. Ibid., 10.

148. Celeste Olalquiaga, *The Artificial Kingdom: A Treasury of the Kitsch Experience* (New York: Pantheon Press, 1998).

149. Abazari and Zakeri, "*Se daheh hamneshini-e deen va Neoliberalism dar Iran*," 39.

150. Zuzanna Olszewska, "Classy Kids and Down-at-Heel Intellectuals: Status Aspiration and Blind Spots in the Contemporary Ethnography of Iran," *Iranian Studies* 46, no. 6 (July 2013): 1–22, at 4.

151. In this assertion I am indebted to Amelia Jones, "Encountering: The Conceptual Body, or a Theory of When, Where, and How Art 'Means,'" *TDR: The Drama Review* 63, no. 2 (Fall 2018): 12–34.

Chapter 3

1. I am grateful to Homayoun Sirizi for bringing this article to my attention.

2. See, for example, Houchang Chehabi and Christina Fotini, "The Art of State Persuasion: Iran's Post-Revolutionary Murals," *Persica* 22 (2008): 1–13.; Behnam Zangi, Habibollah Ayatollahi, and Asghar Fahimifard, "*Barresi-e moghi'yyat-e naghashi divari pas az enghelab dar Iran ba rooykard-e jame'eh shenakhti-e Pierre Bourdieu*" [An analysis of mural paintings after the revolution (based on *Pierre Bourdieu's* anthropological theories)], *Negareh* 24 (Winter 1391 [2011]): 85–101. Also see Peter Chelkowski and Hamid Dabashi, eds., *Staging a Revolution: The Art of Persuasion in the Islamic Republic of Iran* (New York: New York University Press, 1999).

3. Personal interview with Firoozeh Golmohammadi, March 29, 2007.

4. Ibid.

5. Similar trends are detectable in the education of the arts at all levels. See Ali Gholipour, "Training the Eye: New Art against the Instruction of Art," *Mohit Art*, December 13, 2021, https://mohit.art/honar-e-jadid-a-new-art-in-iran/training-the-eye-new-art-against-the-instruction-of-art/#fnrev190397596561bb96e2cdd57-16 (accessed December 16, 2021).

6. Phrase taken from jury statement in *The First Triennial of Volume Works*, exhibition catalog (Tehran: Tehran Museum of Contemporary Art, 1995), 9–10. Cited in Nastaran Saremi, "Sculpture in Post-revolution Iran: A Fertile Ground for a New Art, A Rereading," *Mohit Art*, December 13, 2021, https://mohit.art/honar-e-jadid-a-new-art-in-iran/sculpture-in-the-post-revolution-iran/#ls (accessed December 15, 2021).

7. Personal interview with Keivan Pournasr, June 26, 2020.

8. Personal interview with Mehdi Ghadyanloo, April 10, 2007.

9. For a critique on the poor imitations of Ghadyanloo murals, see Abbas Kazemi, *Amr-e roozmarreh dar jame'eh pasa enghelabi* [*Everyday life in a postrevolutionary society*] (Tehran: Nashr-e Farhang-e Javid, 1398 [2019]), 79–82.

10. Personal interviews with Behzad Khosravi-Noori, May 11, 2021; see also Leila Hosseinzadeh Salavati, "*Gozari bar aseeb shenasi-e mojassamehay-e shahri*" [Pathology of urban sculptures], *Tazarv* 1 (Summer 1395 [2016]): 65–71.

11. Based on interviews with a number of experts in Iran and Clubhouse conversations with the mayor of Tehran.

12. Darabi, "*Fazahay-e Jaygozin*." The focus of Darabi's work is conceptual art. Other such sentiments about short-term public presentations of street rappers and the youth "taboo" activities are articulated in a collected and heavily illustrated volume edited by Malu Halasa and Maziar Bahari, *Transit Tehran* (London: Garnet, 2009).

13. Interview with Ghalamdar.

14. Henri Lefebvre, *Rhythmanalysis*, trans. Stuart Elden and Gerald Moore (London: Continuum, 2004), 88.

15. Ibid., 26. Emphasis in the original.

16. Shiva Biravand in conversation with Gholamhossein Nami, *Nahib Magazine* podcast, December 15, 2020, https://zil.ink/nahibmag (accessed March 10, 2021).

17. Ibid.

18. Ibid.

19. Azimi, "Don't Cry for Me, America," 108.

20. Najafi Ardabili, *Grotowski in Iran*, 27.

21. Carver, "Dead Dogs."

22. Personal interview with Houman Mortazavi, June 27, 2020.

23. Ibid.

24. Ibid.

25. See, for example, Seyyed Saleh Mousavi Khalkhali, "*Jacques Rancière va nezamha-ye shenasai-e honar dar gharb*" [Jacques Rancière and principles of understanding art in the West], *Nahib Magazine* 1, no. 4 (Winter 2020): 155–63.

26 Jacques Rancière, *The Politics of Aesthetics: The Distribution of the Sensible*, trans. Gabriel Rockhill (New York: Continuum, 2004), 13.

27. Personal interview with Jinoos Taghizadeh, July 3, 2020.

28. Ibid.

29. Ibid.

30. Information from Jinoos Taghizadeh's website, http://jinoostaghizadeh.com/2017/02/19/nazr-performance/ (accessed July 7, 2020).

31. *Radio Zamaneh*, "*Negahi beh namayesh-e sim-keshi-e rookar*" [A look at the open wiring exhibition], editorial, 1394 [December 9, 2015], https://www.radiozamaneh.com/250436 (accessed May 24, 2019).

32. Peggy Phelan, *Unmarked: The Politics of Performance* (London: Routledge, 1993), 146.

33. Personal interview with curator Tooraj Khamenehzadeh, February 21, 2021. Also see the interview between Simone Wille and Naiza Khan about her performance in Iran, published in *ArtNow Pakistan*, 2012, http://www.artnowpakistan.com/naiza-khan/ (accessed April 1, 2021).

34. Ibid.

35. Ibid.

36. Ibid.

37. Ibid.

38. Reem Fekri, "Interview with Artist, Naiza Khan," *Art Dubai Journal* 7 (2010): n.p.

39. Mohammad Bagher Ziyayi, statement published on Amir Mobed's 2013 performance, "Repetition," at Azad Gallery in which the artist buried his body chin down, amidst a huge pile of dried dung. Statement available at https://amirmobed.com/work/repetition/ (accessed May 9, 2021).

40. Personal interview with Homayoun Sirizi, April 18, 2021.

41. Ibid

42. Ibid.

43. Ibid.

44. John Gallagher, *Reimagining Detroit: Opportunities for Redefining an American City* (Detroit: Wayne State University Press, 2010).

45. Ehsani, "Survival through Dispossession." Between 2018 and 2021, when the progressive reformist architect Pirouz Hanachi (b. 1963) became the mayor of Tehran, there was more optimism regarding the elimination of *reshveh* and *rant khari* (both roughly translate as bribery), which by his own account were illicit sources of funding for the Tehran municipality for over three decades.

46. Personal interview with Neda Razavipour, July 10, 2020.

47. Ibid.

48. Ibid.

49. Ibid.

50. Ibid.

51. Lighting and sound for the video were created by Keyvan Jahangiri and Masoud Roham, respectively.

52. *Census* is an artistic video that accompanies the project by Neda Razavipour and Shahab Fotouhi, available through Razavipour's personal artist website, https://vimeo.com/79807365 (accessed May 12, 2019).

53. Interview with Razavipour.

54. Ibid.

55. Ibid.

56. Personal interview with Mina Bozorgmehr, April 25, 2015.

57. Fariborz Daraie, "*Te'atre beh ensanhay-e shoja' niyaz darad / Tehran beh*

masabeh sahneh" [Theater needs brave people / Tehran as a stage], *Mehr News*, 1 Ordibehesht 1399 [April 20, 2020], https://www.mehrnews.com (accessed May 20, 2020).

58. Ibid.

59. Ibid.

60. Peter Brook, *The Empty Space* (New York: Scribner, 1968), 7.

61. Interview with Bozorgmehr.

62. Ibid.

63. For more information about Stalker see, for example, Peter T. Lang, "Stalker on Location," in Franck and Stevens, *Loose Space*; Peter Blundell Jones, Doina Petrescu, and Jeremy Till, eds., *Architecture and Participation* (London: Spon Press, 2005), 249–55. The name Stalker originally was an afterthought, when a news reporter who had seen the 1979 film *Stalker* by Andrei Tarkovsky saw affinities between the film's enchanted "zone" and the areas traversed during the walk about Rome.

64. Noir Art Group website, http://noir.ir (accessed May 19, 2016). The story of the rejection is based on a personal interview with Noir in April 2015.

65. Parallel forms of resistance can be seen in other parts of the world. For example, during the thirteenth Havana Biennial, held from April 12 to May 12, 2019, a number of artists felt that they were restricted by the Cuban Ministry of Culture. In response, one community of artists created their own independent, underground art scene. These artists used private homes to exhibit their works. See Lukas Southard, "In Havana, Artists Create Underground Art Show to Confront Government-Backed Exhibit," *Lationousa,* May 13, 2019, https://www.latinousa.org/2019/05/13/latitud/ (accessed May 10, 2020).

66. Interview with Bozorgmehr.

67. Matei Vişniec, *Horses at the Window* (New York: Segal Theatre Center Press, 2010).

68. Talinn Grigor, "Of Metamorphosis: Meaning on Iranian Terms," *Third Text* 17, no. 3 (2003): 207–25; David Douglass-Jaimes, "AD Classics: Azadi Tower / Hossein Amanat," *Archdaily*, September 2018, https://www.archdaily.com/774683/ad-classics-azadi-tower-hossein-amanat (accessed October 10, 2018); Yeganeh Torbati, "Tehran's Azadi Tower, Witness to History, Victim of Neglect," *Reuters*, February 20, 2013, https://www.reuters.com/article/us-iran-azadi/tehrans-azadi-tower-witness-to-history-victim-of-neglect-idUSBRE91J0QU20130220 (accessed October 10, 2018).

69. Suhail Malik, "Occupy," in Hirsch and Miessen, eds., *What Is Critical Spatial Practice?*, 82–83, at 83.

70. Ibid.

71. Daraie, "*Te'atre beh ensanhay-e shoja' niyaz darad.*"

72. Interview with Ghalamdar.

73. Rustin Zarkar, "Making Graffiti an Iranian Art: The Works of Tehran-Based Street Artist Ghalamdar," *Ajam Media Collective,* https://ajammc.com/2014/05/27/making-graffiti-an-iranian-art-ghalamdar/ (accessed April 1, 2018). Also see Zarkar, "A Mural Erased: Urban Art, Local Politics, and the Contestation of Public Space in Mashhad," *Ajam Media Collective*, March 30, 2014, http://ajammc.com/2014/03/30/a-mural-erased-urban-art-mashhad/ (accessed July 20, 2019); Zarkar,"Taking Back the Streets: Iranian Graffiti Artists Negotiating Public Space," *Ajam Media Collective*, November 5, 2012, http://ajammc.com/2012/11/05/taking-back-the-streets-iranian-graffiti-artists-negotiating-public-space/ (accessed July 20, 2020).

74. Interview with Ghalamdar.

75. Siamdoust, *Soundtrack of the Revolution*, 228–31; Ash Koosha in conversation with King Raam, *Masti and Rasti* Podcast, January 10, 2021, https://www.youtube.com/watch?v=_jI2GkboZuA (accessed May 10, 2021).

76. Email correspondence with Blind, July 12, 2020.

77. Hakim Bey, *T.A.Z.: The Temporary Autonomous Zone, Ontological Anarchy, Poetic Terrorism* (Brooklyn, NY: Automedia, 2003).

78. See, for example, the writings of cultural critic Behrouz Safdari, http://www.behrouzsafdari.com/?p=1520 (accessed August 24, 2019).

79. For more on this topic, see Hamid Keshmirshekan, "Saqqa-kana School of Art," *Encyclopedia Iranica,* online edition, 2009, http://www.iranicaonline.org/articles/saqqa-kana-ii-school-of-art (accessed on August 15, 2019).

80. Clare Davies, "The Artist's Map of Tehran, 1956–1966," lecture given at the Watson Institute, Brown University, October 9, 2019.

81. Email correspondence in 2019 with a graffiti artist who does not wish to be named here.

82. Ibid.

83. Rebecca Solnit, *Wanderlust: A History of Walking* (New York: Penguin Books, 2000).

84. Personal interview with Mohammad Khodashenas, July 15, 2019.

85. Ibid.

86. Zohreh Tohidi, "*Tehran shabha dard mikonad*" [Tehran hurts at night], in Kourosh Asef Vaziri, ed., "*Nashriyyeh dakheli sazman-e zibasazi-e shahr-e Tehran: Vijeh nameh hayat-e shabaneh shahri*" [Tehran Municipality Beautification Bureau bulletin, special issue, *Night life in the city*], 1, no. 18 (1394 [2015]): 78–79.

87. Personal interview with Nastaran Safaie, June 19, 2020.

88. Ibid.

89. Anne Friedberg, *Window Shopping: Cinema and the Postmodern* (Berkeley: University of California Press, 1993).

90. Interview with Safaie.

91. For more on the concept of the *flâneuse*, see Anne Friedberg, *Window Shopping: Cinema and the Postmodern.* Also see Nicole Miller, "Following Sophie Calle," *Hyperallergic*, June 18, 2016, https://hyperallergic.com/305869/following-sophie-calle/ (accessed May 19, 2018).

92. Dariush Shaygan, "*Aya Tehran madineh-ie tamsilist?*" [Is Tehran an allegoric city?], *Bokhara* 68, no. 69 (1387 [2008]): 677–88.

93. Ibid.

94. Ibid.

95. Interview with Taghizadeh.

96. Sahar Azad, "*Goftegoo ba Jinoos Taghizadeh*" [A conversation with Jinoos Taghizadeh], *Shargh Daily* 2473, 28 Azar 1394 [December 19, 2015], https://www.magiran.com/article/3282021 (accessed July 8, 2020).

97. See Guy Debord and Asger Jorn, *The Naked City* (screen print, 1957), in Simon Sadler, *The Situationist City* (Cambridge, MA: MIT Press, 1998), 60.

98. Martha Rosler, "Imagination Retakes the Streets," in Hirsch and Miessen, eds., *What Is Critical Spatial Practice?*, 119–20.

99. *Tehran Bureau*, "Taxicab Confessions: Tehran," editorial, PBS, May 7, 2011, http://www.pbs.org/wgbh/pages/frontline/tehranbureau/2011/05/taxicab-confessions-tehran.html (accessed May 10, 2019).

100. Ibid.

101. Azadeh Ganjeh, "Performing *Hamlet* in Modern Iran" (PhD diss., Philosophisch-historischen Fakultät der Universität Bern, 2017).

102. Interview with Azadeh Ganjeh, July 22, 2019.

103. Ibid.

104. Ibid.

105. Haleh Anvari, "Immersive Drama Set in a Tehran Taxi: Iranian Cabs Afford Passengers a Degree of Anonymity, Paving the Way for Uninhibited Conversations and a New Play," *The Guardian: Tehran Bureau*, December 26, 2013, https://www.theguardian.com/world/iran-blog/2013/dec/26/iran-drama-tehran-taxi (accessed May 12, 2015).

106. Ganjeh, "Performing *Hamlet* in Modern Iran."

107. Ibid.

108. Ibid.

109. Urban Art House was a short-lived initiative of the Sabz (Green) Gallery in Gheytariyyeh, a posh neighborhood in northern Tehran. The gallery and its other curatorial and interdisciplinary art initiatives were run by renowned Iranian artist Ali Akbar Sadeghi (b. 1937). Based on a personal interview with digital media artist and filmmaker Aliyar Rasti (b. 1988), June 10, 2019. For more information on Urban Art House and its affiliated branches, see *Honar Online*, "*Khaneh*

honar-e shahri mahalli baray khallaghiyyat va motale'eh ast" [The urban art house is a place for creativity and exploration], editorial, 49318, December 14, 2013, http://www.honaronline.ir/ (accessed May 10, 2019).

110. Marjan Moosavi, "'Unpermitted Whispers': Reflections on the Originality of 'Hopscotch' Performance," *Theatre Times*, January 19, 2018, https://thetheatretimes.com/unpermitted-whispers-reflections-originality-hopscotch-performance/ (accessed July 1, 2019).

111. Anvari, "Immersive Drama."

112. Interview with Ganjeh.

113. *Hamshahri Online*, "*Namayeshi ba gasht-e Taxi dar Tehran*" [A play with a moving taxi in Tehran], editorial, December 7, 2013, www.hamshahrionline.ir/news/241490/ (accessed May 10, 2019).

114. De Certeau, *The Practice of Everyday Life*, xxi.

115. In this I am indebted to discussions of car drivers versus walkers in Tim Dant, *Critical Social Theory: Culture, Society and Critique* (London: Sage, 2004), 78.

116. Interview with Ganjeh. On women's corporal movement in space see Farzaneh Milani, *Words, Not Swords: Iranian Women Writers and the Freedom of Movement* (Syracuse: Syracuse University Press, 2001), 102.

117. Moosavi, "'Unpermitted Whispers.'"

118. *Tehran Bureau*, "Taxicab Confessions."

119. Azadeh Ganjeh, interview with *Hamshahri Online*.

120. Personal interview with Elham Puriya Mehr, June 16, 2020.

121. Ibid.

122. Bita Fayyazi in a 2004 interview with *Bidoun*, in Carver, "Dead Dogs."

123. Interview with Puriya Mehr.

124. Maserrat Amir-Ebrahimi, "*Fazahay-e omoomi dar hesar*" [Captive public spaces], *Honar va me'mari* 64–65 (1381 [2002]): 63–67.

125. Daniel Kötter, "On Hashti Tehran," *Berliner Festspiele on Demand*, 2020, https://vimeo.com/431032326 (accessed June 22, 2020).

126. Julia Gaven, *Best Practices in Inclusive Curating*, 6–9, www.wecurate.eu (accessed July 9, 2018; site discontinued).

127. Interview with Puriya Mehr.

128. Arendt, *The Human Condition*, 63–68.

129. Ibid.

130. Personal interview with Ashkan Zahraie, July 20, 2019.

131. While the often-official and religious *ta'ziyeh* performances could use major public places such as squares, courts, caravansaries, and official venues known as *hoseyniyehs* or *takiyehs*, other secular, entertainment-oriented plays such as *roohowzi* ("over the pool," an informal performance inspired by amateur entertainment activities) were performed in private homes. For more information

on the history of this form of theater, see Erum Naqvi, "Reinventing Ruhowzi Experiments in Contemporary Iranian Musical Theater," *Middle East Journal of Culture and Communication* 13 (2020): 28–48. Additionally, women-only plays, known commonly as *khaleh ro-ro* (Auntie Ro-ro) and *moorcheh dareh* (There Are Aunts), which included acts of striptease and transvestite performances, were performed in the privacy of women's quarters that were inaccessible to adult men. Because of the often vulgar or political nature of some of these improvised performances, in 1930 Reza Shah Pahlavi's censorship officers began to examine major *roohowzi* plays in advance of the performances and eventually clamped down on certain critical characteristics of these plays. In response, entertainers, actors, musicians, and puppeteers would frequently call their performances "private parties." See Farrokh Ghaffary, Arby Ovanessian, and Laleh Taghian, "Iran," in *The World Encyclopedia of Contemporary Theatre, vol. 5, Asia/Pacific*, ed. Don Rubin, Chua Soo Pong, Minoru Tanokura, Ravi Chaturvedi, and Ramendu Majumdar (London: Routledge, 1998), 191–221, at 196; Peter Chelkowski, "Time Out of Memory: Ta'ziyeh, the Total Drama," *Asia Society* archives, https://asiasociety.org/time-out-memory-taziyeh-total-drama (accessed February 10, 2018); see also Kamran Scot Aghaie, *The Martyrs of Karbala: Shi'i Symbols and Rituals in Modern Iran* (Seattle: University of Washington Press, 2004).

132. *The Observers* (France 24), "The Women behind Tehran's Mysterious 'Ladies in Red,'" editorial, October 21, 2011, https://observers.france24.com/en/20111021-iran-women-behind-tehran-mysterious-lady-in-red-performance-art-yaqut-ruby-legend-ladies (accessed May 10, 2014).

133. See examples in "*Banooy-e sorkhpoosh dar Tehran*" [*Lady in Red* in Tehran], *Hodhod*, https://fa.hdhod.com (accessed August 10, 2012).

134. The documentary is available at https://vimeo.com/61951983 (accessed August 24, 2019).

135. *Honar Online*, "*Banooy-e sorkhpoosh beh jashnvareh dastresi-e mahdood amad*" [*Lady in Red* at the Limited Access Festival], January 14, 2013, http://www.honaronline.ir/ (accessed May 12, 2020).

136. Ibid.

137. Mohammad Hosseini, "The Lady in Red," *Akkaskhaneh Vimeo* Channel, October 5, 2013, https://vimeo.com/76218718 (accessed May 10, 2015).

138. *The Observers*, "The Women behind Tehran's Mysterious 'Ladies in Red.'"

139. Ibid.

140. Hosseini, "The Lady in Red."

141. Ibid.

142. Ibid.

143. Text from the January edition of *Tak Magazine*, taken from the personal website of Bavand Behpoor. Bavand Behpoor, "*Aya entezar keshidan ham ejra' ast?*"

[Is waiting performance art?], http://fa.behpoor.com/?p=1397 (accessed May 10, 2020).

144. Personal interview with Saeed Kiaee, May 10, 2021.

145. Andrea Brighenti, *Visibility in Social Theory and Social Research* (New York: Palgrave McMillan, 2010), 39.

146. Alexandru Balaşescu, *Paris Chic, Tehran Thrills: Aesthetic Bodies, Political Subjects* (Bucharest: Zeta Books, 2007), 156–57.

147. Here I am indebted to the work of visual anthropologist Pedram Dibazar, who also contends that invisibility gives a general feeling of security, necessary to the freedom of movement in public urban spaces for women. See Pedram Dibazar, *Urban and Visual Culture in Contemporary Iran: Non-visibility and the Politics of Everyday Presence (London: Bloomsbury, 2021)*, chap. 1.

148. Masserat Amir-Ebrahimi, "Conquering Enclosed Public Spaces," *Cities* 21, no. 6 (2006): 459.

149. Ibid., 460.

150. Ibid., 459.

151. Ibid., 456.

152. Personal interview with Sepideh Zamani, June 25, 2019.

153. Personal interview with Elmira Yousefi, June 27, 2019.

154. Ibid.

155. Interview with Zamani.

156. Ibid.

157. Ibid.

158. Laura Mulvey, "Visual Pleasure and Narrative Cinema," *Screen* 16, no. 3 (October 1975): 6–18.

159. Simon Critchley, *On Humor* (London: Routledge, 2002), 18.

160. *Mikhail Bakhtin, Problems of Dostoevsky's Poetics (Minneapolis: University of Minnesota Press, 1984), 124.*

161. Ibid., 130.

162. On this topic, see Heba Salem and Kantaro Taira, "Al-Thawra al-DaHika: The Challenges of Translating Revolutionary Humor," in *Translating Egypt's Revolution: The Language of Tahrir,* ed. Samia Mehrez (Cairo: American University in Cairo, 2012). On the importance of laughter in political art see George Orwell, "Funny, but Not Vulgar," *George Orwell's Library* (1945), http://orwell.ru/library/articles/funny/english/e_funny; Noël Carroll, *Humour: A Very Short Introduction* (Oxford: Oxford University Press, 2014).

163. Hiyem Cheurfa, "The Laughter of Dignity: Comedy and Dissent in the Algerian Popular Protests," *Jadalyyah*, March 26, 2019, http://jadaliyya.com/Details/38495/The-Laughter-of-Dignity-Comedy-and-Dissent-in-the-Algerian-Popular-Protests (accessed April 10, 2019).

164. Ibid.

165. Karen Rosenberg, "Life in Iran, Etched with Suspicion and Humor," *New York Times,* May 30, 2008, 28.

166. Kim Murphy, "Media: Iran's Revolution Finally Learns to Laugh at Itself: Tehran's Biggest-Selling Magazine Takes Jabs at Parliament Members and Even Mullahs," *Los Angeles Times,* April 28, 1992, https://www.latimes.com/archives/la-xpm-1992-04-28-wr-912-story.html (accessed May 12, 2015).

167. Nikahang Kowsar, "Being Funny Is Not That Funny: Contemporary Editorial Cartooning in Iran," *Social Research* 79, no. 1 (Spring 2012): 117–44, at 141.

168. Michael J. Fischer, *Mute Dreams, Blind Owls, and Dispersed Knowledges: Persian Poesis in the Transnational Circuitry* (Durham, NC: Duke University Press, 2004), 215. For a long of list of hadith examples and popular culture music propagating sadness, see ibid., 418.

169. Meftahi, *Gender and Dance.*

170. Exhibition text from 2013, written by Ali Gholipour. Kindly shared with me by Tehran Carnival. Originally written in English, the text here is slightly tightened and paraphrased.

171. Hamid Naficy, "Iranian Cinema under the Islamic Republic," *American Anthropologist* 97, no. 3 (1995): 555. Cited in Pamela Karimi and Christine Gruber, "Introduction: The Politics and Poetics of the Child Image in Muslim Contexts," *Comparative Studies of South Asia, Africa and the Middle East* 32, no. 2 (2012): 273–93, at 280.

172. Personal interview with Negar Farajiani, September 5, 2018.

173. Personal interview with Fatemeh Sadat Fazael Ardakani, April 30, 2021.

174. Reyhaneh Mirjahani, "Retexture: Traces of Tradition and Contemporary Concerns in Collaboration," *Konesh,* April 22, 2020, https://www.konesh.space/post/retexture-traces-of-tradition-and-contemporary-concerns-in-collaboration (accessed May 1, 2020).

175. Pedram Dibazar, "Leftover Space, Invisibility and Everyday Life: Rooftops in Iran," in *Global Garbage: Urban Imaginaries of Waste, Excess, and Abandonment,* ed. Christoph Lindner and Miriam Meissner (New York: Routledge, 2016), 101–16; Setrag Manoukian, "Where Is This Place? Crowds, Audio-Vision, and Poetry in Postelection Irancomma," *Public Culture* 22, no. 2 (Spring 2010); Hamid Dabashi, *Iranian Cinema: Past, Present, and Future* (London: Verso, 2001), 2; Pakravan, "Territory Jam, Tehran."

176. See, for example, Mahbod Seraji, *Rooftops of Tehran* (New York: New American Library, 2009). Also see Dibazar, *Urban Visual Culture.*

177. Dabashi, *Iranian Cinema: Past, Present.*

178. Manoukian, "Where Is This Place?"

179. Pakravan, "Territory Jam."

180. *BBC News*, “Iranian Parkour Athlete Arrested over a Rooftop Kiss,” editorial, May 23, 2020, https://www.bbc.com/news/av/world-middle-east-52777891 (accessed May 29, 2020).

181. Linda Nochlin, “The Imaginary Orient,” in Nochlin, *The Politics of Vision: Essays on Nineteenth-Century Art and Society* (New York: Harper Row, 1989), 33–59.

182. Elizabeth Grosz, *Becomings: Explorations in Time, Memory and Futures* (Ithaca, NY: Cornell University Press, 1999), 4.

183. Ibid.

184. De Certeau, *The Practice of Everyday Life*, xix.

185. Mikhail Bakhtin, *Rabelais and His World* (Bloomington: Indiana University Press, 1984), 9.

186. Niloofar Rasooli, “*Shahri keh tab-e ma ra nadarad*” [A city that cannot stand “US”], *Etemad Daily* 4696 (29 Tir 1399 [July 19, 2020]): 12

187. Personal interview with Shahin Seyghali, May 9, 2021.

188. Ibid.

189. Ibid.

190. Ibid.

191. Niloofar Rasooli, “*Maremmati dar kar nist, ‘Ma’ ra barchidand*” [There was no restoration plan in place, they simply removed ‘Us’],” *Etemad Daily* 4698 (31 Tir 1399 [July 21, 2020]): 12.

192. The convoluted debates surrounding *Ma* evoke the iconic story of the removal of Richard Serra’s legendary *Tilted Arc* (1981–89) from Lower Manhattan’s Federal Plaza, although Serra’s case involved court appeals, hearings, and copyright discussions rather than the political responses on social media generated by Seighali’s work. For the complete court case story of Serra, see Vilis R. Inde, “Richard Serra: Whose Property Is It Anyway?” in *Art in the Courtroom*, ed. Vilis R. Inde (Westport, CT: Greenwood, 1998), 49–91.

193. Interview with Seyghali.

194. *Louisiana Channel*, “Ulay: How I Stole a Painting,” editorial, 2017, https://channel.louisiana.dk/video/ulay-how-i-stole-painting (accessed May 10, 2021).

195. Hadi Fardanesh in conversation with Reza Daneshmir, December 18, 2020, https://www.instagram.com/p/CI8io3Olwxg/ (accessed March 20, 2021).

196. Reza Daneshmir, “Open Structures, Event Space,” TEDx lecture delivered at Pars University, August 16, 2018, https://www.youtube.com/watch?v=l8IcGhuuJy8 (accessed April 10, 2021).

197. Tim Creswell, *On the Move: Mobility in the Modern Western World* (London: Routledge, 2006), 51.

198. Nicholas Hirsch and Markus Miessen, “Thinking through Space: A Conversation between Nicholas Hirsch and Markus Miessen,” in Hirsch and Miessen, eds., *What Is Critical Spatial Practice?*, 151–61, at 158.

199. Daneshmir, "Open Structures, Event Space."

200. Ali Shariati and Zahra Sarbandi, "*Mo'aser ya vapasgara?*" [Contemporary or reactionary?], *Etemad Daily* 4157, 20 Mordad 1397 [August 11, 2018], https://www.etemadnewspaper.ir/fa/main/detail/107604 (accessed January 20, 2021); *Tasnim News*, "*Negareshi bar me'mari gheir-e eslami masjed-e vali asr*" [A look at the un-Islamic architecture of Vali Asr Mosque], editorial, 28 Esfand 1393 [March 19, 2015], https://www.tasnimnews.com/fa/news/1393/12/28/690886/ (accessed June 10, 2020).

201. *Independent Farsi*, "*Majeray-e 'hesar keshi' mohavvateh te'atr-e shahr chist?*" [What is the purpose of "barracading" the area around the City Theater?], editorial, 17 Esfand 1399 [March 7, 2021], https://www.independentpersian.com/node/128486/ (accessed May 1, 2021).

202. Architecture Discussions Clubhouse group, "Urban Public Space: Censored or Unauthorized?," June 9, 2021.

203. Mojgan Ansari, "*Tab-e plaza dar Tehran*" [Plaza fever in Tehran], *Isna*, 17 Azar 1399 [December 7, 2020], https://www..isna.ir/news/99091712859/تب-پلازا-در-تهران (accessed May 3, 2021).

204. *Avam*, "*Negahi beh tarrahi meidan emam hussein beh bahaneh ayyam-e moharram*" [A look at the design of Imam Hussein Square on the occasion of the month of Muharram], editorial, 19 Shahrivar 1395 [October 10, 2016], https://avammag.com/13069/text-critic/ (accessed May 11, 2021).

205 Miwon Kwon, "Siting of Public Art: Integration versus Intervention," in Ault, *Alternative Art, New York*, 281–320.

206. Personal interview with Kourosh Asef Vaziri, June 15, 2021.

207. Kourosh Asef Vaziri, ed., "*Nashriyyeh dakheli*," 6–9.

Chapter 4

1. Traditionally, the activities of artisans and craftsmen were tied to the operation of guilds (*asnaf*) or royal workshops (*karkheneh or naghashkhaneh*). The first public art exhibition took place through the efforts of the court painter Mirza Abol-Hassan Khan Ghaffari Kashani, better known as Sani ol-Molk (1814–1866). In the early 1840s, Sani ol-Molk was appointed to the painting workshop (*naghashbashi*) of Mohammad Shah's court. He then traveled to Italy to hone his skills, and upon his return, initiated the first public art exhibitions. In a 1862 issue of Iran's first illustrated newspaper, *Dolat-e Elliyeh Iran,* Sani ol-Molk invited readers to view art in the shop on Fridays. Otherwise known as *Majma' dar al-sanaye'* (Assembly of the House of Crafts), the venue was located at the west end of a refurbished open bazaar called *Sabzeh maydan*. Dubbed the painters' shop (*hojreh naghashan*), the venue was also used as an exhibition space. The painter's stall (*dokkan*) was occupied by around forty apprentices and masters. As such the *Majma' dar al-sanaye* became the first alternative institution to the court painting workshops, which also served as places of viewing art by the royals. Sani ol-Molk,

"*Elan-e naghashkhaneh dowlati*" [Announcement about the government painting studio], *Rooznameh vaghayeh' ettefaghiyyeh* (Shaval 1278 [Sunday April 27, 1862]), 11. Cited in Iranpoor, "*Padideh-ie beh nam-e gallery*," 51–55. Also see Maryam Ekhtiar, "From Workshop, to Bazaar, to Academy: Art Training and Production in Qajar Iran," in *Royal Persian Painting: The Qajar Epoch 1785–1825*, ed. Layla Diba (New York: I.B. Tauris, 1998), 50–65, at 50–51.

2. Siamak Delzendeh, *Tahavvolat-e Tasviri-e honar-e Iran: Barresi enteghadi* [Visual transformations in Iranian art: A critical analysis] (Tehran: Nazar Press, 2017), 253–56.

3 See Daftari, *Persia Reframed*, 42–47.

4 Artists Hossein Kazemi and Parviz Tanavoli were also members of the group, but they left later. The Azad Group also invited guest artists such as Hanibal Alkhas (1930–2010), Behzad Hatam (b. 1949), Bahman Boroojeni (b. 1942), Monir Shahroudy Farmanfarmaian (1922–2019), Changiz Shahvagh (1933–1996), Asghar Mohammadi (1938–1984), Ghobad Shiva (1940), Mohammad Saleh Ala (b. 1952), and Mohammad Ehsai (b. 1939). The group organized five exhibitions in total, and each exhibition had a theme: for instance, "volume and environment," "the color blue," and so forth. See Gholamhossein Nami, "*Risheham dar in khak ast* [All My Roots Are Here]," *Shargh Newspaper* 1272, 28 Khordad, 1390 [June 18, 2011], 8; Bavand Behpoor, "Introduction to 'The Nightingale's Butcher Manifesto' and 'Volume and Environment II,'" *ARTMargins* 3, no. 2 (2014): 118–28.

5. Daftari, *Persia Reframed*, 84–85.

6. Pamela Karimi and Michael Vasquez, "Ornament and Argument," *Bidoun: Arts and Culture from the Middle East*, Winter 2008, https://www.bidoun.org/articles/ornament-argument (accessed May 10, 2019).

7. Christiane Gruber, "The Martyrs' Museum in Tehran: Visualizing Memory in Post-Revolutionary Iran," *Visual Anthropology* 25 (2012): 68–97, at 70.

8. Ibid., 68.

9. For more on this institution, see Bajoghli, *Iran Reframed*, 102–4.

10 That TMoCA has hidden away all of its Western collection in the basement is an exaggeration perpetuated by journalistic writings on Iran. Indeed, parts of the collection were consistently, albeit occasionally, on view.

11. Helia Darabi, "Tehran Museum of Contemporary Art as a Microcosm of the State's Cultural Agenda," in *Contemporary Art from the Middle East: Regional Interactions with Global Art Discourses*, ed. Hamid Keshmirshekan (London: I.B. Tauris, 2005), 221–45.

12. Ibid.

13. Personal interview with Sadegh Safaie, June 20, 2020.

14. On this performance, also see Darabi, "Tehran Museum of Contemporary Art," 236–37.

15. Kamrani, "*Hamayesh-e porsesh az honar-e mo'aser-e Iran.*"

16. Darabi, "Tehran Museum of Contemporary Art," 237.

17. Interview with Safaie.

18. For details of these exhibitions, see Darabi, "Tehran Museum of Contemporary Art," 234–39.

19. Yasaman Alipour, "New Media Society," *Arteast* (fall 2017), http://arteeast.org/quarterly/new-media-society/ (accessed March 3, 2019).

20. See Jytte Klausen, *The Cartoons That Shook the World* (New Haven, CT: Yale University Press, 2009).

21. Michael Slackman, "In Tehran, A Riposte to the Danish Cartoons," *New York Times*, August 24, 2006, https://www.nytimes.com/2006/08/24/world/africa/24iht-iran.2585075.html (accessed September 28, 2019).

22. On this performance, also see Darabi, "Tehran Museum of Contemporary Art," 239–40.

23. De Certeau, *The Practice of Everyday Life*, 117.

24. Paul Berliner, *Thinking in Jazz: The Infinite Art of Improvisation* (Chicago: University of Chicago Press, 1994), 2.

25. Ibid., 17.

26. Ibid.

27. See, for example, interviews with Aydin Aghdashloo on *Arte: Tarikh-e shafahi-e farhang va honar-e Iran* [Arte: Oral history of Iran's contemporary culture and art], Fall 2016, https://www.youtube.com/watch?v=GFpKqa5LcQk (accessed May 10, 2021).

28. Imran Khan, "Iranian Artists Negotiate Government Guidelines," *Al Jazeera English*, May 19, 2012, https://www.youtube.com/watch?time_continue=2&v=mE-8emZMENk&feature=emb_logo (accessed June 8, 2020).

29. For these works see the artist's website, http://mehran-saber.net/ (accessed June 17, 2020).

30. Personal interview with Nazila Noebashari, June 17, 2020.

31. Ibid.

32. Personal interview with Behnam Kamrani, June 17, 2020.

33. For the list of sixteen artists participating in this exhibition, see the archives of the Azad Art Gallery, http://azadart.gallery/fa/artistexhibitionsingle.aspx?Id=227 (accessed June 17, 2020).

34. Interview with Kamrani.

35. Personal interview with Mahmoud Bakhshi, June 20, 2020.

36. Ibid.

37. Kamrani, "*Hamayesh-e porsesh az honar-e mo'aser-e Iran*."

38. Tirdad Zolghadr, "Ethnic Marketing: An Introduction," in *Ethnic Marketing*, ed. Tirdad Zolghadr (Tehran: Toseh, 2006; distributed by JRP/Ringier, Zurich), 11.

39. Alipour, "New Media Society."

40. Negar Azimi in conversation with Amirali Ghasemi, "Independent and Artist-Run Initiatives in Tehran, Global Art Forum 2009," https://vimeo.com/showcase/271409/video/6947578 (accessed May 2, 2018).

41. Moeini et al., *Urban Culture in Tehran*, 146.

42. Pamela Karimi in conversation with Amirali Ghasemi, "When Global Art Meanders on a Magic Carpet: A Conversation on Tehran's Roaming Biennale (30 May–6 July 2009)," *Arab Studies Journal* 18, no. 1 (Spring 2010): 288–99.

43. Michael Warner, "Publics and Counterpublics," *Public Culture* 14, no. 1 (Winter 2002): 50.

44. Ghasemi, "Iran: Making Room for New Media."

45. Azimi and Ghasemi, "Independent and Artist-Run Initiatives."

46. Craig Burnett, "The Invisible Curator," *Art Monthly* 291 (November): 1–4.

47. Interview with Bakhshi.

48. Darabi, "*Fazahay-e jaygozin*," 116.

49. Unfortunately, I could not locate any of these photographs for inclusion in this book.

50. Ibid.

51. Interview with Bakhshi.

52. Maud Ellmann, *The Hunger Artists: Starving, Writing, and Imprisonment* (Cambridge, MA: Harvard University Press, 1993), 17.

53. Interview with Bakhshi.

54. Ibid.

55. Personal interview with Shahab Fotouhi, April 27, 2019.

56. For more information on the artistic and architectural activities of Mousavi, see Muhammad Sahimi, "The Political Evolution of Mousavi," *PBS, Frontline*, February 16, 2010, https://www.pbs.org/wgbh/pages/frontline/tehranbureau/2010/02/the-political-evolution-of-mousavi.html (accessed May 10, 2015); *BBC Persian* (*Tamasha* Program), "Mir Hossein Mousavi, the Painter," editorial, November 7, 2013, https://www.youtube.com/watch?v=cLa4wg2p1oI (accessed April 1, 2019).

57. Interview with Fotouhi.

58. Ibid. For more details about these organizations and individuals, see Mehrzad Boroujerdi and Kourosh Rahimkhani, *Postrevolutionary Iran: A Political Handbook* (Syracuse: Syracuse University Press, 2018).

59. Jacques Rancière, *Dissensus, on Politics and Aesthetics* (London: Continuum International, 2010), 187.

60. John Willett, ed. and trans., *Brecht on Theatre* (New York: Hill and Wang, 1964), 91.

61. Rancière, *Dissensus, 142.*

62. Daria Kirsanova, "Articulating Dissensus: Contemporary Artistic Practice in Iran at a Revolutionary Moment," *Ibraaz: Contemporary Visual Culture in North Africa and the Middle East*, August 28, 2013, https://www.ibraaz.org/essays/72 (accessed May 10, 2019).

63. Ziyayi, statement, Amir Mobed's 2013 performance, "Repetition."

64. Kirsanova, "Articulating Dissensus."

65. Quotation retrieved from artist's website, http://www.nedarazavipour.com/2010--alice-in-the-city.html (accessed July 11, 2020).

66. Personal interview with Kourosh Golnari, June 25, 2020.

67. Ibid.

68. Ibid.

69. Personal interview with Ayda (Lili) Vakilian, June 24, 2010. The location of the gallery later changed to Iranshahr Street near the House of Artists (*Khaneh honarmandan*). The gallery halted its activities in 2019, due to the economic downturn resulting from the sanctions.

70. Interview with Vakilian.

71. Hal Foster, "The Artist as Ethnographer," in Foster, *The Return of the Real: The Avant-Garde at the End of the Century* (Cambridge, MA: MIT Press, 1996), 196–97.

72. For example, in his 1961 book, *Ndembu Divination: Its Symbolism and Techniques,* renowned ethnographer Victor Turner famously relied on a single informant for understanding the complex symbolic meanings of the Ndembu rituals. Foster, "The Artist as Ethnographer," 171–204.

73. Grant Kester, "Aesthetic Evangelists: Conversion and Empowerment in Contemporary Community Art," *Afterimage* (January 1995): 5–11, at 6.

74. The word *zan-e asiri* (with possible roots in the Assyrian sexual cults) was popularized via the prominent surrealist novelist Sadeq Hedayat in his novel *Blind Owl*, in which he refers to a seductive woman who is later found dead and whose body is cut to pieces by the protagonist. See Kavoos Hassanli and Siamak Naderi, "*Tabar shenasi-e zan-e asiri dar boof-e koor-e sadeq hedayat*" [Unraveling the origins of ethereal atmosphere women in Sadeq Hedayat's *Blind Owl*], *Literary Text Research Bulletin of Allameh Tabatabaie University* 22, no. 75 (1397 [2018]): 41–60.

75. Original "private" call distributed by Ayda Vakili; emphasis added. But the gist of the text remains the same as the original. Courtesy of the private collection of Igreg Art Studio.

76. Rosi Braidotti, *Nomadic Subjects: Embodiment and Sexual Difference in Contemporary Feminist Theory* (New York: Columbia University Press, 1994), 4.

77. Marina Abramović, Chris Thompson, and Katarina Weslien, "Pure Raw: Performance, Pedagogy, and (Re)presentation," *PAJ: A Journal of Performance and Art* 28, no. 1 (January 2006): 29–50, at 47.

78. Interview with Vakilian.

79. Mohammad Reza Moridi, *Honar-e ejtema'yi*, 222–23. Moridi bases his convictions on a study by Taghi Azad Armaki, *Patogh va moderniteh irani* [*Patogh and Iranian modernity*] (Tehran: Loh-e Fekr Press, 1384 [2005]), 21.

80. *Manshoor*, "About Contemporary Art / The 5th Episode: Conversation with Ali Ettehad, Mohammad Parvizi, and Amir Rad," editorial, 2014, https://www.youtube.com/watch?v=oiO22jGZI4g (accessed June 6, 2020).

81. Joobin Bekhrad, "Street Fighting Man," *Reorient*, June 2, 2015, http://www.reorientmag.com/2015/06/performance-art-iran/ (accessed May 2, 2018).

82. Personal interview with Mohsen Gorji, June 9, 2020.

83. *Deutsche Welle Persian*, "*Honarmandan-e mo'aser dar kafeh Markof-e Tehran*" [Contemporary artists at Tehran's Marcov Café], editorial, January 8, 2013, available at https://www.dw.com/fa-ir/ (accessed June 7, 2020).

84. Ibid.

85. Michael Haldrup, "Choreographies of Leisure Mobilities," in *Mobile Methods*, ed. Monika Büscher, John Urry, and Katian Witchger (London: Routledge, 2011), 54–87, at 46; Cresswell, *On the Move*, 123–46.

86. Nigel Thrift, *Non-Representational Theory* (London: Routledge, 2007), 140.

87. Ibid., 141.

88. Tony Phillips, "Something Like the Sun: Cunningham and His Colleagues Recall 50 Years on the Road," *Village Voice*, July 10–16, 2002, n.p.

89. Sigfried Kracauer, "The Mass Ornament," *New German Critique*, no. 5 (Spring 1975): 67–76.

90. Napier Malcolm, *Five Years in a Persian Town* (London: John Murray, 1905), 135.

91. David Thurfjell, "Emotion and Self-Control: A Framework for Analysis of Shiite Mourning Rituals in Iran," in *Shiite Islam and Identity: Religion, Politics and Change in the Global Muslim Community*, ed. Lloyd Ridgeon (London: I.B. Tauris, 2012), 9–23, at 13.

92. Kourosh Asef Vaziri, ed., "*Nashriyyeh dakheli,*" 26–27.

93. Personal email correspondence with Wafaa Bilal, June 16, 2020.

94. The performance was made in collaboration with curators of the Back Room, Ava Ansari and Molly Kleiman; curator and director of Aaran Gallery, Nazila Noebashari; photographers Aliyar Rasti and Sasan Abri; cinematographer Amir Mousavi; technical director Sohrab Kashani; performance director Hamid Pourazari; choreographer Sara Reyhani; and lighting designer Rodin Hamidi.

95. Personal interview with Nazila Noebashari, June 10, 2020 (interview took place in English). Also see Ava Ansari, "Being There," *Arteeast*, Summer 2012, https://arteeast.org/quarterly/being-there/ (accessed June 16, 2020).

96. Interview with Noebashari.

97. Personal email correspondence with Bilal.

98. See Arta Khakpour, Mohammad Mehdi Khorrami, and Shouleh Vatanabadi, eds., *Moments of Silence: Authenticity in the Cultural Expressions of the Iran-Iraq War, 1980–1988* (New York: New York University Press, 2016).

99. Personal interview with Mohammad Parvizi, June 13, 2020.

100. *Hamshahri Online*, "*Gozaresh neshast-e khabari-e yek performans*" [Report on a press conference about a performance], editorial, 16 Day 1391 [2012], https://www.hamshahrionline.ir/news/196871/ (accessed May 10, 2019).

101. Interview with Parvizi.

102. The content of the interview is taken from the *Aparat* Channel, https://www.aparat.com/v/yXpKd/ (accessed May 10, 2016).

103. Ibid.

104. Mohammad Parvizi, "Come Closer, Closer. Closer than This?" *Akskhaneh* Vimeo channel, https://vimeo.com/75877710 (accessed May 19, 2020).

105. Ibid.

106. Interview with Parvizi.

107. Personal interview with Mahdyar Jamshidi, June 20, 2019.

108. Interview with Parvizi.

109. Teresa Brennan, *The Transmission of Affect* (Ithaca, NY: Cornell University Press, 2004), 5–6.

110. Interview with Parvizi.

111. Nato Thompson, *Seeing Power: Art and Activism in the Twenty-First Century* (New York: Melville House), 39–41.

112. Ibid.

113. Personal interview with Katayoun Karami, May 12, 2021.

114. Ibid.

115. Mehran Mohajer, "*Pareh jomleh hay-e Katayoun Karami: Negahi beh namayeshgah-e pendar-e neek, goftar-e neek, va kerdar neek dar gallery tarrahan-e azad*" [Pseudo-phrases of Katayoun Karami: A look at "Good Thoughts, Good Words, and Good Deeds" at Azad Art Gallery], *Faslnameh herfeh honarmand* 49 (Winter 1392 [2013]): 116–17.

116. Shahab Esfandiari, "*Kutah darbareh festival-e 'Si performance, si honarmand, si rooz'*" [*Regarding 30 performances, 30 artists, 30 days*], *Honar o resaneh* [Art and media] (5 Ordibehesht 1394 [April 2015]), 54–55; *Financial Tribune*, "Performance Arts Festival at TMOCA," editorial, December 7, 2016, https://financialtribune.com/articles/art-and-culture/54921/performance-arts-festival-at-tmoca (accessed May 10, 2019). East Art Gallery allegedly closed its doors after hosting an art project by Mona Zahed in which the poetry of Yaghma Golruyi was used. Golruyi's poems have been used by the renowned US-based Iranian pop singer Siavash Ghomeishi.

117. Alireza Amirhajebi, *Hastishenasi honar-e mafhoomi* [Hermeneutics of conceptual art] (Tehran: Nashr-e Etteffagh, 2019).

118. East Art Gallery, "Performance Art, Euphoria, Alireza Amirhajebi, 2013," https://www.youtube.com/watch?v=hoOqV8WNF4U (accessed September 4, 2015). The work is also addressed in Scheiwiller "Disrupting Bodies, Negotiating Spaces." I am grateful to Scheiwiller for generously offering an earlier draft of this essay.

119. Personal interview with Alireza Amirhajebi, June 15, 2020.

120. Graham's ideas were first presented at the Art Workers' Coalition "Open Hearing" on April 10, 1969. They were then published in Art Workers' Coalition, *An Open Hearing on the Subject: What Should Be the Program of the Art Workers Regarding Museum Reform and to Establish the Program of an Open Art Workers' Coalition* (New York: Art Workers' Coalition, 1969), n.p. Amirhajebi's translation, "*Ettehad-e kargaran-e honar*" [Coalition of art workers], is included in a collection of translated essays, published in 2019 through Ettefagh Press.

121. Scheiwiller, "Disrupting Bodies, Negotiating Spaces."

122. Interview with Amirhajebi.

123. Ibid.

124. Luce Irigaray, *The Sex Which Is Not One*, trans. Catherine Porter (Ithaca, NY: Cornell University Press, 1985), 210.

125. Interview with Amirhajebi.

126. Sylvia Lavin, *Kissing Architecture* (Princeton, NJ: Princeton University Press, 2011), 5–8.

127. Personal interview with Peyman Shafieezadeh, July 11, 2020.

128. The *heya'ti* style was used in the design of the Center for the Eighth Summit of the Organization of Islamic Conference in Tehran in 1997 by architect Yahya Fiuzi. He talked about his use of *heya'ti* for this project with me in a personal interview in 2004. For more information about Fiuzu's design, see Karimi and Vasquez, "Ornament and Argument."

129. W. J. T. Mitchell, "Image, Space, Revolution: The Arts of Occupation," *Critical Inquiry* 39, no. 1 (Autumn 2012): 8–32, at 17.

130. Ibid., 18.

131. For more information about the group see their official website, http://karizarts.com/plays/aras/ (accessed June 02, 2019).

132. Ibid.

133. Personal interview with Hossein Tavazoni Zadeh, June 30, 2019.

134. Behrouzan, *Prozak Diaries.*

135. Interview with Tavazoni Zadeh.

136. Ibid.

137. See, in particular, *Dalan Quarterly, which* launched in 2019. For every

issue the quarterly focuses on a single Tehran street and offers multiple articles that cover mostly the designated street's Pahlavi-era history.

138. For example, see the popular hashtag page *#tarikhshafahimemarimoaser Iran* (oral history of modern Iranian architecture) and many others.

139. Another art group that engages with this architecture in a critical but slightly different way is the New Media Society, an extension of Parkingallery that was created in 1998. Since 2016, the New Media Society has created several projects concerning the spatial dimensions and maps of Tehran. Noteworthy among them is the #MappingKarimKhan project, or simply "Mapping Karimkhan," a visual research project for Iranian artists to reexamine the gentrification of Karimkhan, a neighborhood in central Tehran that New Media Society currently calls home. The neighborhood is now considered part of Tehran's emerging art and culture zone, which is also undergoing a rapid gentrification under the rubric of the capital's "Cultural Rectangle" (*morabba' farhangi*). For more information about the project, see Amirali Ghasemi and Arusha Moshtaghizadeh, "*Mapping-e karimkhan: Naghshehbardari va taghirat-e farhangi va honari dar ghalb-e tehran*" [Mapping Karimkhan: Mapping art and cultural changes at the heart of Tehran], *Tazarv*, no. 5 (Bahar 1397 [Spring 2018]): 94–101.

140. *Honar Online*, "*Asheghaneh-ie dar del-e me'mari*" [A love story in the heart of (historic) architecture], editorial, 8 Dey 1396 [December 29, 2017], http://www.honaronline.ir (accessed May 10, 2019).

141. Ibid.

142. Najafi Ardabili, *Grotowski in Iran*, 30.

143. See Abbas Nalbandian, *Nagahan* (*Tehran: Entesharat-e Television melli-e Iran* [*Iran's national television press*], 1351 [1972]).

144. Personal interview with Tavazoni Zadeh, June 30, 2019.

145. Ibid.

146. Information from the official website of *Kariz*, http://karizarts.com/plays/aras/ (accessed May 28, 2019). I am also grateful to Tavazoni Zadeh for providing additional password-protected recordings of these plays.

147. Nazanin Mousavi, "A Conversation between Tiwall Editorial and Hossein Tavazoni Zadeh about the Amsterdam Play," audio recording, https://www.tiwall.com/podcasts/interview-hosseintavazoni (accessed June 10, 2019).

148. Eve Sedgwick, *Touching Feeling: Affect, Pedagogy, Performativity* (Durham, NC: Duke University Press, 2003), 17.

149. Raymond Williams, "Structures of Feeling," in Williams, *Marxism and Literature* (Oxford: Oxford University Press, 1977), 128–35, at 132–33.

150. Tschumi's work was introduced in Persian as early as 1996, through the translation of Geoffrey Broadbent's *Deconstruction: A Student Guide* (1991) by architectural historian Manouchehr Mozayyeni (1934–2003). Since then, Mohammad

Reza Joadat (b. 1939), Kamran Afshar Naderi (b. 1959), and Mehrdad Iravanian (b. 1957) (to name a few prominent figures) have written about Tschumi or have been indirectly inspired by Tschumi's principles of design.

151. Bernard Tschumi and Robert Young, *The Manhattan Transcripts* (London: Academy Editions, 1994), xxi.

152. Ibid., xxiii.

153. Neil Leach, *Rethinking Architecture: A Reader in Cultural Theory* (London: Routledge, 2005), 306.

154. Reinhold Martin, "Occupy: What Architecture Can Do," in Hirsch and Miessen, eds., *What Is Critical Spatial Practice?*, 89–90, at 89.

155. Architecture Discussions, Clubhouse group, "Urban Public Space."

156. Lefebvre, *The Production of Space*, 191.

157. Azimi and Ghasemi, "Independent and Artist-run Initiatives in Tehran." As of 2018, the private pool studio was in place, with Ave dividing his working time among Tehran, Europe, the United States, and Dubai, providing the next generation of artists with a model to follow when finding themselves in an in-between alternative position.

158. Personal interview with Reza Daneshmir, March 9, 2021.

159. Ibid.

160. Ibid.

161. Personal interview with Benham Kamrani, July 17, 2020.

162. Moeini et al., *Urban Culture in Tehran.*

163. Marco Frascari, "Critical Conversations in Media, Drawing as Theory," *ACSA Annual Meeting,* 2001; cited in Kendra Schank Smith, *Architect's Drawings: A Selection of Sketches by World Famous Architects through History* (Boston: Elsevier, 2005), 1.

164. Hadi Fardanesh in conversation with Reza Daneshmir.

165. Ibid.

166. Personal interview with Alireza Taghaboni, March 2015.

167. Pierre Bourdieu, *The Logic of Practice*, trans. Richard Nice (Stanford: Stanford University Press, 1990), 68.

168. Alice Bucknell, "Behind the Veil," *Architectural Review,* September 6, 2017, https://www.architectural-review.com/essays/viewpoints/behind-the-veil/10022883.article (accessed November 8, 2017).

169. Ibid.

170. Notable examples in this vein are Khorsand Tower, also known as Checker Box Office Complex, by the Arsh Design Studio (2006); The House of 40 Knots by Habibeh Madjdabadi and Alireza Mashhadimirza (2014); Cloaked in Bricks by Admun Studio (2015); Andarzgoo Residential Building by Ayeneh Office (2015); and Orsi Khaneh by Keivani Architects (2016).

171. Personal interview with a contractor in Tehran, July 6, 2019.

172. Personal interview with Atefeh Karbasi, July 2, 2019.

173. Oscar Newman, *Defensible Space: Crime Prevention through Urban Design* (New York: Collier, 1972).

174. Ibid., 2–3.

175. Sarah Chaplin and Alexandra Stara, eds., *Curating Architecture and the City* (New York: Routledge, 2009), 2.

176. The bridge, which is now also known as "the third symbol of Tehran," after the Azadi Monument and the Milad Telecommunication Tower, won three awards in Iran, and many international acknowledgments, notably by Architizer and the Aga Khan Foundation.

177. For example, at one point, an Australian company delayed providing Araghian and her colleagues with the computer software they needed because the project originated in Iran, which is under international sanctions due to its nuclear program. See Saeed Kamali Dehghan, "Take It to the Bridge: The Tehran Architect Striking the Right Chord in Iran and Beyond," *The Guardian*, April 20, 2015, https://www.theguardian.com/world/2015/apr/20/bridge-tehran-architect-iran-leila-araghian-tabiat-sanctions-iranian-designers (accessed April 25, 2015).

178. Personal interview with Leila Araghian, February 13, 2015. The story is also cited in *Al Jazeera*. See Ted Regencia, "The Award-Winning Bridge Connecting Iranians: Project Dubbed as 'The Third Symbol of Tehran' Earns International Recognition for Architect Leila Araghian," *Al Jazeera*, April 16, 2015, https://www.aljazeera.com/indepth/features/2015/04/award-winning-bridge-connecting-iranians-150414121934153.html (accessed May 10, 2016).

179. Ibid.

180. Ibid.

181. Such characteristics are acknowledged by many scholars, most notably Beatriz Colomina. See her "The Split Wall: Domestic Voyeurism," in *Sexuality & Space*, ed. Beatriz Colomina and Jennifer Bloomer (New York: Princeton Architectural Press, 1992), 73–128.

182. Ibid., 83.

183. Interview with Araghian.

184. Ibid.

185. Ibid.

186. Interview with Mehdi Farhadian.

187. Amir Bani Masoud, *Me'mari mo'aser-e Iran* [Contemporary architecture of Iran] (Tehran: Nashr-e Honar va Me'mari Gharn, 1391 [2012]), 152.

188. Saeed Basheertash and Ebrahim Nabavi, "*Si sal-e pish dar chenin roozi: Shahr-e no atash gereft va roospian koshteh shodand*" [Thirty years ago on this day: Shahr-e No caught on fire and prostitutes were killed]," *Radio Zamaneh*, 9

Bahman 1387 [January 28, 2009], http://www.zamaaneh.com/revolution/2009/01/post_218.html (accessed June 20, 2019).

189. Ibid.

190. Ibid.

191. The building was allegedly owned by the *Sepah* (Islamic Revolutionary Guard Corps) since the revolution of 1979.

192. It is noteworthy that in addition to Argo Factory, the foundation also manages the Kandovan and the Café Musée Project. For more information about the activities of the foundation, and especially those that take place in Argo, see http://pejman.foundation/argofactory/category/architecture/ (accessed May 10, 2019).

193. Naghmeh Mazhari, "*Goftegoo ba Ali Shakeri Shemirani darbareh sakhteman-e Argo*" [A conversation with Ali Shakeri Shemirani about the Argo Building], *Memarnet,* January 9, 2017, http://www.memarnet.com/fa/node/3862 (accessed May 21, 2019).

194. Ibid.

195. Nishat Awan, Tatjana Schneider, and Jeremy Till, eds., *Spatial Agency: Other Ways of Doing Architecture* (London and New York: Routledge, 2011), 29.

196. Yasaman Esmaili, "Argo Factory: Contemporary Art Museum & Cultural Centre by Ahmadreza Schricker Architecture–North," *Architectural Record,* November 21, 2021, https://www.architecturalrecord.com/ (accessed November 22, 2021).

197. Ibid.

198. Ibid.

199. These photographs are in the personal collection of Shakeri Shemirani. Due to limits on the number of images, it was not possible to include them in this book.

200. On preservation as critical spatial practice, see Jorge Otero-Pailos, "Subtle Framing," in Hirsch and Miessen, eds., *What Is Critical Spatial Practice?,* 100–102.

201. Personal interview with Homayoun Sirizi, April 7, 2021.

202. Moeini et al., *Urban Culture in Tehran.*

203. Ibid.

204. Azimi and Fotouhi, "Independent and Artist-Run Initiatives."

205. Ave in conversation with AB Gallery.

206. *Setad* was built on the systematic seizure of thousands of properties belonging to former royal family and ordinary Iranians, as well as members of religious minorities, businesspeople, and Iranians living abroad, at times falsely claiming that the properties were abandoned. See Steve Stecklow, Babak Dehghanpisheh, and Yeganeh Torbati, "Khamenei Controls Massive Financial Empire Built on Property Seizures," *Reuters,* December 11, 2013, https://www.reuters.com/investigates/iran/#article/part1 (accessed March 19, 2021).

207. Fereydoun Ave in conversation with *Art Asia Pacific Magazine*, 2017, https://vimeo.com/225382123 (accessed March 8, 2021).

208. Observations based on personal visit. Also see Sohrab Mohebbi, "Homayoun Sirizi," *Bidoun Magazine* Projects, Fall 2007, https://bidoun.org/articles/installations-by-homayoun-sirizi (accessed May 8, 2019).

209. Personal interview with Sirizi, April 18, 2021.

210. Ibid.

211. Henri Neuendorf, "Iranian Art Dealer Sentenced to 27 Years in Prison and 124 Lashes for Morality Offenses," *Artnet News*, January 31, 2018, https://news.artnet.com/art-world/iranian-gallerists-jailed-1212677 (accessed April 19, 2021).

212. Interview with Sirizi.

213. Information regarding collecting other materials comes from personal interview with Sirizi, June 20, 2021.

214. Benjamin H. D. Buchloh, "Gerhard Richter's Atlas: The Anomic Archive," *October* 88 (Spring 1999): 118.

215. I borrow the term from curator Sara Reza. See "The Social Studio," *Guggenheim blog*, January 22, 2016, https://www.guggenheim.org/blogs/map/the-social-studio (accessed May 9, 2019). Reza characterizes Sazmanab as a "social studio" where participatory art takes place.

216. Sazmanab Center for Contemporary Art, http://www.sazmanab.org/about/mission/mission/ (accessed July 26, 2014).

217. Personal interview with Sohrab Kashani, March 20, 2015.

218. Alex Teplitzky, "A Space in Pittsburgh that Transports Visitors to Tehran and Vice Versa," *Creative Capital*, October 15, 2019, https://creative-capital.org/2019/10/15/a-space-in-pittsburgh-that-transports-visitors-to-tehran-iran-and-vice-versa/ (accessed June 02, 2020).

219. Ibid. Also see Moeini et al., *Urban Culture in Tehran*.

220. Beck, "Alternative: Space," in Ault, *Alternative Art, New York*, 256.

221. Ibid.

222. Lefebvre, *The Production of Space*, 170; emphasis in original.

223. Ibid., 73, 94, 85.

224. Ibid., 116.

225. Ibid., 73.

226. Ibid.

227. Ibid., 142.

228. Ibid., 93.

229. Ibid., 191; emphasis in original.

230. Svetlana Boym, "Ilya Kabakov: The Soviet Toilet and the Palace of Utopias," *ARTmargins*, 1999, https://artmargins.com/ilya-kabakov-the-soviet-toilet-and-the-palace-of-utopias/ (accessed May 8, 2020).

231. Claire Bishop, *Installation Art* (London: Tate, 2005), 14.

232. Golnar Yarmohammad Touski, "Two Artists Attempt to Collaborate across Continents, Travel Bans and All," *Hyperallergic*, March 26, 2020, https://hyperallergic.com/547424/two-artists-attempt-to-collaborate-across-continents-travel-bans-and-all/ (accessed April 10, 2020).

233. "The Other Apartment," http://www.theotherapartment.com/information/ (accessed May 10, 2021).

Epilogue

1. Rhonda Richford, "Cannes: 'The Missing Picture' Wins Un Certain Regard Prize," *Hollywood Reporter*, May 25, 2013, https://www.hollywoodreporter.com/news/cannes-missing-picture-wins-regard-558551 (accessed August 8, 2019). On Rasoulof's arrest, see *Radio Zamaneh*, "*Goroohi az honarmandan Mohammad Rasoulof ra ta dadgah-e engelab moshaye'at kardand*" [A group of artists joined Rasoulof on the way to his court appeal], editorial, August 5, 2019, https://www.radiozamaneh.com/j_post_status/ (accessed August 8, 2018).

2. Guy Lodge, "'A Man of Integrity,' 'Wind River,' 'Barbara' Take Un Certain Regard Awards at Cannes: Iranian Filmmaker Mohammad Rasoulof Took the Top Prize from a Jury Headed by Actress Uma Thurman," *Variety*, May 27, 2017, https://variety.com/2017/film/festivals/a-man-of-integrity-wind-river-barbara-win-cannes-un-certain-regard-award-uma-thurman-mathieu-amalric-taylor-sheridan-1202446610/ (accessed May 9, 2018).

3. Gayatri Chakravorty Spivak, "Can the Subaltern Speak?," in *Marxism and the Interpretation of Culture*, ed. Cary Nelson and Lawrence Grossberg (Urbana: University of Illinois Press, 1988), 291.

4. Interview with Razavipour.

5. Recorded interview via Mojtaba Fallahi with Rozita Sharafjahan, January 10, 2019.

6. Negar Azimi, "Iran in Pictures: Social Suffering and Three Sets of Images," in *Sensible Politics: The Visual Culture of Nongovernmental Activism*, ed. Meg McLagan and Yates McKee (New York: Zone Books, 2012), 219–43, at 240.

7. Azimi, "Don't Cry for Me, America," in Azam Zanganeh, *My Sister, Guard Your Veil*, 104–5.

8. Siamak Delzendeh, "Artist Residencies: A Chance for the Micro-narratives to Become Manifest," in *2014–2015 Kooshk Residency*, exhibition catalog (Tehran: Kooshk Residency, 2016), 27–29, at 29.

9. See Sue Curry Jansen, *Censorship: The Knot That Binds Power and Knowledge* (Oxford: Oxford University Press, 1988).

10. *Ocula Magazine*, "Art Underground: An Ocula Report from Tehran," editorial, October 26, 2015, https://ocula.com/magazine/reports/art-underground-a-report-from-tehran/ (accessed November 10, 2018).

11. Ibid.

12. Zuzanna Olszewska, "Classy Kids and Down-at-Heel Intellectuals: Status Aspiration and Blind Spots in the Contemporary Ethnography of Iran," *Iranian Studies* 46, no. 6 (2013): 1–22; Laudan Nooshin, "Whose Liberation? Iranian Popular Music and the Fetishization of Resistance," *Popular Communication* 15, no. 3 (2017): 163–91; Theresa Parvin Steward, "Beyond a Politicization of Persian Cats: Representing Iranian Popular Musicians in the Western Media," *Middle East Journal of Culture and Communication* 13 (2020): 7–27. The work of these scholars draws on those of others in similar sociopolitical contexts; for example, Nooshin references Geoff Baker's study of Cuban rap, in which he argues that seeing rap as political or protest song prevents us from recognizing a whole host of other non-political motivations. See Baker, "La Habana Que No Conoces: Cuban Rap and the Social Construction of Urban Space," *Ethnomusicology Forum* 15, no. 2 (2006): 215–46.

13. John Ward Anderson, "Roll Over, Khomeini! Iran Cultivates a Local Rock Scene, within Limits," *Washington Post*, August 23, 2001, https://www.washingtonpost.com/archive/politics/2001/08/23/roll-over-khomeini-iran-cultivates-a-local-rock-scene-within-limits/. Cited in Nooshin, "Whose Liberation?," 166.

14. Steward, "Beyond a Politicization of Persian Cats," 9.

15. Olszewska, "Classy Kids and Down-at-Heel Intellectuals."

16. Ibid., 3.

17. Olszewska particularly highlights Mahdavi, *Passionate Uprisings*.

18. Ibid., 16.

19. Ibid., 5–6.

20. Personal interview with Amir Mobed, July 13, 2021.

21. Hirokazu Miyazaki, *The Method of Hope: Anthropology, Philosophy, and Fijian Knowledge* (Stanford: Stanford University Press, 2004). Cited in Khosravi, *Precarious Lives*, 14.

22. Jacques Derrida, *Writing and Difference*, trans. Alan Bass (Routledge, 2001), 373.

23. Khosravi, *Precarious Lives*, 15.

24. Personal interview with Ada (tag name), March 16, 2021.

25. Ibid.

26. Personal interview with a prominent artist, art critic, and university professor, who wishes to remain anonymous, March 19, 2021.

27. Ibid.

28. Ibid.

29. Personal interview with a prominent artist, who wishes to remain anonymous, March 10, 2020.

30. Hobsbawm's *Bandits* first appeared in 1969 from Weidenfeld and Nicolson in London. A revised edition appeared in 1981 from Pantheon in New York. See also E. J. Hobsbawm, *Primitive Rebels: Studies in Archaic Forms of Social*

Movement in the 19th and 20th Centuries (Manchester: Manchester University Press, 1959).

31. Interview with aforementioned anonymous artist.

32. Personal interview with Aidin Torkameh, March 8, 2021.

33. On these activities in other global contexts see, for example, Nandini Bagchee, *Counter Institution: Activist Estates of the Lower East Side* (New York: Empire State Editions and Fordham University Press, 2018). See, in particular, "Introduction," 1–2.

34. Art as charity work is a separate genre that is not often considered high art, even if Iranian conceptual artists and high-profile artists with diverse backgrounds often get involved in such benevolent activities. In his book *Honar-e ejtema'yi*, art historian Mohammad Reza Moridi features artists Gizella Varga Sinai (mentioned in chapter 1), Ahmad Nadalian (mentioned in chapter 2), and Maryam Kouhestani (b. 1982), who have worked with what he calls the forgotten (*faramoosh shodegan*), via charitable foundations and other altruistic organizations. Through their often negligible or unpaid labor, these artists lift the morale of marginalized and psychologically or physically disturbed individuals. Mohammad Reza Moridi, *Honar-e ejtema'yi: Maghalati dar jame'eh shenasi-e honar mo'aser-e Iran* [*Social art: Essays on the sociology of contemporary art in Iran*] (Tehran: Aban Press in conjunction with Art University, 1397 [2018]), 90–91. There are also independent social practice projects that directly engage with the environment and pollution for educational purposes. Examples in this vein include works by Negar Farajiani (mentioned in chapter 3). Her best-known long-term social practice project, titled *Tehran Monoxide Project* (2011–15), brought awareness of the need for protection of the environment to local schools and small communities in and around Tehran. Find further information on the artist's website, http://www.negarfarajiani.com/projects/tehran-monoxide (accessed July 12, 2020).

35. Personal interview with Mahmoud Maktabi, August 16, 2020.

36. Ibid.

37. Personal interview with Pouria Jahanshad, August 25, 2019.

38. Bayat, *Life as Politics*.

39. Ibid., 249.

40. Boris Groys, "The Truth of Art," *e-flux* 71, March 2016, https://www.e-flux.com/journal/71/60513/the-truth-of-art/ (accessed May 12, 2017). Also cited in Pouria Jahanshad, "*Honar-e gheyr-e rasmi va gheyr-e rasmi sazi-e honar*" [Informal art and making art informal], in *Bazkhani-e shahr: Hokmrani-e shahr* [*Rethinking the city: Urban governance*] (Tehran: Ruzbahan Press, 2022). I thank Jahanshad for permitting me to read the article in advance of its publication.

41. As an example, consider the 7th Berlin Biennale in 2012 curated by Artur Żmijewski, and the criticism it provoked. Some even went as far as calling it a zoo for art activists. See Olga Kopenkina, "Administered Occupation: Art and Politics

at the 7th Berlin Biennale," *Art Journal Open*, April 18, 2013, http://artjournal.collegeart.org/?p=3457 (accessed May 10, 2016). On ideas of Debord about art versus political activism, see Guy Debord, "The Situationists and New Forms of Action in Politics or Art" (1963), in *On the Passage of a Few People through a Rather Brief Moment in Time*, eds. Peter Wollen et al. (Cambridge, MA: MIT Press, 1989); Sadie Plant, *The Most Radical Gesture: The Situationist International in a Postmodern Age* (London: Routledge, 1992).

42. The outdoor living room has also been featured in Daniel Kötter's film, *Hashti, Tehran* (2016), in which he captures selected peripheral neighborhoods from Tehran and showcases the ways in which the inhabitants interact with these architectural spaces. See Niloofar Niksar, "Public Space: Field of Distinction," *Me'mar* 116 (2019): 40–45; Kaveh Rashidzadeh, *The Book of Tehran, Hashti: Nafar Abad* (Tehran: Bongah Publications in conjunction with Übermut Project, 2017).

43. Thomas Erdbrink, "Cautiously, Iranians Reclaim Public Spaces and Liberties Long Suppressed," *New York Times*, October 5, 2015.

44. Personal interview with Ehsan Rasoulof, July 30, 2020.

45. Ibid.

46. Ibid. On art as civil action, see Philipp Dietachmaire and Pascal Gielen, eds., *The Art of Civil Action: Political Space and Cultural Dissent* (Amsterdam: Valiz, 2017).

47. Lefebvre, *The Production of Space*, 8.

48. Interview with Rasoulof.

49. Ibid.

50. Karl Marx, *The Grundrisse*, trans. Martin Nicolaus (London: Penguin Books in association with *New Left Review*, 1973), 690–712.

51. Henri Lefebvre, "Les nouveaux ensembles urbains (un cas concret: Lacq-Mourenx et les problèmes urbains de la nouvelle classe ouvrière)," *Revue française de sociologie* 1, no. 2 (1960): 186–201. For an in-depth analysis of Lefebvre's ideas concerning space and architecture, see Łukasz Stanek, *Henri Lefebvre on Space: Architecture, Urban Research and the Production of a Theory* (Minneapolis: University of Minnesota Press, 2011); Henri Lefebvre, "From Absolute Space to Abstract Space," in *The Production of Space*, 229–91.

52. These modification strategies of modernist housing projects even emerged in the most sophisticated designs by prominent Iranian architects. Consider, for example, the 1977 Shushtar New Town by the Iranian DAZ architectural group led by Kamran Diba. The complex was carefully composed of intricate brickwork, courtyards, and rooftop spaces for entertaining that resembled the features of native architectural culture. It also emulated modern design in its attempt to push residents to coexist in similar spaces, even forcing them to share parts of their domestic realms with their neighbors. Although highly photogenic, the mere fact that inhabitants of these units altered them to allow for more privacy in their

homes—blocking balconies and dividing shared entrance thresholds—attests to the failure of the idealistic revival of traditional Iranian architecture. Karimi, *Domesticity and Consumer Culture in Iran*, 140.

53. Information taken from the official website of the Mohsen Art Gallery, http://mohsen.gallery/mohsen-projects (accessed August 2, 2020).

54. Ibid.

55. Ibid.

56. Personal interview with Kamrani, March 19, 2021.

57. Interview with Mobed.

58. Ibid.

59. John Keane, *Vaclav Havel: A Political Tragedy in Six Acts* (New York: Basic Books, 2012), 268–86.

60. Alireza Gholami, "*Goftegoo ba Vaslav Havel*" [A conversation with Vaclav Havel], *Mehrnameh* 18 (1390 [2012]). The actual interview took place a few months earlier.

61. Barbad Golshiri, "*Dastgah va tamarrod*" [The system and the rebellion], *Honar-e farda* 4 (1390 [2011]): 10–12.

62. Project description (in English) derived from the Mohsen Gallery website, https://mohsen.gallery/series/disformission/ (accessed June 10, 2021).

63. Interview with Mobed.

64. Project description derived from Mohsen Gallery website.

65. Interview with Mobed.

66. Personal interview with Tooraj Khamenehzadeh and Negin Mahzoon, February 21, 2021.

67. Ibid. Also see Reza Farnam, "1st Rybon International Artists' Workshop Report on the 1st International Artists' Workshop, organized by Rybon Art Center, an Artist-Led Initiative in Tehran," *Nafas Magazine*, November 2012, https://universes.art/en/nafas/articles/2012/rybon-workshop (accessed May 8, 2019).

68. Interview with Rasoulof.

69. On this topic see, for example, Jill Desimini, "Limitations of the Temporary: Landscape and Abandonment," *Journal of Urban History* 41, no. 2 (2015): 279–93.

70. Interview with Rasoulof. Rasoulof's views in some respects align with those of the most vocal supporters of neoliberalism in Iran, who believe that, considering the pressure from international sanctions, it is essential for Iran to "free the economy" and allow the private sector to take over. See, for example, Musa Ghaninejad in conversation with the *Eghtesad negar*, January 1398 [January 24, 2020], http://www.eghtesadnegar.ir/ (accessed August 8, 2020). I am grateful to Azam Khatam for bringing this to my attention.

71. Interview with Rasoulof.

72. Based on several testimonies gathered by artists who work with Rasoulof.

73. In 2011, the platform hosted Rasoulof's Annual Digital Art Exhibition (TADAEX) to open a new window onto digital art and music in Iran, including

work by Amir Sadeghi Konjani (b. 1983), a self-described "post-musician" who combines performance art with avant-garde music.

74. Sandy Narine, "The Institutionalization of Dissent," in *Thinking about Exhibitions*, eds. Sandy Narine, Reesa Greenberg, and Bruce Ferguson (New York: Routledge, 1996), 387–410. Cited in Brian Wallis, "Public Funding and Alternative Spaces," in Ault, *Alternative Art, New York*, 161–81.

75. Simon Sadler, "Drop City Revisited," *Journal of Architectural Education* 59, no. 3 (2006): 5–14.

76. See "Drop City," https://www.spatialagency.net/database/drop.city (accessed May 10, 2019).

77. Brian Wallis, "Public Funding and Alternative Spaces," in Ault, *Alternative Art, New York*, 161–81.

78. Ibid., 174.

79. Ibid.

80. Ibid.

81. For a full list of oppositional voices, see Eric Joseph Van Holm, "The Creative Classes' Greatest Failure," *Journal of Policy Research in Tourism, Leisure and Events* 7, no. 2 (2015): 204–7.

82. Michele M. Hoyman and Christopher Faricy, "It Takes a Village a Test of the Creative Class, Social Capital, and Human Capital Theories," *Urban Affairs Review* 44, no. 3 (2008): 311–33.

83. Gregory Sholette, *Dark Matter: Art and Politics in the Age of Enterprise Culture* (London: Pluto Press, 2011), 188.

84. Stephen Duncombe, *Cultural Resistance Reader* (London: Verso, 2002), 499.

85. While the transfer of internet control to the armed forces is a new phenomenon, other ways that have long regulated the usage of the internet and social media platforms are not. For more information about these activities, see Niki Akhavan, *Electronic Iran: The Cultural Politics of an Online Evolution* (New Brunswick, NJ: Rutgers University Press, 2013).

86. ARCH-GAP Clubhouse group, "*Ma me'maran va internet dar sharayet-e pisheh-e roo*" [We, the architects and the internet under the current circumstances], July 29, 2021.

87. The new "program" (*barnameh*) was published on the ministry's website. The seventy-nine-page document is filled with conservative views. The so-called program was published on the MCIG website. See https://www.farhang.gov.ir/ershad_content/media/image/2021/08/1097720_orig.pdf (accessed August 16, 2021).

88. Artist Instagram post, June 21, 2021. I have withheld the name due to the sensitivity of the comment and its temporary nature.

89. Margaret Mead, *The World Ahead* (New York: Berghahn Books, 2005), 12.

Bibliography

Abazari, Yousof, and Arman Zakeri. "*Se daheh hamneshini-e deen va Neoliberalism dar Iran*" [Three decades of the entanglement of religion and neoliberalism in Iran]. *Naghd-e eghtesad-e siyasi*, February 2019. https://pecritique.com/2019/02/24

Abe, Satoshi. "Conceptions of Nature in Iran: Science, Nationalism, and Heteroglossia." *Journal of Anthropological Research* 69, no. 2 (Summer 2013): 201–23.

———. "Iranian Environmentalism: Nationhood, Alternative Natures, and the Materiality of Objects." *Nature and Culture* 7, no. 3 (Winter 2012): 259–84.

Abrahamian, Ervand. *A History of Modern Iran*. Princeton, NJ: Princeton University Press, 2008.

Abramović, Marina, Chris Thompson, and Katarina Weslien. "Pure Raw: Performance, Pedagogy, and (Re)presentation." *PAJ: A Journal of Performance and Art* 28, no. 1 (January 2006): 29–50.

Abu-Lughod, Leila. "The Romance of Resistance: Tracing Transformations of Power through Bedouin Women." *American Ethnologist* 17, no. 1 (February 1990): 53.

Adjaye, David. "Building Critical Space." In *What Is Critical Spatial Practice?*, edited by Nikolaus Hirsch and Markus Miessen. Berlin: Sternberg Press, 2012.

Afsarian, Iman. "*Nesbat-e mas'aleh dar-e honar va syasat dar honar siyasi Iran*" [The problem of the relationship between art and politics in Iranian political art]. *Herfeh honarmand* 60 (Summer 2016): 64–77.

Afshar, Mahasti. *Shiraz Festival of Arts: Shiraz, Persepolis*. Updated and illustrated version of a paper originally commissioned by the Asia Society for "The Shiraz Arts Festival: A Global Vision Revisited" symposium. New York, Asia Society, 2013. https://asiasociety.org/files/uploads/126files/Festival%20of%20Arts%2C%20Shiraz-Persepolis%201967-77.pdf

Aghaie, Kamran Scot. *The Martyrs of Karbala: Shi'i Symbols and Rituals in Modern Iran*. Seattle: University of Washington Press, 2004.

Ahmed, Sara. "Affective Economies." *Social Text* 79/22, no. 2 (Summer 2004): 117–39.

———. *The Cultural Politics of Emotion*. New York: Routledge, 2004.

———. "Happy Objects." In *The Affect Theory Reader*, edited by Melissa Gregg and Gregory J. Seigworth. Durham, NC: Duke University Press, 2010.

Akcan, Esra. *Architecture in Translation: Germany, Turkey, and the Modern House.* Durham, NC: Duke University Press, 2012.

Akhavan, Niki. *Electronic Iran: The Cultural Politics of an Online Evolution.* New Brunswick, NJ: Rutgers University Press, 2013.

Alipour, Yasaman. "New Media Society." *Arteast* (Fall 2017). http://arteeast.org/quarterly/new-media-society/

Alsaden, Amin. "Alternative Salons: Cultivating Art and Architecture in the Domestic Spaces of Post-WWII Baghdad." In *The Art Salon in the Arab Region: Politics of Taste Making*, edited by Nadia Von Maltzahn and Monique Bellan, 168–208. Beirut: Bergon Verlang Wurzburg in Kommission, 2018.

Amir Arjomand, Said. *The Turban for the Crown: The Islamic Revolution in Iran.* New York: Oxford University Press, 1988.

Amir-Ebrahimi, Samila. "*Ma ba haman: Seyri dar honar-e siyasi ejtema'yi-e Iran-e mo'aser*" [Us and the same: A look at the sociopolitical art of Iran]. *Herfeh honarmand* 60 (Summer 2016): 2–26.

Amir-Ebrahimi, Masserat. "Conquering Enclosed Public Spaces." *Cities* 21, no. 6 (2006): 455–61.

———. "*Fazahay-e omoomi dar hesar*" [Captive public spaces]. *Honar va me'mari* 64/65 (1381 [2002]): 63–67.

Amirhajebi, Alireza, trans. *Ettehad-e kargaran-e honar* [Coalition of art workers]. Tehran: Ettefagh Press, 1398 [2019].

———. *Hastishenasi honar-e mafhoomi* [Hermeneutics of conceptual art]. Tehran: Nashr-e Etteffagh, 2019.

Amirhajebi, Banu. "*Avvalin shabnameh-ie keh dar Tabriz montasher shod*" [The first *shabnameh* that was published in Tabriz]. *Tehran musavvar 397 (*1329 [1950]).

Anderson, John Ward. "Roll Over, Khomeini! Iran Cultivates a Local Rock Scene, within Limits." *Washington Post*, August 23, 2001. https://www.washingtonpost.com/archive/politics/2001/08/23/roll-over-khomeini-iran-cultivates-a-local-rock-scene-within-limits/

Anjo, Liliane. "Contemporary Iranian Theatre: The Emergence of an Autonomous Space." In *Cultural Revolution in Iran: Contemporary Popular Culture in the Islamic Republic*, edited by Annabelle Sreberny and Massoumeh Torfeh, 81–94. London: I.B. Tauris, 2013.

Ansari, Ava. "Being There." *Arteeast* (Summer 2012). https://arteeast.org/quarterly/being-there/

Ansari, Mojgan. "*Tab-e plaza dar Tehran*" [Plaza fever in Tehran]. *Isna*, 17 Azar 1399 [December 7, 2020]. https://www.isna.ir/news/99091712859/تب-پلازا-در-تهران

Anvari, Haleh. "Immersive Drama Set in a Tehran Taxi: Iranian Cabs Afford Passengers a Degree of Anonymity, Paving the Way for Uninhibited Conversations and a New Play." *The Guardian: Tehran Bureau*, December 26, 2013. https://www.theguardian.com/world/iran-blog/2013/dec/26/iran-drama-tehran-taxi

Arendt, Hannah. *The Human Condition*. Chicago: University of Chicago Press, 1998.

———. *The Origins of Totalitarianism*. New York: Harcourt Brace Jovanovich, 1973.

Asef Vaziri, Kourosh, ed. "*Nashriyyeh dakheli sazman-e zibasazi-e shahr-e Tehran: Vijeh nameh hayat-e shabaneh shahri*" [Tehran Municipality Beautification Bureau bulletin, special issue, *Night life in the city*] 1, no. 18 (1394 [2015]): 6–9.

Atwood, Blake. Blake Atwood in conversation with Beeta Baghoolizadeh. "Blake Atwood on the Secret Life of Video Cassettes in Iran." *Ajam Media Collective*, November 29, 2017. https://ajammc.com/2017/11/29/video-cassettes-in-iran/

———, and Peter Decherney, eds. *Iranian Cinema in a Global Context Policy, Politics, and Form*. New York: Routledge, 2015.

Ault, Julie, ed. *Alternative Art, New York, 1965–1985*. Minneapolis: University of Minnesota Press, 2002.

Avam. "*Negahi beh tarrahi meidan emam hussein beh bahaneh ayyam-e moharram*" [A look at the design of Imam Hussein Square on the occasion of the month of Muharram]. Editorial, 19 Shahrivar 1395 [October 10, 2016]. https://avammag.com/13069/text-critic/

Avcioğlu, Nebahat. "A Palace of One's Own: Stanislas I's Kiosks and the Idea of Self-Representation." *Art Bulletin* 85, no. 4 (December 2003): 662–84.

Awan, Nishat, Tatjana Schneider, and Jeremy Till. *Spatial Agency: Other Ways of Doing Architecture*. London: Routledge, 2011.

Azad, Sahar. "*Goftegoo ba Jinoos Taghizadeh*" [A conversation with Jinoos Taghizadeh]. *Shargh Daily* 2473, 28 *Azar* 1394 [December 19, 2015]. https://www.magiran.com/article/3282021

Azad Armaki, Taghi. *Patogh va moderniteh irani* [*Patogh and Iranian modernity*]. Tehran: Loh-e Fekr Press, 1384 [2005].

Azimi, Negar. "Don't Cry for Me, America." In *My Sister, Guard Your Veil; My Brother, Guard Your Eyes: Uncensored Iranian Voices*, edited by Lila Azam Zanganeh, 104–12. Boston: Beacon Press, 2006.

———. "Good Intentions: Art Has a Long History of Engagement with Politics; Does Recent So-Called Socially Engaged or Political Art Effect Change?" *Frieze* 137 (March 1, 2011). https://frieze.com/article/good-intentions

———. "Iran in Pictures: Social Suffering and Three Sets of Images." In *Sensible Politics: The Visual Culture of Nongovernmental Activism*, edited by Meg McLagan and Yates McKee, 219–43. New York: Zone Books, 2012.

———. and Amirali Ghasemi, in conversation. "Independent & Artist-Run Initiatives in Tehran, Global Art Forum 2009." 2009. https://vimeo.com/showcase/271409/video/6947578

Babaie, Sussan. *Isfahan and Its Palaces: Statecraft, Shi'ism, and Architecture of Conviviality in Early Modern Iran*. Edinburgh: University of Edinburgh Press, 2008.

Baghchee, Nandini. *Counter Institution: Activist Estates of the Lower East Side*. New York: Empire State Editions and Fordham University Press, 2018.

Bahari, Maziar, dir. and prod. 1998. *Art of Demolition*. Film.

Bajoghli, Narges. *Iran Reframed: Anxieties of Power in the Islamic Republic*. Stanford: Stanford University Press, 2019.

Baker, Geoff. "La Habana Que No Conoces: Cuban Rap and the Social Construction of Urban Space." *Ethnomusicology Forum* 15, no. 2 (2006): 215–46.

Bakhash, Shaul. *The Reign of the Ayatollah: Iran and the Islamic Revolution*. New York: Basic Books, 1984.

Bakhtin, Mikhail. *Problems of Dostoevsky's Poetics*. Minneapolis: University of Minnesota Press, 1984.

———. *Rabelais and His World*. Translated by Hélène Iswolsky. Bloomington: Indiana University Press, 2009.

Balaghi, Shiva. "Against the Market: The Art of Shirin Neshat." *Ibraaz: Contemporary Visual Culture in North Africa and the Middle East*, 2016. https://www.ibraaz.org/essays/164

Balaşescu, Alexandru. *Paris Chic, Tehran Thrills: Aesthetic Bodies, Political Subjects*. Bucharest: Zeta Books, 2007.

Bani Masoud, Amir. *Me'mari mo'aser-e Iran* [Contemporary architecture of Iran]. Tehran: Nashr-e Honar va Me'mari Gharn, 1391 [2012].

Barthes, Roland. *Camera Lucida: Reflections on Photography*. Translated by Richard Howard. New York: Hill and Wang, 1981.

Basheertash, Saeed, and Ebrahim Nabavi. 2009. "*Si sal-e pish dar chenin roozi: Shahr-e no atash gereft va roospian koshteh shodand*" [Thirty years ago on this day: Shahr-e No caught on fire and prostitutes were killed]. *Radio Zamaneh*, 9 Bahman 1387 [January 28, 2009]. http://www.zamaaneh.com/revolution/2009/01/post_218.html

Bayat, Asef. *Life as Politics: How Ordinary People Change the Middle East*. Stanford: Stanford University Press, 2010.

———. *Street Politics. Poor People's Movements in Iran*. New York: Columbia University Press, 1997.

Bayat, Mongol, Hamid Algar, and W. L. Hanaway, Jr. "*Anjoman*" [Organization]. *Encyclopædia Iranica*, vol. 2, 77–83. http://www.iranicaonline.org/articles/anjoman-gathering-association-society-general-designation-of-many-private-and-public-associations

BBC News. "Iranian Parkour Athlete Arrested over a Rooftop Kiss." Editorial, May 23, 2020. https://www.bbc.com/news/av/world-middle-east-52777891

BBC Persian. "Tamasha: Kargah-e Namayesh, a Conversation with Arbi Avansian." Editorial, Tamasha Program. March 27, 2014. https://www.dailymotion.com/video/x571042

———. "Mir Hossein Mousavi, the Painter." Editorial, Tamasha Program. November 7, 2013. https://www.youtube.com/watch?v=cLa4wg2p1oI

Behdad, Sohrab. "Islamization of Economics in Iranian Universities." *International Journal of Middle East Studies* 27, no. 2 (May 1995): 193–217.

Behpoor, Bavand. "*Aya entezar keshidan ham ejra' ast?*" [Is waiting performance art?]. 31 Tir 1391 [July 21, 2012]. http://fa.behpoor.com/?p=1397

———. "Introduction to 'The Nightingale's Butcher Manifesto' and 'Volume and Environment II.'" *ARTMargins* 3, no. 2 (June 2014): 118–28.

Behrouzan, Orkideh. *Prozak Diaries: Psychiatry and Generational Memory in Iran.* Stanford: Stanford University Press, 2017.

Berliner, Paul F. *Thinking in Jazz: The Infinite Art of Improvisation.* Chicago: University of Chicago Press, 1994.

Bey, Hakim. *T.A.Z.: The Temporary Autonomous Zone, Ontological Anarchy, Poetic Terrorism.* Brooklyn, NY: Automedia, 2003.

Biravand, Shiva, and Gholamhossein Nami. *Nahib Magazine,* podcast, December 15, 2020. https://zil.ink/nahibmag

Bishop, Claire. *Artificial Hells: Participatory Art and the Politics of Spectatorship.* New York: Verso, 2012

———. *Installation Art.* London: Tate, 2005.

Blundell Jones, Peter, Doina Petrescu, and Jeremy Till, eds. *Architecture and Participation.* London: Spon Press, 2005.

Boroujerdi, Mehrzad, and Kourosh Rahimkhani. *Postrevolutionary Iran: A Political Handbook.* Syracuse: Syracuse University Press, 2018.

Bourdieu, Pierre. *The Logic of Practice.* Translated by Richard Nice. Stanford: Stanford University Press, 1990.

Boym, Svetlana. *Another Freedom: An Alternative History of an Idea.* Chicago: University of Chicago Press, 2012.

———. "Ilya Kabakov: The Soviet Toilet and the Palace of Utopias." *Artmargins,* 1999. https://artmargins.com/ilya-kabakov-the-soviet-toilet-and-the-palace-of-utopias/

Braidiotti, Rosi. *Nomadic Subjects: Embodiment and Sexual Difference in Contemporary Feminist Theory.* New York: Columbia University Press, 1994.

Bray, Elisa. "'The Blacks': Genet's Contentious Play Returns." *The Guardian,* October 18, 2007. https://www.independent.co.uk/arts-entertainment/theatre-dance/features/the-blacks-genets-contentious-play-returns-394981.html

Brennan, Teresa. *The Transmission of Affect.* Ithaca, NY: Cornell University Press, 2004.

Breyley, Gay. J. "Between the Cracks: Street Music in Iran." *Journal of Musicological Research* 35, no. 2 (May 2016): 72–81.

Brighenti, Andrea. *Visibility in Social Theory and Social Research*. New York: Palgrave McMillan, 2010.

Brook, Peter. *The Empty Space. New York:* Scribner, 1968.

Buchloh, Benjamin H. D. "Gerhard Richter's At/as: The Anomic Archive." *October* 88 (Spring 1999): 118.

Bucknell, Alice. "Behind the Veil." *Architectural Review*, September 6, 2017. https://www.architectural-review.com/essays/viewpoints/behind-the-veil/10022883.article

Burnett, Craig. "The Invisible Curator." *Art Monthly* 291 (November 2005): 1–4.

Callamard, Agnes, Bethan Grillo, and Sophie Redmond, eds. 2006. *Article 19: Global Campaign for Free Expression: Unveiled, Art and Censorship in Iran*. https://www.article19.org/data/files/pdfs/publications/iran-art-censorship.pdf

Carette, Jeremy. *Foucault and Religion*. London: Routledge, 1999.

Carroll, Noël. *Humour: A Very Short Introduction*. Oxford: Oxford University Press, 2014.

Caruth, Cathy. *Unclaimed Experience: Trauma, Narrative and History*. Baltimore: Johns Hopkins University Press, 1996.

Carver, Antonia. "Dead Dogs: A Decade of Public Art Experiments in Tehran." *Bidoun: Art and Culture from the Middle East* 1 (Summer 2004). https://www.bidoun.org/articles/dead-dogs

Cerwonka, Allaine, and Liisa H. Malkki. *Improvising Theory: Process and Temporality in Ethnographic Fieldwork*. Chicago: University of Chicago Press, 2007.

Chaplin, Sarah, and Alexandra Stara, eds. *Curating Architecture and the City*. New York: Routledge, 2009.

Chehabi, Houchang, and Christina Fotini. "The Art of State Persuasion: Iran's Post-Revolutionary Murals." *Persica* 22, special issue, Tehran Murals (2008): 1–13.

Chelkowski, Peter. "Ta'ziyeh: Indigenous Avant-Garde Theatre of Iran." In *Ta'ziyeh Ritual and Drama in Iran*, edited by Peter Chelkowski. New York: New York University Press, 1979.

———. "Time Out of Memory: Ta'ziyeh, the Total Drama." *Asia Society* Archives, 2002. https://asiasociety.org/time-out-memory-taziyeh-total-drama

———, and Hamid Dabashi, eds. *Staging a Revolution: The Art of Persuasion in the Islamic Republic of Iran*. New York: New York University Press, 1999.

Cheurfa, Hiyem. "The Laughter of Dignity: Comedy and Dissent in the Algerian Popular Protests." *Jadalyyah*, March 26, 2019. http://jadaliyya.com/Details/38495/The-Laughter-of-Dignity-Comedy-and-Dissent-in-the-Algerian-Popular-Protests

Cohen, Gael. *Tarikh-e sansur dar matboo'at-e Iran* [History of censorship in Iran's periodicals]. Tehran: Agah Press, 1360–62 [1981–83].

Colomina, Beatriz, and Jennifer Bloomer, eds. *Sexuality & Space*. New York: Princeton Architectural Press, 1992.

Crawforth, Hannah. "About Kamran Diba." In *Kamran Diba: Good News, Bad News, No News*, edited by Negar Diba, 8–11. Dubai: Gallery Etemad, 2012.

Cresswell, Tim. *On the Move: Mobility in the Modern Western World*. London: Routledge, 2006.

Critchley, Simon. *On Humor*. London: Routledge, 2002.

Crow, Thomas. *The Rise of the Sixties*. New Haven, CT: Yale University Press, 1996.

Croyden, Margaret. *The Centre: A Narrative*. Paris: CICT, 1980.

———. "Peter Brook Learns to Speak Orghast." *New York Times*, October 3, 1971.

Dabashi, Hamid. *Iranian Cinema: Past, Present, and Future*. London: Verso, 2002.

———. *Shi'ism: A Religion of Protest*. Cambridge, MA: Belknap Press in conjunction with Harvard University Press, 2011.

Daftari, Fereshteh. *Marcos Grigorian: Earthworks*, exhibition catalog, September 27–October 29. New York: Leila Heller Gallery, 2011.

———. *Persia Reframed: Iranian Visions of Modern and Contemporary Art*. London: I.B. Tauris, 2019.

Daneshmir, Reza. "Open Structures, Event Space." TEDx talk at Pars University, Tehran, August 16, 2018. https://www.youtube.com/watch?v=l8IcGhuuJy8

Daneshvari, Abbas. *Amazingly Original: Contemporary Iranian Art at Crossroads*. Los Angeles: Mazda, 2014.

Dant, Tim. *Critical Social Theory: Culture, Society and Critique*. London: Sage, 2004.

Darabi, Helia. "Tehran Museum of Contemporary Art as a Microcosm of the State's Cultural Agenda." In *Contemporary Art from the Middle East: Regional Interactions with Global Art Discourses*, edited by Hamid Keshmirshekan, 221–245. London: I.B. Tauris, 2015.

———."*Fazahay-e jaygozin*" [Makeshift spaces]. Hamshahri's *Alef Magazine* 89, special issue, Art and Books (Bahman and Esfand [January and February], 1390 [2012]): 112–17.

———. "*Rokgooyi behtarin rah nist*" [Directness is not the best solution]. *Aseman Magazine* 93 (1390 [2011]): n.p.

Daraie, Fariborz. "*Te'atre beh ensanhay-e shoja' niyaz darad/Tehran beh masabeh sahneh*" [Theater needs brave people / Tehran as a stage]. *Mehr News*, 1 Ordibehesht 1399 [April 20, 2020]. https://www.mehrnews.com

Darling, Cary. "Iran's 127 Uses Net to Beat Repression." *Fort Worth Star-Telegram*, March 16, 2006.

Davies, Clare. "The Artist's Map of Tehran, 1956–1966." Lecture given at the Watson Institute for International and Public Affairs, Brown University, Providence, Rhode Island, October 9, 2019.

Debord, Guy. “The Situationists and New Forms of Action in Politics or Art.” In *On the Passage of a Few People through a Rather Brief Moment in Time*, edited by Peter Wollen et al. Cambridge, MA: MIT Press, [1963] 1989.

De Certeau, Michel. *The Practice of Everyday Life*. Translated by Steven Rendall. Berkeley: University of California Press, 1984.

Degot, Ekaterina. “Performing Objects, Narrating Installations: Moscow Conceptualism and the Rediscovery of the Art Object.” *E-Flux Journal* 19 (November 2011). https://www.e-flux.com/journal/29/68067/performing-objects-narrating-installations-moscow-conceptualism-and-the-rediscovery-of-the-art-object/

Delzendeh, Siamak. *Tahavvolat-e Tasviri-e honar-e Iran: Barresi enteghadi* [Visual Transformations in Iranian Art: A Crtitical Analysis]. Tehran: Nazar Press, 2017.

———. “Artist Residencies: A Chance for the Micro-narratives to Become Manifest.” In *2014–2015 Kooshk Residency*, 27–29, exhibition catalog. Tehran: Kooshk Residency, 2016.

Derrida, Jacques. *Writing and Difference*. Translated by Alan Bass. London: Routledge, 2001.

Desimini, Jill. “Limitations of the Temporary: Landscape and Abandonment.” *Journal of Urban History* 41, no. 2 (2015): 279–93.

Deutsche, Rosalyn. *Evictions: Art and Spatial Politics*. Cambridge, MA: MIT Press, 1996.

Deutsche Welle Persian. “*Honarmandan-e mo’aser dar kafeh Markof-e Tehran*” [Contemporary artists at Tehran’s Marcov Café]. Editorial, January 8, 2013. https://www.dw.com/fa-ir/

Dibazar, Pedram. “Leftover Space, Invisibility and Everyday Life: Rooftops in Iran.” In *Global Garbage: Urban Imaginaries of Waste, Excess, and Abandonment*, edited by Christoph Lindner and Miriam Meissner. New York: Routledge, 2016.

———. *Urban and Visual Culture in Contemporary Iran: Non-visibility and the Politics of Everyday Presence*. London: Bloomsbury Press, 2020.

Diehl, Volker, Maria Popova, Matt Watkins, and Nina Mial, eds. *Glasnost: Soviet Non-Conformist Art from the 1980s*. London: Haunch of Venison in collaboration with Galerie Volker Diehl, 2010.

Dietachmaire, Philipp, and Pascal Gielen, eds. *The Art of Civil Action: Political Space and Cultural Dissent*. Amsterdam: Valiz, 2017.

Donyay-e Eghtesadi. “*Hadaf az tarh-e jame’ Lavasan chist*?” [What is the goal of the Lavasan master plan?]. Editorial, 1394 [August 30, 2015]. https://donya-e-eqtesad.com/بخش-سایت-خوان-62/2965526-هدف-از-تصویب-طرح-جامع-لواسان-چیست

Doyle, Jennifer. *Hold It against Me: Difficulty and Emotion in Contemporary Art*. Durham, NC: Duke University Press, 2013.

Douglass-Jaimes, David. "AD Classics: Azadi Tower / Hossein Amanat." *Archdaily*, September 2018. https://www.archdaily.com/774683/ad-classics-azadi-tower-hossein-amanat

Duncombe, Stephen. 2002. *Cultural Resistance Reader.* London: Verso, 2002.

Dunn, Christopher. *Contracultura: Alternative Arts and Social Transformation in Authoritarian Brazil.* Chapel Hill: University of North Carolina Press, 2016.

Ehsani, Kaveh. "The Politics of Property in the Islamic Republic of Iran." In *The Rule of Law, Islam, and Constitutional Politics in Egypt and Iran*, edited by Said Amir Arjomand and Nathan J. Brown, 153–78. Albany: SUNY Press, 2013.

———. "Survival through Dispossession: Privatization of Public Goods in the Islamic Republic," *Middle East Report* 250 (Spring 2009): 26–33.

———. "'Tilt but Don't Spill': Iran's Development and Reconstruction Dilemma." *Middle East Report* 191 (1994): 16–21.

Eiferman, Pauline. "Creative Disobedience: Q&A with Jeremy Suyker." *Roads and Kingdoms,* February 26, 2015. https://maptia.com/jeremysuyker/stories/iran-s-underground-art-scene

Ekhtiar, Maryam. 1998. "From Workshop, to Bazaar, to Academy: Art Training and Production in Qajar Iran." In *Royal Persian Painting: The Qajar Epoch 1785–1825*, edited by Layla Diba, 50–65. New York: I.B. Tauris.

———, and Marika Sardar. "Modern and Contemporary Art in Iran." In *Heilbrunn Timeline of Art History.* New York: Metropolitan Museum of Art, 2004. http://www.metmuseum.org/toah/hd/ciran/hd_ciran.htm

Ellmann, Maud. *The Hunger Artists: Starving, Writing, and Imprisonment.* Cambridge, MA: Harvard University Press, 1993.

Emami, Farshid. "Coffeehouses, Urban Spaces, and the Formation of a Public Sphere in Safavid Isfahan." *Muqarnas* 33, no. 1 (2016): 177–220.

Entekhab. "Ayatollah midanest keh dar rabeteh ba khatereh sad-e latian janjal khahad shod" [The Ayatollah knew that the memoir of the Latian Dam would create a scandal]. Editorial, 7 Ordibehesht 1395 [April 26, 2016]. https://www.entekhab.ir/fa/news/265292/آیت-الله-می-دانست-که-در-رابطه-با-خاطره-سد-لتیان-جنجال-خواهد-شد-اما-اجازه-سانسور-ندادند.

Erdbrink, Thomas. "Cautiously, Iranians Reclaim Public Spaces and Liberties Long Suppressed." *New York Times*, October 5, 2015.

Esbati, Amir. "*Jonbeshe-e daneshjooyi-e May 1968 va daneshjooyan-e honarhay-e ziba*" [The student movement of May 1968 and the fine arts students]. *Kar va Honar* (1358 [January 1979]): 6–9.

Esfandiari, Shahab. "*Kutah darbareh festival-e: 'Si performance, si honarmand, si rooz'*" [*Regarding 30 performances, 30 artists, 30 days*]. *Honar o resaneh* [Art and media] (5 Ordibehesht 1394 [April 2015]): 54–55.

Esmaili, Yasaman. "Argo Factory: Contemporary Art Museum & Cultural Centre by Ahmadreza Schricker Architecture–North." *Architectural Record*, November 21, 2021. https://www.architecturalrecord.com/

Estefan, Kareem, Carin Kuoni, and Laura Raicovich. *Assuming Boycott: Resistance, Agency, and Cultural Production*. New York: OR Books in partnership with Counterpoint Press, 2017.

Ettehad, Ali, and Joobin Bekhrad. "Street Fighting Man." *Reorient Magazine*, June 2, 2015. http://www.reorientmag.com/2015/06/performance-art-iran/

Ettehadiyeh, Mansoureh. "*Tarikh-e naneveshteh-ha: Barresi elamiyeh-ha va shabnameh-hay-e enghelab-e mashrooteh*" [Unwritten history: Exploring the night letters of the constitutional revolution]. *Shargh Newspaper*, 6 Shahrivar 1383 [August 27, 2004]. http://asre-nou.net/1383/shahrivar/6/m-mashroute1.html

Eyvas Zadeh, Shahla. "*Shabnameh: Resaneh janeshin-e asr-e mashrootiyyat*" [Night letters: Alternative publications in the era of the constitutional revolution]. *Ganjeeneh asnad* 16, no. 2 (Summer 1385 [2006]): 208, 214.

Farnam, Reza. "1st Rybon International Artists' Workshop Report on the 1st International Artists' Workshop, Organized by Rybon Art Center, an Artist-Led Initiative in Tehran." *Nafas Magazine*, November 2012. https://universes.art/en/nafas/articles/2012/rybon-workshop

Farzin, Media. "A Short History of Art Exhibitions in Iran, 1946–78." In *Iran Modern*, edited by Layla S. Diba and Fereshteh Daftari, 67–72. New Haven, CT: Yale University Press, 2014.

———. "The Back Room in Conversation with Media Farzin." *New Museum Six Degrees Blog*, April 9, 2014. https://www.newmuseum.org/blog/view/the-back-room-in-conversation-with-media-farzin

Feeley, Kathleen A., and Jennifer Frost, eds. *When Private Talk Goes Public: Gossip in American History*. New York: Palgrave McMillan, 2014.

Fekri, Reem. "Interview with Artist, Naiza Khan." *Art Dubai Journal* 7 (2010): n.p.

Feniger, Neta, and Rachel Kallus. "Israeli Planning in the Shah's Iran: A Forgotten Episode." *Planning Perspectives* 30, no. 2 (2015): 2–21.

Financial Tribune. "Performance Arts Festival at TMoCA." Editorial, December 7, 2016. https://financialtribune.com/articles/art-and-culture/54921/performance-arts-festival-at-tmoca

Fischer, Michael J. *Mute Dreams, Blind Owls, and Dispersed Knowledges: Persian Poesis in the Transnational Circuitry*. Durham, NC: Duke University Press, 2004.

Floor, Willem. *The History of Theater in Iran*. Washington, DC: Mage, 2005.

Foster, Hal. *The Return of the Real: The Avant-Garde at the End of the Century*. Cambridge, MA: MIT Press, 1996.

Foucault, Michel. *Discipline and Punish: The Birth of the Prison*. Translated by Alan Sheridan. New York: Vintage, 1979.

———. "Of Other Spaces," *Diacritics* 16 (Spring 1986): 22–27.

Fournier, Lauren. *Autotheory as Feminist Practice in Art, Writing, and Criticism.* Cambridge, MA: MIT Press, 2020.

Franck, Karen A., and Quentin Stevens, eds. *Loose Space: Possibility and Diversity in Urban Life.* New York: Routledge, 2006.

Fraser, Ronald. *1968: A Student Generation in Revolt.* London: Chatto & Windus, 1987.

Freud, Sigmund. "Mourning and Melancholia." In *Standard Edition of the Complete Psychological Works*, vol. 12. London: Hogarth Press and Institute of Psychoanalysis, 1953.

Friedberg, Anne. *Window Shopping: Cinema and the Postmodern.* Berkeley: University of California Press, 1993.

Freire, Paulo. *Pedagogy of the Oppressed.* Translated by Myra Bergman Ramos. London: Continuum Press, 2000.

Gallagher, John. *Reimagining Detroit: Opportunities for Redefining an American City.* Detroit: Wayne State University Press, 2010.

Ganjeh, Azadeh. "Performing Hamlet in Modern Iran." PhD diss., Philosophisch-historischen Fakultät der Universität Bern, 2017.

Gaven, Julia. *Best Practices in Inclusive Curating.*" 2019. https://framerframed.nl/wp-content/uploads/2014/04/Best-Practices-on-Inclusive-Curating-by-Julia-Geven-.pdf

Gerould, Daniel. "Jerzy Grotowski's Theatre and Parenthetical Activities as Cosmic Drama." *World Literature Today* 54, no. 3 (Summer 1980): 381–83.

Ghadimi, Ali. "*Sherkat-e khosoolati chist va chera Rouhani ba an mokhalef ast?*" [What is the *khosoolati* agent and why is Rouhani against it?]. *BBC Persian,* May 24, 2017. http://www.bbc.com/persian/iran-features-39993711

Ghaffary, Farrokh, Arby Ovanessian, and Laleh Taghian. "Iran." In *The World Encyclopedia of Contemporary Theatre, vol.* 5, *Asia/Pacific*, edited by Don Rubin, Chua Soo Pong, Minoru Tanokura, Ravi Chaturvedi, and Ramendu Majumdar, 191–221. London: Routledge, 1998.

Ghamari-Tabrizi, Behrooz. *Remembering Akbar: Inside the Iranian Revolution.* New York: OR Books, 2016.

Ghaninejad, Musa. "In Conversation with the *Eghtesad negar.*" Editorial, January 1398 [January 24, 2020]. http://www.eghtesadnegar.ir/

Ghasemi, Amirali. "Iran: Making Room for New Media." Lecture given at Center for Contemporary Art Ujazdowski Castle, Warsaw, Poland, 2014. https://vimeo.com/105141219/514d13d046?

———, and Arusha Moshtaghizadeh. "*Mapping-e karimkhan: Naghshehbardari va taghirat-e farhangi va honari dar ghalb-e Tehran*" [Mapping Karimkhan: Mapping art and cultural changes at the heart of Tehran]. *Tazarv* 5 (Bahar / Spring 1397 [2018]): 94–101.

Gholami, Alireza. "*Goftegoo ba Vaslav Havel*" [A conversation with Vaclav Havel]. *Mehrnameh,* no. 18 (1390 [2012]).

Gholipour, Ali. "Training the Eye: New Art against the Institution of Art." *Mohit Art*, December 13, 2021. https://mohit.art/honar-e-jadid-a-new-art-in-iran/training-the-eye-new-art-against-the-instruction-of-art/#fnrev190397596561bb96e2cdd57-16

Gibbs, Anna. "Contagious Feelings: Pauline Hanson and the Epidemiology of Affect." *Australian Humanities Review,* December 1, 2001. http://australianhumanitiesreview.org/2001/12/01/contagious-feelings-pauline-hanson-and-the-epidemiology-of-affect/

Gitlin, Todd. *The Sixties: Years of Hope, Days of Rage*. Toronto: Bantam Press, 1988.

Giustino, Cathleen M., Catherine J. Plum, and Alexander Vari, eds. *Socialist Escapes: Breaking Away from Ideology and Everyday Routine in Eastern Europe, 1945–1989*. Oxford: Berghahn Press, 2013.

Gluck, Robert. "The Shiraz Arts Festival: Western Avant-Garde Arts in 1970s Iran." *Leonardo* 40, no. 1 (2007): 20–28.

Grande, John K. *Dialogues in Diversity: Art from Marginal to Mainstream.* Italy: Pari, 2007.

Golestan, Lili. "TEDx Talk in Tehran." 2018. https://www.youtube.com/watch?v=lp2N2--nVtA

Golshiri, Barbad. "*Dastgah va tamarrod*" [The system and the rebellion]. *Honar-e farda* 4 (1390 [2011]): 10–12.

Green, Jonathan, and Nicholas Karolides. *Encyclopedia of Censorship.* New York: Facts on File Press, 2005.

Grigor, Talinn. *Building Iran: Modernism, Architecture, and National Heritage under the Pahlavi Monarchs.* New York: Periscope, 2009.

———. *Contemporary Iranian Art: From the Street to the Studio.* London: Reaktion Books, 2014.

———. "Of Metamorphosis: Meaning on Iranian Terms." *Third Text* 17, no. 3 (2003): 207–25.

Grosz, Elizabeth. *Becomings: Explorations in Time, Memory and Futures.* Ithaca, NY: Cornell University Press, 1999.

Grotowski, Jerzy, ed. *Towards a Poor Theatre.* London: Methuen, 1975.

Groys, Boris. "The Truth of Art." *E-flux 71 (March 2016).* https://www.e-flux.com/journal/71/60513/the-truth-of-art/

Gruber, Christiane. "The Martyrs' Museum in Tehran: Visualizing Memory in Post-Revolutionary Iran," *Visual Anthropology* 25 (2012): 68–97.

Hajizadeh, Elaheh, and Seyyed Mahdi Ahmad Panah. "*Salonhatoon arzoonitoon*" [We don't want your theater halls]. *Cheragh Magazine* 11, no. 519 (4 Khordad 1392 [May 25, 2013]): 28–29.

Halasa, Malu, and Maziar Bahari. *Transit Tehran.* London: Garnet, 2009.

Halberstam, Judith. *In a Queer Time and Place: Transgender Bodies, Subcultural Lives*. New York: New York University Press, 2005.

Haldrup, Michael. "Choreographies of Leisure Mobilities." In *Mobile Methods*, edited by Monika Büscher, John Urry, and Katian Witchger, 54–87. London: Routledge, 2011.

Hamkar Parsboom Consulting Engineers for *Vezarat-e rah va shahr sazi* [Ministry of Roads and Urban Planning]. *Tarh jame' shar-e Lavasan* [*Lavasan's master plan*], vols. 1–3 (Winter 1995).

Hamshahri Online. "*Gozaresh neshast-e khabari-e yek performans*" [Report on a press conference of a performance]. Editorial, 16 Day 1391 [2012]. https://www.hamshahrionline.ir/news/196871/

———. "*Namayeshi ba gasht-e Taxi dar Tehran*" [A play with a moving taxi in Tehran]. Editorial, December 7, 2013. www.hamshahrionline.ir/news/241490/

Harcourt, Glenn, Pamela Joseph, and Francis M. Naumann. *The Artist, the Censor, and the Nude: A Tale of Morality and Appropriation*. New York: DoppelHouse Press, 2017.

Harvey, David. "The Right to the City." *New Left Review* 53 (September–October 2008): 23–40.

Hassanli, Kavoos, and Siamak Naderi. "*Tabar shenasi-e zan-e asiri dar boof-e koor-e sadeq hedayat*" [Unraveling the origin of the ethereal atmosphere women in Sadeq Hedayat's *The Blind Owl*]. *Literary Text Research Bulletin of Allameh Tabatabaie University* 22, no. 75 (1397 [2018]): 41–60.

Hauser, Arnold. *The Social History of Art*. London: Routledge & Kegan Paul, 1951.

Hesarloo, Maryam Jafari. "*Honarmand dar roozmarregi mimirad*," [Mundane Life Kills the Artist]. *Iran Newspaper* 5557, no. 19 (23 Day 1399 [January 12, 2021]): 8.

Hirsch, Marianne. *The Generation of Postmemory: Writing and Visual Culture after the Holocaust*. New York: Columbia University Press, 2012.

Hirsch, Nikolaus, and Markus Miessen, eds. *What Is Critical Spatial Practice?* Berlin: Sternberg Press, 2012.

Hobsbawm, Eric. *Primitive Rebels: Studies in Archaic Forms of Social Movement in the 19th and 20th Centuries*. Manchester: Manchester University Press, 1959.

Homing.ir. "*Zendegi dar mahalleh Swiss-e Tehran*" [Life in the Swiss neighborhood of Tehran]. Editorial, 2 *Azar* 1397 [November 23, 2018]. https://homing.ir/mag/area/lavasan-area/ (site discontinued)

Honar Online. "*Asheghaneh-ie dar del-e me'mari*" [A love story in the heart of (historic) architecture]. Editorial, 8 Dey 1396 [December 29, 2017]. http://www.honaronline.ir

———. "*Khaneh honar-e shahri mahalli baray khallaghiyyat va motale'eh ast*" [The urban art house is a place for creativity and exploration]. Editorial, December 14, 2013. Available at http://www.honaronline.ir /

———. "*Banooy-e sorkhpoosh beh jashnvareh dastresi-e mahdood amad*" [*Lady in Red* at the Limited Access Festival]. January 14, 2013. http://www.honaronline.ir/

Hosseini, Mohammad. "The Lady in Red." *Akkaskhaneh Vimeo Channel,* October 5, 2013. https://vimeo.com/76218718

Hosseinzadeh Salavati, Leila. "*Gozari bar aseeb shenasi-e mojassamehay-e shahri*" [Pathology of urban sculptures]. *Tazarv* 1 (Summer 1395 [2016]): 65–71.

Hovian, Andranik. *Kelisahay-e maseehiyan dar Iran zamin* [*Churches of Christians in Iran*]. Tehran: Entesharat-e Moavenat-e Farhangi, 1383 [2004].

Hoyman, Michelle, and Christopher Faricy. 2008. "It Takes a Village: A Test of the Creative Class, Social Capital, and Human Capital Theories." *Urban Affairs Review* 44, no. 3 (2008): 311–33.

Hulpachova, Marketa. "Iran's Economy Struggles to Support Ahmadinejad's Ill-Conceived Housing Vision." *The Guardian*, January 30, 2014. https://www.theguardian.com/world/iran-blog/2014/jan/30/irans-economy-struggles-to-support-ahmadinejads-ill-conceived-housing-vision

Human Rights Watch News. 2020. "Iran: Environmentalists Sentenced Unfair Trial; Continued Due Process Violations." Editorial, November 19, 2019. https://www.hrw.org/news/2019/11/22/iran-environmentalists-sentenced

Inde, Vilis R. *Art in the Courtroom*. Westport, CT: Greenwood, 1998.

Independent Farsi. "*Majeray-e 'hesar keshi' mohavvateh te'atr-e shahr chist?*" [What is the purpose of "barracading" the area around the City Theater?]. Editorial, 17 Esfand 1399 [March 7, 2021]. https://www.independentpersian.com/node/128486/

Iranpoor, Minoo. "*Padidehie taht-e onvan-e gallery: Barresi amalkard-e panj gallery dar Tehran az sal 1375 ta 1380*" [A phenomenon called the gallery: The study of five galleries in Tehran (1375–1380/1996–2002)]. Master's thesis, Honar University / Art University, Tehran, 1380 [2002].

Irigaray, Luce. *The Sex Which Is Not One*. Translated by Catherine Porter. Ithaca, NY: Cornell University Press, 1985.

ISNA (Iranian Students' News Agency). "*Bazgasht-e yek kargardan-e te'atr-e mamnoo' al kar beh sahneh*" [The return of a banned theater director]. Editorial, 31 Khordad 1393 [June 21, 2014]. https://www.isna.ir/news/93033116744

Jackson, Matthew Jesse. *The Experimental Group: Ilya Kabakov, Moscow Conceptualism, Soviet Avant-Gardes*. Chicago: University of Chicago Press, 2010.

Jafarian, Azadeh. 1391 [2012]. "*Bad az chehel sal rahat khabidam*" [I slept well after forty years]. *Shargh Newspaper* 9, no. 1542, 10 Khordad 1391 [May 30, 2012].

Jahanbegloo, Ramin, and Adam Micjnik. "A Conversation between Ramin Jahanbegloo and Adam Micjnik." In *Friendship of Nations: Polish Shiite Showbiz*. Translated by Philip Grant, 45–53. Book Works and Sharja Foundation, 2013.

Jahanshad, Pouria. "Cross-Cultural Interactions: Trend, Deception, or Reality?" In *2017 Kooshk Residency*, exhibition catalog, 25–29. Tehran: Kooshk Residency, 2017.

———. "*Honar-e gheyr-e rasmi va gheyr-e rasmi sazi-e honar*" [Informal art and making art informal]. In *Bazkhani-e shahr: Hokmrani-e shahr* [*Rethinking the city: Urban governance*], edited by Pouria Jahanshad, n.p. Tehran: Ruzbahan Press, 2022.

Jamshidi, Mahdyar. "*Sadeh kardan-e pichidegiha bozorgtarin honar ast*" [The highest form of art is that which simplifies complicated issues]. *Setareh sobh* 7, no. 180 (10 Dey 1394 [December 31, 2015]): n.p.

Jansen, Sue Curry. *Censorship: The Knot That Binds Power and Knowledge*. Oxford: Oxford University Press, 1988.

John-Alder, Kathleen. "Paradise Reconsidered: The Early Design History of Pardisan Park in Tehran." In *Contemporary Urban Landscapes of the Middle East*, edited by Mohammad Gharipour, 120–48. London: Routledge, 2016.

Jones, Amelia. "Encountering: The Conceptual Body, or a Theory of When, Where, and How Art 'Means.'" *TDR: The Drama Review* 62, no. 3 (Fall 2018): 12–34.

Kamali Dehghan, Saeed. "Take It to the Bridge: The Tehran Architect Striking the Right Chord in Iran and Beyond." *The Guardian*, April 20, 2015. https://www.theguardian.com/world/2015/apr/20/bridge-tehran-architect-iran-leila-araghian-tabiat-sanctions-iranian-designers

Kamalvand, Sara. "MesoCity Tehran Workshop, Art, Ecology & the City." *Tavoos Art Magazine, 2020*. http://www.tavoosonline.com/Articles/ArticleDetailEn.aspx?src=163&Page=1

Kamrani, Behnam. 2018. "*Hamayesh-e porsesh az honar-e mo'aser-e Iran*" [A panel on contemporary Iranian art]. Farabi Hall, Art University, Tehran, November 19, 2018. Audio recording.

———, and Setareh Hosseini. "*Honar mo'aser-e Iran va asar-e zist mohiti*" [Contemporary Iranian art and environmental works]. In *Haftomin salaneh honar-e mo'aser-e Persbook, honar-e zist mohiti-e Iran* [*Persbook: The seventh annual festival of contemporary art (Iranian eco art)*], 84–95. Tehran: Nashr-e Bongah, 1396 [2018].

Kanouse, Sarah. "Critical Day Trips: Tourism and Land-Based Practice." In *Critical Landscapes: Art, Space, Politics*, edited by Emily Eliza Scott and Kirsten Swenson, 43–56. Berkeley: University of California Press, 2015.

Kaprow, Allan. *Assemblage, Environments & Happenings*. New York: Harry N. Abrams, 1966.

Karimi, Azadeh. 2018. "Iranian Painter Whose Artworks Were Destroyed in the Revolution Has Berlin Show." *Kayhan Life*, November 30, 2018. https://kayhanlife.com/culture/art/iranian-painter-whose-artworks-were-destroyed-in-the-revolution-has-berlin-show/

Karimi, Pamela. *Domesticity and Consumer Culture in Iran: Interior Revolutions of the Modern Era*. New York: Routledge, 2013.

———, and Amirali Ghasemi. "When Global Art Meanders on a Magic Carpet: A Conversation on Tehran's Roaming Biennale (May 30–July 6)." *Arab Studies Journal 18*, no. 1 (Spring 2010): 294–99.

———, and Christine Gruber. "Introduction: The Politics and Poetics of the Child Image in Muslim Contexts." *Comparative Studies of South Asia, Africa and the Middle East* 32, no. 2 (2012): 273–93.

———, and Michael Vasquez. "Ornament and Argument." *Bidoun: Arts and Culture from the Middle East* (Winter 2008). https://www.bidoun.org/articles/ornament-argument

Karimi-Hakkak, Ahmad. "Censorship." *Encyclopedia Iranica* 5, fasc. 2 (December 15, 1990): 135–42.

Karimi-Hakak, Mahmood. "Exiled to Freedom: A Memoir of Censorship in Iran." *TDR: The Drama Review* 47, no. 4 (Winter 2003): 17–50.

Kasaie, Aria, Studio Kargah, and the AB Projects. *Graphic Design Archive of Kargah-e Namayesh Theatre Workshop*. Tehran: Pejman Foundation Press, 2017.

Kazemi, Abbas. *Amr-e roozmarreh dar jame'eh pasa enghelabi* [*Everyday life in a postrevolutionary society*]. Tehran: Nashr-e Farhang-e Javid, 1398 [2019].

Kazemi, Abbas. *Parsehzani va zendegi-e roozmarreh Irani* [*Iranian strolling and everyday life*]. Tehran: Nashr-e Farhang-e Javid, 1388 [2009].

Keane, John. *Vaclav Havel: A Political Tragedy in Six Acts*. New York: Basic Books, 2012.

Keshmirshekan, Hamid. *Contemporary Art from the Middle East: Regional Interactions with Global Art Discourses*. London: I.B. Tauris, 2015.

———. *Contemporary Iranian Art: New Perspectives*. Los Angeles: Saqi Press, 2014.

———, ed. *Koorosh Shishegaran: The Art of Altruism*. Los Angeles: Saqi Books, 2017.

———. "Saqqa-kana School of Art." *Encyclopedia Iranica*, online edition, 2009. http://www.iranicaonline.org/articles/saqqa-kana-ii-school-of-art

Kester, Grant. "Aesthetic Evangelists: Conversion and Empowerment in Contemporary Community Art." *Afterimage* (January 1995): 5–11.

Khakpour, Arta, Mohammad Mehdi Khorrami, and Shouleh Vatanabadi, eds. *Moments of Silence: Authenticity in the Cultural Expressions of the Iran-Iraq War, 1980–1988*. New York: New York University Press, 2016.

Khalili, Fatemeh. "*Dar naleh ha-ye Damavand cheh razi nahofteh ast*?" [What are the secrets behind Damavand cries for help?]. *Iranian Students' News Agency* (*ISNA*), July 28, 2020. https://www.isna.ir/news/99050704584/چه-دماوند-های-ناله-در-است-نهفته-رازی-

Khan, Imran. 2012. "Iranian Artists Negotiate Government Guidelines." *Al Jazeera English,* May 19, 2012. YouTube channel. https://www.youtube.com/watch?time_continue=2&v=mE-8emZMENk&feature=emb_logo

Khanjani, Ramin S. "Fact, Fiction and Eccentricity in Parviz Kimiavi's Images from 'The Garden of Stones.'" *Offscreen* 19, no. 6 (June 2015). https://offscreen.com/view/garden-of-stones

Khaneh-Saz, Vahid. 1393 [2014]. "*Shoghl-e jadid-e plateau dari*" [The new business of the plateaus]. *IscanNews*, 28 Mordad 1393 [August 19, 2014]. http://www.iscanews.ir/news/29260/

Khatib, Gandom. "Tehran's Underground Speakeasies." *Daily Beast*, July 15, 2014. https://www.thedailybeast.com/tehrans-underground-speakeasies

Khomeini, Ruhollah. *Islam and the Revolution: Writings and Declarations of Imam Khomeini*. Translated by Hamid Algar. Berkeley: Mizan Press, 1981.

Khosravi, Shahram. *Precarious Lives: Waiting and Hope in Iran*. Philadelphia: University of Pennsylvania Press, 2017.

———. *Young and Defiant in Tehran*. Philadelphia: University of Pennsylvania Press, 2008.

Kirsanova, Daria. "Articulating Dissensus: Contemporary Artistic Practice in Iran at a Revolutionary Moment." *Ibraaz: Contemporary Visual Culture in North African and the Middle East*, August 28, 2013. https://www.ibraaz.org/essays/72

Klausen, Jytte. *The Cartoons That Shook the World*. New Haven, CT: Yale University Press, 2009.

Komar, Vitaly, and Sasha Obukhova. *Interview at Garage Museum*, 2017. https://www.youtube.com/watch?v=z5yN2LsVNBg

Kondera, Milan. *Bar-e Hasti*. Translated by Parviz Homayounpur. Tehran: *Nashr-e Goftar*, 1986.

Koocheh Channel. "*Lavasan: Jazireh amn-e kakh neshinan ya zakhmi bar zakhmhay-e Iran?*" [Lavasan: A safe haven for the super rich or another scar on Iran?]. YouTube channel, May 30, 2019. https://www.youtube.com/watch?v=mHjWAHEPCfE

Koosha, Ash. "In conversation with King Raam." *Masti and Rasti* podcast, January 10, 2021. https://www.youtube.com/watch?v=_jI2GkboZuA

Kopenkina, Olga. "Administered Occupation: Art and Politics at the 7th Berlin Biennale." *Art Journal Open*, April 18, 2013. http://artjournal.collegeart.org/?p=3457

Kötter, Daniel. "On Hashti Tehran." *Berliner Festspiele on Demand*, 2020. https://vimeo.com/431032326

Kowsar, Nikahang. "Being Funny Is Not That Funny: Contemporary Editorial Cartooning in Iran." *Social Research* 79, no. 1 (Spring 2012): 117–44.

Kracauer, Sigfried. "The Mass Ornament." *New German Critique*, no. 5 (Spring 1975): 67–76.

Kreuger, Andres. "Thinking-Together Spaces." In *What Is Critical Spatial Practice?*, edited by Nikolaus Hirsch and Markus Miessen, 47–73. Berlin: Sternberg Press, 2012.

Kwon, Miwon. *One Place after Another: Site-Specific Art and Locational Identity.* Cambridge: MIT Press, 2002.

———. "Sitings of Public Art: Integration versus Intervention." In *Alternative Art New York, 1965–1985*, edited by Julie Ault, 281–320. Minneapolis: University of Minnesota Press, 2002.

Ladjevardi, Haleh. *Zendegi roozmarreh dar Iran* [*Everyday life in Iran*]. Tehran: Nashr-e Sales, 1388 [2009].

Lavasan News. 2014. "*Barresi tarh-e jadid-e jame' Lavasan dar gorooh karshenasi*" [Exploring a new master plan for Lavasan with the experts]. Editorial, no. 9 (August 30, 2015). http://www.lavasan.ir/_DouranPortal/documents/No%2009.pdf

Lavin, Sylvia. *Kissing Architecture*. Princeton, NJ: Princeton University Press, 2011.

Leach, Neil. *Rethinking Architecture: A Reader in Cultural Theory.* London: Routledge, 2005.

Lefebvre, Henri. *Le droit a la ville*. Paris: Anthropos, 1968.

———. "Les nouveaux ensembles urbains (un cas concret: Lacq-Mourenx et les problèmes urbains de la nouvelle classe ouvrière)." *Revue française de sociologie* 1, no. 2 (1960): 186–201.

———. *The Production of Space*. Translated by Donald Nicholson-Smith. Oxford: Blackwell, 1991.

———. *Rhythmanalysis*. Translated by Stuart Elden and Gerald Moore. London: Continuum, 2004.

Lenssen, Anneka, Sarah Rogers, and Nada Shabout, eds. 2018. *Modern Art in the Arab World: Primary Documents*. Durham, NC: Duke University Press, 2018.

Lippard, Lucy. "Out of the Safety Zone." *Art in America* 78 (1990): 130–39.

———. *Six Years: The Dematerialization of the Art Object, 1966–1972*. New York: Praeger, 1973.

Lippmann, Walter. *The Phantom Public*. New York: McMillan, 1927.

Lodge, Guy. "'A Man of Integrity,' 'Wind River,' 'Barbara' Take Un Certain Regard Awards at Cannes: Iranian filmmaker Mohammad Rasoulof Took the Top Prize from a Jury Headed by Actress Uma Thurman." *Variety*, May 27, 2017. https://variety.com/2017/film/festivals/a-man-of-integrity-wind-river-barbara-win-cannes-un-certain-regard-award-uma-thurman-mathieu-amalric-taylor-sheridan-1202446610/

Louisiana Channel. "Ulay: How I Stole a Painting." Editorial, 2017. https://channel.louisiana.dk/video/ulay-how-i-stole-painting

Madani, Kaveh. "Iran's Looming Water Crisis." *Middle East in London Magazine* 11, no. 2 (February–March 2015): 9–10.

———. "Urban Planning and Development in Tehran." *Cities* 23, no. 6 (2006): 433–38.

Mahdavi, Pardis. *Passionate Uprisings: Iran's Sexual Revolution*. Stanford: Stanford University Press, 2009.

Mahmoodi, Asma. "*Baghi keh mivehayash sang shod*" [A garden whose fruits turned to stone]. *Mehr News* 9, no. 39 (23 Esfand 1393 [March 20, 2015]). https://www.mehrnews.com/news/2512814/.

Maktabi, Mahmoud. "Eco Avant-Garde Exhibition." In Maktabi, *Nature-Art Variations*, 206–15. Budapest: Musarnok/Kunsthalle, Institution of the Hungarian Academy of Arts, 2016.

Majd, Hooman. "Pride and Prejudice in Tehran: To Understand Iran's Foreign Policy, You Need to Learn a Little Farsi." *Foreign Policy* 229 (July 16, 2018): 8–9.

Malcolm, Napier. *Five Years in a Persian Town*. London: John Murray, 1905.

Malekzadeh, Mehdi. *Tarikh-e enqelab-e mashrootiyat-e Iran* [*The history of the constitutional revolution in Iran*]. Tehran: Sokhan, 1387 [2008].

Malik, Suhail. 2012. "Occupy." In *What Is Critical Spatial Practice?*, edited by Nikolaus Hirsch and Markus Miessen, 82–83. Berlin: Sternberg Press, 2012.

Manoukian, Setrag. *City of Knowledge in Twentieth-Century Iran: Shiraz, History and Poetry*. London: Routledge, 2012.

———. "Where Is This Place? Crowds, Audio-Vision, and Poetry in Postelection Iran." *Public Culture* 22, no. 2 (2013): 237–64.

Manshoor. "About Contemporary Art, the 5th Episode: Conversation with Ali Ettehad, Mohammad Parvizi, and Amir Rad." Editorial, 2014. https://www.youtube.com/watch?v=oiO22jGZI4g

Marcuse, Herbert. *One-Dimensional Man: Studies in the Ideology of Advanced Industrial Society*. Boston: Beacon Press, 1964.

Marriott, John. *The Other Empire: Metropolis, India and Progress in the Colonial Imagination*. Machester: Manchester University Press, 2003.

Martin, Reinhold. 2012. "Occupy: What Architecture Can Do." In *What Is Critical Spatial Practice?*, edited by Nikolaus Hirsch and Markus Miessen, 89–90. Berlin: Sternberg Press, 2012.

Marx, Karl. *The Grundrisse*. Translated by Martin Nicolaus. London: Penguin Books in association with *New Left Review*, 1973.

Mashregh News. "*Basti Hills kojast? Shahri keh vorood beh an baray mardom mamnoo' bood*" [Where is Basti Hills? A city that forbids the public from entering it]. Editorial, 19 Tir 1398 [July 10, 2019]. https://www.mashreghnews.ir/news/973945

———. "*Gasht o gozari dar Lavasan: Jazireh amn-e luxury neshinha* [A stroll in Lavasan: The safe island of luxury tenants]. Editorial, Bahman 1397 [January 2018]. https://www.mashreghnews.ir/news/930512

———. "*Safarhay-e tafrihi-e Hashemi Rafsanjani va Khanevadehash dar daheh Muharram*" [Vacation trips of Hashemi Rafsanjani and his family during Muharram]. Editorial, 12 Mehr 1395 [October 3, 2016]. https://www.mashreghnews.ir/news/638612/سفرهای-تفریحی-هاشمی-رفسنجانی-و-خانواده-اش-در-دهه-محرم.

Mazhari, Naghmeh. "*Goftegoo ba Ali Shakeri Shemirani darbareh sakhteman-e Argo*" [A conversation with Ali Shakeri Shemirani about the Argo Building]. *Memarnet*, January 9, 2017. http://www.memarnet.com/fa/node/3862

Mead, Margaret. *The World Ahead*. New York: Berghahn Books, 2005.

Meftahi, Ida. *Gender and Dance in Iran: Biopolitics on Stage*. New York: Routledge, 2017.

Memari TV. "*Goftegooy-e sareeh ba mohandes Ali Moosapanah, me'mar-e classic kar*" [An honest interview with architect Ali Musapanah, a classicist architect]. Editorial, 1399 [August 22, 2020]. http://memaritv.com

Miessen, Markus, ed. *Crossbenching: Toward Participation as Critical Spatial Practice*. Berlin: Sternberg Press, 2016.

Milani, Farzaneh. *Words, Not Swords: Iranian Women Writers and the Freedom of Movement*. Syracuse: Syracuse University Press, 2001.

Miller, Nicole. "Following Sophie Calle." *Hyperallergic*, June 18, 2016. https://hyperallergic.com/305869/following-sophie-calle/

Mirehsan, Ahmad. "*In yek hazer amadeh ast*" [This is a readymade]. *Etemad Daily* 8, no. 2170 (*Bahman* 1388 [February 6, 2010]): 16.

Mirjahani, Reyhaneh. "Retexture: Traces of Tradition and Contemporary Concerns in Collaboration." *Konesh*, April 22, 2020. https://www.konesh.space/post/retexture-traces-of-tradition-and-contemporary-concerns-in-collaboration

Mirza Saleh, Gholamhossein. *Reza Shah: Khaterat-e Soleiman Behboudi, Shams Pahlavi and Ali Yazdi* [*Reza Shah: According to the memoirs of Soleiman Behboudi, Shams Pahlavi and Ali Yazdi*]. Tehran: Tarh-e Now, 1372 [1993].

Mirzoeff, Nicholas. "Empty the Museum, Decolonize the Curriculum, Open Theory." *Nordic Journal of Aesthetics* 53 (2017): 6–22.

Mitchell, W. J. T. "Image, Space, Revolution: The Arts of Occupation." *Critical Inquiry* 39, no. 1 (Autumn 2012): 8–32.

———. *What Do Pictures Want?* Chicago: University of Chicago Press, 2005.

Miyazaki, Hirokazu. *The Method of Hope: Anthropology, Philosophy, and Fijian Knowledge*. Stanford: Stanford University Press, 2004.

Moeini, Seyed Hossein Iradj, Mehran Arefian, Bahador Kashani, and Golnar Abbasi. 2018. *Urban Culture in Tehran: Urban Processes in Unofficial Cultural Spaces. Urban Book Series*. Cham, Switz.: Springer International, 2018.

Mohajer, Mehran. "*Pareh Jomleh hay Katayoun Karami: Negahi beh namayeshgah-e pendar- e neek, goft ar- e neek, va kerdar neek dar gallery tarrahan-e azad*" [Pseudo phrases of Katayoun Karami: A look at 'Good Thoughts, Good Words, and Good Deeds' at Azad Gallery]. *Faslnameh herfeh honarmand* 49 (Winter 1392 [2013]): 116–17.

Mohd Nasir, Hashim, and Farideh Alizadeh, "A Comparative Study: The Principles of the Distancing Effect in Brechtian Theater and Ta'ziyeh." *Cogent: Arts and Humanities* 7, no. 1 (2020). https://www.tandfonline.com/doi/full/10.1080/23311983.2020.1790195

Mohebbi, Sohrab. "Homayoun Sirizi." *Bidoun Magazine* 12 (Fall 2007). https://bidoun.org/articles/installations-by-homayoun-sirizi

———, ed. *Hotel Theory Reader.* Vancouver: Fillip Editions, 2016.

———. "Rasht 29." *Bidoun Magazine* 20 (Spring 2010). https://www.bidoun.org/articles/rasht-29

———. "Rasht 29 Revisited." In *Into the Night: Cabarets and Clubs in Modern Art*, edited by Florence Ostende and Lotte Johnson, 290–97. London: Prestel and Barbican Art Gallery, 2019.

Mohri, Babak. "*Te'atre baray-e hameh mardom deegar sho'ar nist*" [Theater for all is no longer just a slogan]. *Cheragh Magazine* 11, no. 519 (4 Khordad 1392 [May 21, 2013]).

Montazami, Morad. "Introduction to Amir Esbati, 'The Student Movement of May 1968 and the Fine Art Students.'" *ARTmargins* 6, no. 6 (October 2017): 111–21.

Moosavi, Marjan. "'Unpermitted Whispers': Reflections on the Originality of 'Hopscotch' Performance." *Theatre Times*, January 19, 2018. https://thetheatretimes.com/unpermitted-whispers-reflections-originality-hopscotch-performance/

Moridi, Mohammad Reza. *Honar-e ejtema'yi: Maghalati dar jame'eh shenasi-e honar mo'aser-e Iran* [*Social art: Essays on the sociology of contemporary art in Iran*]. Tehran: Aban Press in conjunction with Art University, 1397 [2018].

Morris, David. "Introduction: Anti-Shows." In *Anti-Shows: APTART 1982–84*, edited by Margarita Tupitsyn and Victor Tupitsyn, 8–21. London: Koeing Books for *Afterall*, 2017.

Mousavi, Nazanin. "A Conversation between Tiwall Editorial and Hossein Tavazoni Zadeh about the Amsterdam Play." Audio file, 1393 [2014]. https://www.tiwall.com/podcasts/interview-hosseintavazoni

Mousavi Khalkhali, Seyyed Saleh. "*Jacques Rancière va nezamha-ye shenasai-e honar dar gharb*" [*Jacques Rancière* and principles of understanding art in the West]. *Nahib Magazine* 1, no. 4 (Winter 2020): 155–63.

Mulvey, Laura. "Visual Pleasure and Narrative Cinema." *Screen* 16, no. 3 (October 1975): 6–18.

Murphy, Kim. "Media: Iran's Revolution Finally Learns to Laugh at Itself: Tehran's Biggest-Selling Magazine Takes Jabs at Parliament Members and Even Mullahs." *Los Angeles Times*, April 28, 1992. https://www.latimes.com/archives/la-xpm-1992-04-28-wr-912-story.html

Naficy, Hamid. "Iranian Cinema under the Islamic Republic." *American Anthropologist* 97, no. 3 (September 1995): 548–58.

———. *A Social History of Iranian Cinema: The Industrializing Years, 1941–1978, vol.* 2. Durham, NC: Duke University Press, 2011.

Najafi, Sina. "Underworld: An Interview with Rosalind Williams." *Cabinet* 30 (Summer 2008). http://www.cabinetmagazine.org/issues/30/najafi.php

Najafi Ardabili, Masoud. *Grotowski in Iran*. Berlin: Peter Lang, 2019.

Nami, Gholamhossein. "*Risheham dar in khak ast* [All My Roots Are Her]." *Shargh Newspaper* 1272, 28 Khordad, 1390 [June 18, 2011].

Naqvi, Erum. "Reinventing Ruhowzi Experiments in Contemporary Iranian Musical Theater." *Middle East Journal of Culture and Communication* 13 (May 2020): 28–48.

Narine, Sandy. "The Institutionalization of Dissent." In *Thinking about Exhibitions*, edited by Sandy Narine, Reesa Greenberg, and Bruce Ferguson, 387–410. New York: Routledge, 1996.

Naser-al-din, Parveen. *Tarikh-e rooznameh negari Iranian va deegar Parsi neveesan* [*The history of Iranian and Persian language newspapers*], vol. 1. Tehran: Markaz nashr-e Daneshgahi, 1377 [1999].

Nasr, Seyyed Hossein. *The Garden of Truth: The Vision and Promise of Sufism, Islam's Mystical Tradition*. New York: Harper Collins, 2007.

Neuendorf, Henri. "Iranian Art Dealer Sentenced to 27 Years in Prison and 124 Lashes for Morality Offenses." *Artnet News*, January 31, 2018. https://news.artnet.com/art-world/iranian-gallerists-jailed-1212677

Newman, Oscar. *Defensible Space: Crime Prevention through Urban Design*. New York: Collier, 1972.

Niksar, Niloofar. "Public Space: Field of Distinction." *Me'mar* 116 (2019): 40–45.

Nochlin, Linda. "The Imaginary Orient." In Nochlin, *The Politics of Vision: Essays on Nineteenth Century Art and Society*, 33–59. New York: Harper Row, 1989.

Nooshin, Laudan. "Underground, Overground: Rock Music and Youth Discourses in Iran." *Iranian Studies* 38, no. 3 (2005): 463–94.

———. "Whose Liberation? Iranian Popular Music and the Fetishization of Resistance." *Popular Communication* 15, no. 3 (July 2017): 163–91.

Nora, Pierre. "Between Memory and History." *Representations* 26, special issue, Memory and Counter-Memory (Spring 1989): 7–24.

Obrist, Hans Ulrich, and Karen Marta, eds. 2011. *Monir Shahroudy Farmanfarmaian: Cosmic Geometry*. Bologna, Italy; Dubai, UAE: Damiani; *The Third Line*.

Observers (France 24). "The Women behind Tehran's Mysterious 'Ladies in Red.'" Editorial, October 21, 2011. https://observers.france24.com/en/20111021-iran-women-behind-tehran-mysterious-lady-in-red-performance-art-yaqut-ruby-legend-ladies

Ocula Magazine. "Art Underground: An Ocula Report from Tehran." Editorial, October 26, 2015. https://ocula.com/magazine/reports/art-underground-a-report-from-tehran/

Ofogh TV. Edalatkhahi-e omid bakhsh [A hopeful quest for justice]. July 2019. https://www.youtube.com/watch?v=cVVf2mRujgg

Olalquiaga, Celeste. *The Artificial Kingdom: A Treasury of the Kitsch Experience*. New York: Pantheon Press, 1998.

Olszewska, Zuzanna. "Classy Kids and Down-at-Heel Intellectuals: Status Aspiration and Blind Spots in the Contemporary Ethnography of Iran." *Iranian Studies* 46, no. 6 (July 2013): 1–22.

Osinski, Zbigniew. *Grotowski and His Laboratory*. Translated and abridged by Lillian Vallee and Robert Findlay. New York: PAJ, 1986.

Osnos, Evan. "Doomsday Prep for the Super-Rich: Some of the Wealthiest People in America—in Silicon Valley, New York, and Beyond—Are Getting Ready for the Crack-up of Civilization." *New Yorker*, January 22, 2017. https://www.newyorker.com/magazine/2017/01/30/doomsday-prep-for-the-super-rich

———. "Rockin' Hard, Rockin' Risky; A Hot Band in Iran Has to Be Furtive, in Part Because It's Fun, Members of the Underground 127 Tell Correspondent Evan Osnos." *Chicago Tribune*, June 20, 2005, 1.4.

Otero-Pailos, Jorge. "Subtle Framing." In *What Is Critical Spatial Practice?*, edited by Nikolaus Hirsch and Markus Miessen, 100–102. Berlin: Sternberg Press, 2012.

Our Man in Tehran (Part Two). Season 36, episode 15 (2018). https://www.pbs.org/video/our-man-in-tehran-part-two-7elm5x/

Pakbaz, Ruin, and Hassan Mourizi Nejad. *Talar-e Ghandriz: Tajrobehyi dar arseh ejtema'yi honar* [Ghandriz Hall: An experiment on the impact of art on society]. Tehran: Herfeh Honarman, 1395 [2018].

Pakravan, Rudabeh. "Territory Jam: Tehran—The Rise of Illegal Satellite TV Has Made the Private Home the True Public Realm." *Places*, July 2012. https://placesjournal.org/article/territory-jam-tehran/

Pepper, David. *Communes and the Green Vision: Counterculture, Lifestyle and the New Age*. London: Merlin, 1991.

Perneczky, Geza. "In the Underground between East and West." In *Promote, Tolerate, Ban: Art and Culture in Cold War Hungary*, edited by Cristina Cuevas-Wolf and Isotta Poggi, 95–109. Los Angeles: Getty Research Institute, 2018.

Phelan, Peggy. *Unmarked: The Politics of Performance*. London: Routledge, 1993.

Phillips, Tony. "Something Like the Sun: Cunningham and His Colleagues Recall 50 Years on the Road." *Village Voice*, July 2002.

Plant, Sadie. *The Most Radical Gesture: The Situationist International in a Postmodern Age*. London: Routledge, 1992.

Plyushteva, Anna. "The Right to the City and the Struggles over Public Citizenship: Exploring the Links." *Urban Reinventors* 3 (November 2009). http://www.urbanreinventors.net/paper.php?issue=3&author=plyushteva

Pui-lan, Kwok. "Elisabeth Schüssler Fiorenza and Postcolonial Studies." *Journal of Feminist Studies in Religion* 25, no. 1 (2009): 191–97.

Radio Zamaneh. "*Goroohi az honarmandan Mohammad Rasoulof ra ta dadgah-e engelab moshaye'at kardand*" [A group of artists joined Rasoulof on the way to his court appeal]. Editorial, 14 Mordar 1398 [August 5, 2019]. https://www.radiozamaneh.com

———. "*Negahi beh namayesh-e sim-keshi-e rookar*" [A look at the open wiring exhibition]. Editorial, 1394 [December 9, 2015]. https://www.radiozamaneh.com/250436

Rahimi, Babak. "Censorship and the Islamic Republic: Two Modes of Regulatory Measures for Media in Iran." *Middle East Journal* 69, no. 3 (July 2015): 358–78.

Rajaee, Farhang. *Islamism and Modernism: The Changing Discourse in Iran*. Austin: University of Texas Press, 2007.

Rancière, Jacques. *Dissensus, on Politics and Aesthetics*. London: Continuum International, 2010.

———. *The Politics of Aesthetics: The Distribution of the Sensible*. Translated by Gabriel Rockhill. New York: Continuum, 2004.

Rashidzadeh, Kaveh. *The Book of Tehran, Hashti: Nafar Abad*. Tehran: Bongah Publications in conjunction with Übermut Project, 2017.

Rasooli, Niloofar. "*Maremmati dar kar nist, 'Ma' ra barchidand*" [There is no restoration plan in place, they removed "Us"]. *Etemad Daily* 4698 (31 Tir 1399 [July 21, 2020]): 12.

———. "*Shahri keh tab-e ma ra nadarad*" [A city that cannot stand 'Us']. *Etemad Daily* 4696 (29 Tir 1399 [July 19, 2020]): 12.

Rasoulof, Ehsan. "Director's Note." In *2016 Koosh Residency*, exhibition catalog, 13. Tehran: Kooshk Residency, 2017.

Rastovac, Heather. "Contending with Censorship: The Underground Music Scene in Urban Iran." *Intersections* 10, no. 2 (2009). http://depts.washington.edu/chid/intersections_Spring_2009/Heather_Rastovac_The_Underground_Music_Scene_in_Urban_Iran.pdf

Ravenscroft, Tom. "ZAV Architects Create Colorful Domed Cultural Retreat on Iranian Island of Hormuz." *Dezeen Magazine*, December 15, 2020. https://www.dezeen.com/2020/12/15/zav-architects-holiday-accomodation-hormuz-iran/

Reddy, William. *The Navigation of Feeling: A Framework for the History of Emotions*. Cambridge: Cambridge University Press, 2001.

Regencia, Ted. "The Award-Winning Bridge Connecting Iranians: Project Dubbed as 'The Third Symbol of Tehran' Earns International Recognition for Architect Leila Araghian." *Al Jazeera*, April 16, 2015. https://www.aljazeera.com/indepth/features/2015/04/award-winning-bridge-connecting-iranians-150414121934153.html

Reilly, Maura, and Lucy Lippard. *Curatorial Activism: Towards an Ethics of Curating*. London: Thames and Hudson, 2018.

Rendell, Jane. *Art and Architecture*. London: I.B. Tauris, 2006.

Restany, Pierre. *Ailleurs: Alex Mlynárčik*. Paris: Galerie Lara Vincy; Bratislava: Galerie Nationale Slovaque, 1994.

Reza, Sara. "The Social Studio," *Guggenheim blog*, January 22, 2016. https://www.guggenheim.org/blogs/map/the-social-studio

Rezaie Rad, Mohammad. *Neshaneh shenasi-e sansoor va sokoot-e sokhan* [*Semiotics of censorship and the silence of words*]. Tehran: Tarh-e Now, 1381 [2002].

Richford, Rhonda. "Cannes: 'The Missing Picture' Wins Un Certain Regard Prize." *Hollywood Reporter*, May 25, 2013. https://www.hollywoodreporter.com/news/cannes-missing-picture-wins-regard-558551

Röder, Kornelia. "Ray Johnson and the Mail Art Scene in Eastern Europe." In *Mythmaking Eastern Europe: Art in Response*, edited by Mateusz Kapustka, *kunsttex-te.de/ostblick* 3 (2014). www.kunsttex-te.de/ostblick

Rogoff, Irit. "Looking Away: Participations in Visual Culture." In *After Criticism: New Responses to Art and Performance*, edited by Gavin Butt, 117–34. London: Blackwell, 2005.

Roozkhosh, Mohammad, and Fereshteh Sadeghi. "*Te'atr-e khosoosi Iran az manzar-e fa'alan-e arseh namayesh*" [Private theater in Iran from the experts' points of view]. *Motale'at-e Farhang va Ertebatat* 77 (1398 [2019]): 57–83.

Rosenberg, Karen. "Life in Iran, Etched with Suspicion and Humor." *New York Times*, May 30, 2008, 28.

Rosenthal, Mark, Sean Rainbird, and Claudia Schmuckli, eds. *Joseph Beuys: Actions, Vitrines, Environments*. New Haven, CT: Yale University Press, 2004.

Rosler, Martha. "Imagination Retakes the Streets." In *What Is Critical Spatial Practice?*, edited by Nikolaus Hirsch and Markus Miessen, 119–20. Berlin: Sternberg Press, 2012.

Roy, Ananya, and Aihwa Ong. *Worlding Cities: Asian Experiments and the Art of Being Global*. New York: John Wiley and Sons, 2011.

Rozak, Theodore. *The Making of a Counterculture*. Berkeley: University of California Press, 1995.

Rubin, Don, ed. *World Encyclopedia of Contemporary Theatre*, vol. 5, Asia/Pacific. London: Routledge, 1998.

Russian TV (RT) News. "Fleeing 1917 Revolution: Orthodox Church in Tehran Maintained by Russian Émigré Descendant." Editorial, November 5, 2017. https://www.rt.com/news/408825-russia-revolution-1917-iran-church/

Sadler, Simon. "Drop City Revisited." *Journal of Architectural Education* 59, no. 3 (2006): 5–14.

———. *The Situationist City*. Cambridge, MA: MIT Press, 1998.

Sahimi, Muhammad. "The Political Evolution of Mousavi." *Public Broadcasting*

Service (*PBS*), *Frontline*, February 16, 2010. https://www.pbs.org/wgbh/pages/frontline/tehranbureau/2010/02/the political-evolution-of-mousavi.html

Saidi Shaygan, Fatemeh. "*Sokhanrani rafeegh madar dar marasem-e yade-yaran yad bad*" [The speech of a comrade mother in memory of her fallen son]. *Payam-e fadayi* 84 (*Ordibehesht 1385* [May 2006]): 2–4. http://www.siahkal.com/index/right%20col/payam84-Sokhan-raniy_Madar.htm

Salem, Heba, and Kantaro Taira. "Al-Thawra al-DaHika: The Challenges of Translating Revolutionary Humor." In *Translating Egypt's Revolution: The Language of Tahrir*, edited by Samia Mehrez. Cairo: American University in Cairo, 2012.

Sani ol-Molk. "*E'lan-e naghashkhaneh dowlati*" [Announcement about the government painting studio]. *Rooznameh vaghayeh ettefaghiyyeh*, 1278 [1862], 11.

Saremi, Nastaran. "Sculpture in Post-revolution Iran: A Fertile Ground for a New Art, A Rereading." *Mohit Art*, December 13, 2021. https://mohit.art/honar-e-jadid-a-new-art-in-iran/sculpture-in-the-post-revolution-iran/#ls

Sarshar, Houman. "Judeo-Persian Communities xi. Music (1)." *Encyclopædia Iranica*, vol. 15/2 (2012), 160–63. http://www.iranicaonline.org/articles/judeo-persian-xi-1-a-general-survey-of-persian-jewish-music

Schank Smith, Kendra. *Architect's Drawings: A Selection of Sketches by World Famous Architects through History*. Boston: Elsevier, 2005.

Schechner, Richard. *Between Theatre and Anthropology*. Philadelphia: University of Pennsylvania Press, 1985.

Scheiwiller, Staci Gem. "Disrupting Bodies, Negotiating Spaces: Performance Art in Tehran." In *Performing Iran: Cultural Identity and Theatrical Performance*, edited by Babak Rahimi, 113–27. London: I.B. Tauris, 2021.

Schwartzstein, Peter. "How Iran Is Destroying Its Once Thriving Environmental Movement." *National Geographic, November 20, 2020*. https://www.nationalgeographic.com/environment/article/how-iran-destroying-once-thriving-environmental-movement

Scott, Felicity. "A Swerve." In *What Is Critical Spatial Practice?*, edited by Nikolaus Hirsch and Markus Miessen, 121–23. Berlin: Sternberg Press, 2012.

Sebti, Saba, Zahra Rahbar Niya, and Mehdi Khabbazi Kenari. "*Mafaheem-e Merleau-Ponty: Bastari baray-e tahleel-e honar-e ta'amoli*" [Merleau-Ponty's views: A context for understanding interactive art]. *Kimia-ye honar* 5, no. 19 (1395 [2016]): 43–52.

Sedgwick, Eve. *Touching Feeling: Affect, Pedagogy, Performativity*. Durham, NC: Duke University Press, 2003.

Seraji, Mahbod. *Rooftops of Tehran*. New York: New American Library, 2009.

Shafi, Sophia Rose. "Glass Palaces: The Role of *Aineh-Kari* in Shi'a Pilgrimage." *Shia Studies*, no. 2 (July–September 2011): 6–9.

Shahrokni, Nazanin. *Women in Place: The Politics of Gender Segregation in Iran.* Berkeley: University of California Press, 2019.

Shamlou, Ahmad. *Ketab-e jom'eh* [*The book of friday*], vol. 1 (1358 [1979]).

Shams, Fatemeh, and Eskandar Sadeghi-Boroujerdi. "Q&A: Head to Head with Abdi Behravanfar, Khorasan Blues Pioneer." *Tehran Bureau, Frontline, PBS,* January 12, 2012. https://www.pbs.org/wgbh/pages/frontline/tehranbureau/2012/01/qa-head-to-head-with-abdi-behravanfar-pioneer-of-the-khorasan-blues.html

Sharafjahan, Rozita, and Saba Mousavi. "*Nasl-e roozhay-e sakht boodeem va zendeh mandeem*" [We were the generation of difficult days and we survived]. *Mo'asseseh farhangi, matboo'ati-e Iran: Iran Newspaper,* n.d. http://www.iran-newspaper.com/newspaper/BlockPrint/157782

Shargh Daily. "*Kasi nist keh Ketabforooshi ra Bekharad*" [There is no one to purchase this bookstore]. Editorial, 1348 (29 Shahrivar 1390 [September 20, 2011]). http://old.sharghdaily.ir/news/90/06/29/33455.html

Shariati, Ali, and Zahra Sarbandi. "*Mo'aser ya vapasgara?*" [Contemporary or reactionary?]. *Etemad Daily* 4157, 20 Mordad 1397 [August 11, 2018]. https://www.etemadnewspaper.ir/fa/main/detail/107604

Shaygan, Dariush (trans. Fatemeh Valiani). "*Aya Tehran madineh-ie tamsilist?*" [Is Tehran an allegorical city]? *Bokhara* 68, no. 69 (1387 [2008]): 677–88.

Sheikh al-Eslami, Pari. *Zanan-e rooznameh negar va andishmand-e Iran* [*Iranian women journalists*]. Tehran: Entesharat-e Zarrin [Zarrin Press], 1351 [1972].

Sheshjavani, Hamidreza. "*Honar dar zamaneh hokmrani-e pool*" [Art in the age of the rule of money]. *Giyumeh,* January 21, 2019.

Shevtsova, Maria. *Robert Wilson.* London: Routledge Performance Practitioners, 2019.

Shirmohammadi, Mehri, and Maedeh Esfandmaz. "*Ru siyahi bar bozorgtarin karkhaneh chay Lahijan*" [A stain on the biggest tea factory in Lahijan]. *Paygah-e khabari va tahleeli farhang va honar* [*Culture and Art News Agency*] (2 *Mehr* 1392 [September 24, 2013]). http://gilmehr.com

Sholette, Gregory. *Dark Matter: Art and Politics in the Age of Enterprise Culture.* London: Pluto Press, 2011.

———. *Delirium and Resistance: Activist Art and the Crisis of Capitalism.* London: Pluto Press, 2017.

Siamdoust, Nahid. *Soundtrack of the Revolution: The Politics of Music in Iran.* Stanford: Stanford University Press, 2017.

Simmel, Georg. "Metropolis and Mental Life." In *Rethinking Architecture,* edited by Neil Leach. London: Routledge, 1997.

Sitar, Sergei. "Four Slogans of 'Collective Actions.'" *Third Text* 17, no. 4 (December 2003): 363–68.

Sjöholm, Cecilia. *Doing Aesthetics with Arendt: How to See Things.* New York: Columbia University Press, 2015.

Slackman, Michael. "In Tehran, A Riposte to the Danish Cartoons." *New York Times,* August 24, 2006. https://www.nytimes.com/2006/08/24/world/africa/24iht-iran.2585075.html

Smith, Anthony Charles H. *Orghast at Persepolis.* New York: Eyre Metheun, 1973.

Sobh-e Sahel. "In Conversation with Pourya Jahanshad: A Place Where Hormoz Ends—Art, a Stage for Disavowing Ownership." Editorial, *Sobh-e sahel* 36, no. 4238 (January 20, 2021): 8–9.

Soleimani, Zohreh. "*Gozareshi az yek namayeshgah-e veejeh dar Tehran: Koodakan-e abi, aseman-e siah*" [A report on a special exhibition in Tehran: Blue children, black sky]. *Golestaneh* 12 (1378 [2000]): 91–94.

Solnit, Rebecca. *Wanderlust: A History of Walking.* New York: Penguin Books, 2000.

Southard, Lukas. "In Havana, Artists Create Underground Art Show to Confront Government-Backed Exhibit." *Lationousa,* May 13, 2019. https://www.latinousa.org/2019/05/13/latitud/

Spivak, Gayatri Chakravorty. "Can the Subaltern Speak?" In *Marxism and the Interpretation of Culture,* edited by Cary Nelson and Lawrence Grossberg. Urbana: University of Illinois Press, 1988.

Sreberny, Annabelle, and Massoumeh Torfeh, eds. *Cultural Revolution in Iran: Contemporary Popular Culture in the Islamic Republic.* London: I.B. Tauris, 2013.

Stanek, Łukasz. *Henri Lefebvre on Space: Architecture, Urban Research and the Production of a Theory.* Minneapolis: University of Minnesota Press, 2011.

Stecklow, Steve, Babak Dehghanpisheh, and Yeganeh Torbati. "Khamenei Controls Massive Financial Empire Built on Property Seizures." *Reuters, December 11, 2013.* https://www.reuters.com/investigates/iran/#article/part1

Sternfeld, Lior B. *Between Iran and Zion: Jewish Histories of Twentieth-Century Iran.* Stanford: Stanford University Press, 2018.

Steward, Theresa Parvin. "Beyond a Politicization of Persian Cats: Representing Iranian Popular Musicians in the Western Media." *Middle East Journal of Culture and Communication 13 (2020): 7–27.*

Stewart, Kathleen. *Ordinary Affects.* Durham, NC: Duke University Press, 2007.

Stoller, Paul. *Sensuous Scholarship.* Philadelphia: University of Pennsylvania Press, 1997.

Suyker, Jeremy. "Iran's Underground Art Scene." *Maptia* (2015). https://maptia.com/jeremysuyker/stories/iran-s-underground-art-scene

Tazarv. "*Bazshenasi mafhoom-e 'heterotopia' dar honar-e shahr*" [Reconsidering the meaning of "heterotopia" in urban art]. Editorial, *Tazarv* 1, no. 1 (Summer 2016): 48–64.

———. "Taxicab Confessions: Tehran." *PBS*, May 7, 2011. http://www.pbs.org/wgbh/pages/frontline/tehranbureau/2011/05/taxicab-confessions-tehran.html

Teplitzky, Alex. "A Space in Pittsburgh That Transports Visitors to Tehran and Vice Versa." *Creative Capital*, October 15, 2019. https://creative-capital.org/2019/10/15/a-space-in-pittsburgh-that-transports-visitors-to-tehran-iran-and-vice-versa/

Terrile, Daniela. "Tehran's Ecological Corridors," *Domus*, February 14, 2010. https://www.domusweb.it/en/news/2010/02/14/tehran-s-ecological-corridors.html

Thompson, Nato. *Living as Form: Socially Engaged Art from 1991–2011*. Cambridge, MA: MIT Press, 2012.

———. *Seeing Power: Art and Activism in the Twenty-First Century*. New York: Melville House, 2015.

Thrift, Nigel. *Non-Representational Theory*. London: Routledge, 2007.

Thurfjell, David. "Emotion and Self-Control: A Framework for Analysis of Shiite Mourning Rituals in Iran." In *Shiite Islam and Identity: Religion, Politics and Change in the Global Muslim Community*, edited by Lloyd Ridgeon, 9–23. London: I. B. Tauris, 2012.

Tofighian, Omid. "Translator's Tale: A Window to the Mountains." In Behrouz Boochani, *No Friend but the Mountains: Writing from Manus Prison*, 4–27. London: Picador, 2018.

Torbati, Yeganeh. "Tehran's Azadi Tower, Witness to History, Victim of Neglect." *Reuters*, February 20, 2013. https://www.reuters.com/article/us-iran-azadi/tehrans-azadi-tower-witness-to-history-victim-of-neglect-idUSBRE91J0QU20130220

Trilling, Ossia. "Robert Wilson's 'Ka Mountain and Guardenia Terrace.'" *TDR: The Drama Review* 17, no. 2 (June 1973): 33–47.

Tschumi, Bernard, and Robert Young. *The Manhattan Transcripts*. London: Academy Editions, 1994.

Tupitsyn, Victor. *The Museological Unconscious*. Cambridge, MA: MIT Press, 2009.

Upton, Dell. "Architecture in Everyday Life." *New Literary History* 33, no. 4 (Autumn 2002): 707–23.

Urry, John. *The Tourist Gaze*. London: Sage, 2002.

Valizadeh, Ali. "*Yadeh aseman-e abi Tehran bekheir*" [Farewell Tehran's blue sky]. *Abrar Newspaper* 2960 (1377 [1999]).

Van Holm, Eric Joseph. 2015. "The Creative Classes' Greatest Failure." *Journal of Policy Research in Tourism, Leisure and Events* 7, no. 2 (2015): 204–7.

Varzi, Roxanne. *Last Scene Underground: An Ethnographic Novel of Iran*. Stanford: Stanford University Press, 2015.

Vişniec, Matei. *Horses at the Window*. New York: Segal Theatre Center Press, 2010.

Wallis, Brian. "Public Funding and Alternative Spaces." In *Alternative Art, New York, 1965–1985*, edited by Julie Ault. Minneapolis: University of Minnesota Press, 2002.

Warner, Michael. "Publics and Counterpublics." *Public Culture* 14, no. 1 (Winter 2002): 49–90.

Watenpaugh, Heghnar. "Deviant Dervishes: Space, Gender and the Construction of Antinomian Piety in Ottoman Aleppo." *International Journal of Middle East Studies* 37, no. 4 (November 2005): 535–65.

Wille, Simone, and Naiza Khan. "In Conversation." *ArtNow Pakistan (2012)*. http://www.artnowpakistan.com/naiza-khan/

Willett, John., ed. and trans. *Brecht on Theatre*. New York: Hill and Wang, 1964.

Williams, Raymond. "Structures of Feeling." In Williams, *Marxism and Literature*, 128–35. Oxford: Oxford University Press, 1977.

Wilson, Robert. "KA MOUNTAIN AND GUARDenia TERRACE: A Story about a Family and Some People Changing." In *Iran Modern*, edited by Fereshteh Daftari and Layla Diba, 93-95. New Haven, CT: Yale University Press in Association with Asia Society, 2013.

Witschge, Loes. "Iran's Gonabadi Dervishes: A 'Long History' of Persecution—Clashes between Members of Iranian Sufi Order and Police Follow More Than a Decade of Increasing Tension." *Al Jazeera*, February 28, 2018. https://www.aljazeera.com/indepth/features/iran-gonabadi-dervishes-long-history-persecution-180227193000395.html

Yarmohammad Touski, Golnar. "Two Artists Attempt to Collaborate across Continents, Travel Bans and All." *Hyperallergic*, March 26, 2020. https://hyperallergic.com/547424/two-artists-attempt-to-collaborate-across-continents-travel-bans-and-all/

Yavari, Houra, ed. *Karim Emami on Modern Iranian Culture, Literature, and Art*. New York: Eisenbrauns, 2014.

Yinger, J. Milton. "Contraculture and Subculture." *American Sociological Review* 25, no. 5 (1960): 625–35.

Zandi, Maryam. *Seemayi az naghashan-e mo'aser-e Iran* [*Portraits of contemporary Iranian painters*]. Tehran: Nashr-e Mo'allef, 1373 [1994].

Zangi, Behnam, Habibollah Ayatollahi, and Asghar Fahimifard. "*Barresi-e moghi'yyat-e naghashi divari pas az enghelab dar Iran ba rooykard-e jame'eh shenakhti-e Pierre Bourdieu*" [An analysis of mural paintings after the revolution (based on *Pierre Bourdieu's* anthropological theories)]. *Negareh* 24 (Winter 1391 [2011]): 85–101.

Zarkar, Rustin. "Making Graffiti an Iranian Art: The Works of Tehran-Based Street Artist Ghalamdar." *Ajam Media Collective,* May 27, 2014. https://ajammc.com/2014/05/27/making-graffiti-an-iranian-art-ghalamdar/

———. “A Mural Erased: Urban Art, Local Politics, and the Contestation of Public Space in Mashhad.” *Ajam Media Collective*, March 30, 2014. http://ajammc.com/2014/03/30/a-mural-erased-urban-art-mashhad/

———. “Taking Back the Streets: Iranian Graffiti Artists Negotiating Public Space.” *Ajam Media Collective*, November 5, 2012. http://ajammc.com/2012/11/05/taking-back-the-streets-iranian-graffiti-artists-negotiating-public-space/

Ziyayi, Mohammad Bagher. Statement published on Amir Mobed’s 2013 performance, “Repetition,” at Azad Gallery (2013). https://amirmobed.com/work/repetition/.

Zolghadr, Tirdad. “The Biotechnical Haruspex.” In *Hotel Theory Reader*, edited by Sohrab Mohebbi, 141–52. Vancouver: Fillip Editions, 2016.

———, ed. *Ethnic Marketing*. Tehran: Toseh; distributed by JRP/Ringier (Zurich), 2006.

Index

Note: Page numbers in italics indicate illustrative material.

Aali, Ahmad, 13; *Self-Portrait* (*Khodnegareh*), 198
Aarabi, Soheil, 83, 84, 85, 128, 130–31
Aaran Gallery, Tehran, 192, 221–22; Bilal's *A Call* performance, 247–49, *248*, 371n94
Abanbar Gallery, Tehran, 96–98, *97*, *98*, 346n203
abanbars (water reservoirs), 97
abandoned and dilapidated buildings (*kolangi*): Bakhshi's *Friends and Enemies* exhibition, 309; *Blue Children, Black Sky* collaborative exhibition, 68–69; Gholhak collaborative exhibition, 67–68; *Independent Contemporary Art Workshop* (*Kargah-e azad-e honar-e mo'aser*): *Project 71/92* collaborative exhibition, 59–61, 62; kitchen utensil factory exhibition, 77–79, *79*; Mortazavi's *Life Accessories* exhibition, 61, 62–65, *63*, *64*; regulation of installations in, 61, 64–65, 66, 68; renovation of, *280*, 280–83, *281*; Shahsavarani's *I Wrote, You Read* exhibition, 73–76, *75*, 101; as spaces for nostalgia and youth refuge, 58–59; tea factory exhibition, 77, *78*, 101–2; *teemi* house exhibitions, 39–40, *40*, *41*; as theater venues, 260–66, *264*, *265*. *See also* leftover urban spaces
Abazari, Yousof, 146, 331n92
Abe, Satoshi, 137
Abedini, Reza, 334n15
Abi Gallery, Tehran, 100
Abramović, Marina, *Rhythm 0*, 240
Abrar Newspaper, 340–41n110
Abri, Sasan, 371n94
abstract art (*honar-e enteza'ie*), 17, 149–50, 297
abstract space, as concept, 24, 302–3
activist art (*honar-e konesh gara*), as category, 8–9, 18
Ada (anonymous graffiti artist), 296
"Adhan to Adhan" (*az azan ta azan*) MCIG program, 246
Adineh, Golab, 283
Adjaye, David, 10
Admun Studio, Cloaked in Bricks, 375n170
affect. *See* feelings and emotions
Afsarian, Iman, 18
Afshar Naderi, Kamran, 375n150
Ag Gallery, Tehran, 124, *125*
aggressive mimicry, 32, 102. *See also* predatory aestheticization
Aghda, Yazd province, 121
Aghdashloo, Aydin, 55, 60, 61–62, 221
agitprop. *See* propaganda
Ahangarani, Pegah, 249–51, *251*
Ahmadinejad, Mahmoud, 73, 76, 167, 219, 228, 230, 232–33, 252–53
Ahmadreza Schricker Architecture–North, 282
Ahmed, Sara, 19, 87
Ahvaz, 58
A.I.R. Gallery, New York, 101
air pollution, 68–69
Ajoudani, Houshang, 214
Akbar Tajvidi, Ali, 222–23

Akcan, Esra, 24
Ala, Mohammad Saleh, 367n4
Alavi, Bozorg, *Fifty-Three Persons* (*Panjah o seh nafar*), 162
Algerian community, 197
alienation (*Verfremdungseffekt*), 12, 233
Ali F.J. One (anonymous graffiti artist), 77, *79*
Ali Khan Vali, 188
Alizade, Mahtabeh, 195
Alizadeh, Ali, 19
Alizadeh, Ayda, 195
Alizadeh, Ghazaleh, 115
Alizadeh, Isa, 212
Al Jazeera (TV network), 221
Alkhansa, Yahya, 49, 53, 337n58
Alkhas, Hanibal, 367n4
alternative art: audiences for, 14–15, 297–98; financial considerations, 295–97; history in Iran, overview, 10–14; by ordinary people, 298–300, 382n42; political engagement, overview, 15–18; research methodology, 27–30; spatial engagement, overview, 19–26; as term, 7, 9–10; Western misunderstanding of, 292–95. *See also* curatorial practices; ephemeral art; escapism and escapist sites; invisible and covert spaces
Al Zahra University (formerly Farah Pahlavi), Tehran, 88
Amanat, Hossein, 172
ambiguity, 133, 252
American Art Workers' Coalition (AWC), 255
Amin-al-Doleh Park, Tehran, 278, *279*
Amir-Ebrahimi, Maserrat, "Public Spaces in Captivity" (*Fazahay-e omoomi dar hesar*), 189, 194
Amir-Ebrahimi, Samila, 18
Amirhajebi, Alireza, *Euphoria* (*Sarkhoshi*), 255–57, *257*
Amirhajebi, Banu, 37
Amir Kabir, 157
Anahita Art Studio, Tehran, *1,001 Afternoons* (*Hezar-o yek asr*) project, 241–44, *243*
Anahita temples, 130
anamorphic drawings, 257–58
Andarzgoo Residential Building, 375n170
Andringa, Melvin, 347n1
Andy (pop singer), 109
Ansari, Ava, 88, 371n94
Antonioni, Michelangelo, 221
Apadana Gallery, Tehran, 214
Apartment Theater (*te'atr-e apartemani*), 55, 80–82, 261
APTART, 7
Arabshahi, Masoud, 215
Arab Spring, 258
Araghian, Leila, 274–77; Tabi'at Pedestrian Bridge, 274–75, *276*, 376nn176–77
Archdaily (website), 140
archeological sites, 129–30, *130*
Architectural Review (magazine), 271
architecture: affective experience of, 256–57, 264–65, 283; of Ave Gallery and Showroom, *268*, 268–70, *270*; complex relationship with economy and politics, 139–40, 267; as curated choreography, 266, 276; curatorial practices, 266–68, 274; façades, 271–73; *hey'ati* style, 258, 373n128; of Imam Hossein Plaza, 210–11, *211*; interdependence between art and, overview, 19–22; of luxury villas, 144–45, *145*; of Majara Residence, 140–42; meaningful narratives in, 169; open spatial plans, 209; and privacy, 271, 273–74, *274*, 277; renovations, *280*, 280–83, *281*; of Sharifi-Ha House, 271, *272*; suspended (*me'mari ta'lighi*), 260; sustainable, 134–37, 142; of Tabi'at Pedestrian Bridge, 274–75, *276*, 376nn176–77; in theater and film, 264–65, 276–77; urban renewal projects, 25–26, 57–58, 164, 165, 302–3, 382–83n52; of Vali Asr Mosque, 209–10, *210*; water temples, *129*, 129–30; workshops in exhibition spaces, 97. *See also* abandoned and dilapidated buildings; leftover urban spaces
Ardakani, Fatemeh Sadat Fazael, *White Cubes* (*Moka'bha-ye sefid*), 201–4, *203*
Arendt, Hannah, 118, 313; *The Human Condition*, 109, 190

Argo Factory, Tehran, *280*, 280–82, *281*
Armenian community, 46–47, 49–52, *51*
Arsh Design Studio, Khorsand Tower, 375n170
Art Bureau of the Islamic Propagation (*Howzeh honari*), 148
art economy (*eghtesad-e honar*), 5
art institution categories, 5–6
The Art of Demolition/Honar-e takhreeb (documentary), 67–68
Arts Foundation (*Howzeh honari*), 335n32
artsy films (*filmhaye honari*), 4
Arya Gallery, Tehran, 66, 89, 159
Aryanpour, Pooya, *Beautiful Virgin*, 20–22, *21*, *22*
Asef Vaziri, Kourosh, 212
Ashena, Mehdi, 131
Asr-e Jadid (New Age) Talent Competition, 102
Assar Gallery, Tehran, 66
assemblies (*anjomans*), underground networks, 36–37
Association of Iranian Artists, 217
Assyrian community, 46–47
A3 art project group, 188
Ati Saz, Tehran, 165–66, *166*
Atrianfar, Mohammad, 231
Atwood, Blake, 4
audiences: absence of, 195, 196; for alternative art, overview, 14–15, 297–98; curated movement of, 250–52, 253–54, 257, 259; distancing effect, 12, 233; ideology of making art for, 64; participation, 21, 84, 104, 127, 132, 200–204, 218, 262, 305–6; passersby, 157, 166, 187–88, 189, 190, 193–94, 200–201, 209; trusted, 5, 61, 79, 80, 102, 126, 159, 227, 237, 238, 269
Aun Gallery, Tehran, 221, 286
AvantTV (YouTube channel), 353n134
Ave, Fereydoun: on art in homes, 55; and regulation of art venues, 284–85; sponsorship of alternative art, 10, 62, 375n157; subterranean art gallery, *268*, 268–70, *270*; on "underground" art, 5. *See also* 13 Vanak Street art space/gallery
Ave Gallery and Showroom, *268*, 268–70, *270*
Av Performance House (*Khaneh Namayesh-e Av*), 84
Av Theater Group: *Ardvi Sura Anahita* performance, *129*, 130; basement venues, 83, 84–85, *85*; black box setting, 83–84; critical reception, 1, 86–87, 131–32, 351n92; establishment, 83; *Gilgamesh* performance, 86; *Ibrahim* performance, 127, 128; *Melpomene* performances, *x*, *86*, *130*, 131–33; and privatization, 82; remote outdoor venues, 126–32
AWC (American Art Workers' Coalition), 255
Ayandegan magazine, 148, *149*
Ayandeh Bank, 301
Ayeneh Office, Andarzgoo Residential Building, 375n170
ayyari partnership, 297
Azad Art Gallery, Tehran: *Ethnic Marketing* (*Bazaryabi-e ghowmi*) exhibition, 225; Fotouhi's and Bakhshi's mock debate, 232–33; Fotouhi's and Fozouni's *By the Horses Who Run Panting* performance, 230–32, *231*; Karami's *Good Thoughts, Good Words, Good Deeds* installation, *253*, 253–54; mentioned, 5, 66; mission as alternative art space, 9–10; Mobed's *Come Caress Me* performance, 234, 304; and Parkingallery, 226, 227, *228*; Razavipour's *Alice in the City* exhibition, 234, *235*; *Rose-and-Nightingale* (*gol-o-bol-bol*) exhibition, 222–23, *223*; *School* (*Madreseh*) exhibition, 222; spatial reconfiguration strategies, 225, 227, 230–34
Azad Group, 154, 215, 367n4
Azadi (Freedom) Tower Complex, Tehran, 87, 172, *173*, *181*, 200–201, *201*
Azghadi, Habib Rahimpour, 19
Azimi, Negar, 294, 340n109

Babajanians, Sanahin, 304
Back Room (digital art platform), 88
Baer, Steve, 110

Bagheri, Maryam, 91
Bagheri, Soodeh, *Dissecting Cadaver* (*Kalbod shekafi*) exhibition, *92*, 93
Bahá'í community, 46, 52, 157, 336n53
Bahá'í Institute for Higher Education (BIHE), 52, 336n53
Bahari, Maziar: *Blue Children, Black Sky* (*Koodakan-e abi, aseman-e siah*) collaborative exhibition, 68; Gholhak collaborative exhibition, 67
Bahman Cultural Center (*Farhangsaray-e Bahman*), 56, 260
Bahrami, Majid, 71
Bajoghli, Narges, 102, 217
Baker, Geoff, 380n12
Bakhshi, Mahmoud, 223–24; *Friends and Enemies* (*Doost o doshman*) exhibition, 309; mock debate (with Fotouhi), 232–33; *Solo Show* (*Namayeshgah-e enferadi*), 228–30; *Tulips Rise from the Blood of the Nation's Youth* (*Az khoon-e javanan-e vatan laleh damideh*), 228
Bakhtin, Mikhail, 197, 204
Balaghi, Shiva, 8
Balaşescu, Alexandru, 194
Bam earthquake (2003), 113–14
Ban, Shigeru, 135
Bani Etemad, Rakhshan, 61
banned art. *See* censorship
Barati, Ehsan, *Ashura* series, 191, *191*
Barba, Eugenio, 125, 169
bare stage, 169
Barobax (music band), 53
Barthes, Roland, 3
basements: as art venues, 56, *57*, 93–94, *95*, 235, *236*; as music recording studios, 51–52; as theater venues, 83–85, *85*
Basiji (militia forces), 84, 142
Basti Hills, Lavasan, 143, 353n134
Bayani, Amir Hossein, 17
Bayat, Asef, 24; *Life as Politics*, 298–99
Bazigah/Playground (theater group), 82
BBC Persian (TV network), 344n167
Beautification Bureau (*Sazman-e ziba sazi-e shahrdari-e Tehran*), 5–6, 26, 150, 165, 210, 212
Beck, Julian, 125
Beck, Martin, 288
Beckett, Samuel, 170
becoming, process of, 204, 244
Behboudi, Mehrnoush, 62–63
Behboudi, Soleiman, 62
Behesht-e Zahra Cemetery, Tehran, 182, *183*
Beheshti, Ayatollah Mohammad, 159
Behpoor, Bavand, 194
Behravanfar, Abdi, 53–54
Behzadi, Alireza, 275
Bel, Jérôme, 245
Belgrand, Eugène, 314
Berlin Biennale, 7th, 381n41
Berliner, Paul, *Thinking in Jazz: The Infinite Art of Improvisation*, 220
Betts, Paul, 54
Beuys, Joseph, 10
Bidoun magazine, 119, 156
BIHE (Bahá'í Institute for Higher Education), 52, 336n53
Bijani, Bijan, 61
Bilal, Wafaa, *A Call* (*Baang*), 247–49, *248*, 371n94
Bishapour, Fars province, 129–30
Bishop, Claire, 111–12
black boxes, 83–84
Black Hand (anonymous graffiti artist): *Offline*, 304, *305*; *teemi* house project, 39
Black Narcissus. *See* Narges Siah
blatant visibility, 172
Blind (anonymous graffiti artist): kitchen utensil factory project, 77, 78–79; portable graffiti, 175–76, *177*; *teemi* house project, *41*; water canal project, 174–75, *175*; wild-style graffiti, 78–79, *79*, 174, *174*
Bloch, Ernst, 296
Boal, Augusto, 16, 169, 232
Bobby Sands Street (formerly Winston Churchill), Tehran, 87
bodily movement. *See* choreography
bomb shelters, as art venues, 94–96, *96*
Bomrani ensemble (music band), 247
Bondi, Liz, 23

Borges, Jorge Luis, "Funes the Memorious," 205
Boroojeni, Bahman, 367n4
Bourdieu, Pierre, 271
Bozorgmehr, Mina, 168–69. *See also* Noir Art Group
Braidotti, Rosi, 240
branded buildings (*sakhtemanhay-e markdar*), 144
brave theater, 172–73
Bread & Puppet theater, 155
Brecht, Bertolt, 12, 233
Brennan, Teresa, 252
breweries, renovation of, *280*, 280–82, *281*
bridges, Tabi'at Pedestrian Bridge (*Pol-e Tabi'at*), 274–75, *276*, 376nn176–77
Broadbent, Geoffrey, *Deconstruction: A Student Guide*, 374n150
Brook, Peter, 11–12, 83, 85–86, 169; *Orghast* (with Hughes), 12
Bruguera, Tania, 245; *Tatlin's Whisper #5*, 247
Buchloh, Benjamin, 287
Burnett, Craig, 228
buses: as gender-segregated, 186–87; Puriya Mehr's *My Own Privacy Policy* exhibition, 187, *188*, 188–90
Byrd Hoffman School of Byrds, 104. *See also* Wilson, Robert

café culture, 241
Café Ferdowsi, Tehran, 241
Café Markof, Qasr Museum, 242–44, *243*
Cage, John, 13
California Institute of Earth Art and Architecture (Cal-Earth), 135, 351n99
Calle, Sophie, 180
calligraphy, 13, 60, *78*, 178. *See also* graffiti art
carnivalesque (literary device), 197, 204
caves, as theater venues, *130*, 130–32, *132*
censorship: of art history books, 277–78; covering inappropriate art, 21–22, *22*, 43, 148; critical commentary on, 74–76; erasure of graffiti, 175; of historical memory, 39–40, 191–92, 205; under Islamic Republic, overview, 42–43; and market economy, 294; of news and journalism, 73, 74, 228–29, 312; of nudity, 42, 43, 44–45, *45*, *46*, 215, 237, 362n131; of political satire, 198; and public-private dichotomy, 4; removal of art, 206; and restricted access to space, 210; sacred *vs.* profane, 21–22; self-censorship, 27, 32, 72, 180, 204, 238, 240; semiotics of, 80; subversion of, 15–16, *16*; of Tehran urban art competition, 6; of Western culture and art, 2, 13, 73
Center for Cooperation of Seminaries and Universities (*Daftar-e hamkari-ye hawzeh va daneshgah*), 42
Central Bank of the Islamic Republic of Iran (*Bank-e markazi*), 301
Central Desert (*Kaveer-e markazi*), 121
Cerwonka, Allaine, *Improvising Theory*, 30
Chaharsad Dasgaah, 260
Chain Murders of Iran (*Ghatlhay-e zanjireh-ie*), 73, 115, 342n133
Changeux, Jean Pierre, *What Makes Us Think?* (with Ricoeur), 250
charity work (*kare- kheiriyyeh*), 298, 381n34
Cheragh magazine, 131–33, *132*
Cheurfa, Hiyem, 197–98
childlike playfulness, 200, 304
children's craftworks (*kardasti*), 65, 220–21
choreography: affective experience of, 247–49, 256–57, 264–65; of architecture, 266, 276; art market criticism, 255–56, *257*; of audience movement, 250–52, 253–54, 257, 259; dance metaphor, 244; political criticism, 247–54, *248*, *251*, *253*, 257–59, *259*; in state propaganda apparatus, 245–46, *246*
Christian community, 47–51, *49*, *50*
churches, Christian, 47–49, *49*, *50*, 50–51
cinema. *See* film (*filmi*) and video (*videoie*)
City Theater (*te'atr-e shahr*), Tehran, 70, 148, 170, 208–9, *210*
Clean Air Day (*Rooz-e havay-e pak*), 138, 352n109
Cloaked in Bricks, 375n170
closet art (*honar-e keshoyi*), 8

Clubhouse (social media platform), 314
Colomina, Beatriz, 275
committed art (*honar-e mote'ahhed*), as category, 215, 224
communism and Marxism, 37, 143, 162, 176, 243, 307, 334n17
community-driven art, 297–300, 301, 381n34
concealed spaces. *See* invisible and covert spaces
conceptual art (*honar-e mafhoomi*), revival in Iran, 14
Conflict Kitchen, Pittsburgh, 290
Constable, John, 278
Constitutional Revolution (1906–9), 36
construal level theory, 123
construction sites: Ati Saz, 165–66, *166*; Tehran International Tower, 167–68, *168*
Cornell, Joseph, 62
corporal action (*konesh-e jesmani*), 81, 133
counterculture, as term, 8, 110, 348n26
covert spaces. *See* invisible and covert spaces
COVID-19 pandemic, 313
Creswell, Tim, 209
Critchley, Simon, 197
critical spatial practice, as concept, 23–26
Cuban alternative art scene, 358n65, 380n12
Cultural Rectangle (*morabba'-e farhangi*), 88–89, 374n139
Cunningham, Merce, 13
curatorial practices: during Ahmadinejad administration, 219; architects as curators, 266–68, 274; collection of relics, *286*, 286–87; global movement of alternative, 34; improvisational strategies, 220–24; during Khatami administration, 217–19; mediator role of curators, 189, 228; post-revolutionary propagandist, 215–17; pre-revolutionary shift from traditional, 214–15; preservation and renovation, 277–83, *279*, *280*, *281*; private assembly (*mahfel-e khosoosi*) model, 236–41, 269–70; public assembly (*patogh*) model, 241–44; during Qajar era, 366–67n1; regulation of, 55, 56, 61, 64 65, 66, 68, 76–77, 98–99, 165, 222, 238, 252, 338n73; replication, *289*, 290–91; spatial reconfiguration strategies, in conventional exhibition spaces, 228–34, 249–52, 253–54, 257–59; spatial reconfiguration strategies, in unconventional exhibition spaces, 89–100, *90*, *92*, *95*, *96*, *97*, *98*, *99*, 225–28, 235–36, 242–44, *268*, 268–70, *270*, 283–84. *See also* choreography

Dabashi, Hamid, 11, 12
Dadaism, 13, 327n44
Dadashi Gallery, Tehran, 223, *224*
Daftari, Fereshteh, 8
Dalan Quarterly (journal), 373–74n137
Daliri, Farzad, 144
dance metaphor, 244. *See also* choreography
Daneshmir, Reza, 209; Ave Gallery and Showroom, *268*, 268–71, *270*
Daneshvari, Abbas, 8
Darabi, Helia, 15–16, 19, 61, 152, 325n25, 340n109
Daraie, Fariborz, 172–73
Dargahi, Mohammad, 162
Darvish Khan, 107–8, 115
Daryabeigi, Abdolreza, 215
Darzi, Neda, *117*, 117–21, *118*, *120*
Dashti, Ali, *Project 71/92* collaborative exhibition, 60–61
Dashti, Gohar, *Home* series, 58–59, *59*
Dashti, Mostafa: *Project 71/92* collaborative exhibition, 59–60; *Roadkill* (*Tasadof-e jaddeh-ie*; with Fayyazi), 155–56
Dastan Basement Gallery (*Zirzamin-e Dastan*), Tehran, 98–99
dates (fruit), 180
Dativ (music band), 175
Davies, Clare, 178
DAZ (architectural firm), Shushtar New Town, 382–83n52
Debord, Guy, 10, 176, 299
decentralization, 123
De Certeau, Michel, 23–24, 33, 34, 204, 220; *The Practice of Everyday Life*, 23, 110, 186
decolonized art history, 27

defiant art, as term, 8
Degot, Ekaterina, 54
Dehghanpour, Yahya, 337–38n67
Dehkordi, Payam, 83
Delgosha Garden, Shiraz, 261
Delzendeh, Siamak, 294
dematerialized art: emergence in Iran, 12–14; as phenomenon, 10
democracy, and theater, 184
demolition, 67–68
Department of Art Affairs (*Mo'avenat-e omoor-e honari*), 43
Derrida, Jacques, 209, 296
dervishes, 32, 137
Desert Dancer (film), 126, 350n79
deserted buildings. *See* abandoned and dilapidated buildings
deserts: Jamshidi's *I Am Here* installation, 119, *121*, 121–24, *122*; *The Red Artery* performance, 119, *120*; as theater venues, 125–26
design projects. *See* architecture
Detroit, Michigan, 164
Deutsche, Rosalyn, *Evictions: Art and Spatial Politics*, 23
Deutsche Welle Farsi News, 243
Dezeen (magazine), 140
Diba, Kamran, 42, 215, 327n44, 382n52; *Clever Waterman* (*Ab-baz-e zebar dast*), 13
Diba Tensile Architecture, 274
Dibazar, Pedram, 363n147
dilapidated buildings. *See* abandoned and dilapidated buildings
distancing effect (*Verfremdungseffekt*), 12, 233
Divan of Hafez, 223
Dolat-e Elliyeh Iran (newspaper), 366n1
Dorcheh, Isfahan province, 120
DOTS (Dancin' on the Street) festival, Detroit, 164
Dowlatabadi, Mahmoud, 47
Drop City, Colorado, 110–11, 310–11
Duncombe, Stephen, 312

East Art Gallery, Tehran, 372n116; *30 Performances, 30 Artists, 30 Days* (*Si performance, si honarmand, si rooz*) festival, 254; Amirhajebi's *Euphoria* performance, 255–57, *257*
Eastern Bloc art. *See* Soviet and Eastern Bloc experience and art
Eco, Umberto, 10
economy: complex relationship with architecture and politics, 139–40, 267; *khosoolati*, 25, 82, 139, 297; and Majara Residence, 140, 141; market-driven art, 10, 58, 159, 241, 255–56, 293, 296–97, 301; participatory budgeting, 93, 309–10; and privatization, 25, 82–83, 102, 310, 383n70; and urban renewal projects, 24–26, 56–58, 164, 165
ecotourism, 127–29
Ehsai, Mohammad, 367n4
Ehsaii, Siamak, 149, *150*
Eisenhower, Dwight D., 87
Eisenman, Peter, 270
Eisenstein, Sergei, 344n167
Ekbatan complex, Tehran, 53
Elahe Gallery, Tehran, 66
Electric Room (*Otagh-e bargh*), Tehran, 99, 99–100
Elf Crew (graffiti art group), 77, *174*, 174–75
El Greco, *Burial of Count Orgaz*, 60
Ellmann, Maud, 229
Emami, Karim, 327n44
Emarat-e Rooberoo/Opposite Building (theater group), 82
embassies, foreign, 46–47, *48*, 51, 120
emotions. *See* feelings and emotions
empty buildings. *See* abandoned and dilapidated buildings
Empty Space Studio, Tehran, 100
Enghelab, Tehran, 179, 180, 299
environmental art (*honar-e mohiti*) and discourse: and ecotourism, 127–29; Mount Damavand as iconic feature of, 137–38, *138*, 139; origins in modern Iran, 108; and *passio*, 303–4; political criticism, 17, 60–61, 68–69, 113, 115–16, 138–39, 146, 352n109; in public interest, 298, 381n34; sustainable architecture, 134–37, 142. *See also* escapism and escapist sites
Environmental Theater (*te'atr-e mohiti*), 104, 169

Enwezor, Okwui, *In/Sight* exhibition, 34
ephemeral art (*honar-e mira*): alternative and indeterminate futures activated in, 203–4; forgotten images in popular imagination, 192–94; humor and playfulness in, 195–202; as institutional critique, 195; as phenomenon, 152–53; revival in Iran, 14; and rhythmanalysis concept, 153–54; state-sponsored, 149–50, *150*, 151. *See also* buses; guerilla style art; leftover urban spaces; mobile art; rooftops; streets and roadsides; taxicabs
Erdbrink, Thomas, 109, 301, 348n20
Esbati, Amir, 334n17
escapism and escapist sites: collaborative spirit formation in, 117–24, 126, 127; concept of "escaping without leaving," 109–10; history in Iran, overview, 32; as institutional critique, 109, 131–32, 133–34; personal soul-searching in, 112–14; rooftops as sites for, 202; for social elite, 142–46; in Soviet context, 111–12. *See also* caves; deserts; environmental art; forests; mountains
Esfahk Mud Center, *136*, 136–37
Eshteiaqee, Athena, 250, 251, *251*
Esmaili, Mohammad Mehdi, 314
Etemad Art Gallery, Tehran, Shafieezadeh's *Negative Positive Space* exhibition, 257–59, *259*
Etemad Daily (newspaper), 77, 204, 206, 209
Etemadi, Parvaneh, 269
ethnic minority spaces, 46–52, *48*, *49*, *50*, *51*, 336n53
ethnographic improvisation, 30
ethnographic turn, 238
Ettehad, Ali, *1,001 Afternoons* (*Hezar-o yek asr*) project, 241–44, *243*
Ettela'at Newspaper, 73, 340–41n110
EUNIC (European Union National Institutes for Culture), 89
Euripides, *Medea*, 126
European embassies, 46–47, *48*, 51, 120
Evin (political prison), 182, 188
exchange programs, Kooshk Art Residency, 89–91, *90*, 301
executive art (*honar-e hokoomati*), as category, 5
experimental art (*honar-e tajrobi*) *vs.* conventional, 10
Ezzati, Elnaz, 195

façades (architecture), 271–73
Facebook, 118–19
factories, abandoned, 77–79, *78*, *79*
Fajrak, Taba, *99*
Fajr Festivals, 161, 170, 192, 219, 260, 263, 297
Farah, Empress, 11, 42, 70, 104
Farajiani, Negar, 188; *Made in China* (*Sakht-e Chin*), 200–201, *201*; *Tehran Monoxide Project*, 381n34
Faramarzi, Ali, 1–2; "A Scar on a Legend" (*Zakhmi bar ostooreh*), 139
Farhadian, Mehdi, 39, 277–78; *Amin-al-Doleh Park in Tehran*, 278, *279*
Farman Farma, Bahman, 61
Farvahar Gallery, Tehran, Golnari's *Feast* installation, 234–36, *236*
Fauré, Gabriel, *Élégie*, 250
Fayyazi, Bita: *Blue Children, Black Sky* (*Koodakan-e abi, aseman-e siah*) collaborative exhibition, 68, 69; Gholhak collaborative exhibition, 67; mobile art exhibition, 187–88; *Roadkill* (*Tasadof-e jaddeh-ie*; with Dashti), 155–56
Fedai Guerrillas (*Chirik-e fadai-e khalgh*), 37
feelings and emotions: and architecture, 256–57, 264–65, 283; distancing effect, 12, 233; embodied experience of, 74–76, 247; humor and playfulness, 195–202; *vs.* logic, 19; and meandering in the city, 176, 178; mourning and grief, 75, 216, 234–36, 247–49; in public spaces, 194, 202, 203, *203*, 256–57; rooftops as safe spaces for, 202; sharing pain of others, 251–52; taxicabs as safe spaces for, 186; therapeutic theater performances, 86–87
Fellini, Federico, 62
Feminist Art Movement, 34
Ferdowsi, Abol-Qasem, *The Book of Kings* (*Shahnameh*), 137–38, 235

Ferdowsi Square, Tehran, 192–94, *193*, 298
57 Group, 334n17
fig-1 program, 99–100
Fighters (*Razmandegan*), 38
Filatov, Nikolay, 340n101
film (*filmi*) and video (*videoie*): architectural engagement, 276–77; Khan's *Metro Beheshti*, 159; during Khatami administration, 66; in leftover urban spaces, 357n52; music in, 52, 53; open distribution of banned, 4; regulation of, 73, 198, 335n32; Soviet and Eastern Bloc, 344n167; and state aggressive mimicry strategy, 102; in taxicabs, 183–84; of women meandering in the city, 179–83, *181*, *182*, *183*
Fin Garden, Kashan, 156–57
Firouz, Eskandar, 134
Fischer, Michael, 198
Fiuzi, Yahya, 373n128
flâneur, 179–80
Florida, Richard, *The Rise of the Creative Class*, 311
Fluid Motion Architects, 209–10, *210*
Font (music band), 175
Food restaurant, New York City, 288
foreign embassies, 46–47, *48*, 51, 120
forests: Maktabi's *I'm Not Political* performance, *115*, 115–16; as theater venues, 125
formal art (*honar-e rasmi*), as category, 18
Forum Theater (*te'atr-e showraie*), 169, 184
Foster, Hal, 238
Fotouhi, Shahab, 17, 227, 233–34; *Census* (with Razavipour), 165–67, *166*, 357n52; *By the Horses Who Run Panting* (*Ghasam beh asbani keh nafashayeshan beh shomareh oftadeh*; with Fozouni), 230–32, *231*; mock debate (with Bakhshi), 232–33; *Orange on Gray: Homage to Mark Rothko* (*Narenji rooy-e Khakestari*; with Razavipour), 167–68, *168*
Foucault, Michel, 23, 27, 112, 122, 160
Fournier, Lauren, *Autotheory as Feminist Practice in Art, Writing, and Criticism*, 100–101
Fozouni, Farhad, *By the Horses Who Run Panting* (*Ghasam beh asbani keh nafashayeshan beh shomareh oftadeh*; with Fotouhi), 230–32, *231*
Francis, Mark, 100
Franklin Furnace, New York City, 311
Freedom Avenue (formerly Eisenhower), Tehran, 87
Freire, Paulo, 10
French alternative art scene, 34, 154–55, 170, 176, 180
Friedberg, Anne, 179
Fuller, Buckminster, 110, 310–11
furnace room performances (*namayeshha y-e motorkhaneh te'atr-e shahr*), 72

Ganjeh, Azadeh, 260; *Unpermitted Whispers* (*Najvahay-e biejazeh*), 184–86, *185*, *187*
garages, as art venues, 225–28, *226*, *228*
The Garden of Stones/Bagh-e sangi (documentary), 107–8, 115
Gardzienice Theater Association, 81, 83, 127, 133
GDR (German Democratic Republic), 54
Geltaftan Foundation, 135
GEM TV, 243–44
gender segregation, 26, 43, 72, 82, 126, 128, 186–87. *See also* men; women
Genet, Jean, 341n122; *The Blacks: A Clown Show*, 70
gentrification (*a'yan sazi*), 88, 374n139
German Democratic Republic (GDR), 54
Germany, Nazi, 245
Gérôme, Jean-Léon, 203
Gerould, Daniel, 12
Ghadirian, Shadi, *Qajar* series, 293
Ghadyanloo, Mehdi, 150–51; *Portrait of the Sky* (*Naghsh-e aseman*), 151, *151*
Ghaffarian, Afshin, 125–26, 350n79
Ghalamdar (Parham Salimy): inspirations for, 334n15; interventionist art project map, 152, *153*; kitchen utensil factory project, 77–78; *teemi* house project, 39–40, *40*, *41*; water canal project, *174*, 174–75; wild-style graffiti, 174, *174*
Ghalibaf, Mohammad Bagher, 150, 217, 274
Ghamari-Tabrizi, Behrooz, 38

Ghandriz Hall, Tehran, 93
Ghanizadeh, Homayoun, 83
Ghasbanpour, Jassem, 247
Ghasemi, Amirali, 73, 77, 225–27
Ghiasi Farahani, Shahrokh, *Project 71/92* collaborative exhibition, 60
Ghobadi, Bahman, 53, 79
Ghodstinat, Soheila, *A Journey to Starland*, 84
Gholipour, Ali, 199
Ghomeishi, Siavash, 372n116
Giacometti, Alberto: *Standing Woman*, 206; *Walking Man*, 206
Gibbs, Anna, 74
Global Art Forum (2009), 227
Golagha magazine, 198
Golestan, Lili, 56, 61, 62, 225
Golestaneh magazine, 68–69
Golestan Gallery, Tehran, 56, 62, 66, 225
Golestan Palace Museum, Tehran: Aryanpour's *Beautiful Virgin* installation, 20–22, *21*, *22*; *Picnic, Iranian Style* exhibition, 20
Golmohammadi, Firoozeh, 148–49
Golnari, Kourosh: *Dream of Bam* (*Khab-e Bam*), 113–14, *114*; *Feast* (*Ziyafat*), 234–36, *236*; *Salatin* (*Sultans*) series, 221
Golruyi, Yaghma, 372n116
Golshiri, Barbad, 18, 305, 306, 328n53
Goodarzi, Milad, 146
Gorbachev, Mikhail, 111
Gorji, Mohsen, "Direct Negotiation" (*Mozakereh mostagheem*), 242–43, *243*
Gottdiener, Mark, *The Social Production of Urban Space*, 25
governmental art (*honar-e dolati*), as category, 5–6, 18
graffiti art: in abandoned kitchen utensil factory, 77–79, *79*; in abandoned *teemi* houses, 39–40, *40*, *41*; in abandoned water canals, *174*, 174–75; audience as broad, 15; map of, 152, *153*; mobile, 175–76, *177*; political criticism, 40, 304; post–Green Movement, 234; privacy and anonymity of artists, 296; wild-style, 79, *79*, *174*
Graham, Dan, 255, 373n120
Graham, Martha, 125
Grand Mosalla mosque of Tehran (Imam Khomeini Mosalla), 258
Grand Palais, Paris, 34
Greek theater, 81, 126, 184
Green Movement (*Jonbesh-e sabz*), 25, 76, 118, 152, 186, 192, 202, 219, 230–36, 306
grief and mourning, 75, 216, 234–36, 247–49
Grigor, Talinn, 8
Grigorian, Marcos, 107
Grosz, Elizabeth, *Becomings: Explorations in Time, Memory and Futures*, 204
Grotowski, Jerzy: *The Constant Prince*, 261; and Gardzienice, 127; influence on Iranian artists, 4, 71, 72, 104, 125, 169, 261; life as art/art as life concept, 86; paratheater concept, 125; poor theater concept, 69–70, 71; and Shiraz Festival of Arts, 11, 125, 261; travels in Iran, 11, 12
Groys, Boris, 299
Gruber, Christiane, 216
guerilla style art (*chiriki*): emergence in Iran, 154; negotiation strategies, 159–60; open political criticism, 161–62; religious imagery, 157–58; subtle political criticism, 155–56, 157; visibility of, 156
guitars, as banned, 52
Gurarzi, Sarah, 348n48
Guyton, Tyree, 164

habitus, 271
Haft Samar Gallery, Tehran, 56, *57*, 66
Haft Tan Mountain, Shiraz, *104*, 104–7
Hajizadeh, Ghasem, 55
Hakim Bey (Peter Lamborn Wilson), 176
Hamedani, Helia, *Displacement* (*Jabejaie*; with Nafisi), 308
Hamidi, Rodin, 371n94
Hamshahri (newspaper), 219, 242
Hanachi, Pirouz, 357n45
Hanaie, Arash, 229
handmade art (*kardasti*), 65, 220–21
Happenings, 10, 169
Harari, Yuval Noah, 313
Hariri, Gisue and Mojgan, 144
Hariri & Hariri Architecture, 144–45, *145*

"harmonious movement" performances (*harakat-e mowzoon*), 13
Harvey, David, 23, 25
Hasheminejad, Ata, Gholhak collaborative exhibition, 67
Hashti, Tehran (documentary), 382n42
Hassanzadeh, Khosrow: *Blue Children, Black Sky (Koodakan-e abi, aseman-e siah)* collaborative exhibition, 68; Gholhak collaborative exhibition, 67
Hatam, Behzad, 367n4
Hatoum, Mona, 218
Hauser, Arnold, *The Social History of Art*, 334n17
Haussmann, Georges-Eugène, 314
Havel, Vaclav, "The Power of the Powerless," 306
hectographs (gelatin duplicators), 36
Hedayat, Sadeq, *Blind Owl*, 370n74
Heidelberg Project, Detroit, 164
Hematian, Hormoz, 99–100
Herfeh honarmand (The Career of the Artist; journal), 18
Heringer, Anna, 135
heterotopia (*deegar makan*), 122
hey'ati (rushed) architecture, 258, 373n128
Hezbollahs, 42
High Council of the Cultural Revolution (*Showra-ye ali-e enghelab-e farhangi*), 42. *See also* MCIG
Hirsch, Marianne, 323–24n7
Hirsch, Nikolaus, 23
Hirst, Damien, 218; *The Physical Impossibility of Death in the Mind of Someone Living*, 195
historic archeological sites, 129–30, *130*
Hobsbawm, Eric, *Bandits*, 297, 380n30
Hockney, David, 150
Hojjat al-Islam Lavasani, Seyyed Said, 144, 145–46
Holbein, Hans, *The Ambassadors*, 257–58
Homayunpour, Parviz, 344n167
homegrown neoliberalism, 25
homes: art classes in, 2, 3, 55; art exhibitions in, 47, *48*, 55; as art venues, officially permitted, 56, *57*, 89–91, *90*, 93–94, *95*, *268*, 268–70, *270*, 301–2, 338nn73–74; as "field of action," 288–90; in modernist urban template, 302–3, 382–83n52; music classes and rehearsals in, 52, 53; as music recording studios, 51–52; *shabnamehs* produced in, 36–37; team/*teemi* houses, 37–38, 39–40, *40*, *41*; as theater venues, 55–56, 79–82, *81*, 261, 361–62n131
Honar va resaneh (newspaper), 242
Hopper, Edward, *New York Movie*, 262, *263*
Hormuz, Majara Residence, 140–42
Hosseini, Mohammad, 191–92; *Women in Red (Banooy-e sorkhpoosh)* performance, 192–94, *193*, 298
House for the Artists of the Revolution (*Khaneh tarrahan-e enghelab*), 151–52
The House of 40 Knots, 375n170
The House of the Artists (*Khaneh honarmandan*), 219, 260
houses. *See* homes
House Theater (*te'atr-e khaneh*), 56, 79–80
House Theater Group (*Gorooh-e te'atr-e khaneh*), 80
Houshyar, Mehran, 218
Hughes, Ted, *Orghast* (with Brook), 12
Hugo, Victor, *Les Miserables*, 314
humor and playfulness, 195–202, 304
Hyrcanian region, 120

ideological art (*honar-e ideologic*), as category, 18
Igreg Art Studio: closure of, 370n69; *Irma* exhibition, 238, *239*, 239–41; Karami's *Resurrected Series*, 237; as private exhibition space, *237*, 237–38
Imam Hossein Plaza, Tehran, 210–11, *211*
improvisation (*bedah-e*), 30, 220. *See also* curatorial practices
Inanlou, Mohammad Ali, 127–28
Indiana, Robert, *Love*, 204
informal art (*gheyr-e rasmi*), as term, 7–8
installation art (*honar-e chideman*), as Zionist, 61
Institute for the Development of Plastic Arts (*Mo'asseseh tose'eh honarha-ye tajassomi*), 217
integrationist art, 211, 212

interactive art (*honar-e ta'amoli*): and audience participation, 21, 84, 104, 127, 132, 200–204, 218, 262, 305–6; defined, 14; Iranian tradition and revival of, 10–14

invisible and covert spaces: minority spaces, 46–52, *48*, *49*, *50*, *51*, 336n53; and "raw" spaces concept, 58; *shabnamehs* distribution in, 36–37; spatial reconfiguration of unconventional exhibition spaces, 89–100, *90*, *92*, *95*, *96*, *97*, *98*, *99*, 283–84; transformation in Iran, overview, 101–3; two types, 44. *See also* abandoned and dilapidated buildings; homes

Invisible Theater, 16, 230, 232

Iran. *See* Islamic Republic of Iran

Iranian Cultural Revolution (1980–87), 42

Iranian People's Fedai Guerrillas (*Chirik-e fadai-e khalgh*), 32, 178

Iranian Radio and Television (*Seda va sima*), 335n32

Iranian Student Protests (1999), 312

Iranian Vaqf Institute (*Sazman-e owghaf*), 139

Iran-Iraq War, 1, 2, 28, 58, 87, 178, 216, 247–49

Iran Khodro, 195

Iravanian, Mehrdad, 375n150

Irigaray, Luce, 256

Irma la Douce/Irma khoshkeleh (film), 238–39

Isfahan, Foad, 186

Islamic Azad University, Tehran, 126

Islamic Republic of Iran: Chain Murders of Iran, 73, 115, 342n133; economic development and urban renewal projects, 24–26, 56–58, 164, 165; establishment, 40–42; feelings *vs.* logic in decision-making processes, 19; Green Movement, 25, 76, 118, 152, 186, 192, 202, 219, 230–36, 306; internet restriction bill (*tarh-e sianat az fazay-e majazi*), 313–14; Iran-Iraq War, 1, 2, 28, 58, 87, 178, 216, 247–49; political prisoners, 139, 161, 162, 229, 235, 250, 286, 306–7; predatory aestheticization and aggressive mimicry strategies, 26, 32, 102, 103, 208, 212; relations with United States, 242–43, 313; renaming practices, 87–88; welfare programs, 54, 331n92. *See also* censorship; propaganda

Islamic Republic Parliament, 182

Islamic Revolution (1979), 1, 39, 41, 87, 161, 172, 216

isolated artist (*honarmand-e monzavi*) myth, 18

Ivanov, Alexander, 340n101

Jahangir, Farid: Gholhak collaborative exhibition, 67; *Project 71/92* collaborative exhibition, 59–60, 62–63

Jahangiri, Keyvan, 357n51

Jahanshad, Pouria, 25–26, 93, 141–42, 298, 299

Jalaiepour, Hamid Reza, 231

Jalali, Bahman, 227, *105*

Jame'i, Ahmad Masjed, 218

Jamshidi, Mahdyar, *I Am Here* (*Man inja hastam*; with Puriya Mehr), *121*, 121–24, *122*, *125*

Japalaghy, Alireza, 202

Jarmusch, Jim, 4

Javadipour, Mahmoud, 214

Javaherian, Faryar, 20

Jeenous (dancer), 61

jellygraphs (gelatin duplicators), 36

Jewish community, 46, 49, 61

Joadat, Mohammad Reza, 374–75n150

Johannesburg Biennale (1997), 34

Jopling, Jay, 100

journalism, censorship of, 73, 74, 228–29, 312

junkyards, as theater venues, 170

Jyllands-Posten (newspaper), 219

Kabakov, Ilya, 290

Kafka, Franz, 170; "A Hunger Artist," 229

Kamali-Moghaddam, Hadi, 168–69, 172–73; *This Is Not an Apple* (*In yek seeb neest*), 170. *See also* Noir Art Group

Kamalvand, Sara, 17

Kamrani, Behnam, 222–23, 225

Karami, Katayoun: *Good Thoughts, Good Words, Good Deeds (Pendar-e neek, goft ar-e neek, kerdar-e neek)*, 253, 253–54; *Resurrected Series (sansoor)*, 237
Karbala, battle of, 126
Karbasi, Atefeh, 273
Karimi-Hakak, Mahmood, 55
Kariz Theater Group (*Gorooh-e te'atr-e kariz*), 260; *Amsterdam* performance, 263, *264*; *Narges* performance, 261–62, 263, *265*
Kashani, Sohrab: and Abanbar Gallery, 97, 346n203; and Bilal's *A Call* performance, 371n94; *The Other Apartment* (with Rubin), *289*, 290–91; and Puriya Mehr's *My Own Privacy Policy* exhibition, 188; Sazmanab studio, 287–88
Kazemi, Abbas, 24
Kazemi, Babak, 188
Kazemi, Hossein, 214, 367n4
Keivani Architects, Orsi Khaneh, 375n170
Keshavarz Boulevard (formerly Elizabeth), Tehran, 87
Keshmirshekan, Hamid, 8
Kester, Grant, 238
Ketab-e jom'eh (magazine), 334n17
Khaju Bridge, Isfahan, 275
Khaledi, Slamak, 337n58
khaleh ro-ro (Auntie Ro-ro) performances, 362n131
Khalili, Nader, 136, 140–41; *Ceramic Houses and Earth Architecture*, 351n99; *Emergency Sandbag Shelter and Eco-Village*, 351n99; *Racing Alone* (*Tanha Daveedan*), 135, 351n99; *Sidewalks on the Moon*, 351n99
Khamenehzadeh, Tooraj, 89–91, 309
Khamenei, Ayatollah, 258
Khan, Naiza, 89; *Metro Beheshti* (*Heavenly Metro*), 159; *Who Makes the Boundary? (Cheh kasi marzha ra ta'een mikonad?)*, 159–60, *160*
Khas, Atefeh, 348n48
Khatami, Hojjat al-Islam Sayyed Mohammad, 14, 66, 74, 80, 150, 217
Khazaeli-Parsa, Pouya, 135–37, *136*
Khodashenas, Mohammad, 77, *78*, 178
Khodorkovsky, Len, 206
Khomeini, Ayatollah Ruhollah, 20, 42, 162, 215, 258
Khoramroodi, Shokoofeh, 99
Khorasan Blues (music band), 53–54
Khorsand Tower (Checker Box Office Complex), 375n170
khosoolati economy, 25, 82, 139, 297
Khosravi, Shahram, 24, 296
Khosravi-Noori, Behzad, 151
Khosroshahi, Maryam, 188
Khosroshahi, Taraneh, 254
Khozoie, Saba, 13, 52
Khrushchev, Nikita, 7, 87
Kiaee, Saeed, 194
Kiarostami, Abbas, 61, 77, 183, 200
Kiesewalter, Georgy, 111
Kieślowski, Krzysztof, 4, 344n167
Kikuo, Saito, 347n1
Killing Mad Dogs/Sag koshi (film), 52
Kimiavi, Parviz, 107–8
Kindergarten (artistic collective), 65–66, 340n101
Kiosk (music band), 50–52
Kirsanova, Daria, 233–34
kissing, 202, 203, *203*, 256–57
kitchen utensil factories, as art venues, 77–79, *79*
kitsch (*mobtazal*), 222–24
Kleiman, Molly, 371n94
Knížák, Milan, *Aktual Walk—Demonstration for All Senses*, 33
kolangi. *See* abandoned and dilapidated buildings
kommunalka (communal apartment, Soviet Union), 7
Konesh-e Mo'aser/Contemporary Interaction (theater group), 82
Koocheh (YouTube channel), 353n134
kooshk (freestanding pavilions), 91
Kooshk Art Residency, Tehran, 89–91, *90*, 301
Kötter, Daniel, 189, 382n42
Kouhestani, Maryam, 381n34
Kovács, András, 344n167
Kowsari, Abbas, 165
Kracauer, Sigfried, 245

Kreuger, Anders, 123–24
Kundera, Milan, *L'Insoutenable légèreté de l'être* (*The Unbearable Lightness of Being*), 344n167
Kurdish community, 190
Kuye Daneshgah Disaster (*Fajaye' kooy-e daneshgah*), 312
Kwon, Miwon, 73, 211

Labor and Art (*Kar va honar*; magazine), 334n17
Laborer's Path (*Rah e kargar*), 38
LACMA, 34
Lahijan Tea factory, 77, *78*, 101–2
Laleh Park (formerly Farah), Tehran, 88, 206
Lalehzar district, Tehran, 282–83
land grabbing/ingestion (*zaminkhari*), 139
Langton, Bacil, *105*
the laughing revolution (*al-thawra al-dahika*), 197
Lavasan, 142, 143–46
Lavasan News, 143
Lavasan Villa, 144, *145*
Lavin, Sylvia, *Kissing Architecture*, 256
Lefebvre, Henri, 23–24, 25, 108, 153–54, 267, 302; *The Production of Space*, 23, 288
leftover urban spaces: generation of, 164; graffiti art in water canals, *174*, 174–75; Razavipour's and Fotouhi's *Census*, 165–67, *166*, 357n52; Razavipour's and Fotouhi's *Orange on Gray*, 167–68, *168*; Tehran Carnival's *Binoculars*, *196*, 196–97; as theater venues, 168–73, *171*, *173*. *See also* abandoned and dilapidated buildings
Leila (film), 276–77
Lemmon, Jack, 238
Lew, Jeffrey, 58
The Limited Access Festival (*Jashnvareh dastresi-e mahdood*), 226
Lippard, Lucy, *Six Years*, 10
lived space, as concept, 24
Living Theater, 125
The Lizard/Marmoolak (film), 198
Loos, Adolph, 209, 276
loose covertness, as concept, 6–7, 26
luxury (*lagjery*) villas and apartments, 143–46, *145*, 167

MacLaine, Shirley, 238
Madani, Kaveh, 146
Madjdabadi, Habibeh, The House of 40 Knots (with Mashhadimirza), 375n170
Magritte, René, *The Healer*, 206
Mahdavi, Sohrab, 119
Maher, Hossein, 108
Mahnia, Elmira, 195
Mahzoon, Negin, 89–91, 309
maintenance art, 255
Majara Residence, Hormuz, 140–42
Majd, Hooman, 330n88
Majma' dar al-sanaye' (Assembly of the House of Crafts), 366–67n1
Makarevich, Igor, 111
makeshift spaces (*fazaha-ye jaygozin*), 19
Maktabi, Mahmoud, 114–15, 298; *I'm Not Political* (*Man siyasi nistam*), *115*, 115–16
Malcolm, Napier, *Five Years in a Persian Town*, *246*
male gaze, 196
Malik, Suhail, 172
Malkki, Liisa, 30
Mandaean community, 46–47
manipulation in urban spaces (*dast kari dar fazahay-e shahri*), 152
A Man of Integrity/Lerd (film), 292
Manuscripts Don't Burn (film), 292
Marcuse, Herbert, 110
marginalized communities, 46–52, 190, 335n37, 336n53
market-driven art, 10, 58, 159, 241, 255–56, 293, 296–97, 301
Markov, Nikolai, 50, 162, 242
Martin, Jean-Hubert, *Carambolages* exhibition, 34
Martin, Reinhold, 267
Martyrs Foundation (*Bonyad-e shahid*), 148, *216*
Martyrs' Museum, Tehran, 216, *216*
Marxism and communism, 37, 143, 162, 176, 243, 307, 334n17
Maryland Historical Society, 34
Mashalak Forest, *115*, 115–16

Mashhad, 58–59
Mashhadimirza, Alireza, The House of 40 Knots (with Madjdabadi), 375n170
Maskoob, Shahrokh, *Mourning for Siavash* (*Soog-e siavash*), 235
Massey, Doreen, 23
Massimo Maffies (engineering firm), 274
Matinfar, Salman, 96–97, 346n203
Matisse, Henri, *The Red Studio*, 1
Matta-Clark, Gordon, 58
Mattress Factory Museum, Pittsburgh, 290
Mazzotta, Matthew, 300
McDowell, Linda, 23
MCIG (Ministry of Culture and Islamic Guidance; *Vezarat-e farhang va ershad-e eslami*): "Adhan to Adhan" (*az azan ta azan*) program, 246; art exhibition regulations, 55, 56, 61, 64–65, 66, 68, 76–77, 98–99, 165, 222, 238, 252, 338n73; artist resistance to collaborations with, 161–62, 314–15; art teacher licensure, 2; establishment, 42; and Fajr Festivals, 161, 170, 219; fluctuating guidelines, 6; Islamicization "program," 314, 384n87; music regulations, 51, 221; noninterventionist approach to independent institutions, 29; performance art regulations, 120, 218; theater regulations, 4, 43, 80, 84, 102, 127, 184
Mead, Margaret, 315
meandering in the city (*parseh zani dar shahr*), 176, 178–83, *181*, *182*, 183
Meftahi, Ida, 198
Mehdizadeh-Jafari, Hooman, *Little Airborne* (*Havadar-e koochak*), 138, *138*
Mehrjui, Driush, 276–77
Mehrnameh (journal), 306
Melehi, Mohammed, 347n13
Memarikahneh (social media platform), 270
memory: collective, 3, 184, 192; and forgetting, 39–40, 192, 199, 205; and nostalgia, 58, 59, 202, 203, 260; and trauma, 40, 114, 236; will to remember, as concept, 39
men: gender segregation, 26, 43, 72, 82, 126, 128, 186–87; male gaze, 196; meandering in the city, 178, 179. *See also* women
Merce Cunningham Dance Company, 245
Mesbah Yazdi, Muhammad Taqi, 42
MesoCity Tehran Workshop: Art, Ecology & the City, 17
Mess Atelier, Tehran, 100
Metro Beheshti (*Heavenly Metro*) station, 159
Miessen, Markus, 23
Mimic Theater Group, 83. *See also* Av Theater Group
Ministry of Cultural Heritage, Tourism, and Handicraft (formerly Organization for Cultural Heritage), 77, 89, 120
Ministry of Culture and Islamic Guidance. *See* MCIG
Ministry of Endowments and Charitable Works, 148
minority spaces, 46–52, *48*, *49*, *50*, *51*, 336n53
Mirehsan, Ahmad, *Lahijan with Bitter Tea*, 77
mirror work (*ayeneh kari*): and heterotopia concept, 122; sculptures, 20–22, *21*, *22*
Mir Tahmasb, Mojtaba, 113
Mirzoeff, Nicholas, 27
Mitchell, W. J. T., 258
Miyazaki, Hirokazu, 296
Mlynárčik, Alex, 112, 118
Mobed, Amir, 309; *Come Caress Me* (*Bia navazesham kon*), 234, 304; *Disformission* (*Kajidan*), *307*, 307–8; *The Killing* (*Keshtzar* or *Field*), 304–6, *306*; "Opening," 15–16, *16*, 304
mobile art: as concept, 173; exhibitions in buses, 187–90, *188*; meandering in the city, 176, 178–80, *181*, *182*, *183*, 222; portable graffiti art, 175–76, *177*; theater performances in taxicabs, 184–86, *185*, *187*
Modern Art Gallery (*Honar-e jadid*), Tehran, 338n74
Mohajer, Mehran, 254, 337n67
Mohammadi, Asghar, 367n4
Mohammadi-Nameghi, Khadije, 188

Mohammad Reza Shah Pahlavi, 1, 41, 59, 87, 107, 161, 172, 192, 215
Mohasses, Ardeshir, 198
Mohasses, Bahman, 148
Mohebbi, Sohrab, 100–101, 337n58; *Hotel Theory Reader*, 101
Mohri, Babak, 83, 127, 132. *See also* Av Theater Group
Mohsen Gallery, Tehran: *Displacement* (*Jabejaie*) installation, 308; establishment and location, 301, 302; *Kitchen* (*Ashpazkhuneh*) exhibition, 304; Mobed's *Disformission* performance, *307*, 307–8; Mobed's *The Killing* performance, 304–6, *306*; *Mohsen Projects* (*Projeha-ye Mohsen*) exhibition, 303–4, *305*; Pelak Project, 308–9; *Scaffolding* (*Darbast*) initiative, 310, 383–84n73; Tehran Carnival's installation, 195
Mojeh No/New Wave (theater group), 82
Moller house, Vienna, 275
Momayez, Morteza, 43, 215
moorcheh dareh (There Are Aunts) performances, 362n131
Moosa Panah, Ali, 144
morality police. *See* censorship; MCIG
Moridi, Mohammad Reza, 241, 381n34
Mortazavi, Houman: influences on, 61–62; *Life Accessories* (*Abzar-e zendegi*) exhibition, 61, 62–65, *63*, *64*; *Parallel* (*Movazi*) project, 156, *157*; Zirpelleh exhibition space, 91–93, *92*, 310; *zirtakhti* collection, 8, *9*, 20
Mosaddeqh, Mohammad, 37
Mostaghel/Independent (theater group), 82
motrebi (light music on streets and social events), 11
mountain grabbing/ingestion (*kooh khari*), 139
mountains: Golnari's *Dream of Bam* sculpture, 113–14, *114*; luxury villas in, 143–46, *145*; Mount Damavand in environmental discourse, 137–38, *138*, 139; as theater venues, 128, *134*; Wilson's *KA MOUNTAIN AND GUARDenia TERRACE* performance, *104*, 104–7
Mount Damavand, 137–38, *138*, 139, 142
mourning and grief, 75, 216, 234–36, 247–49
Mousavi, Amir, 371n94
Mousavi, Mir Hossein, 76, 202, 230–33
movement. *See* choreography; mobile art
Mozayyeni, Manouchehr, 374n150
Muharram religious ceremonies, 11–12, 191–92, 245–46
Mulvey, Laura, "Visual Pleasure and Narrative Cinema," 196
mural paintings: and interactivity, 13; political criticism, 151, *151*; state-sponsored, 148–49, 150. *See also* graffiti art
Museum of Contemporary Art, Isfahan, Seighali's *Ma* commemorative tokens, 207, *208*
music: aboveground venues, 310, 383–84n73; censored Western, 13, 202; experimental performance label, 221; in minority spaces, 49–51, *51*; regulation of, 51, 52, 53, 54, 221, 335n32; religious devotional, 255; "underground," as concept, 4

Nabizadeh, Mohsen, 56
Nabshi Center, Tehran, 94–96, *96*; *Red Paper* (*Kaghaz-e sorkh*) exhibition, 302
Nadalian, Ahmad, 112–13, 115, 349n42, 381n34
Nafar Abad, Tehran, 300, *300*
Naficy, Hamid, 200
Nafisi, Azar, *Reading Lolita in Tehran*, 3
Nafisi, Golrokh, *Displacement* (*Jabejaie*; with Hamedani), 308
Najafi Ardabili, Masoud, 71
Najl-Raheem, Abdol Rahman, 250–51
Najmabadi, Kaveh, 286
nakhl (in Muharram commemoration ritual), 245, *246*
Nami, Gholamhossein, 107, 215
Namjoo, Mohsen, 53, 54
Nancy, Jean-Luc, 10
naqqali (storytelling), 11
Narges Siah (Black Narcissus) Theater Group: *The Blacks: A Clown Show*

performance, *70*, 70–72, 341–42n125; disbanded, 72; Grotowski's influence on, 69–70
Narin, Sandy, 310
narration-based curatorial tactics, 217
Naser, Abdollah, 231
Naser al-din Shah, 36
Nasr, Seyyed Ali, 282
Nasr Theater, Tehran, 282–83
Nassiri, Mehdi, 126, 326n42
Nassiri, Sassan, 59–60, 67–68; *Project 71/92* collaborative exhibition, 59–60
National Endowment for the Arts (NEA), 311
natural sites. *See* escapism and escapist sites
Nature Art Variations (exhibition), 114–15
Nature Institute (*Mo'asseseh Tabi'at*), 128
Navaie (short film), 61
Nazi Germany, 245
NEA (National Endowment for the Arts), 311
negar khaneh (house of embellishments), 56
negative space, 258–59
negotiation strategies, 159–60, 220–24
Neo-Dadaism, 13, 327n44
neoliberalism, homegrown, 25
Neshat, Shirin, *Women of Allah*, 293
new media art (*honar-e neo media*), emergence in Iran, 14
New Media Society, Tehran, 100, 374n139
news and newspapers, censorship of, 73, 74, 228–29, 312
New Theater movement, 104
New York Times, 12
Next Office (architectural firm), 271, *272*
Neyssari, Afarin, 286
Niavaran Cultural Center (*Farhangsaray-e Niavaran*), 161
Nikzar, Niloofar, 300
Nochlin, Linda, 203; *Women Artists* exhibition, 34
Nodjumi, Nicky, 42
Noebashari, Nazila, 221–22, 247, 371n94
Noir Art Group (*Gorooh-e honari-e noir*): brave theater concept, 172–73; establishment and vision, 168–69; *Horses at the Window* performances, 170–72, *171*, *173*; *This Is Not an Apple* performance, 170, *171*
No One Knows about Persian Cats/Kasi az gorbehay-e Irani khabar nadareh (film), 53, 79
Nooshin, Laudan, 294, 295, 380n12
Nora, Pierre, 39
Nostalghia (film), 16–17
nostalgia, 58, 59, 202, 203, 260
nudity, 42, 43, 44–45, *45*, *46*, 215, 237, 362n131
Nyia Theater Group, *81*, 81–82, 133, *134*

object-oriented art, as category, 8
Occupy Movement, 6, 258, 311
Ocula Magazine, 294
Odin Theater (*te'atr-e Odin*), 125, 169
Office of the Expansion of Cultural Spaces of the Tehran municipality (*Sherkat-e tose'eh fazahay-e farhangi-e shahrdari-e Tehran*), 149
Ofogh (TV channel), 145–46
O Gallery, Tehran, Taghizadeh's *Open Wiring* exhibition, 16–17
O-Hum (music band), 49–50, 51, *51*, 52
oil industry, 60–61
Olszewska, Zuzanna, 294, 295
Omar Khayyam, 293
112 Workshop, New York City, 58, 288
127 (music band), 49, 53, 221, 337n58
One Thousand and One Nights, 241–42
Open Palm/Hand (*Panjeh baz*), 115, 349nn48–49
oppositional art (*honar-e moghavemati*), as category, 8, 18
Organization for Islamic Propagation (*Sazman-e tablighat-e eslami*), 148
Organization for Mobilization of the Oppressed (*Basij-e mahalli*), 148
Orsi Khaneh, 375n170
Oslo Opera House, 209
Ossouli, Farah: art exhibitions, 47, *48*; and censorship, 44–45, 47, 336n40; on *Zan-e ruz* cover, 44–45, *45*, *46*
Ossouli, Shahrazad, 47

Ostrovsky, Nikolai, *How the Steel Was Tempered*, 38
outdoor living rooms, 300, *300*, 382n42
Owj Art and Communication Organization (*Sazman-e honari resaneh-ie Owj*), 152

Pac-Man imagery, 227–28, *228*
Pahlavi era, 37, 41, 46, 260–61, 282
Pakdel, Hossein, 70
Pakhomov, Alexei Fedorovich, 39
Pallasmaa, Johani, *The Eyes of the Skin*, 264
Pallett (music band), 310
Panahgah (bomb shelter) Gallery, Nabshi Center, 94–96, *96*
Panahi, Jafar, 183
Panahiha, Pantea, 71
panopticonism, 112
Parastooie, Parviz, 283
paratheater, 125
Parc de la Villette, Paris, 209
Parham, Surena, 335n27
Parkingallery, Tehran, 225–28, *226*, *228*. *See also* New Media Society
participation, audience, 21, 84, 104, 127, 132, 200–204, 218, 262, 305–6
participatory art (*honar-e mosharekati*), 14, 141, 142
participatory budgeting, 93, 309–10
Partovi, Shirin, 252
Parvizi, Mohammad, 308–9; *Come Closer, Closer, Closer Than This?* (*Nazdiktar bia, nazdiktar, nazdiktar az in?*), 249–52, *251*
passersby, 157, 166, 187–88, 189, 190, 193–94, 200–201, 209
passio (patio/greenhouse): Mobed's *Disformission* performance, *307*, 307–8; Rasti's installation at Mohsen, 303–4
passion plays (*ta'ziyeh*), 11–12, 190–91, 326n42, 361n131
Pastoo, Nabshi Center, 96
patogh (hangout) culture, 241
Pazooki, Abdolhamid, 242–43, *243*
pears (religious offering), 157–58
Pejman, Hamidreza, 281, 282
Pejman Foundation for the Arts, *280*, 280–82, 377n192
Pellekan, Nabshi Center, 96
Penn, Richard, *No Signal, Tehran*, 27–28
People's Mujahedin Organization (*Mojahedin-e-Khalq*), 102
performance art (*honar-e ejra'ie*): in abandoned buildings, 61; audience participation, 104, 218, 305–6; and curated choreography, 247–49, *248*, 255–56, *257*; in deserts, 119, *120*; in forests, *115*, 115–16; in mountains, *104*, 104–7; postrevolutionary emergence in Iran, 217–18; in public cafés, 242–44, *243*; regulation of, 120, 218; in spatially-reconfigured galleries, 228–33, *231*; *ta'ziyeh* passion plays, 11–12, 190–91, 326n42, 361n131. *See also* streets and roadsides; theater
Performance Supervision Committee (*Comite-ye nezarat bar namayesh*), 43
Persbook (collaborative art project), 118–21
Persian Wildlife Heritage Foundation, 139
Pesyani, Atila, 62
photography: and memory, 1, 3, 323–24n7; regulated instruction of, 337–38n67; of religious performances, 191, *191*
Pilaram, Faramarz, 13, 215
pincer-movement-like acts (*ejray-e shebh-e gazanbori*), 159
Pirouzram, Pouya, 81, 133
place *vs.* space, 220
plateaus, 81
Platform 28, Abanbar Gallery, 96–98, *97*, *98*; *The Recycling of Socialism* event series, 98
playfulness and humor, 195–202, 304
plaza fever (*tab-e plaza*), 210
plop art (*honar-e teleppi*), 151
Plyushteva, Anna, 25
Polish experimental theater, 81, 83, 127, 133, 344n167. *See also* Grotowski, Jerzy
political art (*honar-e syasi*), direct *vs.* subtle approaches, 15–18. *See also* protest art
pollution, 60–61, 68–69, 340–41n110, 381n34
polyphony, 128

poor theater (*te'atr-e bichiz*), 69–70, 71
Pourassad, Alireza, 337n58
Pourazari, Hamid, 247, 260, 371n94
Pourhang-Ramezani, Jaleh, 42
Pournasr, Keivan, 149–50, *150*, 221
predatory aestheticization, 26, 34, 103, 208, 212. *See also* aggressive mimicry
preservation and renovation, 277–83, *279*, *280*, *281*
prisoners, political, 139, 161, 162, 229, 235, 250, 286, 306–7
prisons and prison-like spaces: Bakhshi's *Solo Show* performance, 228–30; Evin, 182, 188; Golnari's *Feast* installation, 234–36, *236*; Qasr Prison, 161–62; Sirizi's *Total Monument* project, 161–62, *163*
private art (*khosoosi*): as category, 6; private assembly (*mahfel-e khosoosi*) model, 237–41
private-public dichotomy, 3–5, 6–7, 189–90, 226–28, 260, 297, 303
privatization, 25, 82–83, 102, 310, 383n70
profane *vs.* sacred, 20–21
propaganda: artist appropriation of, 223–24, 228; in curatorial practices, 215–17, *216*; emotional control through, 19; Fajr Visual Arts Festival, 161; and negative space, 258–59; post-war thematic shift, 148–49; state choreography of shuffling masses, 245–46; state institutions for, 148, 150, 151–52; in state's aggressive mimicry strategy, 102; state-sponsored *ta'ziyeh* performances, 190–91
protest (*e'teraz*): of elections, 252–53 (*See also* Green Movement); environmental, 107, 138–39; student, 72–73, 312; women's resistance, 299
protest, air of (*bar-e e'terazi*), 206
protest art (*honar-e e'terazi*): as category, 18; designation as, 21, 206; and protest as art, 107–8, 299
public art (*omumi*): as category, 6; public assembly (*patogh*) model, 241–44; state co-opting of, 161, 191, 207–8, 210–12, 215–17, 219. *See also* architecture; curatorial practices; ephemeral art
public-private dichotomy, 3–5, 6–7, 189–90, 226–28, 260, 297, 303
Public Property Bureau (*Edareh koll-e amaken*), 87, 98–99
publics, multiple, 227
Puriya Mehr, Elham, 88; *I Am Here* (*Man inja hastam*; with Jamshidi), *121*, 121–24, *122*, *125*; *My Own Privacy Policy* (*Siyasat-e harim-e shakhsi-e man*) exhibition, 187, *188*, 188–90

Qajar era, 156–57, 261, 278, 366–67n1
qanat (underground water network), 17
Qasr Museum (*Bagh-e moozeh Qasr*), 161–62, 242–44, *243*
Qasr Prison, 161–62
Qur'an, 15, 207, 230
Qurrat al-'Ayn, 157

Rafii, Ali, 86
Rafsanjani, Ali Akbar Hashemi, 56, 57, 217
Raisi, Ebrahim, 6
Ramadan, 149, 246
Rancière, Jacques, 156, 209, 233
Rashidzadeh, Kaveh, 299–300
Rasht 29 Art Club, Tehran, 93, 215
Rasoulof, Ehsan: Annual Digital Art Exhibition (TADAEX), 383–84n73; and Kooshk Art Residency, 89, 301; and Nabshi, 94, 302; on privatization, 310, 383n70; sponsorship of alternative art, 301, 309. *See also* Mohsen Gallery, Tehran
Rasoulof, Jalal, 301
Rasoulof, Mohammad, 292–93
Rasti, Aliyar, 371n94
Rauch, Martin, 135
Ravanbakhsh, Saeed, 242–43, *243*
"raw" spaces, as concept, 58
Raymond, Richard, 350n79
Razavipour, Neda, 164–65, 293; *Alice in the City* exhibition, 234, *235*; *Census* (with Fotouhi), 165–67, *166*, 357n52; *Orange on Gray: Homage to Mark Rothko* (*Narenji rooy-e Khakestari*; with Fotouhi), 167–68, *168*
readymade work (*hazer o amadeh*), 77

reconstruction era (*doran-e sazandegi*), 56–57
The Red Artery (*Rag-e sorkh*), 119, *120*
Reddy, William, 19
religion and religious artistic expression: and architecture, 144–45, 209; *ayeneh kari*, 20; devotional music, 255; in interventionist art, 157–58; processions, 245–46, *246*; Qur'an references, 15, 207, 230; sacred *vs.* profane, 20–21; and Saqqakhaneh group, 176–78; state co-opting of, 191, 207, 245–46; *ta'ziyeh*, 11–12, 190–91, 326n42, 361n131
religious minorities, 46–52, 335n37, 336n53
remote sites. *See* escapism and escapist sites
Rendell, Jane, 23, 26, 329n72
renovation and preservation, 277–83, *279*, *280*, *281*
revolutionary art (*honar-e enghelabi*), as category, 18, 215
Revolutionary Guard(s), 38, 42, 43, 152, 186, 200
Reyhani, Sara, 371n94
Rezaie, Yousef, *Project 71/92* collaborative exhibition, 59–60
Rezaie Rad, Mohammad, 79–80, 254; *Dream of Silent Saints* (*Ro'yay-e taheregan-e khamoosh*), 80; *Semiotics of Censorship and the Silence of Words* (*Neshaneh shenasi-e sansoor va sokoot-e sokhan*), 80
Reza Shah Pahlavi, 37, 162, 190, 362n131
rhythmanalysis (*zarbahangkavi*), 153–54
rhythmic movements (*harakat-e mowzoon*), 217
Richard, Thomas, *At Work with Grotowski on Physical Actions*, 125–26
Richter, Gerhard, 218; *Atlas*, 287
Ricoeur, Paul, *What Makes Us Think?* (with Changeux), 250
Riefenstahl, Leni, 245
Riley, Terry, *Persian Surgery Dervishes*, 255
ritual photography (*akkasi-e a'yini*), 191
rituals, religious. *See* religion and religious artistic expression
The River Still Has Fish/Roodkhaneh hanooz mahi darad (documentary), 113
roadsides. *See* streets and roadsides
Rogoff, Irit, 74
Roham, Masoud, 357n51
Roiter, Andrei, 66, 340n101
Rokhdad-e tazeh mostanad (New Documentary Event), 141–42
Roma Tre University, 169
Rooberoo Building (*Emarat-e rooberoo*), Tehran, 93–94, *95*
rooftops: Ardakani's *White Cubes* installation, 201–4, *203*; Babajanians's installation at Mohsen, 304; as safe spaces, 202
roohowzi ("over the pool" layman entertainment) performances, 11, 361–62n131
Rose, Gillian, 23
Rothko, Mark, 167
Rouhani, Hassan, 25
Roy, Ananya, 25
Rozak, Theodore, 110, 348n26
Rubin, Jon, *The Other Apartment* (with Kashani), *289*, 290–91
Rudafshan Cave, *130*, 130–31

Saba, Roxana, 215
Saber, Mehran, 221–22
Sabz (Green) Gallery, Tehran, 360n109
Sacred Defense Garden and Museum, Tehran, 216–17
sacred *vs.* profane, 20–21
Sadeghi, Ali Akbar, 360n109
Sadighi, Abolhassan, Ferdowsi statue, 214
Sadr, Hamid Reza, 143
Safaie, Nastaran: *Enghelab-Azadi/Revolution-Freedom*, 180; *High Heels* (*Revayathay-e kaf-e khiaban*), 179–80, 222; *In Tehran*, 180, *181*, *182*
Safaie, Sadegh: *And Now Women!* (*Va inak zan!*), 217–18; *The Road Is Under Construction* (*Jaddeh dar dast-e ta'meer ast*), 218
Safavid era, 20, 32, 245
safe (team/*teemi*) houses, 37–38, 39–40, *40*, *41*
Saffari, Bijan, 261
Said, Edward, *Orientalism*, 293
Sajjad, Nadia, 119, *120*

Salam (newspaper), 312
sale of density (*foroosh-e tarakom*), 164
Salimy, Parham. *See* Ghalamdar
Samari, Leyla, 56
Sami-Azar, Alireza, 14, 156, 217, 218
Sandbag Shelters, Ahvaz, 140–41
Sands, Bobby, 87
Sani ol-Molk, 366–67n1
Sapir Hospital, Tehran, 335n37
Saqqakhaneh group, 176–78, 334n15
Sardar Afkhami, Ali, 70
Sarmast, Sardar, 337n58
Satan worship (*sheytan parasti*), 175, 194
satire, political, 198
Sazmanab, Tehran, 287–88
Schechner, Richard, 104, 169
Scheiwiller, Staci Gem, 256
Schlamminger, Karl, 210–11
Schönberger, Sonya, 77
Schumann, Peter, 155
Schüssler Fiorenza, Elisabeth, 330–31n88
Scott, Felicity, 110
sculpture: as banned medium, 2, 43; in basements, 235, *236*; censored, 21–22, *22*, 148, 206; mirror work (*ayeneh kari*), 20–22, *21*, *22*; in mountains, 113–14, *114*; state-sponsored, 149–50, *150*, 151, 207; Tehran biennials, 219
Sedgwick, Eve, 265
Sehgal, Tino, 245
self-censorship, 27, 32, 72, 180, 204, 238, 240
sensible (*mahsoos*), as term, 156
Serial Murders (Chain Murders of Iran), 73, 115, 342n133
Serra, Richard, *Tilted Arc*, 73, 365n192
Setad (Executive Headquarters of Imam's Directive), 285, 377n206
Severi, Hamid, 29, 123
sexual morality, 43, 215, 217, 362n131. *See also* kissing
Seyed Emami, Kavous, 139
Seyghali, Shahin, *Who Are We?* (*Ma keesteem?*), 204–8, *205*, *207*, *208*
Seyhoun Gallery, Tehran, 55, 269
shabnamehs (night letters), 36–37
Shafiabadi, Zahra, 348n48
Shafieezadeh, Peyman, *Negative Positive Space* (*Fazay-e manfi mosbat*), 257–59, *259*
Shahamipour, Shervin, 337n58
Shahbazyar, Ali, 71
Shahnameh-khani (reading of verses of the *Shahnameh*), 11
Shahrokni, Nazanin, 26
Shahroudy Farmanfarmaian, Monir, 20, 338n74, 367n4
Shahrzad (TV series), 260
Shahsavarani, Farideh, *I Wrote, You Read (Neveshtam, khandi)* exhibition, 73–76, *75*, 101
Shahvagh, Changiz, 367n4
Shakeri Shemirani, Ali, *280*, 281–82, 283
Shakespeare, William: *Hamlet*, 184, 185, 186; *Othello*, 185; *The Taming of the Shrew*, 185; *Titus Andronicus*, 182
Shaloui, Mahmoud, 219
Shamlou, Ahmad, 71, 334n17
Sharafjahan, Rozita, 5, 55, 56, 222, 227, 253, 293. *See also* Azad Art Gallery
Sharbaf, Shahram, 49–50, 52
Shargh Newspaper, 192
Sharifi-Ha House, Tehran, 271, *272*
Shato/Chateau (theater group), 82
Shaygan, Dariush: *Afsoon-e zendegi-e jadid* (*The chaos of modern life*), 180; *Dar jostejooy-e fazay-e gomshodeh* (*In search of the lost space*), 180
Sheikh Lotf Allah Mosque, 157, 158
Sheshjavani, Hamidreza, 5
Shevtsova, Maria, 106
Shiite religious artistic expression: *ayeneh kari* in shrines, 20; and battle of Karbala, 126; processions, 245–46, *246*; and Saqqakhaneh group, 176–78; *ta'ziyeh* passion plays, 11–12
Shiraz Festival of Arts: end of, 215; and Grotowski, 11, 125, 261; introduction of choreography in art, 245; introduction of time-based art forms, 13; mentioned, 93; as opportunity to engage in remote natural sites, 104, 108; and Schumann, 155; and *ta'ziyeh*, 11–12; Wilson's *KA MOUNTAIN AND*

Shiraz Festival of Arts (*continued*)
GUARDenia TERRACE performance, *104*, 104–7
Shirin Art Gallery, Tehran, Parvizi's *Come Closer, Closer, Closer Than This?* performance, 249–52, *251*
Shishegaran, Koorosh, *honar-e posti*, 13
Shiva, Ghobad, 367n4
Sholette, Gregory, 32, 312
showroom, as term, 236–37
shrines (*imamzadeh*), 20
Shub, Esfir, 344n167
Shushtar New Town, 382–83n52
siahmashgh (calligraphic practice), 39, 178
Siamdoust, Nahid, 4
Sianie, Khosrow, 344n167
Siin Gallery, Tehran, Mobed's "Opening" performance, 15–16, *16*, 304
Silk Road Gallery, Tehran, 66
Simmel, Georg, "Metropolis and Mental Life," 109
Sinai, Khosrow, 44, 47, 192
Sinclair, Cameron, 135
Siosepol Bridge, Isfahan, 275
Sirizi, Homayoun, 160–61, 285–87; *Total Monument* (*Mojassameh kamel*), 161–62, *163*; *U-Turn* (*Dorbargardan*), *284*, 285
Sitar, Sergei, 111
site-oriented art (*honar-e makan mehvar*), as concept, 14, 19, 73
site-specific art (*honar-e makan vijeh*), as concept, 19, 73
Situationist International group, 176
slacktivism (*koneshgari-e zir lahafi*), 313
Snøhetta (architectural firm), 209
Sobhani, Arash, 50–51, 52
social art (*honar-e ejtema'yi*), as category, 18
social banditry, as concept, 297
social space, as concept, 288
Soheili, Hamid, 62
Soja, Edward, 23
Sokurov, Alexander, 262
Soleimani, Qasem, 153, 258
Solnit, Rebecca, 178
Sontag, Susan, *Regarding the Pain of Others*, 251
Soviet and Eastern Bloc experience and art: escapism, 111–12; fallout shelters, 143; *kommunalka* exhibitions, 7; propaganda, 223, 224; resonance with Iranian artists and resistance groups, 16–17, 38–39, 54, 65, 344n167; use of abandoned buildings, 65–66
Soviet Collective Actions Group (*Kollektivnye Deistvia*), 111
space *vs.* place, 220
Spatial Agency: Other Ways of Doing Architecture, 282
spatial poetry (*she'r-e fazaie*), 169
spatial practices. *See* critical spatial practice, as concept
spatial types. *See specific sites (e.g. abandoned and dilapidated buildings, buses, caves, etc.)*
Spiridonoff, Catherine, 209; Ave Gallery and Showroom, 268, *268*, 269
Spitzweg, Carl, *The Poor Poet*, 207
Staal, Jonas, 301
stair alcoves (*zirpelleh*), as art venues, 91–93, *92*
Stalker (film), 358n63
Stalker collective, 169, 358n63
Steward, Theresa Parvin, 294, 295
Stewart, Kathleen, 87
St. Nicholas Russian Orthodox Church, *50*, 50–51, *51*
Stoller, Paul, 28
strangeness, 233
stream of consciousness, 250
streets and roadsides: Fayyazi's and Dashti's *Roadkill*, 155–56; Hosseini's *Women in Red* performance, 192–94, *193*, 298; Mortazavi's *Parallel* project, 156, *157*; Nami's *Knot*, 154, *155*; women meandering in the city, 179–83, *181*, *182*, *183*. *See also* buses; taxicabs
Street Theater (*te'atr-e khiabani*), 184
Struth, Thomas, 283
student protests, 72–73, 312
Sufis, 32, 104, 106
supreme leader (*velayat-e faqih*), 41–42

surveillance. *See* censorship
Survival Condo Project, Kansas, 142
suspended architecture (*me'mari-e ta'lighi*), 260
sustainable architecture, 134–37, 142
Suyker, Jeremy, *x*, 1, 3
Szabó, István, 344n167

Tabataba, Jazeh, 338n74
Tabatabaie, Shahab, 231
Tabi'at Pedestrian Bridge (*Pol-e Tabi'at*), 274–75, *276*, 376nn176–77
TADAEX (Annual Digital Art Exhibition), 383–84n73
Taghaboni, Alireza, 273, *274*; Sharifi-Ha House, 271, *272*
Taghavi Neja, Seyyed Mojtaba, 206
Taghizadeh, Jinoos: on closet art, 8; environmental initiatives, 352n109; at Mobed's *The Killing* performance, 305; *Oblation* (*Nazr*), 157–59, *158*; *Open Wiring* (*Sim-keshi-e roo kar*) exhibition, 16–17; Qurrat al-'Ayn project proposal, 156–57; *Titus Andronicus*, 181–83, *183*
Taheri, Hamed, 69, 70, 71
Tanavoli, Parviz, 13, 214–15, 367n4; *Farhad and the Deer (Farhad o Ahoo)*, 214
Tantalos Theater, 326n42; *Medea* performance, 125–26
Tarkhani, Nikoo, 241
Tarkovsky, Andrei, 4, 16–17, 262, 344n167, 358n63
Taslimi, Susan, 47
Tasnim News, 209
Tavazoni Zadeh, Hossein, 259–66; *Amsterdam*, 263, *264*; *Narges* (*Narcissus*), 261–62, 263, *265*
Taxi (film), 183–84
taxicabs: Ganjeh's *Unpermitted Whispers* performance, 184–86, *185*, *187*; as safe spaces, 183, 186
ta'ziyeh passion plays, 11–12, 190–91, 326n42, 361n131
tea factories, as art venues, 77, *78*, 101–2
team houses (*khanehay-e teemi*), 37–38, 39–40, *40*, *41*
Tehran Avenue (online art project), 119
Tehran biennials and triennials, 204–5, 215, 217, 219
Tehran Carnival: *Binoculars* (*Doorbeen*), *196*, 196–97; fun and humor, 195, 199–200; *Private Ocean* (*Oghiyanoos-e khosoosi*), 195; *The Urban Greenhouse* (*Golkhaneh shahri*), 200
Tehrani, Atefeh, 71, 72, 341–42n125
Tehran International Tower, 167–68, *168*
Tehran Museum of Contemporary Art. *See* TMoCA
Tehran Today (documentary), 192
Tehran University, 72–73
temporary art. *See* ephemeral art
Ten (film), 183–84
theater (*te'atre*): in abandoned buildings, 260–66, *264*, *265*; audience as broad, 14–15; audience participation, 84, 127, 132, 262; in basements, 83–85, *85*; black box setting, 83–84; in caves, *130*, 130–32, *132*; and democracy, 184; in deserts, 125–26; distancing effect, 12, 233; in forests, 125; in houses and apartments, 55–56, 79–82, *81*, 261, 361–62n131; improvisational, 169; invisible, 16, 230, 232; in leftover urban spaces, 168–73, *171*, *173*; in mountains, 128, *134*; privatization of, 82–83, 102, 310; regulation of, 4, 43, 80, 84, 102, 127, 184; in taxicabs, 184–86, *185*, *187*; therapeutic performances, 86–87; travel (*safar*), 127, 129; "underground," as concept, 4
theater-like art (*honar-e te'atr-e gooneh*), 13. *See also* performance art
Theater Workshop (*Kargah-e Namayesh*), Tehran, 93; *Suddenly* (*Nagahan*) performance, 261
Theatre of the Absurd, 341n122
13 Vanak Street art space/gallery, Tehran: Bakhshi's *Solo Show* performance, 228–30; closure of, 284–86; as invisible, 283–84; mentioned, 62, 66; Razavipour's and Fotouhi's *Census* portraits, 167; relics of, *286*, 286–87; Sirizi's *U-Turn* exhibition, *284*, 285
Thompson, Nato, 252, 340n109

Thrift, Nigel, *Non-Representational Theory*, 244
Thurfjell, David, 245–46
time, and excess of causes, 204
time-based art, emergence in Iran, 13. *See also* ephemeral art
Tirafkan, Sadegh, *Blue Children, Black Sky* (*Koodakan-e abi, aseman-e siah*) collaborative exhibition, 68
TMoCA (Tehran Museum of Contemporary Art): conservative practices during Ahmadinejad administration, 219; freedom during Khatami administration, 217–18; post-revolutionary propagandist curatorial practices, 217; renovations, 287; revival of interactive art, 14; Seyghali's *Ma* installation, 204–5; as theater venue, 260; Western collection, 217, 367n10
Tochal Mountain, 113–14, *114*
Tofighian, Omid, 330n88
Torkameh, Aidin, 24–25, 297
tourism, ecotourism, 127–29
Toward Phoenix/Beh sooy-e simorgh (TV series), 62
Towhid Square (formerly Kennedy), Tehran, 87
translation, challenge of, 24–25, 330–31n88
trauma, 40, 114, 236
travel theater (*safar te'atre*), 127, 129
Trilling, Ossia, 104–6
The Triumph of the Will (film), 245
Trump, Donald, 258, 313, 331n91
trusted audiences, 5, 61, 79, 80, 102, 126, 159, 227, 237, 238, 269
Tschumi, Bernard, 209, 266, 276, 374–75n150
Tudeh (Communist) Party of Iran, 37, 162, 307
Tupitsyn, Victor, *The Museological Unconscious*, 7
Turner, J.M.W., 60
Turner, Victor, 370n72
Twombly, Cy, 5

Ukeles, Mierle Laderman, 255
Ulay (Frank Uwe Laysiepen), 207–8
underground (*zirzamini*), as term, 3, 4–5
underground assemblies (*anjomans*), 36–37
under the bed art (*zirtakhti*), 8
United States: alternative art scene, 58, 101, 110–11, 288, 310–11; luxury apartments, 142; relations with Iran, 242–43, 313
universities: closure and censorship of, 2, 3, 42–43, 55; student protests, 72–73, 312
unofficial art, as term, 8
UpArtMaan, Tehran, 91
Urban Art House (*Khaneh honarha-ye shahri*), Tehran, 184, 360n109
urban imaginaries (*takhayyolat-e shahri*), 25
urban spaces: critical discourse on, 24–25, 67–68, 155, 176, 179; and plop art, 151; renewal projects, 25–26, 57–58, 164, 165, 302–3, 382–83n52. *See also* abandoned and dilapidated buildings; leftover urban spaces; public art
Urry, John, 129

vacated buildings. *See* abandoned and dilapidated buildings
Vafadari, Karan, 286
Vahdat Hall (formerly Rudaki), Tehran, 94, 170
Vakilian, Ayda (Lili), 237–38; *Irma* exhibition, 238, *239*, 239–41
Vali Asr Mosque, Tehran, 209–10, *210*
Vali Asr Avenue (formerly Pahalavi), Tehran, 87, 88, 179, 214, 222, 223
Varga-Sinai, Gizella, 47, 381n34
Varish Mountains, 128
Vaziri Moghaddam, Mohsen, 107
veiled/unveiled women, 43, 44, 72, 80, 102, 126, 159, *160*, 299, 303
Verfremdungseffekt (distancing effect/alienation), 12
Versus Visual Arts Foundation, 62
video. *See* film (*filmi*) and video (*videoie*)
Vinogradov, Garik, 340n101
Vişniec, Matei, *Horses at the Window* (*Paykoobi-e Asbha posht-e panjareh*), 170

Wadsworth Atheneum, Hartford, Connecticut, 255

walking/meandering in the city (*parseh zani dar shahr*), 176, 178–83, *181*, *182*, *183*
Wallis, Brian, 311
Warner, Michael, 227
Washington Post, 295
Water and Fire Park (*Ab-o-atash*), Tehran, 127, 274
water canals, as art venues, *174*, 174–75
water reservoirs, as art venues, 96–98, *97*
water temples, *129*, 129–30
welfare programs, 54, 331n92
Western culture and art: and abstraction, 150; alternative art scene in United States, 58, 101, 110–11, 288, 310–11; as censored and banned, 2, 13, 73, 202; denouncement of, at museums, 215, 219; and kitsch, 223; minority spaces and safe spaces for, 47, 49–52; under Pahlavi dynasty, 41
Wexner Center for the Arts, Ohio State University, 270
Where Is the Friend's Home? (film), 200
Wilder, Billy, 238
wild-style graffiti, 79, *79*, *174*
Williams, Raymond, 265–66
Wilson, Ann, 347n1
Wilson, Fred, *Mining the Museum* exhibition, 34
Wilson, Robert, 13; *KA MOUNTAIN AND GUARDenia TERRACE*, *104*, 104–7
women: anxieties of life in Iran, 250–52; in architecture field, 137; gender segregation, 26, 43, 72, 82, 126, 128, 186–87; and male gaze, 196; meandering in the city, 178–83, *181*, *182*, *183*, 222; regulated appearance in public spaces, 44–45, 189, 194–95; role in establishment of home galleries, 56; sharing secrets, 93; suppressed voices, 157, 158; veiled *vs.* unveiled, 43, 44, 72, 80, 102, 126, 159, *160*, 299, 303; women-only plays, 362n131; *zan-e asiri* concept, 239–40, 370n74
Woolf, Virginia, 59
Worm Brain (anonymous graffiti artist), kitchen utensil factory project, 77, 78, *79*

Yaqat (woman in red), 192
Yarmohammad Touski, Golnar, 290
Y Art Studio. *See* Igreg Art Studio
Yellow Dogs (music band), 53
Yinger, J. Milton, 348n26
Yousefi, Elmira, 195
Youth Palace (*Kakh-e javanan*), Tehran, 344n167

Zabeti Jahromi, Ahmad, 344n167
Zabriskie Point (film), 221
Zaferani, Azadeh, 97
Zahed, Mona, 372n116
Zahmatkesh, Mohammad, 77
Zahraie, Ashkan, 98, 100, 190
Zakeri, Arman, 331n92
Zamani, Sepideh, 195
Zandi, Maryam, *Portraits of contemporary Iranian painters (Seemayi az naghashan-e mo'aser-e Iran)*, 336n40
zan-e asiri concept, 239–40, 370n74
Zan-e rooz (*Women of Today*; magazine), 44–45, *45*
Zarkesh, Shahrnaz, 348n48
Zav Architects, 96, 140–42
Zenderoudi, Charles Hossein, 176–78
Zhivar Tours, 131
Zionist art, 61
Zirpelleh, Tehran, 91–93, *92*, 310
zirzamini (underground), as term, 3, 4–5
Ziyayi, Mohammad Bagher, 160, 234
Żmijewski, Artur, 381n41
Zolghadr, Tirdad, 101; *Ethnic Marketing* (*Bazaryabi-e ghowmi*) exhibition, 225
Zomorodinia, Minoosh, 348n48
Zoroastrians and Zoroastrianism, 46, 106, 253
Zumthor, Peter, *Thinking Architecture*, 264

CPSIA information can be obtained
at www.ICGtesting.com
Printed in the USA
JSHW050812310722
28695JS00001B/1